The Legacy of Pierre

The Legacy of Pierre Bourdieu

Critical Essays

Edited by
Simon Susen and Bryan S. Turner

ANTHEM PRESS
LONDON · NEW YORK · DELHI

Anthem Press
An imprint of Wimbledon Publishing Company
www.anthempress.com

This edition first published in UK and USA 2013
by ANTHEM PRESS
75–76 Blackfriars Road, London SE1 8HA, UK
or PO Box 9779, London SW19 7ZG, UK
and
244 Madison Ave. #116, New York, NY 10016, USA

First published in hardback by Anthem Press in 2011

Chapter 1 originally published as Hans Joas and Wolfgang Knöbl (2009 [2004]) 'Between Structuralism and Theory of Practice: The Cultural Sociology of Pierre Bourdieu', in their *Social Theory: Twenty Introductory Lectures*, trans. Alex Skinner, Cambridge: Cambridge University Press, pp. 371–400. Reprinted with kind permission from Cambridge University Press.

Chapter 4 originally published as Loïc Wacquant (2000) 'Durkheim and Bourdieu: The Common Plinth and its Cracks', in Bridget Fowler (ed.) *Reading Bourdieu on Society and Culture*, Oxford: Blackwell/Sociological Review, pp. 105–119. Reprinted with kind permission from Loïc Wacquant.

Chapter 5 originally published as Pierre Bourdieu (2000) 'Mit Weber gegen Weber: Pierre Bourdieu im Gespräch', in Pierre Bourdieu, *Das religiöse Feld. Texte zur Ökonomie des Heilsgeschehens*, herausgegeben von Franz Schultheis, Andreas Pfeuffer und Stephan Egger, übersetzt von Stephan Egger, Konstanz: Universitätsverlag Konstanz, pp. 111–129. Reprinted with kind permission from Universitätsverlag Konstanz.

British Library Cataloguing-in-Publication Data
A catalogue record for this book is available from the British Library.

Library of Congress Cataloging-in-Publication Data
The Library of Congress has cataloged the hardcover edition as follows:
The legacy of Pierre Bourdieu : critical essays / edited by Simon Susen and Bryan S. Turner.
p. cm.
Includes bibliographical references and index.
ISBN 978-0-85728-768-7 (hbk. : alk. paper)
1. Bourdieu, Pierre, 1930-2002. 2. Sociology–Philosophy. 3. Social sciences–Philosophy. I. Susen, Simon. II. Turner, Bryan S.
HM479.B78L44 2011
301.092–dc22
2011007394

ISBN-13: 978 1 78308 072 4 (Pbk)
ISBN-10: 1 78308 072 8 (Pbk)

This title is also available as an ebook.

CONTENTS

LIST OF CONTRIBUTORS

Lisa Adkins is Professor of Sociology at the University of Newcastle, Australia. Her contributions to Sociology fall into three main areas: the sociology of economic life (especially the sociology of postindustrial economies and the new political economy), social and cultural theory, and the sociology of gender and sexuality. Some key publications include *Revisions: Gender and Sexuality in Late Modernity* (Open University, 2002), *Feminism After Bourdieu* (edited with B. Skeggs, Blackwell, 2005), and a Special Issue (co-edited with Celia Lury) in the *European Journal of Social Theory* on the theme of 'What is the Empirical?' (2009). Her recent work focuses on changing temporalities of labour and value in contemporary capitalism.

Mauro Basaure is Assistant Professor at the Instituto de Humanidades, Universidad Diego Portales, in Santiago de Chile, and he is a member of the Groupe de Sociologie Politique et Morale at the École des Hautes Études en Sciences Sociales in Paris, France. He received his PhD from the Johann Wolfgang Goethe-Universität, Frankfurt, Germany. He was previously at the University of Chile, where he studied sociology (1993–9) receiving his MA in political philosophy (2000–2). He was a Research Fellow at the Institute for Social Research, Frankfurt (2004–9), where he initiated the International Study Group for Critical Theory, and at the Lateinamerika Institut of the Freie Universität Berlin (2003). His areas of research and teaching include social theory, critical theory, contemporary French sociology and political philosophy. He recently edited *Erneuerung der Kritik. Axel Honneth im Gespräch* (New York, Frankfurt: Campus, 2009) (together with Jan Philipp Reemtsma and Rasmus Willig) and *Foucault et la psychanalyse* (Paris: Le Félin, 2009) (together with Emmanuel Gripay and Ferhat Taylan), and he published *Foucault y el psicoanálisis. Gramática de un malentendido* (Santiago: Cuarto Propio, 2011).

Mustafa Emirbayer is Professor of Sociology at the University of Wisconsin–Madison. He is the author of 'Manifesto for a Relational Sociology' (AJS 1997); his most recent articles include 'Bourdieu and Organizational

Analysis' (with Victoria Johnson) and 'What is Racial Domination?' (with Matthew Desmond).

Bridget Fowler is an Emeritus Professor of Sociology at the University of Glasgow. She specialises in social theory, Marxist feminism and the sociology of culture. A long-term interest has been the thought of Pierre Bourdieu, whose ideas she has taken up in various books: *The Alienated Reader* (Harvester Wheatsheaf, 1991); *Pierre Bourdieu and Cultural Theory: Critical Investigations* (Sage, 1997), and (edited) *Reading Bourdieu on Society and Culture* (Blackwell, 2000). She is at present applying Bourdieusian theory to the study of obituaries, addressing critically what is sometimes identified as the contemporary 'golden age of the obituary' (see Fowler, *The Obituary as Collective Memory*, Routledge, 2007).

Bruno Frère is Research Associate at the Fonds National de la Recherche Scientifique (Belgium). He previously worked as a postdoctoral researcher at the University of Cambridge, and he currently teaches at Sciences Po Paris and at the University of Liège. He received his PhD from the École des Hautes Études en Sciences Sociales and has published on a variety of topics: political sociology, political philosophy, social theory, and the history of social sciences. He recently published a monograph on the history of social movements and alternative economy (*Le nouvel esprit solidaire*, Paris: Desclée De Brouwer, 2009) and a book (with M. Jacquemain) on sociological theories in the late twentieth century (*Epistémologie de la sociologie, paradigmes pour le 21e siècle*, Bruxelles: De Boeck, 2008).

Bart van Heerikhuizen is Associate Professor in Sociology at the University of Amsterdam. Along with Nico Wilterdink, he wrote the market-leading 'Introduction to Sociology' textbook in the Dutch language (*Samenlevingen, inleiding in de sociologie*. Groningen: Wolters-Noordhoff, 1985), which is now in its sixth edition.

Hans Joas is Permanent Fellow at the Freiburg Institute for Advanced Studies (FRIAS), University of Freiburg, and Professor of Sociology and member of the Committee on Social Thought at the University of Chicago. He is a regular member of the Berlin-Brandenburg Academy of Sciences, nonresident fellow of the Swedish Collegium for Advanced Study, and Vice President of the International Sociological Association (2006–10). Among his recent publications in English are *Do We Need Religion? On the Experience of Self-Transcendence* (2008), *Social Theory: Twenty Introductory Lectures* (with Wolfgang Knöbl, 2009), and the two coedited volumes, *The Cultural Values of Europe* (with Klaus Wiegandt, 2008) and *Secularization and the World Religions* (with Klaus Wiegandt, 2009).

Bruno Karsenti is Directeur d'études at the École des Hautes Études en Sciences Sociales in Paris and Director of the Marcel Mauss Institute. He has taught in the areas of political philosophy, epistemology, and the philosophy of the social sciences at the Universities of Lyon and Paris-Sorbonne. His most recent publications include *Politique de l'esprit. Auguste Comte et la naissance de la science sociale* (Paris: Hermann, 2006) and *La société en personnes. Études durkheimiennes* (Paris: Economica, 2006). He is Editor of two-book series, *Pratiques théoriques* (Paris: Presses Universitaires de France) and *Raisons pratiques* (Paris: Éditions de l'École des Hautes Études en Sciences Sociales).

Wolfgang Knöbl is Professor of Sociology at the Georg-August-University Göttingen. Together with Hans Joas, he wrote *Kriegsverdrängung. Ein Problem in der Geschichte der Sozialtheorie* (2008) and *Social Theory. Twenty Introductory Lectures* (2009). In 2007, he published *Die Kontingenz der Moderne. Wege in Europa, Asien und Amerika.*

Hans-Herbert Kögler is Professor of Philosophy and Chair of the Department of Philosophy at the University of North Florida, Jacksonville. A frequent guest-professor at the Alpe-Adria University in Klagenfurt, Austria, his work explores the hermeneutic foundations of social science and critical theory, theories of agency, language, and power, as well as intercultural understanding and cosmopolitanism. Major publications include *The Power of Dialogue: Critical Hermeneutics after Gadamer and Foucault*, (1999), *Michel Foucault* (2nd edition, 2004), *Kultura, Kritika, Dialog* (Prague, 2006), and the co-edited volume *Empathy and Agency: The Problem of Understanding in the Human Sciences* (2000). In 1997 the journal *Social Epistemology* dedicated a special issue to Kögler's 'Alienation as Epistemological Source: Reflexivity and Social Background after Mannheim and Bourdieu'.

Bowen Paulle is an Assistant Professor in Sociology at the University of Amsterdam. He is involved in policy ethnography centred around efforts to desegregate schools and is author of *Toxic Schools* (under contract, University of Chicago Press).

Andreas Pfeuffer studied sociology, history, and Latin, and is currently working as a Research Assistant at the Institute for Social Research in Hamburg, where he is involved in a comparative research project on public services in Germany, Austria, and Switzerland. He has translated various works by

Pierre Bourdieu, Robert Castel, Michael Pollak, Serge Paugam, Luc Boltanski, and Laurent Thévenot into German.

Keijo Rahkonen is Adjunct Professor of Social Policy and Head of the Department of Social Research at the University of Helsinki. He is also Director of the research project 'Cultural Capital and Social Differentiation in Contemporary Finland: An International Comparison', which is funded by the Research Council for Culture and Society at the Academy of Finland. He has been Visiting Research Fellow at the London School of Economics and Political Science, UK, and at the European University Institute in Florence, Italy. His recent publications include 'Bourdieu in Finland' (*Sociologica: Italian Journal of Sociology Online*, 2008) and 'Nordic Democracy of Taste? Cultural Omnivorousness in Musical and Literary Taste Preferences in Finland' (with Jukka Gronow and Semi Purhonen, in *Poetics: Journal of Empirical Research on Culture, the Media and the Arts*, 2010).

Derek Robbins is Professor of International Social Theory in the School of Humanities and Social Sciences at the University of East London. He is the author of *The Work of Pierre Bourdieu* (1991) and of *Bourdieu and Culture* (2000). He is also the editor of two four-volume collections of articles on Bourdieu in the Sage Masters of Contemporary Social Thought series (2000 and 2005) and of a three-volume collection of articles on Lyotard in the same series (2004). His *On Bourdieu, Education and Society* was published by Bardwell Press, Oxford, in 2006, and he was the editor of the Special Issue of *Theory, Culture and Society* on Bourdieu (Volume 23, Number 6, 2006). He is currently writing *The Internationalization of French Social Thought, 1950–2000* for publication by Sage.

Franz Schultheis is Professor of Sociology at the University of St. Gallen, Switzerland. He also taught at the Universities of Constance, Paris V, Neuchâtel, and Geneva. He is President of the Bourdieu Foundation and has edited many of Pierre Bourdieu's writings in German. He specialises in the sociology of labour, the sociology of social change, the sociology of popular culture, and the sociology of social structure. Amongst his recent publications are the following: Franz Schultheis, Berthold Vogel and Michael Gemperle (eds.) *Ein halbes Leben: Biographische Zeugnisse aus einer Arbeitswelt im Umbruch* (Konstanz: UVK, 2010) and Franz Schultheis, *Bourdieus Wege in die Soziologie* (Konstanz: UVK, 2007).

Yves Sintomer is Professor of Political Science at Paris 8 University, Guest Professor at Lausanne University, and Invited Researcher at Neuchâtel

University. He received his PhD in Social and Political Sciences from the European University Institute, Florence, and has a Habilitation to direct research (Paris 5 University). He studied at Paris 8, Paris 10, the Johann Wolfgang Goethe-University Frankfurt, and at Harvard University. He was Deputy Director of the Marc Bloch Centre in Berlin, and he has held academic positions in various countries (Switzerland, Germany, Belgium, Italy, and Spain). Together with Hans Peter-Müller, he co-edited *Pierre Bourdieu. Théorie et pratique* (Paris: La Découverte, 2006). He is author of *La démocratie impossible? Politique et modernité chez Weber et Habermas* (Paris: La Découverte, 1999). His work has been translated into thirteen languages.

Simon Susen is Lecturer in Social and Political Theory at Birkbeck College, University of London. He previously worked as a Lecturer in Sociology at Newcastle University (2008–10) and as a Lecturer in Sociology at Goldsmiths College, University of London (2007–8). He received his PhD from the University of Cambridge and studied sociology, politics, and philosophy at a range of international universities and research centres, including the University of Edinburgh, the Colegio de México, the Facultad Latinoamericana de Ciencias Sociales in Mexico City, and the École des Hautes Études en Sciences Sociales in Paris. With John O'Neill and Bryan S. Turner, he is Editor of the *Journal of Classical Sociology*. He is author of *The Foundations of the Social: Between Critical Theory and Reflexive Sociology* (Oxford: Bardwell Press, 2007).

Bryan S. Turner is the Presidential Professor of Sociology at CUNY and Director of the Committee on Religion. He is concurrently the Director of the Centre for the Study of Contemporary Muslim Societies at the University of Western Sydney, Australia. He was the Alona Evans Distinguished Visiting Professor of Sociology at Wellesley College (2009–10), and in recent years he has held Professorships at the National University of Singapore and the University of Cambridge. Together with Engin Isin, he is Editor of the journal *Citizenship Studies*. He recently edited *The New Blackwell Companion to Social Theory* (2009), *The Routledge Handbook of Globalization Studies* (2009), and *The New Blackwell Companion to the Sociology of Religion* (2010).

Loïc Wacquant is Professor of Sociology at the University of California, Berkeley, and Researcher at the Centre de sociologie européenne, Paris. A MacArthur Prize Fellow and the recipient of the 2008 Lewis Coser Award of the American Sociological Association, his interests span urban inequality and marginality, incarnation, the penal state, ethnoracial domination, and social theory and the politics of reason. He is a co-founder and past editor of the interdisciplinary journal *Ethnography* and was a regular contributor to *Le Monde Diplomatique* from 1994 to 2004. His recent books include *Body and Soul: Notebooks of An Apprentice Boxer* (2004), *The Mystery of Ministry: Pierre Bourdieu and Democratic Politics* (2005), *Das Janusgesicht des Ghettos* (2006), *Urban Outcasts: A Comparative Sociology of Advanced Marginality* (2008), and *Punishing the Poor: The Neoliberal Government of Social Insecurity* (2009).

INTRODUCTION

Preliminary Reflections on the Legacy of Pierre Bourdieu

Simon Susen and Bryan S. Turner

Unsurprisingly, the Second World War had separate and distinctive consequences for different national traditions of sociology. After the War, the dominant and arguably most successful of the Western democracies emerged in North America, and its sociological traditions assumed a celebratory and often triumphalist perspective on modernisation. The defeat of the fascist nations – notably Germany, Italy, and Japan – seemed to demonstrate the superiority of Western liberal democratic systems, and North American sociologists took the lead in developing theories of development and modernisation that were optimistic and forward-looking. The examples are numerous, but we might mention Daniel Lerner's *The Passing of Traditional Society* (1958) or S. M. Lipset's *The First New Nation* (1963). At the centre of this post-war tradition stood *The Social System* of Talcott Parsons (1951), which involved the notion that systems could continuously and successfully adapt to environmental challenges through the master processes of differentiation and adaptive upgrading. In many of his short essays, he analysed the problems of German and Japanese modernisation and saw the United States of America as a social system that had successfully adapted to the rise of industrial modernisation. In its assessment of modern society, Parsons's sociology avoided the pessimistic vision of early critical theory – epitomised in Adorno's analysis of mass society – because he looked forward to America as a 'lead society' in large-scale social development (see Holton and Turner, 1986).

It is also the case that, in general terms, North American sociologists did not show much interest in European sociology, especially with regard to its more critical and negative assessments of modern capitalism. Parsons, of course, translated Max Weber's *The Protestant Ethic and the Spirit of Capitalism* and published the first English version in 1930, but he did not focus on Weber's bleak and pessimistic view of the iron cage. He did not perceive the figure of Nietzsche behind Weber. Subsequently, Parsons's reception of Weber was much criticised by writers who sought to 'de-Parsonise' Weber. Later, in 1947, Hans Gerth and C. Wright Mills brought out *From Max Weber: Essays in Sociology*, which showed an increased interest in Weber's writings on the state, bureaucracy, power, and authority. Although other North American sociologists – such as Lewis Coser in his *Masters of Sociological Thought* (1971) – were appreciative of the European legacy, most North American sociologists looked to their own traditions, in particular to the Chicago School, pragmatism, and symbolic interactionism. Their 'founding fathers' were Mead, Park, and Thomas, rather than Marx, Weber, and Durkheim.

This gap between a critical-pessimistic Western European sociology and a progressive-optimistic North American sociology persists to a significant extent today. To take one example, Jeffrey C. Alexander has been at the forefront of the study of the European tradition, but his recent work *The Civil Sphere* (2006) has a characteristic positive conclusion based on the view that various social movements in North American history – notably the women's movement and the civil rights movement – as well as the incorporation of the Jewish community into North American public life testify to the success, flexibility, and robustness of political liberalism in general and American liberalism in particular. There has been a long tradition of critical writing in North American sociology; yet, naturally enough, its focus has been on migration and immigrants, the 'racial' divide, the civil rights movement, and US imperialism in Latin America. By contrast, in European sociology after the mid-twentieth century, the Left was preoccupied with both empirical and conceptual problems that emerged from the legacy of Marxism, such as social class and class consciousness, the role of the state in capitalism, and the role of ideology in class societies – to mention only a few. While 1968 had an impact on both sides of the Atlantic, its meaning in the European context was somewhat different (Sica and Turner, 2005). As shall be explained in the chapter on Pierre Bourdieu's treatment of religion, one clear difference between Western European and North American sociology can be described as follows: whereas Western European sociologists – such as the British sociologist Bryan Wilson – mapped the steady decline of religion in the modern world in the secularisation thesis, North American sociologists were inclined to record the resilience of religion and its essential contribution to the North American way of life, as in the works of Talcott Parsons, Will Herberg, Liston Pope, and Gerhard E. Lenski.

Across the Atlantic, although Britain had emerged successfully from the Second World War, European Anglophone sociology was not especially optimistic or triumphant. The British Empire, which had been in decline since the end of the Victorian period, was finally pulled apart by the war effort, and even the Commonwealth survived only as a fragile reminder of the past. Under the guidance of Harold Macmillan, Britain began to abandon its imperial relationship with its colonies and accepted Macmillan's view of 'the wind of change blowing through the [African] continent', expressed in his famous speech of 1963. Mainstream British sociology was realistic and reformist, rather than optimistic and utopian. In fact, it could be regarded as the parallel of Keynesian economics in focusing on issues around social insurance. Once more, Macmillan had perhaps been prescient in recognising the dawn of modern consumerism in his 1959 election campaign slogan: 'Most of our people have never had it so good'. This mood of gradual reconstruction was captured in sociology by key figures such as Thomas H. Marshall and Richard M. Titmuss, who wrote influential works on social citizenship and welfare reform. Their influence was originally confined to Britain, where the LSE was the dominant institution in the social sciences. Other influential figures within this reformist framework were Michael Young and Peter Willmott, who published their famous investigations of family life in the London East End in the 1950s.

British social science had been blessed by a wave of migrant intellectuals in the twentieth century, particularly by the Jewish refugees who arrived in the 1930s and later, such as Ilya Neustadt and Norbert Elias, both of whom played a major role in creating what became the famous 'Leicester School' (Rojek, 2004). In political philosophy, the dominant figure was Isaiah Berlin, who was fundamentally critical of Marxism and distrustful of sociology, and indeed of any theory that promoted the idea of historical determinism or of the causal priority of 'society' over the 'individual'. By the late 1960s, other émigrés became influential, especially John Rex, who developed conflict theory along Weberian lines, and Ralf Dahrendorf, who combined Weber and Marx in his famous *Class and Class Conflict in Industrial Society* (1959). Both thinkers were deeply critical of Parsons and more generally of North American sociology. Rex's *Key Problems in Sociological Theory* (1961), which contained an important criticism of functionalism, became a basic textbook of undergraduate British sociology. Other critical assessments were delivered by Tom Bottomore (1965) in *Classes in Modern Society* and by David Lockwood (1964) in his article 'Social Integration and System Integration' and, much later, in his book *Solidarity and Schism* (1992). British sociology in the 1960s came to be identified with various radical movements, such as the Campaign for Nuclear Disarmament (CND) and the anti-Apartheid campaign. This political mood of criticism and activism was reflected in Alan Dawe's powerful article 'The Two Sociologies', which was published in the *British Journal of Sociology* in 1970 and in which he argued that Parsons's systems theory ruled out agency and was based on a conservative conception of society. With the principal exception of Roland Robertson, few British sociologists were receptive to North American sociology in general and to Parsonian sociology in particular.

In France, the impact of war was much more profound, and in the post-war period the country was socially polarised and politically divided. The French Left accused many national institutions and traditions of effectively playing the role of the unwelcome and unchanged remainders of Vichy France, while Marxism, as the predominant ideology of the French Communist Party, had a strong impact on post-war French sociology and philosophy. French intellectuals grappled more than most with the issues of politics and ethics to question the relationship of the individual to society and the ultimate bases of ethical responsibility. Jean-Paul Sartre exercised enormous influence over these debates through his lectures at the École normale supérieure, through newspapers such as *Les Temps modernes*, and through the Communist Party. Aspiring French intellectuals had to weigh themselves against the legacy of Sartre. As a consequence, questions about humanism, the self, and power became dominant issues, notably in the works of Michel Foucault and Pierre Bourdieu (Luxon, 2008).

France, unlike Britain, became involved in two major and unsuccessful colonial wars, one in Vietnam and one in Algeria. Whereas Britain abandoned its colonial past without protracted colonial conflicts, France was divided and traumatised by its attempts to secure its presence in Indo-China and North Africa. British colonial struggles in Suez and clashes with native anti-colonial movements such as Mau Mau were, unlike the war in Algeria, relatively short-lived. The result was that Marxist sociology played a far more dominant role in French intellectual life than was the case in Britain and North America. In the post-war period, sociological debate was shaped by key figures such as Louis Althusser (1969 [1965]) and Nicos Poulantzas (1978 [1978]), both of whom developed innovative readings of Karl Marx that were designed to replace 'bourgeois sociology'. While Raymond Aron (2002) was a major figure in both politics and French intellectual life, he had few disciples and did not create a school. In addition, his work has been important in political, rather than in sociological, theory. At a later stage, Michel Foucault (1980) emerged as another significant figure with an international audience.

While French sociology has had enormous influence beyond France, the outside world has had little impact on French sociology and philosophy. Foucault, for example, was largely ignorant of the work of Max Weber, despite certain similarities in their interests and approach: for instance, one can see a parallel between Weber's writings on 'personality and life orders' and Foucault's writings on 'subjectivity and disciplinary orders'. And, of course, both thinkers were heavily influenced by Nietzsche. Few French sociologists worked abroad or seriously engaged with Anglo-American sociology. Exceptions include not only Foucault and Aron, but also Raymond Boudon (1980 [1971]), who worked with Paul Lazarsfeld and Michel Crozier. The only significant French interpretation of Parsons was provided by François Bourricaud (1981 [1977]) in *The Sociology of Talcott Parsons*. French social scientists carved out a rich tradition of their own, but it remained largely sealed off from the rest of the world. In epistemological terms, they were often sceptical about, or hostile towards, Anglo-Saxon traditions based on empiricism or positivism, and in political terms they were often hostile to Anglo-Saxon liberalism. The leading figures of French intellectual life were resolutely anti-American, Sartre being a primary example. Boudon and Aron are the exceptions to this norm. Interestingly, they were both appreciative of Alexis de Tocqueville's interpretation of American democracy. Aron included de Tocqueville in his *Main Currents in Sociological Thought* (1965), and Boudon published a study of de Tocqueville in English. Conversely, it was some time before Americans recognised the value of French sociological work – for example, the importance of Crozier's *The Bureaucratic Phenomenon* (1964 [1963]) and of Bourdieu and Passeron's *The Inheritors* (1979 [1964]).

While it may be argued that French sociology was intellectually isolated from the outside world, it is crucial to acknowledge one curious – and in many respects problematic – exogenous influence: the philosophy of Martin Heidegger. Despite Heidegger's active and complicit involvement in German fascism, he was profoundly influential in post-war French thinking – particularly in philosophy. Heidegger's 'anti-humanism' was influential in the intellectual development of Foucault; and Jacques Derrida, deeply influenced by Heidegger, came to his defence over the persistent accusations of his fascist commitment. In an interview in *Ethos* in 1983, Foucault confessed that '[his] entire philosophical development was determined by [his] reading of Heidegger' (see Didier Eribon's *Michel Foucault*, 1992 [1989]: 30). Sociology was a late development in the French university system, and many academics who became sociologists had been trained in philosophy. Consequently, philosophy has played a much more significant role in Francophone than in Anglophone sociology. It is certainly the case that the often hidden and disguised influence of Heidegger is one of the distinctive features of French sociology.

The differences between Anglophone and Francophone – as well as between North American and Western European – academic traditions are, to a large extent, the outcome of vastly dissimilar experiences of mass warfare, occupation, and liberation. These historical differences between North American and West European sociological traditions continue to produce important forms of divergence in research traditions. North American sociology is supported by a powerful professional body, namely the American Sociological Association; sociology in France and Britain, by contrast, has been more fragmented, devolved, and to some extent even marginalised within the university system. In Britain, sociology remains overshadowed by history departments and historical research, which is reflected in the fact that it has mainly flourished in new universities such as Essex, Lancaster, and Warwick, rather than in the traditional ones. The field of North American sociology is large; national sociology groups in Europe are small. North American sociology is supported by large grants; much European sociology is done with small grants and often depends on observational studies producing qualitative data (Masson, 2008). Although one can list these institutional differences, the divisions between Anglophone and Francophone sociology appear to be the products of long-standing political ideologies and cultural values. This is the socio-historical context within which one has to understand the work of Pierre Bourdieu and the paradigmatic framework within which to discuss his legacy.

Bourdieu was born in Southwest France on 1 August 1930. After training at the École normale supérieure, he was a conscript in the French military in the early years of the Algerian War of Independence (1956–8), but eventually gained a post as an assistant at the University of Algiers. He later published three books relating to his Algerian experiences. These works continue to evoke deep interest in his ethnographic methods, and Bourdieu has been identified subsequently as a 'post-colonial thinker' (see *The Sociological Review – Special Issue: Post-Colonial Bourdieu*, 2009). Unlike that of many previous French sociologists, Bourdieu's work has had a wide and diverse reception. It has played an important part in the 'somaesthetics' developed by Richard Shusterman, who has combined Bourdieu's treatment of practice and habitus with the notion of practice in American pragmatism, notably in his *Pragmatist Aesthetics* (1992) and, to some extent, in his volume *Bourdieu: A Critical Reader* (1999). Bourdieu – in particular since the publication of *Distinction* (1984 [1979]) – has had a major impact on cultural sociology, while his work on the logic of practice has deeply influenced what we may call 'the turn to practice' in anthropology and history. He has had an equally significant role in the development of the sociology of the body (see, for instance, Shilling, 2004; Turner, 1996). In a recent study, Bourdieu's reflexive sociology has been cross-fertilised with Habermas's critical theory (Susen, 2007). In the United States, Bourdieu's work has been promoted and defended, especially by his disciple, Loïc Wacquant, and other major readers have introduced Bourdieu to an American audience – in particular, through the publication of Calhoun, LiPuma, and Postone's edited volume *Bourdieu: Critical Perspectives* (1993). There is also little doubt that, in Britain, Bourdieu's work has had a significant impact on the development of the sociology of education – especially Bourdieu and Passeron's *Reproduction in Education, Society and Culture* (1990 [1970]). In British social theory, this aspect of Bourdieu's reception has been thoroughly analysed by Derek Robbins.

It may appear that Bourdieu's sociology is a successful bridge between the Western European 'critical' tradition and the North American 'professionalised' tradition. In our view, however, this bridge is fragile. Obviously, Bourdieu was largely a product of the forces we have identified in our Introduction. Bourdieu, notably in his political views, was stridently anti-American, particularly in his *The Weight of the World* (1999 [1993]). He was unambiguously a public intellectual of the Left, critical of neoliberal economics in global terms and of French domestic policy (for example, towards immigrants). Various chapters in this study of Bourdieu (see esp. chapters 2 and 3) underline the influence of Marx on Bourdieu's thinking. While Bourdieu was significantly influenced by Marx and Durkheim, he was not particularly receptive to American social science, despite the obvious similarities between his ideas about agency and practice and American pragmatism. And while French philosophy was openly influenced by Heidegger, Bourdieu launched an attack on Heidegger's work and the profound impact of his writings in *The Political Ontology of Martin Heidegger* (1991 [1988]) (see also Bourdieu, 1975). Bourdieu was also influenced, if only to a limited extent, by Weber (see esp. chapter 5). Turner, for instance, examines Bourdieu's deployment of Weber in the sociology of religion (see chapter 10).

Ironically, Bourdieu was, to some extent, the intellectual product of a particular field with its specific cultural capital; in this sense, his sociology was profoundly 'French': his interest in and engagement with Algeria, his sensitivities to migration in general and Muslim migration in particular, his awareness of the competition over political and economic power between Paris and the French regions, and his – at least implicit – anti-Americanism. Yet, Bourdieu also emphasised that *réflexivité* – conceived of as a self-critical position – was an integral component of his own sociological work, and he was conscious of cultural, institutional, and disciplinary boundaries and their tangible impact on the circulation of ideas in the modern world. Was Bourdieu's work able to transcend the French field? And where does his legacy lie? To what extent did he span the divide between classical sociology (Marx, Durkheim, and Weber) and contemporary sociology? Did he cross or provide a bridge between Western European and North American sociology? It is the task of this collection of critical essays to respond to these and similar questions. The volume contains fifteen chapters. The wide range of topics covered in these chapters is indicative of the complexity that characterises Bourdieusian thought in at least five respects.

First, Bourdieu's work is *multithematic*. Bourdieu produced a large number of books and articles on a broad range of topics in various areas of research: cultural sociology, political sociology, economic sociology, the sociology of class, the sociology of gender, the sociology of education, the sociology of language, the sociology of religion, the sociology of power, the sociology of experience, the sociology of time, the sociology of space, and the sociology of knowledge and science – to mention only some of the key research areas in which his sociological writings are situated. The multithematic nature of Bourdieu's oeuvre is indicative of his commitment to the idea that critical social scientists should resist tendencies towards the specialisation of research programmes, the invention of autopoietic research languages, the creation of inward-looking research communities, the institutionalisation of self-referential research units, and the construction of power-driven research empires.

Second, Bourdieu's work is *multidisciplinary*. Given that Bourdieu was a philosopher by training and a sociologist by choice, a multidisciplinary view of things became an integral part of his intellectual development from an early stage. To be exact, there seems to be a consensus in the literature that Bourdieu's work can be considered as multidisciplinary on three levels: in terms of its multidisciplinary *roots*, in terms of its multidisciplinary *outlook*, and in terms of its multidisciplinary *impact*. There can be little doubt that the three disciplines that have played the most important role both in Bourdieu's intellectual development and in his intellectual influence are philosophy, anthropology, and sociology. Some commentators would rightly insist that other disciplines from the human and social sciences need to be added to this list – in particular, economics, politics, linguistics, semiotics, psychoanalysis, and cultural and historical studies, as well as literature, music, and art history. The multidisciplinary – and, indeed, transdisciplinary – nature of Bourdieu's oeuvre is indicative of his firm conviction that critical social scientists should seek to overcome artificial and counterproductive boundaries between epistemically and institutionally separated disciplines.

Third, Bourdieu's work is intellectually *eclectic*. Bourdieu drew on a number of intellectual traditions in his writings. Although one runs the risk of being overly schematic when classifying these traditions and relating the name of Bourdieu to other influential thinkers, it seems appropriate to suggest that the following intellectual traditions (and thinkers associated with these traditions) are particularly important to Bourdieu's oeuvre: in *philosophy*, metaphysics and German idealism (Leibniz, Kant, Fichte, Schelling, and Hegel), phenomenology (Husserl, Heidegger, and Merleau-Ponty), existentialism (Pascal, Heidegger, and Sartre), ordinary language philosophy (Wittgenstein, Austin, and Searle), Marxist philosophy (Althusser), and the philosophy of science (Canguilhem, Popper, and Kuhn); in *anthropology*, structuralist anthropology (Mauss and Lévi-Strauss) and symbolic anthropology (Geertz); and, in *sociology*, materialist sociology (Marx), functionalist sociology (Durkheim), interpretive sociology (Weber), micro-sociology (Mead, Garfinkel, and Goffman), and constructivist sociology (Berger and Luckmann). In other words, there is a long list of different intellectual traditions on which Bourdieu drew in his writings. As is widely acknowledged in the literature, Bourdieu's work not only offers an original synthesis of the 'Holy Trinity' of Marx, Durkheim, and Weber but also illustrates the continuing relevance of their writings to contemporary issues in social and political analysis. The three canonical cornerstones of sociological research – that is, Marxian, Durkheimian, and Weberian thought – are just as crucial to Bourdieu's oeuvre as three of the most influential disciplines in the history of the humanities and social sciences: philosophy, anthropology, and sociology. The eclectic nature of Bourdieu's writings reflects his willingness to engage with different – and, in many respects, competing – currents of social and political thought, indicating his persuasion that critical social scientists should dare to break with canonical patterns of research by cross-fertilising the conceptual tools and theoretical presuppositions of rival intellectual traditions.

Fourth, Bourdieu's work is both *empirically grounded and theoretically informed*. It is no secret that Bourdieu, as he stressed on several occasions, was committed to combining empirical and theoretical research in his own work. More specifically, Bourdieu sought to contribute to overcoming the gap between empirically anchored and practically engaged research, on the one hand, and conceptually driven and theoretically oriented research, on the other. From a Bourdieusian standpoint, truly reflexive social research cannot rely on an artificial division of labour between those who engage primarily in the collection of quantitative or qualitative data 'on the ground' and those who immerse themselves exclusively in the elaboration of sophisticated conceptual frameworks 'from the desk'. Reflexive social research is not simply about either doing ethnological tourism – '*with* the object of study' – through the embodied experience of real life, or embracing a position of philosophical transcendentalism – '*above* the object of study' – through the disembodied experience of scholastic life. In other words, the pursuit of critical social research is not about creating a gulf between data collectors and number crunchers, on one side, and conceptual architects and system builders, on the other. Rather, it is about combining the empirical and the theoretical components of social science and thereby demonstrating their interdependence. If one claims to be committed to the idea of critical social science in the Bourdieusian sense, one must seek to overcome the counterproductive divide between empirical and theoretical research. As a *philosophe* by training and a *sociologue* by choice (Hacking, 2004: 147; Susen, 2007: 246), Bourdieu was convinced that 'research without theory is blind, and theory without research is empty' (Bourdieu and Wacquant, 1992: 162, italics removed). The fact that his writings are not only guided by sophisticated philosophical frameworks but also substantiated by a large variety of empirical studies illustrates that Bourdieu sought to practise what he preached. The empirically grounded and theoretically informed nature of Bourdieu's oeuvre proves his commitment to the view that methodologically rigorous observation and conceptually refined interpretation must go hand in hand if one aims to study the functioning of society in a genuinely scientific manner.

Fifth, Bourdieu's work is *politically committed*. Particularly towards the end of his career, Bourdieu was concerned with establishing a fruitful link between his sociological studies, which were aimed at providing a *deconstructive* grasp of reality, and his various political engagements, which were oriented towards having a *constructive* impact upon society. In this sense, Bourdieusian thought is clearly committed to the Marxist dictum that '[t]he philosophers have only interpreted the world, in various ways; the point is to change it' (Marx, 2000/1977 [1845]: 173). From a Bourdieusian perspective, the social sciences in general and sociology in particular have a normative commitment not only to providing an insightful and critical *understanding* of human reality but also, more importantly, to having a positive and transformative *impact* on the material and symbolic organisation of society. Hence, a critical interpretation of reality should make use of the scientific tools developed by sociology and thereby seek to contribute to the emancipation of society. Precisely, an emancipatory science – in the Bourdieusian sense – needs to confront three essential tasks: first, to *uncover* the underlying mechanisms that perpetuate the reproduction of material and symbolic relations of social domination (Bourdieu and Wacquant, 1992: 14–15); second, to '*universalise* the conditions of access to universality' that generate material and symbolic processes of social emancipation (Bourdieu, 1994: 233, italics added); and, third, to *engage* in a '*Realpolitik* of reason' (Bourdieu, 2001: 32, italics in original), thereby mobilising the empowering resources of critical rationality and making use of them for the consolidation of an emancipatory society. The political nature of Bourdieu's oeuvre is an unambiguous sign of his belief that critical sociologists should not only engage in the scientific study of the relational construction of reality but also aim to have a transformative impact upon the historical development of society.

The fifteen chapters of the present volume illustrate – on different levels and with different emphases – the importance of the aforementioned concerns.

First, similarly to Bourdieu's own work, the selection of essays published in the present volume is *multithematic*. Themes covered in this book range from Bourdieu's cultural sociology (Joas/Knöbl, Rahkonen, and Susen), Bourdieu's political sociology (Basaure, Robbins, and Sintomer), Bourdieu's economic sociology (Adkins), Bourdieu's sociology of language (Kögler), and Bourdieu's sociology of religion (Bourdieu/Schultheis/Pfeuffer and Turner) to Bourdieu's sociology of power (Fowler and Paulle/van Heerikhuizen/Emirbayer), Bourdieu's sociology of experience (Frère and Karsenti), Bourdieu's sociology of time (Adkins), and Bourdieu's sociology of knowledge and science (Robbins, Sintomer, and Wacquant). Unsurprisingly, there is some significant overlap between the thematic foci of these chapters. As much as this overlap is symptomatic of the breadth and depth of Bourdieu's oeuvre, it illustrates the difficulty attached to any attempts to divide his various contributions into key thematic areas. In light of the multithematic complexity of Bourdieusian thought, it may be impossible, and indeed pointless, to pigeonhole his main contributions.

Second, following *l'esprit ouvert* that runs through Bourdieu's writings, the volume is *multidisciplinary*. Even if we accept that all disciplinary boundaries are somewhat artificial and that, as Bourdieu points out, they can have counterproductive effects, we cannot deny that the three disciplinary pillars of Bourdieusian thought – philosophy, anthropology, and sociology – are omnipresent in the following chapters. Although, in the broadest sense, all of the contributions to this volume represent critical studies in social and political thought, they fall into these three main disciplines. We may explore Bourdieu's *philosophically* inspired accounts of the age-old preoccupation with the relationships between history and society (Fowler), being and society (Karsenti), language and society (Kögler), reason and society (Sintomer), faith and society (Turner), polity and society (Robbins), recognition and society (Basaure), resentment and society (Rahkonen), aesthetics and society (Susen), or time and society (Adkins). We may focus on Bourdieu's *anthropologically* motivated analyses of the civilisational functions of culture (Joas/Knöbl), religion (Bourdieu/Schultheis/Pfeuffer and Turner), habitus (Frère), individual and collective experiences (Karsenti), or historical development (Karsenti and Wacquant). And, in fact, we may appreciate the relevance of Bourdieu's *sociologically* grounded studies of a number of themes in literally every chapter: practice and society (Joas/Knöbl), capital and society (Fowler), the body and society (Karsenti), knowledge and society (Wacquant), relationality and society (Bourdieu/Schultheis/Pfeuffer), taste and society (Rahkonen), power and society (Paulle/van Heerikhuizen/Emirbayer), culture and society (Susen), intersubjectivity and society (Basaure), religion and society (Turner), habitus and society (Frère), communication and society (Kögler), politics and society (Robbins), the public sphere and society (Sintomer), or economy and society (Adkins). The wide-ranging disciplinary relevance of Bourdieusian thought to anthropology, philosophy, and sociology, which manifests itself in the diverse thematic foci of this volume, illustrates the fact that Bourdieusian thought transcends canonical boundaries not only in terms of its multidisciplinary roots and outlook but also in terms of its transdisciplinary impact on different areas of research in the humanities and social sciences.

Third, resembling the Bourdieusian approach itself, the volume is intellectually *eclectic*. The book seeks to do justice to the fact that Bourdieu drew on a range of intellectual traditions and on a variety of thinkers whose works are associated with these traditions. Far from covering all of the intellectual schools and paradigmatic trends that influenced Bourdieu's oeuvre, the collection of essays published in the present volume has three main foci. The first set of essays traces the roots of Bourdieu's thought in classical sociology by closely examining his intellectual connections with the writings of the *founding figures of sociology*, that is, with the works of Marx (Fowler and Karsenti), Durkheim (Wacquant), and Weber (Bourdieu/Schultheis/Pfeuffer). The second set of essays is mainly concerned with Bourdieu's relation to *modern social philosophy*, in particular with regard to the works of Nietzsche (Rahkonen), Elias (Paulle/van Heerikhuizen/Emirbayer), Adorno (Susen), and Honneth (Basaure). The third set of essays explores the relevance of Bourdieu's writings to key issues debated in the *contemporary social sciences*, such as the continuous presence of religion (Turner), the transformative power of social movements (Frère), the emancipatory potential of language (Kögler), the political legacy of 1968 (Robbins), the socio-historical significance of the rise of the public sphere (Sintomer), and – particularly important in the current climate – the social consequences of economic crisis (Adkins). The wide range of topics covered in the present volume indicates that it would be a mistake to associate Bourdieu's work exclusively with one particular theme and, in so doing, disregard the fact that intellectual eclecticism constitutes an essential feature of Bourdieu's oeuvre, not only in terms of its roots and points of reference, but also in terms of its overall impact on the contemporary social sciences.

Fourth, in line with one of Bourdieu's deepest convictions, the volume pays tribute to the fact that his work is both *empirically grounded and theoretically informed.* The essays in this book are yet another illustration of the fact that Bourdieu can be praised for practising what he preached in that, in his sociological writings, he was firmly committed to overcoming the divide between 'the empirical' and 'the conceptual', 'the concrete' and 'the abstract', 'the actual' and 'the nominal', and 'the practical' and 'the theoretical'. To be sure, most of the following chapters have a 'theoretical' focus, since they are primarily concerned with the legacy of Bourdieu's work in contemporary social and political thought. Nevertheless, what manifests itself in the contributions to this volume is the fact that we can only make sense of Bourdieu's oeuvre if we consider his conviction that critical social analysis needs to be both empirically grounded and theoretically informed as a central normative position. Indeed, the whole of Bourdieu's famous critique of scholastic thought was motivated by the view that it is the *skholè* – a situation characterised by freedom from necessity – which leads scholastic thinkers to produce scholastic thought, that is, thought which fails to reflect upon the social conditions of its own existence (Bourdieu, 1997: 9, 15, 22, 24, 131, and 143; Susen, 2007: 158–167). According to Bourdieu, scholastic thinkers 'remain trapped in the scholastic dilemma of determinism and freedom' (1997: 131) because their privileged position in the social space permits them to ignore the homological intertwinement of field and habitus. We can look at Bourdieu's fruitful synthesis of the works of Marx, Durkheim, and Weber (chapters 2–5) and his concern with classical sociological categories such as 'social struggle', 'social facts', and 'social understanding'. We can explore Bourdieu's engagement with modern German social philosophy – for instance, with regard to the works of Nietzsche, Elias, Adorno, and Honneth (chapters 6–9) – and his sociological development of concepts such as 'taste', 'power', 'culture', and 'recognition'. And, of course, we can assess the usefulness of Bourdieu's oeuvre for making sense of key issues in the contemporary social sciences, in particular with regard to the sociological significance of religion, language, political change, public debate, and economic transformations (chapters 10–15). All of these themes, which are thoroughly examined in the present volume, were studied by Bourdieu through a fruitful combination of solid empirical data and sophisticated theoretical frameworks. For, as he insisted, only insofar as we do justice to the fact that critical social research needs to be both empirically grounded and theoretically informed can we claim to produce social-scientific knowledge.

Fifth, the contributions to this volume illustrate – some directly, some indirectly – that Bourdieu's sociology is *politically committed*. From a Bourdieusian standpoint, however, sociology can only be politically committed if it is devoted to both providing a critical analysis of social relations and having a transformative impact upon the daily reproduction of power relations. To a greater or lesser extent, Bourdieu's normative commitment to the political nature of reflexive sociology is reflected in each of the chapters of this volume. We shall conclude this Introduction by briefly elaborating upon this political dimension and its relevance to the arguments developed in the following contributions.

In the introductory chapter, Joas and Knöbl remind us of the importance of Bourdieu's experiences in Algeria during a formative time in which Bourdieu gained direct access to the social and political complexities of Algerian colonial and postcolonial realities. In the second chapter, Fowler elegantly shows that, given that he was committed to some of the key presuppositions of historical materialism, Bourdieu not only borrowed powerful conceptual tools and useful methodological frameworks from Marxist social analysis, but he also recognised that the critical study of power relations is pointless if it is not aimed at the emancipatory transformation of social relations. In the third chapter, Karsenti argues, in accordance with both Marx and Bourdieu, that the 'game of theory' is worth nothing if it fails to engage with the 'reality of practice' and that, due to our bodily immersion in a contradictory society, there is no such thing as an innocent form of subjectivity. In the fourth chapter, Wacquant, on the basis of a comparative analysis of the works of Durkheim and Bourdieu, contends that the existence of seemingly ineluctable social facts cannot be dissociated from the existence of relatively arbitrary social norms: the social conditions that appear independent of our will are historically specific arrangements that can and often have to be changed through our will. This position ties in with the thematic focus of the fifth chapter: when interviewed by Schultheis and Pfeuffer, Bourdieu asserts that society can be regarded as an ensemble of relatively arbitrary relations between people and groups of people, whose existence is necessarily shaped by the spatiotemporal specificity of a given cultural reality and by field-differentiated codes of practical legitimacy.

The sixth chapter, written by Rahkonen, seems to suggest that, ultimately, Nietzsche's *Wille zur Macht* and Bourdieu's *Wille zum Geschmack* together form the socio-ontological foundation of our *Wille zur Welt*. Paulle, van Heerikhuizen, and Emirbayer demonstrate in the seventh chapter that if our lives are contingent upon the homological interplay between habitus and field, and therefore upon a constant struggle over different forms of capital, the taken-for-grantedness of social relations is necessarily impregnated with the interest-ladenness of power relations. In the eighth chapter, Susen offers a comparative analysis of Adorno's critique of the culture industry and Bourdieu's account of the cultural economy; the obvious political challenge to be confronted in light of the deep pessimism that permeates both Adornean and Bourdieusian thought is to explore the extent to which there is room for empowering forms of culture within disempowering forms of society. In the ninth chapter, Basaure invites us to take on some difficult tasks from which emancipatory forms of sociology cannot hide away – namely the tasks of giving a voice to the voiceless, of making the unrecognised recognisable, and of shedding light on individual and collective experiences of suffering and disrespect caused by a lack of social recognition and access to social resources.

In the tenth chapter, Turner illustrates that, given that religious practices and belief systems have far from disappeared in modern society, critical sociologists are obliged to reflect upon the normative relationship between secular and religious modes of relating to and making sense of the world. In the eleventh chapter, Frère rightly insists that even if we conceive of people primarily as 'homological actors', who are relatively determined by the various positions they occupy in different social spaces, we need to account for the fact that humans have the capacity to invent and reinvent their place in the world by constantly working and acting upon it. Taking into consideration that, as Kögler elucidates in the twelfth chapter, linguistic interactions are always asymmetrically structured because they are inevitably permeated by power relations, a critical sociology of language needs to explore the extent to which linguistically articulated claims to epistemic validity represent relationally constituted claims to social legitimacy. From Robbins's textual analysis, developed in the thirteenth chapter, it becomes clear that, for Bourdieu, social science and political action have to go hand in hand: a *raisonnement sociologique* that compels us to confront the reality of social domination is, at the same time, a *raisonnement politique* that invites us to contemplate the possibility of social emancipation. As Sintomer explains in the fourteenth chapter, Bourdieu's concept of critical reason is ultimately a form of political reason: just as research without theory is blind and theory without research is empty, politics without critique is edgeless and critique without politics is pointless. Finally, as Adkins convincingly argues in the fifteenth chapter, in Bourdieu's writings we can find powerful resources to make sense not only of the current economic crisis but also of the silent shift from the modern paradigm 'time is money' to the late modern dictum 'money is time': the temporalisation of practice is intimately interrelated with the politicisation of time and, hence, with the restructuring of social life.

We have taken the possibly unusual step of providing an Afterword, which offers the reader a synoptic view of the chapters. We have included this Afterword in part because the chapters, while addressing a common theme, are both diverse and complex. The Afterword contains a clear and concise summary of the overall objectives of this collection. Readers may want to consult both the Introduction and the Afterword before launching into the core of this volume.

Acknowledgements

We are deeply grateful to Elena Knox for her detailed and useful comments on an earlier version of this Introduction.

References

Alexander, Jeffrey C. (2006) *The Civil Sphere*, Oxford: Oxford University Press.

Althusser, Louis (1969 [1965]) *For Marx*, trans. Ben Brewster, Harmondsworth, Middlesex: Penguin.

Aron, Raymond (2002) *Le marxisme de Marx*, Paris: Fallois.

Aron, Raymond, Richard Howard and Helen Weaver (1965) *Main Currents in Sociological Thought*, trans. Richard Howard and Helen Weaver, London: Weidenfeld & Nicolson.

Back, Les, Azzedine Haddour and Nirmal Puwar (eds.) (2009) *The Sociological Review – Special Issue: Post-Colonial Bourdieu* 57(3).

Bottomore, T. B. (1965) *Classes in Modern Society*, London: Allen & Unwin.

Boudon, Raymond (1980 [1971]) *The Crisis in Sociology: Problems of Sociological Epistemology*, trans. Howard H. Davis, New York: Columbia University Press.

Bourdieu, Pierre (1975) 'L'ontologie politique de Martin Heidegger', *Actes de la recherche en sciences sociales* 5–6: 109–156.

Bourdieu, Pierre (1976) 'Le champ scientifique', *Actes de la recherche en sciences sociales* 8–9 [2–3]: 88–104.

Bourdieu, Pierre (1977 [1972]) *Outline of a Theory of Practice*, trans. Richard Nice, Cambridge: Cambridge University Press.

Bourdieu, Pierre (1984 [1979]) *Distinction: A Social Critique of the Judgement of Taste*, trans. Richard Nice, Cambridge, Mass.: Harvard University Press.

Bourdieu, Pierre (1991 [1988]) *The Political Ontology of Martin Heidegger*, trans. Peter Collier, Cambridge: Polity Press.

Bourdieu, Pierre and Terry Eagleton (1992) 'Doxa and Common Life', *New Left Review* 191: 111–121.

Bourdieu, Pierre (1994) *Raisons pratiques. Sur la théorie de l'action*, Paris: Seuil.

Bourdieu, Pierre (1997) *Méditations pascaliennes*, Paris: Seuil.

Bourdieu, Pierre (1999 [1993]) *The Weight of the World: Social Suffering in Contemporary Society*, trans. Priscilla Parkhurst Ferguson [et al.], Cambridge: Polity Press.

Bourdieu, Pierre (2000) 'Mit Weber gegen Weber: Pierre Bourdieu im Gespräch', in Pierre Bourdieu, *Das religiöse Feld. Texte zur Ökonomie des Heilsgeschehens*, herausgegeben von Franz Schultheis, Andreas Pfeuffer und Stephan Egger, übersetzt von Stephan Egger, Konstanz: Universitätsverlag Konstanz, pp. 111–129.

Bourdieu, Pierre (2000 [1997]) *Pascalian Meditations*, trans. Richard Nice, Cambridge: Polity Press.

Bourdieu, Pierre (2001) *'Si le monde social m'est supportable, c'est parce que je peux m'indigner'. Entretien avec Antoine Spire*, Paris: Éditions de l'Aube.

Bourdieu, Pierre and Jean-Claude Passeron (1979 [1964]) *The Inheritors: French Students and their Relation to Culture*, trans. Richard Nice, Chicago: University of Chicago Press.

Bourdieu, Pierre and Jean-Claude Passeron (1990 [1970]) *Reproduction in Education, Society and Culture*, trans. Richard Nice, 2nd Edition, London: Sage.

Bourdieu, Pierre and Loïc Wacquant (1992) *An Invitation to Reflexive Sociology*, Cambridge: Polity Press.

Bourricaud, François (1981 [1977]) *The Sociology of Talcott Parsons*, trans. Arthur Goldhammer, Chicago: University of Chicago Press.

Calhoun, Craig, Edward LiPuma and Moishe Postone (eds.) (1993) *Bourdieu: Critical Perspectives*, Chicago: University of Chicago Press.

Coser, Lewis A. (1971) *Masters of Sociological Thought: Ideas in Historical and Social Context*, New York: Harcourt Brace Jovanovich.

Crozier, Michel (1964 [1963]) *The Bureaucratic Phenomenon*, London: Tavistock.

Dahrendorf, Ralf (1959) *Class and Class Conflict in Industrial Society*, London: Routledge & Kegan Paul.

Dawe, Alan (1970) 'The Two Sociologies', *The British Journal of Sociology* 21(2): 207–218.

Eribon, Didier (1992 [1989]) *Michel Foucault*, trans. Betsy Wing, London: Faber.

Foucault, Michel (1980) *Power/Knowledge: Selected Interviews and Other Writings 1972–1977*, edited by Colin Gordon, translated by Colin Gordon [et al.], Brighton: Harvester Press.

Hacking, Ian (2004) 'Science de la science chez Pierre Bourdieu', in Jacques Bouveresse and Daniel Roche (eds.) *La liberté par la connaissance: Pierre Bourdieu (1930–2002)*, Paris: Collège de France, Odile Jacob, pp. 147–162.

Holton, Robert John and Bryan S. Turner (1986) *Talcott Parsons on Economy and Society*, London: Routledge & Kegan Paul.

Lerner, Daniel (1958) *The Passing of Traditional Society: Modernizing the Middle East*, with the collaboration of Lucille W. Pevsner and an introduction by David Riesman, Glencoe, Ill.: Free Press.

Lipset, Seymour Martin (1963) *The First New Nation: The United States in Historical and Comparative Perspective*, New York: Basic Books.

Lockwood, David (1964) 'Social Integration and System Integration', in George K. Zollschan and Walter Hirsch (eds.) *Explorations in Social Change*, London: Routledge & Kegan Paul, pp. 244–257.

Lockwood, David (1992) *Solidarity and Schism: 'The Problem of Disorder' in Durkheimian and Marxist Sociology*, Oxford: Clarendon Press.

Luxon, Nancy (2008) 'Ethics and Subjectivity: Practices of Self-Governance in the Late Lectures of Michel Foucault', *Political Theory* 36(3): 377–402.

Marx, Karl (2000/1977 [1845]) 'Theses on Feuerbach', in David McLellan (ed.) *Karl Marx: Selected Writings*, 2nd Edition, Oxford: Oxford University Press, pp. 171–174.

Masson, Philippe (2008) *Faire de la sociologie. Les grandes enquêtes françaises depuis 1945*. Paris: La Découverte.

Parsons, Talcott (1951) *The Social System*, London: Routledge & Kegan Paul.

Poulantzas, Nicos (1978 [1978]) *State, Power, Socialism*, trans. Patrick Camiller, London: NLB.

Rex, John (1961) *Key Problems of Sociological Theory*, London: Routledge & Kegan Paul.

Rojek, Chris (2004) 'An Anatomy of the Leicester School of Sociology: An Interview with Eric Dunning', *Journal of Classical Sociology* 4(3): 337–359.

Shilling, Chris (2004) 'Physical Capital and Situated Action: A New Direction for Corporeal Sociology', *British Journal of Sociology of Education* 25(4): 473–487.

Shusterman, Richard (1992) *Pragmatist Aesthetics: Living Beauty, Rethinking Art*, Oxford: Blackwell.

Shusterman, Richard (ed.) (1999) *Bourdieu: A Critical Reader*, Oxford: Blackwell.

Sica, Alan and Stephen P. Turner (2005) *The Disobedient Generation: Social Theorists in the Sixties*, Chicago: University of Chicago Press.

Susen, Simon (2007) *The Foundations of the Social: Between Critical Theory and Reflexive Sociology*, Oxford: Bardwell Press.

Turner, Bryan S. (1996) *The Body and Society*, London: Sage.

Weber, Max (2001/1930 [1904–05]) *The Protestant Ethic and the Spirit of Capitalism*, trans. Talcott Parsons, London: Routledge.

CHAPTER ONE

Between Structuralism and Theory of Practice: The Cultural Sociology of Pierre Bourdieu[1]

Hans Joas and Wolfgang Knöbl
Translated by Alex Skinner[2]

Bourdieu's work was deeply moulded by the national intellectual milieu in which it developed, that of France in the late 1940s and 1950s, a milieu characterised by disputes between phenomenologists and structuralists. But it is not this national and cultural dimension that distinguishes Bourdieu's writings from those of other 'grand theorists'. Habermas and Giddens, for example, owed as much to the academic or political context of their home countries. What set Bourdieu's approach apart from that of his German and British 'rivals' was a significantly stronger linkage of theoretical and empirical knowledge. Bourdieu was first and foremost an empirical sociologist, that is, a sociologist who developed and constantly refined his theoretical concepts on the basis of his empirical work – with all the advantages and disadvantages that theoretical production of this kind entails. We shall have more to say about this later. Bourdieu is thus to be understood primarily not as a theorist but as a cultural sociologist who systematically stimulated the theoretical debate through his empirical work.

Pierre Bourdieu was born in 1930 and is therefore of the same generation as Habermas and Luhmann. The fact that Bourdieu came from a modest background and grew up in the depths of provincial France is extremely important to understanding his work. Bourdieu himself repeatedly emphasised the importance of his origins: 'I spent most of my youth in a tiny and remote village of Southwestern France [...]. And I could meet the demands of schooling only by renouncing many of my primary experiences and acquisitions, and not only a certain accent [...]' (Bourdieu and Wacquant, 1992: 204). Despite these clearly unfavourable beginnings, Bourdieu was to succeed in gaining entry to the leading educational institutions in France, a fact of which many people became aware when he was elected to the famous

Collège de France in 1982. This classic case of climbing the social and career ladder, the fact that Bourdieu had no privileged educational background to draw on, helped legitimise his pitiless take on the French education and university system and on intellectuals in general – a group he investigated in numerous studies over the course of his career. He thus made use of the classical sociological notion of the outsider – the 'marginal man' – in order to lay claim to special and, above all, critical insights into the functioning of 'normal' society.

> In France, to come from a distant province, to be born south of the Loire, endows you with a number of properties that are not without parallel in the colonial situation. It gives you a sort of objective and subjective externality and puts you in a particular relation to the central institutions of French society and therefore to the intellectual institution. There are subtle (and not so subtle) forms of social racism that cannot but make you perceptive [...]. (Bourdieu and Wacquant, 1992: 209)

Yet, Bourdieu's path to the production of a sociology of French cultural institutions and to sociology more generally was anything but straightforward or self-evident – a state of affairs with which we are familiar from the biographies of other major social theorists, such as Habermas and Luhmann, who also took some time to settle on a career in sociology. A highly gifted student, Bourdieu studied at the *École Normale Superieure* in Paris, where he took philosophy – the most prestigious subject in the French disciplinary canon. He initially seems to have wanted to concentrate on this subject, given that he subsequently worked as a philosophy teacher in provincial France for a brief period, as is usual for those who go on to have an academic career in the humanities in France. But Bourdieu was increasingly disappointed by philosophy and developed an ever-greater interest in anthropology, so that he ultimately became a self-taught, empirically oriented, anthropologist, and later sociologist. This process of turning away from philosophy and towards anthropology and sociology was partly bound up with Lévi-Strauss's concurrent rise to prominence. With its claim to a strictly scientific approach, structuralist anthropology began to challenge philosophy's traditional pre-eminence within the disciplinary canon. Bourdieu was drawn towards this highly promising and up-and-coming subject. Structuralism's anti-philosophical tone held much appeal for him (see Joas and Knöbl, 2009 [2004]: 339–370) and often appeared in his own work – for example, when he takes up arms against philosophy's purely theoretical rationality.

It is important, however, to be aware of the fact that Bourdieu's path to anthropology and sociology was also determined by external factors: he was stationed in Algeria during the second half of the 1950s while completing his military service. There, in the undoubtedly very difficult circumstances of the war of independence, he gathered data for his first book, a sociology of Algeria (Bourdieu, 1958) – in which he came to terms intellectually with his experiences in this French colony (see Robbins, 1991: 10 ff.). In this setting, he also carried out field research among the Kabyle, a Berber people of northern Algeria, which led to the publication of a number of anthropological monographs and essays that, in collected and eventually expanded form, appeared as a book entitled *Outline of a Theory of Practice* (1977 [1972]). This work, published in French in 1972, and then expanded greatly for the English (and German) translation, became tremendously famous and influential because Bourdieu departed from the structuralism of Lévi-Strauss, in whose footsteps he had originally followed, and developed his own set of concepts, which held out the promise of a genuine theoretical synthesis.

At around the same time as these basically anthropological studies, Bourdieu began to utilise the theoretical insights they contained to subject *French* society to sociological analysis – particularly its cultural, educational and class system. With respect to the socially critical thrust of his writings, the work of Marx was, in many ways, his model and touchstone, and a large number of essays appeared in the 1960s which were later translated into English – for example, in *Photography: A Middle-Brow Art* (1990 [1965]). In these studies, Bourdieu and his co-authors attempt to describe the perception of art and culture, which varies so greatly from one class to another, and to elucidate how class struggle involves contrasting ways of appropriating art and culture. Classes set themselves apart by means of a very different understanding of art and culture and thus reproduce, more or less unintentionally, the class structures of (French) society. Bourdieu elaborated this thesis in a particularly spectacular way in perhaps his most famous work of cultural sociology, *La distinction. Critique sociale du jugement* (English title: *Distinction: A Social Critique of the Judgement of Taste*, 1984 [1979]).

Bourdieu's subsequent publications merely complemented or completed a theoretical research orientation set at an early stage. In terms of *cultural sociology*, two major studies have become particularly important: *Homo Academicus* (1988 [1984]), an analysis of the French university system, particularly the crisis it faced towards the end of the 1960s, and *Les règles de l'art* (English title: *The Rules of Art*, 1996 [1992]), a historical and sociological study of the development of an autonomous art scene in France in the second half of the nineteenth century. Alongside these works, Bourdieu also published a steady flow of writings that fleshed out his *theoretical* ambitions, *Le sens pratique* (English title: *The Logic of Practice*, 1990 [1980]) and *Meditations pascaliennes* (English title: *Pascalian Meditations*, 2000 [1997]) being the key texts in this regard. But even in these basically theoretical studies, it is fair to say that he expands on the conceptual apparatus presented in *Outline of a Theory of Practice* (1977 [1972]) only to a limited degree; above all, he defends it against criticisms. It is almost impossible, however, to discern any theoretical *development* here. Bourdieu's theory thus distinguishes itself from that of other grand theorists. To deploy the language of the building trade, not only the foundation walls, but also the overall structure and even the roof were in place very quickly, while the later theoretical work related solely to the facade and décor. Ever since it was developed in the 1960s, his theory has thus remained basically the same.

It was solely Bourdieu's identity or role that seemed to change significantly over the course of time. While Bourdieu was always politically active on the left, this generally took a less spectacular form than in the case of other French intellectuals, occurring away from the light of day and basically unnoticed by most people. The fact that he pursued such activities away from the limelight was partly bound up with his frequently expressed critique of high-profile French intellectuals à la Jean-Paul Sartre, who frequently overshot the bounds of their specialisms and claimed a universal competence and public responsibility to which they were scarcely entitled. Yet, Bourdieu abandoned such restraint from the 1990s (at the latest) until his death in 2002. He increasingly emerged as a symbolic figure for critics of globalisation in this period and was almost automatically made the kind of major intellectual he had never wished to be. His book, *La Misère du Monde* (English title: *The Weight of the World: Social Suffering in Contemporary Society*, 1999 [1993]) was conceived as a kind of empirical demonstration of the negative effects of globalisation in different spheres of life and cultures. One has to give Bourdieu credit for having avoided a purely pamphleteering role to the very last. He was too strongly oriented towards empirical research, and his Durkheim-like ambition to strengthen the position of sociology within the disciplinary canon of France and to set it apart from other subjects – especially philosophy and social philosophy – was too strong for him to take on such a role. Bourdieu, so aware of power, had an ongoing interest in developing the kind of *empirical* sociological research which he favoured at an institutional level, as demonstrated in his role as editor of the journal *Actes de la recherche en sciences sociales*, which he founded in 1975 and which was accessible to a broad readership (on Bourdieu's intellectual biography, see the interview in Bourdieu, 1990 [1987]: 3–33).

Our account of Bourdieusian theory will proceed as follows. First, we shall take a closer look at his early work, *Outline of a Theory of Practice* (1977 [1972]), which is of particular theoretical relevance as it features the basic elements of his arguments. Though we shall frequently draw on explanations and more precise formulations from subsequent works, our key aim is to lay bare why, and with the help of which ideas, Bourdieu tackled certain problems at a relatively early stage (1). Always bearing this early work in mind, and while presenting Bourdieu's key concepts, we shall then critically examine the model of action advocated by Bourdieu and the problems it entails (2). We then go on to present the overall architecture of Bourdieusian theory and identify the nodal points within it (3) before presenting, as vividly and as briefly as possible, some characteristic aspects of Bourdieu's works of cultural sociology (4) and shedding light on the impact of his work (5).

1. We therefore begin with the early study of Kabyle society mentioned above, whose programmatic title requires explication: *Outline of a Theory of Practice* (1977 [1972]). Bourdieu – as intimated in our remarks on his intellectual biography – was caught up in the enthusiasm for Lévi-Straussian anthropology in the 1950s and began his anthropological research in Kabylia by focusing on key structuralist topics. Studies of kinship patterns, marriage behaviour and mythology were to provide insights into the logic of the processes occurring within this society and into the way in which it continually reproduces itself on the basis of certain rules. Yet, Bourdieu's research had unexpected results. Above all, these did not confirm the structuralist premise of the constancy of rules (of marriage, exchange, communication) in line with which people supposedly always act. Rather, Bourdieu concluded that actors either play rules off against each other more or less as they see fit, so that one can scarcely refer to the *following* of rules, or follow them only in order to disguise concrete interests. This is particularly apparent in the first chapter of the book, in which Bourdieu scrutinises the phenomenon of 'honour'. In Kabyle society – and in other places as well, of course – honour plays a very important role; it seems impossible to link it with base economic interests because 'honourable behaviour' is directly opposed to action oriented towards profit. A man is honourable only if he is *not* greedy and *cannot* be bought. And, in Kabyle society, the rituals by means of which one demonstrates that one's actions are honourable and that one is an honourable person are particularly pronounced. Bourdieu, however, demonstrates that these rituals of honour often merely mask (profit-related) interests; the actors see this link between honour and interests – or at least unconsciously produce it – and people uphold rituals of honour *because* they enable them to promote their interests.

> The ritual of the ceremony of presenting the bridewealth is the occasion for a total confrontation between the two groups, in which the economic stakes are no more than an index and pretext. To demand a large payment for one's daughter, or to pay a large sum to marry off one's son, is in either case to assert one's prestige, and thereby to acquire prestige [...]. By a sort of inverted haggling, disguised under the appearance of ordinary bargaining, the two groups tacitly agree to step up the amount of the payment by successive bids, because they have a common interest in raising this indisputable index of the symbolic value of their

> products on the matrimonial exchange market. And no feat is more highly praised than the prowess of the bride's father who, after vigorous bargaining has been concluded, solemnly returns a large share of the sum received. The greater the proportion returned, the greater the honour accruing from it, as if, in crowning the transaction with an act of generosity, the intention was to make an exchange of honour out of bargaining which could be so overtly keen only because the pursuit of maximum material profit was masked under the contests of honour and the pursuit of maximum symbolic profit. (Bourdieu, 1977 [1972]: 56)

Rituals of honour thus conceal very tangible interests, which are overlooked if one merely describes the logic of the rules, as do structuralist anthropologists. What is more, for precisely this reason, rules are by no means as rigid and have nothing like the determining effect on behaviour that orthodox structuralist authors assume. As Bourdieu observed, rules that do not tally with actors' interests are often broken, leading him to conclude that an element of 'unpredictability' is clearly inherent in human action with respect to rules and patterns, rituals and regulations (Bourdieu, 1977 [1972]: 9). This places a question mark over the entire structuralist terminology of rules and its underlying premises. Bourdieu puts forward the counter-argument that the following of rules is always associated with an element of conflict. If rules are not, in fact, ignored entirely – which certainly occurs at times – every rule-based act of exchange, every rule-based conversation, every rule-based marriage must *also* at least protect or enforce the interests of those involved or improve the social position of the parties to interaction. Rules are thus consciously instrumentalised by actors:

> Every exchange contains a more or less dissimulated challenge, and the logic of challenge and riposte is but the limit towards which *every act of communication* tends. Generous exchange tends towards overwhelming generosity; the greatest gift is at the same time the gift most likely to throw its recipient into dishonour by prohibiting any counter-gift. To reduce to the function of communication – albeit by the transfer of borrowed concepts – phenomena such as the dialectic of challenge and riposte and, more generally, the exchange of gifts, words, or women, is to ignore the structural ambivalence which predisposes them to fulfil a political function of domination in and through performance of the communication function. (Bourdieu, 1977 [1972]: 14, emphasis in original)

Bourdieu accuses structuralism of having failed entirely to take account of how the action undertaken by social actors is related to interests in favour of a highly idealised description of rules and cultural patterns. People, according to Bourdieu, can manipulate rules and patterns; they are not merely the passive objects of social classification systems. Because actors pursue their interests, we must assume that there is always a difference between the 'official' and the 'regular' (Bourdieu, 1977 [1972]: 38) and between (theoretically) construed models and the *practice* of actors. It may be very helpful to identify social rules, but it is by no means sufficient if we wish to get at actors' *practice*:

> The logical relationships constructed by the anthropologist are opposed to 'practical' relationships – practical because continuously practised, kept up, and cultivated – in the same way as the geometrical space of a map, an imaginary representation of all theoretically possible roads and routes, is opposed to the network of beaten tracks, of paths made ever more practicable by constant use. (Bourdieu, 1977 [1972]: 37)

Ultimately, this is a profound criticism of structuralism (as the title *Outline of a Theory of Practice* indicates), particularly given that Bourdieu also resists applying the Saussurian paradigm of linguistic analysis – so inspiring for structuralists – to the social world (Bourdieu, 1977 [1972]: 24). In this way, he casts doubt on the theoretical and empirical fruitfulness of the structuralist anthropology and sociology of Lévi-Strauss.

> [The only way] the Saussurian construction [...] could constitute the structural properties of the message was (simply by positing an indifferent sender and receiver) to neglect the functional properties the message derives from its *use* in a determinate situation and, more precisely, in a socially structured interaction. As soon as one moves from the structure of language to the functions it fulfils, that is, to the uses agents actually make of it, one sees that mere knowledge of the *code* gives only very imperfect mastery of the linguistic interactions really taking place. (Bourdieu, 1977 [1972]: 25, emphasis in original)

Examining the actual practice characteristic of the 'objects of investigation' more closely, according to Bourdieu, reveals how inappropriate or insufficient structuralist analysis is. To put it in slightly more abstract terms, Bourdieu introduces elements of action theory into his originally structuralist theoretical framework – namely, the idea of conduct at variance with the rules and related to interests. This was to change the structuralist paradigm markedly. As he was to state later in another publication, he objected in particular to the 'strange philosophy of action' inherent in structuralism, which 'made the agent disappear by reducing it to the role of supporter or bearer of the structure' (Bourdieu, 1996 [1992]: 179).

Yet, Bourdieu does not break entirely with structuralism. He always remained attached to structuralist thinking, as evident in the fact that he termed his own approach 'genetic' or 'constructivist structuralism' (see, for example, Bourdieu, 1990 [1987]: 123). The exact nature of this attachment, however, was to become clear only as his oeuvre developed. This is, of course, due to the predominantly empirical orientation of Bourdieu's work, which sometimes makes it appear unnecessary for him to locate and distinguish his own concepts with respect to other theoretical approaches. It is only in his next major theoretical work (Bourdieu, 1990 [1980]: 4) that we find clear evidence of how structuralism 'influenced' him, when, for instance, he praises it for the 'introduction into the social sciences of [...] the relational mode of thought' and having broken with 'the substantialist mode of thought'. Bourdieu's thought leans heavily on structuralism (and, at times, also on functionalism). Thus, for him, it is not the individual actor that is the key analytical lodestone; rather, it is the *relations* between actors or the relations between the positions within a system – that is, in Bourdieusian terms, the positions within a 'field' – which are crucial. 'Fields', to cite a definition provided by Bourdieu, are:

> structured spaces of positions (or posts) whose properties depend on their position within these spaces and which can be analyzed independently of the characteristics of their occupants (which are partly determined by them). There are general laws of fields: fields as different as the field of politics, the field of philosophy or the field of religion have invariant laws of functioning [...]. Whenever one studies a new field, whether it be the field of philology in the nineteenth century, contemporary fashion, or religion in the Middle Ages, one discovers specific properties that are peculiar to that field, at the same time as one pushes forward our knowledge of the universal mechanisms of fields [...]. (Bourdieu, 1993 [1980]: 72)

According to Bourdieu, it is not useful to analyse the behaviour of individual actors in isolation, as many theorists of action do without further reflection, unless one also determines an actor's position within such a 'field', in which action becomes meaningful in the first place. 'Fields' offer options for action, but only *certain* options, which simply means that other options for action are excluded and that the actors are subject to constraints. The logic of action within the religious field is necessarily different from, for example, that in the artistic field because the constraints are different. These constraints and boundaries influence how prone actors – prophets and the faithful, artists and the viewing public – are to take action. This is why it is inevitably quite unproductive to restrict oneself to examining the biography of an actor, prophet, artist or author in order to explain religious or artistic phenomena (Bourdieu, 2000 [1997]: 115 ff.).

In light of this, Bourdieu consciously refrains from referring to 'subjects'; at most, he talks of actors. For him, actors are 'eminently active and acting' – a fact overlooked by structuralism. Bourdieu, however, believes that Foucault's provocative structuralist notion of the 'looming end of man' or the 'death of the subject' is justified in as much as this was merely a way of stating the (structuralist) insight into the crucial significance of relations and relationships (within fields) and expressed the well-founded rejection of the idea, found in the work of Sartre and many other philosophers and sociologists, of a self-creating and autonomous subject (see the foreword to Bourdieu, 1998 [1994]: viii ff.). Time and again, Bourdieu was to defend this structuralist 'insight' with great vehemence; it was also the basis of his attacks on certain sociological or philosophical currents, which, as he puts it, give sustenance to the 'biographical illusion'. Bourdieu mercilessly assails any notion that people create their own biography and that life is a whole, arising, as it were, from the subject's earliest endeavours and unfolding over the course of their life. He repeatedly points to the fact that the 'meaning and the social value of biographical events' are not constituted on the basis of the subject, but on the basis of actors' 'placements' and 'displacements' within a social space, which lends biographical events their meaning in the first place – the meaning which they ultimately take on for the actor (Bourdieu, 1996 [1992]: 258 ff.; see also Bourdieu, 1998 [1994]: 75 ff.). Thus, rather than 'subjects', people are actors in a field by which they are profoundly moulded.

Yet, we wish to avoid getting ahead of ourselves in our discussion of Bourdieu's work. Let us turn once again to his early book, *Outline of a Theory of Practice* (1977 [1972]). Although this text is rather wordy in places, and Bourdieu was to provide a clearer explanation of his position only at a later stage, it undoubtedly sets out his synthetic aspirations. For Bourdieu made it absolutely clear that all action-theoretical perspectives are insufficient *in isolation*: neither symbolic interactionism nor phenomenological approaches within sociology, such as ethnomethodology, are capable of deciphering the really interesting sociological facts. For him, these approaches are too quick to adopt the actor's perspective; they take on his or her *naïve* view of the givenness of the world, forgetting how crucial are *actors' positions in relation to one another* and to the field within which they move. To reinforce his 'objectivist' stance, Bourdieu borrows not only from structuralism, which seems to him overly idealistic in certain respects. He also draws on Marx's 'concrete' materialism when he points, for example, to the conditions of production on the basis of which marriage rituals take place and without which they cannot be understood:

> It is not sufficient to ridicule the more naïve forms of functionalism in order to have done with the question of the practical functions of practice. It is clear that a universal definition of the functions of marriage as an operation intended to ensure the biological reproduction of the group, in accordance with forms approved by the group, in no way explains Kabyle marriage ritual.

> But, contrary to appearances, scarcely more understanding is derived from a structural analysis which ignores the specific functions of ritual practices and fails to inquire into the *economic and social conditions of the production* of the dispositions generating both these practices and also the collective definition of the practical functions in whose service they function. (Bourdieu, 1977 [1972]: 115, emphasis in original)

Critical of the theory of action he describes as subjectivist, Bourdieu ultimately asserts the *pre-eminence of an objectivist form of analysis* in which the structures of a social field are determined *by the sociological observer* – structures that impose constraints on actors, of which they themselves are generally unaware. Loïc Wacquant, a sociologist closely associated with Bourdieu, has put this in the following way, drawing a comparison between the 'objectivism' of the Durkheimian method of analysis and that of Bourdieu:

> Application of Durkheim's first principle of the 'sociological method', the systematic rejection of preconceptions, must come before analysis of the practical apprehension of the world from the subjective standpoint. For the viewpoints of agents will vary systematically with the point they occupy in objective social space. (Bourdieu and Wacquant, 1992: 11)

At the same time, however, Bourdieu regards (objectivist) structuralism on its own as insufficient, just as he does the equally objectivist functionalism, which ignores actors' perspectives. His sociological approach is intended to take full account of actors' power and capacity to act. This means, however, that Bourdieu wishes to sail – and, as he admits, cannot avoid sailing – between the Scylla of 'phenomenology' or 'subjectivism' and the Charybdis of 'objectivism'. For him, all of these forms of knowledge are deficient *in and of themselves*, which is why he wishes to develop a third mode of sociological understanding: his 'theory of practice' – an approach which goes beyond 'objectivism' and takes what actors do seriously. This can succeed only if it is shown that there are '*dialectical* relations between the objective structures [of fields] [...] and the structured dispositions [of actors]' (Bourdieu, 1977 [1972]: 3, emphasis in original; our insertions), that is, that action and structures determine one another through their interrelationship.

What Bourdieu is trying to do here is similar to arguments developed by Anthony Giddens (see Joas and Knöbl, 2009 [2004]: 281–307): Bourdieu also refers to 'structuring' or 'structuration'. Though this active conception never attained the systematic significance that it did in the work of Giddens (in part because Bourdieu was not a 'pure' social theorist and would probably have had no interest in developing the kind of social ontology present in the work of Giddens), it is nonetheless clear that Bourdieu is aiming to develop a stance which, in contrast to functionalists and structuralists, assumes that structures are 'made' and continuously reproduced by actors. In contrast to the ideas supposedly expounded by pure action theorists, however, he also emphasises the profound and causal impact of these structures.

2. So far, we have defined Bourdieu's theoretical approach only vaguely; his cited statements generally represent declarations of intention that underline the need for a theoretical synthesis rather than providing one. When Bourdieu states that he wishes to proceed neither 'phenomenologically' nor 'objectivistically', this is a purely negative definition of his project. The question arises as to *how* he incorporates the action-theoretical elements – the level of actors – into his approach and *how* he conceives, in concrete terms, the actions carried out by actors that drive the process of structuration, which, in turn, structures their actions. Here, there is an evident need to scrutinise Bourdieu's relationship with utilitarianism and its theory of action, particularly in light of the fact that Bourdieu refers so often to actors' 'interests'. And a number of interpreters (see especially Honneth, 1995 [1990]) have, in fact, expounded the thesis that Bourdieu's approach represents an amalgamation of structuralism and utilitarianism – a hypothesis or interpretation of his work which, considering how he reacted to it, certainly infuriated Bourdieu like no other and which he rejected vehemently on numerous occasions. In fact, Bourdieu emerges as a harsh critic of utilitarianism and the rational choice approach in many of his writings – and it is very hard to reconcile key aspects of his work with the basic assumptions of utilitarian or neo-utilitarian arguments. Nevertheless, this does not render superfluous the issue of whether other – perhaps equally important – aspects of his work are not redolent of utilitarianism. What then (see Joas and Knöbl, 2009 [2004]: 94–122) distinguishes Bourdieusian actors from their utilitarian counterparts?

We have already hinted at Bourdieu's *first* criticism of utilitarian thought. Since it places the isolated actor centre stage, it ignores the relational method of analysis, which – according to Bourdieu – is a prerequisite for attaining key insights into the functioning of the social world. This criticism is intended to apply not only to utilitarian theories, but, in principle, to all action-theoretical approaches. His *second* criticism is more specific: Bourdieu assails utilitarian approaches for systematically failing to address the issue of the origin of utility calculations and interests. 'Because it must postulate *ex nihilo* the existence of a universal, pre-constituted interest, rational action theory is thoroughly oblivious to the social genesis of historically varying forms of interest' (Bourdieu and Wacquant, 1992: 125). In addition, in his anthropological studies, Bourdieu showed again and again that the rational-economic calculations typical of modern Western capitalism are not found in other societies in this form.

Thus, according to Bourdieu, utilitarians turn a way of calculating actions that developed in modern capitalist societies into a human universal. More significant and more typical than this very well known criticism is Bourdieu's *third* objection, namely that utilitarians confuse the logic of theory with the logic of practice:

> The actor, as [this theory] construes him or her, is nothing other than the imaginary projection of the knowing subject (*sujet connaissant*) into the acting subject (*sujet agissant*), a sort of monster with the head of the thinker thinking his practice in reflexive and logical fashion mounted on the body of a man of action engaged in action. [...] Its 'imaginary anthropology' seeks to found action, whether 'economic' or not, on the intentional choice of an actor who is himself or herself economically and socially unconditioned. (Bourdieu and Wacquant, 1992: 123)

Here, Bourdieu first of all addresses the fact that utilitarianism has a false notion of real action processes, which are, for the most part, not entirely rational and reflexive. The kind of rationality and reflexivity that utilitarianism takes for granted here is possible only under particular circumstances – for example, in the sheltered world of science –, but is quite rare under normal conditions of practice. Action is indeed concerned with realising interests, but only rarely in the sense of the *conscious* pursuit of these interests. Thus, Bourdieu is advocating a stance similar to that of Anthony Giddens – one close to American pragmatism (see its concept of 'habit'). According to Bourdieu, action generally adheres to a practical logic, which is often shaped by routine requirements and which therefore has no need for the capacity for reflection demanded by rational choice theorists. Determined by socialisation, earlier experiences, etc., certain action dispositions are stamped onto our bodies; for the most part, these can be retrieved without conscious awareness and predetermine what form action takes. Bourdieu captures this idea with the term 'habitus', also to be found in the work of Husserl. A key term within his theory, he developed it at an early stage and was repeatedly to set himself apart from other theoretical schools with its help.

In his *Outline of a Theory of Practice*, he defines the habitus as a 'system of lasting, transposable dispositions which, integrating past experiences, functions at every moment as a *matrix of perceptions, appreciations, and actions* and makes possible the achievement of infinitely diversified tasks, thanks to analogical transfers of schemes permitting the solution of similarly shaped problems, and thanks to the unceasing corrections of the results obtained, dialectically produced by those results [...]' (Bourdieu, 1977 [1972]: 82–83, emphasis added).

This sounds complicated, but is in fact easy to explain. Bourdieu assumes that – from childhood onwards, in the family, school and world of work – we are taught certain schemata of thinking, perceiving and acting, which generally enable us to respond smoothly to different situations, to solve practical tasks, etc. Our physical movements, our tastes, our most banal interpretations of the world are formed at an early stage and then crucially determine our options for action.

> Through the habitus, the structure which has produced it governs practice, not by the process of a mechanical determination, but through the mediation of the orientations and limits it assigns to the habitus's operations of invention. As an acquired system of generative schemes objectively adjusted to the particular conditions in which it is constituted, the habitus engenders all the thoughts, all the perceptions, and all the actions consistent with those conditions, and not others. [...] Because the habitus is an endless capacity to engender products – thoughts, perceptions, expressions, actions – whose limits are set by the historically and socially situated conditions of its production, the conditioned and conditional freedom it secures is as remote from a creation of unpredictable novelty as it is from a simple mechanical reproduction of the initial conditionings. (Bourdieu, 1977 [1972]: 95)

As this quotation indicates, the concept of 'habitus' does not rule out a certain behavioural room for manoeuvre that enables conduct of a creative and innovative nature. On the other hand, however, we cannot step or break out of this habitual behaviour entirely, because the habitus is an aspect of our life story and identity. The attentive reader will discern how this links up with Bourdieu's investigations in cultural sociology and class theory. For it is clear that there is no one habitus in a society, but that *different* forms of perception, thinking and action are inculcated in different classes, through which these classes – and, above all, the differences between them – are constantly reproduced. We are, however, not yet concerned with this aspect. What is important here is that Bourdieu deploys the concept of habitus in the attempt to rid himself of the assumptions of utilitarianism and neo-utilitarianism, which are highly rationalistic and anchored in the philosophy of consciousness.

If, as we have seen, Bourdieu's explicit effort to set himself apart from utilitarianism is unambiguous and there are elements in his theoretical edifice which simply cannot be reconciled with utilitarian thought, why has he so often been accused of being 'close to utilitarianism' – and not only by malicious interpreters or cursory readers? The reason is that, while Bourdieu has certainly criticised thinking in terms of economic utility, *the nature of his criticism is incapable of establishing clear distance between his approach and utilitarian ones.*

Utilitarianism is fairly differentiated internally in that the so-called neo-utilitarians have done away with some of the assumptions of traditional utilitarianism (see Joas and Knöbl, 2009 [2004]: 94–122). Neo-utilitarians have, for example, rid themselves of the concept of utility, replacing it with the neutral term 'preferences', because only very few actions can be explained on the basis of purely economic calculations of utility. It is true that Bourdieu's critique of utilitarianism in its 'original' form goes further than this. The concept of habitus allows him to take leave, above all, of the model of the actor whose deeds are *consciously* rational. Yet, like *all* utilitarians, he continues to adhere to the notion that people (consciously or unconsciously) *always* pursue their interests – or preferences. According to Bourdieu, people are socialised into a 'field', where they learn how to behave appropriately; they understand the rules and internalise the 'strategies' indispensable to playing the game *successfully*. And the aim of these 'strategies' – a (utilitarian) concept used repeatedly by Bourdieu, although he is well aware of how problematic it is in view of his critique of utilitarianism (see Bourdieu and Wacquant, 1992: 128) – is to improve the player's position within a particular field or at least to uphold the status quo.

> It is not enough to say that the history of the field is the history of the struggle for a monopoly of the imposition of legitimate categories of perception and appreciation; it is in the very *struggle* that the history of the field is made; it is through struggles that it is temporalized. (Bourdieu, 1996 [1992]: 157, emphasis in original)

The battle over the realisation of actors' interests is thus a factor driving the historical change of fields. The strategies deployed in the field are not always concerned solely with attaining economic benefits – Bourdieu would roundly reject an economistic or primitive utilitarian perspective of this kind. The way he puts it is that the strategies are intended to procure those goods worth playing for within a particular field. This *may*, as in the field of the economy, be financial profit; in other fields, meanwhile, strategies are oriented towards enhancing one's reputation or honour (which cannot necessarily or immediately be converted into financial gain). The priority, however, will always be to pursue those *interests* relevant within a particular field – in competition with others.

There is no doubt that this line of argument entails a premise backed by typical utilitarian notions, which one can also detect within the context of conflict theory (see Joas and Knöbl, 2009 [2004]: 174–198) and to which

Bourdieu explicitly refers: 'the social world is the site of continual struggles to define what the social world is' (Bourdieu and Wacquant, 1992: 70). The concept of 'struggle' crops up in his work as frequently as that of 'strategy'; in much the same way as in utilitarianism and conflict theory, there is quite often a hint of cynical pleasure in the observation of the hypocritical behaviour of the objects of inquiry, whose subjective motives are by no means to be taken at face value:

> The most profitable strategies are usually those produced, without any calculation, and in the illusion of the most absolute 'sincerity', by a habitus objectively fitted to the objective structures. These strategies without strategic calculation procure an important secondary advantage for those who can scarcely be called their authors: the social approval accruing to apparent disinterestedness. (Bourdieu, 1990 [1980]: 292n.10)

This close connection between utilitarian, conflict theoretical and Marxian arguments is even more clearly apparent in another key Bourdieusian concept, that of 'capital', which complements or completes the concepts of 'field' and 'habitus'.

This concept of capital owes its existence to the following problem. Bourdieu must explain which goods the actors in the various fields struggle over, that is, what they are trying to achieve in deploying their various action strategies. He rejects the notion characteristic of (primitive) utilitarianism that social life is to be understood exclusively as a struggle over (economic) goods. For the same reason, he criticises Marxism, as it tends to focus on the struggle over economic goods, while ignoring or neglecting other forms of dispute (see, for example, Bourdieu, 1985 [1984]: 723).

Bourdieu now takes the logical step already taken in much the same way before him by conflict theorists. *His concern is to bring out how social struggles are about more than just financial utility and economic capital.* Yet, peculiarly enough, the way in which he proceeds – once again, in much the same way as does conflict theory (see Joas and Knöbl, 2009 [2004]: 174–198) – does not entail *a complete break* with utilitarian or Marxian notions. For in order to determine more precisely what is at stake in social struggles, Bourdieu deploys the term capital, which originates in 'bourgeois' and Marxian economics, but he extends its meaning and distinguishes between *different forms* of capital. In *Outline of a Theory of Practice*, Bourdieu criticises Marxism for having utterly neglected what he calls 'symbolic capital' – a consequence of its preoccupation with economic capital. Bourdieu, using language highly redolent of utilitarianism, puts it as follows: Marx only recognised immediate economic interests and these were all he allowed in his theoretical edifice, relegating all other types of interest to the sphere of the 'irrationality of feeling or passion' (Bourdieu, 1977 [1972]: 177). What one must do, however, is apply economic calculations to *all* goods (utilitarians and conflict theorists would say: 'to all resources'):

> [...] contrary to naively idyllic representations of 'pre-capitalist' societies (or of the 'cultural' sphere of capitalist societies), practice never ceases to conform to economic calculation even when it gives every appearance of disinterestedness by departing from the logic of interested calculation (in the narrow sense) and playing for stakes that are non-material and not easily quantified. (Bourdieu, 1977 [1972]: 177)

According to Bourdieu, Marxism entirely disregards the fact that actions which at first sight seem irrational because they are not geared towards immediate financial gain may be a means of acquiring substantial benefits *of other kinds*, which Bourdieu calls 'symbolic profits' and which prompt him to refer to 'symbolic capital' as well as economic capital. Certain deeds – such as generous gifts, extravagant behaviour, etc. – enable people to accrue all kinds of distinction; such deeds are a symbol of one's own (outstanding) position, power, prestige, etc., allowing one to distinguish oneself from those of lower rank. This symbolic form of capital is of relevance to the class hierarchy in a society in as much as it can be converted into 'real' capital in certain circumstances. The great prestige enjoyed by an individual, the good reputation of a particular family, the ostentatiously displayed wealth of a great man often furnishes people with opportunities to attain economic capital as well, in line with the motto: 'to everyone that has (symbolic) capital, (economic) capital shall be given'. Hence, there is nothing (economically) irrational about symbolic capital. Rather, the accumulation of symbolic capital is a clever way of safeguarding one's prospects of obtaining economic capital. This symbolic form of capital is a kind of credit, on the basis of which economic opportunities constantly arise. In this sense, Bourdieu can state that symbolic capital represents a 'transformed and thereby *disguised* form of physical "economic" capital' (Bourdieu, 1977 [1972]: 183, emphasis in original).

> It is thus by drawing up a *comprehensive balance-sheet* of symbolic profits, without forgetting the undifferentiatedness of the symbolic and material aspects of the patrimony, that it becomes possible to grasp the economic rationality of conduct which economism dismisses as absurd: the decision to buy a second pair of oxen after the harvest, on the grounds that they are needed for treading out the grain – which is a way of making it known the crop has been plentiful – only to have to sell them again for lack of fodder, before the autumn ploughing, when they would be technically necessary, seems economically aberrant only if one forgets

> all the material and symbolic profit accruing from this (albeit fictitious) addition to the family's symbolic capital in the late-summer period in which marriages are negotiated. The perfect rationality of this strategy of bluff lies in the fact that marriage is the occasion for an (in the widest sense) economic circulation which cannot be seen purely in terms of material goods [...]. (Bourdieu, 1977 [1972]: 181, emphasis in original)

Nevertheless, this great importance of symbolic capital is not, as this quotation referring to Kabyle society might lead us to presume, restricted to 'primitive' or pre-capitalist societies. It is true, as Bourdieu states, that pre-capitalist economies have a 'great need for symbolic violence' (Bourdieu, 1977 [1972]: 191) insofar as circumstances of unadulterated exploitation and great material inequalities exist and are always papered over symbolically and thus concealed (or, conversely, realised in brutal fashion by means of physical violence). This, Bourdieu suggests, arguing in a very similar way to Marx, has changed in capitalism in that its practice of domination no longer depends on symbolic concealment, but can be legitimised in a very different way (for example, through the ideology of fair exchange between goods, money and labour). This does not mean, however, that symbolic capital plays no role in modern societies. Nothing could be further from the truth. It was to become Bourdieu's core project in the sociology of culture to analyse this 'symbolic capital' in modern societies – particularly modern French society – in a sober and sometimes cynical way. In his view, a convincing analysis of modern societies must go beyond economic forms of capital and pay heed to symbolic capital as well.

Subsequently, when he had more or less ceased to carry out anthropological studies and increasingly devoted himself to the analysis of French society, Bourdieu was to attempt to clarify more precisely this still relatively nebulous concept of 'symbolic capital'. In addition to economic capital, he introduced the distinction between 'cultural' and 'social' capital; sometimes he also refers to 'political capital', prompting observers and critics to refer to the 'inflationary' tendency affecting the concept of capital in his theory. There is no need for us to understand all these extensions and differentiations in detail. It is enough to point out that in his best-known writings, Bourdieu distinguishes between economic, symbolic, cultural and social forms of capital. As the meaning of the term 'economic capital' ought to be fairly clear, we shall briefly clarify the other three types:

- Under the term 'cultural capital' he includes *both* works of art, books and musical instruments, in as much as this capital is present in the form of objects, *and* cultural capacities and cultural knowledge, in as much as these have been 'absorbed' by actors through earlier processes of socialisation, *as well as* titles (such as doctor, along with those conferred by other degrees, etc.), because these demonstrate, as it were, the acquisition of cultural knowledge.

- 'Social capital', meanwhile, covers resources through which one demonstrates membership of or affiliation to a group, one's (distinguished) family background, one's attendance at a particular elite school or university; it refers to networks in the sense of social relationships upon which one may draw in order to realise certain goals, that which is colloquially known as the 'old boys' network' (see Bourdieu's essay, 'The Forms of Capital').
- 'Symbolic capital' is something of a generic term emerging from the interplay of the economic, social and cultural types of capital: all three 'original' capital types lay the foundations for an individual's overall standing, good reputation, renown and prestige in society, thus determining his or her place in the hierarchy.

According to Bourdieu, these concepts of capital enable us to model a society's class structure. In his view, one ought to be aware that the forms of capital may sometimes be exchanged or translated into one another; their conversion is often possible. That is, in determining an individual's position within a society's class structure, it is vital to study both the *volume* of capital available to this individual as well as the *structure* of this capital (which shows which forms of capital this individual's total capital is composed of). To mention one example: professors would generally be located in the middling ranks of a modern society with respect to their economic capital, but at the same time they possess great cultural capital (they have a large number of titles and they not only own lots of books, but have even read many of them) and they often have a fairly large number of social relationships with a diverse range of circles, so that assessing their social position requires a multidimensional approach. To elucidate Bourdieu's mode of analysis, we have provided a model of class developed entirely on the basis of his theoretical framework, but in *simplified form*, as drawn up by Klaus Eder 1989b: 21n.6), taking only the cultural and economic forms of capital into account, for former West Germany. The vertical line is intended to indicate the *absolute* volume of available capital; the horizontal, the *relative* proportion of both forms of capital.

According to this diagram, the volume of capital enjoyed by doctors and members of the independent professions is quite similar, though the composition of this capital is very different: while doctors possess a comparatively small amount of economic capital, their cultural capital is relatively great compared with private sector professionals. Farmers generally have neither particularly great economic nor cultural capital, while in the case of craftspeople, one is struck again by the great discrepancy between

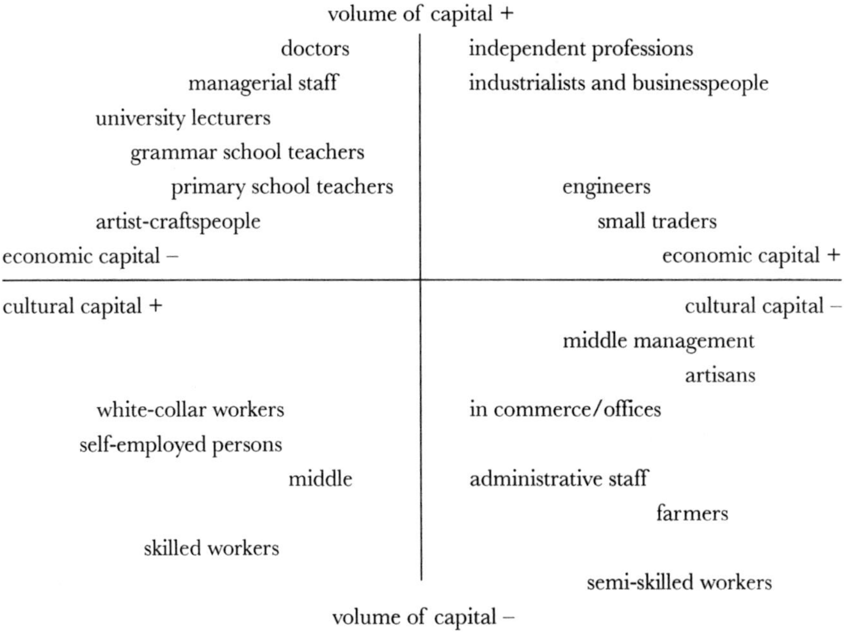

relatively great cultural capital and relatively meagre economic capital, etc. Of course, we could argue endlessly over whether, for example, the cultural capital of craftspeople and professors in relation to one another is 'correct' here, and we would have to look closely at the methodological approach to determining capital that underpins this diagram. This, however, is of no concern to us here.

What we wish to get across is that subtle analyses of social structure of this kind provide a more convincing class theory – and above all one that is more in keeping with the times – than orthodox Marxism. But that is not all. The introduction of differing concepts of capital remedies Marxism's obvious lack of a sociology of culture – and this is a key reason why Bourdieusian theory seemed so appealing to ex-Marxists. The deployment of a sophisticated conception of capital allowed them a *degree* of distance from Marx, without requiring them to enter wholly new theoretical territory.

At the same time – and this brings us back to our initial question concerning the traces of utilitarianism in Bourdieu's theoretical edifice – a concept of capital originating in the economy reinforces the utilitarian (and conflict theoretical) 'feel' of Bourdieusian theory to which we referred earlier: the field of culture is described with fundamentally the same conceptual apparatus as that of the economy. For, in both spheres, actors' interests play the decisive role; it is only the types of capital – and hence the forms of what is a stake – which differ. The main concern is always with profits and losses and the struggles and disputes over them. Bourdieu's model of action – coupled with his concept of habitus – always remains the same and takes fundamentally the same form with respect to the various fields.

> The theory of action that I propose (with the notion of habitus) amounts to saying that most human actions have as a basis something quite different from intention, that is, acquired dispositions which make it so that an action can and should be interpreted as *oriented toward one objective or another* without anyone being able to claim that that objective was a conscious design [...]. (Bourdieu, 1998 [1994]: 97–98, emphasis in original)

It thus comes as no surprise that Bourdieu formulates his ambitions with regard to the production of 'grand theory' in a language that does little to conceal its economistic or utilitarian taproots. The overriding and long-term goal of his work – as he was to express it – was to produce a 'general theory of the *economy* of practices' (Bourdieu, 1996 [1992]: 183, emphasis added) – a theory capable of comprehensively interpreting the logic of the interest-based struggle over specific types of capital in very different fields.

As a result of these echoes of utilitarianism in his theory of action, 'supra-individual' or collective phenomena are also described solely under utilitarian premises: for Bourdieu, 'culture' is no more than a game in which different classes enforce their particular conceptions of aesthetics in an attempt to set themselves apart from other classes. Bourdieu sees the 'public sphere' – the idea of the unconstrained and pluralistic exchange of political arguments, prized so highly by Dewey and Habermas – primarily as something introduced for strategic reasons in the eighteenth and nineteenth centuries by a class of high-ranking bureaucrats as a means of asserting themselves against their competitors (such as the aristocracy) (Bourdieu, 1998 [1994]: 23–24). As Bourdieu sees it, what is invariably at issue here – but by no means only here – is the acquisition of capital, though 'capital' can mean different things. In line with the rules that pertain within specific fields, actors pursue their interests as they relate *to these fields*, though, because they have become habituated to them, actors are not always aware of these interests. This is why, particularly in his later work, Bourdieu also uses the term *illusio* (from *ludus* = 'game') as an alternative to 'interests', to make it clear that these do not refer solely to (conscious) economic interests.

> I much prefer to use the term *illusio*, since I always speak of specific interests, of interests that are both presupposed and produced by the functioning of historically delimited fields. Paradoxically, the term interest has brought forth the knee-jerk accusation of economism. In fact, the notion as I use it is the

> means of a deliberate and provisional reductionism that allows me to import the materialist mode of questioning into the cultural sphere from which it was expelled, historically, when the modern view of art was invented and the field of cultural production won its autonomy [...]. (Bourdieu and Wacquant, 1992: 115–116, emphasis in original)

By deploying the term 'illusio', Bourdieu believes that he has distanced himself sufficiently and conclusively from utilitarianism. He also thinks he can do without a typology of action of the kind produced by Jürgen Habermas, with its distinction between purposive-rational and communicative action. Such a distinction, according to Bourdieu, would merely ignore the existence of different forms of non-material profit in disparate fields. For him, capital exists in various forms, but action does not; actors do their best to accrue the different types of capital within the various fields. Habermas's typology of action is said to be merely an idealistic means of disguising this fact. Despite all his criticisms of utilitarianism, Bourdieu overlooks the fact that this is exactly the position advocated by neo-utilitarians: they too make no mention of different types of action, referring only to actors' attempts to realise their various preferences. They too declare a typology of action absurd or useless, because action in itself is very easy to explain, as it always revolves around obtaining what one wants.

Yet, what is remarkable here is not just Bourdieu's proximity to (neo-) utilitarianism, which was a recurrent feature of his work. What is also of interest in this context is the fact that Bourdieu's position appears not to be entirely consistent. For even if we were to accept his 'theory of habitus', which does not assert that action is entirely determined, we would still be faced with the problem of explaining the actors' *room for manoeuvre* with respect to action, the flexibility of action *within the boundaries set by the habitus*. In concrete terms, within a field that demands a particular habitus, how are the various 'interests' realised by the actors? It should at least be conceivable that normative, affective, etc. forms of action play a role within the variable options for action opened up by the habitus. In fact, a typology of action would be very helpful, if not essential, to shed light on this spectrum of action, because it is the only way of guarding against an overly narrow – perhaps, once again, utilitarian – conception of action. But Bourdieu does nothing to address this issue. He seems rather unaware of it, which suggests a lacuna in his theory. This is also apparent in the fact that, in his studies of art, for example, Bourdieu only illuminates writers' and painters' efforts to establish themselves and obtain distinction along with the constraints upon them, but remains strangely silent about their artistic creativity. This is not to say that this creativity can be described without reference to the logic of the various 'fields'. Bourdieu's critique of idealist notions of the artist's self-creation is entirely justified. If the habitus is not to be understood deterministically, however, the theorist must pay some attention at least to *non-determined* aspects of action, that is, those aspects of social life that are shaped by what we may call the 'creativity of action' (Joas).

3. We have now outlined Bourdieu's theoretical premises from a critical angle and presented his basic concepts of *field, habitus and capital* more or less in isolation from one another. Our concern now is to lay bare how these three concepts *connect* in Bourdieu's thinking and thus to present his theoretical construct in its entirety, as well as identifying the problematic features of its 'architecture'.

The concept of field – or, to be exact, Bourdieu's analysis of fields (plural) – forms the logical starting point of Bourdieusian theory. Social reality is composed of various fields, in which different rules apply; rules which actors have to follow if they wish to succeed in gaining profits – specific forms of capital – within this field. To repeat: the field of science obeys different rules than that of politics, education or sport. This is in a way reminiscent of theorems of differentiation, particularly Luhmann's systems theory. In fact, Bourdieu is fairly close here to the idea advocated by Luhmann and his supporters that the social world has divided into various spheres, which can no longer be straightforwardly unified under conditions of modernity. Thus, Bourdieu is faced with problems which are very similar to those confronted by systems theory. He is unable to convincingly explain *how many fields there are* and *where exactly the boundaries between the fields lie*. (Bourdieu seems to assume that there are a large number of fields, which he believes can be determined only by means of empirical historical investigation, though his references to this process of determination are not particularly helpful and his own research relates only to a few limited aspects of the social world; see Bourdieu, 1990 [1987]: 88.) Theorists of differentiation, and Luhmann in particular, have made detailed theoretical observations in this respect, even though these too failed to satisfy entirely. Bourdieu, by contrast, set about providing his notion of 'fields' with theoretical backup only very late in his career. His comments on the relevant problems are rather thin on the ground and are far from being as systematic as is the case in Luhmann's work. Yet, at least one thing is clear: Bourdieu's 'field theory' can be distinguished from the assumptions characteristic of Luhmannian systems theory in at least two respects. *First*, in contrast to Luhmann, Bourdieu places struggle centre stage, that is, his fields are analysed in terms of conflict theory – a point which was never of any interest to Luhmann in his analyses of 'systems':

> If it is true that, in the literary or artistic field, for instance, one may treat the stances constitutive of a space of possibles as a system, they form a system of differences, of distinctive and antagonistic properties which do not develop out of their own internal motion (as the principle of self-referentiality implies) but via

> conflicts internal to the field of production. The field is the locus of relations of force – and not only of meaning – and of struggles aimed at transforming it, and therefore of endless change. The coherence that may be observed in a given state of the field, its apparent orientation toward a common function [...] are born of conflict and competition, not of some kind of immanent self-development of the structure. (Bourdieu and Wacquant, 1992: 103–104)

Second, in contrast to Luhmann, Bourdieu does not assume that social fields are radically separate and that there is thus no prospect of establishing any kind of unity. It may be no coincidence that the Frenchman Bourdieu – citizen of a highly centralised country – attributed a kind of meta-function to the state. He conceived of the state as a 'meta-field' which is still capable of playing the role of 'arbiter' between the fields owing to its capacity to establish compelling norms (Bourdieu, 2000 [1997]: 127; see also Bourdieu, 1998 [1994]: 33). With this thesis, too, he set himself apart from radical theorists of differentiation and, above all, from Luhmann, but without – we underline – endorsing the idea that societies are integrated by norms, as is the case in the work of Parsons or Münch.

A special habitus is moulded by the rules which apply within the specific fields, and those who enter them inescapably (have to) adapt to this habitus. Scientists, politicians, sportspeople, etc. have a specific habitus detectable in how they talk, gesture, evaluate various issues, walk, etc. This does not mean that all politicians talk, gesture, evaluate, etc. in the same way, which would mean that their behaviour was fully determined. Bourdieu, as we have seen, defends himself against the accusation of determinism so often levelled against him (see, for example, Ferry and Renaut, 1990: 153–184); he repeatedly emphasises that actors adopt a particular habitus only with a certain, if high, degree of probability, and that this habitus also allows for the possibility of behavioural variation:

> Because the habitus is an infinite capacity for generating products – thoughts, perceptions, expressions and actions – whose limits are set by the historically and socially situated conditions of its production, the conditioned and conditional freedom it provides is as remote from creation of unpredictable novelty as it is from simple mechanical reproduction of the original conditioning. (Bourdieu, 1990 [1980]: 55)

Despite all the variability, however, field-specific action, as well as the fields as a whole, are fairly stable. This is because – as a schema of perception, thinking and action (here, Bourdieu draws on ethnomethodological insights) – the habitus tends to be constantly confirmed or reproduced. Since the habitus has entered into people's bodies and become their identity, people (unconsciously) tend to uphold this identity. We wish to see our familiar world confirmed repeatedly and have no interest in destroying this trust in the meaningfulness of the everyday world. This means that through the 'systematic "choices" it makes among the places, events and people that might be frequented, the habitus tends to protect itself from crises and critical challenges' (Bourdieu, 1990 [1980]: 61). As a result, the types of habitus formed in the fields constantly reconfirm the fields in their original form, and the same process of structuration occurs on an ongoing basis.

> Because habitus [...] is a product of a history, the instruments of construction of the social that it invests in practical knowledge of the world and in action are socially constructed, in other words structured by the world that they structure. (Bourdieu, 2000 [1997]: 148)

Nevertheless, the habitus is not only the expression of 'differentiated' social fields, as one (from a systems-theoretical perspective) may suggest. Types of habitus are also the products of specific *class* realities, specific social milieux, which reproduce these realities and milieux:

> One of the functions of the notion of habitus is to account for the unity of style, which unites the practices and goods of a single agent or a class of agents [...]. The habitus is this generative and unifying principle which retranslates the intrinsic and relational characteristics of a position into a unitary lifestyle [...]. (Bourdieu, 1998 [1994]: 8)

Bourdieu's ongoing preoccupation with issues relating to the (French) education system was, among other things, intended to show that this class-based habitus is almost impossible to undo even by means of a seemingly meritocratic education system. In fact, in his view, the opposite applies. The education system continually reinforces these class-specific forms of behaviour, which is why it contributes to the ongoing reproduction of social inequality (see Bourdieu and Passeron, 1977 [1970]) – a thesis which can also be found in the work of conflict theorist Randall Collins (see Joas and Knöbl, 2009 [2004]: 189 ff.).

Of course, this trope of the reproduction of social structures in near-identical form associated with the concept of habitus raises the question of how Bourdieu conceives of *social change* in the first place – especially given that he is cool towards the thesis that ideas or ideologies can do much to influence or change things. This becomes particularly clear in light of the classical sociological concept of the 'legitimacy of domination'. For Bourdieu, this figure of thought, which goes back to Max Weber, is problematic right from the outset because – through the concept of rational-legal domination, for example – it suggests that there can be a somehow *conscious* discourse about the legitimacy of domination. Bourdieu, by contrast, believes that domination functions quite differently. According to him, from childhood onwards, people become accustomed to structures of domination as taken-for-granted features of the world. In institutions – such as nurseries, schools and factories – the lower classes in particular have a self-evident acceptance of social inequality 'drummed into' them, which makes it almost impossible for them to turn these structures into an object of discourse (see Bourdieu, 1998 [1994]: 53–54). And domination is maintained not by means of ideologies or legitimising discourses – of which many people could make neither head nor tail anyway – but by the constant practice of compliance with existing inequalities of power.

> If I have little by little come to shun the use of the word 'ideology', this is not only because of its polysemy and the resulting ambiguities. It is above all because, by evoking the order of ideas, and of action by ideas and on ideas, it inclines one to forget one of the most powerful mechanisms of the maintenance of the symbolic order, the *two-fold naturalization* which results from the inscription of the social in things and in bodies (as much those of the dominant as of the dominated – whether in terms of sex, ethnicity, social position or any other discriminating factor), with the resulting effects of symbolic violence. As is underlined by ordinary-language notions such as 'natural distinction' or 'gift', the work of legitimation of the established order is extraordinarily facilitated by the fact that it goes on almost automatically in the reality of the social world. (Bourdieu, 2000 [1997]: 181)

This stance, though, makes the potential of Bourdieusian theory to contribute to a theory of change a yet more pressing issue, and it inspired some to accuse Bourdieu of (negative) hyperfunctionalism, because according to the logic of his theory, despite ongoing struggles within the fields, the (normatively problematic) unequal power structures are reproduced constantly and stabilised 'automatically', making it seem almost impossible to bring about a new situation. Bourdieu's ideas thus offer few stimuli for a theory of social change. *The Rules of Art* (1996 [1992]: 253), for example, states that processes of change in the fields of literature and painting are most likely to be triggered by those entering a field for the first time – in other words, the *younger generation*. Bourdieu provided historical evidence of this by referring to Flaubert and Baudelaire, demonstrating how, as newcomers to the field of literature, they established and enforced their own new form of aesthetics, restructuring the field significantly. Yet, to a genuine theory of social change this is of very little help. Bourdieu stated that in light of the forms of capital available within it, each field requires its own models of change. Given that his studies focused on only a few fields, however, his work inevitably lacks general statements about social change.

4. The potential of Bourdieu's theory *to cast light on the contemporary situation* is most apparent in his critiques of globalisation and writings in the *sociology of culture*, of which his 1979 book *Distinction* was to become particularly famous. Bourdieu, however, had formulated a conceptual and theoretical programme for this kind of study much earlier. This is perhaps expressed most impressively in the following passage:

> In fact, the least privileged groups and worst-off classes from an economic point of view appear in this game of circulation and distinction, *which is the real cultural game*, and which is objectively organized in line with the class structure, solely as a means of contrast, that is, as the element necessary to highlight the other, or as 'nature'. The game of symbolic distinctions is thus played out within that narrow space whose boundaries are dictated by economic constraints, and remains, in this respect, a game played by the privileged in privileged societies, who can afford to conceal the real differences, namely those of domination, beneath contrasting manners. (Bourdieu, 1970: 72–73, emphasis in original)

Culture, as Bourdieu claims in this quotation, is a game of distinction in which class differences are also expressed or visibly constituted for the first time. Analogously to his concept of cultural capital – which covers a great many things, including objects such as paintings and books, knowledge and skills and even titles – Bourdieu defines culture very broadly indeed; it also refers to aesthetic evaluations. In *Distinction*, he is primarily concerned to assert, provocatively, that even our seemingly most personal predilections – our opinions about how things taste, the aesthetic quality of a piece of music, the 'acceptability' of articles of clothing, etc. – are determined by a class habitus. His simple thesis is that 'taste' or aesthetic judgements classify the very individuals engaged in classification, because they reflect existing economic opportunities or economic constraints.

What is both provocative and fascinating here is not just how distraught we feel when Bourdieu takes such pleasure in casting doubt on our most sublime feelings and perceptions, tracing them back to seemingly banal or profane realities. Émile Durkheim's book *Suicide*, which interpreted what appears to be the freest of all free decisions – to take one's own life – as a *socially determined* phenomenon, was shocking in much the same way. Arguments of this kind contradict utterly our view of ourselves as self-determining beings, which is why they distress us so much. Yet, Bourdieu's writings, especially *Distinction*, are provocative for another reason. Ultimately, he attempts to equate or at least associate aesthetics, the theory of the good and the true (in art), with banal quotidian tastes. Bourdieu wishes to show that what aesthetic theory acclaims as great music, great paintings and great literature is, in reality, nothing other than a form of perception derived from specific economic realities. According to Bourdieu, great art was and is always partly a product of class conflict; the ruling classes have managed to define *their* aesthetic perceptions as 'legitimate' art, concurrently veiling or airbrushing out entirely how this aesthetics is determined by class. The aim of his programme of 'anti-Kantian "aesthetics"' is thus to *expose* and *demystify*.

In this connection, he establishes the dichotomy between so-called 'luxury' and so-called 'necessity-driven' taste. The latter is typical of the lower strata and classes within a society. It is associated with immediate material problems of life, with the everyday experience of lack, with the sense of economic insecurity, etc. Under such circumstances it is supposedly impossible to devote a great deal of time and effort to refining one's behaviour. In line with this, the aesthetic perceptions and everyday behaviour of the lower strata are also very different from those of the ruling classes, as apparent even in their eating habits.

> In the face of the new ethic of sobriety for the sake of slimness, which is most recognized at the highest levels of the social hierarchy, peasants and especially industrial workers maintain an ethic of convivial indulgence. A bon vivant is not just someone who enjoys eating and drinking; he is someone capable of entering into the generous and familiar – that is, both simple and free – relationship that is encouraged and symbolized by eating and drinking together, in a conviviality which sweeps away restraints and reticence. (Bourdieu, 1984 [1979]: 179)

To be sure, it is not only *how* people eat that distinguishes this necessity-driven taste; *what* is eaten is also fundamentally different from that typically consumed by the ruling classes. Bourdieu marshals a mass of statistical evidence and nuanced observational data to demonstrate how variable eating culture is, pointing out that the upper classes always tend, sometimes consciously, but more often unconsciously, to set themselves apart from the eating culture of the lower classes through the refinement of the mealtime experience, in order to develop 'distinction'. The extravagant tastes of the upper strata are always in part an attempt to demarcate themselves from others, to attain *distinction*, which continually reproduces class differences and class boundaries. Intellectuals, businesspeople, journalists, etc. go to Chinese, Vietnamese and Burmese restaurants as a matter of course, something a worker, even if he could afford it, would never dream of doing because his notions of good food are very different. (All such observations, of course, represent snapshots of a particular historical period.) Anyone born into the upper classes is socialised into a particular taste in food and corresponding habitus, through which she almost automatically sets herself apart from individuals of other classes. It is not just their table manners but also their seemingly primal tastes that distinguish the 'aristocrats' from the 'plebeians'. This was true in the past; and, according to Bourdieu, it is also true in the present.

A similar pattern is apparent in the different ways in which members of different classes relate to art. Extravagant tastes and an aesthetics to match, because they are free of economic constraints, have no specific purpose and are seemingly disinterested, which is why members of the upper classes get a good deal more out of *abstract* art – Braque, Delaunay, Malevich, or Duchamp – than the lower classes, who are unfamiliar with disinterested conditions and thus view art in close association with practical tasks of everyday life. They perceive a painting by Braque, for example, as incomprehensible or unappealing and are always more likely to hang a Spitzweg reproduction or one of Caspar David Friedrich's works in their sitting room than a Delaunay. 'Is that what they call art?' – this question is always on the tip of the tongue of the worker or of the petit bourgeois as he or she looks at a Malevich, while artistically inclined intellectuals may see a painting as particularly interesting and expressive precisely because it is rather inaccessible and – as Bourdieu would assume – one can thereby gain distinction, setting oneself apart from the philistines. Much the same applies to the realm of music. If workers listen to classical music in the first place, it tends to be Smetana's *The Moldau* rather than the unmelodic 'noise' of a Shostakovich.

Bourdieu never tires of tracking down similar patterns in the realms of sport, political opinion, film, clothing and leisure time activities. For him, what is always evident here is that the *ruling* classes determine the legitimacy of a particular activity within the various cultural fields: *they* declare, for instance, the latest forms of *avant-garde* art to be *real* art on the basis of their need for distinction, while all that came before takes on an air of triviality, of the not truly artistic, especially if the lower classes begin to appropriate these now 'outdated' forms of art.

Taken together, Bourdieu's investigations cause him to expound the thesis that the habitus acquired within a particular class – as an ensemble of schemata of perception, cognition and action – defines a particular 'lifestyle' by means of which the classes set themselves apart from one another 'culturally'. The different types of lifestyle found within a society point to symbolic conflicts over the efforts made by members of different classes to achieve distinction. According to Bourdieu, this is precisely what we need to grasp, because this is the only way to adequately describe the class structure of a society and its dynamics – something which orthodox

Marxism was incapable of doing as a consequence of its lack of, or blindness to, a theory of culture.

Bourdieu's account, rooted in cultural sociology, is of relevance to the diagnosis of the contemporary era in that his view of the perpetual reproduction of class-based inequality appears to leave little prospect that things will get better. To some extent at least, this is at variance with Bourdieu's role as a public critic of the French education system and of globalisation, to which we alluded at the beginning of this chapter; one may ask how this engagement can be reconciled with his diagnosis of the apparently unalterable and stable nature of social structures. Nonetheless, he himself believes that this 'contradiction' can be resolved by pointing to the fact that freedom is possible only if one knows and recognises the laws governing how a society is structured: '[s]ociology frees by freeing from the illusion of freedom' (Bourdieu, see Dosse, 1997 [1991], vol. II.: 67). Constant references to people's supposed 'free will' may in fact form part of a discourse of power if it ignores either the limits of one's own potential to take action or those applying to 'others'; conversely, the assertion that social relations are determined may be the point of departure for a discourse of liberation. And Bourdieu always claimed that his academic work was advancing just such a discourse of liberation. Especially during the final decade of his life, he tried to mobilise left-wing intellectuals to form a counter-power to what he saw as the ever-advancing and threatening economisation of every aspect of human life and the hegemony of laissez-faire liberalism. No-one engaging in such activities can have an entirely pessimistic worldview. Despite all his references to the constant reproduction of patterns of social inequality, his diagnosis of the modern era must entail an element of hope.

This brings us to the end of our account of Bourdieusian theory. It only remains to investigate briefly its impact.

5. Bourdieu's writings have enjoyed a wide readership, and have exercised a magnetic effect well beyond the bounds of sociology, within which *political sociology* and the *sociology of social inequality* have benefited most from his ideas. In *France*, for example, Bourdieu gathered a large number of collaborators around him who went on to develop his research approach or applied it to new topics. Studies in historical sociology on specific strata and professional groups are the leading case in point, a representative example being Luc Boltanski's *Les cadres. La formation d'un groupe sociale* (English title: *The Making of a Class: Cadres in French Society*, 1987 [1982]). In *Germany*, it is research on inequality that has most often drawn on Bourdieusian theory, with a particular focus on the concept of lifestyle (for an overview, see the anthology edited by Klaus Eder entitled *Klassenlage, Lebensstil und kulturelle Praxis* (1989a) [*Class Situation, Lifestyle and Cultural Praxis*] and Hans-Peter Müller's *Sozialstruktur und Lebensstile* (1992) [*Social Structure and Lifestyles*]. Yet, Bourdieu has been received

in sometimes peculiar fashion: in Germany, the concept of lifestyle (which is not, however, based solely on his ideas) has increasingly been separated out from the arguments of class theory. This has created the impression that people can more or less freely choose their lifestyle, inspiring the dubious assertion that it is thus almost impossible to discern 'real' classes in German society (see, for example, Gerhard Schulze's *Die Erlebnisgesellschaft. Kultursoziologie der Gegenwart* (1992) [*The Experiential Society: A Cultural Sociology of the Present*]). This is an argument quite alien to Bourdieu's way of thinking. Turning to *North America*, a study published in 1992 by the French-Canadian Michèle Lamont (*Money, Morals, and Manners: The Culture of the French and American Upper-Middle Class*) created quite a stir. This was a comparative study of social structure, executed in the spirit of Bourdieu, but which went beyond him in as much as it took seriously the moral discourses of these classes, which Bourdieu tended to neglect, eschewing their immediate reduction to other factors. Lamont (born in 1957) brought out in impressive fashion how much the images and ideas of a morally good life and conduct differ among the upper middle classes of American and French society and how well suited moral stances are to highlighting the boundaries between classes.

Bourdieu's influence on *history* was almost as great. Concepts such as 'capital', 'field' and 'habitus' clearly helped remedy certain theoretical shortcomings. A good example of this is a work which was certainly influenced by Bourdieusian theory and which tackles a topic frequently subject to Bourdieu's attentions – one which we were unable to deal with in greater depth in this chapter. We are referring to Christophe Charle's *Naissance des 'intellectuels': 1880–1900* (1990) [*The Emergence of 'Intellectuals': 1880–1900*], which brings out vividly how the image of intellectuals was constituted during this period of history and the various strategies pursued by these intellectuals to set themselves apart from their 'competitors' and free themselves from state and church.

Notes

1 Originally published as Hans Joas and Wolfgang Knöbl (2009 [2004]) 'Between Structuralism and Theory of Practice: The Cultural Sociology of Pierre Bourdieu', in their *Social Theory: Twenty Introductory Lectures*, trans. Alex Skinner, Cambridge: Cambridge University Press, pp. 371–400.

2 Translation revised by Simon Susen.

References

Boltanski, Luc (1987 [1982]) *The Making of a Class: Cadres in French Society*, trans. Arthur Goldhammer, Cambridge: Cambridge University Press.

Bourdieu, Pierre (1958) *Sociologie de l'Algerie*, Paris: Presses Universitaires de France.

Bourdieu, Pierre (1970) *Zur Soziologie der symbolischen Formen*, trans. Wolfgang Fietkau, Frankfurt am Main: Suhrkamp.

Bourdieu, Pierre (1977 [1972]) *Outline of a Theory of Practice*, trans. Richard Nice, Cambridge: Cambridge University Press.

Bourdieu, Pierre (1984 [1979]) *Distinction: A Social Critique of the Judgement of Taste*, trans. Richard Nice, Cambridge MA: Harvard University Press.

Bourdieu, Pierre (1985 [1984]) 'The Social Space and the Genesis of Groups', trans. Richard Nice, *Theory and Society* 14(6): 723–744.

Bourdieu, Pierre (1986 [1983]) 'The Forms of Capital', in John Richardson, *Handbook of Theory and Research for the Sociology of Education*, trans. Richard Nice, New York: Greenwood Press, pp. 241–258.

Bourdieu, Pierre (1988 [1984]) *Homo Academicus*, trans. Peter Collier, Cambridge: Polity Press in association with Basil Blackwell.

Bourdieu, Pierre (1990 [1987]) *In Other Words: Essays Towards a Reflexive Sociology*, trans. Matthew Adamson, Cambridge: Polity Press.

Bourdieu, Pierre (1990 [1980]) *The Logic of Practice*, trans. Richard Nice, Cambridge: Polity Press.

Bourdieu, Pierre (1993 [1980]) *Sociology in Question*, trans. Richard Nice, London: Sage.

Bourdieu, Pierre (1996 [1992]) *The Rules of Art: Genesis and Structure of the Literary Field*, trans. Susan Emanuel, Cambridge: Polity Press.

Bourdieu, Pierre (1998 [1994]) *Practical Reason: On the Theory of Action*, trans. Randall Johnson, Cambridge: Polity Press.

Bourdieu, Pierre (1999 [1993]) *The Weight of the World: Social Suffering in Contemporary Society*, trans. Priscilla Parkhurst Ferguson [et al.], Cambridge: Polity Press.

Bourdieu, Pierre (2000 [1997]) *Pascalian Meditations*, trans. Richard Nice, Cambridge: Polity Press.

Bourdieu, Pierre, Luc Boltanski, Robert Castel and Jean-Claude Chamboredon (1990 [1965]) *Photography: A Middle-Brow Art*, trans. Shaun Whiteside, Cambridge: Polity Press.

Bourdieu, Pierre and Jean-Claude Passeron (1977 [1970]) *Reproduction in Education, Society and Culture*, trans. Richard Nice, London and Beverly Hills: Sage.

Bourdieu, Pierre and Loïc Wacquant (1992) *An Invitation to Reflexive Sociology*, Cambridge: Polity Press.

Charle, Christophe (1990) *Naissance des 'intellectuels': 1880–1900*, Paris: Minuit.

Dosse, François (1997 [1991]) *History of Structuralism (2 Volumes)*, trans. Deborah Glassman, Minneapolis and London: University of Minnesota Press.

Eder, Klaus (ed.) (1989a) *Klassenlage, Lebensstil und kulturelle Praxis. Theoretische und empirische Beiträge zur Auseinandersetzung mit Pierre Bourdieus Klassentheorie*, Frankfurt am Main: Suhrkamp.

Eder, Klaus (1989b), Klassentheorie als Gesellschaftstheorie. Bourdieus dreifache kulturtheoretische Brechung der traditionellen Klassentheorie', in Klaus Eder (ed.) *Klassenlage, Lebensstil und kulturelle Praxis. Theoretische und empirische Beiträge zur Auseinandersetzung mit Pierre Bourdieus Klassentheorie*, Frankfurt am Main: Suhrkamp, pp. 15–43.

Ferry, Luc and Alain Renaut (1990 [1985]) 'French Marxism (Bourdieu)', in Luc Ferry and Alain Renaut (eds.) *French Philosophy of the Sixties: An Essay on Anti-Humanism*, trans. Mary H.S. Cattani, Amherst and London: University of Massachusetts Press, pp. 153–84.

Honneth, Axel (1995 [1990]) 'The Fragmented World of Symbolic Forms: Reflections on Pierre Bourdieu's Sociology of Culture', in Axel Honneth, *The Fragmented World of the*

Social: Essays in Social and Political Philosophy, edited by Charles W. Wright, Albany: State University of New York Press, pp. 184–201.

Joas, Hans (1996 [1992]) *The Creativity of Action*, trans. Jeremy Gaines and Paul Keast, Cambridge: Polity Press.

Joas, Hans and Wolfgang Knöbl (2009 [2004]) *Social Theory: Twenty Introductory Lectures*, trans. Alex Skinner, Cambridge: Cambridge University Press.

Lamont, Michèle (1992) *Money, Morals, and Manners: The Culture of the French and American Upper-Middle Class*, Chicago: University of Chicago Press.

Müller, Hans-Peter (1992) *Sozialstruktur und Lebensstile. Der neuere theoretische Diskurs über soziale Ungleichheit*, Frankfurt am Main: Suhrkamp.

Robbins, Derek (1991) *The Work of Pierre Bourdieu: Recognizing Society*, Buckingham: Open University Press.

Schulze, Gerhard (1992) *Die Erlebnisgesellschaft. Kultursoziologie der Gegenwart*, Frankfurt am Main and New York: Campus.

CHAPTER TWO

Pierre Bourdieu: Unorthodox Marxist?

Bridget Fowler

Derek Robbins states categorically that '[t]here are no grounds for considering Bourdieu was ever a Marxist' (2006: 513), whilst Brubaker argues that although Bourdieu might appear to be in the Marxist tradition, his critiques of Marxism should make us think otherwise (1985: 761). Although I shall be taking issue with both of these conclusions, I do not want to claim the opposite: that Marx alone influenced him. Bourdieu was unusually inventive in drawing also on Weber, Durkheim, Husserl, Mauss, Elias, and Pascal, not to mention others. Given more space, I would draw out all of these different strands in the texture of his work, whilst acknowledging that, at his best, his syntheses possess a masterly originality. Having rejected 'histmat'[1] or Stalinist orthodoxy (Bourdieu, 1990: 3), however, it is my contention that Bourdieu *is one of the great heirs* of the Western Marxist tradition.[2] It was not simply a youthful flash in the pan that led him to suggest his *lycée* students read *The Communist Manifesto*[3] (Lescourret, 2008: 65–66).

My general proposal is this: a strong case can be made for the influence of Marx on Bourdieu's early writings. A more intricate case needs to be made for the view that Bourdieu *continued* to be influenced profoundly by Marx, despite the development of his distinctive language: the now-familiar concepts of habitus, field, doxa,[4] allodoxia, and so on. *Paradoxically, to defend Marx, Bourdieu chose to wrest some aspects of other theories from idealism – particularly Durkheimian structuralism – aiming to further strengthen historical materialism* (1968 [1968]; 1992: 164).[5] Yet, the reverses of labour after 1968 and the massive impact of the move towards finance capital temporarily discredited Marxism; hence, Bourdieu was impelled to develop a fresh set of terms. Despite this reconceptualisation exercise, it is my view that he effectively operates within the Marxist tradition, demystifying further our understanding of how domination operates and endures. Thus, what he tellingly calls his 'theory of practice' has drawn attention to misrecognised or misunderstood features of social action, particularly those that function analogously *to the extraction of surplus value* in the labour process. Indeed, the title, 'theory of practice' itself evokes the Marxist lineage of the term 'praxis', although Bourdieu has always been careful to distinguish himself from 'trendy Marxism' (1990 [1987]: 22). I am arguing, then, that Bourdieu shares with Marx the hope that by means of such demystification 'the practical relations between man and man [...] [would] generally present themselves in a transparent and rational form' (Marx, 1976 [1867]: 173).

Bourdieu writes memorably of economic, cultural, social, and symbolic capital. The multiplication of these various forms serves to *increase the amount of social energy a family* has at its command: at root, a materialist concern (1996 [1989]: 187; 1998 [1984]: 70–71). Chief amongst such mechanisms is symbolic capital, which legitimates other forms of capital. By conferring reputations along with such symbolic 'baubles' as OBEs, knighthoods, and Nobel Prizes, symbolic capital offers its holders not just recognition but greater *justifications for living* (2000 [1997]: 239). Such legitimacy encourages more investments of energy of the same kind.[6]

Of course, 'symbolic capital' could be said to be the reinvention of Weber's idea of status, and indeed Bourdieu refers to Weber's well-known opposition of class and *Stand* in this context (1992: 237–238). Bourdieu arguably puts this too reductively when he states in *Language and Symbolic Power* that symbolic capital is simply the internalised or incorporated form of 'capital of whatever kind' (1992: 238). In contrast, his later works distinguish sharply between the cultural and symbolic capital possessed by consecrated artists or writers as against the economic capital of businessmen (with or without the addition of reputability or symbolic capital). He thus recognises – in a more classically Weberian fashion – that the historical divergence between the different ruling classes or dominant class fractions leads to *specialised dispositions* towards the various types of capital accumulation (1984 [1979]: 254; 1996 [1989]). Further, young, as yet unrecognised artists – part of the dominated fraction of the dominant class – feel an acute powerlessness, both within the cultural field and within the wider field of power. As a consequence, they are prone to identify with the position of the working class (1993: 44). Nevertheless, suggests Bourdieu, such a transient generational position imparts only a temporary radicalism. Therefore, the alliance of workers with artists or intellectuals is a fraught one, subject to the sabotage of a facile rhetoric and to all the everyday distances of divergences in habitus[7] (1988 [1984]: 179–180; 1993: 44).[8]

Yet, in general – for Bourdieu – symbolic capital reinforces the attraction of the upper hierarchical positions in the division of labour and clears the way for the performance of such practices. For example, the sociology of science discloses that the symbolic capital of being placed in a reputable laboratory within a high-ranking university is associated with greater credibility as an experimenter (2004 [2001]: 20–21). Hence, as Bourdieu saw it, symbolic capital *consolidates a group*, motivates its members to dedicate themselves ascetically to its demands and gives them the same *inner assurance of success* that the Puritan businessman gained from his work (Bourdieu, 1996 [1989]: 47–50 and 110–111; compare Marx, 1976 [1867]: 739 and 741). Bourdieu is evidently referring here to the Weber thesis. Unexpectedly, however, he also intertwines this observation with the words of Marx in *Capital:* 'capital breeds capital', he argues, writing of academic symbolic capital (1988 [1984]: 91).[9]

Bourdieu's whole corpus brilliantly examines a central Marxist idea: the ossification of fluid individuals into a dominant class, with enduring interests and the inheritance of class powers. As everyone knows, he shows that the structures aiding the *reproduction* of class advantages occur across generations (1998 [1994]: 107–108). But, despite his critics' denials, he also demonstrates how such transmission is beset by *contradictions* and *crises*[10] (Boyer, 2003: 274–275). Many such contradictions or conflicts take transfigured forms within contemporary industrial societies. Thus, older struggles persist, like those between priests and prophets or between the *noblesse de robe* (nobles of the gown) and *noblesse d'epée* (nobles of the sword); new clashes also emerge, like those between radical lawyers and law-lords, or between rising avant-gardes and academies (Bourdieu, 1991 [1971]). Crucially, at certain rare moments of catastrophe, authors of allegedly cranky or outlandish ideas may trigger *symbolic revolutions*. In the deepest crises, contradictions in the economic order massively accumulate, bringing widespread poverty and downward mobility. Then these figures of symbolic revolution and creative destruction ignite the flames of political and social revolutions.

Bourdieu may not have theorised at great length any specific transformation – neither the French Revolutions nor the brief Paris Commune. Yet, it is an illusion to conclude that within his theory, there is only 'eternal reproduction'. Surprisingly, however, many very perceptive and cogent writers *have* argued this, in relation to both his theory of class power and his theory of masculine domination (Archer, 2007; Callinicos, 1999a, 2006[11]; Calhoun, 1993: 70; Rancière, 2004 [1983]: 195; Susen, 2007: 221–223 and 312).

If Bourdieu in fact *retains* the major ideas of Marx, it is necessary to reflect on those texts concerning symbolic violence in which Bourdieu upbraids Marxists (1992). I want to clear the ground here initially by arguing that Bourdieu neither abandons the Marxist method of historical materialism as an approach or guiding thread, nor repudiates Marx's own texts. Rather, he seeks first to make historical materialism more complex and to incorporate an analysis of *symbolic power* alongside *economic power*. More about this later.

Second, he wants to draw attention, as he always has, to 'false radicalism'. In his view, such false radicalism rests on a simplistic model of the working class's affinity for revolution, thus resorting too easily to explanatory motifs of seduction by embourgeoisement and consumerism, or to a moralistic rhetoric of betrayal – as in the condemnation of an aristocracy of labour. Such false radicalism springs from a naively realist view of class. Instead, he emphasises not only people's position in the social space (that is, their objective abundance or scarcity of capitals), but also how they subjectively construct the principles of vision and division within the world (Bourdieu, 1987, and 1992: ch. 11). Therefore, in any given conjuncture, national antagonisms or religious divisions – as between Protestant and Catholic – may be substituted for class explanations of suffering (Bourdieu, 1987). Nevertheless, in times of crisis, when the critiques of the proletarianised intelligentsia no longer seem outlandish, the working class becomes full of potential. In Bourdieu's striking phrase, it feels itself to be a 'mystical body' created through 'an immense historical labour of theoretical and practical invention' (1985 [1984]: 742).

In thus acknowledging actors' *active construction* of class solidarities, as opposed to their other forms of solidarity or hierarchy (1992: 241–243), Bourdieu should be aligned not with non-Marxists, but with culturalist Marxists, such as E. P. Thompson and Raymond Williams. These thinkers locate a difficult, protracted, and at times even reversible process in developing a culture of class. Indeed, it should be noted that Bourdieu was first published in Britain by the Birmingham Centre for Contemporary Cultural Studies (CCCS). Both Thompson and Williams were adopted by the CCCS as founding figures.

In a break with mechanical materialism – which recalls Durkheim – Bourdieu also accepts that there are important 'theory effects' that spring from the power of representations as such (1992: 251; also 1990 [1987]: 49). Marxism, he claims, may benefit precisely from its own rhetoric as a doctrine about the future. On the model of a 'self-fulfilling prophecy', such a theory is a particular kind of performative linguistic act. Hence, its heterodox conclusions may come to possess great social force, although – as *Homo Academicus* clarifies – only under certain conditions. Marx, of course, had said as much himself, accepting, in his writing on Hegel, that 'theory also becomes a material force once it has gripped the masses' (Marx, 1975 [1843–4]: 251). Bourdieu rightly goes further in arguing that Marxism ought to possess the reflexivity to understand the precise place of these various determinants (1992: 251).

Paradoxically, Bourdieu provides his most powerful critique of orthodox Marxism ('histmat' or 'diamat') by taking up and extending Marx's own analytical instruments to great sociological effect. In *Distinction*, he explores the Marxist notion of fetishism, daring to apply it to the realm of culture

(1984 [1979]: 250–251).[12] Thus – following Benjamin earlier – he elaborates in many works a theory of the cultural fetishism of consecrated art. In *Language and Symbolic Power*, he takes up a theme that also becomes a constant of several texts: the sociological reality of political fetishism (1992: ch. 9; Wacquant, 2005: ch. 3). In particular, he exposes the mechanisms whereby spokespersons become invested with the 'mystery of their ministry': in Durkheimian fashion, he argues that their power lies in their organic connection to the very social group that mandates them. Yet, such spokespersons acquire their own bureaucratic or apparatchik interests (Bourdieu, 1992: 214–215). Like the great lords of the Church before them, they slowly substitute themselves for the masses they claim to represent. Since factionalism is everywhere denigrated as the worst political sin, Bourdieu wittily reveals that the rank-and-file are often forced to remain powerless – they have only the unhappy options of 'exit' (departure), 'voice' (the censored choice of autonomous protest) or secretly forming another organisation (1992: 208).

As against Brubaker's view that Bourdieu is, in effect, anti-Marxist in these works, certain key points ought to be made. On the one hand, his debt to Marx is in evidence, not least in linking political fetishism back to *Capital*. For example, in this context, he interestingly quotes one of Marx's main discoveries: 'Value does not wear a statement of what it is written on its own brow' (Bourdieu, 1992: 205). On the other hand, it has always been part of the ongoing tradition of Marxism itself that it castigates a facile utopianism in the name of science (Marx and Engels, 1940 [1845]: 180–193). Hence, rather than concluding that Bourdieu intends his sociological analyses to be against Marxism, we could suggest that he writes *in the spirit* of a Marxist critique: one that is wedded to a democratic revulsion against oppressive rule in all its forms (see Nimtz, 2000).

This interpretation is strengthened by Bourdieu's distinctive critique of other leading social theorists. He views these thinkers as having lapsed into divergent forms of idealism. Thus, Derrida has a powerful criticism of Kant but is ultimately too restricted to the philosophical institution and the scholastic attitude (1984 [1979]: 494–498 and 499–500). He consequently has no basis for escaping from the confusion to which Marx himself drew attention – mistaking the world of logic for the order of things (2000 [1997]: 53 and 55). Habermas's model of communicative action with its 'rationalist absolutism' has neglected the strategic pursuit of interest within the lifeworld itself, relegating interest solely to the sphere of instrumental reason characteristic of the capitalist market system (2000 [1997]: 65–66; 2002b: 46, 254, and 271–272).[13] Foucault – whose affectionate obituary he wrote (2002b: 178–181) – nevertheless errs by remaining too much in the 'firmament of ideas' (1993: 33; 1996 [1992]: 197–198): he fails to connect his *épistèmes* to social experiences and structuring structures. Austin correctly understands the extraordinarily transformative power of words, but is curiously silent about the manner in which social roles – power – authorise specific agents' utterances. These social roles provide the conditions underpinning the illocutionary force of significant agents' words, whilst withholding such conditions from poorly placed others (1992: 108–116). One could go on.

Bourdieu's own analysis of language as symbolic power is totally congruent with that of the dissident Marxist, Vološinov (1973 [1930]) – a member of the small group around Bakhtin in the 1920s. Bakhtin himself is also cited favourably by Bourdieu (1984 [1979]: 491–504; 1992: 40 and 88). Both social theorists – Vološinov and Bourdieu (1992: 33–34) – seek to go beyond Saussure. Stressing that the sign is the possession of the whole community, they argue that it is multi-accentual, each speech-act bearing the vibrant but conflicting meanings of different social classes. (Hence Vološinov: 'A sign that has been withdrawn from the pressures of social struggle [...] inevitably loses force, degenerating into allegory, and becoming the object not of live, social intelligibility, but philological comprehension' (1973 [1930]: 23).) The link between a confident and highly articulate use of the hegemonic language and a sense of mastery or ease in one's linguistic habitus is also common to both thinkers (1984 [1979]: 255–256; 1992: 52). Bourdieu stresses that those agents possessing a dominant class habitus may also gain social honour by linguistic 'strategies of condescension', for example, by speaking to local voters in the dialect form, despite their known capacity for great eloquence in the dominant form of French (1992: 68–69). Similarly, Vološinov had suggested that a highly individualistic use of language has its roots in the bourgeois or patrician's sense of self-confidence: such members of the elite feel that the entire social order will be generous to them, since they possess both 'social recognizance' and 'tenability of rights' (1973 [1930]: 89). Bourdieu makes the same point in reverse, citing a Béarn worker's confession that he does not *know how to speak* (in standard French) – a man who is nevertheless very voluble when drinking in the café (1992: 69 and 98–99; see also 2002a).

Brubaker, like others, has dissected the inner kernel of Bourdieu's thought as the attempt to subsume within a new theory the opposites of objectivism and subjectivism (1985: 750–753). This is true, but perhaps Bourdieu is thinking in the tradition of Western Marxism here, rather than as an unfounded innovator. For example, when Marx unveils the 'metaphysical subtleties and theological niceties' (1976 [1867]: 163) of the mundane commodity form, he too is criticising both objectivism and subjectivism. Let us pursue Marx's argument a little longer.

On the one hand, Marx states that we have to explore commodities *beyond their physical objectivity* (that is, the objectivity both of the raw materials from which they are composed and the muscles, brains etc. used in making them). Underpinning this are the varying durations of abstract labour that are embodied in each category of commodity. Of course, such labour can be reduced to 'simple' labour and hence to *average* productivity, but only via the connections that link producers together within the web of the division of labour. Such connections are only revealed where there is no massive fault-line between them, such as the division between slaves and free labour. (Indeed, remarks Marx, this latter division had been so salient in Ancient Greece that even Aristotle had failed to systematically think through the idea he had been the first to entertain intellectually: that labour might be comparable.) Hence, producers may act individually, even privately, but they are affected, willy-nilly, by the whole market. It is this structure of abstract labour – *partly an analytical construct* – which regulates the amount of socially necessary labour needed at any given time to produce a given commodity. Similarly, we might add, individual academics in Britain are regulated by abstract labour to produce their research outputs in a certain period with the imperatives of the RAE or REF[14] in mind.

On the other hand, when individuals try to grasp the form of the commodity, they mistakenly endow the physical form with a nature garnered from their own *subjective interpretations* of the world. Commodities are thus approached in the spirit of necromancy; as Marx says, the objects themselves, when they appear on the market, come to be endowed with an alluring, yet frightening, independence or autonomy, seeming to control the puny men and women who are their own producers. This subjective experience is, of course, inadequate: it makes the commodity into a magical force, and creates a world turned upside down. Hegel had shown how God or Spirit was only a constituent of people's subjective world-construction – 'the products of their own brain' – even if actors had come to see these gods as alienated spirits, dominating them. Marx is arguing that commodities, as the alienated objects of men's own labour, dominate them in similar fashion.

Thus, Marx is waging a war on two fronts. Against taking refuge in 'phantasmagoric' interpretations, he stresses that these fail to confront the historical objectivity of structures within the real world. But these economic tendencies that operate like laws of gravity – i.e. independent of the will of the actors – also hide a secret. This is that it is our own private labour and choice of working practice, whether chiefly intellectual or chiefly manual, that is orchestrated collectively, behind our backs, within a 'socially necessary' duration of labour-time. Each society imposes this changeable norm upon our subjective awareness.

Bourdieu develops analogous critiques to that of Marx vis-à-vis unacceptably objectivist and subjectivist strands in social theory. Against both Althusserianism and structuralism, he stresses that agents are not merely objective bearers of structures, or role-followers (1996 [1989]: 53). Instead (as stressed by Goffman), they are active role-takers, negotiating their performances in the light of back-stage strategies rather than exhibiting dumb conformity to the rules. Conversely, on ethnomethodologists, he censures their incapacity to consider the wider historical arena of structures, the setting for the strategic constructions of actors. Hence, for example, the power of the state in defining the statistical principles of classification detailing '[w]hat is a family?' (1998 [1994]: 66–67 and 72).

In sum, the concepts of field, habitus, fractured habitus etc. can be seen as so many recurrent moves within the theory of practice to steer between the Scylla of objectivism and the Charybdis of subjectivism. In doing so, Bourdieu explores the arenas of modern capitalist society that Marx had rarely addressed, such as modernist art and literature. Not the least among his concerns is their unexpected contribution to the symbolic adornment of the powerful. I shall now consider, under six headings, further instances of his debt to Marx.

Further Textual Evidence for Viewing Bourdieu as a Non-Stalinist Marxist

(1) Algeria

There are references throughout Bourdieu's work to the terms in which Marx characterises economic thought. Marx refers critically to the axiom of classical economic thought, namely that the highest rationality is the pursuit of production and wealth for its own sake: in Bourdieu, this is expressed as the doctrine of 'the economy for the economy's sake'. Like Marx, Bourdieu poses the issue of *when* such an economic rationality is pursued. Far from being a universal outlook, he insists, it is a historical acquisition. The question appears in his well-known work, *Outline of a Theory of Practice* (1977 [1972]). The same points are made earlier in *Le déracinement* (1964), Bourdieu's and Sayad's remarkable study of Algerian ex-peasants and casualised workers, undertaken amidst all the dangers of the Algerian War. This shows the gradual acculturation of Algerian workers to a Western conception of work: the notion that it consists of paid employment. Imbued with this new principle, they become distanced from the peasant ethos, in which the only real work had been labour on the land – a 'semi-artistic' work with nature.[15]

Now, even in 1958, Bourdieu acknowledges the Western mantra of a 'clash of civilisations': he grants that peasants do not readily display the practices summed up in economists' rational choice theory (2008), but he breaks with those 'acculturation theorists' who saw tradition alone as blocking the acceptance of (French) modernity. Rather, the clash is a consequence of domination and especially of domination via the *primitive accumulation* of land. The Algerians' jointly-possessed property was seized from them, starting with the 1863 Sénatus-consulte Law and cemented with the further legalisation of the French colonists' hold over their land in 1873.[16] In brief, Bourdieu's studies of Algeria show how similar processes occurred there to those Marx saw with his own eyes in the Rhineland or discovered, through the Scottish Enlightenment, about the Highland clearances. Indeed, Bourdieu's language with respect to Algeria is of 'social surgery': the 'social vivisection' and fragmentation of a whole society in order to institute individual land ownership, and to legitimate large colonial estates (1961: 105).[17]

Who then are the bearers of the 'economic habitus' in this sense of rational efficiency and rational risk-control? Bourdieu notes that in capitalist modernity this '[John] Stuartmillian view' of economic life is inculcated everywhere, even into the very young. He quotes schoolchildren in Lowestoft in the 1950s who had gone so far as to form their own *insurance society* to protect them against risks: they got four shillings for each caning on the backside (2008: 247).

What stands in the way of rationally maximising gain? He calls this, in 1977 [1972], the *good faith economy* – the gift economy of the peasantry. Ultimately this is founded on 'a whole art of living'. Underneath this familiar anthropological conception is there not also here a covert reference to Marx? Marx had proposed that Aristotle and the ancients had a nobler conception than modern thinkers about what the social world was *for*: the engendering of a good society. In such a society, the entire social order revolved around the production of *men* rather than production *for profits' sake*: '[In Ancient Greece] the human being appears as the aim of production rather than production as the aim of mankind and wealth as the aim of production'. (Marx, 1973 [1857]: 487–488.) In identical terms, Bourdieu invokes Aristotle, depicting the Kabylian Algerians as possessing the 'logic of the philia' – a logic based on community and friendship – rather than a modern 'economic habitus' (2008: 207–208).[18]

Bourdieu's writing on Algeria refers frequently to *time* and to *different experiences of temporality* (for example, 2008: 89–91). Here, he clearly takes issue with the simplistic economic interpretation of Paris intellectuals, such as Fanon, who argues that those who are most impoverished and dispossessed will be the most revolutionary. Explicitly adopting a 'culturalist' theory,[19] he contends instead that the greatest misery – that of the *Lumpenproletariat* – is incompatible with organisation or long-term planning. Rather, such lived experience is felt as a hand-to-mouth existence, where next week's food is precarious – if not today's.

At this point, early in his career, we notice him classifying perceptions of the future and the past, just as Husserl (1970 [1936]) had done.[20] Yet, Husserl's analysis of the underlying phenomena of everyday life provides no clue as to how social structures – such as those of aristocracy, hierarchy or gift exchange – shape experience. For Bourdieu, in contrast, the sense of time has to be grasped as interwoven with the mode of social existence that the group possesses. Thus, there are gulfs in temporal experience dividing various groups. First, traditional peasant communities anticipate the future via a cyclical view of natural and social life: Bourdieu follows Marx in calling this 'simple reproduction' (2008: 93). Second – as we have seen – the deracinated urban sub-proletariat of ultra-precarious workers, cut off from their rural past, are condemned only to experience the present. Third, a more secure section of the proletariat, emerging in great cities, nurtures the conception of an alternative future: one radically different from the past. In other words, the stable working class alone is able to conceptualise their present as an arena of injustice provoked by historically determined structures, rather than seeing the present as the province of a magical fatalism.[21] Here, Bourdieu is enhancing Marxism with a phenomenological awareness of the impact of extreme poverty (cf. Moore, 1973; cf. also Vološinov, 1973: 88–89).

(2) Education and Class

Especially since the Second World War, the role of education in legitimating class has been quite extraordinary. Until very recently, education served to remove from contestation an entire sphere of unequal rewards on the assumption that students were universalistically selected. Now Marx, of course, had criticised as bogus the universalism that Hegel had identified with the German State bureaucracy (Marx, 1970 [1843]: 41–54; 1975 [1843–4]: 99–116).[22] In very similar terms, Bourdieu had become disenchanted with the spurious claims to universalism of the French state. I have referred already to Bourdieu's openly acknowledged debts to Marx. Perhaps the most well-known is *Reproduction*'s famous assessment of the examination, which recycles once more Marx's earlier irony:

> The examination is nothing but the bureaucratic baptism of knowledge, the official recognition of the transubstantiation of profane knowledge into sacred knowledge. (*Marx's Critique of Hegel's Doctrine of the State*, Marx, 1975 [1843–4]: 112, quoted from Bourdieu and Passeron, 1990 [1970]: 141)

Is it not this same 'sacred knowledge' that Bourdieu later calls 'certified cultural capital' or alludes to as the 'consecrated canon of texts'? As all his work reveals, the dominant classes, from the twentieth century on, reproduce themselves not only through material mechanisms, via the inheritance of money and businesses, but also culturally, via privileged access to educational success. Their young people's high recruitment qualifications, conferred by both home and school, are the normal yield of the bourgeois family upbringing.

Bourdieu continues later to extend his gaze to the deeper social realities of class and culture. In particular, he demystifies the elite – especially that section of the French elite that occupies the highest positions in the state, as well as the public corporations. Their rigorous and ascetic training in the Grandes Écoles produces an extraordinary esprit de corps or what he calls a 'social magic'. In the second chapter of *The State Nobility* (1996 [1989]), Bourdieu first subjects this fraction of the dominant class to a statistical analysis, 'objectifying' it to reveal its highly privileged origins. Second, he undertakes a subtle content analysis of teachers' comments on philosophy essays written in the preparatory classes for the Grandes Écoles. Acting without the teachers' knowledge, he undertakes a kind of sociological experiment, matching each set of essay comments to the physically separated records on the students' social backgrounds. The results are surprising: he shows that the essays of children from the higher civil service tend to be praised as 'brilliant' or 'masterly', the essays of petty-bourgeois students are chided for being 'pedestrian' or at best 'solid', while the work of young people from the lower classes – such as cleaners' children – are derided as 'derivative' and 'unoriginal'. These teachers would be horrified if accused of deliberately classifying such students' essays by their class origins. Yet, they have operated such a selection unconsciously, seduced by the more academic culture possessed by the children of the dominant class.

Could we even go so far as to suggest that this 'machine of cognitive misrecognition' – as Bourdieu provocatively calls it – has a parallel place to *Capital*'s paradoxes about the extraction of surplus value (Marx, 1976 [1867]: 279–80, 293–306)? For Marx, in *Capital*, the front stage or bourgeois public space is the sphere of fair contracts between masters and labourers – 'Freedom, Equality, Property and Bentham'. Yet, in the back regions, when the factory door slams shut, the workers know they are going to get 'a tanning' (a skinning) (Marx, 1976 [1867]: 279–280). Similarly, for Bourdieu, the state, front-stage, makes a claim to the universalistic treatment of all its schoolchildren. Yet, back-stage, when the *school* doors bang shut, the proclaimed equality of each pupil can be shown to be paper-thin, undermined by the deeper-laid mechanisms of class reproduction. A symbolic violence is perpetrated towards the ordinary child – creating the irremovable feeling of their *own, individual failure* (1984 [1979]: 156).[23] Such symbolic injury, I might add, supplements the sometimes physical violence of surplus value extraction in the workplace.

(3) The Cultural Field

In late capitalist societies, Bourdieu claims, even art has come to serve ideological functions, similar to religion. Nobody, he comments wryly, has had any reason to unveil the interests behind 'the game of culture' (1984 [1979]: 12). To remedy this, he must demystify the modern aristocracy of culture: the cultivated elite. First, Bourdieu insists that the individual lover of art is drawn to artistic works that are backed by the entire imprimatur or aura of the art-world itself (1984 [1979]: 86). Indeed, what is often seen as the 'natural gift' of a creative subject masks the historical 'privatisation' of artistic production: an artistic production that had once been recognised – even as late as Herder – as founded on collective social property. Furthermore, such art-lovers' discriminating choices confer hidden symbolic profits:

> The denial of the low, coarse, vulgar, venal and [...] in a word, natural enjoyment which constitutes the sacred sphere of culture implies an affirmation of the superiority of those who [are only] satisfied with sublimated, refined, distinguished [...] pleasures. That is why art and cultural consumption are predisposed, consciously or not, to fulfil a social function of legitimating social differences. (1984 [1979]: 7)

In Bourdieu's words, *art* is now the 'spiritual point d'honneur' of the bourgeoisie (1993: 44). At present, consecrated avant-garde art – from surrealism to land art or photorealism, ought to be seen less as a protest and more as a status ornament – a kind of spiritual brooch, which proclaims the higher humanity of its wearer. Now Bourdieu is making a veiled allusion here to the well-known sociological comment by Marx about religion as a spiritual point d'honneur:

> Religion is the general theory of this world, its encyclopaedic compendium, its logic in popular form, its *spiritual point d'honneur*, its enthusiasm, its moral sanction [...] its universal basis of consolation and justification. (Marx, 1975 [1843–4]: 244, my emphasis)[24]

Similarly, Bourdieu:

> The cult of art and the artist [...] is one of the necessary components of the bourgeois art of living, to which it brings a *supplément d'âme*, its spiritualistic point of honour. (1993: 44, italics in original)

I shall show below how Bourdieu's analysis of religion – with its complex character as doxa and heterodoxy, ideology and utopia – becomes important for his theoretical modelling of the secular cultural field.

(4) Struggles Within the University World: Homo Academicus

Homo Academicus contains a chapter on the explosion of contradictions which made up the events of May 1968. Often overlooked within his work, it provides the nearest we have to Bourdieu's theory of revolution. Interestingly, he sees current unrest as engendered by crushed expectations: chiefly, the occupational hopes that had been nurtured within an expanded educational field, only to be dashed later. Direct insurrection of labour against capital is now unlikely, he states.

Nevertheless, despite this apparent break, there are still some parallels with Marx. Marx writes of the concentration of the capitalist class, with small businesses going to the wall in the interests of the wider class; similarly, for Bourdieu, the main discontent triggering the 1968 academic crisis was stemmed by a parallel concentration of cultural capital, within the hands of the few. What does this imply? In an observation that has obvious implications today, he comments that those groups who spent three or four years on a degree and then discovered that they were doomed to *manual or unskilled work* were particularly resentful, caught, as they were, *in a dialectic of qualification and devaluation* ('downclassing'). So also were young lecturers, in 1968 fearful then – as now – that they would never get the promotion that was due to them.

An educational crisis of disappointed aspirations can affect a whole generation, but it does so with an accumulation of crises specific to each field. A contradiction within one field, like the universities, may be linked through a chain reaction to similar contradictions in analogous fields – in radio and television, for example.[25] Then the different senses of time operating within these separate worlds can be brought together: by means of crisis within this *uneven development*, the agents become *contemporaneous*, expressing their different miseries (1988 [1984]: 180). Here you have the preconditions for a successful revolution (1988 [1984]: 172).

In a vivid phenomenological analysis, Bourdieu reveals how at *the critical moment* everything changes. By overturning their usual future, the crisis provokes actors to forget their place. In the festive atmosphere, students use slang even with professors, everything is turned upside down and a sense of 'open time' emerges (1988 [1984]: 162); a vague and almost empty time, *common* to the different fields, seizes everyone (1988 [1984]: 185; cf. Durkheim, 1987 [1897]: 210).

Yet, he also draws attention to the unseen force of the *hierarchy of capitals* separating workers, who are low in cultural capital, from professionals, who are much higher. The alliance forged between workers and intellectuals (as with artists) is thus very fragile – a thing of rhetoric, rarely based on real interaction but nevertheless strengthened by down-classing (1988 [1984]: 164 and 179). We should read this as a realist's warning about *facile* utopias, whilst noting Bourdieu's continued evaluative stand in favour of a 'feasible utopia' (1998 [1997]). Here, I would see Sintomer (1996) as fundamentally right in his analysis of Bourdieu – that he had two phases: a critical 'ethic of suspicion' and a positive ethic of liberty and justice (1996: 91). The first one is a phase of demystification (which subjects ideologies such as the Romantic artistic critique of capitalism to further *disenchantment*). The second is one that *builds* on the concept of 'historical transcendent universals' (such as autonomous scientific experimentation). It sees these as enabling a 'corporatism of the universal': a *Realpolitik* of Reason and Morality which favours liberty, cooperation, and democratic civil rights (Sintomer, 1996: 95–97).

(5) Quixotism: A Different Conception of Agency

Brubaker claims that Bourdieu never uses the Marxist concept of modes or relations of production (1985: 761). Now, while he rarely uses these terms in the orthodox fashion, he does refer to the new 'school-mediated mode of reproduction' (1996 [1989]: 285), in which these same historical divisions are present, but at a deeper level. Another indicator of their persistence is his use of the motif 'Le Mort Saisit Le Vif' (Death Seizes the Living) – a phrase that periodically appears in his work, most evidently in an important article on absolutism (1980). The title of this article, 'Le Mort Saisit le Vif', is again a covert reference to Marx. He comments in *Capital* on the absence of any neat succession of modes of production:

> Alongside the modern evils, we suffer from a whole series of evils arising from the passive survival of archaic and outmoded modes of production, with their accompanying train of anachronistic social and political relations. We suffer not only from the living, but from the dead. *Le Mort Saisit Le Vif*! (Marx, 1976 [1867]: 91)

The suffering provoked by the grip of the dead is never very far away when Bourdieu is debating the nature of peasant society. Indeed, unlike others from the Western Marxist tradition, this 'outmoded [rural] mode of production' is one of his recurrent concerns, contrasting with the concentration on the city within the work of Benjamin, Adorno, Horkheimer, and Lefebvre.[26] Thus, he grasps with great poignancy the sacrifices made by second sons of peasants who often give up even marriage and reproduction (children) in order to preserve their inherited way of life (2002a). The interviews with small farmers in *The Weight of the World* make the same point: their acceptance of protracted hours and a low level of income could be explained only as their 'obligation' to the family farm that had been passed onto them by those brought up in an earlier, agricultural way of life (1999 [1993]: 381–391). As he points out, they have been 'inherited by their heritage' – another reference to Marx (*A Contribution to the Critique of Political Economy*, quoted in 1992: 122; see also 1990 [1987]: 57–58, 2002a: 169).

Further, Bourdieu refers, throughout his early work, to the Don Quixote syndrome. In this, there is a radical discrepancy between the world as the agent's habitus led them to expect it and its real structures. Now in *Don Quixote*, Cervantes alludes to the gulf in seventeenth-century Spain between the idealised chivalric rules of the aristocratic feudal habitus and the actual world of the transition to commercial capital, where money rules supreme. 'Quixotism' as a syndrome is here used as a shorthand by Bourdieu to refer to the clash of expectations with new realities, just as Marx had earlier used it in the same way, referring in many works to the character of the 'Great Don' (Marx, 1976 [1867]: 176 and 179).[27]

After *Distinction* (1984 [1979]: 109), Bourdieu drops his explicit references to Quixote. From his earlier concept of Quixotism, however, he retains a more general type: that of a *fractured habitus (habitus clivé)*.[28] It is this fractured or cleft habitus that leads its bearers to become subversive, capable of artistic and intellectual, or even social, revolutions. Hence, the significance of the fact that Manet, for example, had a subversive habitus, in which his dispositions were in 'dynamic friction' with his position in the field that he had entered. It is this that led him to introduce the break with Academicism in the field of modern art (2002 [2000]: 31–32; Bourdieu and Chartier, 2010: 89–95). Similarly with Beethoven, Flaubert and Heidegger (2002 [2000]: 31–32; Bourdieu and Chartier, 2010: 90–103). In brief, the reference to Quixotism provides another hint – pace Brubaker – that Bourdieu is profoundly influenced by Marx.

(6) Finally, Bourdieu's General Theory of Cultural Power

Bourdieu's demystifying gaze has been stressed, but we can also see the glimmerings in his work of other – more emancipatory – theories. In the little-known *Genesis and Structure of the Religious Field* (1991 [1971]), Bourdieu aims to get beyond the magic circle surrounding the respective sociologies of religion of Marx, Weber and Durkheim. He will integrate them, not eclectically, but by providing the geometrical place where their various perspectives meet (1991 [1971]: 2). Yet, this path-breaking work on fields also possesses a problematic of key significance that comes straight from Marx. In *The Eighteenth Brumaire*, Marx had debated why the 1848 French revolution had failed to take off. Although all the objective prerequisites for a revolution existed – in terms of material inequalities – the absence of a new critique of society and a fresh vision of the future fatally undermined the revolutionaries.

Bourdieu takes this and reworks it into a theory of prophets (1991 [1971], sections 3 and 4). The prophets' critique is of religion – especially of the priests' religion; however, their critique is not without relevance for later popular movements. They demand, for example, the *democratisation* of the gift of grace, and 'autogestion': the workers' control, so to speak, of religious movements. Such prophets, like the proletarianised intelligentsia more widely, often come from a precarious and powerless position within the Church. This makes it easy for them to empathise with the low place of the subordinate classes.[29] The battles they fight within the Church only begin to have any impact on the political order when they are linked to a subversive political doctrine and resonate in a period of *crisis*.

Bourdieu objectifies the conditions of prophetic new ways of seeing and their power:

> If there is, doubtless, no symbolic revolution that does not presuppose a political revolution, the political revolution is insufficient by itself to produce the symbolic revolution, which is necessary to give it an adequate language, the condition for its full accomplishment [i.e. as a political revolution…]. For as long as a crisis is without its prophet, the schema by which one thinks the upside-down world are still the products of the world to be reversed. (1991 [1971]: 37, trans. amended)

He then quotes the famous lines of the *Eighteenth Brumaire*:

> The tradition of dead generations weighs like a nightmare on the minds of the living. And, just when they appear to be engaged in revolutionary transformation, they *timidly* conjure up the spirits of the past to help them, they borrow their names, slogans and clothes […]. Luther put on the mark of the apostle Paul, the revolution of 1789–1814 draped itself as the Roman Republic […]. (Marx: 1974: 146–147)

Bourdieu adds that the

> political revolution finds its fulfilment only in the symbolic revolution that makes it exist fully, in giving it the means to think itself in its truth, that is, as unprecedented, unthinkable and unnameable according to all the previous grids of classification and interpretation […]. (1991 [1971]: 37)

Hence, the power of doxa and heterodoxy in his work, which he regarded – following Husserl – as more fundamental than questions of ideology. Unlike the other poststructuralists influenced by Husserl, however, he notes the underlying social conditions helping to spread the conditions for the break with orthodoxy:

> [J]ust as the priest is allied to the ordinary order, so the prophet is the man for situations of crisis, when the established order is rocked and the whole future is suspended [...] Marcel Mauss noted 'famines [and] wars, instigate prophets, heresies [...] violent contacts broach even the division of the population [...] hybridisations of entire societies [...] necessarily and precisely cause new ideas and new traditions [...]'. (1991 [1971]: 34, trans. amended)

This concern with the social conditions for symbolic and political revolutions recurs throughout Bourdieu's work. We can see it, for example, in his critique of Weber's theory of charismatic leader, which he regards as too individualist (1991 [1971]: 20–21). Weber is still insufficiently aware of the *leaders'* dependence themselves on the masses that they empower, not just the masses' mould-breaking acts when they are supported by the charismatic leader (1987 [1971]; 1991 [1971]: 21).

We can see this same concern for social conditions in Bourdieu's analysis of scientific revolutions and especially his critique of Kuhn's purely internalist account of such revolutions (2004 [2001]: 15).[30] But it flows also through his work on secular, modernist artists and writers, especially those groups positioned inside the restricted cultural field, who act as sources of resistance and transformation. See here his references to Manet (2004 [2001]: 16), to Baudelaire's 'realist formalism' (1996 [1992]: 107), to Virginia Woolf (2001 [1998]), and to Mapplethorpe (Bourdieu and Haacke, 1995 [1994]).

In brief, for Bourdieu, the social structures conducive to conflicting visions or divisions of the world were of key importance in his understanding of the political. Within these, however, he was always especially concerned with those disruptive discourses that denaturalise the social, that reject 'the racism of class' and that refuse to grant an essential necessity to the contemporary arrangements of everyday life. Such heterodoxies can all be seen as vital for a transformative politics. For Bourdieu, a symbolic revolution may flare up within any given cultural field. Yet, unlike the easy substitution of each avant-garde by its successors, such symbolic revolutions do not by themselves remove the more difficult need – from the perspective of the dominated – for a further, politico-economic transformation.

Conclusion

Terry Lovell (2003) has strikingly used the case of the charismatic African-American leader, Rosa Parks, to show how she 'resisted, with authority', the bus segregation of the late 1950s in the Southern States of America. Her quiet courage matched the needs of the forcibly subordinated African-American masses. Lovell uses Bourdieu's critique of Weber's over-individualistic theory of charisma to interpret this case – a development from the *Genesis* article quoted above. Yet, writers like Jeffrey C. Alexander can still state, in *The Civil Sphere*, that Bourdieu has no understanding of 'universalism' or 'cross-sectional solidarity', and hence his theory can throw no light on the epoch-making events of Civil Rights (2006: 562).

The contrary, it seems to me, is true. Bourdieu's *Genesis and Structure of the Religious Field* provides an invaluable account of the symbolic revolutions necessary for such political undertakings, and in this work, allusions to the writings of Marx play a prominent part. Nonetheless, Bourdieu's work does not give us simply new tools for social transformation. It also aids towards a reflexive understanding that could stop revolutions being betrayed (Bourdieu and Wacquant, 1992 [1992]).[31] In particular, we might learn from his grasp of the way personal resentment can draw people towards revolt, whilst also being a poor start for a post-revolutionary epoch. This occurs especially when the revolutionaries are more concerned with 'lopping off the tall poppies', as opposed to a more 'generous' 'ressentiment' (Bourdieu and Wacquant, 1992 [1992]: 212). The ethno-sociologist, he once argued, ought to be a kind of 'organic intellectual of humanity' (2008: 355): in other words, they should be concerned with the social conditions that create the 'social magic' of the present, so to dissolve that magic's subterranean force.

I hope to have shown that far from Bourdieu's 'political turn' having been a feature of the last years of his life – from *The Weight of the World* onwards – he possesses throughout his writings an agenda that was very similar to that of Marx. Indeed, his sociology is a contribution to an enhanced and sophisticated Western Marxism that might restore the power of Marx's original ideas within new social contexts. In this sense, perhaps Verdès-Leroux has a grain of truth in her otherwise ludicrous allegation that Bourdieu is a 'sociological terrorist' (Verdès-Leroux, 1998: 5). He is indeed one of the streams of great social thinkers concerned fundamentally with justice, with the mechanisms of how social injustice becomes customary, and with the transformative consequences of this knowledge.

Notes

1 'Histmat' or 'diamat' were the bowdlerised forms of Marxist thought taken up in the former Eastern European State socialist societies, characterised especially by mechanical materialism, and a strong emphasis on the inevitability of historical progress.

2 Amongst such names I include Lukács, Gramsci, Adorno, Benjamin, Williams, and E. P. Thompson. I cannot go into detail here about the links between these writers and Bourdieu, all of whom have been cited by him.

3 Lescourret (2008: 65–66) gives this account of an episode when Bourdieu taught at the *lycée* in Moulins, before his conscription to the Algerian War.

4 This concept is borrowed from Husserl (1970 [1936]), just as 'habitus' is acknowledged by Bourdieu to have had numerous progenitors.

5 I have no space here to discuss Bourdieu's innovative approach to symbolic forms, that is, to Durkheim's *social* categories as opposed to Kant's transcendental-universal categories. Just as a culturalist Marxist, E. P. Thompson, was to see symbolic forms – such as the idea of the working class – as emergent imagined entities which subsequently became established as part of a 'whole way of struggle' (1968), so also Bourdieu stressed symbolic forms as cultural communications based on classification.

It should be noted here that classification rests on distinctions within a dialectic of superiority and inferiority (or 'culture' and mere 'subcultures'). In this light the whole of *Distinction* could be regarded as a Durkheimian study based on the secular equivalent to that of the sacred and the profane. Divergences in habitus are thus the arena for a disjuncture between celebratory reaffirmations and peremptory dismissals. Yet, whereas Durkheim looked forward to modernity as going beyond the anomic and forced division of labour to centre on the 'sacred individual', Bourdieu shows continued clashes in perspectives on the sacred and profane (1984 [1979]: ch. 1; Durkheim, 1995 [1912]).

6 In British sociological thought, Marx and Weber tend to be opposed. For Bourdieu, in contrast, the great Weberian exploration of legitimation largely strengthens the Marxist conception of domination, much like the Gramscian theme of hegemony. Bourdieu characterises his method in *In Other Words* as analogous to, but broader than, Althusser's deployment of Marx: viz thinking 'with Marx against Marx or with Durkheim against Durkheim, and also, of course, with Marx and Durkheim against Weber, and vice versa' (1990 [1987]: 49).

7 On habitus, see Fowler (1997: 3 and 46).

8 Benjamin's essay on the 'author as producer' makes an analogous argument about the identity of position between workers and cultural producers: Bourdieu, however, also draws out the discrepancies that might lead the alliance to founder (Benjamin, 1973 [1966]).

9 In both these cases – cultural capital in the case of science; the first generation in the case of economic capital – what is at stake, is the life and death struggle to the commitments of the game. Weber is well-known on this, although I prefer Christopher Hill's reassessment. Social theorists sometimes forget, however, that Marx also acknowledged that for the Manchester businessman 'his own private consumption counts as a robbery committed against the accumulation of his capital'. The modernising entrepreneur, he writes 'views accumulation' in tragic terms, as a 'renunciation of pleasure' (Marx, 1976 [1867]: 739 and 741), whilst simultaneously disregarding the structural underpinning: the fact that he chiefly makes his money by the extraction of surplus value (1976 [1867]: 300–301).

10 For example, Calhoun has argued that Bourdieu lacks such an analysis of 'contradiction' or any other 'motor of history' (1993: 70). The term 'crisis' appears most strikingly in the title of a late collection of articles dealing with the 'crisis of peasant society, in the Béarn', or 'the end of a world'. In the crisis and marginalisation of this peasant society, profound social suffering is manifested first and foremost in the relegation of a high proportion of the second sons of peasants to bachelorhood. It is also revealed, secondly, in the low self-esteem and the awkward use of the dominant French language by the middle-aged farm-workers, in notable contrast to the confident Béarn dialect of the older generation of peasants (2002a).

11 In his latest analysis of Bourdieu, Callinicos claims that there is only a 'relatively weak conception of systemic contradiction' (2006: 82).

12 Bourdieu states: 'The value of culture, the supreme fetish, is generated in the initial investment implied in the mere fact of entering the game, joining in the collective belief in the value of the game [...;] the opposition between the "authentic" and the "imitation", "true" culture and "popularization" conceals [...] the fundamental recognition of the cultural game and its stakes' (1984 [1979]: 250). The similarities here between Bourdieu and Adorno, another member of the Marxist tradition, are very striking, especially where Adorno emphasises the contemporary 'hollowing- out' of certain elements crucial to art in earlier epochs: 'The possibility of neutralization – the transformation of culture into something independent and external, removed from any possible relation to praxis – makes it possible to integrate it into the organization from which it untiringly cleanses itself (1991 [1972]: 101)'. Or, much as in *Distinction,* Adorno asserts the need for a relational analysis: 'Culture is viewed as pure humanity without regard for its functional relationships within society' (1991 [1972]: 93). Adorno even links the taste for 'culture' or 'pure art' – including modernism – to high cultural capital: 'Culture long ago evolved into its own contradiction, the congealed content of educational privilege [...], for that reason it now takes its place within the material production process as an administered supplement to it' (1991 [1972]: 109).

13 For an illuminating account of the relationship of Bourdieu vis-à-vis Habermas, see Susen (2007).

14 The United Kingdom's RAE (Research Assessment Exercise) – imposed typically at four-yearly intervals between 1986 and 2008 – was intended to 'produce high quality profiles for each submission of research activity made by [higher educational] institutions [so that the funding bodies may] determine the grant for research to the institutions which fund' (see http://www.rae.ac.uk). Its successor, the REF (Research Exercise Framework), has the same purpose, but bases its allocations on quality – primarily judged by citation numbers – the wider impact of the research, and the vitality of the research environment (see http://www.hefce.ac.uk/research/ref).

15 We might note here, in passing, that the term 'semi-artistic' is also Marx's concept in the *Grundrisse* (Marx, 1973 [1857]: 497).

16 He refers to these Acts as real 'machines of war' designed to disaggregate dangerous economic and political unities (2008: 67).

17 See also citations from Bourdieu in Yacine (in Bourdieu, 2008: 37; cf. Marx, 1973 [1857] and 1976 [1867], I, Part 8.

18 In *The Algerians* (1962 [1958]) Bourdieu introduces a telling phrase, and one that has been misunderstood by those who criticise him as purely cynical. He refers to the good faith gift exchange as operating on a 'double register', possessing elements of 'unavowed self-interest' as well as 'proclaimed generosity' (1962 [1958]: 107). Later, in *Pascalian Meditations,* he clarifies this, invoking as a mistaken 'theoretical monster' the idea that agents might simultaneously give generously and *consciously* expect a useful return (2000 [1997]: 194).

19 Later, in an *Invitation to Reflexive Sociology,* he cites favourably the British culturalist historian, E. P. Thompson (Bourdieu and Wacquant, 1992: 91n.35; 92n.36–37); he also notes Williams' *The Country and the City* as a 'très beau livre' (2002a: 254).

20 However, he also remarks (1991 [1971]: 39n.15) that another source was *Capital,* Volume II.

21 In the later history of the working class, more individuated structures of education and management lead those without capital to experience their futures in the categories of mental illness rather than collective critiques (1984 [1979]: 156).

22 For example, in Marx's *Early Writings* (1975 [1843–4]) the Hegelian notion of the early nineteenth century German bureaucracy as the concrete embodiment of universal rational knowledge is examined and found wanting. Going further, Marx argued that Hegel's claims for universalism on behalf of the Prussian bureaucracy in fact concealed the civil servants' sectional interests:

> The bureaucracy appears to itself as the ultimate purpose of the state [...] The bureaucracy is the imaginary state alongside the real state; it is the spiritualism of the state [...] Within itself, however, *spiritualism* degenerates into *crass materialism*, the materialism of passive obedience, the worship of authority, the mechanism of fixed, formal action [...]. As for the individual bureaucrat, the purpose of the state becomes his private purpose, *a hunt for promotion, careerism* [...]. (Marx, 1975 [1843–4]: 107–108.)

Such criticism of Enlightenment rhetoric as based on a disputable or 'false universalism' was initiated early in Marx's career, in 1842–3 (McLellan, 1973: 66–67). That this well-known critique of Hegel by Marx was familiar to Bourdieu and Passeron is evident from their quotation from it on the nature of examination knowledge, as we shall see. I suggest that this issue is of continuing importance to Bourdieu, who can be seen as exploring further the emphasis that Marx had put on the role of education in his early work on civil society (McLellan, 1973: 74).

23 Bourdieu has two, interlinked views of the school – first, as we have seen, that it is an arena for a rigged competition, where symbolic violence occurs. The second stresses the gender divisions that also come into play, operating alongside pride in a manual worker identity, so as to distance the working-class boy from the school. Instead he will celebrate his toughness, masculinity and nonconformity by various anti-school displays of subversive wit (1992: 95–97). Without wanting to reduce Bourdieu's sociological advances to the effects of a troubled youth, we might guess that he himself was one of these proudly independent school students, distinguished at first mainly for his 'fractured habitus' (2004: 111) and 'bad character' (2004 [2001]: 121). He was, he recalls, indignant about the arbitrary discipline imposed in the *lycée*, which – especially at night in the boarding section, resembled both Genet's penitentiary and Goffman's asylum. Interestingly, he tells us that he was given between 200 and 300 detentions and would have been expelled, save for the weight of his parents' hopes for his future (2004 [2001]: 120–125).

24 The other main axis of relationships to culture is the popular aesthetic: which he christens the 'naïve gaze', evoked in rock and pop music, figurative reproductions of beautiful women, and highly moralistic sentimental literature (or industrial novels). His sources for theorising this popular culture are not just Émile Rousseau, Richard Hoggart and Raymond Williams. They are also writers such as Bakhtin, who represents the earlier 1920s and 30s heterodox Marxism of the Tartu School (cited 1984 [1979]: 604). Bakhtin's *Rabelais and his World* draws particularly on the pithy speech, grotesque realism and gay laughter of workers and peasants, especially during Carnival. Note here, again, that Bourdieu's sociology of cultural consumption is backed by studies which originated in dissident Marxist circles.

25 'The probability that the structural factors which underlie critical tension in a particular field will come to engender a situation of crisis, fostering the emergence of extraordinary events [...] reaches a maximum when a *coincidence* is achieved between the effects of several latent crises of maximum intensity.' (1988 [1984]: 161–162). Bourdieu develops this theory of the interconnected series of field-based changes in relation to crises by using the work of Cournot (1988 [1984]: 174).

26 I am grateful to Georgia Giannakopoulos for general comments and especially for clarifying this point.

27 Don Quixote figures in Marx as a figure who had to learn that certain codes of civilisation (e.g. knightly chivalry) were not eternal: 'And there is Don Quixote who long ago paid the penalty for wrongly imagining that knight errantry was compatible with all economic forms of society' (1976 [1867]: 175, footnote 35 appears on page 176) (see also Prawer, 1976: 240–241 and 292–293). Bourdieu uses Sancho [Panza] as an example of someone who fails to adopt a relational understanding of the modern world, citing Marx's delineation of him in *The German Ideology* to make the point (Bourdieu, 1968 [1968]: 692–693).

28 In *Distinction*, the same idea emerges as a radicalised concept of anomie, hysteresis. In this, the habitus adapted to entry to an earlier professional world is forced to adjust, due to a mismatch of economic opportunities (1984 [1979]: 68).

29 They are especially compelling when their own precarious position within the religious field is accompanied by an earlier contrasting experience, for example, of class privilege (cf. fractured habitus, above) (1991 [1971]: 34).

30 See the vital passage critical of Thomas Kuhn:

> Kuhn's merit [...] is that he has drawn attention to the discontinuities, the revolutions [in scientific knowledge]. But because he is content to describe the scientific world from a quasi-Durkheimian perspective, as a community dominated by a central norm, he does not seem to me to put forward a coherent model for explaining change. It is true that a particularly generous reading can construct such a model and find the motor of change in the internal conflict between orthodoxy and heresy, the defenders of the paradigm and the innovators, *with the latter sometimes reinforced in periods of crisis, by the fact that the barriers between science and the major intellectual currents within society are then removed.* I realize that through this reinterpretation I have attributed to Kuhn the essential part of my own representation of the logic of the field and its dynamic. But this is also, perhaps, a good way to show the difference between the two visions and the specific contribution of the notion of the field [...]. (2004 [2001]: 15–16, my emphasis.)

Bouveresse (2003) has criticised this, arguing that where fields like science have high demands for entry, the homologies with the field of power – and openness to it – are concomitantly *reduced* (see also Lane, 2006). It is a pity that Bourdieu never specified exactly what he meant by the openness of science – at a time of symbolic revolution – to the major intellectual currents swirling more broadly in the field of power, but there is certainly evidence for this in relation to the Newtonian revolution.

31 Lane (2006) has written a scathing indictment of the lacunae of Bourdieu's sociological theory. In my view this is a misleading critique of why Bourdieu strategically supported French Republicanism in 1995, viz, as a bastion of 'civilisation' against neo-liberalism. Lane's assessment of Bourdieu's 'nostalgic' classical canonical modernism hides the fact that his own stance – one that emphasizes the innovative aspects of commerce – may also be a cloak for an uncritical defence of the market. Nevertheless, Lane is right about

three issues, first, Bourdieu's theoretical omissions (as well as insights) in his over-static view of masculine domination, second, his formulaic dismissal of all uneducated voices in the sphere of cultural production, and third, his confusing view of Republicanism. Despite his images of the 'Left Hand' and the 'Right Hand' of the State, Bourdieu's Republicanism retains at least a residue of Durkheim's problematic notion of the State as the social brain of the societal organism.

References

Adorno, Theodor W. (1991 [1972]) *The Culture Industry: Selected Essays on Mass Culture*, trans. Anson G. Rabinbach, edited with an introduction by J. M. Bernstein, London: Routledge.

Alexander, Jeffrey C. (2006) *The Civil Sphere*, Oxford: Oxford University Press.

Archer, Margaret (2007) *Making Our Way Through the World: Human Reflexivity and Social Mobility*, Cambridge: Cambridge University Press.

Benjamin, Walter (1973 [1966]) *Understanding Brecht*, trans. Anna Bostock, introduction by Stanley Mitchell, London: NLB.

Bourdieu, Pierre (1962 [1958]) *The Algerians*, trans. Alan C. M. Ross, with a preface by Raymond Aron, Boston: Beacon Press.

Bourdieu, Pierre (1968 [1968]) 'Structuralism and Theory of Sociological Knowledge', *Social Research* 35(4): 681–706.

Bourdieu, Pierre (1977 [1972]) *Outline of a Theory of Practice*, trans. Richard Nice, Cambridge: Cambridge University Press.

Bourdieu, Pierre (1980) 'Le mort saisit le vif', *Actes de la recherche en sciences sociales* 32–33: 3–14.

Bourdieu, Pierre (1984 [1979]) *Distinction*, trans. Richard Nice, London: RKP.

Bourdieu, Pierre (1985 [1984]) 'Social Space and the Genesis of Groups', *Theory and Society* 14(6): 723–744.

Bourdieu, Pierre (1987) 'What Makes a Social Class? On the Theoretical and Practical Existence of Groups', trans. Loïc Wacquant and David Young, *Berkeley Journal of Sociology* 32(1): 1–18.

Bourdieu, Pierre (1987 [1971]) 'Legitimation and Structured Interest in Weber's Sociology of Religion', in Scott Lash and Sam Whimster (eds.) *Max Weber, Rationality and Modernity*, trans. Chris Turner, London: Allen and Unwin, pp. 119–136.

Bourdieu, Pierre (1987 [1987]) 'Social Space and Symbolic Power', *Sociological Theory*, 7 (1) 14–25.

Bourdieu, Pierre (1988 [1984]) *Homo Academicus*, trans. Peter Collier, Cambridge: Polity Press in association with Basil Blackwell.

Bourdieu, Pierre (1990 [1987]) *In Other Words: Essays Towards a Reflexive Sociology*, trans. Matthew Adamson, Cambridge: Polity Press.

Bourdieu, Pierre (1991 [1971]) 'Genesis and Structure of the Religious Field', trans. Craig Calhoun [et al], *Comparative Social Research* 13: 1–44.

Bourdieu, Pierre (1992) *Language and Symbolic Power*, edited and introduced by John B. Thompson, trans. Gino Raymond and Matthew Adamson, Cambridge: Polity Press.

Bourdieu, Pierre (1993) *The Field of Cultural Production: Essays on Art and Literature*, edited and introduced by Randal Johnson, Cambridge: Polity Press.

Bourdieu, Pierre (1996 [1989]) *The State Nobility: Elite Schools in the Field of Power*, trans. Lauretta C. Clough, Cambridge: Polity Press.

Bourdieu, Pierre (1996 [1992]) *The Rules of Art: Genesis and Structure of the Literary Field*, trans. Susan Emanuel, Cambridge: Polity Press.

Bourdieu, Pierre (1998 [1994]) *Practical Reason: On the Theory of Action*, trans. Randal Johnson [et al.], Cambridge: Polity Press.

Bourdieu, Pierre (1998 [1997]) 'A Reasoned Utopia and Economic Fatalism', *New Left Review* 227: 125–130.

Bourdieu, Pierre (2000 [1997]) *Pascalian Meditations*, trans. Richard Nice, Cambridge: Polity Press.

Bourdieu, Pierre (2001 [1998]) *Masculine Domination*, trans. Richard Nice, Cambridge: Polity Press.

Bourdieu, Pierre (2002a) *Le bal des célibataires*, Paris: Seuil.

Bourdieu, Pierre (2002b) *Interventions Politiques, 1961–2001: Textes et Contextes d'un Mode d'Intervention Politique Spécifique*, textes rassemblés et présentés par Franck Poupeau, Marseille: Agone.

Bourdieu, Pierre (2002 [2000]) 'Habitus', in Jean Hillier and Emma Rooksby (eds.) *Habitus: A Sense of Place*, Aldershot: Ashgate, pp. 27–34.

Bourdieu, Pierre (2004) *Esquisse pour une auto-analyse*, Paris: Raisons d'agir.

Bourdieu, Pierre (2004 [2001]) *Science of Science and Reflexivity*, trans. Richard Nice, Cambridge: Polity Press.

Bourdieu, Pierre (2008) *Esquisses algériennes*, textes édités et présentés par Tassadit Yacine, Paris: Seuil.

Bourdieu, Pierre and Alain Accardo et al. (1999 [1993]) *The Weight of the World: Social Suffering in Contemporary Society*, trans. Priscilla Parkhurst Ferguson [et al.], Cambridge: Polity Press.

Bourdieu, Pierre and Chartier, Roger (2010) *Le Sociologue et L'Historien*, Marseille: Agone.

Bourdieu, Pierre and Hans Haacke (1995 [1994]) *Free Exchange*, Cambridge: Polity Press in association with Blackwell.

Bourdieu, Pierre and Jean-Claude Passeron (1990 [1970]) *Reproduction in Education, Society and Culture*, trans. Richard Nice, 2nd Edition, London: Sage.

Bourdieu, Pierre and Abdelmalek Sayad (1964) *Le déracinement : La crise de l' agriculture en Algérie*, Paris: Minuit.

Bourdieu, Pierre and Loïc Wacquant (1992 [1992]) *An Invitation to Reflexive Sociology*, Cambridge: Polity Press.

Bouveresse, Jacques (2003) *Bourdieu, savant & politique*, Marseille: Agone.

Boyer, Robert (2003) 'L'Art du judoka', in Pierre Encrevé and Rose-Marie Lagrave (eds.) *Travailler avec Bourdieu*, Paris: Flammarion, pp. 267–279.

Brubaker, Rogers (1985) 'Rethinking Classical Theory: The Sociological Vision of Pierre Bourdieu', *Theory and Society* 14(6): 745–775.

Calhoun, Craig (1993) 'Habitus, Field, and Capital: The Question of Historical Specificity', in Craig Calhoun, Edward LiPuma and Moishe Postone (eds.) *Bourdieu: Critical Perspectives*, Chicago: University of Chicago Press, pp. 61–88.

Callinicos, Alex (1999a) *Social Theory: A Historical Introduction*, Cambridge: Polity Press.

Callinicos, Alex (1999b) 'Social Theory Put to the Test of Politics: Pierre Bourdieu and Anthony Giddens', *New Left Review* 236: 77–102.

Callinicos, Alex (2006) *The Resources of Critique*, Cambridge: Polity Press.

Durkheim, Émile (1987 [1897]) *Suicide: A Study in Sociology*, trans. John A. Spaulding and George Simpson, London: Routledge and Kegan Paul.

Durkheim, Émile (1995 [1912]) *The Elementary Forms of the Religious Life*, trans. Karen Fields, New York: Free Press.

Elias, Norbert (2006 [1969]) *The Court Society*, trans. Edmund Jephcott, ed. Stephen Mennell, Dublin: University College Dublin Press.

Fowler, Bridget (1997) *Pierre Bourdieu and Cultural Theory: Critical Investigations*, London: Sage.
Husserl, Edmund (1970 [1936]) *The Crisis of European Sciences and Transcendental Phenomenology: An Introduction to Phenomenological Philosophy*, trans. David Carr, Evanston: Northwestern University Press.
Lane, Jeremy F. (2006) *Bourdieu's Politics: Problems and Possibilities*, London: Routledge.
Lescourret, Marie-Anne (2008) *Pierre Bourdieu. Vers une économie du bonheur*, Paris: Flammarion.
Lovell, Terry (2003) 'Resisting with Authority: Historical Specificity, Agency and the Performative Self', *Theory, Culture & Society* 20(1): 1–17.
Marx, Karl (1970 [1843]) *Critique of Hegel's 'Philosophy of Right'*, trans. Annette Jolin and Joseph O'Malley, edited with an introduction and notes by Joseph O'Malley. Cambridge: Cambridge University Press.
Marx, Karl (1974) *Political Writings (Volume 3)*, ed. David Fernbach, Harmondsworth: Penguin.
Marx, Karl (1975) [1843–4] *Early Writings*, trans. Rodney Livingstone and Gregor Benton, Harmondsworth: Penguin.
Marx, Karl (1976 [1867]) *Capital, Volume 1*, trans. Ben Fowkes, Harmondsworth: Penguin.
Marx, Karl and Friedrich Engels (1940 [1845]) *The German Ideology*, London: Lawrence and Wishart.
Marx, Karl (1973 [1857]) *Grundrisse: Foundations of the Critique of Political Economy*, trans. Martin Nicolaus, Harmondsworth: Penguin in association with New Left Review.
McLellan, David (1973) *Karl Marx: His Life and Thought*, London: Macmillan.
Moore, Barrington (1973) *Social Origins of Dictatorship and Democracy: Lord and Peasant in the Making of the Modern World*, London: Penguin.
Nimtz, August H. (2000) *Marx and Engels: Their Contribution to the Democratic Breakthrough*, Albany, NY: State University of New York Press.
Prawer, Siegbert Salomon (1976) *Karl Marx and World Literature*, Oxford: Oxford University Press.
Rancière, Jacques (2004 [1983]) *The Philosopher and his Poor*, edited Andrew Parker, North Carolina: Duke University Press.
Robbins, Derek (2006) *On Bourdieu, Education and Society*, Oxford: Bardwell Press.
Sapiro, Gisèle (1999) *La guerre des écrivains : 1940–1953*, Paris: Fayard.
Sintomer, Yves (1996) 'Le corporatisme de l'universel et la cité', *Actuel Marx* 20, Deuxième Semestre: 91–104.
Susen, Simon (2007) *The Foundations of the Social: Between Critical Theory and Reflexive Sociology*, Oxford: Bardwell Press.
Thompson, Edward P. (1968) *The Making of the English Working Class*, Harmondsworth: Penguin.
Verdès-Leroux, Jeannine (1996) *Le savant et la politique : Essai sur le terrorisme sociologique de Pierre Bourdieu*, Paris: Bernard Grasset.
Vološinov, Valentin N. (1973 [1930]) *Marxism and the Philosophy of Language*, trans. Ladislav Matejka and I. R. Titunik, New York: Seminar Press.
Wacquant, Loïc (ed.) (2005) *Pierre Bourdieu and Democratic Politics: The Mystery of Ministry*, Cambridge: Polity Press.
Williams, Raymond (1977) *Marxism and Literature*, Oxford: Oxford University Press.

Internet References

RAE http://www.rae.ac.uk (accessed 12.05.10).
REF http://www.hefce.ac.uk/research/ref (accessed 12.05.10).

CHAPTER THREE

From Marx to Bourdieu: The Limits of the Structuralism of Practice[1]

Bruno Karsenti
Translated by Simon Susen[2]

I. Marx

(1) The Question of Anthropological Distinctiveness: The Production of the Means of Subsistence as the Foundation of Society

Let me begin by quoting Marx from the *German Ideology*:

> Men can be distinguished from animals by consciousness, by religion, or anything else you like. They themselves begin to distinguish themselves from animals as soon as they begin to produce their means of subsistence, a step which is conditioned by their physical organization. By producing their means of subsistence men are indirectly producing their actual material life. (Marx and Engels, 2000/1977 [1846]: 177)

From a materialist point of view, the main criterion for distinguishing one species from another is its way of asserting itself as a living species. Thus, *one can distinguish humans from animals on the basis of their capacity to distinguish themselves from other species through the physical organisation of their life forms.* This distinctiveness, which cannot be brought into being by reference to an external force – such as consciousness, thought, or religious sentiment – is rooted in a given activity, namely in production, that is, in *the production of the means of subsistence.* The human body is designed to produce, and reproduce through its production, and thereby ensure its own existence. As the existential importance of the verb 'to produce' suggests, *anthropological specificity* is derived from *human productivity*: in the last instance, to be able to produce means to be able to produce the means of subsistence. Humans do not find themselves immersed in a world where all necessary means of subsistence are always already given, but they have to act – and act collectively – upon the world to produce *their own* means of subsistence, that is, means of subsistence that *they themselves* bring into existence.

It is worth emphasising the centrality of this simple criterion: a species which produces its means of subsistence, and which is therefore capable of *controlling* the process of its own reproduction, affirms its distinctive identity as a species within a given life form. To be more precise, it intervenes *indirectly* upon the process of its own reproduction, that is, from outside by *using the means* that it produced itself to guarantee the reproduction of its own existence. Hence, rather than focusing solely on the act of production – which is central to the Marxist world view – we also need to take into consideration the notion of *means* and, more importantly, the status attributed to it by Marx. Humans live literally *within* their means of subsistence. Their life consists of nothing but the *search for the means of subsistence*, which they produce themselves. To be sure, the relation humans establish with their means of subsistence is far from straightforward. Their means of subsistence are not externally given instruments used exclusively to pursue a previously fixed aim. Rather, their *means of subsistence constitute life as such* – that is, they constitute, in Marx's words, 'life forms' (Marx and Engels, 1968 [1846]: 46). As a consequence, human life is subject to permanent transformation determined by the various means of subsistence produced by humans themselves.

As Marx remarks, technological progress is so dynamic that the human species succeeds in emancipating itself from the cycle of reproduction by which other species are determined. Progress (*Fortschritt*), which literally makes society proceed (*fortschreiten*), situates the human species within a sociohistorical process: what is produced by one generation will be passed on to the next generation; every generation is confronted with the task of acting upon what has been transmitted from the past by generating new means for its subsistence, which it then hands down to the next generation, and so on.

(2) The Question of Anthropological Contradiction: The Critique of the Division between Producers and Non-Producers

In light of the above, one can understand the *importance of critique* in relation to the exploitation of resources derived from the *gradual differentiation of social activity*. Something occurs in the very heart of the activity that is aimed at the production of the means of subsistence: as an activity undertaken by various subjects, *it divides by producing differentiation and differentiates by producing inequality*. At the core of this inequality lies a contradiction – namely, the fact that the very process of social production undermines itself. Production, understood as social production, is divided into *production* and *non-production* – that is, into two *contradictory* processes. Certain agents are 'kept in reserve' through a process which creates a division between those who own and those who do not own their labour power, thereby contributing to the continuous reproduction of their respective existence. The collective agent that is kept in reserve reproduces itself without producing anything, for its conditions of existence depend on its *exclusion* from the production process. Indeed, the production of its means of subsistence is a form of non-production. At the heart of this curious reality lies a paradoxical structure derived from the means of subsistence, through which humans collectively develop their lives and through which their lives are inevitably shaped.

On the basis of the previous reflections, we can understand the particular meaning given to *critique* in Marxian thought. The force of critique, in the Marxian sense, is not rooted in a principle of justice situated *outside* the social process or founded on an *independently* existing ideal order: inequality is not denounced from an *a priori* position of equality; rather, it is conceived as the *effect* – or, to be exact, as the *contradictory effect* – of a sociohistorical process. Based on the social production of means, and reflected in people's capacity to assert themselves as social producers of their means of life (Marx and Engels, 1968 [1846]: 58–60), production is doomed to affirm itself by negating itself and to negate itself by affirming itself. It is in the *paradoxical interdependence of negation and affirmation* that we find a resource not so much of a critical *view* or *interpretation*, but rather of a critical *situation*, that is, of a social state of affairs whose main point of reference is the *capitalist mode of production*.

Social conditions are determined by the division of labour and, in class-divided societies, the evolution of the former cannot be dissociated from the existence of private property, which underlies the constitution of the latter. Social conditions, insofar as they are determined by the division of labour, emerge when producers and non-producers, who are divided in terms of their positionally differentiated relation to the means of production, enter into a determinate relation within a given mode of production. The task of a materialist critique, therefore, is to shed light on the *material foundations of society*. This is precisely what makes it materialist: it is not a critique put forward by an interpreter who observes his or her object from the outside, but it is a critique *anchored* in the reality it describes, thereby facing up to the contradictory movement of society by following the transformations of history. Critique, in the materialist sense, is prepared to confront the contradictory nature of its own existence. In other words, *materialist critique is, by definition, a critique based on contradiction*. Critique, in this sense, is indeterminate, for it exists in the heart of an indeterminate – that is, still-to-be-produced-and-reproduced – reality.

In order to mobilise critique effectively, it needs to accept that it is itself socially embedded.

Thus, the Marxian critique rejects the very idea of a detached interpretation of reality: the main fault of 'ideological' thinkers in Germany was that they failed to take into account their own embeddedness in German reality. In fact, the key mistake of interpreters, no matter how critical they may *claim* to be, is to conceive of critique *regardless* of the situation by which they are themselves conditioned. From a Marxian point of view, this limitation is, first and foremost, an expression of the *socio-material contradiction* that exists *between producer and non-producer*. Given its central importance, this contradiction is a major point of concern in the *German Ideology*, where it is examined in terms of the *opposition between material labour and intellectual labour.*

(3) The Question of Anthropological Development: The Critique of the Division between Material Labour and Intellectual Labour

In order to do justice to the significance of the opposition between material labour and intellectual labour, we need to acknowledge that it plays a pivotal role in the *German Ideology*: by uncovering, and indeed situating himself in the heart of, the opposition between material labour and intellectual labour, Marx immerses himself in the exercise of critique. In so doing, he recognises that *contradiction* is fundamental to the emergence and development of thought – understood as a dynamic dimension, rather than as a static representation, of reality. *Human beings develop their capacity to think always in relation to a determinate stage of production.* When analysing the process of production as well as the intrinsic contradictions of this process, intellectual labour appears as a form of activity that is founded on a gap between its own existence and the existence of the process of production, and consequently on the fact that, paradoxically, intellectual labour remains materially caught up in an already given reality and hence in an already given product.

According to Marx, the ownership of the means of production *marginalises* certain agents *by excluding* them from participating in the production process. Why, then, should it be necessary to conceptualise this process of exclusion in terms of an opposition between material labour and intellectual labour? Should we regard this division as the most crucial source of the segmentation of tasks in modern society? And, if so, how can we make sense of what Marx refers to as 'the production of ideas'? Can, at least under certain conditions, 'the production of ideas' be treated in the same way as 'the production of things'? These questions touch upon a dilemma which Marx, without any doubt, located in the sort of critical activity that is associated with his own endeavour. This dilemma has never ceased to reappear in the history of

Marxism – particularly in recurring charges of theoreticism, which is often regarded as the supreme form of betrayal of the revolutionary project.

The following discussion seeks to explore the ways in which the above problem manifests itself in the way in which critique is conceived of in a sociology that claims to be part of the Marxian heritage: *the sociology of Pierre Bourdieu*. It is worth pointing out, however, that this problem is particularly important with regard to the aforementioned passages from the *German Ideology*, all of which are concerned with the fundamental contradiction arising from the capitalist division of labour. When examined more carefully, it becomes clear that Marx's analysis of the opposition between material labour and intellectual labour is an attempt to develop a critical study of social relations which seeks to be more than a mere interpretation of things, since it is explicitly oriented towards the transformation of reality, or at least clearly aimed at contributing to its transformation.

Yet, in what way does Marx emphasise the importance of the opposition between these *two types of labour*? In essence, he does so by uncovering the *material conditions* which underlie the activity of thinking. As a consequence, the non-producers are considered as specialised agents of thought. Do they, however, regard themselves as non-producers? How exactly should we conceive of the activity of thinking in relation to other activities that are structured by the division of labour? How can we make sense of the activity of thinking in terms of the social contradictions that permeate the production of the means of subsistence? From Marx's point of view, the thought that is generated by non-producers emerges through the contradictory development of production as a process that is always already confronted with its own negation. In this sense, it is not a positive dimension of production to which the producers are materially attached. Non-producing subjects are able to think because of, rather than despite, the fact that they do not produce anything: but *what* do they think?

Let us restate the problem: if the producers are thinking subjects, their thoughts exist necessarily in relation to their productive practices. Yet, if the act of thinking is considered as a privileged practice, we are dealing with something completely different: to conceive of thinking as a process situated *outside* practice means to assume that *production and non-production* continue to be *opposed* to one another within the relational framework of social structures. In the light of this structural opposition, it seems that the *life of non-producers* never ceases to be *dependent*: for them, there is an ineluctable imperative epitomised in a specific form of production of the means of subsistence – as for *every* human being. In addition, the distinctiveness of their own condition, as human beings, continues to be important to them. Their existence, however, has become somewhat paradoxical: *in order to exist, humans need to produce means of subsistence; and, in so doing, they produce and reproduce the very conditions which maintain the contradiction between production and non-production.* To conceive of thought in materialist terms means to consider every reflective activity as being socially embedded. All thought, insofar as it faces up to its own situatedness in the conditions of social existence, has to be oriented towards this objective. This has the following consequence: we have to accept that *the content of all thought is nothing but the content of society*, that is, of a set of social structures, understood as a social totality whose constitutive contradiction is twofold: to be accepted and neglected as well as perceived and concealed by the carriers of its existence.

(4) The Possibility of a Marxist Sociology

Now we are at the heart of the dilemma that concerns the question of the very possibility of a Marxist sociology, understood as a social theory which escapes the logic of dubious ideological methods. *Critique*, in strictly Marxian terms, is suspicious of the *sociological* project in that the former reminds us of the fact that the latter may prove incapable of overcoming its own *ideological* nature. Indeed, it may well be the case that a sociological view can *only* be ideological, entirely produced on the basis of non-producers' thought, oriented towards reproducing a form of structuration that reinforces, rather than undermines, the gap between production and non-production. I do not intend to go into the different ways in which Marxists have portrayed sociology as a bourgeois and conservative science.[3] Marxists certainly have succeeded in developing different forms of protest as well as different ways of rewriting the social sciences. (In France, for example, this applies to the work of Henri Lefebvre.[4]) The issue on which I want to focus here, however, is the *problem of ideology* as it is appears in the *German Ideology* – especially with regard to the sections in which the development of intellectual labour is examined in terms of an integral process of the division of labour.

The act of *theorising* in particular and the act of *thinking* in general are part of a *contradictory* process: the conditions of existence which underlie all acts of theorising and thinking depend on a gap which has to be maintained *even if* it constitutes a source of contradiction. As critical subjects, we have to reflect on this gap in a radical – that is, distrustful – way. One can describe this gesture in the following terms: *to think in terms of contradiction means both to accept and to question the very possibility of contradiction.* The possibility of contradiction is a precondition for the possibility of thinking. Thinking is an activity that seeks to maintain itself within existence; *one must not think of thinking only in terms of its proper content.* Theoretical thinking is permeated by a native perversion: its existence depends on its capacity to *un-realise* its content and thereby perpetuate the contradiction that has brought it into existence in the first place. In order to ensure that the possibility of theoretical thinking is not shattered by its own impossibility, one has to transform the reality of its very possibility, that is, one has to retranslate the reality of contradiction into the possibility of its own condition. *Concealing* the contradiction – in the sense of covering it with a mask that makes it invisible – is *the game of theory*, that is, the game of thinking treated and lived as a *detached form of existence*.

Under these conditions, critique can be contaminated with the perversion of theory. Critique finds its object in contradiction. Yet, in order to avoid contradiction, it has to be treated as real; and, in order to be treated as real, one has to be in a position to see it – that is, one has to be able to push social structures to the conditions of their own impossibility. We need to grasp the power of contradiction in order to comprehend its structuring effect, but without turning away from it. In order to achieve this, one has to fall back upon theory – and this is precisely where the difficulty lies. We need to make sure that theory allows us to see the social structures within which it emerges and by which it is produced, so that it cannot possibly ignore the extent of its own social conditioning. A genuine understanding of social structures, which takes into account the initial contradiction upon which modern society – structured in accordance with the division of labour – is based, contains an *awareness of the division between practice and theory*. This is where Bourdieu comes into play.

II. Bourdieu

(1) Bourdieu's Structuralism of Practice: Beyond Objectivism and Subjectivism

In order to face up to the Marxian challenge, we need to think in terms of *structures*: the contradictions inherent in social activity are embedded in social structures. Critique has to start with a reflection upon *social divisions* and, more importantly, with a reflection upon the *distorting effects* of social divisions. In this sense, critique is concerned with, and seeks to uncover, the very conditions that make a theoretical approach to the social world possible in the first place. A critique that is concerned with the social conditions in which theory is produced is essential to the very project of social theory. For what lies at the heart of critique is the real – however contradictory – object that is always already part of social relations.

Bourdieu's project is marked by a *paradox* that can be described as follows: *the enemies of real thought on structures are the social thinkers who, by focusing on structures, rob society of its real processes of structuration*. Why do they do so? They do so because they think about structure *without* relating it to the most fundamental contradiction – that is, *without* relating it to the source of contradiction outside which structuration cannot take place – and because they conceive of society as a functioning totality – either *objectively*, as a structural process regulated from outside, or *subjectively*, as a set of independently existing wills, each of which can follow its own interests. It does not really matter whether the emphasis is on *objective mechanisms* or on *intersubjective agreements*, for in both cases one fails to grasp the functioning of social reality. As a consequence of this failure, one is forced to reinforce the contradiction, reproduce it, and reproduce one's own existence by reproducing the contradiction. By contrast, to *confront the contradiction* means to go back to the very basis of this contradiction. It means to return to the place itself where the division between practical activity and theoretical activity originates; in short, it means to revisit it theoretically and thereby develop a critical stance through the very process of problematising the fundamental contradiction of society.

To be sure, this task reflects an internal struggle in the social sciences. Bourdieu's contribution consists in the fact that – in one of his masterpieces, namely in the *Outline of a Theory of Practice* (1977 [1972]), written in the 1960s – he put his finger on the nature of this struggle. Sociology, in the Bourdieusian sense, is to be conceived of as *a theory of social structures*; yet, as such, it is to be understood as a *critical sociology*, which, by definition, rejects reductionist forms of sociology (whether they emphasise the alleged power of *objective regulation* or the alleged power of *intersubjective agency*). Such a critical sociology, in the Bourdieusian sense, needs to face up to a *struggle* between two influential paradigms in the social sciences – that is, to a struggle between two antithetical approaches: *sociology and ethnology*. The big enemy of a true sociology of structures is ethnology, or at least the predominant form of ethnology of the 1960s, which was heavily influenced by the work of Claude Lévi-Strauss.

(2) Bourdieu's Structuralism of Practice: The Struggle between Sociology and Ethnology

A sociology that claims to be genuinely committed to the Marxist project can only be *anti-Lévi-Straussian*. Such an approach, however, has to be seriously devoted to the study of social structures. In fact, it can only succeed in sustaining itself on the level of immanent contradiction by confronting, and thereby undermining, the reproductive logic of social structures. That being said, we must not lose sight of one key challenge: *the challenge of moving towards a transformation of the contradiction*. In Marxian thought, *critique* is conceived of in terms of *transformation*, because it embodies the abolition of the division of labour, starting with the *abolition of the separation between manual and intellectual work*. Within the Marxian framework, critique is an integral part, and indeed a cornerstone, of a theory of revolution.

Let us turn our attention to the *opposition between sociology and ethnology*. Sociology, if taken seriously, compels us to oppose a certain *ethnological disposition*. This disposition manifests itself in a particular scientific way of approaching things; it is a *stigmatised disposition*. What does this mean? Going back to the original meaning of the ethnological disposition, one will notice that it lies at the heart of the existence of *the stranger*, understood as the stranger in relation to a given practice. Put differently, *the ethnologist* is a 'type of person': he or she represents the agent who is kept in reserve as a *non-producing agent*. The ethnologist is a stranger who is always already situated one step behind the initial contradiction and who, *within* the structuring process derived from the division of labour, stays, nevertheless, *outside* this very process. Once the division of labour is put in place, ethnologists try to get back on their feet, but without ever achieving this goal.

Bourdieu's work is situated in the thematic horizon of the *German Ideology*, at least in the following sense: to assume that there is a *division of labour* means to suggest that *different individuals do different things*, and that, furthermore, the original way of generating *inequality* based on private property is the creation of a social *gap*. This gap is maintained through the reproduction of life conditions derived from a productive process in which there is a whole group of actors *excluded* from the very process of production. This gap, however, is for the agents themselves a new *existential condition*, namely a new condition shaped by the reproduction of their own lives.

The point is to make this widening gap visible the very moment its reproduction takes place. Every time its reproduction is under way it regenerates its own conditions of existence. How does this work? In relation to this question, Bourdieu seeks to bring together *two different tasks* that he considers to be complementary and mutually supportive: on the one hand, he proposes a theoretical framework for studying the logic of practice; and, on the other hand, he develops a critique of silent and hidden conditions, which escape the theoretical eye. In short, we are dealing with a commitment to both exploring the *production of practice* and questioning the *production of theory*.

The complementarity of these two tasks can be described as follows: *the only thing we know for sure about practice is that its very existence depends on practice and that one cannot, after undertaking a scholastic rupture, project an imagined logic of theory upon a lived logic of practice*. The construction of an autonomised theory is always conditioned by the condition of scholastic theorising itself. The only guarantee that one can find in a solid theoretical critique – understood as a critique of its own limits and of the power it can exercise over practice – is that it allows us to see the paradoxical practice that sustains it whilst trying to escape its own practical attachment to the process of production. It seems, therefore, convenient to have a specific practical logic in mind, which is the kind of logic commonly used to raise theory out of its practical context. This, in many ways, is a *reflexive task*, which needs to be repeated over and over again, and this is where critique – in the Marxian sense, as adopted by Bourdieu – must start.

(3) Bourdieu's Structuralism of Practice: From the Logic of Theory to the Logic of Practice

Lévi-Straussian structuralism has been criticised on a number of counts. One may argue, for example, that it can be converted into an interpretive attitude, similar to those interpretations that Marx had already sought to overcome in his famous eleventh thesis on Feuerbach. According to Bourdieu, Lévi-Straussian structuralism falls into the same trap as interpretive approaches, such as symbolic interactionism and ethnomethodology. The scenario in question is actually rather straightforward and may be described as follows: when ethnologists arrive at a given place or their 'field', their first reaction is to demand three items, which may be given the following tentative titles: *a code*, *a grammar*, and *a map*.

(i) *A code:* It is assumed that *rules* have a meaning *regardless* of their application by concrete subjects, that is, *independently* of the social situations in which subjects find themselves immersed. Against this view, Bourdieu proposes a theory which captures the *determinacy* of social actions by putting forward the idea of *generative schemes of actions* (the habitus), whose existence reflects the *regulative* nature of social action, rather than the normative dimension of rules. This theoretical programme, proposed by Bourdieu, is deeply suspicious of abstract legalism.

(ii) *A grammar:* For Bourdieu, the adoption of a *set of discursive rules* represents an obstacle to a truly sociological point of view, because a sociorelational approach to reality does not permit us to reduce the production of rules to a mere form of discourse. According to Bourdieu, even the notion of *generative* grammar falls into the trap of discursive idealism. Of course, one can say that the notion of grammar gives the speaker a new place within linguistic analysis, a place defined in terms of the separation between *langue* and *parole*. Nevertheless, the conceptual pair *competence/performance* remains trapped in a horizon of abstraction, which removes the speaker from the *context* of enunciation and ignores the social *conditions* that allow linguistic utterances between socially situated and qualified actors to come into existence in the first place. More generally, the linguistic paradigm in the social sciences is caught up in an illusion, comparable to the vision of the arriving stranger, when seeking to comprehend how *one* speaks – that is, the way *everybody* speaks and understands.

The *hypostatisation of language* as the allegedly most *pure* source of meaning is an expression, perhaps the main expression, of the *detachment* which gives rise to the *vision of the stranger*. To be sure, this exogenous approach is typically the strategy of those who situate themselves *outside* the contradiction, *after* the rupture, and who seek to conceal their artificial detachment by suggesting that there is a common language, or at least a common use of language. In this regard, it does not really matter whether one claims to stand in the tradition of Saussure, Jakobson, or Chomsky. The main problem of which we need to be aware, however, is that by converting *language* into the *main paradigm* for understanding *processes of social structuration*, one fails to grasp the contradictory core of these processes. That being said, it is more fruitful to search for evidence in *sociolinguistics*, understood as a social characterisation of linguistic acts, rather than as a social application of linguistics.

(iii) *The map:* The critical reflection on this element is, as far as I can see, central to the theoretical project associated with the work of Bourdieu. The idea of *mapping the space of the investigation* – of having a full grasp of the space where the investigation takes place – is based on the assumption that the *mapped space* of the investigation is isomorphic to the *lived space* of the actor. In fact, it is assumed that the ethnologist moves within this space in the same way as the actor. To ask for, or draw up, a map means to contribute to the *uncoupling of theory from practice*, but on a specific level, which is hardly visible and *appears* to be completely neutral: the uncoupling between producer and non-producer is here conceived of as the uncoupling between producer and non-producer of *movements*.

Practice is productive; in order to produce, it does not cease to engage in constant *movement. Movements are inscribed in a certain space, but a space which is not homogenous or empty.* On the contrary, it is a space whose existence depends on the very movements by which it is produced. It is not a self-contained space, but a space with content, which forms part of movement itself. Yet, *the ethnologist's map* seems to suggest precisely the contrary: it is *an empty and orientationless space*, void of those who move within it, who convert it into a lived space through their practices and whose movements are based on their *tasks* within this space.

I want to insist on the importance of this critique of the map, which, it seems to me, touches upon the epicentre of Bourdieu's thought, at least in relation to the initial stages of his theoretical project. *The map is the privileged space of the thinker*, something that does not shift, or that shifts only with the finger, ideally to project itself towards no matter what point to determine what could be its situation, *if there were any situation at all.* The map constitutes a space where nobody is physically engaged, and where one can reconstruct in a backwards move what one has already constructed forewards, because the backwards and the forwards have no concrete meaning, and because the paths are still reversible. The 'turning back', the 'change of course', and the 'being inclined' do not at all imply the reconfiguration of space. The map, in this sense, is the most tangible instrument for those who do not know the field, because there is nothing to be known in it and because it does not require any major form of commitment; in short, because *one's life is not at stake in it.* It is the instrument of the negation of the logic of practice, inseparable from the effectively undertaken movement. And one sees that ethnologists, the very moment they find themselves immersed in this kind of situation, convert themselves immediately into theoreticians: deceptively homogenous, genuinely indifferent towards the bodies by which they are surrounded, and compulsively obsessed with the search for totality in terms of the 'big picture'.

By contrast, *the space of practice is a space of positions*, where every place is *socially signified* in terms of *social activities*, and where the trajectories do not possess the ideal reversibility for which the indifferent traveller seems to strive. It is a space permeated and reconfigured by the game of positions and by their temporal situatedness, recognised and played as the key action referred to as a singular position. This applies, of course, to both social and temporal space.

(4) Bourdieu's Structuralism of Practice: From Cognitive Detachment to Bodily Engagement

The suspicions one may have about the notions of *grammar* and *code* are fully confirmed at this juncture: Bourdieu's critique, even if it refuses to acknowledge this, points clearly in the direction of a *phenomenological reading*, no matter how vehemently he insists upon the need to study the power of objective structures – a theme which is particularly important not only in Merleau-Ponty's *The Structure of Behaviour* (1942), but also in the work of Goldstein (1934) and in Guillaume's *The Psychology of the Form* (1937). When reflecting upon contemporary forms of social analysis, we have to explore the implications of the tendency to focus on the power of objective structures. According to Marx, the main source of social contradiction is to be found in the *uncoupling process between producer and non-producer.* According to Bourdieu, we need to examine social divisions in relation to *the body*, and we therefore need to provide an *analysis of the body*.

A *critical structuralism* – a structuralism that is critical of both structuralism and structural anthropology, as in the case of Bourdieu – can only be a *structuralism of practice*. Such a structuralism of practice locates the *emergence of contradiction* in *bodily experiences* made by *socially situated subjects*, that is, by subjects who are situated in a space which is theirs and which they absorb subjectively by living and moving in it in different ways and by individuating themselves as situated bodies through these movements.

The return to the place of contradiction is a return to the place of the body. Of course, as Bourdieu knows only too well, there is a lot of room for phenomenological temptations, and he tries hard not to fall into the subjectivist trap. In essence, *phenomenological approaches* conceive of social relations as intersubjective relations between agents who occupy certain positions in the social space and who establish these relations by unfolding a 'natural attitude' derived from the transcendental experience of the world – that is, from an experience that is based on the *subjective* constitution of being in the world. This position, however, is problematic in that it fails to account for the following:

(i) *Social positions are already given* (since, as Marx pointed out, they reflect the very structure of the division of labour), and actors are *constrained* by occupying these conditions. In other words, the social world has an objective structure, and this structure is not the result of a set of subjective acts.
(ii) *The natural attitude is a social attitude*, even though it presents itself as a natural attitude. The subject's adjustment to the world is a construction founded on the collective experience of people who *live* in society. The elimination of this construction presupposes the construction of the means mobilised for this very elimination. We typically encounter this kind of elimination in theories that ignore practice.

From then on, the challenge consists in developing a *theory of the body* capable of addressing the above issues. A sociological theory of the body attributes a *social dimension* to the body – that is, it inserts the body into a space of *social positions*. It is nevertheless a body in the sense that its *socialisation* is not a refusal of the ability to develop a sense of selfhood, but rather a relation to a bodily constituted self that can only be understood as *a socially composed self* – that is, as *a socially mediated self*.

To put it more simply, the socialisation of the body is not accomplished through the mere imposition of external norms (that is, through the repression of a pre-given physical nature in the sense of the repression of a natural body that is subjected to an objectively existing system of cultural norms). Rather, it is to be regarded – at least according to Bourdieu's *Outline of a Theory of Practice* – as a *bodily dialectics*, that is, as a dialectics which proceeds in two directions: *exteriorisation and interiorisation*, representing two movements which must not be conceived of in terms of a linear succession, not even in terms of alternation, but in terms of an overlap between *opposite*, and yet *interdependent*, operations.

(5) Bourdieu's Structuralism of Practice: From Nature without Culture to Culture with Nature

When examining the body – the body of anyone, regardless of their position in the contradictory structure of the social space – Bourdieu does not deny the existence of universal natural characteristics or of fundamental bodily experiences. He insists, however, that these experiences are universal in the sense that 'there is no society that can do without them' (Bourdieu, 1972: 289). It is in this remark that Bourdieu's theory seems to be in line with the structuralist position. At the same time, one can say that it is in this position where Bourdieu remains close to Marx – that is, close to the idea that anthropological distinctiveness originates in the production of the means of subsistence, which equip human beings with the ability to be *creators of their own condition*, whilst remaining exposed to the constraining power of the conditions which they themselves created.

With regard to structuralism, one recognises the echo of what Lévi-Strauss describes, at the beginning of his *The Elementary Structures of Kinship* (1968 [1949]), under the title 'Intervention'. At the level of nature, an empty space is naturally deepened – that which concerns the wedding, which constitutes a *social* vehicle for *biological* reproduction. Yet, whilst representing a source of indeterminacy amongst superior apes (because nature does not determine *with whom*), reproduction amongst humans constitutes a problem that has to be collectively – that is, socially – resolved. One will notice that, similar to Marx's writings, we are essentially dealing with the problem of *means*.

The wedding is the means of reproduction; from a Lévi-Straussian perspective, humans produce this kind of means to ensure their survival as a species. In this sense, *The Elementary Structures of Kinship* represents a genuinely Marxist oeuvre, as it remains loyal to Marx's emphasis on anthropological distinctiveness when examining the cultural 'Intervention' upon seemingly natural processes. How do humans *produce*? This question can be answered only with reference to the concept of *means*. Culture needs to intervene, but it intervenes through a vacuum, this vacuum that nature has dealt with itself, without developing it and, hence, without providing this determination with means necessary for *social existence*, which, by definition, transcends the realm of a purely biological existence. There is an intervention because there is a problem, and *every anthropological problem is a problem of means*.

Bourdieu is firmly situated in this line of argument, emphasising that *society 'takes side'*. The existence of nature poses a challenge to the existence of society, and it constitutes a very complicated challenge indeed. *Human beings are defined by their capacity to confront the challenge of natural indeterminacy by virtue of cultural determinacy.* This explains Marx's emphasis on the means of subsistence, Lévi-Strauss's interest in reproduction, and Bourdieu's reflections on the existence of the body. Social life, insofar as it is concerned with the fabrication of means, is essentially a *response*. That said, it becomes clear that the structural approach – which remains important in Bourdieu's work – excludes an *external* relation between nature and culture, as it is characterised by the *internal* articulation between two levels, starting from the deepened vacuum of the first level. With this in mind, we can understand the extent to which this perspective underlies Bourdieu's *theory of bodily socialisation*, as illustrated in his *Outline of a Theory of Practice.*

When reflecting upon the existence of universal bodily determinations, and thus when examining the existence of a small number of fundamental sensations linked to central bodily functions, the problem of *positioning* emerges. What is *natural* is the space of variability accepted by a small number of sensations; what is *social* is the effectively developed variation. The space of variability is the space of the problem by whose internal nature the answer is determined. How does the problem manifest itself? Bourdieu's response to this question is unambiguous: *the problem manifests itself in practice*, that is, *in bodily practice* – and hence *in the subject's practical involvement in the world*, to which it has to adjust. In order for this to be possible, the subject has to *appropriate* not only *the world* by which it finds itself surrounded, but also *the body* in which it finds itself embedded. Practice, then, has to be reconnected with the original disposition of the *inserted and positioned body*: practice, in this sense, is the natural deepening of the problematic vacuum; it is the filling of, and social solution to, this vacuum. In other words, practice is the natural and unchangeable condition of its own problematic constitution. Given its worldly nature, practice is bound to be *social* and *changeable*, as well as inseparable from *bodily* positions developed in relation to a given world.

(6) Bourdieu's Structuralism of Practice: The Subject's Bodily Existence between Throw and Fall

What connects the invariance of fundamental sensations (their relative resemblance, the limited variability of what a body can and cannot do) to the variation of practices is the fact that *practice is an encounter between the body and the world* – an encounter which is contingent upon the body's position in the world. We can say that this position is, on a primordial level, a *throw*, a *fall*, which is the very first symptom of its *problematic constitution*, of the deepening of the natural problem, which is socially perceived as a problem.

Given that it constitutes the very first symptom of its problematic constitution, we have to start with this *throw* taking into account its contingency. The 'taking side' is indicative of a necessity: 'one has to go there like this and not otherwise'. This necessity acquires meaning on the basis of our existential contingency: one is here and not there. Given its *bodily existence*, the subject is always *a being-thrown-into-existence*. The body has natural dispositions, but what we cannot find in the nature of the body is the solution to the problem of its fall, of its position. The *response*, the 'taking side', is the response which only *society* can give to a problem of the body, that is, to *the body experienced as a problem*. The force of the response lies in the fact that the response itself has a bodily nature, inscribed in the place of the *emptiness of the body* – that is, of the body that senses its emptiness – under the condition of indeterminacy that permeates the position of the body.

Once the emptiness is noticed, this emptiness on which the body turns its back, awaiting and understanding the response, it can be described as the condition of strangeness in the world. *The thrown body is strange, and it seeks to overcome its strangeness through practice.* Surely, this is where practice seeks to respond. It is the place of all primordial necessity (varying according to the places of the fall) based on the *strangeness that needs to be overcome*. In this sense, *practice is the proof of the fall* within the same movement where it tries not to see it as such, to belong to the world where it has taken place, to absorb the irrevocable strangeness of the thrown body.

Thus, we can say that practice is the reduction of the stranger. This can also be understood from an angle that is different from the one previously mentioned. The reduced stranger is not the *theoretical stranger* – who appears as a traitor of practice, guilty of the *disembodiment* of the habitus whilst undertaking an action, and who objectivates the rules, draws the maps, and codifies the languages. Rather, it is a *bodily stranger*, who has a body before having a body – if it is true that the only genuine body is *a simultaneously appropriated and misappropriated body* – within a habitualised and habitualising relation to the world, driven by the eternal 'dialectics of interiority and exteriority' (Bourdieu, 1972: 256). A body that cannot be described as a proper body in this sense first emerges as a stranger to the world into which it has been thrown, and indeed as a stranger to the subject itself, before being formed and reformed through the dialectical interplay between disposition and situation. In short, the *human body* is a *contingent body* and, therefore, a body for which literally nothing is necessary.

Interestingly, Bourdieu talks about this figure only on very few occasions. It seems to serve the function of a *tacit premise* underlying his argument. Whenever he makes it explicit, though, it appears as a source of enlightenment, particularly in his *self-reflexive* writings, which culminate in his plea for a *socio-analysis*. It is open to debate whether or not he lives up to the high standards of a genuine socio-analysis. In any case, he seems to situate himself on a higher level, on the level of *practice as an adjusted response*, as a search for adjustment, triggered by the *encounter between the body and the world* in the moment of their simultaneous emergence. It is worth emphasising that this process takes place between *two levels of strangeness*, that is, between two forms of being strange in the world: on the one hand, the *pre-social state*, which can never be experienced as such and which has the status of an obsessive fear on which we turn our back; on the other hand, the *ideological drift*, which allows us to escape the logic of practice through the logic of theoreticism.

The key question, then, is this: *how is the body extracted from the pre-body?* In other words, *how is the body removed from the situation of the throw?* This is the point where Bourdieu brings the aforementioned return of the place of the contradiction into play – the place where practice separates itself from this very contradiction. This place is regarded as a physical place: it is the place where the 'taking side' occurs.

By acknowledging that this place is physical we can identify a gap in the Lévi-Straussian framework, a gap which is not mentioned in Bourdieu's critique of Lévi-Strauss, but which is nevertheless relevant to measuring both the *distance* and the *proximity* between these two thinkers. What, in Lévi-Strauss, takes place in the *wedding* – and only in the wedding – is tantamount to what, in Bourdieu, is located in the individual *body* as a thrown body impregnated with memory. (From a Lévi-Straussian perspective, the wedding is a socially recognised vehicle for the regulation of sexuality. This link between sexuality and reproduction has recently been re-examined in Luc Boltanski's *La condition fœtale*, published in 2004.) Thus, Lévi-Strauss's initial question concerns the *sexual function of the body*: how can the body be socially formed to ensure the biological mechanisms of breeding? This is the point of incursion of 'Intervention' (Lévi-Strauss 1968 [1949]: 37), and this is what justifies the pivotal role of the prohibition of incest. Bourdieu is concerned with the question of what the body does with itself (and, in this context, it is important to underline the subjectivist nature of the question). This question is relevant not only in relation to other bodies within a set of social relations, but also in relation to the world as a whole. The *social construction of the body* contributes to both the *reproduction of the species* as a collectively adjusted form of being and the *reproduction of the body itself* as an individually adjusted form of being.

We are therefore confronted with a *pre-body*, 'a field universally imposed on social positions' (Bourdieu, 1972: 289). In this regard, the analysis undertaken in *Outline of a Theory of Practice* is unambiguous: the point emphasised by Bourdieu is that, within this 'position-taking' process, the spatial distinctions are established in analogy with the human body. Hence, *the body is a point of reference for the structuration of space*. Put differently, there are 'elementary structures underlying bodily experience' (Bourdieu, 1972: 289). (This statement can be found in full in the *Outline of a Theory of Practice*, and this allusion is unequivocal.) These structures can be described in terms of their coincidence with the principles of structuration of the objective space: inside-outside, up-down, front-back, right-left – these are the *polarities* that structure the space analogically to the experience of the body, within its proper structure. This *co-incidence between two languages* – between the structural language of *the body* and the structural language of *the world* – can be explained in two ways:

(i) One may assume that *everything* is just *projection*. According to this view, we need to focus on the idea of an *innate bodily competence*. This, Bourdieu asserts, would mean to suggest that there is a 'science infused with hidden bodily reactions' (Bourdieu, 1972: 290), which is a view that should be avoided.
(ii) One may claim that the body cannot be said to be situated outside a *network of social relations*. If we recognise that the body is situated in the world, then the body's existence can be proven. Hence, we are dealing with the existence of a *known body*. It is known, however, only because the *knowledge* of its existence and of the world in which it exists is *always already spatially situated*. It is a body capable of enriching itself through self-perception, which it would not be capable of without this *structuration of the world*. In fact, the structuration of the world is, for the body, a way of asserting its existence and *accomplishing its own structuration*.

The question that remains is why the second solution prevails over the first one. The main reason for this is that the *natural experience* of the body is *insignificant*, because the 'small number of fundamental sensations' (Bourdieu, 1972: 289) shared by *all* human beings is a *sparse* material unfit to provide the basis for a genuine experience. This means that the experience of the thrown body, the test of the strange body for every practice, cannot have the positive consistency of a natural bodily experience. *The body is proper only through appropriation, through appropriation in situated action.* Yet, how can we explain the coming into existence of the coincidence, the original scenario of simultaneous emergence? And how can we explain that the body obtains value through structuring themes?

The response to these questions given by Bourdieu is based on a deeply problematic idea: *the body, in its original form, needs to be able to anticipate itself.* According to this view, the world is not an opaque and strange world but a penetrable world, in the sense that it positions itself as a supportive zone for pre-perceptive anticipations (Goldstein's influence, through Merleau-Ponty, is obvious here). Emotions may have the ability to escape this structure of anticipation. At this point, we need to emphasise the influence of Mauss's essays, not only his essay on bodily techniques (1966 [1935]), but also his essay on the expression of emotions, laughter, and tears (1969 [1921]). In short, *the body is emotionally charged* – and so is our bodily relation to the world.

To perceive oneself as a self requires perceiving oneself through one's relation to the outside world – a world in which the perceiving body has anticipated itself, rather than projected itself, as if it had previously embodied the things which it had to absorb from the outside. In this context, 'anticipated' – or 'compelled' – means 'given in advance' or, to be exact, 'a sought-after-given-in-advance' aimed at reincorporating what still has to come into existence.

(7) Bourdieu's Structuralism of Practice: The Subject's Home in Hysteresis

When examined more closely, it becomes apparent that, in its literal sense, the expression '*dialectics of interiorisation-exteriorisation*' (Bourdieu, 1972: 256) is problematic. This is due to the fact that the described relationship is neither about interiorisation nor about exteriorisation – at least not if it is understood within a *sequence of operations*. There is no exteriorisation, because what the body exteriorises is not derived from an interior source in the sense of a place that is tantamount to a home. On the contrary, *if there is anything like a bodily home, it is the body's environment*. From this perspective, strangeness cannot be seen directly, but it is only as a *failure* in the process of integration into the home that the world allows for the *self-anticipation* of the body through practice. *'To be at home' means 'to be in the world', and it means 'to be in the world through anticipation'*. It is only the interiorised body through its adjustment to the world, it is never a structure that is strange to it (an objective rule), but it is what is already put in place, thereby anticipating itself. It is *a structure that already belongs to the actor*, although the former is not the same as the latter.

One will notice that the language of *anticipation* is far from neutral. It puts the emphasis on a certain operation of *time*, from which the body cannot escape. This is what Bourdieu seeks to grasp under a concept of which, unfortunately, he never made use in a more systematic and detailed way: *hysteresis*. This concept can be found particularly in his *Distinction* (1979) and in his *The Logic of Practice* (1980); in its orthodox form, however, the doctrine is relegated to a second level. If there is *anticipation*, this is because *the body is belated* and because *the structuration of the socialised body is a way of escaping its belatedness*, whatever happens. The *human body*, in the Bourdieusian sense, is a *social body*, a body through which society provides the answer to the temporal question of belatedness.

Metaphors permit us to find the answer to the relative problem of the situated being – perceived as a specifically bodily problem – in the *primary experience of the social world*, the situation into which one is thrown. The body presupposes the capacity to adjust: the capacity to adjust to something that is, in fiction, given as something already realised – as something that experiences the world as its own world and, therefore, as its home. What makes this possible is *practice*, but on condition that it *converts the metaphor into metonymy*, thereby accomplishing incorporation. *Education*, which is based on the pedagogy of the body, is the *realisation of metonymy*, which gets under way with its original transformation into metaphor. What this process seems to guarantee is the possibility of not being belated, of giving it the means to fill the gap caused by its belatedness, as a sign of its insurmountable anxiety over the possibility of turning out to be the stranger that the subject has always already ceased to be.

Society has to treat the body as a carrier of memory. Memory is a reminder: a means of a particular sort, indeed – according to Bourdieu – the first means which consists in not having to think and rethink its adjustment, in the sense of experiencing practice, rather than replaying it as a form of belatedness that is still to be accomplished. What lies at the heart of practice is the power of *hysteresis*, which can only be sustained insofar as it is overcome. What is revealed in the pathological figure of the hysterical – suggesting that 'a spoken expression was literally the bodily expression which it expresses' (Bourdieu, 1972: 290) – is precisely the metaphorical failure: this is the one which falls again into the disastrous *hysteresis*, which already looks out for practice due to its capacity to assume and overcome it. Its antonym is the well-adjusted agent, who enjoys living within the limits of his or her *hysteresis*, who is not belated, or – to be exact – whose belatedness is correctly absorbed.

Why is it belated? In essence, it is belated because the body is not of the world, because the dispositions and situations are not homologous. There is a delay because there is a fall, because the birth into the social world happens too quickly, and because the birth process lacks the continuity that would allow for a linear and flawless insertion into the world. *Practice*, therefore, is the *perceived expedient to resolve* what – drawing on both psychoanalytical and biological terminology – may be called a condition of *prematurity*. This is why habituation is first and foremost determined as an available memory – that is, as a stock of already tested physical schematisations. We need to take into account, however, that it is not completely obscure: it belongs to the order of the implicit, a *know-how* on this side of a discursive knowledge, which could be enounced without known rules, applied after having being known. In the logic of practice, memory plays the same role with regard to its application, asserting and consolidating itself by treating novel situations on the basis of situations previously proved and already overcome through the adjustment of dispositions.

Nevertheless, one can see very clearly that the form of memory about which we have been talking here – the one concerning the reminder – conceals another form of memory, which is also quite worrying, and one which is irreducible not only to all know-that but also to all know-how: *the memory of the fall*. The latter, as opposed to the former, is essentially opaque. The only element that makes it visible is *belatedness*, which activates the logic of practice in the temporary activity of research, that is, in its treatment of *hysteresis*. In this regard, the examination of belatedness has a symptomatic value: not as a sign of the fall, and hence of arbitrariness, but of what expresses it in order to conceal it.

(8) Bourdieu's Structuralism of Practice: The Preponderance of Practice and the Need for Socio-Analysis

It is a well-known fact that Bourdieu has always been in close contact with psychoanalysis, whilst at the same time keeping a critical distance from it. In close proximity to psychoanalysis, he elaborates and prescribes a technique called *socio-analysis* (see Bourdieu and Wacquant, 1992: especially chapter 1) – a major procedure of a sociological form of vigilance, to which I have already referred above and which compels us to remove, or at least become aware of, self-imposed barriers characteristic of theoreticist approaches. In opposition to the deviating and – to use Comte's words – digressing theoretician, we play the ideological role of the gravedigger of the structural contradiction. If, following Bourdieu, psychoanalysis has to be revised, this means that, within the framework of psychoanalysis, the *logic of thought* has to be reconnected with the *logic of practice*. What follows from this is that we need to establish a system of thought that arises from a *non-thetical consciousness*, rather than from an unconscious in the Freudian sense.

To put it bluntly: contrary to what has been said and written in the vulgate, *the habitus is not an unconscious disposition in the proper sense of the term*. Rather, it constitutes an *infra-conscience*, composed of both awareness [*connaissance*] and unawareness [*méconnaissance*]. Paradoxically, unawareness is the condition for a certain form of knowledge. The *know-how* is a kind of *knowledge that lacks knowledge* about what it actually does, detaching itself from the very process of doing and treating it as an object. At the same time, anticipation – in its practical fluidity – is a mechanism in which a certain form of consciousness is at work, but a form of consciousness that is not conscious of itself when undertaking actions. This ambiguous regime in which Merleau-Ponty's footprints prevail over those of Freud and Marx, and where the light and the dark sides support one another, authorises a new take on the mode of self-consciousness: it is possible to see its practice on condition that it is possible to see that 'seeing it' means 'ceasing to see it'. We are therefore dealing with an unhappy retake, under the irrepressible form of a 'bad' conscience, which cannot be resisted by the permanent problem of vigilance.

On the conceptual level, this is where it becomes clear that this type of *unconscious* does not have anything to do with the unconscious in the Freudian sense – an unconscious which would not be a non-thetical consciousness, as simply another type of consciousness, but *a mental regime different from consciousness itself, governed by an autonomous logic*. To be sure, this is not just a question of semantics. With the previous emphasis in mind, it is possible to understand what would be analogous to a *true unconscious* in the Bourdieusian sense, namely an unconscious that designates both the unconscious *in* his theory and the unconscious *of* his theory. We are dealing with *an unconscious involved in practice*, which does not necessarily live in practice, because belatedness is always already blamed and because practice out of vocation is to be concealed. If we have to give it a place, it is, rather, the one of *the arbitrary fall* in a certain point of the social space, of the body that is not involved with itself and with its world within its being-thrown-into-existence, and of the body before the proper body. This place cannot be caught up in itself; indeed, from another point of view, it must be possible to put your finger on it, point in its direction, and thereby take a critical position. It is its real force – more profound and more effective than the denunciation of the training that is at work in processes of habituation. It is the last resource of indignation, on this side of practice, and it is this resource that Bourdieu tacitly rediscovers when he uses critique against the other side, for instance, against the theorist who believes to stand above the logic of practice and who has left the home that practice represents.

It occurs to Bourdieu to define habitus as 'making a virtue of necessity' (1972: 260). In order for it to be a *virtue*, however, it first has to become a *necessity*. With the tools offered by Bourdieu concerning this process of 'becoming necessity', the view can only be thrown at a dark foundation, which can be converted into a clear motive of indignation: it is arbitrary, and it appears to be necessary – this is the scandal. Yet, before deciding whether or not we are dealing with a scandal, it remains to be seen if a description can be put in place about what exactly occurs on the level of *experience*.

Let us reconsider the initial scenario: *society*, insofar as it 'takes side', imposes a *determination on the body*, but at the same time it salvages it, precisely by making it proper, appropriated by itself and by the world. Coincidence takes place without having to presuppose the existence of a conductor, without requiring the existence of a big legislator who sets out the rules of adjustment. The body is not initially trained: it trains, or retrains, itself through the resolution of the distance between itself and the world. *Practice is a safeguard*, even if it converts the arbitrary into the necessary, and even if it conceals the vision of the arbitrary. This is where the dilemma lies. In this sense, one could also say that there is such a thing as *a virtue of practice*, which is not so much a virtue made on the basis of necessity which it imposes, but rather a virtue inherent to the salvation which it provides for a body that has to bypass its condition as a thrown body, strange to the world in which – whatever happens – it survives, in an irrepressibly contingent manner.

Therefore, *it is necessary that the body lives its belatedness in a way that allows it not to be belated*, as a form of belatedness charged with dread and confronted by the adjusting efforts which the body never ceases to make. This is where the first visage of *hysteresis* can be found. And this is why the memory-laden experiences, in which the body is heavy, are haunted by another memory, which is still threatening: the memory of the *misadjusted body*. In this light, it is understandable that *every experience of maladjustment is damaging*, but maybe it is for a different reason than the one invoked by Bourdieu. If it is damaging, this is not because practice has failed, or because the situation turns out to be untouchable by the dispositions, but because the social unconscious is affected, because the other situation under every condition seizes the subject and paralyses it in its movement. Thus, the subject would be stopped not by an obstacle which it encounters on its way, but by a type of memory that is different from the naturalised reminder: a memory that is different from the one of the memory-laden body – a body which is filled with accumulated practical knowledge.

Following this interpretation (which we do not find in Bourdieu's oeuvre), *the unconscious* is a matter not so much of practice as such, but rather of the *flaws and failures* of practice – and, more importantly, not so much because they are failures but because they make the *general economy of failures and successes* visible. This process functions not in terms of necessity but in terms of the *arbitrary nature of strangeness in the world*, and of a determination to be there *at all cost*, without any possible justification. As a consequence, however, the notion of the arbitrary ceases to have the same meaning; that is, it does not refer to the idea of indignation: not to be at home does not mean to fail to be at home; rather, it designates the idea of getting hold of oneself at one's side, in discrepant relation to oneself and to the world, on the level of the primary condition that there is both a self and a world, adjusted to the misadjusted, but nevertheless mutually related. This means that, in order to allow for the possibility of an analysis of this kind of relationship, one has to detach oneself.

It must be emphasised that, to a significant extent, these considerations make us *move away from Bourdieu's structuralism of practice* – that is, from the form of structuralism which Bourdieu seeks to make work by drawing upon the structural approach in the sense of what he refers to as the 'elementary structures of bodily experience' (1972: 289). These considerations, then, induce us to turn away from Bourdieusian structuralism, because, in a way, they oblige us to pose the following question: *to what extent are structures really part of practice?* Should we not rather seek to develop a conceptual framework that allows us to understand how the *logic of practice* – through processes of habituation and habitation – supports or expresses an aspect of socialisation which is different from the one that passes through the adjustment of the body itself? On this level, for sure, the *function of the arbitrary* should be envisaged – in itself and not in its recovery – as a *function of structuration.* After all, authentic structuralism, whether it is linguistic or anthropological, does not assert anything else. It is most essentially defined by an *ambitious coarticulation of the arbitrary and the necessary*, which is not tantamount to imposing the existence of the latter with the aim of concealing the existence of the former. It is nonetheless true that, for this reason, it is diverted from the matrix of the body and the practices generated by it.

III. From Marx to Bourdieu

(1) The Enlightening Function of Hysteresis

I think that, in the light of the above reflections, it is pretty obvious that I consider the concept of *hysteresis* to play a pivotal role in allowing us to shed light on some of the main limitations of the Bourdieusian approach. *Hysteresis* – or, if you prefer, *belatedness* – is symptomatic of the *inertia* of the habitus: the proper weight of the body that has to develop the necessary resources to move within a space where it has to find an 'objective sense', allowing it to act upon the outside world – a world in which it has its place and where it is not a stranger. In this sense, *hysteresis* is a feature not of the pre-body but of *the already appropriated body*, engaged in a world where it is *already* disposed of structures that have *already* been tested. Structural dispositions guarantee, retrospectively, the renewal of this incorporation. If the *belatedness* of our subjectivity never disappears and if *hysteresis* is a constitutive component of our habitus, this is so because, as Bourdieu remarks, social life always proceeds through the non-collection of *two distinct levels*: the structural level of incorporated *dispositions* and the structural level of *situations.* Put differently, *hysteresis* is an irreducible component of a *bodily interiorised history.* The habitus, once properly incorporated, is out of touch with short-term history, structuring the situations with which subjects are confronted in the course of their experience.

Here, we are not concerned with the *belatedness* caused by the *fall*; rather, our task consists in showing that *delay represents the temporal mode of the present itself* – that is, of the present in and through which the subject, by virtue of permanent adjustment, establishes a relation to the world. The *social world* defines situations, but it constitutes a world which is structured in its own manner, and which is involved in a process of *transformation*. It is this process which historical materialism, after all, has sought to grasp by developing – with the help of concepts such as mode of production – a science of history and of structural transformation. This history, if it does not have any other base than the one *created* by actors themselves by virtue of their *practices*, evolves in an objective manner that determines what humans do and what they *can* do. Hence, the discrepancy between effective practices and materialist history lies in the *inertia inherent in habituation*. Given that it is structurally determined by the incorporation of schemes of action, practice can never act and react in new situations that contribute to its reproduction. It is disposed, because it is, in fact, *pre*-disposed, under a fundamentally reproductive authority. It is based on the reproduction of the world, which – in accordance with its previously tested schemes – it recognises, questions, and desires. This is how the bodily subject is socially *maintained*. It is, in addition, the reason for its *inevitable delay* with regard to what is *still to occur*, illustrating that the two structural levels – the level of *dispositions* and the level of *situations* – are *not the same*. In brief, it is the task of *dispositions* to respond to *situations* – that is, it is the task of *interior structures* to respond to *exterior occurrences*.

(2) The Social Function of the Habitus

Following Bourdieu's description, the development of the habitus is socially mediated: it is accentuated by *apparatuses of inculcation*, which succeed and reinforce one another in accordance with the principle that a '*structuration of higher level determines that of a lower level*' (1972: 284): from the family to the school, from the school to the profession and to culture. This is how class-based forms of habitus are constructed in terms of social constellations that are homologically related to each other. Solidarity emerges within every class, a solidarity that needs to be conceived of in terms of habituation-habitation processes. If it is true, however, that the higher level determines the lower level, then everything is at stake at the lower level: from there, it becomes obvious that *socio-analysis*, as a *reconstructive* effort, will have a target which remains the same and which will always bring us back to the threshold of the thrown body, to the 'here' rather than the 'there'.

Nonetheless, the proper history of the individual is not the history that takes place. *The habituated body is embodied history*, but precisely for this reason, it is also a *weighty history* – a history reproduced through the body under the form of its social history, which brings it back to its past socialisation: a history that is out of step with situations historically determined by the transformations of the mode of production and the social relations derived from it. Stressing this phase difference, Bourdieu also reveals the limits of the crypto-phenomenological perspective, which he actually shares and which is based on a theory of the body. History makes progress outside the body and trains the bodies through its own development. From this perspective, one can only remain Marxist if one seeks to locate history outside the body, create a profound gap between the two levels, and return to the concepts of mode of production and class relations when examining the practical adjustment of the body.

Put differently, the discrepancy that defines the concept of *hysteresis* on this level only illustrates the difficulties arising from the attempt to collapse practice and production into each other by virtue of an unorthodox interpretation of Marx. From a Marxist standpoint, *practice is a productive activity*. What becomes evident here is that, if we want to understand the extent to which practices are socially determined, the *history of the producer* must not be confused with the *history of production*. The history of the producer is, in this case, the history combined with the past, based on the mode of reproduction of practically incorporated schemes. It is not identical to the history of production, which intercepts with reproduction, testing it in new situations, imposing itself by reviving it, and finding positions in the world which are not delivered by past experiences of already undertaken adjustments. In this sense, *all anticipations are inevitably foiled by history, at least by the agents that have found a home in their own practices*, especially by those whose structuring practices do not possess the sufficient fluidity and lability to situate and *inscribe themselves* in a pertinent manner in the – historically structured – new world.

(3) The Problem of Alienation and the Ethnological Fallacy

At this point, Bourdieu's sociology, conceived of as a form of structuralism of practice, acquires its political meaning. Insisting on the *hysteresis* of the habitus, the problem of bodily expropriation – to which all social subjects are constantly exposed – becomes important. Here we are confronted with the experience of *becoming strange*, becoming strange to both oneself and one's environment. In short, we are confronted with the problem of *alienation*.

This alienation, as we have seen, is founded on a discrepancy between two levels: the level of the habituated body and the level where habituation needs to be produced. This being said, it becomes obvious that the *ethnological fallacy* is not only an *epistemological fallacy*, but also a *political fallacy*: a *blindness* that leads to the *alienation* of the social subject – of the social fact called *hysteresis*. The proper body, understood as a body that is socially tested in a world which itself brings the body into being, converts the world into its own. (At the same time, the proper world – understood as a world that is socially tested in various bodies which themselves bring the world into being – converts the body into its own.) The *proper body* is always, to some extent, an *improper body* – or at least risks being improper – in relation to forms of expropriation producing class domination.

From this perspective, there is no doubt that the ethnologist plays the worst possible game: to put it bluntly, *the ethnological approach reduces the subject to its physical dimension*, treating it from the point of view of the interpreter who acts as a *disengaged interpreter* and, as such, treats the subject as an object. As a consequence, it is not only the ethnologist who is a stranger, but it is also the ethnologist's object which is treated as, and therefore becomes, strange – strange both to the ethnologist and to the ethnologist's environment. Ethnologists project themselves upon the actor. To the extent that they conceive of *themselves* as actors, this projection appears natural to them. Literally speaking, their strangeness does not cost them anything. The cost for the actor, by contrast, turns out to be rather heavy. Acting the way they normally do in their world, ethnologists show not only that they are not willing to pay the actor, but also that they are prepared to do anything in order not to pay the actor. They need to mobilise considerable symbolic and, strictly speaking, incomprehensible resources in order to conceal their strangeness and thereby realise their essential goal – namely, *to be within and to stay there.*

(4) From Ethnological Distance to Sociological Proximity

Within the framework of Bourdieu's structuralism of practice, *the sociologist has to prevail over the ethnologist.* Unlike the latter, the former does not come from far away, but emerges from proximity, like a person who finds herself at home. In the heart of our societies, the ethnologist uncovers strategies of adjustment and maladjustment, turning the construction of the self into a form of destruction – that is, the disappropriation determined by *hysteresis*, the constitutive delay of the habitus. Its object resolves through alienation. In order for the uncovering process to be possible, however, it is crucial that both the proper and the improper can be pulled together. It is therefore necessary that *hysteresis* can be described as a *set of structures* that functions, both despite and through its *disequilibrium.* In short, it is essential to describe the social embeddedness of the body and of the world, allowing for an accurate level of description and thus for an insightful representation of the home.

This home will then be the object of a certain attachment, but of an attachment devoid of ambiguities. If the social construction of the body is based on the ability to overcome the problem of disappropriation, this is because, as we have seen above, the arbitrary remains attached to its beginning. In this sense, *home is a space of incompressible violence.* For Bourdieu, it nevertheless gives rise to an indisputable fascination. For we are certainly dealing with a *home*, in the strong sense of the word, as something that effectively absorbs the *strangeness of the pre-body*, resisting the *alienating processes of disappropriation* caused by a social world that *excludes* subjects from participating in the construction of a proper structural order. In this world, which is based on the *capitalist* mode of production, the discrepancy between the two aforementioned levels is unbearable for the oppressed class. Given its pervasive power, capitalism makes salvation less and less achievable.

This, I think, is where the greatest difficulty concerning Bourdieu's structuralism of practice lies (and concerning the very idea that there is such a thing as a structuralism of practice). The above reflections confirm the view that it makes sense to distinguish between *two forms of society*: on the one hand, *societies of the proper*, of producers, of practical subjects adjusted to the world which belongs to them; and, on the other hand, *societies in which the proper is not achieved in practice itself* by the same producers. To be clear, a distinction is to be drawn between archaic and modern – and, hence, between pre-capitalist and capitalist – societies; and we have to nourish our fascination about the former in order to maintain a critical stance on the latter. Bourdieu's structuralism of practice, then, requires *two types of society*: those in which belonging – the not-being-strange – is experienced; and those in which belonging is no longer experienced – and in which it is no longer worthy of being practically experienced – by the producers. Of course, producers are subjects *involved in life*, that is, they are not freed from life and its necessities as in the case of the people of the *scholé* – these *strangers of practice* who, from now on, tend to be the only ones not to be strange anymore to a world in which practice essentially means alienation.

IV. Concluding Remarks

This strong constraint, which leads Bourdieu to reconsider a grand historical division, has two major consequences that allow us to make sense of the sociological project in relation to other disciplines, such as history and ethnology:

(a) History, as a history of production, can be regarded as a history of practical expropriation, of its denial and its inferiorisation, and hence of a situation which essentially involves the suspension of one's capacity to exercise one's own adjustments necessary for being integrated into a social world considered to be one's home. The particular character of archaic societies, as studied by Bourdieu, hinges on the discrepancy between *two structural levels*: the level of *dispositions* and the level of *situations*. To put this more clearly: it is because history does not alter its self-initiated adjustments that it continues to have a cyclic regularity in archaic societies. From this, however, we must not conclude that nature fixes and determines temporality. As emphasised by

Marx, history is the product of socially appropriated and configured processes, and thus of an external world in which people establish *social relations*. This reflection is expressed in the famous aphorism that appears in the *Grundrisse*: 'the earth is the great laboratory, the arsenal which provides both the means and the materials of labour, and also the location, the basis of the community' (Marx, 1969 [1857–1858]: 437). What we need to add to this insight is the fact that laboratory and arsenal are what they are due to their *inscription in bodies* capable of acting and moving in the world. Social relations are produced and reproduced by *bodies* which are adjusted to the particular place they occupy in the social space – namely, to the position which is theirs and which they aim to maintain.

We are confronted with an *opposition between societies*: on the one hand, *societies which have a history* – that is, societies in which the history of embodiment and the history of production go hand in hand; and, on the other hand, *societies in which history distends all habitation of the world through productive bodies*, because the body is transformed according to a non-reproductive temporality, which is inappropriate for the memorisation of the habituated body. History, located within this horizon of *separation*, becomes *alienation* for the people of practice, whose life conditions are determined by the necessity of production, and specifically by the reproduction of themselves, tied to the act of production. History can conceal its class-divided nature and, therefore, the relations of domination that result from the expropriation of the producers, understood as the expropriation of practice, which is the territory on which the socialisation of the body takes place.

(b) What is also at stake here is *the relation between sociology and ethnology*. Sociology, stretched as far as in Bourdieu's case, cannot conceal its dependence on the analysis of archaic societies. What kind of ethnology are we talking about? Without any doubt, it is not the kind of ethnology criticised above. If the aim consists in shedding light on the logic of practice, one cannot avoid making reference to the concept of pre-capitalist society. This concept is necessary because *living in practical terms* continues to have meaning in this crucial sense of *the belonging of the body to a world in which it is sustained and maintained*. In other words, it is necessary that there be non-strangers, and the theoretically decisive idea can be conceptually grasped and empirically proven by ethnology, rather than sociology. Of course, it contributes to its existence because sociology is successful insofar as it offers good terms for good questions – this it can do only by rejecting the ideology of ethnology in its dominant version (that is, according to Bourdieu, in its Lévi-Straussian version). Thus, another conception of the indigenous – a conception which differs from the cartographer's perspective – becomes acceptable: it is not about the projection of the strangeness of the observer, but about *taking the subject of practice for what it is*, that is, about considering it as a thinking and acting state of practice, produced inside societies in which *hysteresis* is packed, where the question of the delay finds answers in the world and in the temporality of the world.

To be sure, this world, approached by the new ethnologist and haunted by the problem of the structures of practice, is not the *good* world. That is, it is not a world that is intrinsically good. Rather, it is a world in which *the cultural arbitrary* plays a pivotal role. To the extent that this framework works, it is all the better for the subjects not to see it. *It is a world in which, in practice, nobody can be a stranger to the world* – and this is precisely where, according to Bourdieu, its *value* lies. This means that, as is made explicit in certain pages of *Outline of a Theory of Practice*,[5] it is better to live in a world in which practice is concerned with its own disappropriation – with the deconstruction of the body and its capacities to belong to something and to belong to itself. At least this applies to those who do not hide away in the sphere of non-production – that is, in an existence based on the suspension of need to adjust to the world within and through the act of production.

Does this archaic world exist? I really do not know the answer to this question, and I think neither did Bourdieu. What this shows, however, is that one has to understand it from the beginning of its disintegration, expressed in the opposition to the *abstract and disempowering structures of capitalism*. De facto, what applies to this world also applies to the pre-body. One can point in its direction, but one cannot touch it or comprehend it in its proper positivity. We know it in its postcolonial state, just as we know peasant societies in the context of the rise of rural exodus and the urbanisation of the countryside.

It is worth emphasising the heuristic significance of colonisation for Bourdieu's structuralism of practice. It is on the basis of an exogenously triggered maladjustment, an external aggression, and an imposed disembodiment that practical adjustment manifests itself in its resistance to arbitrary power, embodied in the strange perspective of both the ethnologist and the coloniser. Following Bourdieu, it would be fair to say that there is a somewhat *natural complicity between the theoretical disposition of a strange interpretation and the practical disposition of real exploitation* – both having as a vehicle the *disentanglement* of the practical relation to the world, with its adjustment-caused effects, and hence the removal of the home. Practice, with the complicity of the ethnological interpreter, loses its status of habitation-habituation, for becoming the sign of new strangers, in relation to both themselves and their world.

In relation to the ethnology of the Kabyle people, Bourdieu does not cease to denounce this complicity, notably by stigmatising the studies carried out at the beginning of the nineteenth century by civil administrators and the military (see Hanoteau and Letourneux (1872–1873), upon which Durkheim drew in his theory of segmentation). It is remarkable that, in this field, the studies undertaken by contemporary ethnologists, whilst providing painstakingly detailed accounts of the most destructive aspects of the colonial period, have gone back to the initial works, across ethnological studies of the sixties – obsessed with anti-colonialist critique to such an extent that they turned their backs on certain essential dimensions of facts (see Mahé, 2001).

More importantly, however, and this is why Bourdieu's principal epistemological enemy is the ethnological attitude in the Lévi-Straussian sense, one has to remember the inverted story which one finds in the opening pages of *Tristes tropiques* (Lévi-Strauss, 1955: 42–44), ten years before the publication of *Outline of a Theory of Practice*. It seems that, in this oeuvre, Lévi-Strauss starts from an analogous assumption: the tropics are sad, because the object of the ethnologist is involved in a process of death, which turns out to be irresistible. Furthermore, this process has begun by the same power that underlies the ethnological perspective: by the civilisation that has actually colonised other civilisations. Nonetheless, in this book, Lévi-Strauss draws a completely different conclusion from his observation when implying that a way out of this dilemma is to be found in theory – that is, in theoretical forms of interpretation detached from practice.

It is *not* the case that the death of the subject can be prevented, but it *is* the case that *social science* – elevated to a reflection upon structures that depend on the human spirit, rather than on the body – has the resources to take an *alternative perspective on temporality*, and thereby develop *a politics and an ethics*. Undoubtedly, this perspective is opposed to Bourdieu's view, because it presupposes and exploits the resources of the strangeness in practice, not only in relation to the indigenous, but also – and this is a point that Bourdieu does not take into account – in relation to the ethnologist's own world. Social science, as it is conceived here, is not primarily concerned with studying the condition of belonging, the identification of and with the group, or the integration into a realm that it shapes from the inside in the sense of a home. Such a conception of social science prevents it from getting caught up in an illusion and allows it to move uphill by mobilising the power of its critique.

Notes

1 Original Title: 'De Marx à Bourdieu: Les limites du structuralisme de la pratique'. A draft version of this piece was presented in the seminar series of the Groupe de Sociologie Politique et Morale (GSPM) at the École des Hautes Études en Sciences Sociales (EHESS) in Paris, France, on 30th April 2007. The original (French) version of this paper will appear in a forthcoming issue of *Raisons pratiques*.

2 I would like to thank Bryan S. Turner for his detailed comments on this translation. I am also grateful to the author, Bruno Karsenti, for making some useful suggestions.

3 An example of the denunciation of sociology as a 'conservative science' can be found in Rancière (1995).
4 See, for instance, Lefebvre (1958).
5 See Bourdieu (1972: 357–360). This point is particularly relevant to the rural ethos of an 'enchanted' relation to the nature of soil – an idiosyncratic relation that cannot be grasped by the capitalist form of productive labour.

References

Boltanski, Luc (2004) *La condition fœtale : une sociologie de l'engendrement et de l'avortement*, Paris: Gallimard.
Bourdieu, Pierre (1972) *Esquisse d'une théorie de la pratique, précédé de trois études d'ethnologie kabyle*, Paris: Seuil.
Bourdieu, Pierre (1979) *La distinction : Critique sociale du jugement*, Paris: Minuit.
Bourdieu, Pierre (1980) *Le sens pratique*, Paris: Minuit.
Bourdieu, Pierre and Loïc Wacquant (1992) *Réponses. Pour une anthropologie réflexive*, Paris: Seuil.
Goldstein, Kurt (1934) *Der Aufbau des Organismus. Einführung in die Biologie unter besonderer Berücksichtigung der Erfahrungen am kranken Menschen*, Den Haag: Nijhoff.
Guillaume, Paul (1937) *La psychologie de la forme*, Paris: Flammarion.
Hanoteau, Adolphe and Aristide Letourneux (1872–1873) *La Kabylie et les coutumes kabyles*, Paris: Impr. nationale.
Lefebvre, Henri (1958) *Critique de la vie quotidienne*, Paris: L'Arche.
Lévi-Strauss, Claude (1955) *Tristes tropiques*, Paris: Plon.
Lévi-Strauss, Claude (1968 [1949]) *Les structures élémentaires de la parenté*, nouv. éd. revue, Paris: Mouton.
Mahé, Alain (2001) *Histoire de la Grande Kabylie*, Paris: Bouchène.
Marx, Karl (1969 [1857–1858]) *Fondements de la critique de l'économie politique*, trad. par Roger Dangeville, Paris: Anthropos.
Marx, Karl and Friedrich Engels (1968 [1846]) *L'idéologie allemande*, trad. par Henri Auger, Gilbert Badia, Jean Baudrillard et Renée Cartelle, Paris: Ed. Sociales.
Marx, Karl and Friedrich Engels (2000/1977 [1846]) 'The German Ideology', in David McLellan (ed.) *Karl Marx: Selected Writings*, 2nd Edition, Oxford: Oxford University Press, pp. 175–208.
Mauss, Marcel (1966 [1935]) 'Les techniques du corps', in Marcel Mauss, *Sociologie et anthropologie*, 3. éd. augm., Paris: PUF, pp. 363–386.
Mauss, Marcel (1969 [1921]) 'L'expression obligatoire des sentiments (Rituels oraux funéraires australiens)', in Marcel Mauss, *Œuvres III*, Paris: Minuit, pp. 269–278.
Merleau-Ponty, Maurice (1942) *La structure du comportement*, Paris: PUF.
Rancière, Jacques (1995) *La mésentente : politique et philosophie*, Paris: Galilée.

CHAPTER FOUR

Durkheim and Bourdieu: The Common Plinth and its Cracks*

Loïc Wacquant
Translated by Tarik Wareh

For lack of being able to offer here a systematic comparison between Bourdieu's sociology and the thought of Durkheim – which would require an historical-analytic monograph capable of reconstituting the double chain, social and intellectual, of the ramifying causations that link them to each other and to their respective milieu – I would like, by way of selective soundings, to bring out four of the pillars that support their common base: namely, (1) the fierce attachment to rationalism, (2) the refusal of pure theory and the stubborn defence of the undividedness of social science, (3) the relation to the historical dimension and to the discipline of history, and (4) the recourse to ethnology as a privileged device for 'indirect experimentation'.

I am quite conscious of the fact that such an exercise can all too easily take a scholastic turn and fall into two equally reductive deviations, the one consisting in mechanically *deducing* Bourdieu from Durkheim so as to reduce him to the rank of an avatar, the other in *projecting back* the theses dear to Bourdieu into Durkheim's work so as to attest to their intellectual nobility. Its aim is to bring out some of the distinctive features of that French School of sociology, which endures and enriches itself at the cost of sometimes-unexpected metamorphoses.

Far from seeking to reduce Bourdieu's sociology to a mere variation of the Durkheimian score,[1] I would like to suggest that, while he leans firmly on them, Bourdieu imprints each of its pillar-principles with a particular twist, which allows them, ultimately, to support a scientific edifice endowed with an original architecture, at once closely akin to and sharply different from that of the Durkheimian mother-house. This is another way of saying that Pierre Bourdieu is an inheritor who – contrary to Marcel Mauss, for example – could and did, in the manner of an intellectual judoka, use the weight of the scientific capital accumulated by Durkheim to better project himself beyond his august predecessor.

(1) Passio Sciendi, or the Rationalist Faith in Action

Bourdieu shares with Durkheim, first of all, a rationalist philosophy of knowledge as the methodical application of reason and empirical observation to the social realm – an application that demands: on the one hand, perpetual mistrust towards ordinary thought, and towards the illusions, which it continuously generates; and, on the other hand, an endless effort of analytic (de/re)construction, which alone is capable of extracting from the teeming tangle of the real the 'internal causes and hidden impersonal forces that move individuals and collectivities' (Durkheim, 1964: 373). One could go so far as to say that our two authors harbour the same *scientific passion* – in the sense of an irrepressible love for and faith in science, its social value and mission – and the more vigorous their expression of it, the more strongly they are contested.

One recalls that Durkheim's avowed goal, from the inception of his work, was 'to extend to human behaviour the scientific rationalism' that had proven itself in the exploration of the natural world. 'What has been called our positivism', he hammers away in the long reply to his critics that opens the second edition of *The Rules of Sociological Method*, 'is but a consequence of this rationalism' (Durkheim, 1981 [1895]: ix; see also Durkheim, 1982 [1895]: 33). Likewise, Bourdieu forcefully asserts the unity of the scientific method and the membership of sociology in the great family of the sciences:

> Like every science, sociology accepts the principle of determinism, understood as a form of the principle of sufficient reason. Science, which must *rendre raison*, supply explanations for what is, postulates thereby that nothing is without a raison d'être. The sociologist adds *social*: without a specifically social raison d'être. (Bourdieu, 1984: 44; see also Bourdieu, 1993 [1984])

The 'absolute conviction', which he attributes to Flaubert in the task of the writer, Bourdieu himself possesses in the task of the sociologist. Contrary to a number of his contemporaries who have packed up and gone over to the 'postmodern' camp and revel in the abandonment (indeed, the derision) of reason, and whose international vogue has recently given new life to that typically French specialty, the export of designer-label concepts, Bourdieu has remained faithful to the 'party of science, which is now more than ever that of the *Aufklärung*, of demystification' (Bourdieu, 1982: 32).[2]

Durkheim and Bourdieu hold this rationalist faith, besides the national predilection for 'distinct ideas' inherited from Descartes, from their mentors in philosophy, and from their early immersion in the neo-Kantian atmosphere that pervaded their intellectual youth. It was through his personal association with Émile Boutroux – who introduced him to Comte, with Charles Renouvier, whom he regarded as the 'greatest rationalist of our time', and with his colleague at Bordeaux imbued with epistemology, Octave Hamelin (whom he describes nicely as an 'austere lover of right reason') – that Durkheim was led to inscribe his thought in the Kantian lineage. As for Bourdieu, his rationalism is rooted in his assiduous relations with that 'philosophy of the concept' (associated with the names of Georges Canguilhem and Gaston Bachelard, whose student he was) that offered a refuge and recourse against the 'philosophy of the subject' that reigned over the French intellectual field during the years of his intellectual apprenticeship, but also with the German tradition of the philosophy of 'symbolic forms' personified by Ernst Cassirer (whose main works he had translated by Éditions de Minuit, and whose affinities with Durkheimian theory he perceived very early).[3] And if the two are, at a distance of almost a century, deeply marked by Kantianism, it is because, as Durkheim noted on his return from a sojourn of studies across the Rhine, 'of all the philosophies which Germany has produced, [it is] this one that, properly interpreted, can still best be reconciled with the demands of science' (Durkheim, 1887: 330).[4]

For the uncompromising 'empirical rationalism' that gives impetus to the sociologies of Durkheim and Bourdieu is deployed and bolstered in *scientific practice* more than by professions of epistemological faith – even if both perpetrated, in their youth, manifestos of a methodological character. It is in the 'acts of research in the social sciences', to take up the title, which is not innocent, of the journal founded by Bourdieu in 1975 [*Actes de la recherche en sciences sociales*], that its postulates are affirmed and tested. Such is the case with the notion of the 'non-transparency' of the social world and with the priority given to the problematisation of the ordinary sense of the social world: 'Rigorous science presupposes decisive breaks with first-order perceptions' and should therefore not be afraid of 'offending common sense'.[5]

But, whereas Durkheim is content to make a clean sweep of the *praenotiones vulgares* that obstruct sociology, Bourdieu intends to repatriate them in an enlarged conception of objectivity that accords to the practical categories and competencies of agents a critical mediating role between 'the system of objective regularities' and the space 'of observable behaviours'. 'The moment of methodical objectivism – an inevitable but still abstract moment – demands its own transcendence'[6], without which, sociology is doomed to run aground on the reefs of the realism of the structure, or to get stuck in mechanistic explanations unfit to grasp the practical logic that governs conduct. And it is against the neo-Kantian tradition and its vision of the transcendental thinking subject that Bourdieu (re)introduces the concept of habitus in order to restore to the socialised body its function as active operator of the construction of the real.

(2) Impersonal Science, Undivided and Im-Pertinent

Social science is, for Bourdieu as for Durkheim, an eminently serious matter, grave even, because it is the bearer of a great historical 'burden'. Practicing it implies an austere scientific ethic, which is defined by a triple refusal.

Refusal of worldly seductions, first of all, to which Bourdieu attaches, more firmly yet than Durkheim had, the condemnation of the pliancies of intellectual and political prophetism. According to the theorist of anomie, sociology must imperatively 'renounce worldly success' and 'assume the esoteric character that is appropriate to all science'. Bourdieu goes further: the particular difficulty that the science of society encounters in grounding its authority derives from the fact that it is a fundamentally esoteric discipline that presents all appearances of being exoteric, in continuity with 'the vulgar'.[7] This makes of the sociology of the fields of cultural production and of the diffusion of their products, not one chapter among others, but an indispensable tool of sociological epistemology – and of sociological morality. Bourdieu maintains, in addition, that the analysis of the historical process whereby the scientific universe wrenched itself, however imperfectly, from the pull of history, furnishes the means for reinforcing the social bases of the rationalist commitment, which entry into this universe presupposes and produces at the same time (Bourdieu, 1991).

If sociology owes itself to avoid all compromising with the world, it should not, for that, withdraw from it. Bourdieu makes entirely his Durkheim's formula according to which sociological researches would be worth 'not one hour of trouble if they were to have only a speculative interest' and to remain 'an expert knowledge reserved for experts'.[8] To be socially pertinent, and in touch with the sociopolitical reality of its time, social science has a duty to be *im-pertinent*, in the double sense of irreverence to and distance from established powers and established ways of thinking. It must practice that 'ruthless criticism of everything existing' for which the young Marx called in a famous article in the *Rheinische Zeitung*, and first of all a criticism of itself, of its illusions and limitations. Bourdieu departs here from the Durkheimian framework to defend the idea that scientific autonomy and political engagement can grow more intense in concert and give each other mutual support, whenever intellectuals apply themselves to instituting *collective* forms of organisation and intervention liable to put the authority of scientific reason in the service of the 'corporatism of the universal', which, whether they want it or not, is their legacy and for which they are accountable (Bourdieu, 1989a; and Bourdieu, 1987b).

This *refusal of confinement within the scholarly microcosm* is made possible by the reciprocal checks, of which, the scientific community is the support and locus. For Durkheim, science, 'because it is objective, is something essentially impersonal' – which implies that it 'cannot progress except by a collective labour' (Durkheim, 1896–1897: 36). Bourdieu extends this idea by arguing that the true subject of the scientific enterprise, if there is one, is not the individual-sociologist but the scientific field *in toto* – that is, the ensemble of the relations of collision-collusion that obtain between the protagonists who struggle in this 'world apart' wherein those strange historical animals called historical truths are born.

It is also within this collective practice embracing a multiplicity of objects, epochs, and analytic techniques that the *refusal of disciplinary fragmentation and of theoreticism*, as well as of the conceptual mummification fostered by the 'forced division' of scientific labour, is declared. Durkheim and Bourdieu exhibit the same disdain for the scholastic posture that leads those who adopt it – or who are adopted by it – to that cult of the 'concept for concept's sake' which periodically comes back into fashion on one or the other side of the Atlantic according to a pendulum-swing hardly disturbed by the acceleration of the international circulation of ideas.

The 'lack of taste' that Durkheim affected 'for that prolix and formal dialectic', which propels the sociologist into orbit in the pure heaven of ideas, has not always been realised. The unequivocal condemnation of it that he proffers in the course of a review is worth citing *in extenso*:

> Here again is one of those books of philosophical generalities about the nature of society, and of generalities through which it is difficult to sense a very intimate and practical intercourse with social reality. Nowhere does the author give the impression that he has entered into direct contact with the facts about which he speaks [...]. However great the dialectical and literary talent of the authors, one could not go too far in denouncing the scandal of a method that so offends all our scientific habits and yet is still quite widely used. We no longer nowadays admit that one speculates about the nature of life without being first initiated into the techniques of biology. By what privilege could we permit the philosopher to speculate about society, without entering into commerce with the details of social facts? (Durkheim, 1905–1906: 565)

This is a formulation that would not be denied by Pierre Bourdieu, who has stated time and again his disapproval of that 'theoreticist theory', severed from all research activity and unduly reified as an academic specialty, which serves so often as a G-string to cover up scientific nakedness. Theory, as Bourdieu conceives it, is praxis and not logos; it is incarnated and actualised by the controlled implementation of the epistemic principles of construction of the object. Consequently, it feeds 'less on purely theoretical confrontation with other theories than on confrontation with ever-new empirical objects' (Bourdieu, 1992: 251; and Bourdieu, 1985: esp. 11–12).

The key concepts that make up the hard core of Bourdieu's sociology – habitus, capital, field, social space, symbolic violence – are so many *programs of organised questioning of the real* that serve to signpost the terrain of researches that must be all the more detailed and meticulous as one hopes to generalise their results via comparison. Accomplished theory, for the author of *Distinction*, takes after the chameleon more than the peacock: far from seeking to attract the eye to itself, it blends in with its empirical habitat; it borrows the colours, shades, and shapes of the concrete object, located in time and place, onto which it seems merely to hang but which it in fact *produces*.

(3) History as a Sociological Still [*Alambic*]

Durkheim and Bourdieu have in common the fact that they are commonly read as fundamentally ahistorical, if not anti-historical, authors. The 'functionalism' of the former, engrossed with theorising the 'Hobbesian problem' of social order (if one believes Talcott Parsons's canonical exegesis), is alleged to be congenitally incapable of incorporating social change and the irruption of the event. The 'reproduction theory' commonly attributed to the latter is depicted as an infernal machine for abolishing history, and the notion of habitus a conceptual strait-jacket aimed at locking the individual in the eternal repetition of a present frozen in an order of domination at once undivided and inescapable. In brief, Bourdieu and Durkheim are supposed to leave us culpably disarmed in the face of historicity. Nothing, on closer look, could be further removed from both the intent and content of their thought.[9]

Émile Durkheim is an eminently historical sociologist, first, in that all of his investigations partake of a project of *current relevance* (*actualité*), which is to contribute, by way of scientific analysis, to resolving the crisis, diagnosed as 'moral', which is shaking the societies of Europe to their core right before his eyes. The theoretical issue that obsesses him is not to elaborate a conception of social order *in abstracto* but to identify the changing conditions and mechanisms of solidarity in the era of industrial modernity, and thereby to facilitate the maturation of a morality fit for the new social relations. Durkheimian sociology is also historical in the sense that it purports to catch hold of institutions in the movement of their becoming and that its harmonious development requires an active and reflective collaboration with historiography.

For Durkheim, history can and must play 'in the order of social realities a role analogous to that of the microscope in the order of physical realities' (Durkheim, 1970 [1909]: 154). It captures in its nets the particular expressions of the social laws and types which sociology discerns. And only the 'genetic method', which compares the diverse incarnations of a given institution, allows one 'to follow its integral development through all social species', to distinguish the *efficient causes* that have brought it about from the social *functions* that it performs on the synchronic level, and, consequently, to establish its normal (or pathological) character. 'To my knowledge, there is no sociology worthy of the name which does not assume a historical character', Durkheim proclaims during a debate with Charles Seignobos. And he insists he is 'convinced' that sociology and history 'are destined to become ever more intimately related, and that a day will come when the historical spirit and the sociological spirit will differ only in nuances'.[10]

If Durkheim's sociology, judiciously interpreted, must be held to be historical by virtue of its make and its method, that of Bourdieu deserves the qualifier *historicist*.[11] It is no exaggeration to consider that, for Bourdieu, the social is nothing other than history – already made, in the making, or to be made. So much so that one could describe his intellectual project, which some might against his will call philosophical, but after all the label matters little, as a *historicisation of the transcendental project of philosophy* (seen from this angle, Bourdieu would be a sort of anti-Heidegger, since, as we know, Heidegger's ambition was to ontologise history).[12]

Here, again, Bourdieu leans on Durkheimian positions in order better to go beyond them, especially by bringing the historical dimension onto the territory of social ontology and social epistemology. He impugns first of all the distinction, on which the director of the *Année sociologique* sought to found the possibility of a 'true historical science', between 'historical events' and 'permanent social functions' (Durkheim, 1968 [1908]: 212–213), and the artificial antinomies which undergird it, between nomothetic and ideographic approaches, conjuncture and *longue durée*, the unique and the universal. And he calls for working towards a truly unified science of humans, 'where history would be a historical sociology of the past and sociology a social history of the present' (Bourdieu, 1995: 111), starting from the postulate that social action, social structure, and social knowledge are all equally the product of the work of history.

Such a science must, to fulfil its mission, effect a *triple historicisation*. Historicisation of the *agent*, to begin with, by dismantling the socially constituted system of embodied schemata of judgement and action (habitus) that govern her conduct and representations and orients her strategies. Historicisation of the various *social worlds* (fields) in which socialised individuals invest their desires and energies and abandon themselves to that endless race for recognition that is social existence. For, according to Bourdieu, practice no more results from the agent's subjective intentions alone than they flow directly from the objective constraints of the structure. It emerges, rather, in the turbulences of their confluence, from 'the more or less "successful" encounter between positions and dispositions'; it is born from the obscure relation of 'ontological proximity' that weaves itself between these 'two modes of existence of the social' that are the habitus and field, 'history objectified in things' and 'history incarnate in bodies' (Bourdieu, 1981: 313; Bourdieu, 1989b: 59; and Bourdieu, 1982: 38; respectively).

Once the subterranean connections between embodied history and reified history have been elucidated, it remains finally to carry out the historicisation of the *knowing subject and of the instruments of knowledge*, by means of which they construct their own object, as well as of the universe in which the knowledge under consideration is produced and circulates (in this, Bourdieu is infinitely closer to Foucault than to Lévi-Strauss). To summarise:

> If one is convinced that being is history, which has no beyond, and that one must thus ask biological history (with the theory of evolution) and sociological history (with the analysis of the collective and individual sociogenesis of forms of thought) for the truth of a reason that is historical through and through and yet irreducible to history, then one must admit also that it is by historicisation (and not by the decisive dehistoricisation of a sort of theoretical 'escapism') that one may try to wrench reason more completely from historicity. (Bourdieu, 1992: 427–428)

Such a sociology, simultaneously and *inseparably structural and genetic*, can envisage explaining (and not only describing) the unforeseen advent of crisis, the sudden breakthrough of 'genius', the transformational unfolding of action that make for the great social and symbolic revolutions whereby history abruptly redraws its course. Thus, 'it is by historicizing him completely that one can understand completely how [Flaubert] wrests himself away from the strict historicity of less heroic destinies', the originality of his enterprise emerging in full view only as 'one reinserts it in the historically constituted space within which it was constructed' (Bourdieu, 1992: 145).

This historicising sociology can also purport to bring to light, and thus better to curb, the historical determinisms to which, as in every historical practice, it is necessarily submitted. Durkheim asks history to *nourish* sociology; Bourdieu expects it to *liberate* sociology from the historical subconscious, scientific as well as social, of past generations that weighs with all its dead weight on the brain of the researcher. What is instituted by history can be 'restituted' only by history; historical sociology alone, therefore, offers to the sociologist, as historical agent and scholarly producer, 'the instruments of a true awakening of consciousness or, better, of a true *self-mastery*' (Bourdieu, 1980b: 14). Free thinking, Bourdieu holds, comes at this price: it can 'be conquered [only] by a historical anamnesis capable of unveiling everything that, in thought, is the forgotten product of the work of history' (Bourdieu, 1992: 429).

(4) The 'Indirect Experimentations' of Ethnology

Another methodological procedure equally prized by Durkheim and Bourdieu is one in which ethnology is typically entrusted with the lead role: the quest for the *experimentum crucis*, the test-phenomenon or the key-puzzle that will allow one, either to reformulate (and thus to resolve) the great questions bequeathed by philosophy in historical and empirical terms, or to effect a *demonstratio a fortiori*, bearing on the case presumed to be the least favourable, so as to win over the approval of even readers most restive to the model or to mode of reasoning put forth.

Thus it is that, after having – in his dissertation thesis – climbed the rock of morality said to be impregnable by positive study, Durkheim chooses suicide as the object of a 'study in sociology'. This tragic march along the edge of one's interior abyss at the end of which the individual, through an intimate path inaccessible to the gaze 'from outside', comes to deprive herself of that most precious good which is her life, 'would seem to concern psychology alone'. To demonstrate that such an 'individual act which affects only the individual himself' – and which poses in concrete, measurable, terms two of philosophy's perennial enigmas, that of death and that of the will – is the resultant of social forces 'of great generality' is to demonstrate at the same time that there is no behaviour which is not 'the extension of a social state', and that sociological explanation can without harm leave aside 'the individual as individual, his motives and his ideas' (Durkheim, 1930 [1897]: 8, 33, and 148).

Bourdieu's 'suicide' is the aesthetic disposition, the 'love of art' which experiences itself as 'freed from conditions and conditionings', and which properly defines bourgeois culture, or, more generally, taste, that other, but more common, name for habitus.[13] Here again, what is more personal, more ineffable, more in-determinate (and thus seemingly undetermined) than that capacity for discernment which, to borrow the idiom of Kant, claims 'universal validity', although it arises out of that private reaction to the objects of the world, which is the pleasure of the senses and seems, by nature, to exclude all 'decision by means of proof'? *Distinction* draws a vast ethnological tableau of the lifestyles and cultural propensities of social classes in order to establish the structural homology that links, through the mediation of the space of dispositions, the space of positions and the space of position-takings in such varied domains as food and music, cosmetics and politics, furniture, and conjugal love. Whence it turns out that, far from being the inimitable signature of a free individual, taste is the form *par excellence* of submission to social destiny. Now, if things at first glance as insignificant as the manner of drinking one's coffee and wiping one's mouth at the table, the reading of a newspaper and one's favourite sport function as so many marks of distinction, exterior signs of (interior) wealth, (cultural) capitals, what practice can claim to escape this struggle over classifications that is the hidden face of the class struggle?

As Durkheim before him, Bourdieu is fond of supporting his theoretical schemas by means of binary comparisons between so-called 'traditional' or 'precapitalist' societies and 'highly differentiated' social formations (a furiously Durkheimian designation), wherein *recourse to ethnology serves as a technique of sociological quasi-experimentation.*[14] It is well known that Durkheim chose the Australian totemic system as the empirical basis for his quest for the collective foundations of religious belief and, beyond, the social origin of the frameworks of human understanding, because he saw in it 'the most primitive and simple religion that exists' – thus, the one most apt to 'reveal to us an essential and permanent aspect of humanity'. The 'very lack of refinement' of the so-called inferior religions, according to him, made of them 'convenient experiments, where the facts and their relations are easier to make out' (Durkheim, 1960 [1912]: 2 and 11).

The Kabyle society, which Bourdieu, as an ethnosociologist, studied at the height of the Algerian war of national liberation, and, to a lesser degree (or less visibly, owing to a modesty that one suspects is both professional and personal), the Béarn villages of his childhood, are, for him, what the totemic clans of inner Australia were for Durkheim: a sort of 'strategic research site' (as Robert Merton would say), capable of bringing to light in their 'purified' state, as if passed through a filter, mechanisms that it would be too difficult – or too painful – to bring into focus in a more familiar social environment. For Bourdieu, scrutinising the practices and symbolic relations of weakly differentiated societies is the means for effecting a *radicalisation of the socioanalytical intention* – i.e., for exposing the social unconscious nestled in the infolds of the body, cognitive categories, and institutions that seem most innocent and anecdotic.

This radicalising function of ethnology is nowhere more noticeable than in the analysis to which Bourdieu submits 'masculine domination' in the course of a pivotal text that implicitly contains the core of his theory of symbolic violence, as well as a paradigmatic illustration of the distinctive use to which he turns the comparative method (Bourdieu, 1990).[15] The mythico-ritual practices of the Kabyle are distant enough that deciphering them allows for a rigorous objectivation; yet they are near enough to facilitate that 'participant objectivation', which alone can trigger the return of the repressed for which, as gendered beings, we are all depositories. Proof is found in those homologies that one could not make up between the purest categories of the purest philosophical and psychoanalytical thought (those of Kant, Sartre, and Lacan), and the paired oppositions that organise the ritual acts, myths, and oral tradition of the Berber-speaking mountain dwellers. 'Ethnology promotes astonishment before what passes most completely unnoticed – i.e., what is most profound and most profoundly unconscious in our ordinary experience' (Bourdieu, 1994b: 94).[16] In that, it is, not an auxiliary, but an indispensable ingredient of the sociological method. Bourdieu's ethnological detour is not, properly speaking, a detour, but a *bypass* liable to clear for us an access to the social unthought that forms the invisible plinth of our ways of doing and being.

Appendix: Bourdieu's '*Suicide*'[†]

I have entitled my remarks 'Bourdieu's "*Suicide*"' because *Distinction* is to Pierre Bourdieu what *Suicide* was to Émile Durkheim: what Bacon calls an *experimentum crucis*, a 'critical experiment' designed to demonstrate, first, the generic potency of the sociological method – against the claims of philosophy – and, second, the fecundity of a distinctive theoretical schema – the theory of practice anchored by the conceptual triad of habitus, capital, and field.

When Bourdieu undertakes his 'critique of judgement' (the subtitle of *Distinction*, in reference to Immanuel Kant's famous 'Critique of Judgement'), the notion of taste enjoys at best a marginal status in the social sciences. Apart from Max Weber's brief considerations on the 'stylisation' of life, Thorstein Veblen's theory of conspicuous consumption, and Norbert Elias's (then-little known) study of the 'civilising process', the notion has been abandoned to philosophers of mind and aesthetics, on the one side, and to biologists, on the other. It is deemed either too high or too lowly an object for the sociologist to bother with.

In *Distinction*, and in related studies of cultural practices upon which it builds (notably *Photography: A Middle-Brow Art* (1990 [1965]) and *The Love of Art: European Museums and their Public* (1991 [1969])), Bourdieu effects a Copernican revolution in the study of taste. He abolishes the sacred frontier that makes legitimate culture a separate realm and repatriates aesthetic consumption into everyday consumptions. He demonstrates that aesthetic judgement is a social ability by virtue of both its genesis and its functioning. In so doing, Bourdieu offers not only a radical 'social critique of the judgement'. He also delivers a graphic account of the workings of culture and power in contemporary society. And he elaborates a theory of class that fuses the Marxian insistence on economic determination with the Weberian recognition of the distinctiveness of the cultural order and the Durkheimian concern for classification.

(1) A Theory of Perception and Judgement

First, Bourdieu shows that, far from expressing some unique inner sensibility of the individual, aesthetic judgement is an eminently *social faculty*, resulting from class upbringing and education. To appreciate a painting, a poem, or a symphony presupposes mastery of the specialised symbolic code of which it is a materialisation, which, in turn, requires possession of the proper kind of cultural capital. Mastery of this code can be acquired by osmosis in one's milieu of origin or by explicit teaching. When it comes through native familiarity (as with the children of cultured upper-class families), this trained capacity is experienced as an individual gift, an innate inclination testifying to spiritual worth. The Kantian theory of 'pure aesthetic', which philosophy presents as universal, is but a stylised – and mystifying – account of this particular experience of the 'love of art' that the bourgeoisie owes to its privileged social position and condition (this point is revisited in historical fashion in *The Rules of Art*, in which Bourdieu retraces the historical genesis of the artistic field, which is the 'objective' counterpart to the emergence of the 'pure' aesthetic disposition among privileged classes).

(2) Social Judgement as a Relational System of Oppositions and Complementarities

A second major argument of *Distinction* is that the aesthetic sense exhibited by different classes and class fractions, and the lifestyles associated with them, define themselves in opposition to one another: *taste is first and foremost the distaste of the tastes of others.* ('In matters of taste, more than in anywhere else, any determination is negation: tastes are no doubt first and foremost distastes, disgust provoked by horror or visceral intolerance ('sick-making') of the taste of others' (Bourdieu, 1984 [1979]: 56). This is because any cultural practice – wearing tweed or jeans, playing golf or soccer, going to museums or to auto shows, listening to jazz or watching sitcoms, etc. – takes its social meaning, and its ability to signify social difference and distance, not from some intrinsic property it has but from its location in a system of like objects and practices. To uncover the social logic of consumption thus requires establishing, not a direct link between a given practice and a particular class category (e.g., horse riding and the gentry), but the structural correspondences that obtain between two constellations of relations, the space of lifestyles and the space of social positions occupied by the different groups.

(3) A Theory of Social Space

Bourdieu reveals that this space of social positions is organised by *two crosscutting principles of differentiation – economic capital and cultural capital* – whose distribution defines the two oppositions that undergird major lines of cleavage and conflict in advanced society. (We must note here that while Bourdieu's demonstration is carried out with French materials, his theoretical claims apply to all differentiated societies. For pointers on how to extract general propositions from Bourdieu's specific findings on France and to adapt his models to other countries and epochs, see 'A Japanese Reading of Distinction', Bourdieu, 1995).

The first, vertical, division pits agents holding large volumes of either capital (the dominant class), against those deprived of both (the dominated class). The second, horizontal, opposition arises among the dominant, between those who possess much economic capital but few cultural assets (business owners and managers, who form the dominant fraction of the dominant class), and those whose capital is pre-eminently cultural (intellectuals and artists, who anchor the dominated fraction of the dominant class). Individuals and families continually strive to maintain or improve their position in social space by pursuing strategies of reconversion whereby they transmute or exchange one species of capital into another. The conversion rate between the various species of capital, set by such institutional mechanisms as the school system, the labour market, and inheritance laws, turns out to be one of the central stakes of social struggles, as each class or class fraction seeks to impose the hierarchy of capital most favourable to its own endowment. (This is explored further in Bourdieu, 1996 [1989].)

(4) Distinction, Necessity, and Cultural Goodwill: Three Kinds of Class Taste

Having mapped out the structure of social space, Bourdieu demonstrates that the *hierarchy of lifestyles is the misrecognised retranslation of the hierarchy of classes.* To each major social position – bourgeois, petty-bourgeois, and popular – corresponds a class habitus undergirding three broad kinds of tastes.

The 'sense of distinction' of the bourgeoisie is the manifestation, in the symbolic order, of the latter's distance from material necessity and long-standing monopoly over scarce cultural goods. It accords primacy to form over function, manner over matter, and celebrates the 'pure pleasure' of the mind over the 'coarse pleasure' of the senses. More importantly, bourgeois taste defines itself by negating the 'taste of necessity' of the working classes. The latter may indeed be described as an inversion of the Kantian aesthetic: it subordinates form to function and refuses to autonomise judgement from practical concerns, art from everyday life (for instance, workers use photography to solemnise the high points of collective life and prefer pictures that are faithful renditions of reality over photos that pursue visual effects for their own sake).

Caught in the intermediate zones of social space, the petty bourgeoisie displays a taste characterised by 'cultural goodwill': they know what the legitimate symbolic goods are but they do not know how to consume them in the proper manner – with the ease and insouciance that comes from familial habituation. They bow before the sanctity of bourgeois culture but, because they do not master its code, they are perpetually at risk of revealing their middling position in the very movement whereby they strive to hide it by aping the practices of those above them in the economic and cultural order.

(5) Cultural Consumption, the Hidden Dimension of Class Struggle

But Bourdieu does not stop at drawing a map of social positions, tastes, and their relationships. He shows that the *contention between groups in the space of lifestyles is a hidden, yet fundamental, dimension of class struggles.* For to impose one's art of living is to impose at the same time principles of vision of the world that legitimise inequality by making the divisions of social space appear rooted in the inclinations of individuals rather than the underlying distribution of capital. Against Marxist theory, which defines classes exclusively in the economic sphere, by their position in the relations of production, Bourdieu argues that classes arise in the conjunction of shared position in social space and shared dispositions actualised in the sphere of consumption: 'The *representations* that individuals and groups inevitably engage in their practices is part and parcel of their social reality. A class is defined as much by its *perceived being* as by its being' (Bourdieu, 1984 [1979]: 564). Insofar as they enter into the very constitution of class, social classifications are instruments of symbolic domination and constitute a central stake in the struggle between classes (and class fractions), as each tries to gain control over the classificatory schemata that command the power to conserve or change reality by preserving or altering the representation of reality.

To conclude: *Distinction* provides a sociological answer (that is, a historical and empirical answer) to one of the grand questions of philosophy – the question of the origins and operations of judgement. It shows that, just as suicide varies according to social factors, taste, far from being the ultimate repository of spontaneous individuality, is a transfigured expression of social necessity. By revealing taste as simultaneously weapon and stake in the classification struggles whereby groups seek to maintain or improve their position in society by imposing their lifestyle as the sole legitimate *art de vivre*, Bourdieu brings *homo aestheticus* back into the world of the mundane, the common and the contested – i.e. back in the heartland of social science.

In the course of this demonstration, *Distinction* puts forth and illustrates a historicist theory of knowledge (encapsulated by the idea of *practical sense*, which is the original title of *The Logic of Practice*, the companion volume to *Distinction*), a dispositional theory of action (anchored by the notion of habitus) and a relational and agonistic conception of social space (summed up by the concept of field). And it unties the vexed nexus of culture, power, and identity in modern society. All in all, not a bad recipe for attaining classical status.

Summary

This chapter highlights some distinctive features of the French School of sociology by uncovering four principles that support the works of Émile Durkheim and Pierre Bourdieu: (1) the fierce attachment to rationalism, (2) the refusal of pure theory and the defence of the undividedness of social science, (3) the relation to historicity and historiography, and (4) the recourse to ethnology as a privileged device for 'indirect experimentation'. It is argued that Bourdieu both relies on and twists those pillar-principles to support a scientific edifice endowed with an original architecture, at once closely akin to and sharply different from that of the Durkheimian mother-house.

Notes

* Published in Bridget Fowler (ed.) (2000) *Reading Bourdieu on Society and Culture*, Oxford: Blackwell/Sociological Review, pp. 105–119.

1 Bourdieu warned against that 'classificatory functioning of academic thought' (Bourdieu, 1987: 38), which inclined one to wield theoretical labels as so many weapons of intellectual terrorism ('X is a Durkheimian' can be taken to mean 'X is only a vulgar Durkheimian' or again 'X is already entirely contained in Durkheim'). The same caveat would apply to Bourdieu's relations to Marx, Weber, Husserl, Merleau-Ponty, or Wittgenstein.

2 On this point, see also Bourdieu (1994a) and Bourdieu (1998 [1994]) (esp. chapters 3 and 7), and the conference entitled 'La cause de la science', with which Bourdieu opens the issue of the *Actes de la recherches en sciences sociales* devoted to 'The Social History of the Social Sciences' (106–107, March 1995, pp. 3–10).

3 Cf. Bourdieu (1977: 405–411) [Bourdieu (1992 [1977])]; Bourdieu (1987a: 13–15 and 53–54); Bourdieu and Passeron (1968: 162–212).

4 For an interpretation of Durkheimism as 'sociologised Kantianism', see LaCapra (1972); for a Kantian reading of Bourdieu, see Harrison (1993).

5 The first citation is from Bourdieu (1982: 29), the second from Durkheim (1930 [1897]: 349).

6 Bourdieu, Boltanski, Castel and Chamboredon (1965: 22) [= Bourdieu, Boltanski, Castel and Chamboredon (1990 [1965])]; also on this point, Bourdieu (1973: 53–80), and Bourdieu (1980a) [= Bourdieu (1990 [1980])], Book I.

7 Durkheim (1981 [1895]: 144) [= Durkheim (1982 [1895])], and Bourdieu (1982: 25).

8 The first part of the citation is drawn from Durkheim (1930 [1893]: xxxix) [= Durkheim (1984 [1893]): xxvi], the second from Bourdieu (1984: 7).

9 An excellent discussion of Durkheim's relationship to history and historiography can be found in Bellah (1958). For a partial inventory of Bourdieu's views on history, change, and time, see Bourdieu and Wacquant (1992: 79–81, 89–94, 101, and 132–140); Bourdieu (1990 [1980]: chapter 6); Bourdieu (1987a: 56–61); Bourdieu (1994a: 76–80 and 169–174); Bourdieu, Chartier and Darnton (1985); and Bourdieu (1995).

10 Durkheim (1896–1897: 139); Durkheim (1981 [1895]: 137–138) [= Durkheim (1982 [1895]: 157)]; Durkheim (1968 [1908]: 199); and Filloux (1970 [1909]: 157), respectively.

11 As Philip Abrams has rightly suggested in his book *Historical Sociology* (1982).

12 Bourdieu (1988) [= Bourdieu (1991 [1988])]; as well as Bourdieu (1983); and Bourdieu (1994a), *passim.*

13 Bourdieu (1984 [1979]), and Bourdieu, Darbel and Schnapper (1969). (See the analysis of *Distinction* as 'Bourdieu's *Suicide*' in the appendix).

14 Bourdieu says that he conceived his comparative investigations of the matrimonial customs of the peasants of Kabylia and of the Béarn as 'a sort of epistemological experimentation' (Bourdieu, 1987a: 75). See also, for example, Bourdieu (1963) and Bourdieu (1962). On the Durkheimian uses of ethnology, see Karady (1981).

15 One may read in the same vein the superb, if little read, article, 'Reproduction interdite. La dimension symbolique de la domination économique', *Études rurales* 113–114 (1989c): 15–36.

16 The methodical 'ethnologisation' of the familiar world can exercise a similar effect, cf. the 'Preface' to the English edition of *Homo academicus* (Bourdieu, 1988 [1984]) and the conclusion to *La misère du monde* (Bourdieu, 1993) [= Bourdieu (1999 [1993])].

† This appendix was originally prepared for the Panel on Classics of the Twentieth Century, World Congress, International Sociological Association, Montréal, Canada, 28 July, 1999.

References

Abrams, Philip (1982) *Historical Sociology*, Ithaca, N.Y.: Cornell University Press.

Bellah, Robert N. (1958) 'Durkheim and History', *American Sociological Review* 24(4): 447–461.

Bourdieu, Pierre (1962) 'Les relations entre les sexes dans la société paysanne'' *Les Temps modernes* 195: 307–331.

Bourdieu, Pierre (1963) 'La société traditionelle. Attitude à l'égard du temps et conduite économique', *Sociologie du travail* 5(1): 24–44.

Bourdieu, Pierre (1973) 'The Three Forms of Theoretical Knowledge', *Social Science Information* 12(1): 53–80.

Bourdieu, Pierre (1977) 'Sur le pouvoir symbolique', *Annales ESC* 32(3): 405–411.

Bourdieu, Pierre (1979) *La distinction. Critique sociale du jugement*, Paris: Minuit.

Bourdieu, Pierre (1980a) *Le sens pratique*, Paris: Minuit.

Bourdieu, Pierre (1980b) 'Le mort saisit le vif. Les relations entre l'histoire incorporée et l'histoire réifiée', *Actes de la recherche en sciences sociales* 32–33: 3–14.

Bourdieu, Pierre (1981) 'Men and Machines', in Karin Knorr-Cetina and Aaron Victor Cicourel (eds.) *Advances in Social Theory and Methodology: Toward an Integration of Micro and Macro-Sociologies*, Boston: Routledge & Kegan Paul, pp. 304–317.

Bourdieu, Pierre (1982) *Leçon sur la leçon*, Paris: Minuit.

Bourdieu, Pierre (1983) 'Les sciences sociales et la philosophie', *Actes de la recherche en sciences sociales* 47–48: 45–52.

Bourdieu, Pierre (1984) *Questions de sociologie*, Paris: Minuit.

Bourdieu, Pierre (1984 [1979]) *Distinction: A Social Critique of the Judgement of Taste*, trans. Richard Nice, Cambridge, Mass.: Harvard University Press.

Bourdieu, Pierre (1985) 'The Genesis of the Concepts of "Habitus" and "Field"', *Sociocriticism* 2(2): 11–24.

Bourdieu, Pierre (1987a) *Choses dites*, Paris: Minuit.

Bourdieu, Pierre (1987b) 'Für eine Realpolitik der Vernunft', in Sebastian Müller-Rolli (ed.) *Das Bildungswesen der Zukunft*, Stuttgart: Ernst Klett, pp. 229–234.

Bourdieu, Pierre (1988) *L'ontologie politique de Martin Heidegger*, Paris: Minuit.

Bourdieu, Pierre (1988 [1984]) *Homo Academicus*, trans. Peter Collier, Cambridge: Polity Press in association with Basil Blackwell.

Bourdieu, Pierre (1989a) 'The Corporatism of the Universal: The Role of Intellectuals in the Modern World', *Telos* 81: 99–110.

Bourdieu, Pierre (1989b) *La noblesse d'État. Grandes Écoles et esprit de corps*, Paris: Minuit.

Bourdieu, Pierre (1989c) 'Reproduction interdite. La dimension symbolique de la domination économique', *Études rurales* 113–114: 15–36.

Bourdieu, Pierre (1990) 'La domination masculine', *Actes de la recherche en sciences sociales* 84: 2–31.

Bourdieu, Pierre (1990 [1980]) *The Logic of Practice*, trans. Richard Nice, Cambridge: Polity Press.

Bourdieu, Pierre (1990 [1987]) *In Other Words: Essays Towards a Reflexive Sociology*, Cambridge: Polity Press.

Bourdieu, Pierre (1991) 'The Peculiar History of Scientific Reason', *Sociological Forum* 5(2): 3–26.

Bourdieu, Pierre (1991 [1988]) *The Political Ontology of Martin Heidegger*, trans. Peter Collier, Cambridge: Polity Press.

Bourdieu, Pierre (1992) *Les règles de l'art*, Paris: Seuil.

Bourdieu, Pierre (1992 [1977]) 'On Symbolic Power', in Pierre Bourdieu, *Language and Symbolic Power*, edited and introduced by John B. Thompson, translated by Gino Raymond and Matthew Adamson, Cambridge: Polity Press, pp. 163–170.

Bourdieu, Pierre (ed.) (1993) *La misère du monde*, Paris: Seuil.

Bourdieu, Pierre (1993 [1984]) *Sociology in Question*, London: Sage.

Bourdieu, Pierre (1994a) *Raisons pratiques. Sur la théorie de l'action*, Paris: Seuil.

Bourdieu, Pierre (1994b) 'Division du travail, rapports sociaux de sexe et de pouvoir', *Cahiers du GEDISST* 11: 91–104.

Bourdieu, Pierre (1995) 'Sur les rapports entre la sociologie et l'histoire en Allemagne et en France', *Actes de la recherche en sciences sociales* 106–107: 108–122.

Bourdieu, Pierre (1996 [1989]) *The State Nobility: Elite Schools in the Field of Power*, trans. Loretta Clough, Cambridge: Polity Press.

Bourdieu, Pierre (1996 [1992]) *The Rules of Art: Genesis and Structure of the Literary Field*, trans. Susan Emanuel, Cambridge: Polity Press.

Bourdieu, Pierre (1998 [1994]) *Practical Reason: On the Theory of Action*, Cambridge: Polity Press.

Bourdieu, Pierre (1999 [1993]) *The Weight of the World: Social Suffering in Contemporary Society*, trans. Priscilla Parkhurst Ferguson [et al.], Cambridge: Polity Press.

Bourdieu, Pierre, Luc Boltanski, Robert Castel and Jean-Claude Chamboredon (1965) *Un art moyen. Essai sur les usages sociaux de la photographie*, Paris: Minuit.

Bourdieu, Pierre, Luc Boltanski, Robert Castel and Jean-Claude Chamboredon (1990 [1965]) *Photography: A Middle-Brow Art*, trans. Shaun Whiteside, Cambridge: Polity Press.

Bourdieu, Pierre, Roger Chartier and Robert Darnton (1985) 'Dialogue à propos de l'histoire culturelle', *Actes de la recherche en sciences sociales* 59: 86–93.

Bourdieu, Pierre, Alain Darbel and Dominique Schnapper (1969) *L'amour de l'art. Les musées d'art européens et leur public*, Paris: Minuit.

Bourdieu, Pierre, Alain Darbel and Dominique Schnapper (1991 [1969]) *The Love of Art: European Art Museums and Their Public*, trans. Caroline Beattie and Nick Merriman, Cambridge: Polity Press.

Bourdieu, Pierre and Jean-Claude Passeron (1968) 'Sociology and Philosophy in France Since 1945: Death and Resurrection of a Philosophy Without Subject', *Social Research* 34(1): 162–212.

Bourdieu, Pierre and Loïc Wacquant (1992) *An Invitation to Reflexive Sociology*, Cambridge: Polity Press.

Durkheim, Émile (1887) 'L'enseignement de la philosophie dans les universités allemandes', *Revue internationale de l'enseignement* 13: 313–338, 423–440.

Durkheim, Émile (1896–1897) 'Préface', *Année sociologique*, reprinted in *Journal sociologique*, Paris, Presses Universitaires de France, 1969.

Durkheim, Émile (1905–1906) *Année sociologique*, reprinted in *Journal sociologique*.

Durkheim, Émile (1930 [1893]) *De la division du travail social*, Paris: Presses Universitaires de France.

Durkheim, Émile (1930 [1897]) *Le suicide. Étude de sociologie*, Paris: Presses Universitaires de France.

Durkheim, Émile (1960 [1912]) *Les Formes élémentaires de la vie religieuse*, Paris: Presses Universitaires de France.

Durkheim, Émile (1964) 'Sociology', in Kurt H. Wolff (ed.) *Émile Durkheim: Essays on Sociology and Philosophy*, New York: Harper.

Durkheim, Émile (1966/1951 [1897]) *Suicide: A Study in Sociology*, trans. John A. Spaulding and George Simpson, New York: Free Press.

Durkheim, Émile (1968 [1908]) 'Débat sur l'explication en histoire et en sociologie', in Viktor Karády (ed.) *Textes (Vol. 1)*, Paris: Minuit.

Durkheim, Émile (1970 [1909]) 'Sociologie et sciences sociales', in J. C. Filloux (ed.) *La science sociale et l'action*, Paris: Presses Universitaires de France.

Durkheim, Émile (1981 [1895]) *Les règles de la méthode sociologique*, Paris: Presses Universitaires de France.

Durkheim, Émile (1982 [1895]) *The Rules of Sociological Method*, trans. W. D. Halls, First American Edition, New York: Free Press.

Durkheim, Émile (1984 [1893]) *The Division of Labor in Society*, trans. W. D. Halls, 2nd Edition, New York: Free Press.

Durkheim, Émile (2008 [1912]) *The Elementary Forms of Religious Life*, trans. Carol Cosman, edited by Mark S. Cladis, Oxford: Oxford University Press.

Filloux, J. C. (ed.) (1970 [1909]) *La science sociale et l'action*, Paris: Presses Universitaires de France.

Harrison, Paul Raymond (1993) 'Bourdieu and the Possibility of a Postmodern Sociology', *Thesis Eleven* 35: 36–50.

Karady, Victor (1981) 'French Ethnology and the Durkheimian Breakthrough', *Journal of the Anthropological Society of Oxford* 12(3): 166–176.

LaCapra, Dominick (1972) *Émile Durkheim: Sociologist and Philosopher*, Ithaca, N.Y.: Cornell University Press.

Wacquant, Loïc (1995) 'Durkheim et Bourdieu : le socle commun et ses fissures', *Critique* 51: 646–660, translation by Tarik Wareh (Chapter 4 in this volume).

CHAPTER FIVE

With Weber Against Weber: In Conversation With Pierre Bourdieu[1]

Pierre Bourdieu, Franz Schultheis, and Andreas Pfeuffer
Translated by Simon Susen[2]

Question: When did you start to familiarise yourself with the work of Max Weber? If I understand you correctly, this happened during your time in Algeria. What sort of texts were you reading at that time?

Pierre Bourdieu: I began with *Die protestantische Ethik*. During that time, I was working on a book which was intended to summarise my research on Algeria. In *Die protestantische Ethik* there was an abundance of things on the traditional, pre-capitalist 'spirit', and on economic behaviour – wonderful descriptions which were very useful and indeed quite impressive. I drew on Weber's work in order to understand the *M'zab*, a stretch of land in the Arabic desert, inhabited mainly by Kharijites, who are Muslims with a very ascetic – and almost 'Puritan' – lifestyle and whom we might want to call 'the Protestants of Islam', a religious current. This was really mind-boggling; this austerity with regard to sexual morals and self-discipline. At the same time, these are really prosperous and forward-looking traders; in fact, a lot of the small businesses in North Africa belong to them. I was astounded by the typically Weberian connection between religious asceticism and this very smooth adjustment to new conditions. By the way, similar to the Calvinist Puritans, these people are highly educated: they read a lot, they read the *Qur'an*, almost all of the children go to school, and most of them are bilingual in Arabic and French. Then, in *Travail et travailleurs en Algérie*, I described the typical Algerian merchant; the Moabites were the role model.

Question: Where did you get hold of a copy of *Die protestantische Ethik*? I mean, at that time, translations of Weber's work did not exist in France.

Pierre Bourdieu: There were no translations at all. You could not even find the German editions in the libraries. A friend of mine sent me the book, and I started reading it very thoroughly; I learned German and translated entire sections. I did not find the French translations, which were published later, particularly helpful; it seemed to me that the German text was much richer, more precise; the first available translations, especially the one of *Gesammelte Aufsätze zur Wissenschaftslehre*, conveyed a rather distorted view of Weber's work.

Question: How did you come across Weber's work?

Pierre Bourdieu: That was through Merleau-Ponty's *Les aventures de la dialectique*, which I found really impressive. This book had a strong impact on me in my youth, and I remember there being a brief chapter in which he talked about Weber. I think this was the first time I had heard about Weber.

Question: And then, what happened after Algeria? You became an assistant to Raymond Aron, who made Weber famous in France, in his own way…

Pierre Bourdieu: First, I went to Lille, where I gave this strange kind of course on the history of sociological thought: Marx, Durkheim, Weber, Pareto – outrageous, an insane job! Then I met Aron; that's correct. And this appreciation of Weber's work was something we had in common, until I realised that the Weber with whom I was concerned was very different from the Weber in whom Aron was interested. I then began to deal with Weber's writings on science at the Sorbonne.

Question: Was this Weber's *Politik als Beruf* or his *Wissenschaftslehre*?

Pierre Bourdieu: It was his *Wissenschaftslehre*. This was him, Aron's 'neo-Kantian' Weber, preoccupied with the conditions of possibility of 'understanding', and all that kind of stuff. Aron's entire oeuvre goes into this aspect in great detail; but, in those days, this was quite natural, given the omnipresence of the rationalist tradition in French philosophy and given that Aron was one of Brunschvicg's students; this was *his* Weber. He hardly knew Weber's *Religionssoziologie* or his *Wirtschaftsethik der Weltreligionen*. I had already studied, and partly translated, these writings during my time at Lille: the introduction to *Die protestantische Ethik*, some sections of the *Wissenschaftslehre*, and also a few sections from Weber's *Religionssoziologie*. In any case, it soon became clear to me that Aron and I had very different ways of looking at things: my Weber was opposed to Aron's Weber. It is staggering that Aron was hardly familiar at all with Weber's *Wirtschaft und Gesellschaft*.

Question: As a foreign observer, one sometimes gets the impression that there were two 'Webers', two logics of reception: one conservative Weber, who had already been introduced by Aron; perhaps this is a bit exaggerated, but a Weber 'against' Durkheim. Anyhow, Weber seems to have made more of an impression than Durkheim. How was it possible that Durkheim had been so easily eclipsed by this interpretation of Weber?

Pierre Bourdieu: It is not easy to explain this, at least not if one forgets the struggles that were taking place in the French intellectual field at the time. With regard to Durkheim, I am under the impression that behind Weber one senses the full weight of German philosophy: Kant and others. Weber, in this respect, appears to be much more 'aristocratic' than Durkheim, who has always been stigmatised as a 'positivist'. Weber was much more attractive. In Weber there is 'charisma', there is a 'difference'; Durkheim is about 'ethnology', 'the primitive'. Weber wrote about 'world religions', 'advanced civilisations', 'charisma', and '*manna*' – a contrast which may have contributed to the fact that Weber is the more inspiring thinker. Weber is less 'schoolmasterly', less 'prosaic'.

And then we must not forget that, after the Second World War, existentialism and phenomenology began to develop a tremendous power: Sartre, and everything that came after him; a return to 'authenticity', which was opposed to – rationalistically inspired – scholastic philosophy and which at the same time brought, with Sartre, a model of the intellectual into play which has had, and continues to have, an effect until the present day; a certain *radical chic* that coincided with the rediscovery of Hegel and Marx and, hence, with a spectacular expansion of Marxism.

If Weber used to be stigmatised as a 'conservative', then in the sense of a thinker whose work was referred to by the orthodoxy at the time: the 'methodological individualist', the 'bourgeois philosophy'. Their complete ignorance of his oeuvre never prevented French intellectuals from condemning Weber. In support of Marx, one saw in Weber – who says somewhere that whenever he deals with the primacy of 'the economic' he considers himself a Marxist – the advocate of a *spiritualist* philosophy of history. Of course, this interpretation was based on a simplistic reading of *Die protestantische Ethik*. If the orthodoxy referred exclusively to his *Wissenschaftslehre*, then what was left of Weber?

For the philosophers of 'existence', he was 'only' a sociologist. It was clear that amongst Marxists, and many believed to be Marxist at the time, Weber was completely impossible. I remember having conversations – in the early and mid 1960s – in which I often said that it would be barely possible to do sociology without any knowledge of Weber; although this would then be recognised on every occasion – 'yes, sure; Weber is tremendously important' –, when one would try to discuss Weber in a more serious manner, it would soon become apparent that people hardly knew anything about his work. Even Althusser confirmed this when acknowledging that Weber was not taken seriously by Marxists and when confessing that he himself had not read Weber's work. Weber was perceived as 'right-wing'. Obviously, because it was Aron who had made him famous in France, not because of the things that Weber had said himself. That made me mad, given that it had been precisely his marvellous observations that had enchanted me. I said to myself: 'I am not right-wing; Weber is simply good!'

Question: Time and again, the struggles that took place in the intellectual field during that period – between the academic, the traditionally rationalist orthodoxy, on the one hand, and the 'existentialist', intellectual avant-garde, on the other – sought to provoke people into political confessions.

Pierre Bourdieu: And yet, these were utterly artificial oppositions. I believe it is possible to think *with* a thinker and to think, at the same time, *against* him or her. This means that, in a radical way, we have to challenge the classificatory, and hence political, logic in which – almost everywhere – relations with the thoughts of the past are established. 'For Marx', as Althusser wanted it to be, or 'against Marx'. I am convinced that it is possible to think with Marx against Marx, or with Durkheim against Durkheim; and surely also with Marx and Durkheim against Weber, and vice versa. It is not because I have a proclivity for the paradoxical that I want to suggest that Weber accomplished Marxist purposes where Marx was unable to redeem them. This is particularly true with regard to the sociology of religion, which is certainly *not* one of Marx's strengths. Weber, in this respect, develops a genuine 'Political Economy of Religion', an astonishingly materialist view of the phenomenon, but without wanting to deprive it of its curious symbolic nature. When he says, for instance, that the Church presents itself as the 'monopoly' of legitimate distribution of 'sacred goods', he provides us with extraordinarily valuable insights which go far beyond a reductive economistic imaginary.

Question: And the 'right-wing' orthodoxy…?

Pierre Bourdieu: When I wrote my first article on Weber's sociology of religion for the *Archives européennes de sociologie*, I encountered a few difficulties. It was closely related to the *Archiv für Sozialwissenschaften und Sozialpolitik*, and there was a sort of fetishism about the 'great' thinker Weber. The editorial board consisted of eminent people like Aron, Crozier, and Dahrendorf, but I was not a member. It was quite a conservative journal. And I had my article; Aron, however, said to me: 'There is no way you can publish it like this. I really do not agree with it.' In fact, he said I would convert Weber into a 'lefty'. I replied that when I talk about 'the theodicy of privilege' it is not me but Weber who is talking and that everything which appears in inverted commas is Weber's, rather than my, voice. All I had done was to call things, which people refused to take into account, by their real names! Eventually, Aron let the article pass; and some time after its publication I received a long and enthusiastic letter from Randall Collins, in which he wrote that I had wrenched Weber from the conservatives, that I had presented a much more genuine Weber, and that this was extremely important for sociology. By the way, Aron allowed me to teach – primarily – Durkheim, but never Weber, when I would have preferred to give lectures on Weber…!

Question: …subsuming Weber under the title 'sociology of domination', in the broadest sense…

Pierre Bourdieu: …yes, that's exactly right…

Question: …you identify with this notion.

Pierre Bourdieu: Yes, of course. Why shouldn't I? Back then, in Lille, I gave this course on 'From Marx to Durkheim, Pareto, and Weber'; again and again in relation to Marx. Without wanting to overemphasise this point here, it seems to me that the foundational call for all these thinkers came from Marx.

Question: If we take Durkheim and Weber, who deliberately ignored one another: there is no doubt that there are a lot of commonalities between them; in both cases, for example, *religion* was a primary concern. How do you see this key role which the *sociology of religion* plays with regard to the birth of sociology in general? The social sciences come into existence when the 'disenchantment' of the world becomes evident…

Pierre Bourdieu: There are a lot of connections here, but let me reiterate this point; there is something which, at least in Weber, one can see very clearly – and this is what has impressed me the most: the reference to Marx. Weber seeks to close one of the gaps in Marxism. In *Die protestantische Ethik* he asserts, roughly speaking, that he does not claim that his work explains everything, but that it is only aimed at rectifying a picture which Marxism had painted in a somewhat reductive fashion. In essence, Weber is concerned with retrieving *the symbolic dimension* of social life – not as the primary and ultimate dimension, but as a dimension which deserves its legitimate place in history. Not least because of this, religion plays such a pivotal role: religion as 'the symbolic' *par excellence*. Weber explores 'the symbolic'; in fact, he has a try at a materialist theory of 'the symbolic'.

Question: It seems to me that we have now reached a point where you can maybe explain a bit further what lies at the heart of your own works in the *sociology of religion*. Obviously, Weber is of huge importance in this respect; and the article that you wrote for the *Archives européennes de sociologie* focused on Weber's sociology of religion. In your second work on religion you used the concept of 'field', in some detail, for the first time. Was Weber some kind of 'stepping stone' for this project?

Pierre Bourdieu: I got to know Weber's work in Algeria. I found many things in *Die protestantische Ethik* which helped me to understand such traditional societies. When I returned from Algeria, Weber was somebody who had already caught my attention; and then I started to teach Weber's sociology of religion based on his *Wirtschaft und Gesellschaft*. I remember that, during the course, everything just fell into place when covering and comparing different religious 'occupations': the priest, the prophet, the sorcerer, and the laity. I then drew a diagram on the blackboard and tried to capture the relations between them. What does the priest do with the sorcerer and with the prophet? He excommunicates them. What does the prophet do with the priest? He threatens him with the power of 'extraordinariness'. Quickly this became a model of interactions, which seemed very plausible: it was the *relations* between them which defined the respective 'types'.

In a way, Weber had certainly been the main source of inspiration for this whole scheme. Previously, I had run a seminar at the *École Normale*, which focused on the literary field. At that time, I had already used the concept of 'field', which allowed me to get a grip on some of the difficulties. What came out of this seminar was my article *Champ littéraire et projet créateur*, which was published in *Temps modernes* in a number on structuralism, although – ultimately – this article had not really been 'structuralist' at all. It was not until later that, during my course on Weber's sociology of religion, the scales fell from my eyes: we cannot make sense of this in interactionist terms, because we are dealing with *objective relations* – that is, objective structures – which form the base line for the 'typical' behaviour of the participants. After this, when I read Weber's *Das antike Judentum*, everything became more obvious. During that period, I developed my first work on the sociology of religion; it was a certain rupture, an improvement compared to the first attempt, which I had made in *Champ littéraire*.

Question: Did the concept of 'habitus' play a decisive role in this process?

Pierre Bourdieu: Not really; the concept already exists in the works of all the great sociologists: in Durkheim, in Mauss…fair enough, in Weber, the concept is not particularly well developed, but on the other hand in his work you can find immensely powerful descriptions, especially with regard to traditional economic attitudes. For my study of Algeria, this was a real treasure chest.

Question: But was Weber your source of inspiration for the development of the concept of 'field'?

Pierre Bourdieu: Not quite. Starting *from* Weber, the concept of 'field' had to be turned *against* – and indeed go *beyond* – Weber, in order to cope with the difficulty of explaining 'typical' – mutually related – forms of behaviour, which can consolidate themselves *without* real 'interactions'. In Weber, this concept does not really exist; what does exist in his work, however, are these insightful 'personality and life order studies'; and at the end of every section in his *Religionssoziologie* you can find an outline of the relations between 'occupations', not in a 'structuralist' way, but…

Question: …an inspiration…

Pierre Bourdieu: …without any doubt. I have always found Weber inspiring and important. Yet, my work has, from the start, dealt with all sorts of different 'sources'. When I am asked about the development of my work, I cannot overemphasise this point. It is very common to reduce 'Bourdieusian thought' to a few key terms, and usually even just a few book titles, and this then leads to a kind of closure: 'reproduction', 'distinction', 'capital', and 'habitus' – all of these terms are often used in misleading ways, without really understanding what they stand for, and hence they become *slogans*. In reality, however, these concepts – these frameworks – are only *principles* for scientific work, which is usually of mere practical nature; they are *synthetic* or *synoptic* notions, which serve to provide research programmes with scientific *orientations*.

At the end of the day, the important thing is the research itself, that is, the research on the subject matter itself. To be sure, one does have to treat these things carefully; but, when dealing with these concepts, one cannot make any progress without a respectful sense of freedom. *I constantly try to improve my work.* Often, this is perceived as a form of endless repetition; for me, by contrast, these are often tremendously important changes, no matter how insignificant they may appear at first sight.

As far as the 'sources' are concerned, people may be surprised by this, but I really proceed eclectically in this regard: *I am engaged in reflexive eclecticism.* For me, it is not necessarily a contradiction to 'borrow' stuff from everywhere: from Marx to Durkheim via Weber, as long as all this leads to a certain theoretical coherence, which nowadays is castigated as 'totalitarian' by the postmodernists. Besides, this 'eclecticism' is not tantamount to randomness. If, for example, we look at Norbert Elias, it seems to me that he is subject to excessive interpretation by a number of people, precisely because it is not sufficiently clear how much this thinker owes to other thinkers, in particular to Weber. In fact, a lot in Elias is simply a commentary on Weber, and nevertheless this all remains very stimulating.

There is hardly any study by myself that does not owe something, in one way or another, to others; but of course this does not mean that, consequently, nothing has been accomplished. One of the merits for which I really give myself credit is the attempt to shed light on the extent to which these theoretical debates, which often lead to a regrettable barrenness in science, are based on socially 'constructed' oppositions. In this regard, Bachelard used to talk about 'epistemological pairs', which cannot exist independently from one another, but which at the same time impede genuine scientific progress. The opposition between Marx and Weber, for example, is usually a rather artificial one, and there is no reason why their respective contributions should not be subject to cross-fertilisation. The same applies to Durkheim and Weber. We need this conceptual integration, which every forward-looking science is capable of producing.

Question: Let's continue with these three figures: Marx, Durkheim, and Weber. Where do you see their main contributions that have allowed you to make progress in your sociology of religion and, based on it, your conception of 'the field'?

Pierre Bourdieu: As I have already mentioned, religion is certainly not the *forte* of the Marxian oeuvre, and generally of the materialist approach, with which Weber took issue. In Weber, the line of attack is in another direction. Here, religion is the realm in which – more than in any other realm – both the approach and the aspiration of sociology can be illustrated, where what is seemingly most widely separated can be brought together, 'the material' and 'the symbolic', the correspondence of social and mental structures, collective representations – and, eventually, in Weber. In *Die protestantische Ethik*, Weber is primarily concerned with salvaging 'the symbolic' for a materialist conception of history; and his *Religionssoziologie* is an exemplary way of bringing the concrete forms of 'religious labour' together. At some points, they are even a bit too concrete, but precisely the juxtaposition between these 'types' demonstrates very vividly what we are actually dealing with: *the stakes in the struggles over the monopoly of the legitimate power over the sacred goods*. To be clear about this: it is precisely Weber's concrete, sometimes brutal, materialism – that is, his break with the *illusio* – which is so incredibly insightful.

Question: Thus, Durkheim and Weber uncover – each in their own way, in the realm of ideas, which seems to be so 'removed' from the world – the 'worldly' conditionality of our thoughts and actions. Does the religious field lend itself so well to sociology also because it constitutes a realm in which the leap from 'the material' to 'the symbolic' – to a 'theodicy of the conditions of existence' – occurs in such a pure, original form?

Pierre Bourdieu: Of course, in this sense it is very useful. What one sees here is the primitive form of capital accumulation or, if you like, of the accumulation of symbolic capital. I think this is the way in which capital begins to accumulate, initially in its symbolic form, and eventually in order to be converted into other 'types' of capital. This is also the start of the conflicts which then become essential to a given field…

Question: …and which consequently absorb other relations of domination. If one conceives of 'the sacred' and 'the profane' in terms of an opposition, it seems that this 'classical' antagonism crops up again and again in your works on particular fields of cultural production…a continuous semantics…

Pierre Bourdieu: It is true that the religious field provides us with the heuristic model *par excellence* to make sense of these relations – as a kind of realised 'ideal type' of the field. I remember that, during my studies on Weber, I stumbled across a book at some friends' place. They possessed an old library, where I saw this book: a 'guide' through Paris, composed of texts by famous French authors, introduced by Hugo. There was a chapter in it by Sainte-Beuve about the academies; and it said that the academies are like the Church and the prophets, a metaphor, people spontaneously use these metaphors. It talked about the 'incrustation' of these things, of 'everydayness'. This contrast is very powerful, in the struggles of art, politics; and, although it is not always elaborated, it is omnipresent.

Question: Does this also mean that in religion we are confronted with a substantive paradigm? To be exact, how do you conceive of the 'subject matter' religion? Where does religion originate? Is there such a thing as a religious need, about which Schleiermacher used to talk? Is there such a thing as a 'will to faith', some sort of anthropological predisposition?

Pierre Bourdieu: I wrote something about this in my second contribution to the religious field. This is obviously not a simple issue, but the question is whether or not an answer to this problem is actually of any significance. What came first? The need, or the world which – after all, in its own way and in its own order – implants this need in us? I am satisfied with the Weberian definition: religion is a systematic answer to the question of life and death. Actually, this is a beautiful definition. To be sure, there are 'existential' questions that oblige us to reflect upon the 'transcendental' – and, hence, the collective – conditions of the transcendental: questions about life and death; the death of people whom we love; 'ultimate' questions; illness, human suffering. These are all questions that people never manage to answer on their own. Religion gives systematic answers to these questions – or rather quasi-systematic answers, because they are not systematic as, for example, in logic. Religion gives coherence to the 'discontinuous' events of our life; it bestows abstract contingence with concrete coherence; in this respect, it resembles philosophy, a 'total' explanation of the world…

Question: …which is smashed to pieces under the 'dull compulsion' as we know it today…in this regard, Weber is more radical than Marx…

Pierre Bourdieu: …and he is right! In Algeria this became very clear to me: people who lived in a religious universe, and who were unexpectedly confronted with an economic universe; all of a sudden they had to resolve ineluctably difficult questions, questions to which religion provided ready answers. 'Should I wear a tie?' 'And, if I wear one, do I subjugate myself to the colonisers?' Or the haircut: 'If I choose the imported haircut, do I then look like somebody "from yesterday"?' In this respect, the Turkish haircut was a solution; since Ataturk, the Turks belonged to the 'modern people'; and, at the same time, it was in accordance with Islamic tradition – although, at the end of the day, in such a historical setting everything causes difficulties, everything becomes a problem…

Question: …the contact with a foreign culture…

Pierre Bourdieu: …exactly. Everything seems to indicate that the great philosophical revolutions emerged out of such situations; in the Greek societies, the big controversies over what is determined by nature or law; this comes to the surface when people – ultimately, tribes, which have different laws – encounter one another. If some do certain things in one way, and others do these things in another way, then you start having doubts: it does not *have to be* – that is, it is not *necessarily* – like this or like that. I have seen societies in which all of the behavioural patterns were consecrated by the power of truth; and suddenly others arrive who do it not only differently, but who do not even have an idea of how 'true' this is. Traditional societies have no idea of other traditions.

Question: Like us…

Pierre Bourdieu: Like us; there are things that hardly change. Yet, when you suddenly encounter people whose behaviour and 'self-ordering' are different, then the philosophers emerge: there are those who say 'no, it must remain as it was' and others who say 'no, this is true'. This is the origin of philosophy. In these situations, religions are very important, because they tell you what needs to be done and how it needs to be done: a selective practice that permeates even the smallest things, which then acquire an overriding importance. If you do not wear a head covering, you run the risk of being beaten to death, and this is not an anecdote…

Question: …because one facilitates the cultivation of a kind of 'sociological awareness'. One drags religious symbols, which have an abstract nature, into the light of social relations and thereby makes sense of them within a 'sociological' framework.

Pierre Bourdieu: Exactly. Maybe this definition is a bit reductive, but I have described religion as relations of *feelings*, which have to be experienced, and of *meanings*, which do have meaning. In Algeria this was better than living with the agony of having to be 'experienced'…

Question: …a theodicy of 'the negatively privileged'. It is even more astonishing that this dimension of domination, which is omnipresent in Weber's work, has hardly contributed to a 'left-wing' – i.e. a critical – reading of Weber.

Pierre Bourdieu: Perhaps this is because, as a 'foreigner', I had fewer reservations. The dance of the autochthons for their great ancestors is performed with much more doggedness, but I am not an exegete. I did not want to say what 'the truth' is about Weber. This is not my job; I conceive of myself as a researcher; I search for 'food for thought', for research 'tools'. Weber may well have said a few stupidities, but what I read of him was rather insightful. Or, for example, Simmel, who is perhaps not a 'great' thinker, but there are some thrilling and powerful elements in his work, some reflexive devices; I gladly accept such propositions…as long as the person was not a monster. I have been told that Weber was a conservative; this, however, has not particularly impressed me. What I read by him – for instance, his work on the East Elbian peasants – had been written in a context which might have given rise to a 'conservative' reading of his work. Yet, against the background of political history, it seemed rather progressive. I was not very familiar with these things at the time; this was not my history. Had I been German, this might have been different: I would have been in a better position to judge Weber's role in the academic world and in the political world. But never mind, this gave me a sense of freedom to which many German sociologists were not entitled. In addition, when – after a few years – I returned from Algeria, I was even a bit of a stranger myself in France: the classificatory fervour, with which the struggles within the intellectual field were fought there, this was – after everything I had experienced – incomprehensible.

Another aspect which has always impressed me about Weber is the fact that he granted himself incredible liberties in relation to the scholarly world. In *Wissenschaft als Beruf*, Max Weber said some extraordinary things of an almost brutal sincerity. When I was selected by the CNRS to be honoured for my work, I quoted a few sentences from Weber in my speech – sentences which were quite fierce. After this event, some people told me: 'What you have just poured out there is unbelievable. You cannot say this sort of thing in the presence of all the dignitaries, of the ministers, of the director of the *École Normale*, of the *Collège de France*' – in the presence of all of my colleagues! Phrases of such ruthless and brutal candour! It is mindboggling that Weber really said these things at the time. The scholarly world is full of people who behave like *revolutionaries* when they deal with things that do not concern them directly and like *conservatives* when they have a personal stake in the matter. In any case, I was fully invested in these lectures, and I delivered them with passion. In former times, I was not very familiar with the cultural background. It was not until I started to engage with the work of Heidegger that a lot of these things became clear to me. It was easier for me to understand what it actually meant to say these things at the time, and I admire Weber more and more for that reason, as he was really very courageous.

Question: Weber used to say a lot of things against his own 'status group'…

Pierre Bourdieu: …tremendously radical. Often one is called 'right-wing' when one says the truth about the 'left'. I have already suggested some time ago that intellectuals are the dominated stratum amongst the dominant groups; but this was inconceivable, because intellectuals were regarded as 'out of the game', 'sublime', 'free', 'disinterested', 'creative' – anything you want. Maybe this explains the label of the 'right-winger'. Weber says things about intellectuals…but what is 'conservative' in his writings?

Question: The 'context' played a much less significant role in the reception of Nietzsche in France; quite the opposite…

Pierre Bourdieu: What applies to Durkheim in relation to Weber also applies to the perception of the relation between Weber and Nietzsche. The latter is much more suitable for grandiose philosophical platitudes than the former. If the epistemological meta-discourse, which has also been forced upon Weber, has for a long time – maybe up to the present day – obscured scientific practice (such as Weber's extraordinary effort to provide an outline of a historical sociology or sociological history of religion, the economy, and law), then Weber's 'charisma', this 'miracle' of the German University, stands behind the philosophical autodidact Nietzsche. Nietzsche is engulfed by the *radical chic* – by the way, in France even more so than in Germany itself. Weber, who has been – not only for me – a sort of intellectual shock, has had such a tremendous impact because what lingers behind his fundamental questions is a whole universe of worldwide knowledge about all kinds of cultures. Weber is the incarnation of comparative method, with all its array of social premises. In any case, Weber refers to reflexive scientific practice – an exercise with which French post-war philosophy refused to engage. You could draw on Hegel's *Grundlinien der Philosophie des Rechts* or on Nietzsche's *Genealogie der Moral*, but on Weber? And all this despite the fact that, in more than one respect, Weber goes far beyond these works…

Question: …maybe this is yet another issue concerning the relationship between Weber and Nietzsche. Recently, there have been a number of studies which have presented Weber much more definitely against this background, against this 'mood of the time', which was not least shaped by Hegel. The impression that Nietzsche made on Weber seems rather essential in this respect.

Pierre Bourdieu: Weber and Nietzsche share a number of views and opinions. Of course, there are also some objective connections. What I have in mind, for instance, is Nietzsche's philosophy of resentment – which is, by the way, itself nourished by resentment – but also the way in which Weber describes the religions of redemption: all those things about 'the feeling of dignity', 'the way of life', most likely perhaps the whole vocabulary about power, of struggle, 'the heroic'. Yet, one should not allow oneself to be deceived by all this, by the commonality of 'attitude'. In Weber, this is all much more thought out, more organised, more saturated. In Nietzsche, by contrast, the concept of power is so shapeless and vague. In Weber's *Wirtschaft und Gesellschaft* there is a section in which, when putting forward his concept of 'domination', he discards the concept of power, which – as he sees it – is of no use for a sharp sociological concept formation…

Question: …as a 'spontaneous sociologist', however, Nietzsche is quite remarkable…

Pierre Bourdieu: …and yet, this is precisely what has never really impressed the Nietzscheans – at least not in France. I remember a conversation with Foucault in which he tried to identify the main sources of his own intellectual passions – in his search for a way out of the cul-de-sac of traditional philosophy. For him, the great shock was caused by Nietzsche's *Genealogie der Moral*. In my case, this was not the same: I had different inclinations, which were derived from Weber and Durkheim. To be sure, it is possible to read Nietzsche in a 'positivist' way, as a moral sociology, but to me this seemed to be too limited, very intuitive. This sort of thing had much more of an 'impact' on the philosophers; Hegel, Marx, Nietzsche, Heidegger. There were not many philosophers who remained unimpressed by this. I found Merleau-Ponty more inspiring; and, in his work, Weber was not presented as an 'epistemologist' or as an 'interpretive' sociologist. The whole phenomenological obscurantism; Sartre and existentialism; the heroic aesthetics in Nietzsche; the salvation of a philosophy of the subject – I have always found all of this quite dumb. I have never really been on this *trip*. For me, Weber is about science, and in the best sense of the term!

Notes

1 Original Publication: Pierre Bourdieu, 'Mit Weber gegen Weber: Pierre Bourdieu im Gespräch', in Pierre Bourdieu, *Das religiöse Feld. Texte zur Ökonomie des Heilsgeschehens* (herausgegeben von Franz Schultheis, Andreas Pfeuffer und Stephan Egger, übersetzt von Stephan Egger, Konstanz: Universitätsverlag Konstanz, 2000), pp. 111–129. The interview was conducted by Franz Schultheis and Andreas Pfeuffer and took place in a café on Boulevard Saint-Germain in Paris in the spring of 1999.

2 I am grateful to Bryan S. Turner and Loïc Wacquant for their detailed comments on this translation. I would also like to thank William Outhwaite for making many useful suggestions. I am deeply indebted to Stephan Egger for providing me with the original (French) audio version of this interview.

CHAPTER SIX

Bourdieu and Nietzsche: Taste as a Struggle

Keijo Rahkonen

> The sociologist's privilege, if he has one, is not that of trying to be suspended above those whom he classifies, but that of knowing that he is classified and knowing roughly where he stands in the classifications. When people who think they will win an easy revenge ask me what are my tastes in paintings or music, I reply, quite seriously: those that correspond to my place in the classification. (Bourdieu, 1993 [1984]: 44–45)

This chapter makes a comparison, which from a sociological perspective might appear a little surprising: it is between Pierre Bourdieu's and Friedrich Nietzsche's respective conceptions of 'power' and 'taste'. The aim is to show that there is an interesting resemblance between the two with regard to these conceptions in general, and to 'struggle for power', 'ressentiment' and 'will to power' in particular, and thus to shed light on some key aspects of Bourdieu's thinking. The order of the *dramatis personae* in this analysis is no accident: Bourdieu and Nietzsche. This alludes to the fact that the discussion that follows is primarily about what lies behind Bourdieu's sociological, rather than Nietzsche's philosophical, conceptions of taste and power. Thus, Nietzsche is read, first and foremost, from a sociological perspective.

Pierre Bourdieu's Taste

There were no sociological disputes about the concept of taste before the publication of Pierre Bourdieu's studies on the subject. Thus, one has good reason to argue that his *Distinction* (1984 [1979]) and the preliminary studies from the 1960s (Bourdieu et al., 1990 [1965]; Bourdieu et al., 1991 [1966]; Bourdieu, 1968; and Bourdieu and de Saint Martin, 1976) were the first attempts to provide a genuinely sociological interpretation. Max Weber's remarks about the 'stylisation of life', Georg Simmel's studies on fashion and

'*Vornehmheit*', or 'distinction' as Tom Bottomore and David Frisby translated it in Simmel's *Philosophy of Money* (Simmel, 1990 [1900]), Thorstein Veblen's theory of 'conspicuous consumption', and Norbert Elias's interpretation of the 'civilisation process' do touch on the question of taste, but none of these accounts deal with it in an explicit, let alone systematic fashion (Elias, 1994 [1939]). It has been studied and commented on more in the fields of aesthetics, philosophy and art history. For example, the entry on taste published in the *International Encyclopaedia of the Social Sciences* (Wenzel, 1968) describes it – together with smell – merely as a physico-chemical phenomenon. It would thus appear to be justified to characterise – as Loïc Wacquant does – Bourdieu's *Distinction* as a 'Copernican revolution in the study of taste' (Wacquant, 1993: 663).

Generally speaking, Bourdieu extends Durkheim's programme in arguing that '[t]here exists a correspondence between social structure and mental structures' (Bourdieu, 1989: 7; Wacquant, 1992: 12–14). In so doing he converts Immanuel Kant's *Third Critique* – in other words the *Kritik der Urteilskraft* – into a sociological programme or, to be exact, into a 'sociology of aesthetics', as Hans-Peter Müller calls it (Müller, 1992a: 300).

Bourdieu considered taste to be one of the main battlefields in the cultural reproduction and legitimation of power. Taste represents the concealed exercise of power; it is a 'matter of course', the 'natural difference' that has grown apart from the social. Attempts at a sociological explanation of these self-evident relations are usually denounced as pointless by people who have something to gain in mystifying the relation between taste and education (or some other social factors).

Bourdieu conceives of everyday life as a constant struggle over the final word in determining what is 'good' taste, taste that claims to be 'universal'. This struggle is a cultural game that no one can escape: '[…] taste is the basis of all that one has – people and things – and all that one is for others, whereby one classifies oneself and is classified by others' (Bourdieu, 1984 [1979]: 56). He indentifies three different kinds (universes) of taste, which 'roughly correspond to educational levels and social classes' (Bourdieu, 1984 [1979]: 16). At best, these different 'universes' or distinctions manifest themselves in the field of music, which he uses as an illustrative example (see Bourdieu, 1984 [1979]: 13–18).

The first universe refers to the *'pure' taste*, in other words the taste whose cultural objects are 'legitimate', as expressed in 'highbrow culture'. It is most often found in the factions of the dominant class with the greatest educational capital. The second universe concerns the *'middle-brow' taste* (*le goût 'moye'*), directed to more common and less valuable objects, and the third manifested in *'popular' or 'vulgar' taste*, which is represented by objects that lack all artistic ambition (e.g. 'pop culture'). This kind of taste is spontaneous like 'anti-Kantian aesthetic'; it is 'barbaric' in the very sense that Kant gave it (Kant, 1966 [1790]: 99; in English: Kant, 1987 [1790]: 69; § 13; cf. Bourdieu, 1984 [1979]: 41–43). There is another important feature here: the self-exclusion of this third taste from 'taste' itself. It does not (re)present itself as taste at all – except in the specific case of the artistic aestheticising of kitsch, but then it moves to the side of good taste or 'avant-garde'. As the Rolling Stones put it briefly and pithily: 'It's only rock 'n roll (but I like it)'.

Correspondingly, Bourdieu identifies three general attitudes or 'dispositions' towards culture, each connected to a given class position. The dominant class has a 'sense of distinction', the middle class (the 'new petty bourgeoisie') has 'cultural goodwill' ('*bonne volonté culturelle*'), and the lower classes ('*classes populaires*') are left with the 'necessary choice'. The dominant class strives to distinguish itself from those representing other taste categories: the line of demarcation runs between 'good' and 'bad' – that is, between 'sophisticated' and 'barbarian' – taste. Which distinction is most refined at any moment of time is defined by the avant-garde. At the stage when popular taste finally comes to embrace what used to be good taste, taste has turned from 'pure' to 'vulgar'. This mechanism thus appears to bear a certain resemblance to Simmel's description of fashion (Simmel, 1983 [1895]) although, interestingly, Bourdieu makes no reference to Simmel in *Distinction*.

Bourdieu's Critique of Kant

As the Kant-sounding subtitle of Bourdieu's *La distinction* – namely, *Critique sociale du jugement* (in the English translation[1] the word 'taste' is added to the subtitle: *A Social Critique of the Judgement of Taste*) – indicates, the book is a direct critique – a 'vulgar critique', as Bourdieu puts it – of Immanuel Kant's aesthetics in general and of Kant's *Critique of Judgement* in particular (Kant, 1966 [1790]; in English: Kant, 1987 [1790]). It is a social or sociological critique of judgement. (Let us ignore the critical remarks of commentators such as Crowther [1994] and Fowler [1994] about Bourdieu's critique of Kant, given that the aim in this chapter is not to evaluate its validity.)

It is worth bearing in mind that Bourdieu's 'vulgar' (in other words sociological) critique goes beyond Enlightenment philosophy. Indeed, it takes a stand against it, questioning the very possibility of universal judgement. Yet, he does not take a stand in favour of 'vulgar' taste, which may well lead to a sociological version of 'prolet-cult' or 'proletarian science'.

In Kantian terms, aesthetic judgement anticipates 'common sense' (*sensus communis*) – or a kind of aesthetic community (on *sensus communis*, see also Lyotard, 1991 [1987]) – judgement shared by everyone (Kant, 1966 [1790]; Kant, 1987 [1790], § 40; cf. also Gronow, 1997 and Müller, 1992b). Bourdieu transforms this into a social community, or rather a social field, and Scott Lash calls it a 'reflexive community' (Lash, 1994: 161).

In essence, Bourdieu argues that every aesthetic judgement is socially determined. He thereby turns Kant's antinomy concerning the principle of taste – referring to the idea that taste is both subjective and objective – into social antinomy: taste that is represented as both subjective and objective in fact corresponds to one's relationally defined position in the social universe. This is precisely what Bourdieu criticises Kant for having neglected. Nevertheless, Bourdieu's theory of distinction is not a mere sociology of class. Indeed, as he emphasises (see Bourdieu, 1989 [1988]: 407–409), it was never meant to be, although at first sight it appears to be and has even been referred to be as 'sociological reduction'. It rather resembles 'reflexive sociology' (cf. the title of Bourdieu and Wacquant, 1992: *An Invitation to Reflexive Sociology*), the aim of which is to explore the unconscious of the social in terms of people's habitus and practices, and thereby uncover the 'unthought' (*impensée*).

At the end of *Distinction*, Bourdieu presents a systematic critique of Kant under the title 'Postscript: Towards a "Vulgar" Critique of "Pure" Critiques' (Bourdieu, 1984 [1979]: 485–500). He also argues passionately against Jacques Derrida's 'pure' reading of Kant (Derrida, 1987), criticising him for taking a position both inside and outside of the game (although one could criticise Bourdieu for the same reason). Bourdieu (1984 [1979]: 499–500) writes:

> In short, the philosophical sense of distinction is another form of the visceral disgust at vulgarity which defines pure taste as an internalised social relationship, a social relationship made flesh, and a philosophically distinguished reading of the Critique of Judgement cannot be expected to uncover the social relationship at the heart of a work that is rightly regarded as the very symbol of philosophical distinction.

This 'pure' and 'disinterested' taste is distance-taking: it 'asserts the absolute primacy of form over function' (Bourdieu, 1984 [1979]: 30 and 56). What is more, taste – 'i.e., manifested preferences' (Bourdieu, 1984 [1979]: 56) – is determined by negation, that is, by disgust:

> In matters of taste, more than anywhere else, all determination is negation; and tastes are perhaps first and foremost distastes, disgust provoked by horror or visceral intolerance ('sick-making') of the tastes of others. 'De gustibus non est disputandum': not because 'tout les goûts sont dans la nature', but because each taste feels itself to be natural – and so it almost is, being a habitus – which amounts to rejecting others as unnatural and therefore vicious. (Bourdieu, 1984 [1979]: 56)

Bourdieu thus considers Kant's principle of pure taste 'nothing other than a refusal, a disgust – a disgust for objects which impose enjoyment and a disgust for the crude, vulgar taste which revels in this imposed enjoyment' (Bourdieu, 1984 [1979]: 488).

It is interesting that Jean Baudrillard, one of the French 'essayists' Bourdieu despised (Bourdieu, 1988 [1984]: xvi-xxvi and 279), stresses disgust à la Bourdieu, even – à la Baudrillard indeed – extending his thesis further to herald the end of tastes:

> Nowadays, only dislike [*dégoût*] is determined, tastes do not come into it any more [...]. The only source of what is beautiful and of renewal in fashion is ugly. (Baudrillard, 1986: 5–6)[2]

Taste and Power

On a more general level, then, what lies behind Bourdieu's own thinking is his sociology of power in general and his sociology of symbolic power in particular. Of course, taste is only one, albeit important, element of it (as in the academic field; cf. Bourdieu, 1988 [1984]). As Loïc Wacquant, one of his closest colleagues and interpreters (cf. Bourdieu and Wacquant, 1992; and Bourdieu and Wacquant, 1999 [1998]), puts it:

> Classes and other antagonistic social collectives are continually engaged in a struggle to impose the definition of the world that is most congruent with their particular interests. The sociology of knowledge or of cultural forms is *eo ipso* a political sociology, that is, a sociology of symbolic power. (Bourdieu and Wacquant, 1992: 14)

The struggle for (good) taste is a (symbolic) struggle for power, and this is even true of truth itself: 'if there is a truth, it is that truth is the stake of struggles (*enjeu des luttes*)' (Bourdieu, 1990: 297).

There is still one concept of Bourdieu that should be mentioned in this context, and that is his concept of the 'field' (*champ*). He uses the notion 'field of power' to avoid the problematic – arguably 'substantialist' – concept of the 'ruling class' (Bourdieu and Wacquant, 1992: 76n 16). He offered perhaps the most explicit definition of this notion in his lecture 'The Field of Power', which he delivered in English at the University of Wisconsin at Madison in April 1989:

> The field of power is a field of forces defined by the structure of the existing balance of forces between forms of power, or between different species of capital [...]. It is also simultaneously a field of struggle for power among the holders of

> different forms of power. It is a space of play and competition [...]. The field of power is organised as a chiasmatic structure: the distribution according to the dominant principle of hierarchisation (economic capital) is inversely symmetrical to the distribution according to the dominated principle of hierarchy (cultural capital). (Bourdieu and Wacquant, 1992: 76n.16)

The concept of 'field' permeates Bourdieusian thought: it is a 'system of objective forces', similar to a magnetic field. At the same time, however, Bourdieu emphasises that sociology is not reducible to 'social physics' (Bourdieu and Wacquant, 1992: 17 and 100n 52). Bourdieu's analogy of a field game (*champ-jeu*) goes back to the work of Maurice Merleau-Ponty. Merleau-Ponty's concept of 'field' does not have major theoretical significance, however, but simply denotes the field of sports (Bourdieu and Wacquant, 1992: 22n 39). Bourdieu points out that there is a major difference between 'a game' and 'a field':

> We can indeed, with caution, compare a field to a game (*jeu*) although, unlike the latter, a field is not the product of a deliberate act of creation, and it follows rules or, better, regularities, that are not explicit and codified. (Bourdieu and Wacquant, 1992: 98)

The game itself is tantamount to a form of (social) poker rather than roulette: although both demand a certain amount of (social, economic, and cultural) capital, poker demands accumulation and strategies plus a 'poker face' (habitus?).

Lash's interpretation of Bourdieu's reflexive sociology and of the field as a 'reflexive community' is referred to above. According to Lash, Bourdieu's sociology could be described as the sociology of the unconscious – the unconsciousness not only of taste but also of habits and practices – and, as a consequence, as the examination of taken-for-granted and unproblematised categories and presuppositions (Lash, 1994: 153). This sociology of the unconscious has had an influence on so-called reflexive anthropology, which denounces objectivism, the realism of Lévi-Strauss and functionalism. It means learning and knowing through habitus (which has the same root as the French verb '*habiter*'). Moreover truth is neither conceptual nor mimetic; it manifests itself in shared practices. Lash claims that Bourdieu operated 'in a fully different terrain than [...] aesthetic (Adorno, Nietzsche) reflexivity' (Lash, 1994: 156).

As Lash put it, Bourdieu's 'fields' are not filled with structures, agents, discourses, subjects, or objects, but rather comprise habits, unconscious and bodily practices, and 'categories of the unthought'. The implication is that classes and class fractions are involved in a struggle over background assumptions, concerning habits and tastes, for example (which Lash – not Bourdieu – calls 'the ontological foundations of ideology'). In Bourdieu's view – following Lash's argumentation – it is not class as a collective actor that is involved in the struggle, but class as a collective habitus and a 'form of life'. Conceived of in this sense, class is not an organised actor with conscious aspirations. It is rather a question of the 'logic of practices', which operates not through institutional organisations but through shared meanings and habits. Such meanings and habits do not constitute structures in any way (Lash, 1994: 166).

Power and Ressentiment

Thus, there is something a rather paradoxical in Bourdieu's thinking: on the one hand he dismisses the idea of Kant's 'pure aesthetics' on the basis of his 'vulgar' sociological critique, and on the other he develops his own 'reflexive sociology' – similar to a 'Münchhausian trick' – making a case for disinterest. He writes:

> I believe that sociology, when it is reflexive, enables us to track down and to destroy the last germs of ressentiment. [...] Sociology frees you from this kind of sickly strategy of symbolic inversion because it compels you to ask: Do I not write because [...]. Isn't the root of my revolt, my irony, my sarcasm, of the rhetorical vibration of my adjectives when I describe Giscard d'Estaing playing tennis [Bourdieu refers to his *Distinction*] the fact that, deep down, I envy what he is? Ressentiment is for me the form par excellence of human misery; it is the worst thing that the dominant impose on the dominated (perhaps the major privilege of the dominant, in any social universe, is to be structurally freed from ressentiment). Thus, for me, sociology is an instrument of liberation and therefore of generosity. (Bourdieu and Wacquant, 1992: 212)

As to Bourdieu's Münchhausian trick – significantly, one of his 'intellectual heroes' is Karl Kraus (Bourdieu and Wacquant, 1992: 212) – it is apparent in the citation above that he is presenting his own version of disinterested and 'pure' sociology. Reflexive sociology – understood as the sociology of knowledge and power – implies that nothing, including aesthetics, is disinterested except sociology. As a sociologist Bourdieu did not think that he stood above all classifications (cf. the motto of this chapter), but his sociology does not take a stand in favour of any class. Free from ressentiment he could afford to look at things disinterestedly – in other words scientifically and reflexively – from the viewpoint of truth. This is realised *in concreto* in his gigantic project on 'the misery of the world' (*La misère du monde*; Bourdieu et al., 1999 [1993]). He thus appears to be a 'positivist' in two senses of the term: first, he gives his reflexive sociology the status of a queen among sciences, and secondly he presents his own extensive research programme for empirical sociology.

In an interview on his book *Homo Academicus*, Bourdieu formulated perhaps his most explicit standpoint concerning the sociological truths that underlie objectively existing situations in the social world. It is also his most explicit anti-autobiographic statement (cf. Bourdieu, 1986):

> [T]he most intimate truth about what we are, the most unthinkable unthought [*impensée*], is inscribed in the objectivity, and in the history, of the social positions that we held in the past and that we presently occupy. (Bourdieu, 1989 [1988]: 25)

Yet, it is unclear how sociology in the Bourdieusian sense could avoid this reduction back to social positions, or stand outside this objectivity, even as a 'free-floating' sociology. In any case, Bourdieu appears to believe in the possibility of a disinterested sociology, situated neither beyond good and evil nor beyond truth and untruth (Bourdieu's personal communication to the author, 22 June 1993).

Nietzsche's Taste

> Philosophical taste neither replaces creation nor restrains it. On the contrary, the creation of concepts calls for a taste that modulates it. The free creation of determined concepts needs a taste for undermined concept. Taste is this power, this being-potential of the concept [...] Nietzsche sensed this relationship of the creation of concepts with a specifically philosophical taste [...]. (Deleuze and Guattari, 1994: 78–79)

Despite the fact that there is an interesting 'family resemblance' – although not in the strictly Wittgensteinian sense – between Bourdieu and Nietzsche with regard to the concepts of power, taste and knowledge, it would be erroneous to assume that everything in Bourdieu goes back to Nietzsche. He refers to Nietzsche's writings on several occasions, but none of his remarks – in *Distinction*, for example – is relevant to the question of taste. In this sense one cannot say that Bourdieu is Nietzschean. One could suggest, however, that in Bourdieu's thinking are some interesting elements that resemble to Nietzsche's conceptions of taste and power. It is not an entirely novel idea to claim that Nietzsche had a significant influence on the history of sociology. In fact, he had a strong impact particularly on the classic German scholars Tönnies (who later became one of his critics), Simmel (see e.g. Lichtblau, 1984) and Weber (Stauth and Turner, 1988; and Turner, 1992). As the saying goes: they were all 'sociologists after Nietzsche'.

On the other hand, traditionally Nietzsche has not been included in the classics of sociology. In this sense it is interesting that – perhaps for the first time in its 100-year history – the *American Journal of Sociology* published an article (Antonio, 1995) dealing with the absence of Nietzsche from sociological theory, especially in the United States. His influence is widely recognised in Germany and France, as Louis Pinto's analysis of the reception of Nietzsche in France shows, for example (Pinto, 1995; see also Goldman, 1993), even though Pinto has nothing to say about Bourdieu's relation to Nietzsche.

However, it is quite difficult to promote the idea of a specifically Nietzschean conception of taste, although Deleuze and Guattari claim that it was 'philosophical'. For one thing, Nietzsche's style is anything but systematic, it is fragmented and aphoristic (cf. Deleuze, 1965; and Nehemas, 1985). Secondly, to this writer's knowledge no study has been undertaken on Nietzsche's 'philosophy of taste'.[3]

Nietzsche occasionally refers to taste in his books: in *Beyond Good and Evil* (Nietzsche, 1990 [1886]), *The Gay Science* (Nietzsche, 1974 [1882]), *On the Genealogy of Morals* (Nietzsche, 1967 [1887]), *Nietzsche Contra Wagner* (Nietzsche, 1968 [1895]), *Thus Spoke Zarathustra* (Nietzsche, 1961 [1883 1885]) and the so-called *The Will to Power* – i.e. his *Nachlaß* of the 1880s – as well as in his aphoristic way of speaking. Nevertheless, there is much more material about power than about taste in his literary production.

The key quotation from Nietzsche – which could serve as a motto for Bourdieu's *Distinction* – is to be found in *Thus Spoke Zarathustra* ('Of the Sublime Men'):

> And do you tell me, friends, that there is no dispute over taste and tasting? But all life is dispute over taste and tasting!
>
> Taste: that is at the same time weight and scales and weigher; and woe to all living creatures that want to live without dispute over weight and scales and weigher! (Nietzsche, 1961 [1883–1885]: 140)

It is clear from the above quotation that Nietzsche conceived of 'all life' as a dispute about taste, and that one should not contest but rather accept and admit that this is an incontrovertible fact. One could say that Bourdieu agrees with Nietzsche to a large extent in considering taste to be a perpetual struggle in modern society. For both of them it is 'eternal' and everlasting, and there can be no reconciliation. This view is not far from Max Weber's conception of struggle, which expressed as follows in his speech 'Science as Vocation' (1919):

> And, since Nietzsche, we realise that something can be beautiful, not only in spite of the aspect in which it is not good, but rather in that very aspect. [...] It is commonplace to observe that something may be true although it is not beautiful and not holy and not good. Indeed it may be true in precisely those aspects. But all these are only the most elementary cases of the struggle [*Kampf*] that the gods of the various orders and values are engaged in. I do not know how one might wish to decide 'scientifically' the value of French and German culture; for here, too, different gods struggle [*streiten*] with one another, now and for all times. [...] Many old gods ascend from their graves; they are disenchanted and hence take the form of impersonal forces. They strive to gain power over our lives and again they resume their eternal struggle [*ewigen Kampf*] with one another. (Weber, 1970 [1919]): 139–149; Weber, 1992 [1919]): 99–101)

Nietzsche and Bourdieu

There is little doubt that Nietzsche, like Bourdieu, could be regarded as an anti-Kantian thinker. He attacks Kant's aesthetic conception in his *Genealogy of Morals*, especially the 'predicates of beauty': non-personality and universality. Like Schopenhauer, he dismissed Kant's definition of 'beautiful' as something that pleased audiences in a disinterested fashion (*ohne Interesse*) (Nietzsche, 1967 [1887]: 844).

According to Nietzsche, one cannot watch 'without interest' because every perception of the world is necessarily perspective-laden. Kant's fundamental mistake was thus to consider aesthetics from the viewpoint of the spectator, and to include the spectator in the concept of 'the beautiful'. Nietzsche confronts Kant with the 'experience of the artist (the creator)'. This is the view of a real 'spectator' and artist, and Nietzsche preferred Stendhal's definition of beautiful as '*une promesse de bonheur*' to Kant's disinterestedness. Interestingly, Bourdieu – in his *Logic of Practice* – quotes exclusively and sympathetically from this section of Nietzsche's critique of Kant (see Bourdieu, 1990 [1980]: 58).

Nietzsche deals with the change in common taste in the *Gay Science* (First book, chapter 39; Nietzsche, 1963 [1882], 64f). He considers it more important than change in opinion, which is only a symptom of changed tastes. How then, does taste change? According to Nietzsche, it happens when influential people project their own opinions and carry them through. Thus, when they say that something is ridiculous and absurd, they are following the dictates of their own taste and disgust. They subordinate people under power that gradually takes in increasingly large numbers and finally becomes indispensible

(Nietzsche, 1963 [1882]: 64f). This interpretation of changing tastes is rather unsubtle, but there are similar elements here and in Bourdieu's analysis, such as the implementation of 'legitimate taste' by the dominant faction, and especially the manifestation of taste judgements through negation and disgust.

Nietzsche writes: '[T]heir *hoc est ridiculum, hoc est absurdum* [...]. They [i.e. powerful and influential persons] thereby lay a constraint upon many people, out of which there gradually grows a habituation for still more, and finally a necessity for all' (Nietzsche, 1963 [1882]): 64). A sociological interpretation of 'constraint' (*Zwang*) as an abstract social pressure brings Nietzsche's conception close to Bourdieu's thinking. The same applies to Nietzsche's conceptions of 'habituation' (*Gewöhnung*) and 'necessity' (*Bedürfnis*), which are somewhat similar to Bourdieu's conceptions of 'habitus' and 'practice'. Furthermore, Nietzsche recognises that individuals sense and taste things differently because they are embedded in different ways of life, and because they have different bodies (*physis*).[4] Correspondingly, Bourdieu conceives of social class in terms of a collective habitus and lifestyle, which is articulated bodily (*fait corps*) (Bourdieu and Wacquant, 1992: 149), and even physionomically (cf. Simmel: *Nasenfrage*). According to Nietzsche, aesthetic and moral judgements are the 'finest tunes' of the body. Bourdieu refers to Nietzsche (his so-called 'will to power') in his *Distinction*, and to the 'body language' of class habitus (Bourdieu, 1984 [1979]: 177). In another connection he borrows from Marcel Mauss in stating that '[l]anguage is a technique of the body' (Bourdieu and Wacquant, 1992: 149).

Despite the substantial differences between respective viewpoints, it is remarkable that Bourdieu's and Nietzsche's conceptions of the social determination of taste are surprisingly similar. Of course, from a sociological perspective, Bourdieu's interpretation is more sophisticated.

The two also share similar views on ressentiment. In fact, Bourdieu refers directly to Nietzsche when he explains the notion of a 'reflexive sociology' in relation to the concept of ressentiment:

> Ressentiment is not, as with Scheler [Bourdieu refers to Max Scheler's book *Ressentiment*] (who wrote truly awful things about ressentiment), synonymous with the hatred of the dominant experienced by the dominated. It is rather, as Nietzsche, who coined the term, suggested, the sentiment of the person who transforms a sociologically mutilated being – I am poor, I am black, I am a woman, I am powerless – into a model of human excellence, an elective accomplishment of freedom and a *devoir-être*, an ought-to-be, a fatum, built upon an unconscious fascination with the dominant. (Bourdieu and Wacquant, 1992: 212)

It was this very freedom from ressentiment nurtured Bourdieu's disinterested sociology.

Where does this leave Nietzsche's 'will to power' (*Wille zur Macht*), which has led so many misunderstandings? At first glance there seems to be no connection with Bourdieu. By way of contrast, Nietzsche ridicules the 'bad taste' of philosophy, its 'will to truth' (Nietzsche, 1967 [1885]: 9; see also Nietzsche, 1967 [1886]: 567 and 1967 [1887]: 886–887).

Nietzsche makes an interesting distinction between 'strong' and 'weak' forces and 'times' in his posthumous *Will to Power* of the 1880s.[5] 'Strong' here does not necessarily refer to those in power, and 'the will to power' does not denote the idea of 'greed for power', as Gilles Deleuze (1965: 70–77) points out. 'Strong people' act and create, 'weak people' react according to their ressentiments. According to Bourdieu in *Distinction*, the lower classes and the 'new petty bourgeoisie' supposedly similarly go along with the distinctions made by the dominant faction.

Is it sheer coincidence that *Der Wille zur Macht* is translated into French as *La volonté de puissance* (Deleuze, 1965: 89)? It had an obvious influence on Michel Foucault's history of sexuality in *La volonté de savoir* (Foucault, 1976; Foucault, 1990), and perhaps on Bourdieu's concept of 'good cultural will' (*bonne volonté culturelle*)?

The viewpoint of the creative artist (cf. Nietzsche's critique of Kant above) also coincides with Nietzsche's personal artistic programme. Does this also apply to Bourdieu's reflexive sociology, or is there at this point a genuine difference between the two? Nietzsche's mission was to act as an individual avant-garde, to create taste and new values, among other things, and not to judge them (this is something he calls 'women's aesthetics'; see Nietzsche, 1966: 717). On the other hand, Bourdieu gives the artist a special status in his discussion with Hans Haacke: above all, an artist has a specific competence, namely to cause a sensation and to express something that scientific research is not able to say (Bourdieu and Haacke, 1995 [1994]: 36).

Since, as Nietzsche claims (1966: 489 and 484), Kant and his criticism have deprived us of our right to interpretation, the will to power must essentially interpret, outline and define grades and power differences. Although both Nietzsche and Bourdieu are very critical of Kant, Nietzsche describes the will to power as an affirmative and positive force, allowing us – as Michel Maffesoli (1993) remarks – to say 'yes to life'. Bourdieu, however, sees it as something negative. It is nevertheless productive sense, but neither in the Nietzschean sense of 'producing values' nor in the Foucauldian sense of 'producing knowledge'. Furthermore, 'good cultural will', which is typical of the 'new petty bourgeoisie', is a more descriptive term in Bourdieu's writing.

Nietzschean thought is not only anti-Kantian but also anti-sociological (Lichtblau, 1984: 236–238). Nietzsche claimed that nineteenth-century sociology in France and England (especially 'Herr Herbert Spencer') represented the spirit of decadence and general mediocrity (Nietzsche, 1967 [1889]: 981). What lay behind this decadence and mediocrity was the process of Western rationalisation, together with the emergence of the 'social question' and the growth of the socialist movement – all of which could supposedly be considered 'decadent' phenomena.

Nietzsche's anti-sociology was a moral and cultural critique. It was a kind of 'positive counter-sociology', and his radical thought had a strong impact on German sociology, particularly on Simmel (Lichtblau, 1984: 238) and Weber (Stauth and Turner, 1988: 120–121). This counter-sociology was an aristocratic and affirmative 'pathos of distance'. Nietzsche's description of this phenomenon in *Beyond Good and Evil* in the chapter 'What is noble?' is, as such, not so far from Bourdieu's analysis:

> Without the pathos of distance such as develops from the incarnate differences of classes, from the ruling caste's constant looking out and looking down on subjects and instruments and from its equally constant exercise of obedience and command, its holding down and holding at a distance, that other, more mysterious pathos could have developed either, that longing for an ever-increasing widening of distance within the soul itself, the formation of ever higher, rarer, more remote, tenser, more comprehensive states, in short precisely the elevation of the type 'man' [...]. (Nietzsche, 1990: 192; Nietzsche, 1967 [1886]: 604)

Nietzsche's and Bourdieu's conclusions are clearly substantially different, however. It would be reasonable to assume that Bourdieu would not be prepared to accept the characterisation of his sociology as aristocratic. Furthermore, in contrast with Nietzsche's positive tone, he makes a rather critical remark about distancing, in other words the primacy of form over content, which is a central feature of aristocracy in his analysis (Bourdieu, 1984 [1979]: 56). Nonetheless, his sociology *is* aristocratic in that it is noble and generous (cf. the above-mentioned 'sociological generosity'), and it allows a certain distance-taking as disinterested attitude. If the question for Nietzsche, on the one hand, concerned the artist-philosopher's productive capacity or power to create new values, for Bourdieu, on the other, it is about a producer-sociologist's capacity – a matter of *poiesis*. Yet, Nietzsche placed the emphasis on form over content in his artist programme and, for him, philosophy was primarily a matter of style.

In *Will to Power* (Nietzsche, 1966: 560) Nietzsche makes the claim that sociology should be replaced by the 'study of power configurations' (*Herrschaftsgebilden*) and society by the 'cultural complex'. Although this remark is open to interpretation, it does not sound entirely unfamiliar and could be applied to Bourdieu's sociology of symbolic power (although it might be closer to Weber's sociology of domination).

Moreover, it seems that, for Bourdieu, symbolic struggle is a more or less continuous and endless process. There is no harmonious state or stage to be attained – quite the opposite. Nietzsche promoted the idea of the 'eternal recurrence of the same' (*ewige Widerkunft*), which was – as he saw it – 'the highest formula of affirmation' (Nietzsche, 1979: 99; Nietzsche, 1967 [1888]: 1155). This does not imply a simple cycle of the 'same', nor does it mean the repetition or recurrence of historical events or suchlike. It is 'selective'. Moreover, it is doubly selective, like thinking (cf. Deleuze, 1965: 37). It meant 'will' freed from all morality: whatever I want, I have to want so much, as if I also want the eternal recurrence of it (cf. Kant's categorical imperative). Simmel considers Nietzsche's theory of 'eternal recurrence' the highest form of 'individual law' in the ethics of responsibly: we should live as if we will live for ever, in other words as if there were eternal recurrence (Lichtblau, 1984: 261). This kind of positive will to power is not evident in Bourdieu's thought, although perhaps in the case of Bourdieu one could refer to the sociologist's ethics of responsibility.

Conclusion

What, then, was the world to Nietzsche? The *Will to Power* gives us a clear answer:

> And do you know what the world is to me? Shall I show it to you in my mirror? [...] *This world is the will to power – and nothing besides.* And you yourselves are also this will to power – and nothing besides! (Nietzsche, 1966: 916–917; Nietzsche's italics; quoted in English in Nehemas, 1985: 75)

Bourdieu would probably agree with this statement (cf. Rahkonen, 2006). In claiming that 'there is no way out of the game of culture' he portrays society as a battlefield of symbolic power, a struggle from which one cannot disengage. He quotes Horace's aphoristic statement 'De te fabula narratur' – the same phrase Marx used in his preface to *Das Kapital* (Bourdieu1984 [1979]: 12; Marx, 1867: ix).

To paraphrase Nietzsche, Bourdieu might say that 'society is the will to power' – and you yourselves are also this will to power. Nevertheless, there is for his[6] *will to truth*, which, pace Bourdieu, is in my opinion 'positive' – if not 'positivist' – in the very sense in which Comte implied (cf. his *capacité positive*). In the end, Bourdieu has not been able to overcome this dilemma, and has ended up with his own version of the Saint-Simonian programme: 'La sociologie est un sport de combat' (Bourdieu, 2007).[7]

Acknowledgements

This article is a revised and enlarged version of my article 'Le goût vu comme une lutte: Bourdieu et Nietzsche', published in *Sociétés* 53 (1996): 283–297.

Many thanks are due to Joan Nordlund, the University of Helsinki Language Centre, and Simon Susen for discerning language revision.

Notes

1 There is another interesting difference between the French and English cover illustrations of Bourdieu's *Distinction*. Bourdieu chose the picture for the cover of the French edition (Bourdieu, 1979) after having seen it in Budapest (Bourdieu's personal communication to the author, 16 March 1994). It is an old painting by Godfried Schalken, *Le gourmet*, which hangs in the National Gallery of Prague, and portrays a fat man, a gourmand, taking great pleasure in stuffing his mouth.

The picture on the cover of the English edition, about which Bourdieu had no say (in fact he did not like it; Bourdieu's personal communication to the author, 16 March 1994), is a detail from the well-known painting, *Sunday Afternoon on the Island of La Grande Jatte* by Georges Seurat (cf. Rahkonen, 1989: 272–74; Bloch, 1986 [1959]): 953). It portrays (with irony?) a bourgeois Sunday, but a boring one without any joie de vivre whatsoever.

Perhaps these differences in the cover pictures manifest the cultural differences between the French and British societies. Does the picture on the cover of the English editions just reflect the stereotypical British image of France? One interpretation would be that there are genuine social and cultural differences between British and French societies. Britain could be considered more straightforward or rough, whereas in France there may be more sophisticated, 'hidden' class distinctions.

There is another astonishing feature in the original cover picture, and that is the old-fashioned gourmand himself. This, of course, goes back to the genealogy of taste (cf. Falk, 1994: 13–15; Gronow, 1997). However Bourdieu's conclusions suggest rather that the biggest differences in taste are in music. In this sense a more suitable picture on the cover might have reflected this fact.

2 Gerhard Schulze has brought an interesting new viewpoint to this discussion. In his ingenious book *Die Erlebnisgesellschaft* (1992), he discusses *Erlebnis*, which could be translated as subjective experience, as opposed to *Erfahrung*, objective experience (cf. Lash, 1994: 163). He points out that *Erlebnis* is directed at beauty in particular. He argues that beauty (no longer used in the Kantian sense of the word as a judgement) is a uniting concept for valued experience (in German '*schön*'; in English e.g., 'nice'). 'Beautiful' may just as well refer to washing one's car, or Rilke's sonnets, or both of them might be equally banal. In another context (Schulze, 1993: 15–16) Schulze maintains that there has been a change in ways of speaking and discussing. The new form of talk about arts and culture is laconic. Speech is limited more and more to 'how I feel', and to expressions such as 'great', 'fine', 'super', 'hype' and 'cool' (cf. above the Rolling Stones: '[…] (but I like it)'). The same vocabulary characterises one's holiday, a friend's new girl- or boyfriend or a cocktail party.

Responses to questions concerning the judgement or valuation of culture or the arts sound the same as answers to the question: 'How are you?' When we are asked how we value a piece of art – in fact the very question has a colloquial ring to it: did we like or fancy it –, we say how we feel about it. Basically, we do not really talk about art, we talk about ourselves; it is not about the piece of art, but about its effect on us. We do not discuss the quality of art in the objective sense, it is just a question of like or dislike. The subjectivity becomes clear in differences of opinion: I like that film, you do not. It is enough that we know and state this – there is no need for an aesthetic or theoretical dispute about the subject. The subjectivity of opinions is approved as such; thoroughly subjective aesthetics has won. Something appeals to one person, but not to another. There is clearly no longer any dispute about taste! (See also Müller, 1992b)

Bourdieu might accept Schulze's analysis of everyday anti- or a-aesthetics, but he would perhaps like to add that sociological subjectivity goes back to objective social and basically hierarchical positioning. The difference between Bourdieu and Schulze is that, for Schulze, consumption creates classes, 'milieus' and 'scenes' (*Szenen*), whereas for Bourdieu it is vice versa.

3 To my knowledge the only scholar who has dealt thoroughly with Nietzsche and taste (in connection with a theory of consumption) is the Danish historian of ideas Lars-Henrik Schmidt (see Schmidt, 1989: 85–111 and Schmidt, 1990).

4 'Das diese einzelnen aber anders empfinden und "schmecken", das hat gewöhnlich seinen Grund in einer Absonderlichkeit ihrer Lebensweise [...], kurz in der Physis.' – Schrift (1990, 38–40), referring to Heidegger's interpretation, calls Nietzsche's aesthetic theory a 'physiology of art' resting on 'biological values' (for 'bios' read life).

5 According to Heidegger, after *Thus Spoke Zarathustra* (1961; 1967 [1883–1885]) 'Nietzsche never did publish what he really thought' (Heidegger, 1968 [1954]: 73; cf. Schrift, 1990). What he really thought is to be found in his *Nachlaß*, although only in the form of 'unthought':

'What is un-thought in a thinker's thought is not a lack inherent in his thought. What is un-thought is there in each case only as the un-thought. The more original the thinking, the richer will be what is unthought in it' (Heidegger, 1968 [1954]: 76).

Note that Bourdieu uses the same term 'unthought' (impensée) above, but he gives it quite another connotation.

6 Bourdieu's personal communication to the author, 22 June 1993. – In a conversation we once had in Paris Bourdieu suggested to me that I could do the same to Nietzsche as he had done to Heidegger (cf. Bourdieu (1991 [1988]). (Bourdieu's personal communication to the author, 5 October 1995.)

7 In English: 'Sociology is a Martial Art': 'Je dis souvent que la sociologie c'est un sport de combat, c'est un instrument de self defense. On s'en sert pour se défendre, essentiellement, et l'on n'a pas le droit de s'en servir pour faire des mauvais coups.' (Bourdieu, 2007.)

References

Baudrillard, Jean (1986) 'La puissance du dégoût', *Traverses* 37: 5–13.

Bloch, Ernst (1986 [1959]) *The Principle of Hope*, Vol. 3, trans. Neville Plaice, Stephen Plaice and Paul Knight, Oxford: Blackwell.

Bourdieu, Pierre (1979) *La distinction. Critique sociale du jugement.* Paris: Minuit.

Bourdieu, Pierre (1984 [1979]) *Distinction: A Social Critique of the Judgement of Taste*, trans. Richard Nice, Cambridge, Mass.: Harvard University Press.

Bourdieu, Pierre (1986) 'L'illusion biographique', *Actes de la recherche en sciences sociales* 62/63: 69–72.

Bourdieu, Pierre (1988 [1984]) *Homo Academicus*, trans. Peter Collier, Cambridge: Polity Press.

Bourdieu, Pierre (1989 [1988]) 'Antworten auf einige Einwände', in Klaus Eder (ed.) *Klassenlage, Lebensstil und kulturelle Praxis. Theoretische und empirische Auseinandersetzung mit P. Bourdieu's Klassentheorie*, Frankfurt am Main: Suhrkamp, pp. 395–410.

Bourdieu, Pierre (1989) 'For a Socio-Analysis of Intellectuals: On Homo Academicus: An Interview with Pierre Bourdieu', *Berkeley Journal of Sociology* XXIV: 1–29.

Bourdieu, Pierre (1990 [1980]) *The Logic of Practice*, trans. Richard Nice, Cambridge: Polity Press.

Bourdieu, Pierre (1990) 'Animadversiones in Mertonem', in Jon Clark, Celia Modgil and Sohan Modgil (eds.) *R. K. Merton: Consensus and Controversy*, London, New York & Philadelphia: Falmer Press, pp. 297–301.

Bourdieu, Pierre (1991 [1988]) *The Political Ontology of Martin Heidegger*, trans. Peter Collier, Cambridge: Polity Press.

Bourdieu, Pierre (1993 [1984]) *Sociology in Question*, London: Sage.

Bourdieu, Pierre (ed.) (1993) *La misère du monde*, Paris: Seuil.

Bourdieu, Pierre (1999 [1993]) *The Weight of the World: Social Suffering in Contemporary Society*, trans. Priscilla Parkhurst Ferguson [et al.], Cambridge: Polity Press.

Bourdieu, Pierre (2007) *La sociologie est un sport de combat.* Un film de Pierre Carles sur Pierre Bourdieu, en partenariat avec *Le Monde diplomatique*, 150 min/DVD, Montpellier: C-P Productions et VF Films.

Bourdieu, Pierre and Monique de Saint Martin (1976) 'Anatomie du goût', *Actes de la recherche en sciences sociales* 5: 2–112.

Bourdieu, Pierre, Luc Boltanski, Robert Castel, and Jean-Claude Chamboredon (1990 [1965]) *Photography: A Middle-brow Art*, trans. Shaun Whiteside, Stanford, CA: Stanford University Press.

Bourdieu, Pierre, Alain Darbel, and Daniel Schnapper (1991 [1966]) *The Love of Art: European Art Museums and Their Public*, trans. Caroline Beattie and Nick Merriman, Cambridge: Polity Press.

Bourdieu, Pierre and Loïc Wacquant (1992) *An Invitation to Reflexive Sociology*, Cambridge: Polity Press.

Bourdieu, Pierre and Loïc Wacquant (1999 [1998]) 'On the Cunning of Imperialist Reason', *Theory, Culture & Society* 16(4): 1–58.

Bourdieu, Pierre and Hans Haacke (1995 [1994]) *Free Exchange*, trans. Randal Johnson and Hans Haacke, Cambridge: Polity Press.

Crowther, Paul (1994) 'Sociological Imperialism and the Field of Cultural Production: The Case of Bourdieu', *Theory, Culture & Society* 11: 155–169.

Deleuze, Gilles (1965) *Nietzsche*, Paris: PUF.

Deleuze, Gilles and Pierre-Félix Guattari (1994) *What is Philosophy?* London & New York: Verso.

Derrida, Jacques (1987) *The Truth in Painting*, trans. Geoff Bennington and Ian McLeod, Chicago: University of Chicago Press.

Elias, Norbert (1994 [1939]) *The Civilizing Process*, Vol. 1–2, trans. Edward Jephcott, Oxford: Blackwell.

Falk, Pasi (1994) *The Consuming Body*, London: Sage.

Foucault, Michel (1990 [1976]) *The History of Sexuality, Vol. 1: An Introduction*, trans. Robert Hurley, New York: Vintage Books.

Fowler, Bridget (1994) 'The Hegemonic Work of Art in the Age of Electronic Reproduction: An Assessment of Pierre Bourdieu', *Theory, Culture & Society* 11(1): 129–154.

Goldman, Harvey (1993) 'Knowledge Production among Contemporary French Intellectuals, with an Eye toward the Appropriation of Nietzsche', paper presented at the Centenary Congress of the Institut Internationale de Sociologie, Paris, July 1993 (unpublished paper).

Gronow, Jukka (1997) *The Sociology of Taste*, London & New York: Routledge.

Heidegger, Martin (1968 [1954]) *What is Called Thinking?* Transl. J. Glenn Gray, New York: Harper & Row.

Kant, Immanuel (1966 [1790]) *Kritik der Urteilskraft*, Stuttgart: Reclam.

Kant, Immanuel (1987 [1790]) *Critique of Judgement*, trans. Werner S. Pluhar, Indianapolis: Hackett.

Lash, Scott (1994) 'Reflexivity and its Doubles: Structure, Aesthetics, Community', in Ulrich Beck, Anthony Giddens and Scott Lash, *Reflexive Modernisation: Politics, Tradition and Aesthetics in the Modern Social Order*, Cambridge: Polity Press, pp. 110–173.

Lichtblau, Klaus (1984) 'Das "Pathos der Distanz": Präliminarien zur Nietzsche-Rezeption bei Georg Simmel', in Heinz-Jürgen Dahme and Otto Rammstedt (eds.) *Georg Simmel und die Moderne: Neue Interpretation und Materialen*, Frankfurt am Main: Suhrkamp, pp. 231–281.

Lyotard, Jean-François (1991 [1987]) 'Sensus Communis: The Subject in *statu nascendi*', in Eduardo Cavada, Peter Connor and Jean-Luc Nancy (eds.) *Who comes After the Subject?* New York & London: Routledge, pp. 217–235.

Maffesoli, Michel (1993) 'Body and Postmodernity', paper presented at the International Conference on the Sociology of Consumption, Helsinki, 14–19 June (unpublished).

Marx, Karl (1867) *Das Kapital: Kritik der politischen Ökonomie*, Bd. 1. Hamburg: Otto Meissner Verlag.

Müller, Hans-Peter (1992a) *Sozialstruktur und Lebenstile: Der neuere theoretische Diskurs über soziale Ungleichgeit*, Frankfurt am Main: Suhrkamp.

Müller, Hans-Peter (1992b) 'De gustibus non est disputandum? Bemerkungen zur Diskussion um Gesmack, Distinktion und Lebensstil', in Reinhard Eisendle and Elfie Miklautz (eds.) *Produktkulturen: Dynamik und Bedeutungswandel des Konsums*. Frankfurt am Main & New York: Campus, pp. 117–34.

Nehemas, Alexander (1985) *Nietzsche: Life as Literature*. Cambridge, Mass.: Harvard University Press.

Nietzsche, Friedrich (1961 [1883–1885]) *Thus Spoke Zarathustra: A Book for Everyone and No One*, trans. R. J. Hollingdale, Harmondsworth: Penguin.

Nietzsche, Friedrich (1963 [1882]) 'Die fröhliche Wissenschaft (La gaya scienza)', in his *Werke in sechs Banden; dritter Band*, herausgegeben von Karl Schlechta, München: Carl Hanser Verlag, pp. 7–274.

Nietzsche, Friedrich (1966) 'Aus dem Nachlaß der Achtzigerjahre', in his *Werke in sechs Banden; sechster Band*, herausgegeben von Karl Schlechta, München: Carl Hanser Verlag, pp. 471–925.

Nietzsche, Friedrich (1967 [1883–1885]) 'Also sprach Zarathustra', in his *Werke in sechs Banden; dritter Band*, herausgegeben von Karl Schlechta, München: Carl Hanser Verlag, pp. 277–456.

Nietzsche, Friedrich (1967 [1885]) 'Vorrede zur zweinten Ausgabe (Die fröhliche Wissenschaft)', in his *Werke in sechs Banden; dritter Band*, herausgegeben von Karl Schlechta, München: Carl Hanser Verlag, pp. 7–274.

Nietzsche, Friedrich (1967 [1886]) 'Jenseits von Gut und Böse', in his *Werke in sechs Banden; vierter Band*, herausgegeben von Karl Schlechta, München: Carl Hanser Verlag, pp. 563–759.

Nietzsche, Friedrich (1967 [1887]) 'Zur Genealogie der Moral', in his *Werke in sechs Banden; vierter Band*, herausgegeben von Karl Schlechta, München: Carl Hanser Verlag, pp. 761–900.

Nietzsche, Friedrich (1967 [1888]) 'Ecce homo: Wie man wird, was man ist', in his *Werke in sechs Banden; vierter Band*, herausgegeben von Karl Schlechta, München: Carl Hanser Verlag, pp. 1063–1159.

Nietzsche, Friedrich (1967 [1889]). 'Götzen-Dämmerung: Streifzüge eines Unzeitgemäßen', in his *Werke in sechs Banden; vierter Band*, herausgegeben von Karl Schlechta, München: Carl Hanser Verlag, pp. 939–1033.

Nietzsche, Friedrich (1968 [1895]) 'Nietzsche Contra Wagner', trans. Walter Kaufmann, in Walter Kaufmann (ed.) *The Portable Nietzsche*, New York: Viking Press, pp. 661–683.

Nietzsche, Friedrich (1974 [1882]) *The Gay Science*, trans. Walter Kaufmann, New York: Vintage Press.

Nietzsche, Friedrich (1979 [1888]) *Ecce homo: How One Becomes What One Is*, trans. R. J. Hollingdale, Harmondsworth: Penguin.

Nietzsche, Friedrich (1990 [1886]) *Beyond Good and Evil*, trans. R. J. Hollingdale, London: Penguin.

Pinto, Louis (1995) *Les neveux de Zarathoustra: Le réception de Nietzsche en France*, Paris: Seuil.

Rahkonen, Keijo (1989) 'Utopia (on utopia)/A Utopia (is a utopia)', in Timo Valjakka (ed.) *Synnyt – nykytaiteen lähteitä / Sources of Contemporary Art*, Helsinki: Museum of Contemporary Art, pp. 266–286.

Rahkonen, Keijo (1996) 'Le goût vu comme une lutte: Bourdieu et Nietzsche', *Sociétés* 53: 283–297.

Rahkonen, Keijo (2006) 'Pierre Bourdieu – l'homo academicus : Étude de la pensée de Bourdieu dans une perspective bourdieusienne', in Fred Dervin & Elina Suomela-Salmi (éds.) *Communication et éducation interculturelles : Perspectives*, Bern: Peter Lang, pp. 207–226.

Schmidt, Lars-Henrik (1989) *Der Wille zur Ordnung*, Aarhus: Aarhus universitets forlag.

Schmidt, Lars-Henrik (1990) 'Smagens analytik', in Kurt Ove Eliassen and Tore Eriksen (eds.) *Smag, sansning, civilisation: En antologi*, Aarhus: Aarhus universitets forlag, pp. 118–155.

Schrift, Alan D. (1990) *Nietzsche and the Question of Interpretation: Between Hermeneutics and Deconstruction*, New York & London: Routledge.

Schulze, Gerhard (1992) *Die Erlebnisgesellschaft. Kultursoziologie der Gegenwart*, Frankfurt & New York: Campus.

Schulze, Gerhard (1993) *Auf der Suche nach dem schönen Leben. Glücksmodelle, Kunst und Publikum der Gegenwart*, Bamberg (unpublished manuscript).

Simmel, Georg (1983 [1895]) 'Die Mode', pp. 26–51 in his *Philosophische Kultur. Über das Abenteuer, die Geschlechter und die Krise der Moderne, Gesammelte Essais*, Berlin: Wagenbach.

Simmel, Georg (1990 [1900]) *The Philosophy of Money*, London: Routledge.

Stauth, Georg and Bryan S. Turner (1988) *Nietzsche's Dance: Resentment, Reciprocity and Resistance in Social Life*, Oxford: Blackwell.

Turner, Bryan S. (1992) *Max Weber: From History to Modernity*, London & New York: Routledge.

Weber, Max (1970 [1919]) 'Science as Vocation', in Hans H. Gerth and C. Wright Mills (eds.) *From Max Weber: Essays in Sociology*, London: Routledge, pp. 129–156.

Weber, Max (1992 [1919]) ‚Wissenschaft als Beruf', in his *Gesamtausgabe*, Vol. 17/1. Tübingen: J.C.B. Mohr (Paul Siebeck), pp. 71–111.

Wacquant, Loïc (1993) 'Taste', in William Outhwaite and Tom Bottomore (eds.) *The Blackwell Dictionary of Twentieth-Century Social Thought*, Oxford: Blackwell, pp. 662–664.

Wenzel, Bernice M. (1968) 'Taste and Smell', in *International Encyclopaedia of the Social Sciences*, Vol. 15, New York: Macmillan & Free Press, pp. 514–516.

Other Sources

Bourdieu's personal communication (letter) to the author, 22 June 1993.
Bourdieu's personal communication to the author, 16 March 1994.
Bourdieu's personal communication to the author, 5 October 1995.

CHAPTER SEVEN

Elias and Bourdieu

Bowen Paulle, Bart van Heerikhuizen, and Mustafa Emirbayer

The deeper one penetrates the universes of Norbert Elias and Pierre Bourdieu, the clearer it becomes: the similarities between their visions of society are striking. While the two sociologists always showed great sympathy for one another,[1] there are no indications that they were fully aware of how fundamental the subterranean intellectual affinities were.[2] And even though many social scientists combine a high regard for some of Elias's works with great admiration for several works by Bourdieu, thereby showing an instinctive sense of the affinities between these authors, until now it seems that no one has noticed the degree to which Bourdieu and Elias are intellectual siblings. The contributions of each has been highlighted in convincing work – in the case of Elias, for example, by Goudsblom (1987), and, in the case of Bourdieu, by the likes of Wacquant (2006). Even in such careful and judicious accounts, however, important connections between the two authors have remained either hidden or implicit. Engaging in some degree of excavation, this chapter brings to light why Bourdieu and Elias can be viewed as contributors to a single theoretical approach. The most important finding here is that both relied heavily on the same triad of core concepts, and both deployed those concepts in relentlessly relational and processual fashion. Our first goal, therefore, is to uncover these deep-seated conceptual affinities.

Our second goal is to demonstrate that, when taken together, the two authors' perspectives yield a vision more far-reaching and powerful than either considered separately. More concretely, we hope to show that researchers drawing simultaneously upon Elias and Bourdieu can systematically overcome decades of misguided dichotomies in social thought, dichotomies such as those between individual and society, subject and object, the internal and the external, reason and emotion, the soul and the flesh.

One can easily imagine why the deep-seated affinities and compatibilities between Elias and Bourdieu might have been overlooked.[3] To begin with, Elias's seminal works were written in German in the years leading up to the Second World War. Bourdieu started producing his most important contributions in French roughly a quarter-century after the War. Their at times poorly (and belatedly) translated works appear quite different from one another and seem to refer to very different networks of conceptual resources, or to what Elias (1978 [1970]: 111–113) later in life would term 'means of speaking and thinking'. More importantly, Elias was associated primarily with the study of grand historical developments spanning several centuries. Bourdieu is most famous for his work on socio-cultural reproduction during the 1970s. Elias felt that our stocks of sociological knowledge are still too primitive to be of much practical use in political matters (cf. Elias, 1956 and 1987). Although a staunch defender of a genuinely reflexive sociological field, Bourdieu did engage openly in political debates during various episodes of his life.[4] No wonder, then, that most (if not all) of the profound similarities between these authors continue to escape so many standard textbook accounts (e.g. Ritzer and Goodman, 2004) and remain implicit even in more thorough and discerning studies (Van Krieken, 1998; Kilminster, 2007; Shusterman, 1999).

Yet, the affinities between the two social thinkers should come as no surprise. To a significant extent, Elias and Bourdieu were exposed to the same intellectual currents during their formative years. They studied the works of Marx and Weber, felt the influence of philosophers such as Husserl, Cassirer, and Heidegger, and – perhaps most crucially – evinced a deep understanding of Durkheimian thought. In their biographies, one can also detect similarities. Both men felt in certain periods of their lives the sting of being outsiders. Both showed a tremendous energy in fighting their way into the castles of academic excellence. Both experienced, body and soul, how processes of inclusion and exclusion can restrict one's freedom of movement in various social fields. And, when the time came to collect the highest rewards the academic community has to offer, both discovered that such accolades do not alleviate the pain of scars for which there is no healing process. These parallels along biographical, social, and intellectual dimensions all help to explain the affinities between them.

What immediately follows is an introduction to the three core concepts re-crafted and deployed by both authors: habitus, field, and power. While this is not the place to investigate the formation of these concepts in a systematic fashion, we think it is useful to begin with a brief discussion tracing their intellectual roots. In the main body of this chapter, we examine how each of our two authors deployed his three main conceptual devices to interrogate a range of empirical phenomena. We do not offer here a thorough exposition of these authors' theories or an exhaustive overview of their empirical engagements. We do, however, direct attention to various convergences that until now have been left largely out of account, showing how themes developed by Bourdieu and Elias are actually expressions of one common way of depicting the social world. After drawing attention to this common perspective, we move to a direct example of both the two authors' complementarity and their important differences of emphasis. Specifically, we reflect on their respective approaches to the rather anti-intellectual and body-centred world of sport. We conclude by discussing how the basically harmonious outlook demonstrated in this article might have a bearing on relational and processual theorising in the future.

Identifying (the Roots of) the Triad[5]

> [T]he pretension to be what one is not [leads to] insecurity of taste and conduct, 'vulgarity'. [...] The attempt does not succeed [...]. [T]he attempt to achieve the poise of the upper class leads in most cases to a particular falseness and incongruity of behavior which nevertheless conceals a genuine distress, a despair to escape the pressure from above and the sense of inferiority. (Elias, 1994 [1939]: 508)

Despite some confusion on this topic, which will be cleared up below, it remains the case that Elias was working extensively with a concept of habitus long before Bourdieu had ever heard of the term. The idea was crucial to both thinkers. Throughout most of their major writings, both used the term habitus or some similar notion – such as 'second nature' (or, in Bourdieu's case, a 'feel for the game') – frequently and in prominent fashion (e.g. Elias 1994 [1939]: 447 and 1983 [1969]: 241, Bourdieu 1990 [1980]: 66 and 2000 [1997]: 211.

As terms like 'second nature' make plain, Elias and Bourdieu sought to emphasise the importance of taken-for-granted ways of perceiving, thinking, and acting on the part of (more or less) competent actors immersed in their everyday practices. Both focused on practical action and knowledge because they understood that, in real time and space, human conduct tends to be orchestrated from 'within' by dispositions functioning primarily beneath the level of discursive consciousness. Understanding habitus as a system of acquired dispositions allowed them to act upon their belief that, at bottom, our responses and practices are based on prediscursive familiarity with the social worlds we inhabit. It helped both authors systematically to address how incorporated dispositions can be triggered – and to some degree reconstituted (especially early in life) – by networks of unfolding solicitations and sanctions.[6]

The concept of habitus allowed both Elias and Bourdieu to escape the subject-object dichotomy and to get beyond the myth of the self-contained knowing subject. It enabled them to explore the social constitution as well as the largely unconscious here-and-now functioning of 'self steering apparatus(es)', to use one of Elias's (1994 [1939]: 456) alternative terms for habitus, of agents absorbed into, and to varying degrees remade by, influences emanating from the 'outside' world. Crucially, both authors saw that the responses generated from 'within' by the habitus tend not to be the responses of thinking (let alone calculating) subjects standing apart from explicitly conceptualised objects. Both rejected the view that real-time actions of living agents require the mediation of self-contained and explicit mental representations. For Elias as well as for Bourdieu, the practical appraisals of the habitus-in-action tended to be those of the 'open' or 'exposed' person who has gradually come to feel so at home in (or at least prediscursively absorbed by) an objective situation that time- and energy-consuming explicit mental representations might only get in the way.

Aspects of this kind of thinking are reminiscent of any number of philosophical streams, such as American pragmatism (Emirbayer and Schneiderhan, forthcoming). Above all, however, we find evidence here of massive influence from someone who, along with Elias, was studying with Husserl in Freiburg during the 1920s: Martin Heidegger.[7] Even in the case of Bourdieu, who was much more forthcoming about his intellectual inheritance than Elias, there is no mystery about the fundamental influence of Heidegger and of the 'philosopher of the flesh': Merleau-Ponty.[8] Thinkers like Heidegger and Merleau-Ponty not only broke with Cartesian thinking about self-contained agents existing somehow outside social structures, but they did this in terms that anticipated the sociological language that Elias and Bourdieu would later come to speak fluently. Armed with sociologically grounded versions of what – in these predecessors – had been phenomenological and ontological concepts, Elias and Bourdieu got past the problematic division of 'inner' (and somehow static) selves, on the one hand, and bounded flows of moods, meanings, and mechanisms operating in various social contexts, on the other.

Of course, much of the thinking that we might associate with beings-in-the-social-world preceded even Heidegger. In his treatise on *The Rules of the Sociological Method*, published originally in 1895, Durkheim warned against the tendency to reduce '*les faits sociaux*' to the level of individual consciousness. The realm of the social, he argued, has a dynamic all of its own vis-à-vis that of psychological facts. The social dimension constitutes '*une réalité sui generis*'. Durkheim (1966 [1895]: 103) was outspoken in claiming that '[s]ociety is not a mere sum of individuals. Rather, the system formed by their association represents a specific reality which has its own characteristics.'[9] In his later masterpiece, *The Elementary Forms of Religious Life* (1995 [1912]), he maintained not only that society was the driving force behind religion but also that, through their (effervescent) religious practices, people actually worshiped society. Look into the heart of the individual, he contended, and you will find the social.

In part because Elias and Bourdieu knew their Durkheim so well, they saw the need for reasonably identifiable social worlds 'apart' and characterised by their own internal logics. Both grasped, as Mead had also done before them, that 'human nature' is social through and through. Nevertheless, 'society' was, for both our students of Durkheim, far too blunt an instrument.

Enter Max Weber, the theorist of life orders. Whether they opted for field or figuration, Elias and Bourdieu were empirically and theoretically at their best when they put Weber's concept of life orders to work by meticulously examining specific bundles of shifting social relations among interdependent people, positions, and institutions within a broader society. As our discussions below will document, particular social microcosms (court society, the field of cultural production, the world of sport) embedded in larger social universes (e.g. France) served as our authors' most useful units of analysis.

Using Weber's (as well as Durkheim's) notions of relatively autonomous social contexts, Elias and Bourdieu systematically investigated how specific social configurations, conceptualised both on micro and on macro levels, serve as the sources of second natures and as the dynamic contexts in which habitus (plural) function. Both stressed that the social forces generated in relatively autonomous relational contexts tend to be more compelling than the second natures of even the most powerful individuals constituting them. They also demonstrated, however, that it ultimately makes no sense to analyse in isolation either figurational dynamics or the functioning and formation of habitus.

Introducing the dialectic of second natures and social structures, we have already hinted at the two authors' concepts of power, or, as Bourdieu called it, capital. (Their shared inclination to focus on objective distributions of power brings to mind, of course, the materialist sociology of Karl Marx.) Elias and Bourdieu understood that individuals and groups accumulate different amounts and types of (non-economic) power resources; both stressed that these power resources always emerge out of, function within, and restructure unfolding social configurations. Albeit in diverging contexts, both documented how second natures well suited to specific settings often serve as indispensable assets. No matter what terms they used (power ratios, species of capital), it was impossible for either author to conceptualise social structural dynamics (or the formation and workings of habitus) outside objective distributions of power resources.

The Triad as Deployed by Bourdieu

> Such notions as habitus, field, and capital can be defined, but only within the theoretical system they constitute, not in isolation. (Bourdieu and Wacquant, 1992: 96)

Bourdieu's analytic approach is based on a triad of interdependent core concepts. As he (like Elias) never tired of reminding us, this theoretical system arose gradually out of ongoing 'confrontations' with diverse empirical realities. These confrontations began in the late 1950s and early 60s both in Algeria (during the war of independence) and in his native Béarn (during a period when protourbanisation was forcing even the more intelligent, handsome, and landed men of his rural village into celibacy). Then, after the early 1960s, Bourdieu (with Passeron) shifted to other questions such as why the children of secondary school teachers tend to do better in the French educational system than the offspring of bankers. Dealing first and foremost with empirical questions related to structural change and reproduction, he felt impelled to start thinking about relations to 'legitimate' culture as themselves a vitally important source of power. Early studies of cultural capital and education would lead, of course, to Bourdieu's attack – in *Distinction* (1984 [1979]) – on Kantian notions of context-free discriminations and relations to culture. More convincingly (or at least more provocatively) than any sociological study up to that moment, his investigation in that latter work of a specific field – class relations in France during the 1970s – would link aesthetic dispositions to ongoing forms of 'naturalised' class-based oppression.

Unfortunately, some of his early works – such as *Reproduction in Education, Society, and Culture* (Bourdieu and Passeron, 1977 [1970]) – and some of his mid-career works – such as *Distinction* – are frequently misinterpreted as arguing (at least implicitly) that social reproduction works in the form of a closed loop, with objectively unequal social structural positions generating more or less 'legitimate' cultural skills and dispositions that, in turn, regenerate the same basic socioeconomic inequalities. The label used to characterise Bourdieu on these grounds was 'reproduction theorist'. Truth be told, Bourdieu was a sociologist of shifting configurations of power. Bourdieusian fields are 'spaces' of ongoing historical contestation *temporarily* objectified in the form of hierarchical positions (occupied, for example, by agents or institutions).[10] To interrogate the sets of dispositions operating largely beneath the surface of discursive consciousness among the people making up these social fields, Bourdieu relied on his reworked notion of 'history turned flesh': habitus. As terms like 'second nature' and 'feel for the game' imply, habitus was basically the effect of previous conditionings associated with specific (class) positionings and understood as 'social injunctions addressed not to the intellect but to the body' (Bourdieu, 2000: 141). Because people socialised into specific classes (or, better yet, into specific regions of the larger social space) tended to be exposed to similar conditions and conditionings, this approach made it possible to bring macro-level realities (e.g. the class structure of France) into analyses of micro-level dynamics (e.g. taken-for-granted feelings about what is appropriate for 'our kind' in specific educational, residential, or economic contexts). Our 'primary' and 'specific' second natures were the embodied effects of our social trajectories though specific (positions within specific) fields. Once crystallised, these durable systems of dispositions would govern our responses to unfolding situations in the here-and-now as well as our (preconscious) orientations to the future.[11] Here again, the guiding principle was not that of habitus formation necessarily leading to social reproduction but, rather, that of more and less empowering habitus formation processes leading to better or worse 'fits' within emerging social realities.

Crucially, then, Bourdieu argued that second natures can operate as forms of capital (specifically, cultural capital in the embodied form). Yet, capital – whether in its embodied form or in any other form – can *exist* only within specific fields and during specific intervals. Power resources are scarce and therefore distinctive, not because of possessing any timeless or essential attributes, but because they are the temporary effects of symbolic struggles (that is, struggles over valuations of various species and amounts of capital) that took place in the past. Shifting and largely unconscious or habituated valuations can create, temporarily maintain, and destroy capitals. They can set up, preserve, and redefine the boundaries and principles of division of a Bourdieusian field.

After *Distinction*, Bourdieu deployed his triad of core concepts in investigations of empirical objects as diverse as sport, French housing markets, and shifting modes of masculine domination. He also continued to deal with culture, for example, in *The Rules of Art* (1996 [1992]) and *The Field of Cultural Production* (1993). Upon closer examination of these important works, what is most striking is the unwaveringly relational and processual deployment of all three of his main concepts.

Bourdieu's studies of power dynamics and culture all rest on a certain understanding of social space. The latter was, for this son of a sharecropper-turned-post-office worker from south-western France, a universe of ongoing struggle. Privileging economic and cultural capital, Bourdieu postulated atop the social space a more delimited 'field of power' – that is, an arena within which 'dominant dominants' were engaged in continual struggles with 'dominated dominants'. Those most advantaged in these struggles were people, organisations, and fields (e.g. the field of corporate law firms and the field of high finance) associated with relatively greater amounts of economic capital and relatively lesser amounts of cultural capital. Those least advantaged were people more or less like ourselves, the readers of this paper (social scientists, although Bourdieu also mentioned artists), organisations like the ones we belong to (universities, but also various other cultural institutions), and fields such as our own (sociology, but more broadly the field of cultural production).

The nature of the power struggle and ongoing dynamics of this field of power, as of all Bourdieusian fields, are clear from the moment this picture is sketched. Social life is inherently processual, even if the current state of affairs is mapped out two-dimensionally and even if it is pointed out that, ultimately, the ministry of culture carries less weight than the ministry of finance. The question is always who (or what) is anchored into which more or less dominant positions because of which species and amounts of capital. This, in turn, is always related to the questions of how habitually ('naturally') recognised valuations of various forms of capital emerge, how they are reproduced, and how they are (or might be) altered.[12]

Immediately we see, then, that the big picture has to do with (symbolic) struggle, ongoing oppression, (potential) resistance, and perpetual change. The next step in the study of fields of cultural production is perhaps the most theoretically inspired. Examining fields of practice within this overall dynamic structure, we find, yet again, spaces of 'play'. Even if Bourdieu at times gave the impression that his objects of study were reified structures at rest, he in fact saw fields as sites of ongoing contestation on the part of differently positioned and empowered actors. To get a better sense of this, let us focus here on the French literary field so carefully examined in *The Rules of Art*.

Highlighting the space of possible moves presented to and (to some degree) created by Flaubert, Bourdieu theorised and documented the genesis and increasing autonomy of the French literary field in the nineteenth century. Within what eventually emerged as the modern literary field, he drew our attention to the ongoing struggle between avant-garde and established artists (i.e. the people and organisations occupying the two main poles of the field, poles organised around different types of assets and capitals). For Bourdieu, there was no possibility of understanding what goes on at one or the other of these two poles in abstraction from what goes on in the rest of the relational context (understood as itself a referential totality). For example, because of their positions within the overall field as well as their unique relation to forces outside it, the established tended to favour more conservative symbolic strategies and position-takings – especially those associated with 'bourgeois' literature (but also, at times, those identified with 'social art'). In the 'economic world inverted' that he was helping to create even as it created him, Flaubert lambasted these artists who tried to make their aesthetic intentions clear to potential audiences and congratulated those who remained inaccessible. 'I do not know if there exists in French a more beautiful page of prose', he declared to a lesser-known revolutionary (quoted in Bourdieu, 1996 [1992]: 79). 'It is splendid and I am sure that the bourgeois don't understand a word of it. So much the better.' Members of the avant-garde – sensing the relative positions of all involved, as well as where their field as a whole stood in relation to the broader *espace social* – gravitated towards position-takings that challenged the authority of established writers, institutions, styles, and conventions (e.g. political and aesthetic detachment). Hence, we see the ongoing dynamic. As a result of becoming too commercial according to a pre-existing yardstick for judging such matters, or perhaps due to a fall from grace precipitated by the introduction of new valuations, or possibly even because of death, the once-established would either leave the field or lose their grip on superior positions. Some members of the (more or less marginal) avant-garde would then ease into those more established positions, where the temptation to 'sell out' would become harder to resist. This, in turn, would open up space for still more newcomers to the avant-garde.

Flaubert offers a perfect example of how early socialisation (in his case, the formation of an aristocratic primary habitus) could trigger an initial belief in the game – the faith or 'illusio' that entering the field is worth the trouble – and serve as itself a crucial power resource. Disgusted by bourgeois styles no less than by literature 'for the people', Flaubert was predisposed towards risks that others would never have dreamed of taking. The logic of the field he so heavily influenced (i.e. the expectations, valuations, desires related to different positions and distributions of power) seeped into all the subjectivities of those who paid the price of admission and entered the field for an extended period. Those who became familiar with the field's internal dynamics – those who were deeply and durably shaped by it – tended to acquire an additional specific habitus that could only result from extended exposure to such a specific set of everyday conditions and conditionings. Thus is explained the inclination towards art that is authentically and exclusively for art's sake, even and perhaps especially when it is inaccessible to 'the people' or 'the bourgeoisie' – an inclination that appears 'irrational' to those caught up in the logics of other fields.

The Triad as Deployed by Elias

> From the interweaving of countless individual interests and intentions […] something comes into being that was planned and intended by none of these individuals, yet has emerged nevertheless from their intentions and actions […]. The understanding of a formation of this kind requires a breakthrough to a still little-known level of reality: to the level of the immanent regularities of social relationships, *the field of relational dynamics*. (Elias, 1994 [1939]: 389, italics added)

As these closing sentences of the penultimate empirical chapter of *The Civilizing Process* indicate, Elias liked to end his arguments with a bang. Interestingly, the key term here was not *figuration* but *field*.[13] What did he mean by this term? The best way to show how Elias deployed it is to bring it to life.

The paradigmatic illustration of the field of relational dynamics, as Elias understood it, is found in his repeated discussions of Louis XIV. Even in the case of this person who may have believed himself to be the state (*'L'état c'est moi'*), Elias looked not at the single entity but all around it, beneath it, and beyond it. Feelings, thoughts, and actions were always depicted in relation to shifting balances of power at the macro-level (the position of nobles vis-à-vis the bourgeoisie), at various institutional meso-levels (dynamics within court society, bourgeois families), and in micro-level here-and-now experiences (ways of interacting during various ceremonies of the court). While the Sun King managed to remain at the centre of a tension-filled and multisided balance of power, Elias showed that even this absolute monarch was effectively pushed and pulled by figurational pressures emanating from all quarters (e.g. competing factions of rising and declining dominant groups, and pressures from subdominant groups).

In both *The Court Society* and *The Civilizing Process*, Elias detailed the most important effects of the lengthening 'chains of interdependence' creating and sustaining radical levels of inequality during the Sun King's reign. One especially compelling image illustrates this point. Successful (and ascending) members of the king's court did not merely resist the impulse to draw their swords when challenged, as their forefathers had almost automatically done. In many cases, the adequately socialised members of this new kind of dominant class resisted the impulse even to raise an eyebrow. Often they took insults in their stride as they plotted possible future retaliations. Yet, given that they *were* – effectively – the networks of relations and intrigue in which they had been formed, they almost automatically grasped that temporary alliances with enemies could help them defeat an even more important enemy (or avoid being undone by a more important challenge) down the road.

In these early yet seminal works, Elias also showed that chains or 'webs' of interdependence produced such intense fantasies about the inherent superiority of the aristocracy – and such intense collective fears about downward mobility – that all the social dominants found themselves trapped in tedious postures and ceremonial displays of etiquette. On and beneath conscious levels, all involved were fundamentally influenced by the courtly social relations and repeated experiences into which they had been thrust. Crucially, even the Sun King himself was ultimately powerless to bring about adaptations in this state of affairs. Here we might cite a passage from Elias's *The Court Society*, one that Bourdieu (1996 [1989]: 129) also found important enough to quote at length:

> In the last analysis this compelling struggle for ever-threatened power and prestige was the dominant factor that condemned all those involved to enact these burdensome ceremonies. No single person within the figuration was able to initiate a reform of the tradition. Every slightest attempt to reform, to

> change the precarious structure of tensions, inevitably entailed an upheaval, a reduction or even abolition of the rights of certain individuals and families. To jeopardize such privileges was, to the ruling class of this society, a kind of taboo. The attempt would be opposed by broad sections of the privileged who feared, perhaps not without justification, that the whole system of rule that gave them privilege would be threatened or would collapse if the slightest detail of the traditional order were altered. So everything remained as it was.

A central point here is that the king and his court were basically held hostage by the very figurational dynamics they temporarily dominated. Elias's primary interest, however, was not in how dominant groups were dominated by their own positional advantage. His point was that potent figurational pressures (such as those related to distributions of power, 'courtly' behavioural norms, collective ways of feeling, and worldviews) predated the absolute monarch, governed the king and his court for a time, and then carried on after the Sun King and his courtiers were dead. Indeed, Elias showed how the very sociogenetic (i.e. structural) pressures the Sun King dominated would, in altered form, ultimately lead some of the king's own kind to the guillotine.

Even in this case characterised by some of the most extreme power differentials ever recorded, for Elias the question was never 'Who is in control?'; rather, the properly sociological question was how particular responses (socialisation pressures, feelings, thoughts) temporarily emanate from specific figurational developments (conceptualised across more macro- and micro-domains and in terms of longer- or shorter-term processes). The key features ostensibly 'of' the individuals and groups Elias examined (e.g. natural poise in elite social gatherings, refined tastes, relatively high degrees of emotional self-control) did not exist outside the social networks in which the king and his courtiers found themselves. And none of these open human beings (*homines aperti*) could possibly have remained essentially unchanged throughout their ongoing interrelations.

From this perspective, it makes no sense to think about some 'true', deep down, non-social 'self'. For Elias at least, these early studies of 'courtisation' put the nail in the coffin of the eternal soul, the transcendental subject, the utility-maximising individual with a fixed preference schedule. Using the more or less intentional and meaningful actions of the Sun King and his court as the limiting case, he argued that nearly all 'our' actions and attributes are actually produced *within* dynamic chains of interdependence in which we are temporarily caught. The focus, therefore, must remain on shifting networks of interdependent actors. Social relations and pressures operative in the kinds of figurations worthy of our sustained attention are the very stuff of the passions, worldviews, and levels of emotional self-control 'of individuals'.

Hence, the notion of figurational dynamics helped Elias to escape the grip of 'naïve egocentricity' – as well as to decontextualise substantialist categorisations more generally – and therefore to arrive at ways of speaking and thinking based on the fundamental interdependence of human beings within continually unfolding social settings just as real as the individuals constituting them.[14] Elias's notion of penetrating, yet fluid-like, social structures helped him to grasp how self-restraint and a predisposition towards the use of a good deal of foresight were associated with 'civilising' pressures (as well as 'decivilising' surges) that could fruitfully be examined over the course of many centuries.[15]

Elias's approach to fields of relational dynamics was based on the assumption that not even the effects of the enculturation process for which he is most famous could be decontextualised (i.e. understood outside specific social configurations) and reduced to some kind of substance that is inherently advantageous or disadvantageous. As he and Scotson (1994 [1965]: 10) argued, 'every element in a configuration and all of its properties are what they are only by virtue of their position and function within a configuration'. Sensing the utility of his approach to figurations, Elias (1978: 116) never stopped advising sociologists to 'work out' from these shifting relational wholes 'to the elements involved in them'. Aware of how difficult it would be to break with modes of substantialist thinking which had become embedded in the very languages we speak, he (1978: 98) reiterated that it 'is a scientific superstition that in order to investigate them scientifically one must necessarily dissect processes of interweaving into their component parts'. In his more polemical remarks, Elias associated substantialist thinking with *Zustandreduktion*, the reduction of what are in fact unfolding processes to frozen states (cf. Goudsblom and Mennell, 1998: 143), and he accused many of his colleagues of 'retreating into the present' (Elias, 1987).

Let us now shift our focus from social configurations to habitus. Elias, like many other intellectuals in inter-bellum Germany, used this term frequently. This is often overlooked in part because 'habitus' was translated in the English version of *The Civilizing Process* as 'personality structure' or 'personality make-up'.[16] There can, however, be no doubt about Elias's reliance on his notion of habitus in all his writings, from his early masterpiece, *The Civilizing Process*, to *The Germans* – a book, written towards the end of his life, in which he attempted to deal with the deeper causes of the 'breakdown of civilisation'. As Elias (1996 [1989]: 19) wrote in the introduction to that latter work, which featured the term 'habitus' in its subtitle, '[t]he central question is how the fortunes of a nation over the centuries became sedimented into the habitus of its individual members'. Instead of slavishly sticking to poor translations and awkward terms, we need to take a closer look at what the concept of habitus allowed Elias to accomplish.

It is true that Elias's analyses of habitus formation often stretched back to the 'dark ages'. And he is most famous for connecting state formation and other longer-term, macro-level processes to structural transformations in everyday social relations that exerted more or less 'civilising' influences.[17] Yet, he was by no means interested exclusively in longer-term socialisation processes. There is another – less well-known – Elias, who had a sharp eye for processes related to contemporary child-rearing techniques, adolescent-socialising practices, and the extended and specialised training now required for a reasonable chance at success in 'fields of adult activities' (Elias, 1991 [1987]: 123; see also Elias, 1996: 268; Elias and Dunning, 1986; Elias and Scotson, 1994 [1965]).[18]

Whether he was taking the long view or not, as we mentioned at the outset, Elias relied on habitus largely because it helped him to arrive at a more fundamental understanding of how internal steering mechanisms function. For the most part, second natures operate not only *in situ* but also beneath the level of consciousness. Expressing this crucial insight early in his career, Elias (1994 [1939]: 485–486, italics in original) argued that '[c]ivilization [...] is not a process within a separate sphere of "ideas" or "thought". It does not involve solely changes of "knowledge", transformations of "ideologies", in short alterations of the *content* of consciousness, but changes in the whole human makeup, within which ideas and habits of thought are only a single sector [...] [E]very investigation that considers only the consciousness of men, their "reason" or "ideas", while disregarding the structure of drives, the direction and form of human affects and passions, can be from the outset of only limited value.'

Elias saw that, in specific cases and during certain periods, habitus development could lag behind social structural transformations. Here we might return to the gradual 'courtisation' of the warrior class in late medieval Europe. For the first warriors undergoing transitions into new types of social spheres – contexts in which outbursts of violence (or otherwise 'giving free play to the emotions') put one at a distinct disadvantage – courtly manners were far from automatic. Elias argued that the ways of being required by the new situation were far from second nature to these newly 'civilised' warriors. Only if one took a longer view on courtisation could one grasp that habitus formation and social structural transformations are interdependent aspects of the same underlying development.[19]

So even if the concept of figuration can be treated as the first among equals, in Elias's scheme, there is another interpretation that is no less compelling. Thinking in terms of a unified process encompassing both structural dynamics and habitus formation processes, it would be senseless to say that either the first or the second is the prime motor of social development. Indeed, we find

Elias using habitus-in-figurations – just as Bourdieu did – to reject the very dichotomy between internal and external worlds.[20]

Although Bourdieu certainly elaborated on Elias's ideas about power, both authors can also be treated essentially as sociologists of *shifting configurations of power*. Elias never assumed that people would be able adequately to appraise, let alone put into words, the ways in which power relations emerge and operate within the figurations they comprise. Much like Bourdieu, he regarded a staunchly realist (objectivising) delineation of changing power imbalances to be the primary task of the sociologist. For him, it often went without saying that social configurations are always configurations of power and that the second natures operating in them (and to varying degrees produced by them) are by definition more or less empowering. After all, shifting 'power ratios' (or ever-changing 'balances' or 'distributions' of 'power chances') were, for Elias, the very stuff of human interdependence. From his perspective, people do not just need other people (for everything from physical and emotional contact to cognitive orientations); they need others – and are naturally oriented towards others – who are *objectively* more or less powerful than themselves. There are no feelings or thoughts about group formation (e.g. I or we are 'Irish') outside of power relations (e.g. with 'the English'). It would be absurd, Elias believed, to consider the habitus of a person or group as somehow separate from the (longer- or shorter-term) effects of specific experiences within specifically structured configurations of power. And to thematise a person's (or a group's) habitus was always already to discuss what is at least potentially a scarce power resource.

One of the clearest treatments of power resources in Elias came in his work with Scotson (1994 [1965]), *The Established and the Outsiders*. In this book, which now includes an introduction entitled 'A Theoretical Essay on Established and Outsider Relations' (added in 1976), Elias showed how newcomers to a working-class neighbourhood in 'Winston Parva' (a pseudonym for a city in the British midlands) were effectively forced into feeling inferior, as a group, to the more 'established' residents of the same neighbourhood. The key here was that emotionally charged group-formation processes took place despite the fact that the newer and older sets of residents had the same socioeconomic, ethnic, and religious backgrounds. True to form, Elias documented how feelings of 'group disgrace' no less than fantasies of 'group charisma' could not possibly be understood unless the overall field of relational dynamics served as the point of departure and the basic unit of analysis. Power was more explicitly thematised here than in other works because none of the usual suspects (income level, education, gender, ethnicity, religion, or sexual orientation) could help one to get a grip on the basic social divisions structuring the field of relational dynamics under interrogation.

Although this theoretical introduction showed how established and outsider figurations could be analysed by reference to long-term developments, *The Established and the Outsiders* itself was not based on the *longue durée*. After relating current visions and divisions to slightly longer-term developments (the newcomers had 'only' been living in Winston Parva for at most two or three generations), Elias and Scotson focused on the directly observable present. While the element of time remained crucial to their overall argument, their detailed analyses were based on here-and-now manifestations of the time-bound conflict. However, the conceptual approach taken in this study of unexpected power differentials was just as processual as those taken in studies based on developments over the course of several centuries. While delving into here-and-now aspects of a single community's (dis)integration issues, Elias based his analyses on ongoing transactions in a well-defined relational context of action, rather than on static entities presumed to exist before their interactions with one another. For Elias, focusing on self-enclosed individuals, the attributes of a given social group, or some disembedded belief system was never an option. And, of course, objective differences in position and prestige, too, had to be approached relationally as well as processually.

So what was the difference that made the difference in this particular setting? Why would the 'established' working-class residents see themselves as a 'group' over and above the 'group' of working-class residents who had 'only' been living in an adjacent part of the same neighbourhood for two or three generations? Most importantly, why were the newcomers effectively forced to measure themselves with a yardstick based on 'established' behavioural norms? The answer is that, relative to 'outsiders', the 'established' group displayed relatively high degrees of social cohesion and integration. A higher degree of social control and a more tightly-knit network allowed members of the established group to maintain myths about their intrinsic superiority as well as about the inherent, and therefore all the more shameful, inferiority of the newcomers.

Crucially, then, Elias and Scotson found that 'outsiders' were effectively unable to make up their own minds. They were forced by the compelling logic of the overall figuration and by virtue of the power wielded by the established residents to accept a stigmatising view of their 'kind' and themselves. Yet, because of their positions vis-à-vis the less powerful outsiders, the established in Winston Parva were also led into collective fantasies about their own superiority and about the need to maintain a certain distance from members of the inferior group. They were led by the structure and logic of figurational dynamics to adopt ideas and practices that seem to us no less absurd than the powdered wigs of eighteenth century France.[21]

The Established and the Outsiders contains still more theorising about how different types of power worked in this conflicted community. For instance, Elias and Scotson (1994: 155) explained why the mud that 'established' residents were successfully slinging would sooner or later stop sticking to the wall: 'Without their power', they wrote, 'the claim to a higher status and a specific charisma would soon decay and sound hollow whatever the distinctiveness of their behaviour'. In other words, neither utterances nor modes of behaviour (i.e. visible interactions) really drove the dynamics of stigmatisation. Less visible yet objective power differentials prestructured the dynamics of stigmatisation and the overall pattern of community relations.

Elias's empirical investigation of Winston Parva seems to have deeply influenced his thinking about the properties of figurations more generally. As the 1976 introduction indicates, he stressed that, whether or not extreme power inequalities were obviously present, figurations were marked by more established (dominant) and less established (dominated) poles. Indeed, he (1994: xxvi) claimed to see evidence of the selfsame 'pattern of stigmatisation used by high power groups in relation to their outsider groups [...] all over the world in spite of [...] cultural differences [...] [and even in settings where such dynamics] may at first be a little unexpected'. Drawing from an array of historical examples in that introduction, he argued that different kinds of power inequalities generate basically similar types of fantasies about the innate inferiority of groups characterised by less positional power. He held that, despite what one might see at first glace, the most fundamental power inequalities are never really based on such dimensions as race, caste, or ethnicity. If one goes back far enough, one finds that underlying forms of interdependence marked by objective power imbalances are precisely what prestructures social constructions of racial, caste, or ethnic groupness and otherness. These underlying, objective power inequities are what ensure that stigmatising attributions and classifications will be effective – in the minds of both the established and the outsiders. In setting after setting, it is 'the very condition of their outsider position and the humiliation and oppression that go with it' (Elias, 1994: xxvi) that enable and reproduce myths about (biological) attributes related to so-called racial, caste, or ethnic groups.[22]

In *The Established and the Outsiders* we arrive at something very close to Bourdieu's notions of social and symbolic capital. And similarities in terms of their thinking about power do not end here. In *An Invitation to Reflexive Sociology*, Bourdieu claimed that Elias was insufficiently sensitive to the properly *symbolic* power of the state and that the older master 'always fail[ed] to ask who benefits and suffers' from a state's monopoly over the use of legitimate violence (Bourdieu and Wacquant, 1992: 92–93). Yet, Elias's depiction of state formation in *The Civilizing Process* was explicitly and repeatedly linked to emerging class structures, most importantly in what would eventually become France. One of the main ideas here was that, to survive during the late Middle Ages, socially dominant groups had to monopolise the legitimate use of physical violence over ever-larger populations and tracks of land. Elias showed in detail that some stood to gain, while others were killed or forced to suffer as this process unfolded.

Elias and Bourdieu can, therefore, be treated as sociologists of power. And, on closer examination one finds profound similarities even in the ways they expressed their notions of (non-economic) power resources. The concept of the state monopoly over the 'means of violence' in the work of Elias was intended to counteract the economic determinism in Marx's theory, the notion that the bourgeoisie monopolised the 'means of production'. (Although Weber's definition of the state centred on the 'monopoly of the legitimate use of violence', he did use the term 'means' in this context.) Bourdieu tried to escape from a similar kind of Marxist 'economism' by adding to the classical concept of economic capital other types of capital: cultural, social, and symbolic types of assets being the most noteworthy. Thinking with and against Marx, both Elias and Bourdieu based their analyses on objective power differentials yet steered away from an approach that exaggerated the pervasiveness of economic forces in social life. Furthermore, their understanding of context-specific forms of power – in Elias's case, continua between poles analogous to those in Bourdieu's field based approach to power struggles – should be seen as one of their primary analytic insights, right alongside those of figuration and habitus.

As this discussion of power vis-à-vis habitus and field has documented, in Elias's hands these three main concepts merged into one extremely fruitful point of view. Therefore, just as with Bourdieu, when considering Elias's work we ought rather to speak of a triune than of a triadic approach to the study of social life.

Sport: Twists and Turns Towards a Hand-in-Hand Approach

Elias and Bourdieu were the only major sociologists of the twentieth century to take sport seriously. This is not the place to go into any great detail regarding this matter, but even a brief sketch of their overlapping approaches to the topic – combined with some summary reflections on what an Elias- and Bourdieu-inspired approach to sport might look like – can offer examples of uncanny and far-reaching complementarity.

In his 'Essay on Sport and Violence', Elias's theoretical sensitivities led him to investigate the '"sportization" of pastimes' in England as a particularly noteworthy example of a 'civilizing spurt' (1986: 22).[23] Starting in times when life and leisure seemed especially nasty and brutish – and then citing examples of the increasing pacification of the dominant classes in England during the eighteenth century (Whigs and Tories engaging in nonviolent political contests, peaceful transfers of power, and the institutionalisation of opposition as part and parcel of a functioning government) – Elias concluded that the '"parliamentarization" of the landed classes of England had its counterpart in the sportization of its pastimes' (Elias, 1986: 34). Fear and violence were once again central to Elias's simultaneously macro-, meso-, and micro-level analysis. And yet again, Elias's structuralist as well as constructivist approach highlighted the emerging positions and generative tastes of the dominant class (i.e. the established strata symbolically powerful enough to serve as a model for the more or less marginalised masses of outsiders). Here we see, again, in a nutshell, his triadic approach to sociological inquiry and his openness to longer-term historical perspectives.

Explicitly citing Elias's essay, Bourdieu stated that Elias was 'more sensitive than I am to continuity' (Bourdieu and Wacquant, 1992: 93). To some degree, he was convinced by Elias's arguments about broad structural transformations and corresponding shifts in habitus formation going back to the late Middle Ages. At the same time, he warned that longer-term analyses – such as those of Elias on sport – 'carry the danger of masking' (Bourdieu and Wacquant, 1992: 93) crucial historical breaks. Bourdieu seemed to think that longer-term analyses carry the risk of hiding as much as they reveal. He pointed out, for example, that from the eighteenth to the twentieth centuries, terms like athlete (or artist, dancer, etc.) took on ever-changing meanings. Because new fields (sport, literature) emerged and were fundamentally transformed – the world of sport became increasingly commercial and autonomous, and 'California sports' were introduced – such terms could be extremely misleading when used in more far-reaching historical analyses. He therefore questioned the validity of Elias's longer-term perspective on trends in leisure activities and sport. 'There is nothing in common', he (Bourdieu and Wacquant, 1992: 93, italics in original) argued, 'between ritual games such as medieval *soule* and American football'.

This was not Bourdieu, however, at his most convincing. His own analyses in *Masculine Domination* (2001) spanned both sides of the Mediterranean and reached back to antiquity. It is certainly true that longer-term perspectives can blind even the greatest of researchers to important aspects of the developments they address. For example, by treating them like any other institutional restraints, Elias seems to have downplayed the potentially 'civilising' effects of the church (Kempers, 1992; Turner, 2003). Bourdieu's own work and comments on Elias indicate, however, that he recognised the potential utility of longer-term analyses.

Furthermore, whether one finds this line of reasoning convincing or not, what Bourdieu left out of his comments on Elias's work on sport is as revealing as what he mentioned. It is Elias's eye for longer-term processes as well as his systematic thematisation of steadily increasing levels of emotional self-control (and feelings of shame with regard to physical violence) that make Elias's approach to sport potentially such a useful companion to the one devised by Bourdieu. Elias saw that, in sports as well as in many other fields, emotional-bodily self-control tends to operate as the most fundamental power resource and as a prerequisite to the sedimentation of all kinds of abilities and forms of knowledge. From this perspective, it makes perfect sense to ask how longer-term structural transformations made the development of increasingly regulated regimes of sport possible in the first place. It also makes sense to question how increasingly regulated regimes of sport might engender empowering levels of emotional stability and productive increases in self-discipline (cf. Wacquant, 2004). By contrast, when Bourdieu thematised bodily regulation through rituals of sport (and other disciplining rituals), it usually led him to discussions about the generation of docility – in the dual sense of becoming disposed to learning and becoming passive and easily manipulated (cf. Bourdieu, 1990a: 166–167). In terms of both the longer-term processes related to what are indeed increasingly regulated regimes of sports and the ways in which 'civilising' pressures emanating from rituals of sport can turn into *empowering* emotional self-constraints incarnate, Bourdieu seems to have missed out on a promising opportunity to score.

At the same time, Bourdieu's application of field theory to sport is an indispensable extension of Elias's work. Bourdieu showed much greater appreciation not only for important historical cleavages (think of 'professional football' in the early and late twentieth century) but also for how more or less convertible and distinctive forms of capital related to sport can operate in broader social (and especially class-based) conflicts. Another aspect of Bourdieusian thought that deserves special attention here is his sensitivity to body-based learning, knowledge, skills, and practical action. This – largely Merleau-Pontian – vision of the situated and lived body as the fundamental source of perceptions and preinterpretive 'strategies' is especially noteworthy because it makes advances on even Elias's vividly incarnated theorising about habitus formation and sport.

We can now pull these thoughts together and demonstrate how a combined approach to sport is more productive than one that relies exclusively on either Elias or Bourdieu. Let us take tennis as an example. From an Elias- and Bourdieu-inspired perspective, we can see that tennis is a prime example of an originally upper (middle) class sport that requires relatively high degrees of precision and, above all, socialised self-restraint. Even the occasional smash requires a modicum of restraint. And every successful serve-and-volley requires an (almost) automatically well-tempered touch. Using the original (sexist) language of the game, we can say that the stiff stances of the 'linesmen' during serves and the rigidly synchronised movements of the 'ballboys' between points are meticulously orchestrated and perpetually monitored. And no matter how large the crowd, there is silence before a serve even during the tensest of moments. Civility goes far beyond the fact that the players almost never fight. If a ball is hit hard and directly towards an opponent, or even if one unwittingly profits from the ball hitting the net, apologies are often offered by means of a rather subtle hand gesture. And no matter what is at stake, the ritual always closes down with handshakes over the net and with the appropriately elevated umpire symbolising legitimate authority. ('He is on high because he needs to see!') This final nod to the ultimate authority of the elevated is often accentuated by bows to any royalty that may be looking down from one of the appropriate boxes. After the fleeting and more or less intense emotional release, the timeless moral order is restored. Even if they do occasionally smash one of their many rackets or scream at an umpire, advanced tennis players never really let it rip; and one must wonder if they would be able to do so even if they tried.

From our combined theoretical approach, tennis appears to be an extremely restrained sport devised by, and played in front of, established groups. As surely as strength or speed, emotional self-restraint and social distinction seem the name of the game. Questions about how longer-term sociogenetic transformations – e.g. state formation, pacification, and shifting distributions of economic power – relate to the evolution of tastes and abilities in such a regulated pastime seem just as appropriate as questions about who has benefited, more recently, from enculturation processes centred on the old (and young) boys (and girls) network known in many contexts simply as 'the club'. More specifically, one might ask which types of people have been able to convert economic, cultural, and social capital (money for membership, knowledge of the 'right' sport and the 'appropriate' clubs, and connections with people who can help attain access to the club) into empowering socialisation processes for their children. On the outcome side, one might also think here of the development of middle- and upper-class ways of speaking, moving, feeling, and thinking as well as the building of social capital (business networks and opportunities) for adults and eventually their offspring. How does repeatedly moving together in time, in a bounded and in many cases elite microcosm, engender carnal connections and passionate group solidarities? Might these seemingly meaningless mutual reconstitutions among people with a good first serve be central to the formation of fantasies about self-made men, natural distinction, and the inherent inferiority of those who engage in less 'refined' sports like football, wrestling, darts, and auto racing? Drawing simultaneously from Elias and from Bourdieu also helps us to focus more closely on lived bodily coping in the here-and-now. Micro-situational pressures and a practical sense of the 'space of possible moves' infiltrate the whole being of (good) tennis players. For example, if a ball flies towards you while your opponent on the other side of the net is deep in her own territory, you are drawn – especially if you are an authentically competent player – immediately to the right comportment. Were it not for its disembodying connotations, 'feelings first, second thoughts' might be a good motto for what actually happens here. The main point is that your response is initiated quickly enough because it is *not* mediated by any time-consuming explicit mental representations. Certainly, you were already on the alert because you are playing tennis; now that this ball is screaming towards you, you cannot be accused of any conscious strategising as you react to this specific aspect of the flowing mix of injunctions. The new stance called forth by this emerging configuration of sanctions and invitations (e.g. the way you bend your knees before you lurch forward or the way you start to shift your grip on the racket) itself also influences your next feeling, movement, or 'position-taking'. Conscious thinking, if any finally occurs, should be considered the tip of the iceberg. In the heat of the moment, you almost certainly are not thinking consciously about what the lines on the court mean, why you care about winning, why you have invested time in such a sport, how you should move in the next instant, and so forth. At the very moment the ball charges towards you, your emerging responses are infused with projections based on countless previous experiences.

Zooming in allows us to see what social being in real time is actually like. It allows us to interrogate the workings, in Bourdieusian and Eliasian terms, of one's feel for an exceptionally distinctive and civilised game. That game is in you because you have been in the game. Along with others, you have been formed by the ongoing patterning we call tennis. It would be pointless to draw any sharp demarcations between internal and external, the mind and the body, reasonable projections into the likely future and emotional dispositions moulded in the past, the subjective sense of the player and the objective regularities of the game. We are in the flow now; what to play next?

Conclusion

We have specified some underlying similarities in the theoretical perspectives of Elias and Bourdieu. These similarities – or subterranean affinities, as we have also described them – centre around these thinkers' common deployment of three important concepts: habitus, field, and power. Despite outward differences in terminology (at times due to the vagaries of translation) – such as Elias's idea of habitus being rendered as 'personality structure' or as 'make-up', his notion of field as 'figuration', or Bourdieu's concept of power as 'capital' – the two thinkers effectively converged at least on the basic meanings of these concepts. They also thought in similar terms about the interrelation of these key ideas, as we have illustrated in our final substantive section on their respective analyses of sport. More importantly still, Elias and Bourdieu shared an emphasis on relational and processual thinking. Both reacted strongly against the substantialist tendencies pervasive in sociological theorising and research, and in place of these tendencies they elaborated an approach concerned primarily with situating their objects of study in ever-shifting and evolving webs or configurations of relations – in Harrison White's (1997: 60) felicitous phrase, 'processes-in-relations'. A century and a half ago, Marx opened the way for sociologists to think in relational and processual terms by analysing capital as a dynamic system not of 'things' but of social relations. In the early twentieth century, classical sociologists such as Simmel, classical pragmatists such as Dewey and Mead, and phenomenologists such as Heidegger and Merleau-Ponty further developed this theoretical perspective. In the mid to late twentieth century, it was arguably Elias and Bourdieu who most effectively served as the torch-bearers of this way of thinking.

It is important today that we recognise the deep commonalities and affinities in their approaches to sociological inquiry not merely as an intellectual or scholastic exercise but because it potentially serves as a stimulus to new advances in relational and processual analysis (see Emirbayer, 1997; Paulle, 2005). As we mentioned, Elias criticised long ago the tendency of sociologists (in this respect, he observed, they are like lay persons) to think in static and reified terms, that is, to engage in 'process-reduction'. This struggle against substantialism could never conclusively be won. Indeed, tendencies towards entity-based analysis are not uncommon in sociology even today, whether in the area of stratification research, where, as Bourdieu (1991: 381) pointed out, an 'alliance' reigns between quantitative methodology and 'modernized versions of methodological individualism, that is, the theory of rational action', or in areas of qualitative inquiry where, for example, racial and ethnic categories are sometimes still conceptualised as insular, bounded groups. (Brubaker, [2004] called the latter way of thinking 'groupism'.) Elias and Bourdieu provide, with their field-theoretic, power-centred, and habitus-based approaches, a valuable corrective to such tendencies, a way of doing sociology that serves us well as we move into the second decade of the twenty-first century.

To be sure, the shared theoretical orientation of Elias and Bourdieu needs to be generatively extended into a wide range of substantive fields of inquiry in the social sciences if it is to retain its relevance. We have seen the contributions their ideas can make to a sociology of sport – an enterprise that, however, still does not feature many of those ideas in its market-leading textbooks and anthologies. What might an Elias- or Bourdieu-inspired approach to comparative and historical sociology look like? Elias is widely regarded as an important contributor to that field, but his deeper theoretical insights have hardly been plumbed, not to mention Bourdieu's own ideas, especially since the latter are widely depicted as reproduction theory. What might an Elias- or Bourdieu-inspired organisational sociology look like? What impact might their ideas regarding habitus have in the present-day field of social psychology, where research agendas such as attribution theory, expectation states theory, and the like, often make it into the indexes of leading textbooks while 'Elias', 'Bourdieu', and 'habitus' merit nary a mention?[24] To date, whenever the strikingly unified and coherent systems of ideas of these two thinkers have been appropriated, it has been in piecemeal fashion, one concept at a time. How many thousands of studies have cited Bourdieu on 'cultural capital' without ever coming to terms with the larger framework of thought within which that concept does its work? A thorough engagement is surely necessary with the different subfields and research agendas currently dominant in sociology if the promise in Elias's and Bourdieu's sociologies is to be fully realised.

It is important in this regard that the academic divide between qualitative and quantitative inquiry be superseded, and, in particular, that formalised approaches be developed that 'think relationally' as Bourdieu once said of correspondence analysis – and, indeed, also processually. Social network analysts on the spatial side and sequence analysts on the temporal side have sought to elaborate new ways of furthering this goal on the quantitative and mathematical end of the standard divide. Elias never really attempted to move in such a direction himself. Bourdieu, by contrast, did – and his life's work manifested a long-term fascination with French-style data analysis in the tradition of Benzecri, a mode of analysis serving as the empirical basis of much of his analyses in *Distinction* and *The State Nobility*, among other major writings. Whether correspondence analysis as Bourdieu practised it is truly the best way to proceed is an open question, but sociology can surely benefit from other formal approaches that allow the field-, habitus- and power-oriented ideas of Elias and Bourdieu to be generalised. With his openness to formal modelling, Bourdieu certainly had the right intuition, even if the mathematical and statistical means of realising that vision were not yet fully available in his day (and might not be still in ours).

Largely unbeknownst to one another, and in implicit fashion primarily, Elias and Bourdieu complemented each other and pointed sociological inquiry in similar directions. They take their place as crucial figures in an ever-unfolding tradition of thought that needs generatively and creatively to be renewed with each passing decade if it is to remain living and vital. Much as these social thinkers each selectively appropriated from his predecessors in seeking to move sociology forward, so too must we take stock of their important theoretical contributions and then do something genuinely new upon that basis. Only then will this look back at the writings of Elias and Bourdieu have positive significance for theorisation and research in future sociology.

Notes

1 Indeed in 1991, the author of *State Nobility* expressed his indebtedness to the elder master at a memorial service in Amsterdam honouring the originality of Elias's contributions. An expanded version of this tribute would later be published under the title 'Rethinking the State: Genesis and Structure of the Bureaucratic Field' (Bourdieu, 1994).

2 We thank the Elias Foundation, and in particular Stephen Mennell, for allowing us access to Elias's and Bourdieu's personal correspondence.

3 Among others, Quilley and Loyal (2005: 812) and (Heinich, 2002) have also taken serious looks at the (dis)similarities between Elias and Bourdieu.

4 Another noteworthy difference between Elias and Bourdieu is that the former thematised (control over) ecological processes. This inspired Johan Goudsblom's (1992) *Fire and Civilisation* as well as his later work on the 'expanding anthroposphere' (De Vries and Goudsblom, 2002; see also Quilley, 2004).

5 The term triad might readily be associated with the most relational of all classical sociologists: Simmel. Among those acquainted with Elias's work, this term will also conjure up the 'triad of basic controls' in *What is Sociology* (1978 [1970]: 156–157). All earlier usages of the term are unrelated, however, to the way we are using 'triad' here.

6 Elias and Bourdieu foreshadowed the current interest in the lived body, the emotional brain, and neuroplasticity. This is not the place, however, to bring in how developments in neurobiology and cognitive science – e.g. those popularised by Damasio (2003: 55–56) – have effectively reinforced the (at times) overlapping arguments made by these two scholars long before the breakthroughs enabled by new generations of brain scans.

7 While Heidegger's role in Nazi Germany may make many Elias followers uncomfortable, and while Elias was notoriously uncomfortable about admitting where he got even his most profound ideas, Kilminster (2007: 19) is dead on when he notes that 'the attack on Cartesian rationalism, Kantianism, and conventional historiography in the work of Heidegger [...] was highly significant for Elias's development'. Furthermore, as Kilminster (2007: 20) notes, '[h]aving been on friendly terms [...] with [the likes of Hannah] Arendt (a pupil of Heidegger) [...] Elias must have had direct experience (and even insider knowledge) of the two dominant philosophical currents of the time in Freiburg – phenomenology and fundamental ontology.'

8 In Wacquant's dense yet tidy formulation, Bourdieu 'builds in particular on Maurice Merleau-Ponty's idea of the intrinsic *corporeality of the preobjective contact between subject and world* in order to restore the body as the source of practical intentionality, as the fount of intersubjective meaning grounded in the preobjective level of experience' (Bourdieu and Wacquant, 1992: 20, italics in original).

9 Or, as Durkhiem (1895: 127) originally phrased it: 'la société n'est pas une simple somme d'individus, mais le système formé par leur association représente une réalité spécifique qui a ses caractères propres.'

10 A field, for Bourdieu (Bourdieu and Wacquant, 1992: 97), can be defined as 'a network, or a configuration, of objective relations between positions. These positions are objectively defined, in their existence and in the determinations they impose upon their occupants, agents or institutions, by their present and potential situation (*situs*) in the structure of distribution of species of power (or capital) whose possession commands access to the specific profits that are at stake in the field, as well as by their objective relation to other positions (domination, subordination, homology, etc.).'

11 Wacquant (in Bourdieu and Wacquant, 1992: 18, italics in original) calls our attention to how Bourdieu described habitus as 'a *structuring mechanism* that operates from within agents, though it is neither strictly individual, nor in itself fully determinative of conduct […]. As the result of the internalization of external structures, habitus reacts to the solicitations of the field in a roughly coherent and systematic manner'.

12 This notion that the social space should be conceptualised primarily as a site of ongoing struggle becomes utterly clear in Bourdieu's various writings on the state. There he shows how the left hand of the state is associated primarily with the dominated dominants (academia and the arts, agencies pushing for better education and health care, and social workers), while the right hand of the state is associated primarily with the dominant dominants (the military and the monetary, agencies pushing for fiscal discipline at least for the poor, and the police). These weaker and stronger 'hands' correspond respectively to the upper-left quadrant (lower economic capital and greater cultural capital) and the upper-right quadrant (greater economic and lower cultural capital) of social space, as Bourdieu's diagrams often made clear.

13 In the original version, the final words were 'ins Feld der Beziehungsdynamik' (1997 [1939]: 230).

14 As Elias put it, in one of his many memorable passages from *The Civilizing Process* (1994 [1939]: 213–214), '[s]uch interdependencies are the nexus of what is here called the figuration, a structure of mutually oriented and dependent people. Since people are more or less dependent on each other first by nature and then through social learning, through education, socialization, and socially generated reciprocal needs, they exist, one might venture to say, only as pluralities, only in figurations'.

15 We wish to reiterate that this approach to social structures did not generate insights into processes associated with '(de)civilizaiton' alone. Elias (1994 [1939]: 482) exhibited the same type of thinking when, for example, he discussed the schoolchild who is assumed to possess 'creative intelligence' and to be a 'very special individual "natural talent"'. The very way of being that is singled out here, he argued, 'is only possible at all within a particular structure of power balances; its precondition is a quite specific social structure. And it depends further on access which the individual has, within a society so structured, to the kind of schooling [experiences] […] which alone permit […] capacity for independent individual thought to develop.'

16 Cf. original text (Elias, 1997 [1939] I: 76, 78, 82, 351; II: 49, 326, 330–331, 344).

17 In the following passage, Elias (1994 [1939]: 448) summed up his findings on *The Civilizing Process*: 'In general […] societies without a stable monopoly of force are always societies in which the division of functions is relatively slight and the chains of action binding individuals together are comparatively short. […] The moderation of spontaneous emotions, the tempering of affects, the extension of mental space beyond

the moment into the past and future, the habit of connecting events in terms of chains of cause and effect – all of these are aspects of the same transformation of conduct which necessarily takes place with the monopolization of physical violence, and the lengthening of chains of social action and interdependence. It is a "civilizing" change of behavior.'

18 In essays originally penned in the 1940s and 50s, although they were published much later, Elias (1991: 115–116 and 122–123) developed ideas quite similar to Bourdieu's notions of 'specialised' or 'secondary' habitus (e.g. the pugilistic habitus that Wacquant [2004] acquired in a boxing gym as an adult).

19 From this vantage point, as Elias (1989: 336) wrote, one cannot 'clearly recognize the connections between – whatever it is – "society" and "culture", "state" and "individual", "external" and "internal" steering mechanisms, unless ones conceptualizes them as something in movement, as aspects of social processes that are themselves processes, indeed as functionally interdependent processes involving varying degrees of harmony and conflict.'

20 It would be incorrect, however, to deduce from this that Elias was out to destroy 'the agent' or, as the expression goes, that he left too little 'room for agency'. Elias stressed time and again that individuals acquire 'dispositions' of their own. Exploring this idea before the Second World War, he (in Mennell and Goudsblom, 1998: 73) pointed out: 'Of course, the dispositions which slowly evolve in the new-born child are never simply a copy of what is done to him by others. They are entirely his. They are his response to the way in which his drives and emotions, which are by nature oriented towards other people, are responded to and satisfied by the others'. To this, Elias (in Mennell and Goudsblom, 1998: 73) added elsewhere: 'However certain it may be that each person is a complete entity in himself, it is no less certain that the whole structure of his self-control, both conscious and unconscious, is a product of interweaving formed in a continuous interplay of relationships to other people.'

21 Here again, Elias exhibited a sharp eye for the short-term socialisation pressures exerted on adolescents. Because of countless everyday injunctions, youth growing up 'on the wrong side of the tracks' could not help but experience themselves as members of a group deemed 'inferior by "nature" to the established group' (Elias and Scotson, 1994: 159). More specifically, greater social cohesion and control (mediated in many cases through gossip) ensured that established working-class residents could typically induce outsider youth to accept an image of themselves modelled on the 'minority of the worst' and an image of themselves modelled on a 'minority of the best'.

22 Trying to express his ideas about power more clearly, Elias repeatedly returned, in his more theoretical remarks (e.g. a chapter entitled 'Game Models' in *What is Sociology?*), to the shifting power differentials in various kinds of games. Sticking to reflections on a football match, he (1978: 131) asserted that 'the concept of power has [to be] transformed from a concept of substance to a concept of relationship': 'At the core of changing figurations', he wrote, '[…] – indeed at the very hub of the figuration process – is a fluctuating, tensile equilibrium, a balance of power moving to and fro, inclining first to one side and then to another. This kind of fluctuating balance of power is a structural characteristic of the flow of every figuration.'

23 This essay was first published (in French) in 1976, in the journal founded a year earlier by Bourdieu, *Actes de la recherche en sciences sociales*. It was later reprinted in shorter form in Elias and Dunning's (1986: 150–174) *Quest for Excitement*.

24 Anyone wishing to verify this statement might peruse, for example, the index of Michener et al.'s Fifth Edition of *Social Psychology* (2004).

References

Bourdieu, Pierre (1984 [1979]) *Distinction: A Social Critique of the Judgement of Taste,* trans. Richard Nice, London: Routledge & Kegan Paul.

Bourdieu, Pierre (1986) 'The Forms of Capital', in John G. Richardson (ed.) *Handbook of Theory of Research for the Sociology of Education*, New York: Greenword Press, pp. 241–258.

Bourdieu, Pierre (1990 [1980]) *The Logic of Practice,* trans. Richard Nice, Cambridge: Polity Press.

Bourdieu, Pierre (1990a) *In Other Words: Essays Towards a Reflexive Sociology,* trans. Matthew Adamson, Stanford: Stanford University Press.

Bourdieu, Pierre (1991) 'Epilogue: On the Possibility of a Field of World Sociology', in Pierre Bourdieu and James S. Coleman (eds.) *Social Theory for a Changing Society*, Boulder: Westview, pp. 373–378.

Bourdieu, Pierre (1993) *The Field of Cultural Production: Essays on Art and Literature*, Cambridge: Polity Press.

Bourdieu, Pierre (1994) 'Rethinking the State: Genesis and Structure of the Bureaucratic Field', *Sociological Theory* 12(1): 1–18.

Bourdieu, Pierre (1996 [1992]) *The Rules of Art: Genesis and Structure of the Literary Field,* trans. Susan Emanuel, Stanford: Stanford University Press.

Bourdieu, Pierre (1998) *Acts of Resistance: Against the New Myths of Our Time,* trans. Richard Nice, New York: New Press.

Bourdieu, Pierre (2000 [1997]) *Pascalian Meditations*, trans. Richard Nice, Stanford: Stanford University Press.

Bourdieu, Pierre (2001 [1998]) *Masculine Domination*, trans. Richard Nice, Cambridge: Polity Press.

Bourdieu, Pierre and Jean-Claude Passeron (1977 [1970]) *Reproduction in Education, Society, and Culture*, trans. Richard Nice, London: Sage.

Bourdieu, Pierre and Loïc Wacquant (1992) *An Invitation to Reflexive Sociology*, Cambridge: Polity Press.

Bourgois, Philippe (1995) *In Search of Respect: Selling Crack in El Barrio*, Cambridge: Cambridge University Press.

Brubaker, Rogers (2004) *Ethnicity Without Groups*, Cambridge: Harvard University Press.

Damasio, Antonio (2003) *Looking for Spinoza: Joy, Sorrow, and the Feeling Brain*, New York: Harcourt.

Durkheim, Émile (1895) *Les Règles de la méthode sociologique,* Paris: Felix Alcan.

Durkheim, Émile (1966 [1895]) *The Rules of Sociological Method*, trans. W. D. Halls, New York: Free Press.

Durkheim, Émile (1995 [1912]) *The Elementary Forms of Religious Life*, trans. Karen E. Fields, New York: Free Press.

Elias, Norbert (1956) 'Problems of Involvement and Detachment', *British Journal of Sociology* 7(3): 226–252.

Elias, Norbert (1978 [1970]) *What is Sociology?*, trans. Stephen Mennell and Grace Morrissey, New York: Columbia University Press.

Elias, Norbert (1983 [1969]) *The Court Society*, trans. Edmund Jephcott, Oxford: Basil Blackwell.

Elias, Norbert (1987 [1983]) *Involvement and Detachment*, trans. Edmund Jephcott, Oxford: Blackwell.

Elias, Norbert (1987) 'The Retreat of Sociologists into the Present', *Theory, Culture & Society* 4(2–3): 223–249.

Elias, Norbert (1994 [1939]) *The Civilizing Process: The History of Manners and State Formation and Civilization*, trans. Edmund Jephcott, Oxford: Blackwell.

Elias, Norbert (1996) *The Germans: Power Struggles and the Development of Habitus in the Nineteenth and Twentieth Centuries*, trans. Eric Dunning and Stephen Mennell, New York: Columbia University Press.

Elias, Norbert (1997 [1939]) *Über den Prozeß der Zivilisation*. Bazel: Haus Zum Falken.

Elias, Norbert and Eric Dunning (1986) *Quest for Excitement: Sport and Leisure in the Civilizing Process*, Oxford: Basil Blackwell.

Elias, Norbert and John Scotson (1994 [1965]) *The Established and the Outsiders: A Sociological Enquiry into Community Problems*, London: Sage.

Emirbayer, Mustafa (1997) 'Manifesto for a Relational Sociology', *American Journal of Sociology* 103(2): 281–317.

Emirbayer, Mustafa and Erik Schneiderhan (forthcoming) 'Dewey and Bourdieu on Democracy', in Philip S. Gorski (ed.) *Bourdieuian Theory and Historical Analysis*, Durham: Duke University Press.

Goudsblom, Johan (1987) *De sociologie van Norbert Elias*, Amsterdam: Meulenhoff.

Goudsblom, Johan and Stephen Mennell (1998) *The Norbert Elias Reader: A Biographical Selection*, Oxford: Blackwell.

Heinich, Nathalie (1997) *La sociologie de Norbert Elias*, Paris: La Decouverte.

Kempers, Bram (1992) *Painting, Power and Patronage: The Rise of the Professional Artist in Renaissance Italy*, New York: Allen Lane.

Kilminster, Richard (2007) *Norbert Elias: Post-philosophical Sociology*, London: Routledge.

Krieken, Robert van (1998) *Norbert Elias*, London: Routledge.

Lukes, Steven (1973) *Emile Durkheim: His Life and Work*, Harmondsworth: Penguin.

Mennell, Stephen and Johan Goudsblom (eds.) (1998) *Norbert Elias: On Civilization, Power and Knowledge*, London: University of Chicago Press.

Michener, H. Andrew, John D. DeLamater, and Daniel J. Myers (2004) *Social Psychology*, Fifth Edition, Belmont: Thomson Wadsworth.

Paulle, Bowen. (under contract) *Toxic Schools*. Chicago: University of Chicago Press.

Quilley, Stephen (2004) 'Ecology, "human nature, " and civilizing processes: Biology and Sociology in the Work of Norbert Elias', in Steven Loyal and Stephan Quilley (eds.) *The Sociology of Norbert Elias*, Cambridge: Cambridge University Press.

Quilley, Stephen and Steven Loyal (2005) 'Eliasian Sociology as a "Central Theory" for the Human Sciences', *Current Sociology* 53; 807–828.

Ritzer, George and Douglas J. Goodman (2004) *Sociological Theory*, Fifth Edition, Boston: McGraw Hill.

Shusterman, Richard (ed.) (1999) *Bourdieu: A Critical Reader*, Oxford: Blackwell Publishers.

Turner, Bryan (2003) 'Warrior Charisma and the Spiritualization of Violence', *Body and Society* 9(4): 93–10.

Vries, Bert de and Johan Goudsblom (eds.) (2002). *Mappae Mundi - Humans and their Habitats in a Socio-Ecological Perspective: Myths, Maps, Methods and Models*, Amsterdam: Amsterdam University Press.

White, Harrison C. (1997) 'Can Mathematics Be Social? Flexible Representations for Interaction Process and its Sociocultural Constructions', *Sociological Forum* 12(1): 53–71.

Wacquant, Loïc (2004) *Body and Soul: Notebooks of an Apprentice Boxer*, Oxford: Oxford University Press.

Wacquant, Loïc (2006) 'Pierre Bourdieu' in Rob Stones (ed.) *Key Contemporary Thinkers*, Second Edition, London and New York: Macmillan.

CHAPTER EIGHT

Bourdieu and Adorno on the Transformation of Culture in Modern Society: Towards a Critical Theory of Cultural Production

Simon Susen

Introduction

This chapter examines the transformation of culture in modern society by drawing upon the works of Pierre Bourdieu and Theodor W. Adorno. Far from intending to embrace the entire complexity of Bourdieusian and Adornian thought, the analysis focuses on some key dimensions that are particularly relevant to understanding the relationship between modern culture and modern society. This study seeks to show that comprehending the transformation of culture in the modern world requires taking into account the transformation of society as a whole. In order to demonstrate this, the chapter is structured as follows.

The first section briefly elucidates *the concept of culture*. Given the central importance of the concept of culture for the analysis of this chapter, it seems sensible to clarify its different meanings. If the concept of culture can be used and defined in several ways, it is necessary to specify with which of its various meanings the present study is mainly concerned.

The second section centres upon *Bourdieu's analysis of culture*. More specifically, the Bourdieusian approach to culture allows us to understand the transformation of culture in modern society in terms of three significant tendencies: (i) the differentiation of culture, (ii) the commodification of culture, and (iii) the classification of culture. Taken together, these three social processes are indicative of the complexification of culture in the modern world, which manifests itself in the emergence of an increasingly powerful 'cultural economy'.

The third section gives an overview of some of the key elements of *Adorno's analysis of culture*. Similarly to the methodology of the previous section, the

Adornian approach to culture is scrutinised by differentiating three tendencies that are symptomatic of the transformation of culture in modern society: (i) the heteronomisation of culture, (ii) the commodification of culture, and (iii) the standardisation of culture. In essence, these three social developments are due to the colonisation of culture by industrial capitalism, leading to the rise of the 'culture industry'.

The fourth section offers a brief *comparison* between the Bourdieusian and the Adornian accounts of the transformation of culture in modern society. Instead of opposing Bourdieusian and Adornian strains of thought to one another, this section suggests that the similarities between the two approaches permit us not only to compare them, but also to integrate them and thereby to enrich our understanding of the transformation of culture in modern society.

I. Preliminary Reflections on Culture

The concept of culture is far from unambiguous, for it can be used and defined in different ways. Despite the variety of its meanings, we can distinguish three main conceptions of culture: culture as a *sociological* category, culture as a *philosophical* category, and culture as an *aesthetic* category.

First, as a sociological category, the concept of culture refers to a specific *form of life* produced and reproduced by a given group of people. From this perspective, 'culture is a description of a particular way of life, which expresses certain meanings and values not only in art and learning but also in institutions and ordinary behaviour' (Williams, 1994: 48). In this sense, culture can be regarded as a sociological, and indeed an anthropological, category which describes a particular – that is, a spatiotemporally specific – way in which a given form of human coexistence is organised.[1]

Second, as a philosophical category, the concept of culture can be conceived of as a human *ideal*, that is, as a distinctively human quality to which all mature subjects should aspire. According to this conception, the formation of humanity depends on the creation of culture. Thus, the notion of culture describes 'a state or process of human perfection, in terms of certain absolute or universal values' (Williams, 1994: 48). This view is situated in the German tradition of idealist thought, which suggests that culture can be identified with the realm of 'the mind' or 'the spirit'. From this perspective, the existence of the transcendental realm of culture manifests itself in the existence of the material realm of society: 'the cultural spirit' of humankind is embodied in the consolidation of ever more sophisticated social institutions, constituting evolutionary expressions of the transcendental quality of culture. In this sense, culture can be seen as a philosophical category which captures the species-constitutive properties of human civilisation. In other words, the project of society is driven by the anthropological quest for the development of humanity through the creation of culture: the *Bildung der Gesellschaft* (the formation of society) depends on the *Bildung der Menschen* (the education of the people).[2]

Third, as an aesthetic category, the concept of culture denotes a distinctively human expression of *artistic creativity*. Hence, 'culture is the body of intellectual and imaginative work, in which, in a detailed way, human thought and experience are variously recorded' (Williams, 1994: 48). From this point of view, culture constitutes a vehicle for creativity and imagination, capable of challenging and developing both the rational and the emotional potentials of human existence. Human subjects are capable of elevating themselves above their own existence through the existence of culture: it is by virtue of culture that the distinctively human exercise of artistic transcendence can be realised. In this sense, culture can be considered as an aesthetic category which refers to the human capacity to attribute meaning to the world through the expressive power of artistic production.

It is this third – that is, the aesthetic – perspective that is particularly important for the analysis of culture developed in the present chapter. This does not mean that the sociological and philosophical approaches to culture are irrelevant or that they can be ignored. On the contrary, all three interpretations have to be taken into account: the sociological, philosophical, and aesthetic meanings of culture are closely interrelated and should not be regarded as mutually exclusive. Every human form of life is permeated by ideals and allows for artistic creativity; human ideals are influenced by particular forms of life and can be articulated through artistic creativity; and artistic creativity is situated in specific forms of life and often inspired by human ideals. In short, the *sociological*, *philosophical*, and *aesthetic* potentials of culture are symptomatic of the *normative*, *purposive*, and *creative* nature of human life.

Whatever theoretical approach to culture one may wish to defend, the transformation of culture in the modern world cannot be fully understood without accounting for the transformation of society in modern history: the rise of mass culture is inextricably linked to the emergence of bourgeois society. To suggest that cultural criticism is necessarily a form of social criticism is to recognise that culture is embedded in society. As remains to be shown, Bourdieu and Adorno articulate two diverging but complementary accounts of the relationship between culture and society. In the following sections, the transformation of culture in modern society shall be explored by looking at the theoretical approaches developed by these two thinkers.

II. Bourdieusian Reflections on Culture: The Cultural Economy

Bourdieu's sociological theory can also be regarded as a cultural theory in that it presupposes that the comprehensive study of society must be committed to the critical examination of culture.[3] Put differently, there is no general theory of society without a general theory of culture. In order to understand the transformation of culture in the modern world from a Bourdieusian perspective, we need to examine three social processes: (i) the *differentiation* of culture, (ii) the *commodification* of culture, and (iii) the *classification* of culture.

i) The Differentiation of Culture

Inasmuch as Bourdieu's general sociology of society is a general theory of the economics of material practice, 'his general sociology of culture is a general theory of the economics of symbolic practice' (Lash, 1993: 193). A critical sociology of human practices must strive to understand both the economy of material practices *and* the economy of symbolic practices, for the former and the latter are intimately interrelated. If we acknowledge that cultural relations are necessarily embedded in material relations just as material relations are unavoidably situated in cultural relations, then we also need to recognise that every society produces its own cultural economy.

The power of *social stratification* depends on society's capacity to reproduce itself through an economy of *cultural differentiation*. The reproduction of class relations cannot be dissociated from the reproduction of cultural relations: in order to comprehend how social hierarchies are consolidated and sustained we need to account for the ways in which they are symbolically mediated and legitimated. To be more precise, economic and cultural relations are both interdependent and interpenetrative power relations: as *interdependent* power relations, they function in relation to one another to ensure their efficiency; as *interpenetrative* power relations, they colonise one another to guarantee their ubiquity.[4] This is not to suggest that class relations can be derived from, or even reduced to, cultural relations; rather, this is to accept that the material power of class relations is inconceivable without the symbolic power of cultural relations.

The rise of capitalism led to the 'autonomization of intellectual and artistic production' (Bourdieu, 1993 [1971/1985]: 112). For one consequence of capitalist modernisation is the emergence of relatively independent fields of cultural production. The modern world is characterised by the appearance of two main cultural fields: 'the *field of restricted production*' and 'the *field of large-scale cultural production*' (ibid.: 115, italics in original). Both constitute social arenas which are aimed at the production of cultural goods. Yet, whereas the cultural creations of the former are 'objectively destined for a public of producers of cultural goods' (ibid.), the cultural creations of the latter are 'destined for non-producers of cultural goods, "the public at large"' (ibid.).

Hence, the transformation of the cultural sphere in modern society manifests itself in the *binary differentiation* between the 'restricted production' and the 'large-scale production' of cultural goods. The more the former succeeds in separating itself from the latter, the more profound 'the dialectic of cultural distinction' (ibid.) turns out to be. To the extent that the restricted fields of cultural production can claim relative autonomy from the universally accessible fields of cultural production, the heterodoxy and idiosyncrasy of the former must be distinguished from the orthodoxy and conventionality of the latter. In this sense, the autonomisation of the cultural sphere in the modern world constitutes a particular characteristic of 'the field of restricted production', since it is capable of functioning independently of the imperatives that govern the mass-oriented nature of 'large-scale production'. A relatively autonomous field is a relationally constructed social realm able to assert its existence by virtue of its own logic of functioning. Therefore, 'the autonomy of a field of restricted production can be measured by its power to define its own criteria for the production and evaluation of its products' (ibid.). Autonomous culture can only be created by its own creators, judged by its own judges, and appreciated by its own appreciators.

The autonomy of every field is based on its capacity to create and maintain its own codes of legitimacy, through which it distinguishes itself from the imperatives that govern the logic of other fields of social reality. 'Thus, the more cultural producers form a closed field of competition for cultural legitimacy, the more the internal demarcations appear irreducible to any external factors of economic, political or social differentiation' (ibid.). It is the gradual liberation from the constraints of economic reproduction which allows the cultural field to generate conditions of social refraction.

If the 'degree of autonomy of a field has as a main indicator its power of refraction, of retranslation' (Bourdieu, 1997a: 16)[5], the degree of heteronomy of a field has as a main indicator its power of assimilation, of absorption. The relative autonomy of the field of restricted cultural production is inconceivable without the relative heteronomy of the field of large-scale cultural production. Contrary to the former, the latter 'principally obeys the imperatives of competition for conquest of the market' (Bourdieu, 1993 [1971/1985]: 125). Thus, it is not only largely dependent upon the logic of the market, but it is in fact driven by it. The autonomisation of cultural production in the privileged sphere of the *société distinguée* goes hand in hand with the heteronomisation of cultural production in the popularised sphere of the *société massifiée*. Whereas the former is granted the power to bypass the imperatives of the market, the latter is largely governed by them. The conquest of artistic autonomy can challenge the ubiquity of economic instrumentality; the surrender to artistic heteronomy confirms the absorbability of culture by economic functionality.

To be sure, all cultural fields – that is, both the field of restricted cultural production and the field of large-scale cultural production – are *irreducible* to other social fields (see Susen, 2007: 289). Even the ubiquitous power of the economic field cannot eliminate the potentiality of culture towards autonomous reproduction. It would be naïve to assume that the fields of artistic production are completely independent from the economic organisation of society, but it would also be misleading to suggest that the fields of artistic production depend entirely on the economic constitution of society. By definition, the relation between fields of artistic production and fields of economic production is characterised by both relative autonomy and relative heteronomy: the former are relatively *autonomous* insofar as they can never be totally determined by the latter; at the same time, the former are relatively *heteronomous* insofar as they cannot exist independently of the latter. Nevertheless, whereas the field of large-scale cultural production depends directly on the imperatives of the market, the field of restricted cultural production derives its relative autonomy from its capacity to circumvent the logic of economic functioning that prevails in modern capitalist societies. The autonomisation of culture, then, is both a reality and a potentiality: as a reality, it is *always already* existent, challenging the hegemonic universality of large-scale cultural production; as a potentiality, it is *always still* to be realised, affirming the self-sufficient particularity of restricted cultural production.

The binary differentiation of culture is symptomatic of the historical shift from traditional to modern society. In traditional societies, artistic production is largely controlled and regulated 'by a small number of very powerful legitimising forces or agents' (Jenkins, 1992: 135). In advanced capitalist societies, by contrast, artistic production is increasingly divided between the realm of large-scale cultural production, which is driven by the imperatives of the economy, and the realm of small-scale cultural production, which is shaped by the quest for symbolic autonomy.

ii) The Commodification of Culture

Cultural production under capitalism leads to the creation of *symbolic goods*, a term standing for 'a two-faced reality, a commodity and a symbolic object' (Bourdieu, 1993 [1971/1985]: 113). Symbolic goods can be described as the ambivalent carriers of both cultural and economic values that are only *relatively* independent from each other, since the cultural sanction may come to reinforce their economic consecration, just as 'the economic sanction may come to reinforce their cultural consecration' (ibid.). The potential autonomy of these goods is reflected in their symbolic nature; their potential heteronomy, on the other hand, manifests itself in their commodity character. In other words, under capitalism the cultural *use value* of symbolic goods is gradually colonised by their economic *exchange value*. The commodification of culture represents a central feature of late capitalist society, illustrating the ineluctable entanglement of use value and exchange value which permeates every market-driven 'economy of cultural goods' (Bourdieu, 1984 [1979]: 1).

The economy of cultural goods can be regarded as an integral component of late capitalist reproduction. Inasmuch as commodities are increasingly culturalised, culture is increasingly commodified in late capitalism. The ambivalence of symbolic goods consists in the simultaneous articulation of their *autonomy*, rooted in the power of cultural creativity, and of their *heteronomy*, regulated by the logic of economic functionality. As symbolic objects, they reaffirm the undeniable strength of cultural forces; as material objects, they illustrate the inescapable presence of economic forces. To the extent that symbolic objects cannot break away from the parameters of the material world, economic objects cannot escape from the parameters of the cultural world. In capitalist society, symbolic goods are unavoidably absorbed by the imperatives of market forces. The particularity of symbolic goods stems from their cultural idiosyncrasy, just as the universality of symbolic goods derives from their systemic commodifiability.

Both the production and the consumption of culture require that subjects are equipped with a subjectively internalised system of collectively constructed schemes of perception, appreciation, and action: the *habitus*.[6] To be more precise, the habitus constitutes 'an acquired system of generative schemes objectively adjusted to the particular conditions in which it is constituted' (Bourdieu, 1977 [1972]: 95). Hence, the habitus forms a dynamic conglomerate of generative classificatory structures subjectively internalised and intersubjectively developed: the habitus exists inside subjects' subjectivities, but it 'only exists in, through and because of the practices of actors and their interaction with each other and with the rest of their environment' (Jenkins, 1992: 75). As a *sens pratique* – literally, a 'practical sense' (see Bourdieu, 1976 and 1980) – the habitus represents 'a structured and structuring structure'[7] by virtue of which actors shape their environment whilst at the same time being shaped by it. To the extent that society is driven by the functional imperatives of the cultural economy, human agency is permeated by the power of symbolic determinacy. A market of symbolic goods cannot be divorced from a market of symbolic capacities; a market of cultural fields cannot dispense with a market of a cultural habitus.

To be sure, the *commodification* of culture is not limited to the *creation* but extends to the *consumption* of culture. For not only the *production* but also the *perception* and *reception* of culture become increasingly commodified in capitalist societies. The power of culture is only conceivable as 'symbolic power' (Bourdieu, 1992 [1977])[8], that is, as a form of power which determines how we make sense, or how we fail to make sense, of reality by virtue of cultural codes. The more commodified the symbolic world in capitalist societies, the more our capacity to participate in the cultural world becomes subject to the force of exchange value. The more the market succeeds in imposing itself as the ultimate source of social legitimacy, the more it manages to transform our habitus into a subjective appendage of systemic commodifiability.

The commodification of culture reinforces 'the affirmation of the primacy of form over function, of the mode of representation over the object of representation, [...] of the saying over the thing said' (Bourdieu, 1993 [1971/1985]: 117), of the signifiers over the signified, in short, of appearance over substance. Cultural struggles are always struggles over the parameters of social legitimacy. In advanced industrial societies, a commodified culture is quasi-naturally legitimated by the systemic hegemony of the capitalist mode of production. The degree of commodification of culture indicates the degree of colonisation of society by the market. In order for a cultural product to succeed in a market-driven society, it needs to prioritise its external form and representational transcendence over its internal content and social immanence. A cultural commodity draws its symbolic power not from its material substance but from its social significance. When we buy into the symbolic power of cultural commodities we are subject to both the powerful nature of the symbolic and the symbolic nature of power: we seek to acquire the value the commodity *represents*, and we aim to obtain the authority the commodity *contains*. To feel both represented and empowered by a cultural commodity means to identify with and subscribe to it. The commodifiability of culture confirms the ubiquity of the market.

iii) The Classification of Culture

'If modernization entails the differentiation of an autonomous aesthetic field, then the appreciation of (modern) art that this brings about entails the inculcation of a "differentiated" habitus' (Lash, 1993: 197). The complexification of cultural fields manifests itself in the emergence of increasingly differentiated forms of cultural habitus. In order for a relatively autonomous aesthetic field to be created and appreciated by the 'distinguished' parts of society, its members need to develop and share a 'distinguished' form of collective habitus, allowing them to articulate their cultural idiosyncrasy by virtue of their codified legitimacy. The legitimacy of every social field depends on the legitimacy of its actors. Without necessarily being aware of their field-specific determinacy, human actors have a tendency to reproduce the legitimacy of the specific social fields in which they find themselves immersed.

In order to convert themselves into effective carriers of legitimacy, social actors need to be capable of translating the schemes of classification and distinction which are imposed upon them *by* the world into parameters of differentiation and stratification which are projected by them *upon* the world. There are no reliable forms of social reproduction without effective patterns of social identification: identifying with particular codes of legitimacy, we situate ourselves in the world as reproductive participants of society. Powerful forms of legitimation require efficient types of classification. Hence, to the extent that the social world is divided by different fields with multiple codes of legitimacy, social actors are divided by different forms of habitus with various types of capital. In order to participate in a cultural field, we need to acquire cultural capital. In order to play a part in the economic field, we need to attain economic capital. In order to be involved in society, we need to dispose of social capital. Our habitus is composed of different forms of capital, which enable us to position ourselves in different fields of society. In short, *a legitimately situated actor is a legitimately classified and classifying actor.*

The struggle for and against classification is dialectical in that 'economic *and* cultural capital are both the objects *and* the weapons of a competitive struggle between classes' (Jenkins, 1992: 142, italics in original). The functionalisation of cultural capital by economic capital and the functionalisation of economic capital by cultural capital constitute two complementary social processes which lie at the heart of the cultural economy. Inasmuch as the differentiation of economic capital contributes to the reproduction of social stratification, the differentiation of cultural capital reinforces the classificatory power of symbolic domination.

The economic and cultural reproduction strategies of society stem from a 'competitive struggle' (ibid.) over power and resources, that is, from a struggle which defines the separation between the dominated and the dominant classes. This '[c]ompetitive struggle is the form of class struggle which the dominated classes allow to be imposed on them when they accept the stakes offered by the dominant classes. It is an integrative struggle and, by virtue of the initial handicaps, a reproductive struggle, since those who enter this chase, in which they are beaten before they start [...], implicitly recognize the legitimacy of the goals pursued by those whom they pursue, by the mere fact of taking part' (Bourdieu, 1984 [1979]: 165). Hence, class struggle is a struggle over the legitimacy of a given form of social reproduction.

'Productive interests in the artistic field [...] find "homologies" with class interests in the social field' (Lash, 1993: 197)[9]. Essentially, cultural classification systems reflect the socio-economic division of the class system (cf. Fowler, 1997: 48–49). The division of labour manifests itself in the division of culture: economic forms of social segregation go hand in hand with cultural forms of social classification. The instrumentalisation of culture as both a target and a vehicle of legitimacy is due to the fact that 'art and cultural consumption are predisposed, consciously and deliberately or not, to fulfil a social function of legitimating social differences' (Bourdieu, 1984 [1979]: 7). Since cultural forms do not constitute invariant and natural categories, they can be efficiently integrated into the social construction of structural differences between human subjects. In other words, inasmuch as cultural forms are socially constructed, their contingency can be efficiently functionalised by the contingency of the class system of a given society. The spatiotemporally determined contingency of social domination is symptomatic of the relative arbitrariness of social classification.

The consumption of culture depends on subjects' capacity to absorb and interpret culture. Yet, our capacity to make sense of the cultural world reflects a socially acquired, rather than naturally given, competence: our perception *of* the world is shaped by our social engagement *with* the world. Just as the internalisation of our external world cannot be separated from the externalisation of our inner world, the externalisation of our inner world cannot be divorced from the internalisation of our external world.

Our perceptive faculty (*Wahrnehmungsvermögen*) is both a capacity (*Vermögen* in the sense of *Fähigkeit*) and a property (*Vermögen* in the sense of *Besitz*): as a capacity, it ensures *that* we are able to absorb and interpret the world; as a property, it determines *how* we absorb and interpret the world. Put differently, our perceptive faculty is based both on our ability to comprehend the world and on our mastery of the field-specific tools that determine the ways in which we comprehend the world. Thus, the consumption of culture through our perceptive apparatus is never a neutral but always an interested act, that is, it constitutes a social performance that is permeated by relationally determined schemes of legitimacy.

Authoritative 'talents of perception' emanate from powerful 'programmes for perception' (Bourdieu, 1984 [1979]: 2). Culture and art can be systematically transformed into instruments of social distinction (cf. Robbins, 1991: 121). Even the seemingly most personal taste and even the ostensibly most individual form of aesthetic judgement contain implicit references to socially pre-established patterns of appreciation and perception. The perceived is never simply 'out there' but it is always also 'in here': that is, *in* the eye of the perceiver. By definition, every perception of reality is composed of both a perceived object and a perceiving subject. The perceived object allows for the fact *that* something is to be perceived; the perceiving subject determines *how* it is to be perceived. Certainly, perception is not a solitary affair. Even the most personal perceptions are shaped by collectively constructed patterns of classification assimilated by socialised individuals. The perceiver exists never simply 'in himself' or 'in herself', but always 'in relation to other selves'. Legitimacy is a product not of individual determinacy but of social acceptability. We become who we are in relation to what surrounds us. Our perception *of* the world is not absolved from our determination *by* the world. Only if the act of perception is understood in terms of its social and historical contingency can we succeed in comprehending the nature of culture in terms of its collective determinacy.

Patterns of consumption need to create corresponding patterns of perception in order to generate successful patterns of legitimation. The omnipresence of socially constructed codes of legitimacy, which induce us to make sense of the world in accordance with pre-established modes of appreciation, destroys any illusions about the possibility of a 'natural empathy' between the perceiver and the perceived, of a 'disinterested relationship' between the consumer and the consumed, or of a 'horizontal exchange' between subject and object. Our capacity to consume culture is always dependent on our ability to be consumed by it. There is no cultural empathy without social legitimacy. The empathy *with* a cultural object is inconceivable without the sympathy *of* a cultural subject, for the legitimacy of cultural objects depends on their acceptability by cultural subjects.

Every act of consumption presupposes an act of acceptance; every act of cultural integration is accompanied by an act of cultural classification. In order to consume, we need to be able to classify. As consumers, we classify what we like and what we dislike, what we appreciate and what we deprecate, what we accept and what we reject. 'Consumption is [...] a stage in a process of communication, that is, an act of deciphering, decoding, which presupposes practical or explicit mastery of a cipher or code' (Bourdieu, 1984 [1979]: 2). All cultural struggles constitute classificatory struggles over historically contingent forms of perception. Put differently, all cultural struggles are concerned with both the construction and the destruction of legitimate and illegitimate forms of classification.

As shown above, the *differentiation*, *commodification*, and *classification* of culture constitute pivotal features of the transformation of culture in modern society. They represent overlapping and complementary processes which illustrate that the structural conditions of the production and consumption of culture have been profoundly transformed under late capitalism. (i) The *differentiation* of culture implies the gradual separation between the field of restricted cultural production and the field of large-scale cultural production: 'culture as a source of human *creation*' competes with 'culture as a source of social *distinction*'. (ii) The *commodification* of culture has created a situation in which the use value of symbolic goods is colonised by their economic exchange value: 'culture for the sake of the *created*' is confiscated by 'culture for the sake of the *market*'. (iii) The *classification* of culture is based on the imposition of different codes of legitimacy which reveal the historical contingency of different schemes of appreciation and perception: 'culture motivated by individual *creativity*' exists in relation to 'culture programmed by collective *legitimacy*'. Hence, in modern society cultural struggles are struggles over the differentiation, commodification, and classification of culture.

III. Adornian Reflections on Culture: The Culture Industry

Adorno's analysis of culture is highly complex and, as stated in the introduction, this chapter does not intend to offer an exhaustive account of the Adornian approach. Rather, it centres on three social processes which, from an Adornian perspective, are indicative of the changing nature of culture under late capitalism: (i) the *heteronomisation* of culture, (ii) the *commodification* of culture, and (iii) the *standardisation* of culture.

i) The Heteronomisation of Culture

The term 'mass culture' should not be conceived of as synonymous with the term 'culture industry'. The former may evoke positive connotations, depicting 'the mass' or 'the people' as legitimate creators and responsible carriers of an autonomous culture. The latter, on the other hand, brings to mind negative connotations, portraying 'the mass' or 'the people' as manipulated buyers and alienated reproducers of a heteronomous culture. Mass culture – if it is not imposed 'from above' but emerges 'from below' – has at least the potential of producing autonomous individuals able to construct their lives as creative subjects. The culture industry, by contrast, is based on the necessity of producing heteronomous individuals condemned to degenerate into instrumentalised objects. In short, whereas mass culture is not necessarily antithetical to the empowerment of subjects, the culture industry is only possible through their disempowerment.[10]

One of the great paradoxes of modern society consists in the fact that 'culture is taken over by the very powers it had criticized. Consumer culture is the degradation of culture' (Bernstein, 1991: 15). In other words, the term 'culture industry' contains a dialectical irony: on the one hand, the notion of 'culture' can, in principle, be associated with human autonomy, social emancipation, and improvisational creativity; on the other hand, the notion of 'industry' cannot be dissociated from human heteronomy, social domination, and instrumental rationality. The culture industry robs culture of its ontological foundation, namely its *raison d'être sans raison d'être*. For, under capitalism, 'culture has come to function as a mode of ideological domination, rather than humanization or emancipation' (Kellner, 1989: 131). The emergence of the culture industry has led to the gradual abolition of radical criticism, since it is precisely radical criticism which could jeopardise its existence. From an Adornian perspective, however, culture needs criticism as an integral component of its very existence, since culture 'is only true when implicitly critical' (Adorno, 1967 [1955]: 22).

The culture industry is the epitome of non-criticality, for its existence depends on the uncritical reproduction of its own imperatives. 'The power of the culture industry's ideology is such that conformity has replaced consciousness' (Adorno, 1991 [1975]: 90). Society's conflicts are allowed to be solved in appearance, in a world of surface only, since the solution of people's substantial problems in their real lives would inevitably imply the dissolution of the culture industry as such. It is precisely because the culture industry manages to *appear* to have the capacity to solve people's real problems that its social reproduction can be guaranteed. The domination of the dominated through the culture industry is nourished by the illusion that the dominated are the dominators of their own fate. As long as the ideological substance of this creed can be sustained, the material substance of the culture industry will hardly be dissolved. People's structural heteronomy, imposed by late capitalist society, is maintained through the belief in individual autonomy, allegedly granted by the culture industry. In the culture industry, appearance is everything whereas substance is nothing, just as heteronomy is everything whilst autonomy is nothing. As long as the appearance of autonomy is controlled by the essence of heteronomy, the culture industry does not have to fear the dissolution of its own solutions.

According to Adornian parameters, the only true social function of art is its functionlessness: 'the necessity of art [...] is its nonnecessity' (Adorno, 1997 [1970]: 251). Since art is precisely defined by its capacity to transcend from the mundane materiality of social life, it is the very quality of standing above the functionality of reality which characterises the functionlessness of art. To go beyond reality through art, however, does not mean to escape from reality. The illusory escape from reality forms part of the false promises of the culture industry. In the culture industry, art is not 'functionless' (*funktionslos*) but 'functionfull' (*funktionsvoll*), since its existence is degraded to the functional reproduction of the social system in place. Conversely, the functionlessness of truly autonomous art is rooted in its structural independence from the systemic reproduction of society based on the liquidation of autonomy. This is not to assert that art can be deployed and interpreted independently of the material conditions of society, as an idealistic perspective may suggest. Rather, this is to acknowledge that truly free and emancipated art is only a viable possibility if it is not completely absorbed and colonised by the material conditions of society. The potential social functionlessness of art consists in its capacity to transcend the mundane reality of material life while at the same time standing within this reality. It is the transcendent immanence and immanent transcendence of art which enable art to autonomise itself through its very functionlessness from the heteronomy of the functionality of social reality. Removed from the functionality imposed by society, art stands in the centre of its own reality.

'If art were to free itself from the once perceived illusion of duration, were to internalize its own transience in sympathy with the ephemeral life, it would approximate an idea of truth conceived not as something abstractly enduring but in consciousness of its temporal essence' (Adorno, 1997 [1970]: 28–29). Heteronomous art believes, and makes one believe, in its ahistorical and detached, or at least detachable, existence. The culture industry reinforces this systemic illusion by detaching itself ideologically from its material attachment to the foundation of capitalist society: class antagonism.

The 'relative' autonomy of art is always an autonomy which exists in 'relation' to its material existence. Heteronomous art and heteronomous culture, as produced and celebrated by the culture industry, can *pretend* to escape the material determinacy of society; yet, the more art and culture pretend to be autonomous by ideologically detaching themselves from their material determinacy, the more slavish and erroneous they turn out to be. Real artistic transcendence faces up to its own societal immanence. We can only transcend our societal immanence by accepting it, since going beyond the givenness of reality presupposes being situated within it. The preponderance of the object can be challenged but never overcome by the subject. A subject that is critical of its own functions, a *funktionskritisches Subjekt*, is a subject that is critical of its historical situatedness, a *geschichtskritisches Subjekt*. The culture industry is uncritical *both* of its own function as a systemic conglomerate capable of instrumentalising culture *and* of its own history as a systemic missionary capable of maintaining capitalism. The real falseness of the culture industry emanates from its false realness: even the quest for 'functionlessness' (*Funktionslosigkeit*) fulfils a function and even the quest for 'historylessness' (*Geschichtslosigkeit*) has a history. To the extent that the function of the culture industry needs to be historicised in order to relativise the appearance of its functionlessness, the history of the culture industry needs to be functionalised in order to uncover the essence of its functionladenness.

Inasmuch as any 'artwork that supposes it is in possession of its content is plainly naïve in its rationalism' (Adorno, 1997 [1970]: 27), any culture that makes the human subjects believe they are in possession of their identity is caught up in a dangerous game of existential self-sufficiency. The culture industry does not undermine but reinforces the illusion of worldly completeness by virtue of systemic effectiveness: by autonomising the industry and heteronomising culture it invites us to industrialise our autonomy and cultivate our heteronomy. In the universe of the culture industry, *Aufklärung* (enlightenment) asks not for an *Erklärung* (explanation) but for a *Verklärung* (transfiguration) of reality: under the unwritten law of the culture industry, the idea that everything can be sold is sold to us as the order of things. The order of the market is converted into the order of things.

'Art, even as something tolerated in the administered world, embodies what does not allow itself to be managed and what total management suppresses' (Adorno, 1997 [1970]: 234). The structural integration of art into the totally administered world (*die total verwaltete Welt*) destroys any illusions about the innocence of culture: there is no culture beyond society, just as there is no society beyond culture. By definition, culture is situated in society and society is situated in culture. Our – tacit or overt – complicity with the givenness of reality always precedes our possible but by no means unavoidable – break with the reality of the given.

Even the most subversive work of art cannot escape its immersion in society. Nonetheless, true art always refuses to be the tolerated appendage of the tolerating totality. What suppresses art is what invigorates the culture industry, and what suppresses the culture industry is what invigorates art. The administration of art is just as contradictory as the improvisation of administration: both are ultimately impossible. 'Modern art is questionable not when it goes too far – as the cliché runs – but when it does not go far enough' (Adorno, 1997 [1970]: 34). Administration *is* questionable when it goes too far,[11] but it is not questionable when it does not go far enough, when it does not aim at its proper abolition. The questionableness of the culture industry derives from its ontological non-self-questioning. It ought to be the task of art, as a form of critical culture, to challenge the self-ontologisation of the culture industry, a form of uncritical *Unkultur*.

'Neutralization is the social price of aesthetic autonomy. [...] In the administered world neutralization is universal' (Adorno, 1997 [1970]: 228–229). The neutralisation of the culture industry consists in the simultaneous heteronomisation of culture and autonomisation of the industry. The neutralisation is universal, but this universalisation is not neutral: it attacks the heart of artistic autonomy. 'The categories of artistic objectivity are unitary with social emancipation when the object, on the basis of its own impulse, liberates itself from social convention and controls' (Adorno, 1997 [1970]: 231). The only convention of autonomous art is its non-conventionalism; the only control over itself is its non-control; its identity is its non-identity with social reality; its breaking through society is achieved through its breaking free from the chains of reality; in short, its immanence in-itself rests on its transcendence beyond-itself.[12]

ii) The Commodification of Culture

'The principle of idealistic aesthetics – purposefulness without a purpose – reverses the scheme of things to which bourgeois art conforms socially: purposelessness for the purposes declared by the market' (Adorno and Horkheimer, 1997 [1944/1969]: 158). The heteronomisation of culture is not limited to its administration but intensified by its commodification. The functionlessness of art is functionalised for the functionality of the imperatives of the market. As the purposefulness without a purpose has been transformed into purposelessness for purposes, the artistic character of art and the cultural character of culture have been overridden by the commodity character of society. To acknowledge that art and culture become gradually commodified means to recognise that even the most autonomous spheres of society can be heteronomised by the market. It is not the autonomy of the market that has been heteronomised by culture, but, on the contrary, the autonomy of culture that has been heteronomised by the market. Since the most inner quality of art, autonomy, has been confiscated by the market, the potentialities of culture have been degraded to a state of impotence, of apparent powerlessness. The omnipresence of the market in every single social sphere seems to reveal its omnipotence.

'Culture is a paradoxical commodity. So completely is it subject to the law of exchange that it is no longer exchanged; it is so blindly consumed in use that it can no longer be used' (Adorno, 1997 [1944/1969]: 161). In the culture industry, culture is systemically – by capitalism – and systematically – by its administration – transformed into a centralised commodity. The culture industry has made culture lose its integrity and sovereignty, its autonomy and spontaneity. This is why it is the notion of *Kulturindustrie*, not the notion of *Industriekultur*, which characterises the commodification of culture in late capitalism: whereas the former implies that it is the industry, the market, which dominates culture, the latter could misleadingly suggest that it is culture which predominates over the industry, the market. In the concept *Kulturindustrie*, however, *Kultur*, the 'ideological prefix' of society, unambiguously depends on *Industrie*, the 'material suffix' of society. For symbolic relations are always embedded in the economic realm of society. Hence, it is not so much culture that penetrates the market, but, on the contrary, the market that penetrates culture.

It is worth pointing out that the notion of *Kulturindustrie* stems from a Marxist interpretation of society: although culture, as part of the ideological superstructure of society, must not be reduced to a mere reflection of the market, as the economic base of society, the former cannot be fully understood without taking into account the latter. Culture should not be conceived of as a completely independent realm existing merely 'in-itself', as an idealistic perspective might suggest; nor should it be reduced to an epiphenomenon of an omnipresent material base, as an economistic perspective might assume. The conceptual dichotomisation of society does not allow for its ontological binarisation. The holistic concept of *Kulturindustrie* indicates that social reality constitutes a unity of – directly and indirectly – interconnected particularities. In this sense, culture is a social particularity that cannot be divorced from the social whole. To the extent that the relationally constructed conglomerate of society is increasingly commodified by the market, culture – as a *relatively* autonomous social sphere – cannot escape its penetration by the economy. The most autonomous social microcosm can be colonised by the macrocosmic force of the market.

A central problem of art under late capitalism consists in its incapacity to overcome the power of commodity fetishism as long as the predominance of the market is not ideologically challenged and materially undermined. Given its ineluctable situatedness in society, art cannot avoid this contradiction unless the contradiction itself is resolved. It is part of the nature of art to be part of the nature of society. 'If art cedes its autonomy, it delivers itself over the machinations of the status quo; if art remains strictly for-itself, it nonetheless submits to integration as one harmless domain among others. The social totality appears in this aporia, swallowing whole whatever occurs' (Adorno, 1997 [1970]: 237). Regardless of whether art is consciously opportunistic or deliberately self-sufficient, it cannot escape its absorption by the market machinery. Even the most anti-integrationist art is only food for the chronic integrationism of the culture industry. All artistic 'ways out' end up in 'ways in', all artistic circumvention remains trapped in social convention, all artistic solutions can be disarmed by social convolution, and all artistic euphoria can be converted into social aporia.

The commodity fetishism of late capitalist societies describes 'a situation in which things only have substance and value insofar as they can be exchanged with something else' (Jarvis, 1998: 117). It turns society upside down in such a way that the objects created by the human subjects become subjects that transform the human subjects into objects. The objectification of human relations goes hand in hand with the subjectivisation of economic relations. The gradual disempowerment of society emanates from the increasing empowerment of the economy. 'The source of art's power of resistance is that a realized materialism would at the same time be the abolition of materialism, the abolition of the domination of material interests. In its powerlessness, art anticipates a spirit that would only then step forth. [...] A liberated society would be beyond the irrationality of its *faux frais* and beyond the ends-means-rationality of utility. This is enciphered in art and is the source of art's social explosiveness' (Adorno, 1997 [1970]: 29 and 227).

Materialism cannot be transcended without realising it, nor can it be realised without transcending it. As long as the categorical imperative of society is the market imperative of material interests, art in particular and culture in general will remain unable to slip out of the omnipresent reification of society. A realised capitalism necessarily involves the thingification of society (*Verdinglichung der Gesellschaft*); a realised materialism inevitably requires the socialisation of things (*Vergesellschaftlichung der Dinge*). Art carries the negation of exchange value inside its humanised and humanising subjectivity. Its repudiation of fetishised social relations is a core element of the sociability intrinsic to art. The splendour of the market is the mutilation of art. The splendour of art is the mutilation of the market. To realise materialism means to abolish it.

iii) The Standardisation of Culture

The consolidation of the totally administered world is expressed in the rationalisation, centralisation, and homogenisation of society, that is, in its gradual standardisation. The triumph of standard is the defeat of the individual. The regress of autonomous art is complementary to the progress of industrialised mass culture. The heteronomisation and commodification of culture is perfected through its standardisation. '[W]hile critical philosophy is inadequate without aesthetic experience, this experience needs critical philosophy' (Jay, 1984: 158); while the culture industry is adequate without critical aesthetic experience, this experience does not need the culture industry, for the pervasiveness of aesthetic autonomy is antithetical to the preponderance of social heteronomy. Genuine art, as the epitome of cultural transcendence, needs individuality and spontaneity; the culture industry, as the embodiment of systemic immanence, needs conformity and standard.

'Culture is the condition that excludes the attempt to measure it' (Adorno, 1967: 91).[13] The only control of art is its non-control. Authentic art cannot be controlled by any external systemic force; it cannot even be controlled by itself. Controlled art could hardly overcome a state of compulsory improvisation, of monopolised plurality, of standardised individuality.[14] The culture industry is based on the economic necessity to measure culture, since it is its exchange value that is most relevant to the market-driven standardisation of society. The culture industry forces culture to wear the standardised corset of the standardising market. Only by destroying the corset of systemic standardisation, however, can culture become truly free and emancipatory. The standard of the culture industry is norm, its general feature is its generalisability, and its particularity is its universality. The standard of true art is its non-standard, its general feature is its non-generalisability, and its universality is its particularity. The market does not know any limits in imposing its own limits. Art does not know any limits in transcending its own limits.

Art is about the possibility of expressing the disunity of our internal world with the unity of our external world. Art allows us to articulate the non-identity of our subjective world with the identity of our objective world. A creative subject does not necessarily intend to rebel against society, but it seeks to assert its individuality by acting upon and shaping the world. The creative subject will never leave the world as it is, but will always strive to explore what the world could – or even should – be. Our distinctively human capacity to reverse the universe is inextricably linked to our distinctively subjective ability to unify ourselves with ourselves through our disunity with the world. Human beings do not only have a deep-seated need to *create* their own creations; they also have a deep-rooted tendency to *abandon* their own creations. We are at peace with ourselves as long as we know that we can abandon ourselves. We affirm our unity with ourselves most poignantly when we insist upon our disunity with the world. The world is ours only insofar as we are of the world. We are of the world only insofar as we create our own world. We feel at home in the house of being as long as we remain the architects of the house of being. The space of humanity is a place of reconstructability. We are what we become.

Our unity with ourselves depends on our potential disunity with our existence. 'The question is not whether culture has lost its unity, but whether the possibility of expressing disunity may have been lost' (Rose, 1978: 116). Standardised culture unifies art to such an extent that art is robbed of its ontological cornerstone, disunity. To unify art with the market means to divide art from art. 'Illusory universality is the universality of the art of the culture industry, it is the universality of the homogeneous same, an art which even no longer promises happiness but only provides easy amusement as relief from labour' (Bernstein, 1991: 6). The more standardised this domination, the more dominated culture becomes. Ideology, including standardised culture, is a business, for '[a]musement under late capitalism is the prolongation of work' (Adorno and Horkheimer, 1997 [1944/1969]: 137). Culture is transformed into mere entertainment. Entertainment ossifies into boredom, guaranteeing that its perception by the masses does not require excessive creative or intellectual efforts.

Art becomes artificial, as the unadorned Adornian critique reveals: '[m]ass culture is unadorned make-up' (Adorno, 1991 [1981]: 67–68). By virtue of its monopolistic artificiality, it aims at the constant monopolisation of society. As 'consummated conflictlessness' (ibid.: 67), art conceals the basic antagonisms of society. Art itself is translated into a decisive moment of the material reproduction of society. As a consequence, it has lost its capacity to transcend the systemic immanence of social reality, because in the empire of the culture industry it is not culture that has transcended the market but, on the contrary, the market that has transcended culture. Culture appears as the standardised and standardising appendage of the administered world. The forcing-into-line of society (*die Gleichschaltung der Gesellschaft*) leads to the total synchronisation of culture, equalling the factual liquidation of its normative potentiality. Standardisation is pseudo-individualisation, since it allows difference to exist only as long as it fits into the overall picture. The standardisation of culture is realised through the systemic and systematic 'promotion and [...] exploitation of the ego-weakness to which the powerless members of contemporary society, with its concentration of power, are condemned' (Adorno, 1991 [1975]: 91). The subtle totalitarianism of a standardised society degrades culture to a reliable vehicle of standardised domination.

As shown above, the *heteronomisation*, *commodification*, and *standardisation* of culture can be regarded as complex manifestations of the transformation of culture in the modern world. (i) The *heteronomisation* of culture reflects a colonising process which attacks the autonomy of culture: 'culture as a source of *artistic creativity*' is replaced with 'culture as a vehicle of *systemic functionality*'. (ii) The *commodification* of culture constitutes a colonising process which degrades culture to a functionalised appendage of the imperatives of the market: 'culture as an expression of *purposefulness without a purpose*' is converted into 'culture as *purposelessness for the purposes of the market*'. (iii) The *standardisation* of culture stands for a colonising process which subjugates culture to a steering medium of an increasingly synchronised and synchronising society: 'culture as a realm of *transformative individuality*' becomes more and more of a fiction in the face of 'culture as a machine of *reproductive sociality*'. Thus, in the modern world cultural struggles are struggles over the heteronomisation, commodification, and standardisation of culture.

IV. Comparative Reflections on Culture: Between Bourdieu and Adorno

The above analysis has sought to demonstrate that the transformation of culture in the modern world needs to be understood in the context of the transformation of society as a whole. Despite the existence of substantial differences between Bourdieusian and Adornian thought, the two approaches share some fundamental assumptions (cf. Karakayali, 2004). This is not to suggest that the two perspectives can be considered congruent; rather, this is to acknowledge that they possess some striking affinities. It is the purpose of this section to elucidate these points of convergence and thereby to put forward a critical theory of cultural production which sheds light on the relationship between (i) *culture and economy*, (ii) *culture and domination*, (iii) *culture and legitimacy*, (iv) *culture and history*, and (v) *culture and emancipation*.

i) Culture and Economy: The Commodification of Culture

Culture cannot be divorced from the material reality in which it is embedded. One central feature of modern society is the commodification of culture, constituting a powerful social process which is driven by the market economy. Both Bourdieu's concept of *cultural economy* and Adorno's concept of *culture industry* imply that culture becomes gradually commodified in late capitalist societies.

To be sure, both concepts are indicative of a theoretical shift from the classical Marxist insistence on the material nature of reality to the neo-Marxist emphasis on the interpenetration of the material and the cultural realms of society. In advanced capitalist societies, the material economy is intimately entangled with the cultural economy. Metaphorically speaking, base and superstructure do not collapse but they are more and more intertwined, indicating how the material and the cultural dimensions of social life become almost indistinguishably interwoven. Due to its socially contingent and historically variable character, culture fits into the logic of an economic system whose existence depends on the production of socially contingent and historically variable commodities:

> By an effect of circular causality, the structural gap between supply and demand contributes to the artists' determination to steep themselves in the search for 'originality' [...], ensuring the incommensurability of the specifically cultural value and economic value of a work. (Bourdieu, 1993 [1971/1985]: 120)
>
> The abstractness of the new is bound up with the commodity character of art [...], artworks distinguish themselves from the ever-same inventory in

> obedience to the need for the exploitation of capital. [...] The new is the aesthetic seal of expanded reproduction, with its promise of undiminished plenitude. (Adorno, 1997 [1970]: 21, translation modified)

Given their potential for 'originality' and 'incommensurability', as well as for 'distinctiveness' and 'newness', cultural products meet the capitalist need for novelty and exploitability embodied in the commodity. The resourceful contingency of culture can be smoothly absorbed by the purposeful contingency of the market. Artistic creativity is thereby degraded to a cultural commodity. In capitalism, the symbolic value of culture is subdued by the exchange value of the market.

ii) Culture and Domination: The Functionalisation of Culture

Every form of culture can be transformed into a constitutive component of social domination. One pivotal characteristic of modern society is the functionalisation of culture by the established social system. Both Bourdieu's concept of *competitive struggle* and Adorno's concept of *social struggle* are based on the assumption that culture and domination are closely interrelated in late capitalist societies.

Again, both notions are symptomatic of a theoretical shift from the classical Marxist concern with class domination and class struggle to the neo-Marxist preoccupation with cultural domination and cultural struggle. Just as different forms of economic domination are entangled with different forms of cultural domination, different forms of class struggle are intertwined with different forms of cultural struggle. There are no efficient modes of material domination without effective modes of symbolic domination. In late capitalism, economic domination is increasingly mediated by, although not replaced with, cultural domination. Base and superstructure are not dissolved, but economic and cultural mechanisms of domination superimpose themselves upon one another; their functional reciprocity reveals their ontological unity. The social functionality of culture matches the systemic elasticity of the capitalist economy:

> Competitive struggle is the form of class struggle which the dominated classes allow to be imposed on them when they accept the stakes offered by the dominant classes. It is an integrative struggle and, by virtue of the initial handicaps, a reproductive struggle, since those who enter this chase, in which they are beaten before they start [...], implicitly recognize the legitimacy of the goals pursued by those whom they pursue, by the mere fact of taking part. (Bourdieu, 1984 [1979]: 165, already referred to above)

> Social struggles and the relations of classes are imprinted in the structure of artworks [...]. (Adorno, 1997 [1970]: 232.) But the secret doctrine [...] is the message of capital. It must be secret because total domination likes to keep itself invisible: 'No shepherd and a herd'. Nonetheless it is directed at everyone. (Adorno, 1991 [1981]: 81)

Domination in late capitalism is mediated by culture. In advanced capitalist societies, culture constitutes both a vehicle *and* a motor of class domination. As a vehicle of class domination, culture is an instrument of power; as a motor of class domination, culture is a source of power. Domination through culture is subtle but total, since it penetrates every single sphere of society far more efficiently and reliably than the most perfected totalitarian political regime ever could. The systemic mechanisms of cultural domination in late capitalism do not abolish the economic division of society; they only conceal this division.

iii) Culture and Legitimacy: The Classification of Culture

The power of every form of culture depends on its degree of legitimacy. One important element of modern society is the classification of culture for the maintenance of social order. Both Bourdieu's concept of *affirmation* and Adorno's concept of *justification* allow us to understand how the legitimacy of culture can contribute to the legitimacy of society:

> Any act of cultural production implies an affirmation of its claims to cultural legitimacy [...]. (Bourdieu, 1993 [1971/1985]: 116.) [T]he field of production and diffusion can only be fully understood if one treats it as a field of competition for the monopoly of the legitimate exercise of symbolic violence. (Ibid.: 121.) [A]rt and cultural consumption are predisposed, consciously and deliberately or not, to fulfil a social function of legitimating social differences. (Bourdieu, 1984 [1979]: 7)
>
> No ideology even needs to be injected [...], art becomes a form of justification [...]. (Adorno, 1991 [1981]: 57.) Mass culture allows precisely this reserve army of outsiders to participate: mass culture is an organized mania for connecting everything with everything else, a totality of public secrets. (Ibid.: 72)

The stability of any social system depends largely on the degree of legitimacy it is able to obtain. The most legitimate legitimacy is a form of legitimacy that is not forced to be legitimated because it is based not only on tacit consent and implicit approval but also on integrative opportunism and doxic complicity. The legitimacy of symbolic violence is nourished by the outsiders' participation in the cultural legitimisation of their own domination. Classified culture classifies classified people, just as much as classified people classify classified culture. The consecration of culture in modern society is a manifestation of the classificatory division of society as a whole.

iv) Culture and History: The Contextualisation of Culture

Every form of culture is historically situated. One crucial facet of modern society is the resignification of culture according to the imperatives of the market. Both Bourdieu's concept of *reference* and Adorno's concept of *immanence* point towards the fact that the power of culture is always contingent upon the horizon of meaning in which it finds itself historically situated:

> Science can attempt to bring representations and instruments of thought [...] back to the social conditions of their production and of their use, in other words, back to the historical structure of the field in which they are engendered and within which they operate. [...] [O]ne is led to historicize these cultural products, all of which claim universality. But historicizing them means not only [...] relativizing them by recalling that they have meaning solely through reference to a determined state of the field of struggle [...]; it also means restoring to them necessity by removing them from indeterminacy (which stems from a false eternalization) in order to bring them back to the social conditions of their genesis, a truly generative definition. (Bourdieu, 1993 [1987]: 263–264)
>
> The immanence of society in the artwork is the essential social relation of art, not the immanence of art in society. (Adorno, 1997 [1970]: 232)

To contextualise culture means to accept its contingency by facing up to its intrinsic historicity. The constitution of culture in the modern world cannot be understood without taking into account the constitution of society as a whole. The situatedness of culture *within* society destroys any illusions about the possible indeterminacy of culture *beyond* society. The creative transcendence of culture is possible because of, rather than despite, its societal immanence, for what seeks to write its own history needs to face up to its own determinacy.

v) Culture and Emancipation: The Liberation of Culture

Culture contains an emancipatory potential. One significant aspect of modern society is that it challenges us to exploit the emancipatory core of culture in order to abolish the emancipation of exploitation. Both Bourdieu's concept of *open work* and Adorno's concept of *the unspeakable* seem to suggest that the quest for the autonomy of human culture cannot be separated from the quest for the autonomy of human existence:

> The production of an 'open work' [...] [is] the final stage in the conquest of artistic autonomy [...]. To assert the autonomy of production is to give primacy to that of which the artist is master [...]. (Bourdieu, 1984 [1979]: 3)
>
> [T]here is no art without individuation, [...] art must be and wants to be utopia, and the more utopia is blocked by the real functional order, the more this is true; [...] only by virtue of the absolute negativity of collapse does art enunciate the unspeakable: utopia. (Adorno, 1997 [1970]: 32.) The categories of artistic objectivity are unitary with social emancipation when the object, on the basis of its own impulse, liberates itself from social convention and controls. (Ibid.: 231)

The individuation of artistic openness is the opening of artistic individuation. Art liberates the subject just as much as the subject liberates art by speaking the unspeakable. The categories of liberating art are uncategorical for the categorical imperative of liberation is the abolition of categories, just as much as the realisation of materialism is the abolition of materialism. The impulse that drives the conquest of artistic autonomy can only be fully realised through the realisation of the quest for human sovereignty, which is always already existent in social objectivity. There is no realised individuation without a realised society, just as there is no realised society without realised individuation. As long as art can go beyond society, society will be able to go beyond itself.

Conclusion

Drawing upon the works of Bourdieu and Adorno, this chapter has explored the transformation of culture in modern society. Rather than seeking to embrace the entire complexity of Bourdieusian and Adornian thought, the chapter has deliberately focused on some key dimensions that are particularly relevant to the critical analysis of the relationship between modern culture and modern society. As demonstrated above, the transformation of culture in the modern world cannot be understood without taking into account the transformation of society as a whole.

The 'cultural economy' constitutes a market of symbolic goods driven by economic and cultural struggles. In essence, it is shaped by three simultaneous social processes: the differentiation, commodification, and classification of culture. (i) The *differentiation* of culture is embedded in a binary separation between the field of restricted cultural production and the field of large-scale cultural production: in modern society, culture oscillates between its symbolic independence from and its material dependence upon the ubiquitous power of the market economy. (ii) The *commodification* of culture cannot be dissociated from the culturalisation of commodities: inasmuch as culture is increasingly commodified, commodities are increasingly culturalised in modern society. (iii) The *classification* of culture is an expression of the stratification of society: cultural struggles are basically struggles 'about' social classification 'through' representational classification, reflecting the deep material and symbolic divisions of modern society.

The 'culture industry' represents both the product and the vehicle of an increasingly synchronised and synchronising society. Its powerful influence upon the constitution of modern society manifests itself in three simultaneous social processes: the heteronomisation, commodification, and standardisation of culture. (i) The *heteronomisation* of culture stems from the subjugation of artistic creativity to systemic functionality: the culture industry feeds the empowerment of the economy and contributes to the disempowerment of humanity by autonomising the industry and heteronomising culture. (ii) The *commodification* of culture is symptomatic of the omnipresent power of the capitalist economy, in which the symbolic value of culture is subdued to the exchange value of the market: the culture industry liquidates the autonomous core of culture by commodifying it. (iii) The *standardisation* of culture illustrates the homogenising power of totally administered societies: to standardise culture means to deculturalise culture; it means to unify the ontological disunity of art; in short, it means to divide culture from culture and art from art. The subtle totalitarianism of late capitalist society is equipped with the unwritten recipe of standardised domination.

Despite the substantial differences between Bourdieusian and Adornian social theory, the two approaches offer complementary, rather than antithetical, perspectives on the transformation of culture in modern society. As shown above, the two accounts converge on five levels, allowing us to make a case for a critical theory of cultural production. (i) Both approaches are concerned with the *relationship between culture and economy* in that they explore the social implications of the *commodification* of culture. The search for originality and novelty, which is essential to the creation of artwork, matches the need for invention and reinvention, which is fundamental to the reproduction of the 'cultural economy' and the 'culture industry'. (ii) Both approaches highlight the *relationship between culture and domination* in that they study the social implications of the systemic *functionalisation* of culture. Social antagonisms seem to disappear behind the make-up of the unadorned adornment of systemic domination. (iii) Both approaches shed light on the *relationship between culture and legitimacy* in that they draw our attention to the social implications of the *classification* of culture. Cultural authority is one of the most powerful vehicles of social legitimacy. (iv) Both approaches emphasise the *relationship between culture and history* in that they study the social implications of the *contextualisation* of culture. Just as we need to recognise the historicity of society, we need to face up to the contingency of culture. (v) Both approaches insist on the *relationship between culture and emancipation* in that they reflect on the social implications of the possible *liberation* of culture. Emancipatory forms of society cannot dispense with emancipatory forms of culture. To reappropriate society would mean to reappropriate culture.

Acknowledgements

I am grateful to Bryan S. Turner and Elena Knox for their helpful comments on an earlier version of this chapter.

Notes

1 On the concept of culture as a socio-ontological foundation of the human condition, see, for example, Susen (2007: 287–292).
2 The German term *Bildung* has several meanings. In the most general sense, it refers to the 'formation' or 'shaping' of something. In a more specific sense, it can also signify 'education', that is, literally the 'formation' or 'shaping' of a person.
3 See, for example, Bourdieu (1984 [1979]), Bourdieu (1993), Bourdieu and Passeron (1990 [1970]), and Bourdieu and Wacquant (1992a: esp. 87–89). See also Bohman (1999), Fowler (1997), Lash (1993), LiPuma (1993), Swartz (1997), and Wacquant (2002).
4 On the polycentric nature of social power, see, for example, Susen (2008a) and Susen (2008b).
5 On the autonomy of the field, see also Susen (2007: 176–177).
6 See, for example: Bourdieu (1977 [1972]: 83), Bourdieu (1980: 28, 90, and 122), Bourdieu (1982: 16), Bourdieu (1982: 84), Bourdieu (1997: 44, 166, 205, and 222), Bourdieu (1998: 102), Bourdieu (2001: 129), Bourdieu, and Chamboredon and Passeron (1968: 46). See also Susen (2007: 188, 255, 296, and 299).
7 On the notion of the habitus as 'a structured and structuring structure', see, for example: Bourdieu (1976: 43), Bourdieu (1980: 87–88 and 159), Bourdieu (1997b: 118, 172, and 219), and Bourdieu (2001: 154). In the secondary literature, see, for example: Bonnewitz (1998: 62), Dortier (2002: 5), Jenkins (1992: 141), Knoblauch (2003: 189), Lewandowski (2000: 50), Liénard and Servais (2000 [1979]: 87), Vandenberghe (1999: 48), and Wacquant (2002: 33).
8 See also Bourdieu and Wacquant 1992b. In the secondary literature, see, for example, Lash (1993: 196) and Susen (2007: 142–145).
9 Cf. LiPuma (1993: 16): '[…] an "almost perfect homology" between the structures of culture and those of social organization'.
10 See Adorno (1991 [1975]: 85). Adorno writes: 'In our drafts we spoke of "mass culture". We replaced that expression with "culture industry" in order to exclude from the outset the interpretation agreeable to its advocates: that it is a matter of something like a

culture that arises spontaneously from the masses themselves, the contemporary form of popular art.' On the concepts of empowerment and disempowerment in contemporary critical theory, see, for example, Susen (2009a: 84–105) and Susen (2009b: 104–105).

11 In Adorno's writings, Auschwitz epitomises the dark side of a totally administered world.

12 On Adorno's insistence upon the emancipatory nature of art, see, for example, Susen (2007: 107–111).

13 Cf. Jay (1984: 118 and 181n.22).

14 Adorno's arguments against the artistic legitimacy of Jazz are particularly relevant to his notion of compulsory improvisation. See Jay (1973: 186–187). Cf. Adorno 1991 [1981: 76]. See also Kodat (2003: 114).

References

Adorno, Theodor W. (1967) 'Thesen zur Kunstsoziologie', *Kölner Zeitschrift für Soziologie und Sozialpsychologie* 19(1): 87–93.

Adorno, Theodor W. (1967 [1955]) *Prisms*, trans. Samuel and Shierry Weber, London: Spearman.

Adorno, Theodor W. (1991 [1975]) 'Culture Industry Reconsidered', in Theodor W. Adorno, *The Culture Industry: Selected Essays on Mass Culture*, trans. Anson G. Rabinbach, edited and introduced by J. M. Bernstein, London: Routledge, pp. 85–92.

Adorno, Theodor W. (1991 [1981]) 'The Schema of Mass Culture', in Theodor W. Adorno, *The Culture Industry: Selected Essays on Mass Culture*, trans. Nicholas Walker, edited and introduced by J. M. Bernstein, London: Routledge, pp. 53–84.

Adorno, Theodor W. (1997 [1970]) *Aesthetic Theory*, trans. Robert Hullot-Kentor, London: Athlone Press.

Adorno, Theodor W. and Max Horkheimer (1997 [1944/1969]) 'The Culture Industry: Enlightenment as Mass Deception', in Theodor W. Adorno and Max Horkheimer, *The Dialectic of Enlightenment*, trans. John Cumming, London: Verso, pp. 120–167.

Bernstein, J. M. (1991) 'Introduction' in Theodor W. Adorno, *The Culture Industry: Selected Essays on Mass Culture*, edited and introduced by J. M. Bernstein, London: Routledge, pp. 1–25.

Bohman, James (1999) 'Practical Reason and Cultural Constraint: Agency in Bourdieu's Theory of Practice', in Richard Shusterman (ed.) *Bourdieu: A Critical Reader*, Oxford: Blackwell, pp. 129–152.

Bonnewitz, Patrice (1998) *La sociologie de P. Bourdieu*, Paris: Presses Universitaires de France.

Bourdieu, Pierre (1976) 'Le sens pratique', *Actes de la recherche en sciences sociales* 7 [1]: 43–86.

Bourdieu, Pierre (1977 [1972]) *Outline of a Theory of Practice*, trans. Richard Nice, Cambridge: Cambridge University Press.

Bourdieu, Pierre (1980) *Le sens pratique*, Paris: Minuit.

Bourdieu, Pierre (1982a) 'L'économie des échanges linguistiques', in Pierre Bourdieu, *Ce que parler veut dire. L'économie des échanges linguistiques*, Paris: Fayard, pp. 11–21.

Bourdieu, Pierre (1982b) 'La formation des prix et l'anticipation des profits', in Pierre Bourdieu, *Ce que parler veut dire. L'économie des échanges linguistiques*, Paris: Fayard, pp. 59–95.

Bourdieu, Pierre (1984 [1979]) *Distinction: A Social Critique of the Judgement of Taste*, trans. Richard Nice, London: Routledge & Kegan Paul.

Bourdieu, Pierre (1992 [1977]) 'On Symbolic Power', in Pierre Bourdieu, *Language and Symbolic Power*, edited and introduced by John B. Thompson, translated by Gino Raymond and Matthew Adamson, Cambridge: Polity Press, pp. 163–170.

Bourdieu, Pierre (1993) *The Field of Cultural Production: Essays on Art and Literature*, edited and introduced by Randal Johnson, Cambridge: Polity Press.

Bourdieu, Pierre (1993 [1971/1985]) 'The Market of Symbolic Goods', in Pierre Bourdieu, *The Field of Cultural Production: Essays on Art and Literature*, trans. Rupert Swyer, edited and introduced by Randal Johnson, Cambridge: Polity Press, pp. 112–145.

Bourdieu, Pierre (1993 [1987]) 'The Historical Genesis of a Pure Aesthetic', in Pierre Bourdieu, *The Field of Cultural Production: Essays on Art and Literature*, trans. Charles Newman, edited and introduced by Randal Johnson, Cambridge: Polity Press, pp. 253–266.

Bourdieu, Pierre (1997a) *Les usages sociaux de la science. Pour une sociologie clinique du champ scientifique*, Paris: INRA.

Bourdieu, Pierre (1997b) *Méditations pascaliennes*, Paris: Seuil.

Bourdieu, Pierre (1998) *La domination masculine*, Paris: Seuil.

Bourdieu, Pierre (2001) *Science de la science et réflexivité*, Paris: Raisons d'agir.

Bourdieu, Pierre, Jean-Claude Chamboredon and Jean-Claude Passeron (1968) *Le métier de sociologue. Préalables épistémologiques*, Paris: Éditions de l'École des Hautes Études en Sciences Sociales/Mouton.

Bourdieu, Pierre and Jean-Claude Passeron (1990 [1970]) *Reproduction in Education, Society and Culture*, trans. Richard Nice, 2nd Edition, London: Sage.

Bourdieu, Pierre and Loïc Wacquant (1992a) 'The Unique and the Invariant', in Pierre Bourdieu and Loïc Wacquant, *An Invitation to Reflexive Sociology*, Cambridge: Polity Press, pp. 75–94.

Bourdieu, Pierre and Loïc Wacquant (1992b) 'Language, Gender, and Symbolic Violence', in Pierre Bourdieu and Loïc Wacquant, *An Invitation to Reflexive Sociology*, Cambridge: Polity Press, pp. 140–174.

Dortier, Jean-François (2002) 'Les idées pures n'existent pas', *Sciences Humaines*, Numéro Spécial: L'œuvre de Pierre Bourdieu: 3–8.

Fowler, Bridget (1997) *Pierre Bourdieu and Cultural Theory: Critical Investigations*, London: Sage.

Jarvis, Simon (1998) *Adorno: A Critical Introduction*, Cambridge: Polity Press.

Jay, Martin (1973) *The Dialectical Imagination: A History of the Frankfurt School and the Institute of Social Research, 1923–1950*, London: Heinemann.

Jay, Martin (1984) *Adorno*, Cambridge, Mass.: Harvard University Press.

Jenkins, Richard (1992) *Pierre Bourdieu*, London: Routledge.

Karakayali, Nedim (2004) 'Reading Bourdieu with Adorno: The Limits of Critical Theory and Reflexive Sociology', *Sociology* 38(2): 351–368.

Kellner, Douglas (1989) *Critical Theory, Marxism and Modernity*, Cambridge: Polity Press.

Knoblauch, Hubert (2003) 'Habitus und Habitualisierung. Zur Komplementarität von Bourdieu mit dem Sozialkonstruktivismus', in Boike Rehbein, Gernot Saalmann and Hermann Schwengel (eds.) *Pierre Bourdieus Theorie des Sozialen: Probleme und Perspektiven*, Konstanz: UVK, pp. 187–201.

Kodat, Catherine Gunther (2003) 'Conversing with Ourselves: Canon, Freedom, Jazz', *American Quarterly* 55(1): 1–28.

Lash, Scott (1993) 'Pierre Bourdieu: Cultural Economy and Social Change', in Craig Calhoun, Edward LiPuma and Moishe Postone (eds.) *Bourdieu: Critical Perspectives*, Chicago: University of Chicago Press, pp. 193–211.

Lewandowski, Joseph D. (2000) 'Thematizing Embeddedness: Reflexive Sociology as Interpretation', *Philosophy of the Social Sciences* 30(1): 49–66.

Liénard, Georges and Émile Servais (2000 [1979]) 'Practical Sense', in Derek Robbins (ed.) *Pierre Bourdieu. Volume I*, London: Sage, pp. 83–92.

LiPuma, Edward (1993) 'Culture and the Concept of Culture in a Theory of Practice', in Craig Calhoun, Edward LiPuma and Moishe Postone (eds.) *Bourdieu: Critical Perspectives*, Chicago: University of Chicago Press, pp. 14–34.

Robbins, Derek (1991) *The Work of Pierre Bourdieu: Recognizing Society*, Milton Keynes: Open University Press.

Rose, Gillian (1978) *The Melancholy Science: An Introduction to the Thought of Theodor W. Adorno*, London: Macmillan.

Susen, Simon (2007) *The Foundations of the Social: Between Critical Theory and Reflexive Sociology*, Oxford: Bardwell Press.

Susen, Simon (2008a) 'Poder y anti-poder (I-III)', *Erasmus: Revista para el diálogo intercultural* 10(1): 49–90.

Susen, Simon (2008b) 'Poder y anti-poder (IV-V)', *Erasmus: Revista para el diálogo intercultural* 10(2): 133–180.

Susen, Simon (2009a) 'Between Emancipation and Domination: Habermasian Reflections on the Empowerment and Disempowerment of the Human Subject', *Pli: The Warwick Journal of Philosophy* 20: 80–110.

Susen, Simon (2009b) 'The Philosophical Significance of Binary Categories in Habermas's Discourse Ethics', *Sociological Analysis* 3(2): 97–125.

Swartz, David (1997) *Culture and Power: The Sociology of Pierre Bourdieu*, Chicago: University of Chicago Press.

Vandenberghe, Frédéric (1999) '"The Real is Relational": An Epistemological Analysis of Pierre Bourdieu's Generative Structuralism', *Sociological Theory* 17(1): 32–67.

Wacquant, Loïc (2002) 'De l'idéologie à la violence symbolique : culture, classe et conscience chez Marx et Bourdieu', in Jean Lojkine (ed.) *Les sociologues critiques du capitalisme : en hommage à Pierre Bourdieu*, Paris: Collection Actuel Marx Confrontation, Presses Universitaires de France, pp. 25–40.

Williams, Raymond (1994) 'The Analysis of Culture', in John Storey (ed.) *Cultural Theory and Popular Culture: A Reader*, New York: Harvester Wheatsheaf, pp. 48–56.

CHAPTER NINE

The Grammar of an Ambivalence: On the Legacy of Pierre Bourdieu in the Critical Theory of Axel Honneth

*Mauro Basaure**

In the mid-1980s, Axel Honneth – successor to Jürgen Habermas, and now considered the most prominent representative of the Frankfurt School's third generation – made an important contribution to the socio-philosophical reading of Pierre Bourdieu's work that fundamentally shaped its German reception (see Behr, 2001). This contribution is marked by a clear ambivalence. On the one hand, it is obvious that it was in no way gratuitous. Honneth knew from the beginning that Bourdieu's work was to play a key role in his own project to renew the tradition of critical theory (Honneth, Basaure, Reemtsma and Willig, 2009). At the centre of this project was a reappropriation and revitalisation of the Hegelian concept of the 'struggle for recognition' (Honneth, 1995 [1992]; 2000; 2003; 2007 [2000]). On the other hand, Honneth's early texts, which contribute to the German reception of Bourdieu, are eminently critical of Bourdieu's work. In a monographic article presented in the early 1980s, Honneth (1984) advances the critique that Bourdieu's social theory tends to ignore the normative structuring of social life and instead takes up a utilitarian, strategic understanding of social action. This charge similarly dominates the interview Honneth and his colleagues conducted with Bourdieu, which was published two years later (Bourdieu, Honneth, Kocyba and Schwibs, 1986). I want to argue that this ambivalence cuts across Honneth's entire relationship with Bourdieu's work. Whilst Honneth rejects what he considers to be the socio-ontological foundations of Bourdieu's sociological theory, he draws upon the Bourdieusian approach and considers it as an expression of an exemplary sociology.

As shall be illustrated below, this ambivalence can only be understood in light of the structure of Honneth's theory of the struggle for recognition.

The first section demonstrates that this ambivalence does not constitute a contradiction because Honneth's assessments of Bourdieu's sociology – one negative and one positive – correspond to two key argumentative axes within this theory, which are very different from one another and unequally developed. The second section uses this analysis to explain why the existing body of literature has taken up Honneth's negative assessment of Bourdieu's sociology, while largely ignoring the former's affirmative critique of the latter. Intervening in this discourse, the third section engages in more substantive reconstruction by exploring the impact of Bourdieu's legacy on Honneth's work. Finally, the fourth section provides a systematic account of the various ways and contexts in which Honneth turns to Bourdieu, suggesting that the basic requirements of the former's theory of the struggle for recognition cannot be dissociated from the latter's theoretical framework. Such an analysis permits us to identify the fundamental elements that constitute the grammar underlying the ambivalent relationship between Honneth's critical theory and Bourdieu's critical sociology.

1. Bourdieu's Sociology Between the Key Axes of Honneth's Theory of the Struggle for Recognition

Theories that are concerned with the nature of social struggles tend to ignore one – arguably fundamental – analytical distinction: the distinction between sociological research devoted to explaining the motives for contestatory action and sociological research devoted to studying the preconditions of contestatory action. In fact, if we apply this distinction to Honneth's theory of the struggle for recognition (1995 [1981]; 1984; 1995 [1992]; 2000; 2003; 2007 [2000]), we can make sense of his ambivalent assessment of Bourdieu's sociology.

A brief but methodical reconstruction of Honneth's theory allows us to identify two intimately related argumentative axes: a *moral-sociological axis* and a *historico-philosophical axis.* The first axis represents the conceptual effort to provide an explanation for the moral motives of subjective action that lie at the heart of social struggles and conflicts. Drawing on a reinterpretation of Hegel and Mead, Honneth employs a non-utilitarian moral-sociological explanation of social conflicts which suggests that the motives for engaging in social struggle can be traced back to experiences of a lack of recognition which cause negative moral feelings. Their objective and cognitive nature resides in their expression of the breakdown of the system of reciprocal expectations of behaviour based on values anchored in intersubjective structures of mutual recognition that underlie individual identity development. Honneth's theory of recognition is concerned with the construction of an intersubjective concept of subjectivity that is not only sensitive to forms of moral damage but also capable of reacting to this damage with negative moral feelings. These feelings could provide the motivational basis for social struggles. Such a moral-sociological perspective, which is based on the link between conflict and normativity, is captured in the subtitle of Honneth's (1995 [1992]) book *The Struggle for Recognition: The Moral Grammar of Social Conflicts*.

The historico-philosophical axis proposes a context of historical interpretation for a process of moral construction within which the struggles for recognition can be inscribed as part of a historical process of normative development and learning. In this way, struggles lose their contingent nature and cease to be separate episodes. They are instead understood in the context of a historical deployment and broadening of the moral structures of reciprocal recognition (Honneth, 1995 [1992]). It is important to note that both axes assume a moral perspective and that, as stated above, they are intimately related to one another. Since morally motivated social struggles develop and broaden the normative structures of reciprocal recognition, these struggles possess historical significance, implying ever-greater levels of inclusion as well as moral demands.

Although it is not self-evident, it is possible to identify a third axis in the conceptual architecture of Honneth's theory. This third axis, which I will refer to as the *political-sociological axis*, exists within the conceptual space constituted by the two main axes mentioned above and is concerned with the phenomenon of social struggle as such. In other words, it represents the concept of struggle as the process of constructing antagonistic collectives. The political-sociological axis, therefore, does not directly address the moral-sociological explanation of the motives of social struggles or their inscription within a philosophical historical context of moral development. To put it another way, it does not address the motivational causes of the social struggle or their consequences for the deployment of moral learning. Rather, it focuses on the way in which collectives are antagonistically constructed and on their ability to shape political public spaces and transform the order, values and practices that regulate social recognition and the rights of individuals. Conceived in this way, the political-sociological axis is inserted between the moral-sociological axis and the historico-philosophical axis.

As shall be demonstrated below, the political sociology of Pierre Bourdieu plays a key role in Honneth's development of the political-sociological axis. It is worth mentioning this at this point because, along with the previous reconstruction, it allows us to understand the fundamental ambivalence that characterises Honneth's assessment of Bourdieu's work. My argument is that, with respect to the moral-sociological axis, Honneth (1995 [1984]) rejects the nucleus of economic and utilitarian theory, which – as he sees it – is essential to Bourdieu's theory of symbolic struggles. Referring to the motivations for contestatory action, Honneth asserts that a moral normative logic undergirds contestatory action and argues against all exclusively utilitarian strategic explanations for such motivations (Honneth, 1995 [1984]; 1995 [1992]), which – correctly or not – he sees reflected in Bourdieu's work. To put it another way, Honneth rejects Bourdieu's sociology as incomplete because the phenomenon of the moral does not play a significant role in its sociological explicative frame. To illustrate this, I will establish Honneth's position by condensing into a single quotation the four central pages of his argument:

> Bourdieu is guided by utilitarian motifs in overcoming structuralism […] the concept of «habitus» is its [critique of anthropological structuralism] logical extension. The concept of habitus provides the means by which we can move from the view of a profit motive permeating social life in its entirety to the level of actual social practices and orientation of action. For to avoid having to assume, as a consequence of an underlying utilitarian theory of action, that acting subjects possess the actual intention of utility maximization, Bourdieu proceeds from the idea that the contingently located utility calculus of social groups are manifest in their collective perceptual and evaluative schemata on an unconscious level. Bourdieu called these group-specific dispositions and modes of action orientations which project beyond the individual's horizon of meaning forms of *habitus.* One of the presuppositions of this concept […] is that Bourdieu could now claim that even if they subjectively orient their actions in other ways, social subjects act from the economic viewpoint of utility which had been deposited in the modes of orientation, classificatory schemes and dispositions binding to their group. The subjectively conscious plan of action therefore does not have to coincide with the habitually intended aim of action, which is in principle determined by utility maximization […]. The utilitarian concept of social action then is at the basis of Bourdieu's social theory and analysis of culture. […] social groups incessantly strive to better or at least hold on their social position. (Honneth, 1995 [1984]: 186–190)

In contrast to this critical reading, and in accordance with what we may characterise as the political-sociological axis of his work, Honneth (1995 [1992]; 2003) turns to Bourdieu's political sociology in a largely affirmative way. While he rejects it with respect to the moral explanation of the motivations of belligerent action, he takes up Bourdieu's political sociology when discussing the preconditions of collective action and considers it to be exemplary.

Given my previous assertions, it is important to note that the ambivalence in Honneth's assessment of Bourdieu does not constitute a contradiction: indeed, the two values of ambivalence – the positive and the negative – correspond to the two axes of the Honnethian theory of the struggle for recognition which are independent of one another.

2. The Asymmetrical Assessment of Bourdieu's Sociology

In modern social theory, there is some confusion about the nature of social struggles, that is, there is a failure to differentiate between conceptual proposals geared towards explaining the subject's willingness to enter into conflict – that is, the moral-sociological axis, if we are to use Honneth's theory as an example – and proposals oriented towards explaining these struggles as such, that is, as an integral component of social life (the political-sociological axis).

In Honneth's theory of the struggle for recognition, this fundamental confusion manifests itself in the unequal development of the aforementioned axes which causes this approach to suffer from a lack of balance. In fact, when Honneth talks about the struggle for recognition, he does so almost exclusively in reference to the motivations behind it and, thus, to the 'why' rather than the 'how' of this struggle. To elaborate, the former dimension – the 'why' – concerns the moral-sociological axis, while the latter dimension – the 'how' – refers to the political-sociological axis. Although Honneth mainly works to explain the normative logic underlying the motivational forces that lead people to engage in struggles for recognition, he does not aim to develop a theory of social struggles as such. What is problematic, however, is that the political-sociological axis remains underdeveloped in Honneth's writings.

If – as suggested above – Honneth's negative assessment of Bourdieu corresponds to the painstakingly developed moral-sociological axis, while his positive critique addresses the deficiently developed political-sociological axis of his theory, it is no mystery that Honneth makes more of an effort to flesh out his negative critique of Bourdieu through a monographic article (Honneth, 1995 [1984]), whereas his positive assessment of Bourdieu is not reflected in an equal manner in any part of his work, but is instead evident in scattered remarks throughout his writings.

This further explains why Honneth's negative assessment of Bourdieu's sociology has been taken up so often in the literature on Bourdieu's work. There is a direct relationship between what is recognised and thematised in Honneth's negative assessment of Bourdieu and the central, predominant nature of the moral-sociological axis in Honneth's work as well as between the unexplored nature of the affirmative aspect of Honneth's critique of Bourdieu and the underdeveloped nature of the political-sociological axis in Honneth's work.

For those familiar with the secondary literature on Bourdieu's sociology, there is a well-established intellectual relationship between Honneth and

Bourdieu. Working from a moral-sociological perspective, Honneth is the theorist from the Frankfurt School who, like others, has criticised the presence of a strategic economic perspective of action and a utilitarian nucleus in Bourdieu's work (Wacquant, 1992; Swartz, 1997), despite his interest in and open admiration for the critical theory of society and the exemplary conjunction between it and the empirical social research Bourdieu developed (Honneth and Schiller, 1994; Bourdieu, Honneth, Kocyba and Schwibs, 1986; Honneth, 2007).

According to this understanding, Honneth forms part of a group of authors (Jenkins, 1982; Joppke, 1986; Caillé, 1992; Miller and Branson, 1987; Miller, 1989; Gartman, 1991) who, in one way or another, denounce the presence of a utilitarian strategic perspective in the concepts of habitus, capital and field. It is these writers who, in defence of Bourdieu, respond to this critique, citing the profoundly flawed nature of Honneth's interpretations of Bourdieu's work (Wacquant, 1992). In this context, he is directly linked to the anti-utilitarian undertakings of Alain Caillé (1981; 1992; 1994; 2000).

As is clear in the secondary literature, this discussion about the more or less utilitarian strategic perspective present in Bourdieu's works centres on the interpretation of the Bourdieusian concept of interest (Honneth, 1995 [1984]; 1995 [1992]; Bourdieu, 1993; Bourdieu and Wacquant, 1992; Calhoun, 1993; Swartz, 1997). While Honneth recognises Bourdieu's attempt to revive the concept of the subject of action without abandoning a structuralist perspective, he feels too high a price is paid when the subject is assumed to be not only over-socialised but also as a mere carrier of the unconscious interests associated with class positions. In other words, Honneth asserts it is too costly to reintroduce or reappropriate – even in revised terms – a utilitarian perspective based on the idea of utility maximisation. Thus, for Honneth, the notion of unconscious strategy represents not an alternative to utilitarianism (1995 [1984]; 1995 [1992]) but rather an innovative conceptual variation within it. Due to this key difference at the socio-ontological level, Honneth, according to his own reconstruction, cannot take up Bourdieu's concept of the symbolic struggles for recognition or the model of social conflict that informs it. Those who defend Bourdieu (Wacquant, 1992) – including Bourdieu himself (Bourdieu and Wacquant, 1992) – continue to argue that the concept of interest and alternative concepts such as illusio, libido, commitment (Bourdieu, 1998 [1994]) do not necessitate an intentionalist or utilitarian perspective. The fact that this defence sees in that critique an understanding of the concept of interest and strategy in intentionalist terms – that is, conscious strategies – leaves no room for doubt that there is a lack of understanding, conceptual precision and clarity in this debate which raged during the late 1980s and early 1990s.

While the scope and objectives of this chapter make it unfeasible to reconstruct this lengthy discussion or adjudicate on Honneth's critique of Bourdieu, I wish to demonstrate it is not coincidental that the literature on this subject has largely ignored Honneth's assessment of Bourdieu's sociology as exemplary. This is because the argumentative axis on which Bourdieu constitutes a fundamental contribution is not fully developed in the conceptual architecture of Honneth's theory. On that axis Bourdieu's sociology is Honneth's only resource. As such, the affirmative references to it match exactly with what has thus far been the embryonic development of the political-sociological axis of Honneth's theory of recognition. This affirmative and exclusive relationship with Bourdieu in the context of that axis implies that when Honneth's affirmative recourse to Bourdieu is researched, one is also researching the political-sociological axis of Honneth's theory of the struggle for recognition. The following section examines the dual nature of such an endeavour.

3. *Political Recognition* and the Bourdieusian Space within a Moral-Sociological Theory of the Struggle for Recognition

The political-sociological axis is not only less developed than, but also housed or located within, the moral-sociological axis in Honneth's work. To put it differently, the development of this axis is not just highly diminished but also relatively invisible. As a result, in order to identify it, one must extract political-sociological arguments from the broad moral-sociological field that houses this axis.

Perhaps the most appropriate context in which to initiate such an analysis is Honneth's discussion of social struggles for recognition as social esteem (*soziale Wertschätzung*) (Honneth, 1995 [1992]; 2003). I will reconstruct this context in part by employing my own analytical categories. According to Honneth's analysis of the structure of social relationships of recognition, external negative situations in the sphere of recognition as social esteem – that is, situations which entail a lack of recognition and therefore cause moral suffering – are those that result in an unjust or inadequate social appraisal of the contributions people make to society through their activities or their individual capacities and characteristics.[1]

According to this moral-sociological model of social conflict, the struggle for recognition as a struggle over social esteem goes back to moral experiences characterised by the feeling of social disrespect (*soziale Mißachtung*). Honneth defends the relevance of this moral-sociological explicative model, recommending that it not only be acknowledged for its distinctiveness with respect to other explicative models based on the notion of interest, but also that it be placed alongside or even in a condition of superiority over these other models because of its explicative potential (Honneth, 1995 [1992]).

These assertions are evident in Honneth's debate with Fraser, during which he gives attention and credence to the social struggle to make female labour visible (Honneth, 2003). Honneth argues that the underestimation of the value of women's activities is not due to the content of the work itself, but due to the fact that when an activity is carried out mainly by women it automatically loses value in the social hierarchy. To put it another way, the social value of an activity is not an objective, technical issue related to its content but rather a matter dependent on the cultural significance of the gender of those who perform it. Honneth thus explains that domestic work and childcare are not even considered to be labour. This negative external situation unleashes a feeling of injustice which results from seeing the real contribution one makes to society unjustly undervalued. At the same time, this feeling can become the motivational basis for structuring one's subjectivity around a commitment to social struggle.

At least in this context, Honneth is not interested in the strictly political-sociological issue of how these individual and subjective experiences come to be articulated as collective experiences that constitute the basis for shared social struggles. He does, however, productively examine the goals and objectives which can be identified in these struggles. One such objective is the calling into question of dominant forms of social esteem in order to change them, thereby transforming the social recognition of women's work and leading to the establishment of more equitable material (Honneth, 2003). Used here as an example, the feminist movement clearly established this link between a specific type of unjust experience and a goal such as the transformation of the standards by which society accords social esteem, as seen in the systemic, objective and structural nature of the negative exterior situations which provoke unequal treatment.

As explained above, Honneth's argument addresses the identification of a negative external situation that raises negative experiences or feelings of injustice which potentially constitute the motivational basis of social struggles, whose goals are oriented towards transforming the dominant symbolic systems of social esteem. For Honneth, identifying the moral nature of these objectives is important because it is the only way he can theoretically anticipate the moral justifiability of the demands for recognition. This is because, to the degree that these demands are based on the socially accepted value of equality of merits, they must be publically justifiable. It is doubtful, however, whether or not the justifiability (or non-justifiability) of a demand for recognition can be based solely on this pre-political aspect. Rather, justifiability also occurs in the strictly political sphere, that is, in the sphere linked to the political-sociological axis, where practices of justification and public validation take place.

Notably, Honneth does not explain the causal nexus between these experiences and goals. That is, he does not focus on which complex social technology comes into play so that these collective goals can be constituted on the basis of experiences that are initially singular and unarticulated. Instead, Honneth reconstructs this nexus starting from a paradigmatic example of the feminist struggles in which these goals are already explicit.

It is precisely in relation to that 'practical habitus' – which takes place between singular negative experiences and the formulation of collective goals that are discursively articulated and sustained through stable collective work – that a fundamentally political-sociological argument develops. Through this process, individual or singular forms of social suffering can be articulated, cognitively and politically represented, and expressed through adequate language, such as that of the construction of goals. I want to argue that this is the phenomenal field to which the political-sociological axis refers in general – an axis that, as I have stated, is underdeveloped and barely perceptible in Honneth's work.

As I have shown, Honneth's argument with respect to the struggle for recognition as social esteem emphasises the moral-sociological issue regarding the goals that a collective borne of systematic experiences of injustice sets for itself. These goals include transforming dominant forms of social esteem considered to be symbolic sources of the social disrespect in question. In so doing, Honneth refers, though superficially, to the prerequisites for achieving such a goal (recognition as social esteem). Honneth briefly frames these prerequisites in Bourdieusian vocabulary. From early on, he has been interested in Bourdieu's assertion that the symbolic dimension of social life acquires relevance without implying a denial of the significance of the material nature of class situations and the mechanisms by which these situations are reproduced. In fact, Honneth borrows the concept of symbolic struggles from Bourdieu to describe the political means by which social groups try to force a reinterpretation of the dominant system of social classifications in order to elevate their own positions in the system of prestige and social power.

> [S]ince the content of such interpretations depends in turn on which social groups succeed in publicly interpreting their own accomplishments [*Leistungen*] and forms of life in a way that shows them to be especially valuable, this secondary interpretive practice cannot be understood to be anything other than an ongoing cultural conflict. In modern societies, relations of social esteem are subject to a permanent struggle, in which different groups attempt, by means of symbolic force [*mit den Mitteln symbolischer Gewalt*] and with reference to general goals, to raise the value of the abilities associated with their way of life. (Honneth, 1995 [1992]: 126–127, the German words in italics are mine)

Honneth clearly posits this issue in terms of means and ends. The end is to achieve a reinterpretation of the dominant forms by which social esteem is accorded which, at the same time, is a means for achieving greater *social recognition*, but the means to this end is the symbolic violence that a group likely accumulates as it constitutes an effective instance of cognitive and political representation. These means can be understood in terms of the *political recognition* of a group and the demands that it can manifest in the political public space. It is further necessary to differentiate between social recognition, understood here as an objective and possible result of a social struggle, and the political recognition of that struggle, which is a prerequisite for social recognition to be demanded, sought and potentially reached. This difference is implicit when Honneth notes that

> [t]he more successful social movements are at drawing the public sphere's attention to the neglected significance of the traits and abilities they collectively represent, the better their chances of raising the social worth or, indeed, the standing of their members. (Honneth, 1995 [1992]: 127)

What I identify here using the term political recognition corresponds to the political-sociological axis, as identified above. When Honneth talks of recognition, he is clearly not talking about political recognition but rather the lack of recognition – that subjects, who are morally sensitive, develop feelings of resentment and then react by expressing these feelings. Honneth further refers to social recognition as a moral political objective of struggles that can be traced back to these moral feelings. And, if these moral feelings lead individuals to band together and form common goals which are eventually met, they can provide their subjects with the ability to enjoy change at the level of social structures.

Political recognition or the lack thereof is part of the political-sociological axis because the sociological question does not refer directly to the explanation of the motivational sources at the root of social struggles or to the goals that the organised and networked actors propose in order to overcome unjust situations. It refers instead to the potential development of complex interpretative processes of intersubjective articulation through which the actors, by their own practices, manage to objectify an intersubjective movement that allows a simple, uncoordinated and diverse collection of subjects and subjective experiences – a *simple collectio personarum plurium*, to use Bourdieu's words (Bourdieu, 1992) – to come into being as a collective, a social agent able to represent interests and demands in an antagonistic manner in the political public space. Bourdieusian concepts (Bourdieu, 1992) such as representation, delegation, substitution and ministerium revolve around the political-sociological axis in that they refer to the social technologies that make political recognition possible.

Honneth is able to turn to Bourdieu precisely because the political-sociological axis is independent of the moral-sociological axis and because there is no necessary continuity between them. To put it another way, in the context of the political-sociological axis, it is not decisive whether the motivations for social struggle correspond to a utilitarian strategic model of social action – such as the one Honneth argues Bourdieu supports – or to a moral-sociological model. The independence of the political-sociological axis is based on the fact that it can, in principle, correspond to either model. As I see it, this independence explains how Honneth can selectively inherit the Bourdieusian theory of the symbolic struggles for recognition, taking only that which fits with his own moral-sociological theory. Even as Honneth criticises Bourdieu's sociology for relying on an economic theory of action model to explain social actors' motivations for committing to social struggles, he can still take up Bourdieu's political-sociological conception. Bourdieu's political sociology can be removed from its original utilitarian strategic framework and relocated within a moral-sociological model. The supposition is that this kind of grafting does not pose an obstacle to or contradict the general framework of an elementally moral-sociological theory such as Honneth's. It is far from clear, however, if such an operation can be realised without generating conceptual problems of compatibility, that is, without generating a certain degree of ambivalence. Yet, rather than evaluating the consequences of such an operation, I will instead proceed with identifying the limited space in which certain key aspects of Bourdieu's political sociology find traction within Honneth's critical theory.

4. Bourdieu in Honneth's Political Sociology of Recognition

Once I have identified the argumentative field to which the political-sociological axis in Honneth's work specifically refers, I can touch upon some of the general characteristics of the Bourdieusian political-sociological representation to which Honneth turns in his discussions of social theory.

Honneth (1995 [1992]) states that it is not only the availability of symbolic violence to social groups but also their ability to influence the political public space – hegemonised by other groups and by those forms of social esteem that cause systemic experiences of a lack of recognition – that will decide the group's chances of achieving greater social recognition. Here the term 'greater' refers to the negative meaning of repairing damage rather than to the purely positive meaning of maximising status (model of conflict based on the notion of interest). In the context of this argument, which rests directly on Bourdieu's vocabulary, there are two fundamental argumentative vectors which I see as being intimately related and as structuring the phenomenal space of the political-sociological axis of Honneth's theory: the *vector of the continuum* and the *vector of conceptual sensibility*.

The vector of the continuum refers to Honneth's understanding of the notion of social struggles in terms of the different levels of collective association and cognitive and political representation that actors can achieve through their own practices. Influenced by Bourdieu, Honneth has a complex understanding of struggle. It is broad in the sense that it covers the different states of representation and organisation of social struggles. It covers the phenomenal space ranging from those forms of social suffering that are not thematised as such, that are minor, or that are comprised of individual struggles, initially invisible and not linked with one other, to collectively articulated political struggles, like the social movements that act discursively in the political public sphere, demanding reparation for suffering conceived of as a collective experience. Honneth conceives social struggle as a dynamic phenomenon in the sense that singular and plural experiences can always be represented and articulated collectively and that processes of collective articulation and cognitive representation can be developed and generalised by passing through the discursive filter of the dominant public thematisation.

Both characteristics of this political-sociological representation can be said to exist on a continuum between different 'states' of the objectification of social struggles according to the levels of generalisation, collective association and organisational and discursive density that are reached. Based on this notion of a continuum, the vector of conceptual sensibility refers to Honneth's argument that critical theory should not reduce the breadth of its gaze to social struggles which, having reached a relatively high level of articulation and cognitive and political representation, reside over the threshold of thematisation and public visibility. His argument is that theoretical analysis should instead focus on – or at least not lose sight of – experiences of suffering and forms of struggle whose existence, whether real or theoretically postulated, reside below the threshold given their low level of association, generalisation and cognitive and political representation.

The interconnection of these two vectors provides a system of reference in which it is possible to situate most, if not all, of Honneth's limited arguments involving the political-sociological axis. He concentrates on the section of the continuum of articulation and public visibility with respect to subjective expressions of criticism and social struggles that reside below the threshold of thematisation and public visibility. He demands that critical theory not forget the phenomenal field in which experiences of social suffering, and subjective reactions to them, have not acquired a level of association to the degree that they can be politically represented in the political public sphere, as they are often not even represented cognitively. In addressing this demand, Honneth finds that Bourdieu's sociology is exemplary as a critical sociology.

There is a certain parallelism in the logic that underlies both the moral-sociological axis and the political-sociological axis in Honneth's work. The first axis assumes a perspective relative to the negativity of the social world in the sense that it starts from negative moral experiences of a lack of recognition or social rejection. Honneth requires that theory and social research do the same with respect to the political-sociological axis – i.e. not to concentrate only on the social struggles that already enjoy political recognition, but on those that are not yet politically recognised. To put it another way, the concern with the lack of social recognition in the moral-sociological axis corresponds to a concern over the lack of political recognition in the political-sociological axis.

This appraisal is especially evident when Honneth perceives that there is a tendency to detract from the phenomenal field in other developments of critical theory. To support this argument, I will refer to two metatheoretical critiques Honneth offers in this regard. The first one appears very early on against Habermas (Honneth, 1995 [1981]), and the other one, more recently, against Fraser (Honneth, 2003).

Honneth (2000) has criticised the fact that Habermas's theory of communicative action abstracts the phenomenal field of negative moral experiences. Early on, Honneth rejected the abstracting of all forms of negative experiences, social suffering and social struggles, which – given their lack of discursive and political organisation and thus their lack of cognitive and political representation – are not represented in the democratic public sphere where the collective will is formed. These two critiques are related but different, and I am interested in the latter rather than in the former.

By the early 1980s, Honneth (1995 [1981]) was using Bourdieu's sociology to criticise the effects of theoretical insensitivity that the Habermasian perspective produced. Rather than refute the assertion that a moral practical interest capable of promoting historical moral learning accumulates in culturally advanced and economically privileged groups – a thesis that, according to Honneth, Habermas would defend – Honneth tried to demonstrate that this kind of theoretical representation provoked a strong cognitive insensitivity within critical theory. In a certain sense, this critique challenged the Arendtian separation between political equality and economic inequality which, despite great differences, Honneth (2007 [1999]) seems to identify, at least residually, in Habermas. To conceive, as Habermas would have done, that the potential for rationality and the moral development of modern societies is concentrated only in critiques of the consequences of instrumental rationality carried out by certain socio-cultural vanguards – the privileged, cultural and socially advanced groups that issue their demands directly in the political public space – would imply for Honneth that we must ignore the moral-sociological explicative concern regarding the moral practical interest expressed by those groups who develop such an interest precisely because of their systematic experiences of deprivation and economic dependence. Viewing this situation from a political-sociological perspective, it becomes clear that these struggles, unlike those faced by the aforementioned socio-cultural vanguards, take place in political and social invisibility. In other words, they are deployed below the threshold of public thematisation because they are experiences of suffering that are not collectively or discursively expressed through an adequate moral vocabulary or politically represented through a collective in struggle (Honneth, 1995 [1980]; 1995 [1981]; Iser, 2008).

At the same time, assuming what I have called the continuum vector, Honneth (1995 [1981]) uses Bourdieu to assert that Habermas's perspective is blind to the fact that the public expression of feelings of social injustice by dispossessed and economically dependent classes is hindered or impeded by the ideological effectiveness of social control in the context of symbolic domination. In a certain sense, this coincides with the fact that Honneth reaffirms that the tradition of critical theory has always imposed an extra task upon itself. That is, in addition to offering a critique of unjust or pathological social conditions, it thematises certain states of consciousness and practices of social suffering and structurally determined forms of conflict even when the actors themselves do not describe their practices and experiences in these terms (Honneth, 2007 [1994]). The practical moral expressions of these classes would be invisible in any theory focused on the discourses that hegemonically occupy the political public space and do not thematise the effects of symbolic domination or prerequisites of cultural and symbolic power necessary for participation in that sphere. Honneth tends to assume, with Bourdieu, that differences at the level of symbolic cultural capital are intimately related to differences in the power to intervene in the political public space, to the extent that the focus of Habermas's theory on culturally advanced groups would necessarily imply a focus on a conceptual field that exists over the threshold of visibility and perceptibility.

Although he does so with different objectives and in ways that depart from those seen in the context of Habermas's critique, Honneth – in the framework of a discussion entitled 'Redistribution and/or Recognition?' (Fraser and Honneth, 2003) – criticises Nancy Fraser's theory as being insensitive not only to experiences of social suffering that are not politically represented but also to the everyday struggles carried out by actors in reaction to their experiences. Even more clearly than in his critique of Habermas, Honneth makes use of the concept of the political-sociological axis in order to advance an argument in which Bourdieu's sociology is valued as exemplary. The aspect of Fraser's critique that is most relevant here relates back to the characteristics of broadness and dynamism which figure prominently in the Bourdieusian socio-political representation with which Honneth operates.

Consistent with what I call the breadth of his concept of politics, Honneth criticises the fact that Fraser's theory tends to limit its attention to those negative experiences and social struggles that are expressed and operate only in the political public sphere. This is because they already enjoy political recognition as such or, as Honneth puts it, they have already crossed the threshold of perceptibility (Honneth, 2003). In this regard, Honneth claims that one of the biggest problems with Fraser's critical theory is that she is satisfied with reducing its cognitive abilities to demands that have already been expressed by social movements. In so doing, it loses the autonomy necessary to cognitively represent that which is not yet represented cognitively or politically but is nonetheless important from the standpoint of critical theory (Honneth, 2003), given that it refers to experiences of suffering as well as to practically and morally significant reactions to it.

Honneth uses his analysis of the dynamic character of social struggle to advance a critique against Fraser, charging her with taking a static or objectified view of social struggles. Whether she wants to or not, Honneth argues, by fixing her theoretical perspective on the realm of social movements that are hegemonically operative in the political public space, Fraser focuses on the mere result of struggles for social recognition. In other words, she concentrates on the most elevated space of objectification in the context of a dynamic process of association and representation that, if thought of as a continuum, embeds its roots far below the threshold of public visibility. Honneth also speaks of Fraser's fascination with social movements. This fascination prevents her from adopting the perspective of continuum, which would allow her to see that what is politically represented at a given moment is established by a complex process of association that involves great effort on the part of many actors, the majority of whom are below the level of public recognition.

During the 1980s, Honneth turns mainly to Bourdieu's *Distinction* (1984 [1979]) to inform his critique of Habermas while, at the beginning of this century, he primarily cites *The Weight of Our World* (1999 [1993]) in his critique of Fraser. Nonetheless, Honneth's affirmative references to Bourdieu are marked by the same political-sociological cognitive interest – a cognitive interest of a fundamentally moral-sociological explicative order. No matter how different they appear or how far apart they are in time, the same demand can be appreciated in both argumentative contexts. Honneth contends that critical theory should be sensitive to the phenomenal field that exists below the perceptual threshold of the political public sphere (Honneth, 2003; Cooke,

2009). This demand clearly has a moral-sociological explicative aspect: not to lose sight of the moral practical expressions that are not directly within reach as empirical objects because they are not found in the space of visibility and public thematisation. I want to argue that this demand also has a political-sociological aspect in that it refers to a specific representation of the complex phenomenon of social struggles as such and of the experiences of political recognition that take place in the field.

As shown above, this demand becomes a critique of other expressions of critical theory (those of Habermas and Fraser). Above all, however, it refers to the person who asserts the demand. This is surely linked to a specific concept of critical theory and social research and, as such, should be found in one way or another in Honneth's research projects at the Frankfurt *Institute for Social Research*, which he has directed since 2001. Clearly, an evaluation of the degree to which Honneth's intellectual project also aims to meet this Bourdieusian demand is beyond the scope of this chapter. The arguments presented here are simply meant to be a first step – one that is less substantively theoretical but more analytical and pertinent to conceptual architecture, thereby leading us to a more comprehensive understanding of the relationship between two important modern social theories of social struggles and an exploration of the fields of analysis in which this relationship may be evaluated. Having taken this first step, we unfurl an extensive array of questions which should continue to be explored.

Acknowledgements

I am grateful to Nora Sieverding and Luc Boltanski for their generous comments on my ideas. In addition, I would like to thank Katherine Goldman, Simon Susen, and Jonathan Trejo-Mathys for their support in the development of this text.

Notes

* Instituto de Humanidades, Universidad Diego Portales – Santiago de Chile. Also Groupe de Sociologie Politique et Morale, École des Hautes Études en Sciences Sociales, Paris.

1 With Hegel's help, Honneth (1995 [1992]) describes the structure of the social relationships of recognition within modern societies as a differentiated structure in three modes of recognition: emotional attention, respect, and social esteem. Each one of those forms of recognition refers to a dimension of the personality: the nature of needs and affectivity, moral responsibility, and a person's specific skills and qualities, respectively. There are also three forms of recognition that are implied there: those that take place in primary relationships such as love and friendship; legal relations among

individuals, expressed specifically in individual rights; and community values, which constitute relationships of solidarity. While positive experiences in each of these spheres generate self-confidence, self-respect and self-esteem, respectively, each is also related to a specific form of negative moral experience. These are mistreatment and violation, the dispossession of rights and exclusion and indignity and injury. In each of these spheres exists a component of the personality that is threatened where such negative moral experiences effectively take place: physical integrity, social integrity and, lastly, honor and personal dignity.

References

Behr, Hartmut (2001) 'Die politische Theorie des Relationismus: Pierre Bourdieu', in André Brodocz and Gary Schaal (eds.) *Politische Theorien der Gegenwart II. Eine Einführung*, Opladen: Leske + Budrich, pp. 378–397.

Bourdieu, Pierre (1984 [1979]) *Distinction: A Social Critique of the Judgement of Taste*, trans. Richard Nice, Cambridge, Mass.: Harvard University Press.

Bourdieu, Pierre (1992) *Language and Symbolic Power*, edited and introduced by John B. Thompson, translated by Gino Raymond and Matthew Adamson, Cambridge: Polity Press.

Bourdieu, Pierre (1993) 'Concluding Remarks: For a Sociogenetic Understanding of Intellectual Works', trans. Nicole Kaplan, Craig Calhoun and Leah Florence, in Craig Calhoun, Edward LiPuma and Moishe Postone (eds.) *Bourdieu: Critical Perspectives*, Chicago: University of Chicago Press, pp. 263–275.

Bourdieu, Pierre (1998 [1994]) *Practical Reason: On the Theory of Action*, Cambridge: Polity Press.

Bourdieu, Pierre (1999 [1993]) *The Weight of the World: Social Suffering in Contemporary Society*, trans. Priscilla Parkhurst Ferguson [et al.], Cambridge: Polity Press.

Bourdieu, Pierre, Axel Honneth, Hermann Kocyba and Bernd Schwibs (1986) 'Der Kampf um die symbolische Ordnung', *Ästhetik und Kommunikation* 16(61/62): 142–164.

Bourdieu, Pierre and Loïc Wacquant (1992) *An Invitation to Reflexive Sociology*, Cambridge: Polity Press.

Calhoun, Craig (1993) 'Habitus, Field, and Capital: The Question of Historical Specificity', in Craig Calhoun, Edward LiPuma and Moishe Postone (eds.) *Bourdieu: Critical Perspectives*, Chicago: University of Chicago Press, pp. 61–88.

Caillé, Alain (1981) 'La sociologie de l'intérêt est-elle intéressante?' *Sociologie du travail* 23(3): 257–274.

Caillé, Alain (1992) 'Esquisse d'une critique de l'économie générale de la pratique', *Cahiers du LASA* 12/13: 109–219.

Caillé, Alain (1994) *Don, intérêt et désintéressement. Bourdieu, Mauss, Platon et quelques autres*, Paris: La Découverte.

Caillé, Alain (2000) *Anthropologie du don. Le tiers paradigme*, Paris: Desclée de Brouwer.

Cooke, Maeve (2009) 'Wertepluralismus und Selbstverwirklichung. Überlegungen zu einer postuniversalistischen Politik der Anerkennung', in Rainer Forst, Martin Hartmann, Rahel Jaeggi and Martin Saar (eds.) *Sozialphilosophie und Kritik. Axel Honneth zum 60. Geburtstag*, Frankfurt am Main: Suhrkamp, pp. 17–39.

Fraser, Nancy and Axel Honneth (2003) *Redistribution or Recognition? A Political-Philosophical Exchange*, trans. Joel Golb, James Ingram and Christiane Wilke, London: Verso.

Gartman, David (1991) 'Culture as Class Symbolization or Mass Reification: A Critique of Bourdieu's *Distinction*', *American Journal of Sociology* 97(2): 421–447.

Honneth, Axel (1984) 'Moralischer Konsens und Unrechtsempfindung. Zu Barrington Moores Untersuchung über *Ungerechtigkeit. Die sozialen Ursachen von Unterordnung und Widerstand*', in *Suhrkamp Wissenschaft. Weißes Programm im Frühjahr 1984. Ein Almanach*, Frankfurt am Main: Suhrkamp, pp. 108–114.

Honneth, Axel (1995 [1980]) 'Work and Instrumental Action: On the Normative Basis of Critical Theory', trans. Mitchell G. Ash and Charles W. Wright, in his *The Fragmented World of the Social*, edited by Charles W. Wright, Albany: State University of New York Press, pp. 15–49.

Honneth, Axel (1995 [1981]) 'Moral Consciousness and Class Domination: Some Problems in the Analysis of Hidden Morality', trans. Mitchell G. Ash, in his *The Fragmented World of the Social*, edited by Charles W. Wright, Albany: State University of New York Press, pp. 205–219.

Honneth, Axel (1995 [1984]) 'The Fragmented World of Symbolic Forms: Reflections on Pierre Bourdieu's Sociology of Culture', trans. T. Talbot, in his *The Fragmented World of the Social*, edited by Charles W. Wright, Albany: State University of New York Press, pp. 184–201.

Honneth, Axel (1995 [1990]) *The Fragmented World of the Social. Essays in Social and Political Philosophy*, edited by Charles W. Wright, Albany: State University of New York Press.

Honneth, Axel (1995 [1992]) *The Struggle for Recognition: The Moral Grammar of Social Conflicts*, trans. Joel Anderson, Cambridge: Polity Press.

Honneth, Axel (2000) 'Anerkennungsbeziehungen und Moral. Eine Diskussionsbemerkung zur anthropologischen Erweiterung der Diskursethik', in Reinhard Brunner and Peter Kelbel (eds.) *Anthropologie, Ethik und Gesellschaft. Für Helmut Fahrenbach*, Frankfurt am Main, New York: Campus, pp. 101–111.

Honneth, Axel (2003) 'Redistribution as Recognition: A Response to Nancy Fraser', in Nancy Fraser and Axel Honneth (2003) *Redistribution or Recognition? A Political-Philosophical Exchange*, trans. Joel Golb, James Ingram and Christiane Wilke, London: Verso, pp. 110–197.

Honneth, Axel (2007 [1994]) 'Pathologies of the Social: The Past and Present of Social Philosophy', trans. Joseph Ganahl, in his *Disrespect: The Normative Foundations of Critical Theory*, Cambridge: Polity Press, pp. 3–48.

Honneth, Axel (2007 [1999]) 'Democracy as Reflexive Cooperation: John Dewey and the Theory of Democracy today', trans. John Farrell, in his *Disrespect: The Normative Foundations of Critical Theory*, Cambridge: Polity Press, pp. 218–239.

Honneth, Axel (2007 [2000]) *Disrespect: The Normative Foundations of Critical Theory*, Cambridge: Polity Press.

Honneth, Axel (2007) *Pathologien der Vernunft. Geschichte und Gegenwart der Kritischen Theorie*, Frankfurt am Main: Suhrkamp.

Honneth, Axel and Hans-Ernst Schiller (1994) 'Aktualität des Adornoschen Denkens: Ein Gespräch mit Axel Honneth und Hans-Ernst Schiller', *Links* 7/8: 27–31.

Honneth, Axel, Mauro Basaure, Jan-Philipp Reemtsma and Rasmus Willig (2009) *Erneuerung der Kritik. Axel Honneth im Gespräch*, Frankfurt am Main, New York: Campus.

Iser, Mattias (2008) *Empörung und Fortschritt. Grundlagen einer kritischen Theorie der Gesellschaft*, Frankfurt am Main, New York: Campus.

Jenkins, Richard (1982) 'Pierre Bourdieu and the Reproduction of Determinism', *Sociology* 16(2): 270–281.

Joppke, Christian (1986) 'The Cultural Dimension of Class Formation and Class Struggle: On the Social Theory of Pierre Bourdieu', *Berkeley Journal of Sociology* 31: 53–78.
Miller, Max (1989) 'Die kulturelle Dressur des Leviathans und ihre epistemologischen Reflexe', *Soziologische Revue* 12(1): 19–24.
Miller, Don and Jan Branson (1987) 'Pierre Bourdieu: Culture and Praxis', in Diane Austin-Bross (ed.) *Creating Culture: Profiles in the Study of Culture*, Sydney: Allen and Unwin, pp. 210–225.
Swartz, David (1997) *Culture and Power: The Sociology of Pierre Bourdieu*, Chicago: University of Chicago Press.
Wacquant, Loïc (1992) 'Toward a Social Praxeology: The Structure and Logic of Bourdieu's Sociology', in Pierre Bourdieu and Loïc Wacquant, *An Invitation to Reflexive Sociology*, Cambridge: Polity Press, pp. 1–59.

CHAPTER TEN

Pierre Bourdieu and the Sociology of Religion[1]

Bryan S. Turner

Introduction: The Secularisation Thesis

Whereas in recent years many of sociologists and philosophers have come to the conclusion that religion has to be taken seriously in debates about modern politics and the public sphere, such was not the case with many post-war social theorists. Louis Althusser, Luc Boltanski, Ralf Dahrendorf, Norbert Elias, Anthony Giddens, David Harvey, Edward Said and Göran Therborn either ignored religion or paid little attention to it, rather than treating it as a central aspect of modern society. Michel Foucault was probably alone in his consistent interest in religion – for example, in his essays on medieval Christian teaching on chastity and in his view of the Iranian Revolution as a form of spiritual politics. On a more personal note, he spoke about 'spirituality', that is, the 'search, practice and experience through which the subject carries out the necessary transformations on himself in order to have access to the truth' (Foucault, 2005 [2001]: 15). The majority of public intellectuals on the Left in the post-war period ignored religion as a spent force in modernity. What has changed? The obvious answer is that there are various transformations of social and political life that have placed religion as an institution at the centre of modern society. Religion now appears to be closely related to identity politics and has been the ideological driving force behind social movements such as Solidarity, 'engaged Buddhism' and Hindu nationalism.

The earlier post-war generation of social scientists accepted the secularisation thesis that, with modernisation, religion would inevitably decline and hence there was little point investing research effort into an institution that was going to disappear. In Europe, there was the additional factor of Marxist social and political theory, which was in France and elsewhere an influential tradition. For these critical theorists, there was no assumption that religion could continue to exercise significant ideological influence over secular modernity, especially in the West. As the 'heart of a heartless world' religion might have some lingering influence in the Third World, but religion was simply a set of false beliefs that comforted the disinherited and legitimised the rich and powerful. Religious ideologies would disappear with the spread of secular science, urbanisation, literacy, working-class struggles and the emancipation of women.

The dramatic collapse of organised communism in the early 1990s and the decline in Marxist-Leninist ideology allowed religion to flourish once more in European societies, especially in Eastern European countries such as Poland, the Ukraine and what used to be Yugoslavia. In Russia, the Orthodox Church has become closely associated with nationalism. In Vietnam, while the Communist Party has not disappeared, the modern Renovation Period has seen a modest return of religion (such as Roman Catholicism) to public life, and Protestant sects have been successful in missionary work among the ethnic minorities. Spirit possession cults are also attracting members of an emerging middle class from the expanding capitalist sector. Globalisation and the Internet have created new opportunities for evangelism even in societies where the Party still attempts to regulate or suppress the flow of information and interaction. In China, Charter 08 calls for, among other things, freedom of religious assembly and practice. While these dissident movements are unlikely to shake the control of the Party or its authoritarian responses to religious revivalism, these developments are likely to see a significant growth in religious activity across both the existing communist and the post-communist world. As a result of such social transformations, there is a need to rethink many aspects of modern secularity (Taylor, 2002 and 2007). Pentecostalism and charismatic churches have also enjoyed phenomenal growth in South America and Africa.

One obvious feature of globalisation has been the growth of flexible labour markets, mass migration and permanent settlement producing the world-wide emergence of diasporic communities in societies with expanding economies. These diasporic communities are typically held together by their religious beliefs and practices in such a way that in modern societies the distinction between ethnicity and religion begins to become irrelevant. Indeed the 'Turks' in Germany have become 'Muslims', and around the world Chinese minorities – for example, in Indonesia and Malaysia – are almost automatically called 'Buddhists'. The result is that religion has become a major plank of public culture and 'the politics of identity'. Consequently, religion has often emerged as the principal site of ethnic and cultural contestation, and states have become involved in the management of religions, thereby inevitably departing from the traditional separation of state and religion in the liberal framework. Paradoxically, by intervening to regulate religion in the public domain, the state automatically makes religion more important and prominent. In societies as different as the United States and Singapore, the state intervenes to regulate Islam in the name of incorporating 'moderate Muslims' into mainstream society (Kamaludeen, Pereira and Turner, 2009). Throughout the modern world, there is a complex interaction between religion and national identity – from Hinduism in India to Catholicism in Poland to Shinto in Japan – whereby religion becomes part of the fabric of public discourse.

Perhaps the critical event of modern religious history was the Iranian Revolution in 1978–9. The fall of the secular state, which had promoted a nationalist vision of society as a Persian civilisation over a traditional Islamic framework, provided a global example of a spiritual revolution. It offered a singular instance of the mobilisation of the masses in the name of religious renewal. The message of the Iranian intellectual Ali Shariati against what he called 'Westoxification' was embraced by a wide variety of religious movements outside the specific Iranian context (Akbarzadeh and Mansouri, 2007). Islam became at least one conduit of the political idea that modernisation could take many forms and that the domination of North American capitalist society could be opposed (Halliday, 2003). Reformed Islam came to encapsulate the notion that secularism was not the inevitable shell of modernity. The other defining moment was the 9/11 attack on the Twin Towers – the very symbol of the financial dominance of the West over the developing world. This attack has come to be interpreted as a symbolic as much as a terrorist event (Gole, 1996). In a similar fashion, the cultural and social ambiguities of veiling stand for the problematical status of women in modern secular cultures (Lazreg, 2009).

By now there is considerable attention to the limitations and failures of the conventional secularisation thesis and much has consequently been written about religious renewal and revival. Whereas in the 1960s sociologists of religion such as Bryan Wilson (1966 and 1976) described the decline of religion as a necessary outcome of modernisation, the secularisation thesis is now seen to be narrow and culturally specific rather than a general account of social change (Demerath, 2007). Northern Europe, rather than the United States, is seen to be the principal example of 'exceptionalism' in the sense that religious decline in terms of church membership, attendance and religious belief may have been characteristic of many European societies in the second half of the twentieth century but these developments have not been typical – albeit for very different reasons – of the United States, Africa and much of Asia.

The rekindling of academic interest in religion and modernity has been sparked off by the (unexpected) attention shown by Jürgen Habermas (2002 [1981, 1991, 1997]) in his *Religion and Rationality*. For academics working in the sub-discipline of the sociology of religion, Habermas's reflections on religion do not provide any new insights or conclusions that are not already familiar to social scientists working in the sociology of religion. He has claimed that the secularisation thesis rested on the assumption that the 'disenchanted world' rests on a scientific outlook in which all phenomena can be explained rationally. In addition, there has been a differentiation of society into specialised functions in which religion becomes increasingly a private matter. Finally, the transformation of society from an agrarian basis has improved living standards and has reduced risk, removing the dependence of individuals on supernatural forces and reducing their need for religious meaning and psychological support.

Habermas notes, however, that the secularisation debate is based on a narrow European viewpoint. North America, by contrast, appears to be a vibrantly religious society, in which religion, prosperity and modernisation have sat comfortably together for decades. In more global terms, Habermas draws attention to the spread of fundamentalism, the growth of radical Islamic groups, and the presence of religious issues in the public sphere. The privatisation of religion – the cornerstone of the liberal view of tolerance in the legacy of John Locke – is thought by many observers to be no longer a viable political strategy in the separation of state and religion (Spinner-Halevy, 2005). Habermas's solution to the problems surrounding radical fundamentalism and radical secularism is to propose a dialogue involving the inclusion of foreign minority cultures into civil society, on the one hand, and the opening up of subcultures to the state in order to encourage their members to participate actively in political life, on the other. Both religious and secular citizens are called upon to give a public account of their beliefs and to engage in public debate; secularists can no longer marginalise religious belief, while religious citizens have an equal obligation to make their beliefs available to public reasoning (Habermas, 2008 [2005]).

In some respects, Habermas's debate about the pre-political foundations of the liberal state with Joseph Ratzinger (subsequently Pope Benedict XVI) at the Catholic Academy of Bavaria on 19 January 2008 was a revealing encounter. Both men were in a conciliatory mood (Habermas and Ratzinger, 2006). Habermas recognised that religion had preserved intact values and ideas that had been lost elsewhere and that the notion of the fundamental equality of all humans was an important legacy of the Christian faith. Habermas has also shown himself to be aware of, and possibly sympathetic to, much of the Jewish quest for otherness in the first generation of critical thinkers in the Frankfurt School. In retrospect, it is very clear that, for example, Walter Benjamin's interpretations of modern secular culture were deeply coloured by Jewish messianism (Wolin, 1994). This issue raises important questions not only about the continuities and discontinuities between the early and the late members of the critical tradition, but also about the notions of secularity,

Enlightenment rationality, and modernity. Indeed, it poses a problem about the continuity of Habermas's own philosophical work, which at the beginning had relatively little to say about the place of religion in civil society or about the idiosyncratic nature of religious discourse.

Habermas's response to Ratzinger can be understood against the German background of *Kulturprotestantismus*, in which there is a general respect for religion and where religion is far more prominent in public life than is the case in the United Kingdom or Scandinavia. Habermas's response may have been generous, but it does rest upon the idea that political institutions, and in particular the state, cannot really function without a robust civil society and without a set of shared values. Contrary to much critical theory and contrary to the secularisation thesis, the main role of religion may consist in supporting social life as such through the creation of shared meaning. This view of the public nature of religion was encapsulated in the idea of civil religion from Jean-Jacques Rousseau to Robert Bellah.

There is therefore discontent with the common emphasis in mainstream sociology of religion on the decline in belief and church membership in the conventional approach to secularisation. There is no necessary or simple connection, for example, between Christian belief and religious practice. In Britain, Grace Davie (1994 and 2006) pioneered the phrase 'believing without belonging' to capture these discontinuities between belief, church membership and worship. In retrospect one of the most important sociological interventions in this debate was José Casanova's *Public Religions in the Modern World* (1994), which provided a general framework for understanding key developments that had put religion at the centre of political life in many societies. Although there is a strong temptation to abandon the secularisation thesis in its entirety, Casanova does not support any premature abandonment of the entire argument about secularity but instead proposes that we can think of secularisation as simply a sub-theme of the more general notion of modernisation and that modernity involved the differentiation of the religious and the secular sphere. He has been critical of the idea that secularisation means simply the decline of religious belief and practice. He therefore identified three components of secularisation: (i) *differentiation* of various spheres of the social system (such as religion, state and market), (ii) *rationalisation* as the decline of religious belief and practice, and (iii) the *marginalisation* of religion to the private sphere. Consequently, an adequate sociology of religion has to evaluate these three components separately and independently. Following these global developments, sociologists of religion have been forced to review their assumptions about secularisation with the eruption of 'public religions' in the 1980s. Yet, his critical contribution was to identify important developments in what he called the 'deprivatisation' of religion. His examples of public religions included the Iranian Revolution, the liberation theologies of Latin America, the Solidarity movement in Poland, and the rise of the Moral Majority and the Christian Right in North America.

There is much discontent among contemporary sociologists of religion with traditional approaches to religion, and Casanova's work pushed the debate in important new directions, but there is still much turmoil in the subfield and some degree of uncertainty about what might come after the secularisation debate. As a result, sociologists of religion have started to look towards the work of Pierre Bourdieu to give them a more adequate framework for understanding religious practice, ritual and habitus (Furseth, 2009). Although Bourdieu's actual production of essays in the sociology of religion was slight, his influence can be seen in recent work such as Terry Rey's *Bourdieu on Religion* (2007). Other writers have also begun to draw on Bourdieu's notion of symbolic capital and field to study religion (Bell, 1990; Braun and McCutcheon, 2000; Engler, 2003; Schwartz, 1996; Taylor, 1998; Verter, 2003). There has also been interest in his early work on Algeria, in which one can find some discussion of religion (Loyal, 2009).

In this chapter I want to ask whether Bourdieu's work holds out any significant interest or new conceptual frameworks for the student of religion. My answer is somewhat paradoxical. What Bourdieu actually says about religion in his small oeuvre of essays on religion is not very interesting and most of it appears to depend on Max Weber explicitly and Louis Althusser implicitly. Having said that, his conceptual framework – capital, field, hexis and habitus – does provide a powerful perspective; avoiding many of the pitfalls arising from the exaggerated attention to religious beliefs, rather than embodied practices, in the work of both sociologists and philosophers of religion. Although Bourdieu's contribution to the sociology of practice is considerable, insights into practice and embodiment are obviously present in alternative traditions such as pragmatism (Barbalet, 2006).

In this chapter I develop a critical view of Bourdieu's interpretation and use of Weber's sociology of religion. These critical remarks on this aspect of Bourdieu's work need to be set within the context of recognising Bourdieu's clearly enthusiastic response to Weber's sociology as a whole; the enthusiasm was self-evidently present in his interview with Franz Schultheis and Andreas Pfeuffer (2000). Bourdieu's interpretation of Weber as salvaging the symbolic in Marx's economic sociology provided an important alternative to both Talcott Parsons and Raymond Aron, who – while themselves occupying different positions in politics – sought to distance Weber from Marx. Weber's writings became useful at various stages in Bourdieu's development. For example, Bourdieu notes that reading Weber's *Protestant Ethic* gave him a genuine insight into the economic ethics of the Kharijites in his Algerian research. Bourdieu also recognised the importance of Weber in his development of the concept of 'field', allowing him to capture the existence of social struggles over symbolic capital. Finally, Bourdieu acknowledged the value of Weber's work for putting forward the idea of 'character studies'. I would prefer to use Weber's own expression, 'personality and life orders', in order to develop the notion that Weber was constructing a sociology of piety, where we can see immediately the connections between piety, habitus, disposition and Aristotle's notion of virtue or excellence. From Bourdieu's interview it is clear that, avoiding the futile debate about whether Weber was on the left or the right of European politics, he made good use of Weber in his various works on distinction, symbolic violence, practice and so forth. Having recognised Bourdieu's appreciation of Weber, we need to turn to what Bourdieu actually has to say about religion.

Bourdieu on Religion: A Preliminary Critique

There is no need here to present an account of Bourdieu's general sociology. I shall merely select here certain aspects that are germane to a discussion of religion. According to Rey (2007), Bourdieu produced some ten essays on religion which were mainly confined to Roman Catholicism in France and to Islam in Algeria. His early work on the Kabylia in Algeria became the basis of a critique of the anthropological structuralism of Claude Lévi-Strauss. When Islam does appear in his work on Algeria the main influence on Bourdieu appears to be Weber's comparative sociology of religion, including Weber's commentaries on the sociology of law. Bourdieu's analysis of the differences between *Shari'a* and Kabyle customary law with respect to women and inheritance was probably influenced by Weber. Bourdieu did not pursue any subsequent ethnographic research that engaged with religion, with the possible exception of the study of Catholic bishops with M. de Saint Martin in 1982, and his ethnographic account of the Kabylia has been subsequently criticised (Goodman, 2003). Bourdieu undertook an empirical study of his home town Denguin in France in 1959 and 1960, publishing the work later as a collection of essays (Bourdieu, 2002). Although this work subsequently led Bourdieu to think more seriously about the emotional relations between biography and research, his study of marriage strategies in Denguin did not involve any significant discussion of the role of religion in peasant life (Jenkins, 2006).

Rey (2007: 57) has summed up Bourdieu's legacy in the study of religion by suggesting that his contribution was based on two firm convictions: 'that religion in the modern world is in decline; and that the ultimate function is to help people make sense of their position in the social order'. These two notions could be said to be a crude combination of Marx's view of religion as an opium of the people and Weber's treatment of religion as an aspect of power struggles between social groups over legitimacy. In this respect, the dominant influence was Weber, rather than Marx, and unsurprisingly the attention of most commentators has been focused on 'Une interprétation de la théorie de la religion selon Max Weber' (Bourdieu, 1971), a revised version of which was translated as 'Legitimation and Structured Interests in Weber's Sociology of Religion' (Bourdieu, 1987 [1971]).

Bourdieu's sociological reflections on religion have to be seen within the larger context of French secularism, that is, within the tradition of *laïcité* and French republicanism. For the Left, religion has meant in practice Roman Catholicism, which, for obvious reasons, has represented French conservatism, both in its political and in its cultural form. This critical view of Catholicism is associated with the French Revolution, with Rousseau's expression of Deism and with the conflicts between the Church and liberalism throughout the nineteenth century. The fact that France has been more deeply divided between left and right is reflected in the development of a tradition of 'religious sociology', rather than the 'sociology of religion'. In this French tradition, religious sociology often served as an arm of the pastoral reach of the Catholic Church, providing useful sociological data on church attendance, recruitment, belief and so on. These data were then used, for example, to make the missionary work of the Church more effective. Given that, in France, belief and investigation seem to have become hopelessly entwined, there has been the justifiable suspicion that the sociological study of religion has not been – and possibly cannot be – a neutral or objective inquiry.

This situation led Bourdieu to the conclusion that a science of religion was a contradiction in terms and that, as a result, religion was not a suitable topic for sociology. In a lecture to the French Association of Religious Sociology, which was later published as 'Sociologues de la croyance et croyances de sociologues', Bourdieu (1987) cast doubt on any sociological capacity to understand the institutions of religion without the intervention of the screen of belief. Those sociologists who were Catholic could by definition not study the Church, while those who had left the Church might be equally 'contaminated' by belief – or more so. Finally, those sociologists who had never had any connection with the Church would either not be interested in the topic or would miss important aspects of the phenomena out of ignorance. It follows that, from this point of view, religion cannot be studied by sociologists. As Danièle Hervieu-Léger (2000 [1993]: 14) points out, Bourdieu's lecture was a clever intervention, but not a convincing account of the issues involved. The same arguments might apply, for example, to the study of sexuality. It would mean that gay sociologists could never study homosexuality or that prisons could never be studied by sociologists with a record of incarceration. And, in any case, Bourdieu himself went on to publish some thirteen articles on religion – just to disprove his own argument?

One key problem with Bourdieu's approach to religion – in particular with regard to his study of the Church – is that he concentrated too much on formal positions, institutions and organised churches (Dillon, 2001). Bradford Verter (2003: 151) made a similar criticism when he observed that 'Bourdieu perceives religion almost exclusively in organisational terms [...]. This leaves little room for imagining lay people as social actors capable, for example, of manipulating religious symbols on their own behalf'. In addition, Bourdieu had, unlike Weber, relatively little interest in undertaking the comparative study of religion, and hence his observations on religion were to a large extent confined to Western Christianity. It might be more appropriate to suggest that his thinking about religion was confined to French Catholicism. Bourdieu's actual interests did not engage with the issues of explaining religious revivalism globally, the religions of the dispossessed, liberation theology in Latin America, Solidarity in Poland and so forth. While Bourdieu was influenced by Marx – writing, for example, an article called 'La sainte famille' (Bourdieu, 1982) after Marx and Engels's *The Holy Family* – he appeared to have suppressed Marx's equally important notion that religion is 'the sigh of the oppressed creature'. Religion is as much about protest against inequality and opposition to oppression as it is about the legitimacy of power. In arguing that a modern capitalist society is fundamentally secular, he borrowed from Weber in thinking about struggles over symbolic capital. In fact, he appropriated Weber's notions about the struggles between priest, prophets and sorcerers as a general model of the conflicts over status within the cultural field.

Religion, for Bourdieu, defines people and situates them in the social order. The idea that religion functions to define and insert people in the social structure is similar to the arguments put forward by Louis Althusser regarding the general character of ideology. Although there may be no direct or sustained intellectual connection between Althusser, structuralist Marxism and Bourdieu, there is some analytical similarity between Althusser's theory of ideology and Bourdieu's interpretation of religion. In his development of Marx's theory of ideology, Althusser constructed the idea of the 'interpellation' of the subject. For Althusser, the functions of ideology are unchanging throughout human history or, as he famously put it, 'ideology has no history' (1971: 150). The purpose of ideology is simply to constitute a subject and Althusser explained this process in terms of the notion of hailing a subject or interpellation. For example, when a teacher shouts out to a pupil 'Pay attention!' and the students turns towards the teacher, then this event of hailing forms a subject. Yet, this very recognition as a subject is already a 'misrecognition' (*méconnaissance*), since the individual is always already born as the subject of an ideology. Althusser illustrated this notion from Christianity by noticing that, in hearing the Voice of God, an individual receives instruction about his or her place in the world and what that person must do to become reconciled with Jesus Christ (Althusser, 1971: 166). By becoming subjected to themselves, individuals become subjects. Althusser, in this respect, conceived of ideology in terms of an imaginary relationship representing the connections between individuals as their actual or real conditions of existence (Althusser, 1971: 153). Finally, Althusser refused to see ideology as merely a collection of ideas, insisting instead that ideology is *embodied in actions and behaviours* that are governed by certain dispositions. In fact, ideas simply disappear, so to speak, in the material practices of persons in specific material settings. This idea of interpellation appears to coincide with Bourdieu's view of how religion functions in relation to the individual.

By interpreting ideology in terms of the dispositions that determine social actions, Althusser's theory of ideology appears to anticipate Bourdieu's notion of habitus fairly exactly. In short, to understand religion – for instance, religious orthodoxy – we should not attend to the formal *beliefs* (or doctrines) which individuals may or may not hold, but consider the ensemble of *practices* by which individuals occupy a position within a religious field. I see no reason, therefore, to accept David Swartz's assertion that 'Bourdieu is not fundamentally Althusserian' (Swartz, 1996: 73). The problem with this relationship to Althusser is that it suggests that Bourdieu has not in fact resolved the traditional conceptual problems of sociology such as the agency/structure division. Similar concerns have been expressed about Bourdieu's interpretations of literature where it is claimed that he reduces literature to a power struggle. In relation to Bourdieu's commentary on Flaubert, Jonathan Eastwood (2007: 157) complains about Bourdieu's 'excessive reductionism' and claims, reasonably enough, that '[l]iterary activity is clearly more than a battleground for the control of power resources' (Eastwood 2007: 166). Similar problems are raised about Bourdieu's theory of exchange and especially with respect to the idea of the gift where Bourdieu struggled unsuccessfully to deal with the possibility of the disinterested character of gift-giving (Silber, 2009).

While Bourdieu borrowed from the legacy of a structuralist Marxism, he also incorporated much from Weber, especially his analysis of charisma. The general notion of a religious field, within which different social groups compete for control and domination, is explicitly derived from Weber's general sociology. For Weber, all social relations are relations of power. Bourdieu, however, was critical of what he believed was Weber's psychological treatment of charisma. Allegedly, Weber interprets charisma as a *property* that belongs to an individual, rather than undertaking an examination of the social *relations* within which charismatic power resides.

Bourdieu (1987 [1971]: 129) contended that 'Max Weber never produces anything other than a psycho-sociological theory of charisma, a theory that regards it as the lived relation of a public to the charismatic personality'. Such a model is, for Bourdieu, defective because it ignores the interaction between prophet and laity. Social change can only take place when prophecy 'has its own generative and unifying principle a habitus objectively attuned to that of its addressees' (Bourdieu, 1987 [1971]: 131). While Bourdieu accepts the notion that charisma is a source of social transformation, it can only be so when the charismatic message is completely attuned to the dispositions or habitus of disciples and followers. Nevertheless, such an argument appears to rob charisma of its transformative agency by, for example, making it look more like traditional authority, that is, a form of authority that is compatible with existing dispositions (customs, values, and mores). The New Testament account of Jesus shows how he overthrows traditional authority: 'It is written but I say unto you.' We have, of course, to take into account that the New Testament wants to show how both Jesus and Paul overturned Jewish institutions in order to create a new dispensation, namely how the law is replaced by grace.

This interpretation of Weber is in fact completely misplaced and misleading. To take one crucial feature of the analysis of charisma in *The Sociology of Religion* (1966 [1922]), Weber recognised that disciples or followers of a charismatic figure want demonstrable and tangible proof of charismatic powers. The authority of charisma tends to get confirmed by the capacity of the leader to provide health, wealth or political success for his (and rarely her) followers. Thus, Weber (1966 [1922]: 47) observed that 'it was only under very unusual circumstances that a prophet succeeded in establishing his authority without charismatic authentication, which in practice meant magic. At least the bearers of a new doctrine practically always needed such validation'. In other words, in a struggle within the religious field, leaders seek social vindication from followers typically through magical means. To understand charisma, we need to appreciate its manifestations in social relationships. Weber identified an interesting paradox here. The charismatic leader desires a 'pure' commitment from his followers – 'Follow me because I come with the authority of God!' –, but the followers ask for clear evidence of such powers that are in concrete terms beneficial to them. Hence, in Weber's view, there is a constant *social* pressure for 'pure' charisma to become 'mundane' or practical charisma as a consequence of the conflicting interests of leader and followers. Commentaries on these charismatic demonstrations have noticed that the accounts of magical activities in the confirmation of Jesus's authority in the New Testament account are absent from the Acts of the Apostles, where Paul concentrates on one single event – Christ is resurrected (Badiou, 2003 [1997]).

These magical activities serve to show how the reception of charisma can often transform its contents in response to an audience. Weber was obviously aware of these pressures.

This tension is intensified by the frequent competition between charismatic figures for domination. These issues are evident in the New Testament account of Jesus, whose pure charisma is illustrated by his rejection of the Pharisees' interpretation of the Law. Nonetheless, Jesus's pure charisma is demonstrated by various magical *acts*: walking on water, the transformation of water into wine and the feeding of the five thousand. Although the New Testament portrays John the Baptist as preparing the way for Jesus and thereby subordinating himself to Jesus's ministry, we can interpret the relationship between them as an example of *charismatic competition*. Weber's analysis of charisma is parallel to his understanding of virtuoso and mass religion in which the superior charismatic status of the virtuoso remains parasitic upon the material gifts of the followers, in turn for which they can bestow a charismatic blessing. Weber's analysis of Buddhist monks in relation to the laity is another illustrative example of the exchange relationship (both competitive and co-operative) between laity and specialist (Weber, 1958 [1921]).

Within the competitive field, some charismatic leaders will become sorcerers, that is, religious agents who provide services to an audience – healing through magical activity. Over time, other forms of charismatic activity will be subject to routinisation, being thereby converted into priestly roles. Yet, some charismatic leaders, although subject to pressure from their followers to perform magical acts, will *transcend* the immediate habitus of their followers to issue a message that is both an act of transgression and an act of innovation. It is only when the message and the audience are not wholly 'attuned' that a charismatic breakthrough can occur at all. Interpretations of the actions of Jesus in the New Testament are obviously deeply divided, but one version would suggest that his followers expected him to take on the messianic role of a king, in the line of David, who would drive out the occupying Roman forces. His crucifixion was totally incompatible with those expectations. It is only when a charismatic leader stands over and against the routine expectations of an audience that a radical message can emerge and only in such circumstances can one speak about 'the Other' in history. Bourdieu's attempt to 'sociologise' charisma distorts Weber's typology of prophet, priest and sorcerer. Weber had to retain some notion of the difference between genuine and compromised charisma in order to recognise the difference between the radical transformation of history by charismatic intervention and the magical manipulation of charisma for mundane ends. We might reasonably compare Weber's notion of 'charismatic breakthrough' with Alain Badiou's notion of 'the event' (2005 [1988]) as that moment that divides history in two through the 'evental' statement that he explores in the life of Saint Paul 'Christ is Risen!' (Badiou, 2003 [1997]). Without some notion of an eventful charismatic breakthrough, we are left with the rather uninteresting definition of charisma as an empowering feature of any person who is presumed to have extraordinary qualities. In brief, Bourdieu transforms Weber's theory of charisma into a rather conventional theory of religious institutions.

Bourdieu and the 'New Paradigm' in the Sociology of Religion[2]

In the last couple of decades, a novel set of assumptions, commonly referred to as the 'new paradigm' or the 'economic interpretation of religion', has been heavily promoted in North American sociology. This 'new paradigm' – which has been influenced in many ways by rational choice theories – is associated with figures such as Rodney Stark, Roger Finke, Laurence Iannaccone and R. Stephen Warner. This 'new' approach is often contrasted disparagingly with 'old' European theories of religion. European sociology, it is alleged, has been too narrowly focused on the symbolic dimensions which social actors require to make sense of life; the new paradigm, by contrast, is primarily concerned with the economic dimensions of religious behaviour, including both demand for and supply of religious beliefs, practices and objects. On the whole, the religious markets approach favours supply-side explanations, taking particular note of how state responses to religious pluralism may or may not encourage religious competition. This approach to religion and politics has often produced valuable insights into how states manage religious diversity (Gill, 2008). The economic approach to religion has also generated important insights into how the decline of communism has given rise to flourishing religious markets in, for example, post-communist China (Yang, 2007).

Although Bourdieu interpreted religions and religious groups as existing within a competitive field, he clearly rejected the economic interpretation of religion prevalent in North American sociology (Hamilton, 2009). Here again it is difficult to see how his criticisms of this approach and his attempt to distance himself from it can be sustained. I shall turn now to a more complete account of the development of what is variously known as the rational choice model of religion or the economic approach to religion.

What are the principal theoretical claims of this new paradigm? First, whereas traditional European social theory emphasised the centrality of secularisation to modernisation alongside urbanisation, increasing literacy and democratic politics, the new paradigm takes note of the *resilience* of religion – not only in the United States but also globally. In his *Contemporary Transformations of Religion* (1976), Wilson argued that religion (that is, Christianity) had survived in North America at the cost of its orthodox theological content. Wilson sought to explain the prominence of Christian belief and practice in North America by saying that it had simply accommodated belief and practice to the predominant values and life-styles of a consumer society. In short, the form of Christianity survived but only at the costs of its contents. Such a theory of religion implies that modern religious cultures are inauthentic and make few demands on their followers. One might suggest that religion, in this secularisation theory, has become merely religiosity. An alternative to this version of secularisation can be found in Robert Bellah's account of the growth of a civil religion in North America in his 'Civil Religion in America' (1967). Through a subsequent series of influential publications (Bellah and Tipton, 2006) Bellah argued that, alongside Christianity, there was a vibrant national religion drawing upon North American values which treated North American history as an unfolding of salvation. Christianity remained influential in public life when refracted through the lens of a civil religion. Bellah did not imply, however, that 'civil religion' was somehow less religious or less authentic than traditional Christianity. The new paradigm tends to bypass any discussion of the authenticity of religion, because it concentrates not on the meaning or importance of religion in the lives of individuals, but on the institutional framework within which religion is provided. It is therefore regarded in economic terms as a supply-side, rather than a demand-side, theory of religious growth and decline.

Second, the new model directs research attention towards the *function* of religious or spiritual markets in which there is a competition for 'brand loyalty' from consumers of religious meaning, practices and objects. The notion of spiritual markets has been explored empirically and systematically by Wade C. Roof in his *Spiritual Marketplace* (1999). In any historical understanding of religion and modern society, it is impossible to understand religious behaviour without taking into account the impact of the post-war generation (the 'baby boomers') in North American culture, especially on religious practice and consciousness. Roof made an important contribution to the study of religion and generational change in his *A Generation of Seekers* (Roof, 1993), in which the post-war generations were defined as religious seekers, but also regarded as eclectic in their religious 'tastes'. The 'culture wars' of the post-war period reorganised the map of mainstream religion in North America just as they challenged establishment culture generally. North American denominational pluralism as a spiritual marketplace in the absence of an established church continues to encourage organisational innovation and cultural entrepreneurship. The new paradigm emphasises the importance of the absence of an established church in American constitutional history and hence the importance of an open religious market in which competition is endemic.

The implication of the theory is that, paradoxically, the more a religion demands from its adherents, the more they will give to religious organisations. In terms of a theory of the costs of commitment, the specific contents of a religious message are less important for success than the demands for commitment that it places on its members (Kelley, 1977). Ultimately the costliness of commitment is measured by control over members' life-styles, the development of a strong church, and the seriousness of religious involvement. In his *The Resilience of Conservative Religion* (2002), Joseph Tamney provides some support for the strong church thesis. For example, conservative congregations support a traditional gender division of labour and conventional gender identities. In a society which is deeply divided over gender issues, such ideological reassurance can be psychologically attractive. Furthermore, given the general uncertainties of everyday life in modernity, the certainties of religious teaching on morality can also be psychologically supportive and comforting.

Third, the paradigm has several interesting substantive claims, such as the notion that the religious demand for meaning is more or less constant across time – that is, the demand for meaning will remain more or less static (Finke and Stark, 1992; Stark and Finke, 2000). One cannot explain religious change by reference to the demand for meaning which is seen to be constant. Hence variations in religious behaviour are influenced by supply, rather than by demand. Religious pluralism in North America, by offering innumerable outlets for religious taste, promotes greater involvement. The theory in making a useful distinction between demand for and supply of religious products, effectively explains the proliferation of religious groups in the United States, switching between denominations by customers, the inflationary character of the market, and the resulting hybridisation and experimentation that is characteristic of modern religiosity. Unlike popular forms of spirituality, fundamentalist churches succeed because of their strictness, that is, by the exacting demands they make on their members. Religions of high-demand, such as Jehovah's Witnesses, aim to avoid the free-rider problem – joining without paying – by monopolising the commitment of their followers (Iannaccone, 1994).

In summary, the economic model of religious behaviour states that institutional pluralism – such as in the North American situation – strengthens and sustains the religious economy and that monopoly – such as an established church – is inefficient. There are in fact no truly effective monopolies, only situations where religious markets are regulated. Historical variations in religious behaviour over time are best explained by institutional variations in the supply, rather than by changes in individual religious needs for meaning and other religious services.

The economic model of religious behaviour has been subject to considerable theoretical and empirical criticisms and qualifications. These are too numerous to discuss here (Bruce, 1999; Bryant, 2000; Lechner, 2008). There are, however, two significant criticisms which are worth mentioning in this context: one is *theoretical*, relating to the inability of rational-choice models to explain the institutional framework within which markets operate and consumer choices are made, and the other one is *empirical*, to do with the historical claims of the new model about European patterns of established religion. Rodney Stark's assumption that a society with a state church gives that church a monopoly position is questionable, and the assumption that monopoly is an imposition on a society is dubious. If we look at the Catholic Church in Poland and the Orthodox Church in Russia, we can see that in the religious field the monopolistic status of established churches is in fact very variable and dependent on context. Steve Bruce's criticisms demonstrate that the empirical claims of the market model of religious institutions, especially about the relationship between religious activity and competition or deregulation, are subject to numerous empirical qualifications. Competition in North America may have been associated with religious vitality, but a situation closer to monopoly in Poland has been a context for significant religious survival and vitality.

The idea that competitive religious markets, like secular economic markets, automatically enhance choice of services, quality of products and efficiency of services is questionable. The majority of Pentecostal sects work in an unregulated institutional vacuum where other organised denominations and established churches are often absent. The religious field of charismatic movements, fundamentalist groups and Pentecostal sects is a market which is highly deregulated and in many respects free of competition. These evangelical or charismatic churches often flourish in economically depressed areas where other more institutionalised denominations are simply absent. Lack of competition in these inner-city areas with a clientele from the underclass may be the context in which these charismatic groups flourish. In brief, there is no obvious relationship between competition and religious dynamism.

We might, despite these criticisms, concede that the new paradigm has important, and testable, features (Beckford, 2003; Warner, 2004). It has produced some interesting insights intro the deregulated Chinese market in a period of post-communist regulation. But is it a new model? The idea of a religious supermarket was originally developed by Peter Berger in his analysis of the crisis of religious plausibility. The crisis of these 'plausibility structures' was produced by individuals 'shopping around' to satisfy their spiritual needs. Berger (1969: 137) wrote that 'the religious tradition which previously could be authoritatively imposed now has to be *marketed*. It must be "sold" to a clientele that is no longer constrained to "buy". The pluralistic situation is, above all, a *market*' (italics in original). In other words, the transition from monopoly to competition seriously undermined authority. This approach provides creative ways of understanding the relationship between the state and religion, because the supply side of religion is often dependent on state policies towards religious competition in civil society. Although the new paradigm has produced interesting insights into many aspects of religious markets, the paradigm has also been criticised precisely because of its emphasis on free markets, individual choice and subjectivity (Bastian, 2006; Robertson, 1992).

Since Bourdieu also concentrated on the competition over symbolic capital in the religious field, it might be argued that there is a strong parallel between his notion of a religious field and the rational model of religious markets. The counterargument would hold that Bourdieu's theory is somewhat different because it does not assume the rational social actor of micro-economics who makes individual consumer choices in a free market. The distinctive characteristic of Bourdieu's theory is the idea of 'structuring structures' shaping the dispositions of the social actor. Therefore, a sympathetic view of the contributions of Bourdieu to the sociology of religion draws attention to the idea of religious interests and the role of institutions in organising the field. In my view, however, his essays on religion actually serve to pinpoint the real problem in Bourdieu's work, namely its failure to overcome the traditional dichotomies of sociological theory action and structure, on the one hand, and materialism and idealism, on the other. We might frame this comment by asking whether his sociology of religion was shaped more by the *economic sociology* of Marx and Weber or more by the *cultural sociology* of Émile Durkheim, Mauss and Maurice Merleau-Ponty?

I have already suggested that there is little to distinguish Bourdieu's notion of religion as the consecration of economic inequality through the 'illusio' of theological dogma and existing Marxist theories of ideology and that for Bourdieu, as for Althusser, the individual is inserted into a place in the social field by the interpellations of religion. This legacy of Marxist sociology points to the deterministic undercurrent of Bourdieu's work. To quote again and at some length from the essay on Weber and religious interests, '[c]ompetition for religious power owes its specificity [...] to the fact that what is at stake is the monopoly of the legitimate exercise of the power to modify, in a deep and lasting fashion, the practice and world-view of lay people, by imposing on and inculcating in them a particular religious habitus' (Bourdieu, 1987: 126). This formulation of religion as ideology suffers from all the problems that have attended 'the dominant ideology thesis' in Marxist sociology (Abercrombie, Hill and Turner, 1980). It takes the effective functioning of a dominant ideology for granted; it assumes ideologies are primarily directed at the subordinate class; it assumes that the subordinate class cannot effectively understand their exploitation and subordination; and, finally, it cannot easily explain resistance and opposition except in a circular functionalist fashion, namely in terms of some failure of ideology. It neglects the alternative possibility, identified by Marx, that the dull compulsion of everyday life – such as the need of embodied agents for sleep and food – is sufficient to limit sustained resistance. On the one hand, Bourdieu wants to recognise the constraining force of social structures; on the other hand, he seeks to acknowledge the liberating force of social agency. He attends to have both determinacy and agency – that is, both necessity and freedom – through the idea of structuring structures and the general characterisation of his work as a contribution to reflexive sociology, but he provides few convincing examples of such an outcome.

In rejecting the social actor of classical economics and developing his own analysis of hexis, habitus and practice, can we argue that there is an alternative component in Bourdieu's theory that is not the legacy of mechanistic interpretations of religious ideology? Can we argue that, in his notion of practice and habitus, Bourdieu drew on a tradition that included Wittgenstein, Durkheim, Mauss and Merleau-Ponty and as a result formulated a more sophisticated view of religious practice? Can the concept of habitus lift Bourdieu's theory out of simple determinism? While Bourdieu gives us, through his emphasis on embodied action, a much richer and more satisfying description of the social actor than what one can find in the world of economic theories of rational action, Bourdieu's concept of habitus fails to escape the problem of determinism. Bourdieu allows for the fact that social actors are reflexive and that they engage in strategies that involve choice, but the reflexivity of social actors does not allow them to escape from the ultimate logic of the situation – from the structural determination of the game within which strategies are played out. He provides no example of how and where social actors might change the structuring structures within a field of competition. No charismatic breakthrough can be explained by Bourdieu's sociology of religion, and hence it is difficult to see to what extent in his approach to the sub-discipline of religion the principle of reflexive sociology operates.

To conclude, a persistent problem in the sociology of religion is the status of conversion and the actor's reflexivity about such a transformation of the self. The majority of sociological and historical accounts of such religious phenomena deny or ignore the actor's accounts. Conversion is normally seen as driven by social considerations relating to social status and material gain. Mass conversions are related, for example, to the role of the state in supporting different religions in a competitive environment or they are the effect of prior socialisation. I propose that the sociology of conversion would be a test case of structuring structures in which case Bourdieu would, one assumes, argue that conversion is simply an effect of the nature of competition between groups with the social field. It is difficult to see what a reflexive sociology of conversion would look like, because Bourdieu's sociology is geared not to the analysis of subjective and intersubjective agency but to the analysis of institutional and ideological determinacy.

Conclusion: Making Use of Bourdieu

Much of the debate about religion in modern society has been dominated by philosophers who typically neglect anthropological and sociological research on religion. Philosophical commentary on religion, as offered by intellectuals such as Richard Rorty and Gianni Vattimo, has no feel for the ethnographic character of modern social scientific accounts of religion. In particular, they neglect religious *practice* in favour of the idea that the problem of religion is a question of *belief*. Whereas the analysis of religion in Durkheim and the late Wittgenstein pinpointed the importance of religious practices, the concentration on belief to the exclusion of religious practice is a major defect of these philosophical approaches, and vitality resides in practice. Belief can only survive if it is embedded in practice, and practice can only survive if it is embodied in the everyday world (Turner, 2008). This argument seems to me to be the central but unintended conclusion of twentieth-century anthropology, particularly in the work of Mary Douglas (1970). What emerges from the development of the sociology of the body is the notion that conscious embodiment is situated in the taken-for-granted rituals that constitute the everyday habitus. The conclusion of Douglas's anthropology of religion is that the micro-rituals of this everyday world can only be sustained if they are underpinned by the rituals of a shared (sacred) community. Because Bourdieu perceives the social as a secular field of endless struggle and contestation, his understanding of the social somewhat precludes any insight into the religious roots of the rituals that sustain it. According to Douglas, religion in Western society is weak because it has become de-ritualised, cut off from a collective calendar and disconnected from the human life-cycle. Bourdieu did not make a major contribution to the sociology of religion. Nevertheless, his key conceptual tools, such as embodiment, habitus, practice and field, offer a fruitful way of thinking about religion, which avoids many of the shortcomings that one finds in recent philosophical approaches to religion. Ultimately, however, Bourdieu failed to resolve some of the central problems that he so skilfully identified in classical sociological theory, notably the problem of the relationship between structure and agency, and his actual contribution to the study of religion was little more than a gloss on Weber's analysis of charisma and its eventual rountinisation into ecclesiastical institutions.

Notes

1 A version of this chapter will appear in Bryan S. Turner (forthcoming) *Religion and the Modern World. Secularization, Citizenship and the State*, Cambridge: Cambridge University Press.

2 Some aspects of this argument about rational choice and religious behaviour first appeared in Bryan S. Turner (2009)' Goods Not Gods: New Spiritualities, Consumerism and Religious Markets' in Ian Rees, Paul Higgs and David J. Ekerdt (eds) *Consumption and Generational Change*, New Brunswick: Transaction Publishers, pp. 37–62.

References

Althusser, Louis (1971) *Lenin and Philosophy and Other Essays*, trans. Ben Brewster, London: New Left Books.

Badiou, Alain (2003 [1997]) *Saint Paul: The Foundation of Universalism*, trans. Ray Brassier, Stanford, California: Stanford University Press.

Badiou, Alain (2005 [1988]) *Being and Event*, trans. Oliver Feltham, New York: Continuum.

Barbalet, Jack (2000) 'Pragmatism and Symbolic Interaction', in Bryan S. Turner (ed.) *The Blackwell Companion to Social Theory*, 2nd Edition, Oxford: Blackwell, pp. 199–217.

Bastian, Jean-Pierre (2006) 'La nouvelle économie religieuse de l'Amérique latine', *Social Compass* 53(1): 65–80.

Beckford, James A. (2003) *Social Theory and Religion*, Cambridge: Cambridge University Press.

Bell, Catherine (1990) 'The Ritual Body and the Dynamics of Ritual Power', *Journal of Ritual Studies* 4(2): 299–313.

Bellah, Robert N. (1964) 'Religious Evolution', *American Sociological Review* 29: 358–374.

Bellah, Robert N. (1967) 'Civil Religion in America', *Daedalus* 96 (Winter): 1–21.

Bellah, Robert N. and Steven M. Tipton (eds.) (2006) *The Robert Bellah Reader*, Durham, NC: Duke University Press.

Berlinerblau, Jacques (1999) 'Ideology, Pierre Bourdieu and the Hebrew Bible', *Semeia* 87: 193–214.

Bourdieu, Pierre (1971) 'Une interprétation de la théorie de la religion selon Max Weber', *Archives européennes de sociologie* 12(1): 3–21.

Bourdieu, Pierre (1977 [1972]) *Outline of a Theory of Practice*, trans. Richard Nice, Cambridge: Cambridge University Press.

Bourdieu, Pierre (1987) 'Sociologues de la croyance et croyances de sociologues', *Archives de sciences sociales des religions* 63(1): 155–161.

Bourdieu, Pierre (1987 [1971]) 'Legitimation and Structured Interest in Weber's Sociology of Religion', in Scott Lash and Sam Whimster (eds.) *Max Weber, Rationality and Modernity*, trans. Chris Turner, London: Allen and Unwin, pp. 119–136.

Bourdieu, Pierre (2000) 'Mit Weber gegen Weber: Pierre Bourdieu im Gespräch', in Pierre Bourdieu, *Das religiöse Feld. Texte zur Ökonomie des Heilsgeschehens*, herausgegeben von Franz Schultheis, Andreas Pfeuffer und Stephan Egger, übersetzt von Stephan Egger, Konstanz: Universitätsverlag Konstanz, pp. 111–129.

Braun, Willi and Russell T. McCutcheon (eds.) (2000) *Guide to the Study of Religion*, London: Cassell.

Bruce, Steve (1999) *Choice and Religion: A Critique of Rational Choice Theory*, Oxford: Oxford University Press.

Bryant, Joseph (2000) 'Cost-Benefit Accounting and the Piety Business. Is *Homo Religiosus* at Bottom *Homo Economicus*?', *Method and Theory in the Study of Religion* 12: 520–548.

Casanova, José (1994) *Public Religions in the Modern World*, Chicago: University of Chicago Press.

Davie, Grace (1994) *Religion in Britain Since 1945: Believing Without Belonging*, Oxford: Blackwell.

Davie, Grace (2006) 'Religion in Europe in the 21st Century: The Factors to Take into Account', *Archives européennes de sociologie* XLVII(2): 271–296.

Demerath III, Nicholas Jay (2007) 'Secularization and Sacralization Deconstructed and Reconstructed', in James A. Beckford and Nicholas Jay Demerath III (eds.) *The SAGE Handbook of the Sociology of Religion*, London: Sage, pp. 57–80.

Dillon, Michele (2001) 'Pierre Bourdieu, Religion and Cultural Production', *Cultural Studies* 1(4): 411–429.

Douglas, Mary (1970) *Natural Symbols: Explorations in Cosmology*, London: Barrie & Rockliff Cresset Press.

Eastwood, Jonathan (2007) 'Bourdieu, Flaubert, and the Sociology of Literature', *Sociological Theory* 25(2): 149–169.

Eisenstadt, S. N. (2000) 'The Reconstruction of Religious Arenas in the Framework of "Multiple Modernities" Millennium', *Journal of International Studies* 29(3): 591–611.

Engler, Steven (2003) 'Modern Times: Religion, Consecration and the State in Bourdieu', *Cultural Studies* 17(3/4): 445–467.

Finke, Roger and Rodney Stark (1992) *The Churching of America, 1776–1990: Winners and Losers in our Religious Economy*, New Brunswick, N.J.: Rutgers University Press.

Foucault, Michel (2005 [2001]) *The Hermeneutics of the Subject: Lectures at the Collège de France, 1981–1982*, London: Palgrave Macmillan.

Furseth, Inger (2009) 'Religion in the Works of Habermas, Bourdieu and Foucault', in Peter B. Clarke (ed.) *The Oxford Handbook of the Sociology of Religion*, Oxford: Oxford University Press, pp. 89–115.

Göle, Nilüfer (1996) *The Forbidden Modern: Civilization and Veiling*, Ann Arbor: University of Michigan Press.

Goodman, Jane E. (2003) 'The Proverbial Bourdieu: Habitus and Politics of Representation in the Ethnography of Kabylia', *American Anthropologist* 105(4): 782–793.

Habermas, Jürgen (2002 [1981, 1991, 1997]) *Religion and Rationality: Essays on Reason, God, and Modernity*, trans. Ciaran P. Cronin, Eric Crump, Peter Dews, Peter P. Kenny, Frederick G. Lawrence and Max Pensky, edited and with an introduction by Eduardo Mendieta, Cambridge: Polity Press.

Habermas, Jürgen (2008 [2005]) *Between Naturalism and Religion: Philosophical Essays*, trans. Ciaran Cronin, Cambridge: Polity Press.

Habermas, Jürgen and Joseph Ratzinger (2006 [2005]) *Dialectics of Secularization: On Reason and Religion*, trans. Brian McNeil, edited by Florian Schuller, San Francisco: Ignatius Press.

Halliday, Fred [1995] (2003) *Islam and the Myth of Confrontation: Religion and Politics in the Middle East*, New ed Edition, London: I.B. Tauris.

Hamilton, Malcolm (2009) 'Rational Choice Theory: A Critique', in Peter B. Clarke (ed.) *The Oxford Companion to the Sociology of Religion*, Oxford: Oxford University Press, pp. 116–133.

Hervieu-Léger, Danièle (2000 [1993]) *Religion as a Chain of Memory*, trans. Simon Lee, Cambridge: Polity Press.

Iannaccone, L. R. (1994) 'Why Strict Churches are Strong', *American Journal of Sociology* 99(5): 1180–1211.

Jenkins, Tim (2006) 'Bourdieu's Bearmais Ethnography', *Theory, Culture & Society* 23(6): 45–72.

Kelley, Dean M. (1972) *Why Conservative Churches are Growing: A Study in Sociology of Religion*, New York: Harper & Row.

Lazreg, Marnia (2009) *Questioning the Veil: Open Letters to Muslim Women*, Princeton: Princeton University Press.

Lechner, Frank J. (2007) 'Rational Choice and Religious Economics', in James A. Beckford and Nicholas Jay Demerath III (eds.) *The SAGE Handbook of the Sociology of Religion*, London: Sage, pp. 81–97.

Loyal, Steven (2009) 'The French in Algeria, Algerians in France: Bourdieu, Colonialism and Migration', *The Sociological Review* 57(3): 406–427.

Rey, Terry (2004) 'Marketing the Goods of Salvation: Bourdieu on Religion', *Religion* 34(4): 331–343.

Rey, Terry (2007) *Bourdieu on Religion: Imposing Faith and Legitimacy*, London: Equinox.

Robertson, Roland (1992) 'The Economization of Religion? Reflections on the Promise and Limitations of the Economic Approach', *Social Compass* 39(1): 147–157.

Robertson, Roland and Bryan S. Turner (eds.) (1991) *Talcott Parsons: Theorist of Modernity*, London: Sage.

Roof, Wade Clark (1993) *A Generation of Seekers: The Spiritual Journeys of the Baby Boom Generation*, San Francisco: Harper.

Roof, Wade Clark (1999) *Spiritual Marketplace: Baby Boomers and the Remaking of American Religion*, Princeton, N.J.: Princeton University Press.

Silber, Ilana F. (2009) 'Bourdieu's Gift to Gift Theory: An Unacknowledged Trajectory', *Sociological Theory* 27(2): 173–190.

Spinner-Halevy, Jeff (2005) 'Hinduism, Christianity and Liberal Religious Tolerance', *Political Theory* 33(1): 28–57.

Stark, Rodney and Roger Finke (2000) *Acts of Faith: Explaining the Human Side of Religion*, Berkeley: University of California Press.

Swartz, David (1996) 'Bridging the Study of Culture and Religion: Pierre Bourdieu's Political Economy of Symbolic Power', *Sociology of Religion* 57(1): 71–85.

Tamney, Joseph B. (2002) *The Resilience of Conservative Religion: The Case of Popular, Conservative Protestant Congregations*, Cambridge: Cambridge University Press.

Taylor, Charles (2002) *Varieties of Religion Today: William James Revisited*, Cambridge, Mass.: Harvard University Press.

Taylor, Charles (2007) *A Secular Age*, Cambridge, Mass.: Belknap Press of Harvard University Press.

Turner, Bryan S. (ed.) (2008) *Religious Diversity and Civil Society: A Comparative Analysis*, Oxford: Bardwell Press.

Verter, Bradford (2003) 'Spiritual Capital: Theorizing Religion with Bourdieu Against Bourdieu', *Sociological Theory* 21(2): 150–174.

Warner, R. S. (2004) 'Enlisting Smelser's Theory of Ambivalence to Maintaining Progress in Sociology of Religion's New Paradigm', in Jeffrey C. Alexander, Gary T. Marx and Christine L. Williams (eds.) *Self, Social Structure and Beliefs: Explorations in Sociology*, Berkeley: University of California Press, pp. 103–121.

Weber, Max (1958 [1921]) *The Religion of India: The Sociology of Hinduism and Buddhism*, translated and edited by Hans H. Gerth and Don Martindale, Glencoe, Ill.: Free Press.

Weber, Max (1966 [1922]) *The Sociology of Religion*, trans. Ephraim Fischoff, introduction by Talcott Parsons, London: Methuen.

Wilson, Bryan R. (1966) *Religion in Secular Society: A Sociological Comment*, London: C.A Watts.

Wilson, Bryan R. (1976) *Contemporary Transformations of Religion*, London: Oxford University Press.

Wolin, Richard (1994) *Walter Benjamin: An Aesthetic of Redemption*, Revised Edition, Berkeley: University of California Press.

Yang, Fenggang (2007) 'Oligopoly Dynamics: Official Religions in China', in James A. Beckford and Nicholas Jay Demerath III (eds.) *The SAGE Handbook of the Sociology of Religion*, London: Sage, pp. 635–653.

CHAPTER ELEVEN

Bourdieu's Sociological Fiction: A Phenomenological Reading of Habitus

Bruno Frère[1]

Between Genetic Structuralism and Phenomenology: The Complex Constitution of Habitus

For nearly thirty years now, the critical sociology of Pierre Bourdieu has been used in an increasingly large number of studies in the social sciences. It is remarkable, however, that it has had a rather weak impact on my own field of research: the study of new social movements. This chapter argues that the reason for this anomaly lies with Bourdieu's theory of habitus (a central element of Bourdieusian thought) and the particular problems that this theory poses for researchers of new social movements. As original and powerful as it can be, the theory of habitus is, first and foremost, a theory of reproduction and determination. As such, its ability to help us to understand the creativity and radical innovations of the actors who constitute new social movements is severely limited. Thus, whilst immersed in my own research, I found that I had to choose between two options: one option was to abandon the Bourdieusian approach to the social all together; the other option was to stay within the Bourdieusian paradigm and, in the light of its substantial shortcomings, seek to transcend its limitations. Preferring to pursue the latter – somewhat more optimistic – project, the question to be confronted was whether or not it is possible to move Bourdieu's paradigm forward, beyond its conventional applications, in order to render it operational in other areas, such as my own, where it is has not contributed a great deal. This chapter aims to demonstrate that it is possible to do so. Although Bourdieu's sociological framework in general and his conceptual tools in particular have often been used in a rather orthodox fashion, this chapter seeks to show that Bourdieusian social theory is sufficiently open for us to maintain much of its contribution whilst looking elsewhere to overcome some of its substantial shortcomings.

Thomas Kuhn's concept of 'paradigm' is often used out-of-hand, but it can certainly be employed to describe the framework which Bourdieu's work gave rise to. If we acknowledge that 'paradigms consist of scientific discoveries that are universally recognized and which, for a time, provide a community of researchers with certain types of problems and solutions' (Kuhn, 1983 [1962]: 11), then Bourdieu's 'constructivist structuralism' (which is also described as 'genetic structuralism') can be considered to be paradigmatic. Indeed, the Bourdieusian paradigm has opened a space for reflection between the two poles that dominated twentieth-century sociology for a long time: objectivism and subjectivism. Given this ambition, Bourdieusian thought has allowed for a conceptualisation of the relation between individuals and their social environment in a way that, when it was proposed for the first time, was entirely new (Kuhn, 1983 [1962]: 11).[2] To be sure, with the term 'structuralism' Bourdieu refers to the idea that there are objective structures in the social world which exist independently of the consciousness and the will of actors. These structures are capable of orienting and restraining social practices in, and social representations of, the world. When using the term 'constructivism', on the other hand, Bourdieu suggests that actors' schemes of perception, thought and action have a social origin. These predispositional schemes are constitutive of actors' habitus, and always exist in relation to positional schemes of external social structures, such as fields, groups and social classes (Bourdieu, 1987: 147).

The synthesis of structuralist and constructivist traditions can be regarded as a solution to the question (or, in Kuhnian terms, to the 'enigma') which was at stake during the 1960s and which neither tradition has ever been able to resolve. Both Luc Boltanski's 'pragmatic sociology' and Bruno Latour's 'actor network theory' are firmly situated in the debate concerning a possible synthesis of these aforementioned traditions. In particular, this debate obliges us to reflect upon the 'place of culture': the place where the constructions of culture by its agents, and of agents by their culture, are woven together. This place corresponds to the notion of habitus, a notion which found a role in the field of scientific sociological innovation and, indeed, did have an important impact on the discipline in general for a time (Boltanski, 2003: 159). Yet Boltanski does not align himself with those who make use of the term habitus in its 'strong' sense (for example, the researchers of the Centre for European Sociology, which Bourdieu used to run: Champagne, Pinto, Sapiro, and Accardo – to mention only a few of them). For, according to Boltanski, an orthodox Bourdieusian use of the term habitus remains trapped in a determinist understanding of the social, which fails to account for the sociological significance of situational contingency.[3] From a Boltanskian perspective, individuals often find themselves in situations where they are compelled to 'improvise' or 'invent' their behaviour. In this context, Boltanski poses the following question:

> The analyst considers that he has reached the end of his task when he can show that, when immersed in different situations, the actor responds by actualising schemata that are written in his habitus, that is to say, predictably – which tends to mean the question of action itself fades away. But what remains of action once we have eliminated the uncertainty an actor must be faced with even in the most apparently routine of situations: that uncertainty that contains the possibility of something new occurring, that is to say an eventful dimension? (Boltanski, 2003: 160)

In other words, how can an actor – or, to use the language of genetic structuralism, an agent – 'invent' something? And, daring to push the question further, how can an actor innovate because, not in spite, of the weight of their habitus? This is the fundamental question that constructivist (or genetic) structuralism has left aside and that this chapter aims to address. This question ought to have been addressed a long time ago, both by those who see only 'determinism' in the notion of habitus (and, instead of seeking to resolve the problem, dismiss it as a concept that deprives the actor of freedom) and by those who defend it in an orthodox fashion (and who, instead of refining it, have until now subsumed an ever-increasing quantity of material from different domains of research under this analytic category, in order to prove its validity).

Just as it is necessary to transcend the limits of the notion of habitus, it is essential to push both theoretical and empirical investigations of this notion further than Bourdieu did himself. Genetic structuralism has been considerably reconfigured and strengthened since the publication of Bourdieu's Kabyle ethnology (1972) and his *Sens pratique* (1980; translated into English as *The Logic of Practice*, 1990). This is partly due to the work of two authors who are particularly widely read in the contemporary field of French social science: Philippe Corcuff and Bernard Lahire. They can be seen both as the least orthodox representatives of the Bourdieusian paradigm and as two scholars who have made substantial contributions to its fruitful development. We should therefore pay tribute to the existence of Corcuff's and Lahire's respective approaches. It is this type of work, situated at the edge of the Bourdieusian paradigm, which prevents that paradigm from becoming rigid and sterile. Their contribution shall therefore be discussed at some length in the first two sections of this chapter, assuming – with Boltanski – that their respective contributions can be regarded as firmly established (Boltanski, 2003: 159–160).

From the outset, Lahire and Corcuff situate Bourdieu's genetic structuralism in an area of overlap between psychology and philosophy. In so doing, they allow us to see clearly the potential in the notion of habitus, whilst laying the foundations necessary to resolve the enigma with which we are concerned: how can something new arise out of habitus? Both authors put forward the notion of 'the plural individual', a concept that does not easily find its place in Bourdieu's genetic structuralism. This theory – in associating the habitus with social fields, groups or classes – seeks to demonstrate the regularity of behaviour in a given situation. As we will see further in the argument below, both Lahire's and Corcuff's approaches are largely convincing, although it must also be said that they diverge in some respects. Nonetheless, their success comes, in the case of Corcuff, at the price of a partial abandonment of the notion of habitus and, in the case of Lahire, at the price of embracing an arguably excessive empiricism.

The methodological usefulness and conceptual forcefulness of the notion of habitus stem from the fact that habitus allows us to conceive of human subjectivity in terms of an ensemble of social norms converted into individual dispositions. To be sure, subjectively internalised norms are not explicit rules of behaviour but unconsciously assimilated – and thus 'socially naturalised' – tendencies to act in one way rather than another. The concept allows us to extract the 'unconscious' from the psychic straightjacket to which psychoanalysis had consigned it and by virtue of which the unconscious is considered a purely mental phenomenon (Frère, 2004: 88). The concept of the schemata (or dispositions) of habitus, however, does not refer to an existing representation of mental life of which we are unconscious (and which may be detached from the mind, and of which we become conscious *a posteriori*); rather, it refers to social injunctions that are 'addressed not to the intellect but to the body' (Bourdieu, 1997: 169).[4]

As a consequence, it seems that we are confronted with a curious paradox: habitus is unconscious, and yet the concept of habitus does not describe a merely mental, psychic or psychological state of affairs. This paradox is fundamental to the analytical value of the concept; at the same time, however, it has proved to be perceived as somewhat challenging by various scholars. It is probably this paradox which troubles Lahire, who searches for a correspondence of dispositions on a psychological level. According to Lahire, habitus can essentially be regarded as a psychological apparatus that functions mechanically and whose creative potential is limited. Corcuff on the other hand, without rejecting the notion of habitus altogether, seeks to abandon the emphasis on the allegedly 'unconscious' nature of habitus. In so doing, he attempts to develop a notion of a creative habitus. Drawing on Paul Ricoeur's concept of ipse-identity, Corcuff has sought to demonstrate that the human agent possesses a subjectivity (or, if one prefers, ipse-identity) that works independently of, and potentially contrary to, exogenous determinations. In opposition to this view, this chapter aims to show that, if the agent is capable of both 'inventing a situation' and 'inventing itself in and through a situation', this is *because of*, rather than *despite*, exogenous determinations arising from the social world.

The paradigm of genetic structuralism has been enriched by the elaboration of the notion of habitus via the concept of the 'plural actor' (which was first developed by Lahire and then adopted by Corcuff). Yet, we should not omit the unconscious dimensions of habitus (as Corcuff does), nor should we seek to reduce the predispositional schemes of habitus to a matter of the psyche (as Lahire does). This is why, in the fourth section of this chapter, the notion of habitus is referred to as a 'fiction'. Although habitus as such may be conceived of as immaterial and unlocalisable, it constitutes a tangible and powerful element of the social world in general and of social agents in particular. It seems essential to conserve the idea of an ensemble of unconscious social habits incarnated in each one of us in the form of behavioural dispositions, just as it is important to conceive of the magma of these dispositions without reducing the carrier of these dispositions to a purely psychological mechanism. For Lahire, the adaptation of the actor to a range of fields is made possible through the field-dependent development and mechanical reproduction of acquired skills. For Corcuff, this – somewhat determinist – conception of habitus needs to be revised in the light of the creative potentials of human subjectivity and the power of ipse-identity, which liberates the agent from the weight of social habits. In neither case, however, is it ever a question of the agent actually *inhabiting* the space: consciously or unconsciously, agents simply 'adapt' to the social spaces by which they find themselves surrounded. Neither Corcuff nor Lahire resolve the fundamental problem of the inertia of habitus. Even if we put forward a complex, rather than a monolithic, conception of habitus, and even if we are prepared to acknowledge that an individual is both plural and unique, how is it possible to account for the existence of human characteristics such as creativity or social ingenuity? Can the habitus be something *other* than the weight of personal history that conditions the activity of the actor? This question is frequently raised by sociologists studying aspects of human reality where the idea of innovation is essential to a proper understanding of social action; unsurprisingly then, this question is particularly important in the sociology of culture, the sociology of art, the sociology of knowledge, and the sociology of social movements.

By way of response, the final section of this chapter attempts to bring some elements of phenomenology to the paradigm of genetic structuralism in order to complete the redefinition of habitus introduced by Lahire and Corcuff.

Here then, the concept of habitus is not based on the Husserlian intellectual stream, which arguably feeds the sociology of Schütz; rather it is founded on a tradition that is still relatively unexplored in sociology, a tradition that focuses on the body, rather than on consciousness: the phenomenology of Maurice Merleau-Ponty[5] – in particular his philosophical works on culture – and the political philosophy of Cornelius Castoriadis. As shall be demonstrated below, the analytical framework proposed in this chapter conceives of habitus as a creative capacity, that is, as a competence which allows for the construction of something new and hitherto non-existent. As a result of this conception, it is possible to envisage a habitus that is multiply-determined, unconscious and able to escape the mechanistic logic of social reproduction. The chapter draws to a close by referring to my empirical research on social movements. It seems that a collective work on the intellectual legacy of a thinker is the ideal place to move beyond the theoretical and practical limitations of this legacy; in addition, it provides an opportunity to consider the continuous relevance of this legacy to new areas of empirical research. The chapter concludes by arguing that a phenomenological elaboration of the Bourdieusian paradigm can help to extend its usefulness in the sociological study of activists engaged in new forms of social struggle.

Two Paths for a Genetic-Structuralist Sociology of the Plural Actor

Lahire begins his critical analysis of Bourdieu's approach by demonstrating the lack of precision with which certain key notions are used in critical sociology. He asserts that Bourdieu must have been unaware of the fact that, in the 1970s and 1980s, the field of psychology provided precise definitions of terms such as 'disposition' and 'psychological reproduction of social structures'. This omission on Bourdieu's part leaves his system – which is aimed at identifying relationally defined patterns in social behaviour and categorising them in terms of a particular habitus – relatively powerless. Indeed, the significance of this omission is reflected in the fact that Bourdieu's framework does not allow us to answer a number of fundamental questions such as the following: how can various individual and social experiences coexist in the same body, and what is their impact on the individual's life? Given that the Bourdieusian framework is not really concerned with the nature and development of individual dispositions, 'we have no example of the social construction of the incorporation or transmission of these dispositions. We have no indication as to the way they may be constructed nor the way they behave' (Lahire, 1999b: 129). Thus, within a Bourdieusian framework of social analysis, it is difficult – if not, impossible – to understand why and how actors are able to incorporate objective structures and, more importantly, how these structures can be converted into mental and cognitive structures (Lahire, 1999a). The idea of the inscription of social structures in the brain, which take the form of mental structures, is problematic unless we succeed in explaining how cognitive structures and social structures are homologically interrelated. When we stand back and consider this issue more carefully, it becomes obvious that different sets of mental structures vary between different individuals.

The sociological acknowledgement of the existence and importance of psychological internalisation processes manifests itself in terms such as matrices, schemata and dispositions. Yet, the usage of these terms in sociology does not necessarily imply that their underlying ways of functioning have been adequately understood. In reality, genetic structuralism has reproduced these concepts in a reified, undigested and uncritical manner for the last twenty years. These concepts are, however, 'just a kind of resume of the most advanced psychological works of the era' (Lahire, 1998: 105; see also Lahire, 1999b: 124–125). Since the 1980s, researchers who study the incorporation of objective structures have failed to make sense of this dialectic; that is, they have not shown themselves capable of capturing the construction of multiple types of dispositions and schemata through social experience. Had they been able to do so, they would have confronted the challenge of exploring the diversity and irreducibility of individuals and, therefore, the diversity and irreducibility of schemata and dispositions. In order to do so, they would have had to refine their conceptual and methodological frameworks.

Lahire's project can be described as a psychological sociology inspired by the work of Jean Piaget (1999). As such, it makes extensive use of concepts such as 'schemata', 'dispositions', and 'matrices', that is, of concepts employed by structural-constructivist sociologists to give meaning to the social organisation of the actor's (or agent's) modes of thought, behaviour and action. These concepts, then, permit us to capture different modes and instances of interiorisation and, more importantly, the extent to which actors have the ability to adapt to different social contexts. Lahire's reconceptualisation of habitus allows us to conceive of the individual as a multiply socialised, multiply determined, and unique entity. As social beings, we are all confronted with an ensemble of local situations which have different degrees of impact on the composition of our dispositional baggage.

To be sure, there is nothing inevitable about the conversion of the objective structures of society into the subjective structures of the individual. Given its relative inability to take on board the work of psychologists, sociology has had a tendency to take the existence of schemata and dispositions, and in particular their relative social determinacy, for granted. This has allowed it to construct a typology of individuals' responses in terms of a generalisation of arbitrarily chosen schemata.

> In fact, the regime of generalised transferral, not discussed and not adequately tested, prevents us from conceiving (and therefore observing) the existence of schemata or dispositions that are local (specific to social situations or areas of particular practices) modes of categorisation, perception, or appreciation attached to specific objects and areas. It reduces the process of exteriorisation of complex inner nature to a simple unique function, that of assimilation/accommodation: assimilation of situations to incorporated schemata, and accommodation (correction) of previously established schemata to variations and changes of situation. (Lahire, 1999b: 136)

Thus, according to Lahire, our dispositional baggage is composed of a set of schemata, some of which can be inhibited or which may become dormant to leave room for the development or activation of others. They can be delimited as specific social dispositions, activated only in a precisely defined area of relevance, with a given individual learning to develop dispositions that differ in different contexts. Individuals do not simply engage in the constant transfer of dispositional structures; they carry a plurality of dispositions – corresponding to a plurality of social contexts – within themselves. Indeed, the more an individual is exposed to non-homogenous, complex and diverse social contexts, the more likely he or she is to possess a variegated legacy of adapted dispositions, habits or abilities that are non-homogenous and not unified. For the sociologist, working to discover this legacy is tantamount to restoring the individual's particularity, diversity and complexity. In fact, it is precisely one of Piaget's main achievements to have shown that mental categories are not static and transcendental but dynamic and situated components of every individual (Piaget, 1970: 80).

A significant amount of fieldwork which combines qualitative and quantitative data has broadened the Bourdieusian research programme. Without, in this case, drawing on the work of Piaget, but supported by several statistical studies, Lahire sets out a number of strong hypotheses. One example is his idea of 'dissonant profiles', which concerns individuals whose attitudes, practices and tastes do not necessarily correspond to the characteristics of their socio-professional or socio-cultural backgrounds (Lahire, 2004: 175–203). In light of the solid empirical evidence for these hypotheses, there is no need to make vague and speculative statements about the rise of individualism or to give in to the – ideologically biased – rejection of the notion of social class, of which contemporary thinkers such as Marcel Gauchet, Alain Renaut, Ulrich Beck, Charles Taylor, and Gilles Lipovetsky may be accused. What is at stake here concerns another issue: the prospect of a rupture with certain Durkheimian intellectual habits leads to a fear of the 'psychologisation of social relations' and of the 'regression to atomism'. According to Lahire, this kind of fear can be found in contemporary forms of constructivist (or genetic) structuralism (Lahire, 2004: 696).

Notably, Corcuff is inspired by this area of overlap between psychology and constructivist structuralism, that is, by the kind of overlap that Lahire's psychological sociology attempts to sketch out (Corcuff, 2003: 82–86). Their position is close to Bridget Fowler's stance with regard to her concern with the popularisation of Bourdieu's work in the field of British cultural studies. In her work, Fowler emphasises the importance of the formation of plural identities in advanced societies, which reflects a social process that cannot be reduced to a mechanical interplay between internal and external structures and to the notion that the individual is a malleable entity completely determined by external structures (Fowler, 1997: 132). It is by insisting on this very idea of a plural singularity (or plurality of identity) that Corcuff tries to construct his alternative framework to a determinist conception of habitus 'which *a priori* unifies the dispositions and constructs a permanence of the person' (Corcuff, 2003: 70, emphasis in original).

Where Lahire turns to psychology and Piaget in order to specify which schemata compose the variable content of habitus, Corcuff turns to Ricoeur. The concept of ipse-identity (*identité-ipséité*) developed by Ricoeur refers to the moment when a person asks the question '*Who* am I?' This concerns the subjective element of personal identity, which is opposed to the objective element responding to the question of *what* that person is – idem-identity (*identité-mêmeté*).

This corresponds to the 'durable dispositions' of habitus (Corcuff, 1999: 98, and 2003: 62). Thus, here we are dealing with what may be described as the 'objective aspects' of a subject's identity. The ipse-identity, however, is closer to the notion of role distance favoured by Erving Goffman and to the idea of the sedimentation of a 'personal reserve' which is irreducible to the social roles taken on and internalised by the individual. Most researchers working within the structural-constructivist paradigm – for which the reflexivity of the actor is a biographical illusion (Bourdieu, 1994: 81–90) – do not account for the existence, let alone the significance, of the 'subjective sense of the self'. Some of them may go so far as to consider this sense null and void, or simply non-existent. It could seem that only a sociologist who is equipped with concepts such as 'domination', 'field' and 'habitus' is able to shed light on the real meaning and constitution of an individual's identity. This sociological hypothesis, although it is not false, is certainly inadequate. In their study of the social world, it is crucial for sociologists to explore the symbolic and material impacts of social identities, and thus it is essential to study the power of habitus to make agents behave and act in one way or another.

Corcuff and Lahire on the Dilemmas of Consciousness, Empiricism and Habitus

The advantage of these two attempts to move beyond the limits of Bourdieu's paradigm is that their refusal to conceive of habitus as a set of 'durable, transposable dispositions, structured structures predisposed to function as structuring structures' (Bourdieu, 1980: 88) does not lead them to reject his genetic-structuralist hypothesis in its entirety – unlike other theorists such as, for example, Raymond Boudon in France and Jeffrey C. Alexander in the United States. It is because these schemata and dispositions are more than simply the 'incorporation of the same objectivised history in habitus and [mental] structures' (Bourdieu, 1980: 97) that they do not always produce identical behaviour that would be 'mutually understandable and immediately adjusted to structures' (Bourdieu, 1980: 97). In this regard, Bourdieu's intuition is accurate, and Corcuff and Lahire are right to take it on board and to develop it further.

Of all the recent models and approaches that draw on Bourdieu's genetic sociology, these two positions belong to the most convincing ones. Yet, one remark should be made in this regard. Both authors, in aiming to 'reform' Bourdieu's conception of habitus, introduce difficulties that Bourdieu's original model had avoided. Corcuff, for example, is right to insist upon his sociological interest in individual consciousness in general and in individuals' capacity to reflect upon their various identities and actions in particular. As a result, however, he partly closes the door that was left open to account for the richness of our socially constituted unconscious. Thus he implies that, if the actor is capable of creativity, this innovative competence must be understood only as peculiar to that ipse-identity, which is constructed as though existing in parallel to habitus.

Yet, it is Corcuff who leads us to the path of what may be described as the 'dynamic habitus'. He does so by drawing a distinction between an individual and a social habitus. According to Bourdieu, we cannot use these terms interchangeably because

> [...] that would mean assuming all representations produced according to identical schemata are impersonal and interchangeable which [...] reflects nothing about the particularity of the empirical self. [...] Each individual system of disposition is a structural variant of the others, in which the singularity of the position within class and trajectory are expressed. [...] The principle of differences

> between individual habitus lies in the singularity of social trajectories to which a series of chronologically ordered determinations – which are irreducible to each other – corresponds: the habitus, which at any given moment achieves a unique integration, structuring new experiences according to the structures produced by prior experiences, which affects these structures in the limits defined by their powers of selection. (Bourdieu, 1980: 101)[6]

Corcuff is aware of the fact that here is an opportunity to use a conceptual archaeology in order to demonstrate, once and for all, that the notion of habitus is not a case of a collectivity acting as a bulldozer against the singular; rather, it is a term that permits us the irreducible nature of an individual's subjectivity. Bourdieu's genetic structuralism tends to conceive of habitus primarily in terms of its relation to a social field (that is, in relation to a social space within which actors acquire particular social characteristics and dispositional schemes). Given Bourdieu's emphasis on the field-specific constitution of habitus, Corcuff concludes that 'it is not possible to make the notion of habitus the end point for a sociology of singularity' (2003: 62).

From a Bourdieusian point of view, this is where Corcuff goes wrong. Having drawn attention to both the existence and the significance of the 'singular habitus', he himself avoids the question and does not pursue it any further. In fact, although he claims to account for the singularity of every habitus, he does not do justice to the full complexity of individual aspects of habitus. Considering the notion of habitus as 'inert' or as a 'receptacle for determinisms', corresponding to Ricoeur's idem-identity, Corcuff refers to the ipse-identity in order to speak more easily of subjective identity. Such an approach allows us to recognise actors' self-reflective and self-critical capacity, which they mobilise in their daily actions. Equipped with the conceptual tools that Boltanski forged in his *L'amour et la justice comme compétences* (1990), and with Laurent Thévenot in their *De la justification* (1991), Corcuff asserts that habitus is merely a 'facet of singularity' (2003) which ought not to monopolise the researcher's attention at the expense of the actor's reflexive capacities.

These capacities are testimony to the inalienable creativity of social actors. In spite of the weight of habitus, social actors are able to create and develop their identities themselves. The reflexivity of the actor allows 'identity' to emerge in response to the question 'Who am I?', and the practical response to this question can be found in the existence of a fundamentally dynamic and self-reflexive consciousness, that is, of a type of consciousness that is not merely unconscious of itself. Within Bourdieu's framework of genetic structuralism, habitus and creativity tend to be conceived of as mutually exclusive, rather than mutually inclusive, features of subjectivity. Ultimately, it seems as though Corcuff abandoned the question of individual habitus immediately after raising it, for he seems to favour another concept, namely Ricoeur's concept of ipse-identity.[7]

Lahire, on the other hand, remains committed to the sociological framework of structuralist constructivism. According to this framework, actors acquire certain dispositions through their exposure to and participation in diversified social fields. These dispositions are nevertheless embedded in the unique structures of our subjectivity, defining who we are and what kind of identities we develop throughout life; and these identities always have a deep, indelible and quasi-genetic imprint. Lahire's approach permits us to understand why communication and coordination between differently socialised people is possible: for instance, a worker and a CEO who play cards together, the son of an opera singer and the son of a rapper who have a similar passion for Beethoven's concertos, and so forth (see Boltanski, 2003). Yet, the notion of the plural actor does not always allow us to understand how the determinisms that make up this figure comprise a wealth of unconscious abilities that are easily mobilised in the 'invention' of singular behaviour.

Arguing for a psychological test against 'Bourdieu's inclination to decide theoretical questions based on philosophical quotations', Lahire concludes by limiting his research to the discovery of the psychological products of habitus (Lahire, 1998: 187). He almost reaches the point of asking what the schemata and dispositions of habitus correspond to *materially* in the neurones of an individual brain. In this respect, his approach comes close to an anti-intellectual empiricism that is no longer capable of posing the question in the following terms: are we dealing with an empirically existing concept, or are we dealing with a 'mystic reality' and an 'additional space' (between structure and practice) that the sociologist needs in order for the theory to come full circle (Lahire, 1998: 63)?

In order to move towards an understanding of habitus that, metaphorically speaking, does not portray subjectivity as a collective bulldozer crushing all forms of singularity, it is necessary to avoid conceiving of the relationship between philosophy and empirical psychology in dichotomous terms. Objectivist approaches to the social have been criticised by early phenomenological sociologists such as Alfred Schütz, who – along with Scheler –argues that whatever form it adopts, 'empirical psychology supposes the objectifiability of the psychological as such, and includes the unfounded assumption that the same psychological events can reappear in a multitude of different subjects and can be reproduced through experimentation' (Schütz, 1962: 157; see also Scheler, 1993: 166).

This suggests that it is necessary to dissect the schemata and dispositions that we incorporate in the form of habitus. Yet, if we aim to determine their psychological location and content, we run the risk of producing simplistic categories of social groups (that is, categories according to which individuals belonging to a specific group can be basically treated as identical). Lahire puts forward a 'psychological multi-determinism', rather than a 'sociological determinism'. Such a multi-dimensional approach permits us to understand why particular individuals may appreciate classical music even though their working-class habitus does not predestine them to such a choice. In principle, this applies to all dispositions that make up habitus. Each disposition corresponds to a field of socialisation, even if these dispositions turn out to be contradictory, as in the case of the working-class lover of classical music. Yet, the challenge of subjective singularity still needs to be confronted: how can we make sense of the notion of an individual habitus?

If the social agent is nothing more than the sum of dispositions, then how is it possible that social action is more than simply the exteriorised outcome of previously interiorised dispositions? More specifically, how can we explain the rise of new forms of behaviour in a given situation and the social ability to make something 'new' happen? If, following Corcuff, we explain processes of individuation in terms of actors' reflexive and creative capacities, it is far from clear how such capacities can be located in habitus. For the concept of habitus becomes easily dissociated from social acts by which individuals manage to construct their own identities. According to Corcuff, there are essentially two types of identity: first, an identity based on an individual habitus; and second, an identity based on free subjectivity, that is, an ipse-identity based on relative self-sufficiency.

In contrast to this position, I want to argue that the notion of individual habitus allows us to combine ipse-identity and idem-identity. If the former and the latter can be combined, then there is no reason to believe that they have to be separated from each other and that Bourdieu's genetic structuralism has to be completely abandoned. In fact, we may propose to embark on a third research project, which conceives of habitus neither as a merely empirical reality nor as a merely conceptual tool. From this perspective, habitus can be defined as a sociological fiction which may be considered as legitimate within sociology, similarly to the fiction of Kant's transcendental ego in philosophy (Frère, 2005).

If we reduce the concept of habitus to an indecipherable 'black box' (Boudon, 1998) or to a set of mental and cognitive structures (Lahire, 1998, 1999a, and 1999b), we end up imposing somewhat problematic – namely, positivist – parameters upon the sociological study of social action. Habitus, however, is not a box materially incorporated within the individual or a mechanically driven set of thoughts and actions. Rather, it is an intellectual abstraction, a sociological fiction which allows us to understand the individuation of collective schemata in the form of individually embodied dispositions. The use of phenomenology comes into play here as a way of promoting a more adequate conceptualisation of this 'sociological fiction'. The principal goal of this approach to the nature of habitus is to conceive of habitus as a powerful conceptual and methodological tool for the sociological study of human reality.

Phenomenology and Sociological Fiction: A Third Genetic-Structuralist Programme for a Dynamic Habitus

It should be remembered that the term 'habitus' appeared for the first time in the writings of Aristotle, but then also in the work of Edmund Husserl, the founding father of phenomenology. He described the self 'as Me subsisting by durable habitus' and further articulated an idea of durable habitus as the foundation of the 'Me', or self (1994 [1950]: 114). Indeed, behind Bourdieu's use of the notion of habitus (considered as a corollary to the history of individual social life), Husserl's idea of retention is sporadically visible. According to this idea, our life is a succession of moments with other social subjects which, once they have happened, leave an imprint on us that 'still remains there' (1964 [1928]: 44). In his writings, Husserl seeks to understand why and how the traces of our past experiences can continue to influence our present ones. Ultimately, however, the notion of habitus is a concept of peripheral status in Husserl's writings, referring to a transcendental identity deeply hidden in the self. Retention, conversely, refers to a process that only concerns conscious events. For Husserl, it is the task of the phenomenological project to undertake the 'transcendental reduction' (the *epoché*) enabling us to regress to the level of 'pre-social subjectivity', and thus to the level of 'that which the personal subject can originally experience', that is, to their pre-social confrontation with the world (1982 [1952]: 278–279). Yet, consciousness is largely inoperative within the Bourdieusian framework of genetic structuralism.[8]

Similar to Bourdieu's emphasising the corporeal, rather than the cognitive, nature of habitus, Merleau-Ponty 'changed the nature of the Husserlian enterprise by centring his phenomenology on the body rather than on the consciousness' (Wolff, 1978: 499). In his work, the body is what puts us in contact with the (social) world, independently of our thoughts and consciousness. In this sense, the body epitomises a kind of original intentionality, a way of relating to our social environment that is distinct from reflexive knowledge (1945: 444)[9]: it is intertwined with the substance (*la 'chair'*) of the world; it sinks into it and merges with it. In the texts contained in *In Praise of Philosophy*, *Signs*, or *The Prose of the World*, Merleau-Ponty clearly leads the way for Bourdieu's genetic structuralism, as he conceives of our entanglement with the world and our ineluctable situatedness in our bodies as 'cultural'. (By the way, this is the 'place of culture' upon which Boltanski insists in his writings.[10]) This view is based on the assumption that 'the unity of culture extends above the limits of an individual life the same kind of envelope that captures in advance all the moments in that life, at the instant of its institution or its birth' (Merleau-Ponty, 1960a: 111). In this, Husserl joins others who err in seeking 'in the mind the guarantee of unity which is already there when we perceive' the world and the meaning that one's culture (one's social universe) has deposited as sediment (Merleau-Ponty, 1960a: 111). Through the action of culture, in a certain sense I inhabit lives that are not mine, because the significations that the objects in the world take on for me are the significations that were forged by those who 'preceded my present' (Merleau-Ponty, 1960a: 111).[11] This present becomes what Merleau-Ponty calls the 'social-mine' (*social-mien*); that is to say, the raw material of my being-in-the-world that I will then be able to sculpt (Frère, 2005: 248).

At various points in his work it is possible to see a nod in the direction of sociology – a discipline he was one of the few philosophers to believe in at that time.[12] He describes, for example, a social fact not as a 'massive reality' (clearly directed at Durkheimian objectivism) but as 'embedded in the deepest part of the individual' (1960c: 123–142). Every life has 'a social atmosphere' which precedes and conditions the reflexive gaze we can turn on it. Because the work of Merleau-Ponty was interrupted by his sudden and unexpected death, this atmosphere, this social-mine (*social-mien*), 'has found no name in any philosophy', according to Claude Lefort.[13] It did, however, emerge in sociology. In moving from a philosophy that evacuates the substance of the consciousness to a sociology that does the same (as we can observe in Bourdieu's genetic structuralism), the being-in-the-world – the social-mine (*social-mien*) – is called habitus.

This interrelation between the individual and their cultural world is not reflexive. If it were reflexive, it would be similar to Corcuff's model, which applies the ipse-identity of Ricoeur to the notion of habitus.[14] The individual habitus, understood in the light of Merleau-Ponty's work, allows us to envisage the idea of a plural actor, that is, of an actor with a potential for creation and transformation. It thus becomes a fruitful, rather than a deterministic, concept.

One of our main questions is whether or not there is any legitimate room for the role of actors' creative capacity within Bourdieu's framework of genetic structuralism. Put differently, the question remains whether or not, within Bourdieu's social theory, there is such a thing as a subjective identity capable of creative activity. We can draw on the works of Corcuff and Lahire in order to understand how habitus is uniquely and, at the same time, unconsciously constructed. Yet, Corcuff and Lahire do not allow us to understand how habitus therefore enables actors to construct themselves and the world by which they find themselves surrounded. In their writings, habitus remains a kind of blank slate, destined to be shaped by the outside world. Nevertheless, we need to recognise that habitus has a dynamic nature and creative potential; otherwise we are unable to conceive of individuals as unique entities with unique identities. Of course, in some parts of Bourdieu's writings, it is possible to find references to the idea of a habitus that, although it is socially constructed, is equipped with the capacity to act upon the social world. In fact, such a view portrays the relationship between habitus and the social world as a relationship of mutual and continuous transformation. Yet, we also need to recognise that in most parts of his writings Bourdieu has, to a large extent, neglected the existence – and consequently the significance – of the creative and transformative nature of habitus. Such a deterministic conception of habitus portrays actors as heteronymous entities condemned to reproduce the social conditions of their domination. This somewhat fatalistic perspective is particularly seductive when studying the situation of the working classes in advanced societies. For, according to this view, these classes 'learn' to like watching television, rather than reading books, and they 'learn' to disengage from, rather than to engage with, politics; in short, they 'learn' to accept their alienation.

With the phenomenology of the body, it becomes possible to use the concept of the plural actor, as proposed by Lahire, without discarding the existence of an individual habitus, which is largely ignored by Corcuff. Thus, we need to account for the fact that the existence of 'social determinations' and the existence of 'cultural richness' are not necessarily mutually exclusive. Socially complex individuals are not necessarily aware of the main elements of their cultural identities, and may be even less so of their creative capacity that allows them to 'invent' themselves and the world in which they find themselves situated. In other words, *all individuals are plural even if their personalities are structured by an unconscious habitus*. And 'the presence of a habitus' does not necessarily imply 'the absence of competences': individual actions are always shaped, but not necessarily determined, by the predispositional schemes of habitus.

Towards a New Approach of Activism

Merleau-Ponty uses the example of a painter to show how the 'being-in-the-world' is a source of creativity. In *L'œil et l'esprit* (1964; in English: *The Eye and the Mind*), he states that it is 'through the act of offering himself (his body) to the world' that the painter is through that very process of creation transformed into a painting of that reality, becoming as it were 'its echo' (see Merleau-Ponty, 1964: 16 and 22). Castoriadis follows in the footsteps of the phenomenology of the body constructed by Merleau-Ponty, giving it a political application.[15] In *L'institution imaginaire de la société* (1975; in English: *The Imaginary Institution of Society*), he argues that

> […] the support of the subject and non-subject in the subject (i.e. what comes to him or her from his or her social influences) is the body: the point of articulation between the Self and the Other is the body, that material structure full of potential meaning. The body is not alienation – that would mean nothing – but participation in the world. Meaning attachment and mobility constitute the pre-constitution of a universe of meaning that is prior to any reflexive thought. (Castoriadis, 1975: 157)

Castoriadis's description of 'the subject' overlaps with both Lahire's and Corcuff's respective accounts of 'the social actor'. The subject is not that abstract moment of a removed form of disembodied subjectivity; rather, it constitutes an active and embodied entity situated in different spheres of the social world. In this sense, the subject is not an 'absolute self'. Rather, it is an individual conditioned by social contents; and as such it is the 'active authority that constantly reorganises these contents by using them' (Castoriadis, 1975: 158). Autonomy is thus no longer, as the critical (or genetic) school would have it, seeking to prevent or control 'the effects of the oppressive structure of society on our lives' (1975: 161) Autonomy is precisely that structure itself, from the moment actors transform it by 'acting'.

What Castoriadis calls the radical imagination of the *psyche* corresponds to the description of habitus as sociological fiction outlined above. There is no point in trying to localise the psyche; it can be regarded as a magma of social determinisms. Castoriadis puts this as follows:

> [M]an is deep psyche; man is society. He is only in and by society, his institution and the socially imagined meanings that make the psyche adapted to life. Beyond biology [...] man is a psychological and socio-historic being. It is on these two levels that we will regain the capacity of creation that I have called imaginary and imagination. There is radical imagination in the *psyche*. (Castoriadis, 1996 [1978]: 112, emphasis in original)

The psyche is the ability to combine pre-given elements (habits) to create new forms of activity. Through the body, the psyche receives impressions that it gives shape to unconsciously in order to bring about discourses and action. According to Castoriadis, the psyche – that is, as our individual habitus – is 'the ability to bring to light things that are not real', but this ability is possible thanks to elements provided by reality. The magma, of which the components are unconscious, is our pre-subjective world, 'a compact mass, blind and deaf and which leads to the "flowering of the imaginary"' (Castoriadis, 1997 [1978]-b: 95).

Castoriadis allows us to move forward considerably. Following Castoriadis, we can view the agent both as a proper subject and as a social actor with a psyche. From this perspective, we are no longer trapped in a determinist understanding according to which actors 'have no choice'. To be sure, actors do not really understand their actions because they do not understand the different social mechanisms by which their habitus is determined, but it would be erroneous to reduce the habitus to a dispositional apparatus aimed at the mere reproduction of an established order. Such a view would be equivalent to considering the habitus as purely passive. Instead, it is the task of a truly critical sociology to account for both the passive *and* the active, both the unconscious *and* the conscious aspects of the habitus. From this perspective, it becomes possible to regard the habitus as both an internalised social unconscious and a cradle of creative imagination that, rather than veiled in ignorance, is inhabited by a vision of dynamic magma.

Thus society is not simply a conglomerate of structures that restrict our freedom, but it is also a space of opportunities that facilitates our actions and thereby turns us into creative and complex beings, who are exposed to various experiences and who are capable of developing new modes of expression and action. New ways of being together can emerge without actors, involved in the construction of these new ways of being, necessarily being aware of this emergence. New social movements are a tangible illustration of what can come of such creative processes: largely random forms of habitus that are close to each other and yet dissonant. If, for instance, we look at the appearance of the social forums in Porto Alègre, Bombay, Paris and London, we can observe the emergence of groups of actors who come together periodically and who have developed a shared militant habitus through which people from different social and professional backgrounds manage to agree on particular political aims, such as the aim to 'combat neo-liberalism'. In their own way, individually or in small groups, they each innovate and invent new models of political contestation, new political justifications, or even new economic models such as cooperatives, mutual companies and so forth. They 'institute' propositions for 'an alternative world' inspired by the rejection of the existing one. Of course, each member of the movement has certain militant dispositions incorporated into their own history and life-course. Everyone is rich in determinations, and different people are embedded in different life forms, even if actors are not conscious of the exact extent to which their lives are shaped by external factors. 'Why engage in one association rather than in another one?', the activist may wonder when questioned by the sociologist. The question provokes hesitant and diverse responses that illustrate the complexity of the various reasons that people may have when deciding to engage in a particular form of collective action.

Given the complexity of the issue, it would be difficult to come up with a 'proper' definition, let alone an exhaustive analysis, of political activism. In the contemporary world, activists seem to be increasingly reluctant to claim an affiliation to a trade union or an institutional federation. Instead, they engage only sporadically in political action, often through several different associations at once, to conserve their 'autonomy' (Ardizzone, 2007). This is not to suggest, however, that their engagement is 'weak'. Those present at the anti-globalisation summits become – as Merleau-Ponty would say – 'the body' of the event. They may identify themselves with different associations (for instance, Attac, Greenpeace, or No Logo) and sympathise with different discourses (for example, environmentalist, feminist, or anti-capitalist) at different moments in time. For some of them, this means that they engage in political actions and discourses with which they were not, or were hardly, familiar in the past; more importantly, this means that such collective events can lead to the *creation* of political actions and discourses which did not exist in the past. The fact that these forums exist as *new* forms of social struggle is indicative of the *creative* potential of social action. Yet, neither the traditional notion of habitus, in the strictly Bourdieusian sense, nor the critical use made of it by other theorists, such as Corcuff or Lahire, seem to be able to capture the emancipatory potential of social creativity, embodied, for example, in the existence of a 'militant habitus'.

It is highly probable that these forms of dynamic habitus, themselves the result of socialisation processes, have consequences of which the actors are not conscious. Whatever the future of the anti-globalisation movement, the combination of different encounters and processes will lead to new forms of institutionalisation at the macro-social level, and – both for activists and sociologists – it will be difficult to predict the exact nature of these institutionalisation processes.

Conclusion: A Sociology of Contingency

On the basis of the analysis developed above, it would be fair to suggest that sociological approaches which stand in the tradition of Bourdieu's genetic structuralism need to develop conceptual and methodological tools which allow us to account for the power of social contingency. The assumption that there is such a thing as a dynamic habitus is largely dependent on the idea that social innovation is unpredictable. As explained above, it is not possible to make sense of the existence of a dynamic habitus if we rely exclusively on Bourdieu's social theory, as Bourdieu – following Émile Durkheim – conceived of sociology primarily as a science aimed at uncovering the underlying causal mechanisms that determine the course of social life. My own fieldwork, by which this analysis is inspired and which is based on my active participation in different social movements, suggests that it is intellectually worthwhile to try to develop genetic structuralism by drawing on issues of everyday life and the opaqueness of the magma of ordinary social action. Facing up to the contingencies of everyday life may indeed be necessary to prevent the Bourdieusian paradigm from falling into the trap of structuralist determinism. Of course, more work needs to be done to develop the ideas presented in this chapter further. It seems essential to explore the creative aspects of actors' 'militant habitus' if we seek to shed light on the resources mobilised in pursuit of social and political innovation. Creative imaginaries and creative action are indispensable components of creative societies. Thus, we may conclude by asking the following question: what is the radical imaginary, the cultural magma, the substance which brings actors together and allows for the possibility of collective action?

Notes

1 I am grateful to Simon Susen and Elena Knox for their detailed comments on this chapter.

2 In addition to the terms 'constructivist structuralism' and 'genetic structuralism', the term 'critical structuralism' is used in the Bourdieusian literature. Bourdieu's preference for the term 'constructivist structuralism' is symptomatic of the fact that he sought to distinguish himself from the 'relativist constructivism' of Bloor or Latour, with whom he disagreed on various points (see, for example, Bourdieu, 2001: 41). In this chapter, I use the terms 'genetic structuralism' and 'constructivist structuralism' interchangeably.

3 On this point, see, for example, Alexander (1995: 131).

4 On Bourdieu and psychoanalysis, see also, for example, Fourny (2000).

5 It is no accident that Merleau-Ponty had a tremendous influence on Bourdieu's intellectual development in general and on his conception of habitus in particular. In French sociology it is common to conceive of Bourdieusian structuralism in opposition to the phenomenological project (see, for example, Bénatouïl, 1999). We can endorse this reading on the condition that we take into account the fact that Bourdieu's reticence is essentially directed at the intellectualist prologue of this tradition, initially forged by Husserl (see the discussion in the last section of this chapter). According to Bourdieu, this intellectualist and anti-genetic tradition prevents us from posing 'the question of the social construction of the structures or schemata that the agent employs to construct the world' (Bourdieu, 1980: 44; on this point, see also Bourdieu, 1987: 47, Bourdieu, 1997: 175, and Bourdieu, 2001: 182).

6 Parts of this section are also quoted in Corcuff (1999: 103) and Corcuff (2003: 56). One cannot but notice that Bourdieu's conception of habitus was deeply problematic, as it largely constrained the notion of class habitus. Indeed, the homological interpretation of habitus of members of the same class reappears in most parts of his writings. This is indicative of Bourdieu's attempt to 'build hidden analogies' in order to identify

specific rules and regularities that determine the constitution of habitus, similar to the – positivistically inspired – attempt to establish rules and regularities for the objects of science (Bourdieu, Chamboredon and Passeron, 1968: 78).

7 The sociological questions arising from the concern with reflexivity and rational competence, a concern which is of crucial importance in Corcuff's writings, oblige us to reflect upon the concept of individual habitus.

8 In *Réponses. Pour une Anthropologie Réflexive*, Wacquant argues that, in Bourdieu's work, the term 'habitus' is a phenomenological concept. Quoting Merleau-Ponty, Bourdieu defines it as 'the intrinsic corporality of pre-objective contact between subject and object so as to reproduce the body as a source of practical intentionality, as a source of signification [...] rooted at the pre-objective level of experience' (Bourdieu and Wacquant, 1992: 27). In this regard, Bourdieu was opposed to the 'deep intellectualism of European philosophers who have overlooked the potential advantages of addressing the body' (Bourdieu and Wacquant, 1992: 98).

9 We 'know' the world intuitively through our bodies before we become 'aware' of the world in a reflexive sense, and we know it with a knowledge that is shared with others and which stems from community. Indeed, our body allows us to be 'deaf to the world, in an initiation to the world upon which rests the relationship between a thought and its object, and which is always already complete when the reflexive return of the subject takes place' (Merleau-Ponty, 1945: 57).

10 Boltanski (2003).

11 I am immersed in the world before becoming aware of the world. Merleau-Ponty put this as follows: 'When I awake in me the consciousness of this social-mine (*social-mien*), it is my whole past that I am able to conceive of [...], all the convergent and discordant action of the historical community that is effectively given to me in my living present' (Merleau-Ponty, 1960b: 12).

12 On this point, see esp. Bourdieu (1987: 15).

13 Lefort (1978: 110).

14 This was best expressed in Merleau-Ponty's later writings: '[T]he body overflows into a world of which he carries the schemata [...] which continuously provokes in him a thousand wonders' (Merleau-Ponty, 1960a: 108). It is important to keep in mind Merleau-Ponty's insistence on the unconscious nature of the habitus: an '*unconscious* incorporation of specific social dispositions in practice, as an individual or socialised biological body, or as a social entity biologically individuate by incarnation' (Merleau-Ponty, 1997: 186). Thus, it develops on a daily basis through the subject's constant exposure to the social world. This essentially means that 'my body has its world, or understands its world without having to pass through representations, without submitting itself to an objectivising function' (Merleau-Ponty, 1997: 164).

15 See also Castoriadis (1997 [1978]-a).

References

Alexander, Jeffrey C. (1995) *Fin de siècle Social Theory: Relativism, Reduction, and the Problem of Reason*, London: Verso.

Ardizzone, Leoisa (2007) *Gettin' my Word Out: Voices of Urban Youth Activists*. Albany: State University of New York Press.

Bénatouïl, Thomas (1999) 'Critique et pragmatique en sociologie: quelques principes de lecture', *Annales, Histoire, Sciences Sociales* 54(2): 281–317.

Boltanski, Luc (1990) *L'amour et la justice comme compétences*, Paris: Métailié.

Boltanski, Luc (2003) 'Usages faibles, usages forts de l'habitus', in Pierre Encrevé and Rose-Marie Lagrave (eds.) *Travailler avec Bourdieu*, Paris: Flammarion, pp. 153–161.

Boltanski, Luc and Laurent Thévenot (1991) *De la justification. Les économies de la grandeur*, Paris: Gallimard.

Boudon, Raymond (1998) 'Social Mechanisms Without Black Boxes', in Peter Hedström and Richard Swedberg (eds.) *Social Mechanisms: An Analytical Approach to Social Theory*, Cambridge: Cambridge University Press, pp. 172–203.

Bourdieu, Pierre (1972) *Esquisse d'une Théorie de la Pratique, Précédé de Trois Études d'Ethnologie Kabyle*, Paris: Seuil.

Bourdieu, Pierre (1980) *Le sens pratique*, Paris: Minuit.

Bourdieu, Pierre (1987) *Choses dites*, Paris: Minuit.

Bourdieu, Pierre (1994) *Raisons pratiques. Sur la théorie de l'action*, Paris: Seuil.

Bourdieu, Pierre (1997) *Méditations pascaliennes*, Paris: Seuil.

Bourdieu, Pierre (2001) *Science de la science et réflexivité*, Paris: Raisons d'agir.

Bourdieu, Pierre, Jean-Claude Chamboredon and Jean-Claude Passeron (1968) *Le métier de sociologue. Préalables épistémologiques*, Paris: Éditions de l'École des Hautes Études en Sciences Sociales / Mouton.

Bourdieu, Pierre and Loïc Wacquant (1992) *Réponses. Pour une Anthropologie Réflexive*, Paris: Seuil.

Castoriadis, Cornelius (1975) *L'institution imaginaire de la société*, Paris: Seuil.

Castoriadis, Cornelius (1996 [1978]) 'Anthropologie, philosophie, politique', in Cornelius Castoriadis, *La montée de l'insignifiance, les carrefours du labyrinthe IV*, Paris: Seuil, pp. 105–124.

Castoriadis, Cornelius (1997 [1978]-a) 'Merleau-Ponty et le poids de l'héritage ontologique', in Cornelius Castoriadis, *Fait et à faire, les carrefours du labyrinthe V*, Paris: Seuil, pp. 157–195.

Castoriadis, Cornelius (1997 [1978]-b) 'De la monade à l'autonomie', in Cornelius Castoriadis, *Fait et à faire, les carrefours du labyrinthe V*, Paris: Seuil, pp. 85–107.

Corcuff, Philippe (1999) 'Le collectif au défi du singulier : en partant de l'habitus', in Bernard Lahire (ed.) *Le travail sociologique de Pierre Bourdieu : dettes et critiques*, Paris: La Découverte & Syros, pp. 95–120.

Corcuff, Philippe (2003) *Bourdieu autrement : fragilités d'un sociologue de combat*, Paris: Textuel.

Fourny, Jean-François (2000) 'Bourdieu's Uneasy Psychoanalysis', *SubStance* 29(3): 103–112.

Fowler, Bridget (1997) *Pierre Bourdieu and Cultural Theory: Critical Investigations*, London: Sage.

Frère, Bruno (2004) 'Genetic Structuralism, Psychological Sociology and Pragmatic Social Actor Theory: Proposals for a Convergence of French Sociologies', *Theory, Culture & Society* 21(3): 85–99.

Frère, Bruno (2005) 'Quelle phénoménologie pour une sociologie du consensus ?', *Études phénoménologiques* 41–42: 243–266.

Husserl, Edmund (1964 [1928]) *Leçon pour une phénoménologie de la conscience intime du temps*, trans. Granel Gérard, Paris: PUF.

Husserl, Edmund (1982 [1952]) *Idées II, recherches phénoménologiques pour la constitution*, trans. Eliane Escoubas, Paris: PUF.

Husserl, Edmund (1994 [1950]) *Méditations cartésiennes*, trans. Marc de Launay, Paris: PUF.

Kuhn, Thomas (1983 [1962]) *La structure des révolutions scientifiques*, trans. Laure Meyer, Paris: Flammarion.

Lahire, Bernard (1998) *L'homme pluriel : les ressorts de l'action*, Paris: Nathan.

Lahire, Bernard (1999a) 'Esquisse du programme scientifique d'une sociologie psychologique', *Cahiers internationaux de sociologie* 106: 29–55.

Lahire, Bernard (1999b) 'De la théorie de l'habitus à une sociologie psychologique', in Bernard Lahire (ed.) *Le travail sociologique de Pierre Bourdieu : dettes et critiques*, Paris: La Découverte & Syros, pp. 121–152.

Lahire, Bernard (2004) *La culture des individus. Dissonances culturelles et distinction de soi*, Paris: La Découverte.

Lefort, Claude (1978) 'Réflexions sur de premiers commentaires', in Claude Lefort, *Sur une colonne absente*, Paris: Gallimard.

Merleau-Ponty, Maurice (1945) *Phénoménologie de la perception*, Paris: Gallimard.

Merleau-Ponty, Maurice (1960a) 'Le langage indirect et les voix du silence', in Maurice Merleau-Ponty, *Signes*, Paris: Gallimard, pp. 63–135.

Merleau-Ponty, Maurice (1960b) 'Le philosophe et la sociologie', in Maurice Merleau-Ponty, *Éloge de la philosophie*, Paris: Gallimard, pp. 97–122.

Merleau-Ponty, Maurice (1960c) 'De Mauss à Claude Lévi-Strauss', in Maurice Merleau-Ponty, *Éloge de la philosophie*, Paris: Gallimard, pp. 123–142.

Merleau-Ponty, Maurice (1964) *L'œil et l'esprit*, Paris: Gallimard.

Piaget, Jean (1970) *Psychologie et épistémologie : Pour une théorie de la connaissance*, Paris: Denoël.

Ricœur, Paul (1965) *De l'interprétation : essai sur Freud*, Paris: Seuil.

Scheler, Max (1993 [1926]) *Problèmes de sociologie de la connaissance*, trans. Sylvie Mesure, Paris: PUF.

Schütz, Alfred (1962) 'Phenomenology and the Social Sciences', in Alfred Schütz, *Collected Papers, Volume I*, The Hague: Martinus Nijhof, pp. 97–203.

Wolff, Kurt (1978) 'Phenomenology and Sociology', in T. B. Bottomore and Robert A. Nisbet (eds.) *A History of Sociological Analysis*, New York: Basic Books, pp. 499–554.

CHAPTER TWELVE

Overcoming Semiotic Structuralism: Language and Habitus in Bourdieu

Hans-Herbert Kögler

Pierre Bourdieu's conception of habitus marks a theoretical step which no adequate understanding of social reality can ignore. By introducing habitus, Bourdieu is able both to integrate and to transcend major insights of the linguistic turn in philosophy, most prominently the idea that conscious intentional understanding necessarily relies on a host of implicit, practical, and holistic background assumptions which constitute meaning while being themselves unrepresented (Searle, 1989). The concept of habitus incorporates this idea since it shows that individual agency and its self-understanding are constituted by relying on an acquired social sense, the cognitive habitus, which defines how an agent understands, acts, and perceives itself and its environment. At the same time, it transcends the philosophical thematisation of a constitutive yet implicit background because it makes this hidden continent of pre-understanding susceptible to empirical-analytic social science.

This major step is hailed in traditional social theory as well as by Bourdieu himself as the mediation of agency and structure. It consists in reconstructing how specific social environments (that is, the structural conditions of agency) relate to and shape the internal sense of intentional agency (that is, the individual first-person dimension of agency) (Bourdieu, 1977 [1972]; 1990 [1980]). Habitus connects the two via a realm of pre-structured, schematised modes of understanding that define the specific cognitive accomplishments that any particular agent is capable of performing. Social analysis shows that those cognitive performances can be typified, that they are quasi-determined by the relationally constituted environments in which agents are situated, and that therefore the realm of intentional reflexivity and decision-making is to a large extent pre-figured (or literally 'pre-conceived') in terms of the environmentally inculcated schemes that agents have previously acquired. The trick of this mediation of agency and structure is to show that agents require the habitus *to enact* the embodied typified pre-conceptions that derive from social situations. Thus, the habitus is not itself just a form, scheme, or structure, but rather the agent-based capability to enact, to bring into play, to launch forward a certain understanding vis-à-vis an objective event or situation – and yet, its capabilities can only be enacted via the drawing on certain inculcated schemes, and thus remain in the end tied to an objectively existing social context. The social-empirical study of intentional cognitive attitudes has thus become possible.

Yet, the way in which Bourdieu conceives of the connection between the symbolic-practical schemes and the capabilities that activate them does not leave enough room for intentional and reflexive agency (Kögler, 1997; Bohman, 1997; see also Turner, 1994). This is not, as has been said regarding such criticisms, to deny that Bourdieu includes an account of consciously strategic agency, even though its acts and practices are nevertheless largely dependent on pre-accomplished modes of understanding (Foster, 2005). Agents are indeed very much capable of reflexively adjusting their acts and intentions to situations, albeit always on the basis of pre-structured schemes of understanding. The real question, however, is how agency can come to affect those interpretive schemes themselves, how the pre-accomplished modes of self-understanding can be challenged such that (a) specific ways of conceiving of something as something can be transformed and effectively criticised, that is, how it can be challenged such that different ways of understanding, feeling, and action become possible for the reflexively engaged agent, and (b) the strategic functionalist mode of investing those capabilities for an advantage for oneself in a situation or context could itself be challenged, meaning that one's existing mode of action for an agent could be seriously evaluated in light of value assumptions that do not have merely strategic value, but count intrinsically.

I will set out to show that Bourdieu's mediation of agency and structure owes too much to its departure from an overcoming of the one-sidedness of semiotic structuralism. Bourdieu's critique of Levi-Strauss's neglect of the temporal structure of gift exchange, which leads to the incomprehensibility of structures-in-action, as it were, emphasises the focus on agency, which – to avoid to complementary reduction of a free non-situated individual – remains socially grounded via the habitus (Bourdieu, 1977 [1972]). Yet, if we focus specifically on Bourdieu's account of language, we will see that his departure from semiotic structuralism, which rightly needs to be overcome through a more contextualist and pragmatic account, nevertheless fails to account fully for the *relatively autonomous realm of linguistic world-mediation*. I will argue that the capabilities related to habitus are capabilities operating always at both a pre-linguistic and a post-linguistic level, that is, they can only be understood as involving both pre-conceptual practical skills and linguistically mediated conceptual frameworks. The way agents adjust their pre-understanding to a situation owes to practical as well as linguistic moments, and the way in which a socially inculcated habitus can disclose reality is itself dependent in part on the linguistic level. Thus, to suggest a base-superstructure model between social and linguistic habitus, to which Bourdieu appears to adhere, fails to do justice to the co-constitution between practical and conceptual moments in achieving an intentional approach to understanding. Yet, as we will see, the linguistic dimension itself needs still to be understood in a practically acquired and schematically mediated way, suggesting that overly conceptualist or cognitivist accounts of linguistic understanding leave out the imaginative perspective-taking based on socially situated meanings which define much of social dialogue and understanding.

Accordingly, I will reconstruct how Bourdieu's conception of habitus relates to language. Specifically, this will involve an analysis and critique of how a socially inculcated pre-linguistic habitus is supposed to relate to the linguistic habitus, or to our linguistically mediated intentional pre-understanding. While Bourdieu's account in the end only illuminates one side of the equation – the grounding relation between the social dimension vis-à-vis the linguistic one – his analysis helps to build a richer conception. By doing so, we can hope to make Bourdieu's immensely rich empirical analyses accessible to a reflexive account of agency that sees habitus-based conditions as sources of agency and transformation. We can also hope to integrate the fruitful concept of habitus into a body of social theory that is finally free from the traditional dualisms of agency and structure, freedom and determinism, individual and society, to conceive of social situations as mediated possibilities to interact creatively so as to enhance the realm of options and opportunities. The mediating power of the *symbolic imagination*, activated in intersubjective encounters wherein agents release the creative force of empathetic and dialogical understanding, is thus mobilised against an overly static and conservative understanding of habitus as the arbiter of previously acquired meanings as self-identity.

1. The Limits of the Semiotic Model of Communication

In Saussure we find perhaps the best, and certainly the classic, expression of semiotic structuralism, exemplified in his code-model of mutual understanding. The guiding idea is that in order for two (or more) speakers to communicate intelligibly with one another, their thoughts and beliefs have to be expressed in a *symbolic medium* in which the speakers participate, or according to which they articulate and structure their thoughts and beliefs. According to this reading, substantiated by the early introduction of the speech circuit as the model of his semiotics, Saussure's semiotics sets out to explain the possibility of successful communication (Saussure, 1983 [1915]; see also Lee, 1997, Taylor, 1992).[1] An intentional speech act – inasmuch as it is oriented towards making an intelligible statement – presupposes the existence of a shared medium of expression.[2]

Saussure claims that it is essential for a sign *as a sign* that it has an identical meaning for the speakers; historical or etymological knowledge is irrelevant for this function. In order to understand the possibility of shared symbolic meaning, it is thus necessary to leave the genetic point of view behind.[3] To understand the meaning of 'house', for instance, the knowledge regarding its 'origin' as a term is superfluous. Identical meaning can simply be defined as a shared understanding of certain symbols pertaining to the same ideas for the individual involved in the communicative interaction. 'All the individuals linguistically linked in this manner will establish among themselves a kind of mean; all of them will reproduce – doubtless not exactly, but approximately – the same signs linked to the same concepts' (Saussure, 1983 [1915]: 13). The speaker, assuming that he or she can communicate with another speaker by means of symbols, has to presuppose the possibility of being understood. This means that Saussure privileges, albeit in a very general and structural fashion, the perspective of the language-user. It is ultimately the idealised first-person perspective of the speaker (who presupposes 'the same signs linked to the same concepts') that determines the need for a structural linguistics.

Such a structural linguistics has the task to reconstruct precisely what kind of system, or *code*, speaker and hearer rely on in order to explain the success of communication. The genetic or 'diachronic' view has thus to be replaced by a 'synchronic' view that analyses the functional properties and relations that allow signs to have a meaning, that is, to be precise, a *shared* meaning. This view alone allows us to capture the *structural links* that symbols establish between different individuals communicating the *sameness* of the symbols used: 'It is clear that the synchronic point of view takes precedence over the diachronic, since for the community of language users that is the one and only reality [...]. Synchrony has only one perspective, that of the language users' (Saussure, 1983 [1915]: 13). Yet, this does not imply that speakers are conscious of the structural properties of signs or symbolic orders on which they necessarily draw in order to communicate. For Saussure, the essential task of a structural linguistics, indeed the very birth certificate of this discipline as an autonomous science, is precisely to reconstruct 'objectively' the underlying features of such symbolic systems.[4]

In order to determine the nature of the code, Saussure rightly excludes the physical-physiological aspects from consideration. We are interested not in sounds as such, but in the 'experienced' sound-patterns that are endowed with meaning. Similarly, we have to exclude *individual speech* from our consideration. Saussure motivates this point, far less controversial, with the argument that speech only 'executes' the underlying structure of language, while the *shared* understanding can only be made possible – by definition – by a dimension that is prior to, and both transcends and surpasses individual intentional acts. Saussure understands that the question of shared meaning forces one to consider language as a *social phenomenon*, and therefore feels entitled to exclude the mere individual actualisation of the underlying, meaning-enabling mechanism from semiotics. A *speech act* (*parole*) is defined as 'an individual act of will and intelligence' in which speakers make use of the underlying *code* provided by language; *language-structure* (*langue*) instead creates and establishes a common medium, the *code*, as a sort of intermediary ground between the speakers on the basis of which they can make themselves understood to one another.

There is no space – and probably no need – to go into all the well-known details of Saussure's semiotics. Suffice it to recall that language-structure (*langue*) is defined as a social, holistic, synchronic, and formal system. Language can be defined as a system of signs. A sign can be defined as a material carrier that 'indicates' or stands for something else (see also Cassirer, 1955 [1923]). Hence, meaning is determined by a conceptual and by a material side. *A sign is a unified duality between signifier and signified, or sound image and concept/idea.* The association between a single signifier with a signified, however, is only made possible by its difference to other signs. This is Saussure's novel point. The identity or meaning of a sign is thus determined neither by the prior articulation of a thought nor by its reference to some fixed entity or thing, but only by its difference to other symbolic units.[5] We can identify two important consequences following from this: first, *the principle of arbitrariness*, according to which every sign system or language defines meaning through 'arbitrary' distinctions[6]; and second, *the principle of internal differentiation*, according to which all the differences within a language are produced by the internal differences of sound patterns that distinguish conceptual meanings and by conceptual meanings that in turn define the differences between sound patterns.[7]

It is now crucial that a *conventional system of signs* mediates between communicators so as to allow for shared meaning. As mentioned above, Saussure grounds this thesis by submitting the more radical claim that the very thought to be communicated would be impossible without a material carrier, a symbolic articulation that structures the otherwise 'amorphous mass' (of thought) into 'articulated' and thus meaningful units (as in Cassirer, 1955 [1923]).[8] This means that a Platonic conception of pre-linguistic conceptual meaning is excluded; and since languages exist as conventional systems of meaning, thought itself bears a conventional marker.

Before noting several problems with this model, a remark is in order. The claim that the speaker's consciousness is symbolically structured does not mean, as Dummett suggests, that Saussure never escaped an empiricist psychology of association (Dummett, 1990: 131ff.). Symbolic relations are 'associated' in the mind of the speaker and express their meaning by being structured by syntagmatic and paradigmatic patterns of meaning. Yet, those symbolic forms are, in a Durkheimian fashion, rendered as previously constituted social media into which the self is socialised and out of which each speaker builds up an 'accumulated stock' of patterns, thus defining his or her specific linguistic competence. Accordingly, Saussure argues as a *social externalist* by placing the meaning-constitution in the in-between of speaker and hearer who are participating in the shared realm of symbolic structuration, and not within a psychological realm of mental associations.[9] Thus, an important step towards the mediation of language and meaning has been undertaken. Nevertheless, despite these clarifications, three major problems of the code-model remain.

1. Even though Saussure claims that the codes are constructed through speech, (implying that the linguistically reconstructed code is in fact an abstraction from embedded rules and norms), the social embeddedness of linguistic competence is not adequately taken into account. The code is presented as a formal and holistic grid that ultimately exists in a strictly demarcated sphere of internal differences. In this lies its function of guaranteeing meaning. Yet, a concept of symbolic sequence (such a syntagmatic or paradigmatic semiotic relations (Saussure, 1983 [1915]: 121 ff.) needs to be *understood* – and thus applied – in practical contexts, an application which cannot be controlled or determined by the code itself (Stern, 2003; Dreyfus, 1980; Wittgenstein, 1953). Since a formal rule can be interpreted in a variety of ways, agents must already know how to understand the rule. A new *rule* that would fix the interpretation cannot exist, because it could be read in different ways; for the supposed 'rule-of-application', the same problem (that is how exactly to understand it) would arise. What *is* essential, however, is to know how to apply the rule. Accordingly, agents have to possess some kind of practical know-how in order to account for understanding here. This Wittgensteinian argument – echoed by Gadamer's thesis of the intertwinement of interpretation and application (Gadamer, 1989 [1960]) – is evidenced by cultural studies that show how processes of 'encoding' – producing a formal and analysable structure of a text, a movie, an artwork, or a speech – do not predetermine the 'decoding' of the intended meaning (Hall, 1980). Interpretive understanding rather arises from an embedded, *context-sensitive* sense

that draws on a symbolico-practical background understanding which is both more elusive and more pervasive than the mere application of 'rules'. Bourdieu has a very clear grasp of this dimension of meaning, as his concept of *habitus* is developed to render the intuitive, practical, and embedded disclosure of meaning accessible to sociological analysis.

2. Saussure's model does not entirely separate the code from the intentional consciousness of the speaker, inasmuch as that code is introduced as a quasi-transcendental presupposition of successful communication. This general relation, however, does not translate into an *interpretive connection* between background-code and interpretive performance. Owing to the rigid methodological separation between *langue* and *parole*, between code and speech act, linguistic change – albeit considered as 'emanating' from individual speech – is never able to exert any intended or conscious influence on meaning. Echoing Durkheim, Saussure claims that *langue* exists 'external to the individual, who by himself is powerless either to create it or to modify it' (Saussure, 1983 [1915]: 14). While this statement is plausible regarding the formal features of language, it leaves unaccounted all processes of conscious adjustment and transformations of meanings that agents derive from interactions with the world and others. In this regard, Bourdieu follows in the questionable footsteps of the Saussurian structuralist approach. As we will see, Bourdieu rejects and overcomes the conceptualisation of language as *langue* or structure, which he replaces with the notion of habitus; nonetheless, he retains a quasi-foundational relation between habitus and agency, according to which intentional and reflexive agency is seen as the dependent product and 'actualisation' of the structural/schematic resources provided by habitus (Bohman, 1997; Kögler, 1997).
3. Saussure's model conceives of communication as a process enabled through a *shared structure*, but the 'sharedness' is not understood as a *mutual and intersubjective bond* of which the language-users are somewhat aware, i.e. as an *implicit normative order* that binds speakers to certain (however implicit) expectations and rules. Rather, the production of shared meaning is explained in terms of a somewhat parallel actualisation of similarly structured semiotic stocks. These objectively identical structures are supposed to explain the sameness of meaning. This means that the *experience* of shared meaning – that is, the fact that participants have an intuitive knowledge of the norms and expectations that are 'implied' in the social use of language – goes wholly unexplained. In fact, Saussure emphatically rejects a 'normative' understanding of semiotic codes: 'Synchronic laws are general, but not imperative. It is true that a synchronic law is imposed upon speakers by the constraints of communal usage. But we are not envisaging

> here an obligation relative to the language users [...]. A synchronic law simply expresses an existing order' (Saussure, 1983 [1915]: 91). Saussure entirely misses the implicit normativity that inheres in linguistic usage. Participation in linguistic practices, as we will see below, entails indeed a normative dimension, it compels speakers to behave and express themselves in specific ways, and it entails presuppositions that speakers, by use of linguistic means, can be held accountable for. Instead of rendering the sharedness of meaning solely in terms of *regularity*, the intersubjective performance of language asks for an analysis of the *normativity* of the rules that are followed.

Here, Bourdieu equally fails to include the intentional normative sense of rules and assumptions inherent in linguistically mediated practices, such that their violation – that is the *experience* of someone or something running counter to what is expected and demanded by normal language use – is greeted with a critical response. Often, such violations may lead to a demand for justification, such that the unexpected behaviour becomes understandable action in light of new reasons that are provided for it (Brandom, 2000). Bourdieu understands that there is a certain inherent normativity in language use, but analyses this mainly in terms of symbolic power, i.e. in light of a normal and normalised order that is – à la Saussure – conventionally imposed onto an existing situation. The internal organisation of the symbolic order is then explained via disproportionally available resources, which define different social positions, and thus different access-relations to differently constituted social environments, including different socially inculcated skills and practices, which coalesce to a social habitus. The sharedness of meaning is thus fully explained by the structural-holistic organisation of the background of an intentional speaker.

This analysis is based on an agency-structure model for which the intersubjective relation is a later result, which in turn can be explained via the different habitus formations that are involved, and which in turn respond and are reconfigured through the experience of agents with different resources and habitus. In the social context as a whole, habitus functions as capital, as skills and cognitive-social capabilities, which are agent-based and agent-incorporated resources to advance one's social position (Bourdieu, 1977 [1972]; 1990 [1980]; 1985) [1984]). They function as means for the realisation of one's interests and goals which are themselves essentially shaped by one's habitus, as one generally attempts to reach that which is within one's reach. The intentional orientation at one's interests or values is thus *conceptualised* vis-à-vis the socially encountered other, with whom one may assess the legitimacy of one's claims, but it is *explained* by means of socially produced, causally induced background structures that produce an intuitive, practical, embedded self-understanding via habitus. Accordingly, while Bourdieu's practical move advances significantly over the semiotic structuralism of Saussure, he retains some of the methodological baggage of structuralism in the way in which he conceptualises habitus as the underlying resource of intentional agency. To situate our post-Saussurian analysis and critique of Bourdieu in this context, however, we have to situate it more explicitly alongside with the normative post-Wittgensteinian approach to communicative meaning.

2. Two Models of Linguistic Meaning: Validity Claims versus Practical Dispositions

Our critique of Saussure's code-model provides us with a sense for the necessary desiderata of a revised conception of shared linguistic meaning, and thus a linguistically mediated reflexive agency. Such a conception would have to be able to include the context-sensitive applications of terms and sentences, it would have to account for reflexive transformations of meanings, and it would certainly have to account for the implicit normative dimension that inheres in language-use. Yet, at the same time, such a theory would still have to be able to designate 'something' as the common ground, it still requires a *medium* that accounts for shared meaning. The perhaps obvious move, in fact undertaken by the currently dominating turn toward performativity, is to locate the *rules* that speaker and hearer follow *within the performative practices themselves*. Instead of projecting (through a methodological objectification of underlying intuitive presuppositions such as 'sharing a code') an external system of symbolic relations, the rules and structures that bind agents to one another are now seen as existing 'within', as being internal to communicative practices. The turn from the code-model to the paradigm of performativity consists precisely in the translocation of rule or structure – or, to be exact, structuration (cf. Giddens, 1994) – into interpretive performance itself.

Now that this practical-communicative move has been undertaken, we may follow an ideal-typical path, in two highly divergent and yet somewhat complementary ways. On the one hand, we find the approach of *speech act theory* which takes its cues from the late Wittgenstein, but attempts to systematise the idea of rule-following in communicative contexts so as to derive some universal *presuppositions* of meaning, truth, and understanding (Wittgenstein, 1953; Searle, 1969; 1995; Habermas, 1983/1987 [1981]). This paradigm assumes that speakers reach communicative understanding through a set of standardised uses understood as shared counterfactual norms. On the other hand, the post-structuralist approach, as found in Foucault and Bourdieu, sets out to analyse the ways in which speakers are constrained by implicit discursive rules or practices (as it were, 'normalising norms') that shape perception, conception, and action. Instead of aiming at *universal conditions* that would in counterfactual idealisation be able to account for the success of our meaning-intentions and truth-claims, this approach shows how the *actual success* (or failure) of particular speech acts is grounded in underlying grids of speech performances. We thus witness a dramatic split, indeed a deep internal rift in the approaches toward linguistic performativity. The internal reconstruction of 'underlying' performance-rules is either taken to account for the possibility of intersubjective communication and shared meaning; *or* it is employed as a critical means to unmask the necessary myths and misrecognitions that precisely inhere in the universal value-orientation which defines, among others, the speech act approach. While speech act theory aims at a reconstruction of the universalist presuppositions that it takes to underlie our truth-oriented sense of shared meaning, the discourse-theoretical approach uses the reconstruction of implicit rules of performative acts as a critique of the symbolic-social power that is usually exercised within such practices.[10]

The speech act approach claims to save our universalist and truth-oriented intuitions by providing a new 'performative' basis for intersubjective meaning. The basic idea is that a speaker, much like the idea that drove Saussure in the first place, can only avoid a 'performative self-contradiction' (that is, a conflict between intentional content and their speech performance) by assuming that shared meaning is possible. A closer analysis shows that the sameness of meaning is not sufficiently guaranteed by syntactical or semantic rules, but requires a pragmatic understanding of the context in which terms and sentences are used (Habermas, 1992). Yet, the pragmatic grounding does not open the door to contextualism or relativism, since it is possible to reconstruct types or standards inherent in language-use that define literal meaning.[11]

Habermas's version of speech act theory, the 'theory of communicative action', is particularly instructive in this respect (Habermas, 1983/1987 [1981]). Habermas argues that a speaker, by entering into communicative contexts, *willy nilly* comes to participate in a normatively structured situation in which he or she is taken, however implicitly, to raise exactly three validity claims. The idea is that speakers usually assume that what they say is true, that it follows rationally acceptable moral norms, and that it expresses an authentic intention on the side of the speaker. Such normative orientations are *latent* in everyday speech, and become *manifest* once one or several of the claims are contested: then the speaker has to provide reasons for why she said what she said – and the broken intersubjective understanding can only be *redeemed* by filling in the gaps interrupting the sharedness of sense. The sharedness of meaning is thus, in a certain sense, based on the counterfactual assumption that valid reasons can be provided in case of need. For Habermas, this shows that *meaning and validity* are mutually presupposing concepts, because the understanding of an utterance can be explained by 'knowledge of the conditions under which a hearer may accept it. *We understand a speech act when we know what makes it acceptable* [i.e. what assumed conditions of validity make it acceptable, HHK]' (Habermas, 1983 [1981]: 297, italics in original).

Habermas's communicative theory does take into account the *contextual embedding of meaning* by granting that every speech act must, in order to make sense, draw on an implicit horizon of pre-understandings. Those *background assumptions* – which, according to Habermas, are situated in what he calls the 'lifeworld' – form a context in which statements are usually embedded, in which they initially are defined and developed. For Habermas, however, the intended meaning of utterances is not encapsulated in – that is, it is not bound by – their *initial* contexts of use. Habermas assumes that this is the case because, even in the most concrete circumstances, statements are uttered with the (however implicit) communicative understanding of being true, right, and authentic; they thus imply, by definition of their context-transcending validity claims, a wider, in fact an ultimately 'endless' or universal context of meaning. Because the initial assumptions are intertwined with context-transcending claims, the meaning that is first shaped in particular circumstances is taken to be capable of being 'transmitted' to any other context.

Now it is precisely this claim of the *possibility of context-transcendence* that the competing paradigm of performance-rules by Foucault and Bourdieu puts into question. In order to not miss the exact point of the opposition, however, it is important to see that the contextual embeddedness in rule-governed contexts is in fact not so much an issue just of 'rules' – rules the discourse-analyst is capable of reconstructing – but rather one of the *practical capabilities*, the embodied dispositions and skills that form the background for the application of rules in contexts. These contextual rules are considered *formative of meaning* by Foucault and Bourdieu. Following Wittgenstein, rules are not defining meaning-contexts 'on their own', but are deeply ingrained into, and operative through, the cognitive and interpretive skills and practices of situated agents. Foucault's attack on the humanistic self-understandings of modern institutions – including modern concepts of 'madness', 'health', 'man', 'punishment', and 'sexuality' (Foucault, 1979 [1975]; 1990 [1966]; 1994 [1976]) – as much as Bourdieu's reconstruction of the class-bases of certain cognitive capacities draws on the claim that social practices and its related practical sense pre-structures and thus pre-directs all conscious, if you wish, rule-governed behaviour (Bourdieu, 1977 [1972]). Bourdieu defines the practical sense as 'habitus', as a generative capacity to produce certain statements and utterances; it always already organises the perceptions, thoughts and actions of agents according to an implicit grid that has been acquired in specific social circumstances:

> The conditionings associated with a particular class of conditions of existence produce habitus, systems of durable, transposable dispositions, structural structures, that is, as principles which generate and organise practices and representations that can be objectively adapted to their outcomes without presupposing a conscious aiming at ends or an express mastery of the operations necessary in order to attain them. (Bourdieu, 1977 [1972]: 15)

To be sure, Habermas might reply to such a form of 'practical reductionism' that the actual communicative capacities of speakers are misconstrued if rendered 'grounded' in contextually circumscribed understandings. Yet, the claim that agents are in fact capable of transcending their contextually acquired boundaries – boundaries that are assumed to be now operating from within the agent – needs to be cashed in by more than just a repeated reference to the inherent universal validity claims. This is so because the fact that discourse is oriented towards truth, morality, and authenticity is not an assumption that Foucault or Bourdieu leave on the side. Rather, it is part of their theories that the practical and power-laden dispositions work as effectively as they do precisely because agents consider their communicative performances as usually being true, right, or correct; the implicit 'modus operandi' that distributes the contextual resources differently so that certain statements and assumptions are 'true', while others are 'false' (and 'illegitimate', 'subcultural', 'abnormal', etc.) are, literally, in the background. The 'misrecognition' of statements is being guided by a socially inculcated sense that reproduces power; it works on the basis of – and not despite – the assumption that we are all oriented towards truth and validity, and that such truth and validity is, at least in principle, attainable for everyone.

Habermas had already in the seventies presented a theory of moral and cognitive development that was supposed to show how the speaker reaches, through maturing through different stages of cognitive and moral understanding, a universal standpoint (Habermas, 1979: 69 ff.; Habermas, 1990). Yet, the claim of such a formal reconstruction – that uses the normative ideal of a trans-contextual perspective to reconstruct the empirical emergence of such an understanding in each individual speaker – is subject to the very criticism as the communication theory itself. It is remains unclear how the universal standpoint is capable of disentangling itself from the practically acquired modes of self-understanding, given that such modes are more deeply ingrained in the communicative background – or the self for that matter – than discursive rules. The reference to the normative dimension is by itself incapable of convincing us that situated speakers are capable of actualising its force, that they are up to the normative implications that their discourse demands – granted that communications implies such value-orientation. This problem is intrinsic to the universalist theory of speech performance, since the communicative coordination of action through speech is taken to be embedded in, and to arise from, concrete cultural and social contexts.[12]

The discussion has shown that each side has to defend a certain understanding of the background in order to make its position work. For Habermas, the meaningful background of communication cannot be considered resisting its communicative representation; whatever the initial assumptions are, it must be possible to articulate and explicate them in discursive communication so as to reach possible agreement about what's at stake and what's justifiable. For Foucault and Bourdieu, on the other hand, the background must essentially resist such reflexive explication, at least if their position is understood as implying inescapable power relations. Here, the critical theoretical explication of the structures of the social world never really catches up with its true nature and operating principle, which continues to belief in the pro-claimed normative value-orientations. Habermas's position must assume that the promise of possible understanding within language can (in whatever regulative manner) be fulfilled, whereas the poststructuralist position suggests we abandon this promise in order to see through its illusion. Yet, how intentional and critical agency may then be possible presents a major challenge for poststructuralist perspectives.

At this point I suggest that we should agree that we cannot simply dismiss the practical embeddedness of intentional agents, but that we also need to do justice to the relative autonomy of intersubjective communication, to the capacity of an agent as well as an interpretive social theorist to understand and exchange views regarding oneself and the other within a shared medium of meaning. We need to preserve this dimension of our shared everyday as well as theoretical understanding without denying that meaning entails in its background dimensions relations of power. If this is granted, the task becomes to show how the contextual embeddedness pointed out by Foucault and Bourdieu doesn't undermine the capacity of interpretive dialogue and intersubjective communication, and that intentional agency is capable of a reflexive self-understanding within a medium of theoretical articulation which entails the reconstruction of power without reducing to its exercise. If we want to find a way out of the dialectic of normative reason and practical power, we have to find a conception of understanding that is able to mediate between, on the one side, normative orientations and their intentional self-understanding and, on the other side, the contexts of their embeddedness which entail power relations through inculcated practical dispositions. In order to prepare the ground for such a new understanding, we will now take a closer look at how Bourdieu conceives of the relation between language and power. In particular, we will reconstruct how the conception of habitus is employed to make sense of the linguistic mediation of reality and experience as grounded in social existence, i.e. power.

3. Language, Habitus, and Symbolic Power

Bourdieu assumes that an agent's capacity to speak – including the capacities to perceive, to think, and to act – are built up in the context of symbolic social practices that shape an implicit sense, a hermeneutic pre-understanding. Bourdieu can thereby sketch a theory of symbolic power in which the role of language is conceived in terms of the concrete social contexts that establish a speaker's authority and guarantee shared intersubjective understanding. Accordingly, Bourdieu does not define the construction of an agent's or speaker's identity vis-à-vis truth-oriented discourse (as Habermas does), but suggests that the overall *competence* to perform any speech act, in specialised discourses as well as in the social lifeworld, depends on the acquisition of skills and capabilities that are embodied in a linguistic habitus that in turn is grounded in social practices of power. Accordingly, with Bourdieu we can further pursue the most pressing questions of our inquiry at this point: to what extent are speakers shaped and constituted by the language they speak, inasmuch as this language reflects the social conditions of their existence, including relations of power and domination? More generally, how do social practices and institutions shape the symbolic meaning through which speakers make sense of the world and of themselves?

My thesis is that as a basic approach to these questions, Bourdieu grounds the linguistic habitus (the *symbolically mediated* background assumptions, values, and skills) in the social habitus (the *socially inculcated and context/class-specific knowledges, skills, and practices*) which leads ultimately to a problematic and under-analysed identification of both background dimensions. While this move establishes a crucial connection between intentional linguistic understanding and practices with social background structures, it disregards – or, at least, underestimates – the creative, reflexive, and critical potential that agents possess via the medium of language as such. Bourdieu fails to explore the critical gap that exists between the background inculcation of certain attitudes and assumptions, and the potential, which is grounded in their *symbolic form*, of transcending those assumptions in order to explore different attitudes, alternative interpretations, and contrasting viewpoints. Nonetheless, his discussion of habitus, both in its social and its linguistic form, clarifies the dimension of the social background for any further theory of situated social agency.[13]

Regarding language, Bourdieu argues that what linguistics takes to be a natural product, or the essence of language as such, is in fact the production of political and social efforts at the unification or 'normalisation' of linguistic practices (Bourdieu, 1994, esp. 1994a). The process of 'codification' involves that unruly and open linguistic practices, which are spread out into many different contextual forms, are subjected to some kind of 'streamlining' procedure. What grammarians are analysing is thus not a mental or biological given, but a social product produced in part by the very activity claiming to discover its inherent structures. Accordingly, language as a Saussurian code, as a set of rules that exists in terms of strict syntactic mechanisms and fixed lexical meanings, is nothing but a fiction – albeit, since the birth of the national state and its educational system, a real because realised one: 'Linguists merely incorporate into their theory a pre-constructed object, ignoring its social laws of construction and masking its social genesis' (Bourdieu, 1994a: 44). Opposing what linguists take to be the underlying essential reality of language, that it is a code, Bourdieu claims that the law-like nature of 'language' is (a) a *symbolic construction* that produces what it claims to find, i.e. it is a codification of what exists in plural and practical contexts in a pragmatic and open-ended manner; and (b) a *social imposition* that has, once 'grammatically' established, been opposed to the everyday speech practices in order to normalise the social and cognitive behaviour of its agents:

> Produced by authors who have the authority to write, fixed and codified by grammarians and teachers who are also charged with the task of inculcating its mastery, *the language is a code*, in the sense of a cipher enabling equivalences to be established between sounds and meanings, but also *in the sense of a system of norms regulating linguistic practices*. (Bourdieu, 1994a: 45, italics added)

The code in Saussure (or for that matter 'depth grammar' in Chomsky) is in fact produced by the social context which brings about the transformation of linguistic practices into structured and codified entities. The concrete social context which functions as the causal site of this particular creation is the nation state, in the course of which local linguistic practices become subjected to the norm created via an official national language. Thus, 'dialects' become possible only against the official establishment of, say, 'French'. Bourdieu can show how the development of the modern state produced the need and politics of a unified national language. In this context, normative grammar is established, and the micro-practices of teaching and supervising linguistic norms and conventions – such as spelling, pronunciation, and style – help to produce a legitimate language.

> [In France], the imposition of the legitimate language in opposition to the dialects and patois was an integral part of the political strategies aimed at perpetuating the gains of the revolution through the production and the reproduction of the 'new man'. [...] To reform language, to purge it of the usages linked to the old society and impose it in its purified form, was to impose a thought that was itself purged and purified. [...] The conflict between the French of the revolutionary intelligentsia and the dialects of the patois was a struggle for symbolic power in which what was at stake was the formation and re-formation of mental structures. (Bourdieu, 1994a: 47–48)[14]

For grammarians, these accountants of national languages thus help to create the socially recognised reality of a normed, and thus 'normal', language, which was also used to generate new universal forms of thinking. The new French, however, needed to be imposed on the dialect-speaking subjects; and, as critical sociologists, we need to examine how this was possible.[15] If there are different attitudes with regard to language and how to speak, we need to explain how subjects who speak patois are able to accept French as the legitimate language, how they come to perceive themselves as speaking 'dialect'. How is it that speakers subordinate their own identities to the ones imposed by the state, especially if they do not gain but lose symbolic recognition in this process?

Bourdieu's answer is prepared by the rephrasing of this problem, which entails that *symbolic power requires the cooperation of the oppressed.* In other words, the speakers themselves have to accept the view of 'French' as the legitimate language, so as to allow the symbolic (state) power to take hold of them: 'All symbolic power presupposes, on the part of those who submit to it, a form of complicity which is neither passive submission to external constraint nor a free adherence to it' (Bourdieu, 1994a, 50–51). The question is now how this *complicity* is brought about, what makes it possible, since it is obviously against the interests of those who submit to it because it denigrates them to a subordinate position. In order to explain this phenomenon, Bourdieu introduces a set of theoretical concepts, the most important of which is the social habitus and its derivative form, the linguistic habitus. It is here that we find the core thesis of Bourdieu's theory of symbolic power which consists in the grounding of intentional linguistic self-understanding in a prior cognitive mode, the habitus, which acquires a quasi-foundationalist meaning with regard to reflexive agency.

Bourdieu rightly rejects the (itself one-sided and problematic) view that the social world is constitutively created by the conscious and intentional use of linguistic symbols. He rather assumes that agents acquire, in the context of *early childhood socialisation*, a social habitus that pre-schematises their perception, thought and action by internalising structural features of their social environment. The general capacity of selves to adjust creatively and spontaneously to the ever-changing demands of social situations are thus not the free or conscious project of the subject, acting either alone or 'intersubjectively'. They are rather made possible by general, yet flexible, *interpretive schemes* that equip agents with the necessary skills to cope with their immersion in different social situations. Being relieved from the impossible task to always interpret anew, agents acquire a pre-conscious sense of how to react, how to perceive, how to speak, etc., i.e. their social habitus. These habitus formations or schemes are socially differentiated, since they are acquired and shaped by the social situation within which agents grow up, and thus reflect or represent the economic, educational, cultural, gendered etc. relations that define the respective social environments. Those objective conditions are nonetheless transformed into embodied schemes and skills that enable agents to smoothly adjust and react to the present. As such, habitus provides the agents with different skills, with a different form of 'capital', to participate in social institutions, or 'fields'. The habitus provides a precondition of one's successful participation in public life, one which is nonetheless differently shaped according to social background (Bourdieu, 1977 [1972]; 1990 [1980]).

For our context, the aspect of the *unconscious and pre-linguistic nature of habitus* is most important. For Bourdieu, the habitus is acquired *prior to the conscious use of symbols*, indeed to any use of linguistic symbols at all:

> There is every reason to think that the factors which are most influential in the formation of the habitus are transmitted *without passing through language and consciousness*, but through suggestions inscribed in the most apparently insignificant aspect of the things, situations and practices of everyday life. Thus the modalities of practices, the ways of looking, sitting, standing, keeping silent, or even of speaking ('reproachful looks' or 'tones', 'disapproving glances' and so on) are full of injunctions that are powerful and hard to resist precisely because they are silent and insidious, insistent and insinuating. (Bourdieu, 1994a: 51, italics added)

The fact that in many ways *the sense of the situation* – that is, of what is appropriate, expected, adequate, acceptable – is not conveyed through the explicit and conscious use of symbols, but in an insinuating and holistic manner, suggests for Bourdieu that a *pre-linguistic* habitus builds up as a fixed and thus extremely effective stabilisation of meaning.

> The power of suggestion which is exerted through the things and persons and which, instead of telling the child what he must do, tells him what he is, and thus leads him to become durably what he has to be, is the *condition of the effectiveness of all kinds of symbolic power that will subsequently be able to operate on a (thereby created) habitus predisposed to respond to them.* (Bourdieu, 1994a: 52, italics added)

Accordingly, a social habitus is built up 'without passing through language and consciousness' (Bourdieu, 1994a: 51). It is pre-linguistically created in holistically structured social situations, and importantly, it pre-structures the linguistic habitus, that is, the way a subject speaks, expresses itself, and thinks with and through a language. The basic social habitus is defined as an internalised scheme of meaning that adjusts the subject to the situation; it is made up of embodied 'assumptions' derived from former experiences within the objective environment; the experiences are thus organised as a quasi-worldview.[16] Because this adjustment gets incorporated into a bodily scheme, it does not require reflective or explicit application; subjects are, on the contrary, always already attuned to the power-defined and hierarchical structures they know best because they grew up in them. Agents know practically and intuitively (and in this way much better than by means of reflexive thematisation) what to say, to think, to do, or to perceive:

> The conditionings associated with a particular class of conditions of existence produce habitus, systems of durable, transposable dispositions, structural structures, that is, as principles which generate and organise practices and representations that can be objectively adapted to their outcomes without presupposing a conscious aiming at ends or an express mastery of the operations necessary in order to attain them. (Bourdieu, 1977 [1972]: 15)

We thus encounter a theory close to Heidegger's 'practical holism', as understood by Hubert Dreyfus, according to which meaning, in our case the social sense of the situation as well as the capacities to think and speak, is preformed and basically anchored to provide a meaningful ground for the use of linguistic symbols in intentional, conscious and intersubjective speech (Dreyfus, 1980; 1993; Heidegger, 1962 [1927]). The habitus is supposed to explain how agents internalise what we could call a symbolic inferiority complex: they cannot but speak the socially based idiolect which defines, via the world-disclosing function of language, their self-understanding. At the same time, the agents cannot fail but recognise their own difference to the official code, and thus must assess the value and acceptability of their own speech practices in light of the legitimate languages: 'All linguistic practices are measured against the legitimate practices, i.e. the practices of those who are dominant' (Bourdieu, 1994a, 53). Thus, the linguistic habitus is supposed to explain both the enduring nature of dialects, which are based on different social conditions of existence, and the universal acceptance of the legitimate code, which is inculcated through all sorts of micro-practices like school-teaching, media, etc., and which helps to maintain the power-differentiated status quo of the social order.

Yet, the question is whether we can assume that the linguistic habitus – and therefore the very notion of *linguistic agency* – is as strongly tied to particular social conditions, including specifically defined cognitive competences, as Bourdieu claims. If it is true, this claim would suggest a full constitution of speakers by social power. If the use of language is grounded in a linguistic habitus, which in turn relies on a social habitus formed through unconscious, practical interaction with one's environment, then speech practices can be nothing but the *expression* of that underlying disposition. It is hard to see then how speakers could critically reassess or change their habitual structures, since they are inculcated into a level of 'understanding' that escapes the conscious and intentional use of symbols.[17]

4. Linguistic Habitus and the Social Sources of Agency

Bourdieu's intended overcoming of the agency/structure divide can appear to be reductionist vis-à-vis agency due to its subordination of linguistic habitus to social habitus. Indeed, assuming that a habitus forms fully on the level of pre-linguistic and unconscious processes of agency-development deprives the reflectively acting subject of a major tool: namely, the capability to not only orient his or her actions or beliefs towards something directly encountered (so to speak, in front of it), but also the ability to engage in a *reflexive restructuration and reconfiguration* of those background assumptions and schemes that disclose something as something in the first place. While the social theorist in Bourdieu's case is capable of unearthing the habitus formations as the implicit background actor that pre-configures what appears as meaningful and real in a social context, the agents themselves remain subject to the capital they received due to prior socialisation that they are bound to invest as is. Precisely this division, however, would cut off the critical force that social theory could unleash with regard to the reflexive agency of which agents themselves could prove capable. And precisely this move, I suggest, comes about by unduly reducing the role of language in the mediation of individual agents with their objective environments, or in the constitution of habitus.[18]

This can be shown by going back to what habitus can possibly mean in the context of a theory of agency, Bourdieu's social theory included. If a social habitus is integrated into a conception of human agency, it must entail a constitutive relation to intentional agency, because without intentional concepts agency cannot be made sense of (Winch, 1991 [1959]). Bourdieu's important and convincing move is to sacrifice any Cartesian assumption of pre-existing capacities for a methodological socialism that assumes that capabilities emerge within the context of social relations. Those relations, however, are always already situated in objective contexts that determine how the emergent capabilities are de facto constituted. The cognitive resources on which agents can draw, their cognitive accomplishments as individual bearers of intentional processes, carry the irrevocable stamp of their environments, their relative wealth or poverty, with regard to certain conditions that enable the development of certain cognitive processes. Since we cannot assume any objective or independent access to the objects of intentional disclosure, the capacities are defined relative to their contextual usefulness, which in turn is defined in terms of the established contexts or fields which make some capacity relevant and important. As explained above, Bourdieu conceives the contextual structures such that they shape the social habitus – the agent-based capabilities – which thereby become (a) an objective reflection of the existing social environments and (b) a subjectively incorporated scheme of understanding that directs the intentional cognition of the respective individual agent.

The important step beyond and advantage over semiotic structuralism consists in the designation of the habitus as agent-based intentional capabilities. Thereby, the structures are not externally patched onto an otherwise unaffected individual, but they are shown to function as internal resources, as inner-cognitive dimensions of self-understanding, as true symbolic forms that define what counts for an agent as his or her self-understanding, because only thus can it delimit what he or she can possibly think, perceive, feel or do. Yet, the problematic feature of this move is that the meaning-constitutive force of linguistic concepts and assumptions in the constitution of habitus is not sufficiently taken into account, which means that the thematisation of the structuring forces on the habitus must remain, via methodological fiat, one-sided. This critique is not based on an individualist or normative truth-oriented intuition; rather, it draws on a reconstruction of how a habitus, understood as agent-based capabilities, must be formed so that it can *internally relate to the self-understanding of the agent.* To do so, it must entail capabilities that *define the agent's self-understanding.* It must track on the level at which an agent can possibly relate to herself or himself as such-and-such an individual. To do so, however, it must entail linguistic concepts and assumptions. It must entail a symbolically mediated dimension that cannot be fully constituted prior to that level, because then the agent would not be an agent that is constituted at least in part via that self-understanding, which itself is part of the conceptual idea of being a human agent (Taylor, 1985; Humboldt, 1988 [1836]). Human agency is essentially defined by being constituted of having a reflexive relation to oneself, which needs to be taken into account when one is to mediate the intentional and reflexive understanding with an agent's dependency on external conditions and structures (Mead, 1934; Sokal and Sugarman, 2010).

Agency entails consciousness of oneself as an agent in the context of a given identity and situation. It also entails the assumption that one can distinguish between self-chosen and externally caused phenomena and events. Only if an agent is capable of establishing a self-relation in which his or her own understanding can be susceptible to an analysis where the agent can have an effect on the beliefs and actions of the agent himself or herself can we speak of human agency (Kögler, 2010). Yet, since the agent is essentially situated in a social context from which his or her capabilities emerge, we must name a *medium* in which the agent can define his or her agency with regard to himself or herself and the environment. In other words, it must be possible for an agent to reconstruct his or her own identity, to analyse how one is situated socially, how one can aim for certain goods, project certain goals, all in light of an assessment of the situation. And this analysis must (potentially) include a reconstruction of the agent's own limits vis-à-vis the encountered challenges. Thus, only if the linguistic mediation of an agent's self-understanding is taken into account can those demands be fulfilled. The fact that the linguistic habitus is a schematised pre-understanding that derives from an accumulated stock of experiences and encounters that coalesced into a pattern of habits and expectations, of skills and assumptions, allows for a reflexive thematisation of agency via its own intentional focus. It is important to note, however, that the very idea of habitus as an internally operative background of intentional cognition itself requires that it is intrinsically connected to language or linguistically mediated concepts and values. This is because only if it affects these beliefs and assumptions does it really concern the level that in turn shapes an agent's self-understanding.[19]

To insist, this is not an external point against Bourdieu's conception of agency, but amounts to an immanent criticism and even constructive explication of the implications of his position that attempts to mediate between agency and structure. The capabilities that define habitus can only come into play if actualised in the context of social fields, in which they function both as competence and as capital. Nevertheless, agents must be capable to orient their input at the value-orientations in the respective fields, which requires a practico-conceptual grasp of their intentional structure. Clearly, the value themselves as much as their substantive and socially shared interpretations are not consciously represented; an unconscious grasp, however, is therefore not pre-conceptual, as the disclosure within which the actions take place is already saturated by the understanding of the values (Weber, 1978 [1914]; Winch, 1991 [1959]; Dilthey, 2004 [1910]). This becomes clear when their normative-intentional orientation is not fulfilled, such as when expectations are disappointed and agents make claims explicit. While the critical disruption of existing practices may thus help to bring to light – both in the practice itself as well as for the theorist – that they indeed entail a normative infrastructure, this fact cannot, as illustrated in the above critique of Habermas, lead one to idealise the practice in terms of formally abstract rules and apart from the embodied and inculcated forms of practical skills and capacities that define its local grounding. The fact that human agency is intentionally structured does not challenge the deeply social grounding, but it anchors within the symbolically mediated contexts the basic capability to reconstruct how a particular practice understands itself in light of its linguistically articulated concepts as well as its practical contexts. That the understanding of human agency requires intentional concepts, which in turn require linguistic mediation, can be made clear by three arguments (see also Kögler/Stueber, 2000).

1. The interpretive identification of an action as an action requires the bringing into play of what the action intends to realise, what it is aiming at. If we lack a purpose or value or goal at which an action aims, we are hard pressed to identify it as an action at all (Stueber, 2004). Yet, such a purpose or goal must be one that can be articulated, and thus can only exist in a linguistically mediated form (Gadamer, 1989 [1960]; Kögler, 1999). This is a *quasi-transcendental argument* which suggests that the medium of identification of an action forces us to attribute some conceptual structure to its nature (Habermas, 1988 [1968]).
2. The concrete identification that is attributed to an action as such-and-such has to be formulated by the social scientist or interpreter who develops a conceptual-linguistic account of what goes on. By assuming that this account captures, at least to an extent, the action at stake, and by means of the need to only thus be able to identify the act, the linguistic mediation and thus *articulation* inheres intrinsically within action. This means that the *methodological requirement* to be able to account for how one is able to identify the action which one is reconstructing requires that they can be explicated. This requirement would be undercut if we were to attribute the full meaning constitution to a pre-conceptual level which would resist any explication. In that case, any account of the social scientist would be but an arbitrary projection upon a practical continent forever withdrawn from our eyes, and therefore an account as good as any other, or none. Moreover, if this pre-conceptual level would be meaning-constitutive, and

as such form the background understanding of the social scientist, his or her explicit understanding would (a) remain encapsulated in his or her own habitus, and (b) never catch up with the explicit meanings that it portrays as the other's self-understanding. Bourdieu can claim, as he does, that in addition to the conceptual articulation of aesthetic habitus formations, as so brilliantly executed in *Distinction* (1985 [1984]), a practical skill-based level persists. Yet, he must grant that the symbolic interpretation of those attitudes as intentional attitudes – that is, as aesthetic perspectives in the full experiential sense – also captures a layer which is itself of meaning-constitutive importance.

3. The acquisition of a social habitus is not accomplished pre-symbolically but goes hand-in-hand with symbolic means. This is exemplified by developmental accounts of human agency (Sokal and Sugarman, 2010; Mead, 1934; Kögler, 2010). Far from suggesting that there is such a thing as a neatly separated sphere of practical, pre-conceptual, and unconscious meanings on the one hand, and linguistic, conceptual, and conscious meanings on the other, the creation of socially grounded meaningful attitudes is a symbolic-practical co-constitution. Mead's emergence of a communication of significant symbols adequately embedded this process in a gradual process which can include stages of play and game, i.e. the *imaginary perspective-taking* where an agent assumes in pretence the social perspectives of other agents, which always puts into play a mix of practical and conceptual dimensions (Mead, 1934; Sokal and Sugarman, 2010). Subsequently, the orientation at general rules that apply to all represents a more advanced form of abstraction, but really remains grounded in the capacity to represent all possible roles and put oneself imaginatively into the role of the generalised other. A widely shared *developmental account* of how intentional agency emerges from basic practical and pre-conceptual intersubjective settings strongly suggests that linguistic self-understanding, and with it the capacity to reflect and transform modes of self-understanding in a critical and creative fashion, belong to the core features of human agency (Clement, 2010).

The transcendental presupposition of understanding human agency is obtained via the intersubjective process of perspective-taking, which equips the social-scientific interpreter with the necessary capabilities to make sense of situated agents. The fact that linguistic elements are now seen as equally constitutive for the agent's self-understanding does not diminish the importance of the – differentially acquired – social habitus. Those background schemes of pre-understanding represent the contextually defined resources for agents to make sense of their environment in a pre-structured manner. Nonetheless, the fact that these schemes are symbolically synthesised via the basic concepts and assumptions widens the options with regard to critical and reflexive agency. Now the ray of subjective intentionality is not fully preformed by an implicit holistic grid defining in advance its internal elements. Rather, the schemes themselves are potentially accessible, agents can relate not only to phenomena within their worlds, but reflectively thematise the world structures that define them *a tergo*.

The emergence of habitus from intersubjective perspective-taking means that the capabilities which brought about understanding can always be (re-) activated to advance beyond the hitherto acquired and established schemes of understanding. Intentional understanding is therefore not conceptually tied to specifically defined habitus, as if they operate only within a given frame, as if they are incapable of being utilised to challenge outworn ones, to transcend existing ones, and to disclose new ones. By emphasising the linguistic dimension of the background, the conceptual self-understanding is not severed from its practical, embodied, power-based source; rather, we now introduced a mediating level that allows agents to self-engage in an ongoing restructuration of their socially constituted selves. Agents will not just transcend their inculcated identities by means of idealised validity claims, but neither do they remain imprisoned in the sense-making structures they inherited from early childhood. By taking up, within their own agency, the otherness which social practices instilled in them, they unleash the developmentally acquired potential to go beyond an existing frame to understand others, to relate to oneself critically, and to project oneself in light of value-orientations that have a normative status and can be defended with reason. Only if the symbolic dimension of habitus is given its due can it be reconciled with ethical agency and, thus, with human agency as such.

Notes

1 According to the model of the *speech circuit*, one individual (A) makes conscious states that are represented by linguistic signs known to another individual (B). The communication of ideas is here undertaken by using vocal gestures that ‘transport’, by means of physical air waves, certain sounds to the receiver who thereby ‘understands’ the thoughts which were formerly present to individual (A). The basic question is: what makes the ‘transportation’ of meaning from (A) to (B) possible? What has to be considered an essential part of the process of creating or enabling a mutually shared symbolic understanding between (A) and (B)?

2 More radical than his empiricist predecessors, however, such success is not only explained by the ‘subsequent’ transposition of thought into the social medium of ‘language’ for the purpose of communication; rather, the very possibility of thought itself is attributed to symbolic mediation.

3 The 'genetic' point of view would reconstruct the historical genesis of how a term came to possess a certain meaning, that is how a certain 'sound' came to be 'associated' with a certain conceptual or cognitive understanding.

4 While from the 'intuitive' perspective of a language user meaning is 'simultaneously' in both participants, the structural properties that make such a 'miracle' of shared meaning possible usually remain altogether hidden. Only a 'structuralist' perspective that analyses the very nature of the symbols involved can explain how it is possible.

5 This point is supported by two reflections. First, we can only distinguish linguistic units by knowing their meaning. By hearing a foreign language, we are unable to distinguish how many words there are. In order to do so, we have to know the meaning of the words. However, on a more basic, phonetic level, each language defines internally which phonetic differences are to count as meaningful. Japanese, for instance, does not differentiate between j and r, German does not between w and v, but both are significant, that is, meaning-constitutive, in English. 'Jay' and 'ray' mean different things, but this could not be expressed in Japanese, and the difference between 'wheel' and 'veil' does not track phonetically in German. Second, the differentiation of phonetic sounds into meaningful differences within a sound pattern, which makes the fixation and identification of conceptual differences possible, is arbitrary and conventional. Thus, while the difference between 'cow' and 'now' (and to all other units) allows us to fix symbolically the idea of a cow, there is no intrinsic reason why 'Kuh' or 'vache' are not just as good. The systems that make meaning identifiable are thus arbitrary.

6 What is crucial, however, is that within the system the use of differences is absolutely determined, and thus, for the individual user, necessary in order to achieve meaning. In contrast to the idea of arbitrariness, this can be called the *conventionality* of the sign-system. While the symbolic order is arbitrary with regard to the thought (and ultimately the reality) that it expresses or represents, it is necessary within its system of distinctions, because only the established order of differences (as being the same for each sign and sign-user) can establish the identity of meaning.

7 The reference to objective differences in meaning is excluded, because of the restriction to meaning which in turn was justified by the orientation toward the 'psychological' side of meaning (we know that this 'psychologism' does not contradict Saussure's social theory of meaning, since the speaker becomes a speaker only as participant in the social world of meaning, which is due to socialisation). Similarly; the reference to objective phonetic differences is excluded, because natural languages establish conventional systems of phonological differentiation that internally 'decide' what counts as a meaningful sound-distinction. Thus, the identification of any positive term in a language is only possible on the basis of knowing its *difference* within the linguistic or symbolic system. This is the point behind Saussure's claim that language is a form, not a substance, because it is defined by the internal differences, and its law is the establishment of the rules that distinguish 'signifiers' and 'signifieds' from each other.

8 This idea goes back at least to Humboldt, who saw language equally as a necessary medium for thought. He defined language as the 'formative organ of *thought* [...]. The inseparable bonding of *thought, vocal apparatus*, and *hearing* a language is unalterably rooted in the original constitution of human nature [...]' (Humboldt, 1988: 54 and 55). Cassirer's philosophy of symbolic forms is based on the same thought (Cassirer 1955 [1923]).

9 One might also defend Saussure against such criticisms of the code as 'mentalistic' by pointing out that codes are taken to be constituted in the course of *intersubjective speech*

practices. As such, they seem to be tied back to the 'real' social practices of communicating agents. Yet, this defense would already reach beyond what Saussure himself supplies as theoretical means, as the following criticisms should show.

10 My analysis does not attempt a full scale comparison of social theories that are either based on speech act theory or on poststructuralist assumptions. Rather, I specifically focus on the issue of explicating the implicit social background assumptions with regard to their normative versus power-based implications. For a much needed analysis of the respective contributions of Habermas and Bourdieu, see the much needed book by Simon Susen (2007). For a critical comparison of Foucault and Habermas with regard to hermeneutic reflexivity, see Kögler (1996).

11 Far from giving up the game, à la late Wittgenstein, and accept an uncontrollable multiplicity of contexts and uses, certain standard-types of use can be filtered out – or reconstructed from the intuitive pre-understanding of speakers engaged in social communication. Such reconstructions will not repeat the positivist mistakes of the tradition by remaining focused solely on truth and reference; rather, the orientation at shared meaning deriving from intersubjective rules broadens the spectrum to include social value-orientations in a variety of fields.

12 Habermas is a far cry from a traditional liberal or action-theoretical position that assumes a 'free-floating' and disembedded agent. Yet, a final defensive move – the switch toward the macro-perspective of a theory of modernity that assumes that the inherent value-orientations have historically been fleshed out by constituting social fields like science, moral and legal discourse, and modern art – is equally bound to fail. This is because just as much as those spheres (or 'discourses') can be shown to be guided by normative rules, just as much do they exemplify underlying patterns of privilege and power, of unaccounted hierarchies and new modes of domination. The role of power-laden habitus props up, as it were, from within the rational public sphere like the tortoise to the hare in the fairy tale.

13 To suggest that language and linguistic habitus are ultimately grounded in social habitus seems to be contradicted by statements where Bourdieu acknowledges 'that social science has to take account of the autonomy of language, its specific logic, and its particular rules of operation' (Bourdieu 1994: 41). Yet, the 'autonomy of language' is explicated as a 'formal mechanism whose generative capacities are without limits', only to suggest that those generative capacities will themselves be employed to determine social power relations: 'Rituals are the limiting case of situations of *imposition* in which [...] a social competence is exercised – namely, that of the legitimate speaker, authorised to speak and to speak with authority' (Bourdieu 1994: 41). At stake is whether the symbolic surplus, the 'originative capacity – in the Kantian sense – which derives its power to produce existence by producing the collectively recognised, and thus realised, representation of existence' (Bourdieu 1994:42) can be turned against power and reflexively appropriated by agents to realise normatively acceptable value-orientations.

14 Before going on, I should point out an ambiguity in this explanation. Bourdieu wants to show that the grammatical structure of language is due to the fact of the codification by grammarians, which shaped what is known as explicit grammars. Those grammars then helped to establish a national code, a national language – and suppressed all the dialects. However, the fact that one code was established and used to suppress and denigrate other languages, which then came to be seen as mere dialects, does not show as such that languages don't contain an implicit grammatical structure, as Chomsky or Saussure would claim. Bourdieu thus seems to conflate two issues: First, there is the question of whether languages should be seen as being constructed on the basis of

rules and codes (we have seen in our critique of Saussure that there are good reasons to question such an approach); and second, the question of how one specific rule system, the one associated with modern French in France, came to be seen as the legitimate language, and was used to integrate the population into the new ideology of the state. Here Bourdieu gives a plausible account of how conceiving a certain code as the legitimate 'grammar' of (a) language helped establish a sense of national identity and distinction.

15 Just as in Saussure, the idea is that the linguistic code forms the 'amorphous mass of thought' – even though now that amorphous mass is itself already linguistic mediated in terms of the unruly speech practices which later become known as dialects.

16 Bourdieu, however, criticises the concept of worldview because of its cognitivist overtones (Bourdieu 1990: 56).

17 As the previous remarks made clear, our interest is here to probe whether Bourdieu develops a one-sided notion of reflexivity, one which remains – by all its stringent and highly important critique of Saussure's structural semiotics – attached to a model of *reflexive objectification* that is taken from the representation of a natural fact, or an object. The alternative model is one of a *reflexive expressivism*, where the reflexive project is related to explicating and articulating the inherent conceptual, normative, and value-orientational beliefs and assumptions that define an agent's perspective vis-à-vis the other, the world, and the self. Yet, any such alternative account requires a more developed account of the role of language.

18 There is no doubt that Bourdieu, especially towards the end of his career, became very interested in the transformative powers given to agency. Our reflections were intended to bring to light the implications of his systematic analyses regarding the intertwinement of agency, language, and habitus, with a special emphasis on how the intentional meaning that agents attach to their self-understanding as well as value-oriented social struggles can be mediated with a social analysis of agency. In this regard I hold that the basis of Bourdieu's philosophy of language is too narrow to account for the complex meanings and potentials opened up by the linguistic mediation of reality. For a very sympathetic reading of Bourdieu in this regard, see the essay by Bridget Fowler in this volume.

19 If you drug or shoot someone, you do affect their cognition – you create weird and uncontrolled beliefs and images, or you entirely stop any cognition at all from happening – but you do not affect their *intentional self-understanding*. For that, the beliefs have to be incorporated into the stock of beliefs and values that consciously, and over the span of an agent's life-activities, define his or her self-identity. Drug experiences may later affect one's overall self-understanding, as they can be consciously appropriated. In any event, what counts as *real and fictional* is relative to the established symbolic frameworks of the social contexts in which a self-understanding emerges, but is nevertheless a real distinction within any such framework.

References

Bohman, James (1997) 'Reflexivity, Agency, and Constraint. The Paradoxes of Bourdieu's Sociology of Knowledge', *Social Epistemology* 11(2): 171–186.

Bourdieu, Pierre (1977 [1972]) *Outline of a Theory of Practice*, trans. Richard Nice, Cambridge: Cambridge University Press.

Bourdieu, Pierre (1985 [1984]) *Distinction*, trans. Richard Nice, Cambridge, MA: Harvard U.P.

Bourdieu, Pierre (1990 [1980]) *The Logic of Practice*, trans. Richard Nice, Stanford, CA: Stanford University Press.

Bourdieu, Pierre (1994) *Language and Symbolic Power*, edited and introduced by John B. Thompson, trans. Gino Raymond and Mathew Adamson, Cambridge, MA: Harvard U.P.

Bourdieu, Pierre (1994a) 'The Production and Reproduction of Legitimate Language', in *Language and Symbolic Power*, trans. Gino Raymond and Mathew Adamson, Cambridge, MA: Harvard U.P., pp. 43–65.

Brandom, Robert (2000) *Articulating Reasons*, Cambridge, MA: Harvard U.P.

Cassirer, Ernst (1955 [1923]) *The Philosophy of Symbolic Forms*, trans. Ralph Manheim, Vol. 1: New Haven: Yale U.P.

Clement, Fabrice (2010) 'To Trust or Not to Trust? Children's Social Epistemology', *Review of Philosophy and Psychology*, Springerlink, published online: 6 March 2010.

Dilthey, Wilhelm (2002 [1910]) *The Formation of the Historical World in the Human Sciences*. Edited with an Introduction by Rudolf A. Makkreel and Frithjof Rodi. Princeton: Princeton University Press.

Dreyfus, Hubert (1980) 'Holism and Hermeneutics', *Review of Metaphysics* 34(1): 3–24.

Dreyfus, Hubert (1993) *Being-in-the-World: A Commentary on Heidegger's Being and Time*. Cambridge, MA: The MIT Press.

Dummett, Michael (1990) *Origins of Analytical Philosophy*, Cambridge, Mass.: Harvard U. P.

Foucault, Michel (1979 [1975]) *Discipline and Punish*, trans. Alan Sheridan, New York: Pantheon Books.

Foucault, Michel (1990 [1966]) *The Order of Things*, trans. unknown, New York: Vintage Books.

Foucault, Michel (1994 [1976]) *History of Sexuality: An Introduction*, trans. Robert Hurley, New York: Vintage Books.

Foster, Roger (2005) 'Pierre Bourdieu's Critique of Scholarly Reason', *Philosophy & Social Criticism* 31(1): 89–107.

Gadamer, Hans-Georg (1989 [1960]) *Truth and Method*, translation revised by Joel Weinsheimer and Donla G. Marshall, New York: Crossroads.

Giddens, Anthony (1984) *The Constitution of Society*, Berkeley and Los Angeles: University of California Press.

Habermas, Jürgen (1979) 'Moral Development and Ego Identity' in *Communication and the Evolution of Society*, trans. Thomas McCarthy, Boston, MA: Beacon Press, 69 ff.

Habermas, Jürgen (1983/87 [1981]) *Theory of Communicative Action*, trans. Thomas McCarthy, Vol. 1 and 2. Boston: Beacon Press.

Habermas, Jürgen (1988 [1970]) *On the Logic of the Social Sciences*, trans. by Shierry Weber Nicholsen and Jerry A. Stark, Cambridge, MA: The MIT Press.

Habermas, Jürgen (1990) 'Moral Consciousness and Communicative Action' in *Moral Consciousness and Communicative Action*, trans. by Christian Lenhardt and Shierry Weber Nicholsen Cambridge, MA: The MIT Press, pp. 116–194.

Habermas, Jürgen (1992) 'Toward a Critique of the Theory of Meaning', in *Postmetaphysical Thinking*, trans. Mark Hohengarten, Cambridge, MA: The MIT Press, pp. 57–87.

Hall, Stuart (1980) 'Encoding/Decoding', in Stuart Hall, Dorothy Hobson, Andrew Lowe, and Paul Willis (eds.) *Culture, Media, Language, Working Papers in Cultural Studies*, Hutchinson, London, pp. 128–138.

Heidegger, Martin (1962 [1927]) *Being and Time*, trans. John Macquarrie and Edward Robinson, New York: Harper & Row.

Humboldt, Wilhelm von (1988 [1836]) *On Language: The Diversity of Human Language-Structure and its Influence on the Mental Development of Mankind*, trans. Peter Heath, ed. Michael Losonsky, introduction by Hans Aarsleff, Cambridge: Cambridge University Press.

Kögler, Hans-Herbert (1996) 'The Self-Empowered Subject: Habermas, Foucault, and Hermeneutic Reflexivity', *Philosophy & Social Criticism* 22(4): 13–44.

Kögler, Hans-Herbert (1997) 'Alienation as Epistemological Source: Reflexivity and Social Background after Mannheim and Bourdieu', *Social Epistemology* 11(2): 141–164.

Kögler, Hans-Herbert (1999 [1992]) *The Power of Dialogue: Critical Hermeneutics after Gadamer and Foucault*, trans. Paul Hendrickson, Cambridge, MA: The MIT Press.

Kögler, Hans-Herbert (2010) 'Agency and the Other: On the Intersubjective Roots of Self-Identity', in Sokol and Sugarman 2010, Human Agency and Development, *New Ideas in Psychology* (NIP) (in press).

Kögler, Hans-Herbert and Karsten Stueber (eds.) (2000) *Empathy and Agency: The Problem of Understanding in the Human Science*, Boulder, CO: Westview Press.

Lash, Scott (1998) *Another Modernity, A Different Rationality*, London: Blackwell Publishers.

Lee, Benjamin (1997) *Language, Metalanguage, and the Semiotics of Subjectivity*, Durham, NC/London: Duke University Press.

Mead, George Herbert (1934) *Mind, Self, and Society*, Chicago: University of Chicago Press.

Saussure, Ferdinand de (1983 [1915]) *Course in General Linguistics*, trans. Roy Harris, La Salle: Open Court Publishing House.

Searle, John (1969) *Speech Acts*, Cambridge: Cambridge University Press.

Searle, John (1989) *Intentionality*, Cambridge: Cambridge University Press.

Searle, John (1995) *The Construction of Social Reality*, New York: The Free Press.

Sokal, Bryan and Jeff Sugarman (2010) 'Human Agency and Development', editors, special issue in *New Ideas in Psychology* (NIP), Elesevier.

Stern, David (2003) 'The Practical Turn', in Stephen Turner and Paul Roth (eds.) *The Blackwell Guide to the Philosophy of the Social Sciences*, Malden, MA/Oxford, UK: Blackwell, 185–206.

Stueber, Karsten (2004) 'Agency and the Objectivity of Historical Narratives', in William Sweet (ed.) *The Philosophy of History: A Reexamination*. Aldershot, UK: Ashgate Press, 197–222.

Susen, Simon (2007) *The Foundations of the Social: Between Critical Theory and Reflexive Sociology*, Oxford: Bardwell Press.

Taylor, Charles (1985) *Human Agency and Language*, Cambridge: Cambridge University Press.

Taylor, Talbot (1992) *Mutual Misunderstanding*. Durham, NC/London: Duke University Press.

Turner, Stephen (1994) *The Social Theory of Practices: Tradition, Tacit Knowledge, and Presuppositions*. Chicago, IL: University of Chicago Press.

Turner, Stephen and Paul Roth (eds.) (2003) *The Blackwell Guide to the Philosophy of the Social Sciences*. Malden, MA/Oxford: Blackwell.

Weber, Max (1978 [1914]) 'Basic Sociological Terms', in Guenther Roth and Claus Wittich (eds.) *Economy and Society*, trans. Ephraim Fischoff et al., Berkeley/Los Angeles: University of California Press, 3–62.

Winch, Peter (1991 [1959]) *The Idea of a Social Science and Its Relation to Philosophy*, London: Routledge.

Winch, Peter (1964) 'Understanding a Primitive Society', in Bryan Wilson (ed.) *Rationality*, New York: Harper and Row, 78–111.

Wittgenstein, Ludwig (1953) *Philosophical Investigations*, trans. Elizabeth Anscombe, Cambridge: Cambridge University Press.

CHAPTER THIRTEEN

Social Theory and Politics: Aron, Bourdieu and Passeron, and the Events of May 1968[1]

Derek Robbins

The purpose of this contribution is to explore historically the relationship between the social theory emerging at the Centre de sociologie européenne in Paris during the 1960s and the Parisian events of May 1968. Adopting the terminology of an article of 1981 by Pierre Bourdieu himself ('Décrire et prescrire. Note sur les conditions de possibilité et les limites de l'efficacité politique' ['Describing and Prescribing. A Note on the Conditions of Possibility and the Limits of Political Effectiveness'] (Bourdieu, 1981), my purpose is to consider in what ways the work of the Centre de sociologie européenne could be said to *describe* or *prescribe* the May 'events'. This consideration is a vehicle for an assessment of the diverging positions of Aron, Bourdieu and Passeron at the time, particularly by reference to their responses to the work of Weber.

The Centre de sociologie européenne was established by Raymond Aron in 1960. I shall explore the development of Aron's view of sociology in the context of his prior commitment to engaged historical observation and then consider his influence on Bourdieu and Passeron. My purpose is to ask what it meant (and might still mean) to regard objective phenomena or events as either *social* or *political*.

Mise-En-Scène

Raymond Aron was born in 1905 and was one of a famous cohort of entrants to the École normale supérieure in 1924, which also included Jean-Paul Sartre. His training was predominantly philosophical. In 1930, he obtained a post as Teaching Assistant at the University of Cologne. He spent almost three years in Germany. After one year in Cologne, he moved to Berlin, leaving in 1933. In Germany, he decided that he would undertake doctoral research on the philosophy of history. This was not to be a consideration of idealist philosophy of history but, instead, a philosophical analysis of the practice of writing history and, increasingly, an exploration of what it might mean to be an historian of the present. It was by chance that Célestin Bouglé invited him to write an account of contemporary German sociology, which Aron published in 1935 as *La sociologie allemande contemporaine* [*Contemporary German Sociology*] (Aron, 1935). The largest part of that book was devoted to a celebration of the work of Max Weber. Aron was the first French intellectual to give detailed attention to Weber's work, but at the time he was interested primarily in Weber's philosophy of history and his philosophy of social-scientific method, rather than in Weber as a sociologist. Aron completed and published his main and complementary doctoral theses in 1938. The effect of the arguments of the two theses was that Aron developed a view of the 'participant historian'. He followed Weber in being committed to retaining a division between the roles of politicians and the roles of scientists, but what was unclear was whether his scientific historical observation of the present was essentially a form either of social or of political science. Historical events caused Aron to begin to identify social reality with politics. Shortly before the French surrender to the Germans early in 1940, Aron travelled to London, where he was soon recruited to write a regular monthly column, 'Chronique de France', for *La France libre*. His engaged historical observations took the form of political commentary. After the War, Aron carried on with his journalism, becoming an employee of *Le Figaro* for which he wrote regularly from 1947 until 1977.

During the period between 1944/5 and 1955, in which Aron appeared to have chosen a career in journalism, he maintained university contacts, teaching both at the École nationale d'administration and at the Institut d'études politiques de Paris as well as giving lectures abroad. In these years, he also published *Le grand schisme* (Aron, 1948) and *Les guerres en chaîne* [*Bounded Wars*] (Aron, 1951). As Aron states in his *Mémoires*, these were linked to the intellectual position he had reached in his research theses in that they were 'an attempt at a kind of immediate philosophy of history in the making intended to serve as a framework and a basis for my daily or weekly commentaries and for the positions I took' (Aron, 1990 [1983]: 199). Notice that Aron had come to assume that 'history in the making' is virtually synonymous with politics and international relations. In June 1955, Aron made it known that he wished to be appointed to a Chair at the Sorbonne, and he was successful in his application in competition with Georges Balandier. Aron was instrumental in institutionalising the teaching of sociology for a *licence* within two years of his election to the Chair at the Sorbonne. The lecture courses which he gave in 1955–6, 1956–7, and 1957–8 were initially roneographed for distribution by the Centre de documentation universitaire, but Aron agreed to their more extensive publication and they appeared, respectively, as *Dix-huit leçons sur la société industrielle* [18 lectures on industrial society] in 1962 (Aron, 1962); *La lutte des classes. Nouvelles leçons sur les sociétés industrielles* [*Class Struggle: New Lectures on industrial societies* in 1964 (Aron, 1964); and *Démocratie et totalitarisme* [*Democracy and Totalitarianism*] in 1965 (Aron, 1965). In addition, two other courses were published in two volumes in 1967 as *Les étapes de la pensée sociologique* [The stages of sociological thought] (Aron, 1967). Throughout, Aron maintained his commitment to the work of Weber. Julien Freund's translations of Weber's two lectures of 1918 – *Wissenschaft als Beruf* [*Science as Vocation*] (Weber, 1919, and 1922: 524–555) and *Politik als Beruf* [*Politics as Vocation*] (Weber, 1921: 396–450) – published, together with an introduction by Aron in 1959, as *Le savant et le politique* [*Science and Politics*] (Weber, int. Aron, 1959) were the only texts of Max Weber available in French in 1960. Freund was to translate some articles from Weber's *Gesammelte Aufsätze zur Wissenschaftslehre* [*Collected Essays on Scientific Theory*] (Weber, 1922) in 1965 as *Essais sur la théorie de la science [Essays on the theory of science] (Weber, trans. Freund, 1965)* and also to publish his *Sociologie de Max Weber* [*The Sociology of Max Weber*] in 1966 (Freund, 1966). Aron's *La sociologie allemande contemporaine*, first published in 1935, was re-issued in 1950 and 1966.

Turning now to Jean-Claude Passeron, he had been teaching at a lycée in Marseille since 1958, when, in 1961, he received a phone call from Aron inviting him to become his research assistant at the Sorbonne. Passeron had been born in a mountain village in the Alpes-Maritimes in 1930 and received his secondary education at the lycée in Nice before gaining entry to the Lycée Henri IV in Paris prior to entry to the École normale supérieure in 1950. At the École, he gained a licence de philosophie, certificat de psycho-physiologie. He was particularly friendly with Foucault and Althusser and was associated with the communist cell organised at the École by Le Goff. He gained a Diplôme d'études with a thesis entitled 'L'image spéculaire' [the mirror image] written under the supervision of Daniel Lagache, who was appointed Professor of Psychology at the Sorbonne in 1951 and who also created a Laboratoire de psychologie sociale at the Sorbonne a year later. Passeron had remained at the École until 1955, when he was conscripted to serve in the army in Algeria. He had remained there until 1958, before returning to France to take up his teaching post at Marseille. Bourdieu had been a Maître de conférences at the University of Lille for two years when he was invited by Aron to become the secretary to the Centre de sociologie européenne in Paris. It appears that the paths of the two men (Bourdieu and Passeron) had not crossed significantly either at the École normale or in Algeria, but their social backgrounds and trajectories were remarkably similar. Bourdieu had been born in 1930 in the Béarn and had moved early on to a mountain village in the Hautes-Pyrénées. From the age of 7, he was a boarder at the lycée at Pau before gaining entry to the other main Parisian lycée preparing students for entry to the École normale supérieure – the Lycée Louis-le-Grand. Bourdieu entered the École in 1950. He left in 1954, having acquired his licence and having gained his Diplôme d'études supérieures with a dissertation under the supervision of Henri Gouhier, which involved making a translation of, and a commentary on, Leibniz's critique of Descartes entitled *Animadversiones in partem generalem Principiorum cartesianorum*. Bourdieu had taught at the lycée in Moulins for two years before he too was conscripted to serve in the army in Algeria. Whilst at Moulins, he registered to undertake doctoral research on 'Les structures temporelles de la vie affective' ['The Temporal Structures of Affective Life'] under the supervision of Georges Canguilhem, but this never commenced. Bourdieu had managed to get himself a post in military intelligence in Algeria, which enabled him to become associated with the collection of official statistics. He was appointed to a post at the University of Algiers in 1958, when he published his first book: *Sociologie de l'Algérie* [*Sociology of Algeria*] (Bourdieu, 1958). By the time that Aron invited Bourdieu to become secretary to his Research Group, the second edition of *Sociologie de l'Algérie* had been published (Bourdieu, 1961) and this was followed by the English translation which was published by Beacon books, Boston in 1962 as *The Algerians*, with a Preface by Aron (Bourdieu, 1962).

Aron's Conception of the Relationship between Social Science and Political Action

In the first paragraph of the introduction to *Le savant et le politique*, Aron could have been writing about himself:

> Max Weber a été un homme de science, il n'a été ni un homme politique ni un homme d'Etat, occasionnellement journaliste politique. Mais il a été, toute sa vie, passionnément soucieux de la chose publique, il n'a cessée d'éprouver une sorte de nostalgie de la politique, comme si la fin ultime de sa pensée aurait dû être la participation à l'action. (Weber, int. Aron, 1959 [1919/1922]: 7)
>
> [Max Weber was a man of science. He was neither a politician nor a statesman, but occasionally a political journalist. All his life he was passionately concerned about public issues and never ceased showing a kind of nostalgia for politics, as if the ultimate goal of his thought ought to have been participation in action.]

Aron's introduction to Weber's lectures is self-regarding, but it also offers some critique. Aron explains that Weber insisted that it is not possible 'en même temps' [at the same time] to be a scientist and a politician but that, equally,

Weber asserted that 'on peut prendre des positions politiques en dehors de l'université' [political positions can be adopted outside the university]. In other words, the activities had to be kept separate, but they had to impinge on each other. There are logical grounds for this reciprocity, because the pursuit of causal explanation in science relates to purposive action. As Aron summarises Weber's view:

> Une science qui analyse les rapports de cause à effet [...] est donc celle même qui répond aux besoins de l'homme d'action. (Weber, int. Aron, 1959 [1919/1922]: 8)
>
> [A science which analyses the relations between cause and effect [...] is therefore one which responds to the needs of the man of action.]

There is, however, no necessary causal connection between science and action. Aron says:

> La compréhension de l'action menée par les autres dans le passé ne conduit pas nécessairement à la volonté d'agir dans le présent. (Weber, int. Aron, 1959 [1919/1922]: 10)
>
> [Understanding actions taken by others in the past does not necessarily lead to the will to act in the present.]

In other words, Aron is tacitly making it clear that his view of the function of history is not at all historicist. He preserves human freedom by insisting that our historical perceptions of the past do not determine future events. Importantly for our purposes, Aron tries to insist on the separation of the man of science from man in his everyday humanity. He continues:

> Il n'y en a pas moins, philosophiquement, et, pour employer le jargon à la mode, existentiellement, un lien entre la connaissance de soi et celle des autres, entre la résurrection des luttes que se sont livrées les hommes disparus et la prise actuelle de position. (Weber, int. Aron, 1959 [1919/1922]: 10)
>
> [There is nonetheless, neither philosophically nor, to use fashionable jargon, existentially, no link between self knowledge and knowledge of others, between resurrecting the struggles in which past men were involved and taking positions in the present.]

And, a little further on, he elaborates:

> La réciprocité entre la rencontre avec l'autre et la découverte de soi est donnée dans l'activité même de l'historien. La réciprocité entre la connaissance et l'action

> est immanente à l'existence non de l'historien, mais de l'homme historique. (Weber, int. Aron, 1959 [1919/1922]: 10)
>
> [The reciprocity between the encounter with the other and self-discovery is a given in the very activity of the historian. The reciprocity between knowledge and action is intrinsic to the existence of man in history and not of the historian.]

Thus, Aron is arguing that the knowledge of somebody acting as a scientist does not dictate their behaviour as a person. People have multiple identities, and there is no necessary integration of knowledge acquired in following the rules of autonomous intellectual discourses with the behaviour inducing personality of the scientist. It is significant that Aron has a swipe at existentialism in this context. The opposite view to the one Aron is upholding would argue that, as individuals, we are involved in a process of self-totalising self-construction and that the acceptance of multiple identities manifest in fragmented and discrete roles is evidence of a lack of authenticity and of bad faith. Aron is tacitly advancing the argument against Sartre, which he was to make in full in *D'une Sainte Famille à l'autre*, published in 1969 (Aron, 1969).

I do not want to discuss whether Aron accurately represents Weber here, but he immediately raises some theoretical objections to Weber's position, the first of which I want to consider. Aron continued with these three sentences:

> On s'est demandé dans quelle mesure la pensée propre de Max Weber s'exprime adéquatement dans le vocabulaire et les catégories du néo-kantisme de Rickert. La phénoménologie de Husserl, qu'il a connue mais peu utilisée, lui aurait, me semble-t-il, fourni l'outil philosophique et logique qu'il cherchait. Elle lui aurait évité, dans ses études sur la compréhension, l'oscillation entre le 'psychologisme' de Jaspers (à l'époque où celui-ci écrivait sa psycho-pathologie) et la voie détournée du néo-kantisme qui n'arrive à la signification qu'en passant par les valeurs. (Weber, int. Aron, 1959 [1919/1922]: 10–11)
>
> [The question is raised to what extent Max Weber's own thought is adequately expressed in the vocabulary and categories of the neo-Kantianism of Rickert. The phenomenology of Husserl, which he knew but used little, would, it seems to me, have provided him with the philosophical and logical tool for which he was searching. It would have enabled him to avoid, in his studies of understanding, oscillation between the 'psychologism' of Jaspers (at the time when the latter was writing his psycho-pathology) and the neo-Kantian detour which only reaches meaning by passing through value judgement.]

Aron seems to be implying that the problem with Weber's adherence to Rickert's neo-Kantian epistemology is that, in imitation of Kant's *Critique of Pure Reason*, the boundaries of historical understanding are situated categorically within a logically a priori 'historical reason'. If, however,

Weber had lived to know both Husserl's *Cartesian Meditations (Husserl, 1977 [1950])* and his *The Crisis of the European Sciences (Husserl, 1970 [1954])*, he would have had the possibility of recognising that categories of thought derive pre-predicatively from the lifeworld. Aron seems to be implying that he has the advantage over Weber in this respect and that although he has followed Weber's thought, he has replaced the transcendental idealism that he derived from the work of Rickert with a transcendental phenomenology based on the work of Husserl. This is what Aron appears to be saying, but I want to suggest that it was Bourdieu who was to deploy phenomenology descriptively, deprived of its transcendentalism, whereas Aron's thinking continued to rely on a neo-Kantian framework. This point is apparent in Aron's discussion of what he calls the continuation of Weber's notion of the disenchantment of the world by science in which he considers two kinds of threat posed by contemporary science. The first is that scientists, particularly natural scientists, have become intimidated by the consequences of the exploitation of their science. The second is that totalitarian political states insist on the nation-state allegiance of their scientists and seek to control the pursuit of objective truth.

Aron argues that the fallacy inherent in this second menace is that it ignores, as he puts it, that there is a 'République internationale des esprits qui est la communauté, naturelle et nécessaire, des savants' ['international republic of minds which is the natural and necessary community of scientists'] (Weber, int. Aron, 1959 [1919/1922]: 15). This community operates according to its own rules and 'les problèmes à résoudre leur sont fournis par l'état d'avancement des sciences' ['the problems to be resolved are generated by the stage of development of the sciences'] and not by any political state. Aron then takes the example of his friend Jean Cavaillès to illustrate both this point and the point that we all have multiple identities or live plurally in a range of contexts. As a French soldier, Cavaillès fought against the occupying Germans, but, as a man of science or logician, he remained a disciple of international mentors – Cantor, Hilbert and Husserl. Aron concludes that, when a state tries to dictate to science what should be its objects or its rules of activity, what we have is the 'intervention illégitime d'une collectivité politique dans l'activité d'une collectivité spirituelle, il s'agit, en d'autres termes, du totalitarisme, saisi à sa racine même' ['illegitimate intervention of a political collectivity into the activity of a spiritual collectivity, which, in other words, is a question of totalitarianism in its essence'] (Weber, int. Aron, 1959 [1919/1922]: 16). The important point to note here is that Aron assumes that these two kinds of collectivities are categorially different. Whilst he makes no comment whether the political collectivity is socially constructed, he uses the word '*spirituelle*' to show that a scientific collectivity has transcendental status, i.e. that its social existence reflects a logical necessity. Aron proceeds to commend Simmel for having described brilliantly 'La pluralité des cercles sociaux auxquels chacun de nous appartient, et il voyait dans cette pluralité la condition de la libération progressive des individus' ['the plurality of social circles to which each of us belongs, seeing in this plurality the condition for the progressive liberation of individuals'] (Weber, int. Aron, 1959 [1919/1922]: 16–17), and he contrasts this celebration of plurality with the fundamental totalitarian impulse:

> Ce souvenir nous permet de juger les tentatives de totalitarisme pour ce qu'elles sont : des efforts proprement réactionnaires pour ramener les sociétés au stade primitif où les disciplines sociales tendaient à embrasser tous les individus et les individus tout entiers. (Weber, int. Aron, 1959 [1919/1922]: 17)
>
> [This memory enables us to judge the endeavours of totalitarianism for what they are: efforts which are properly called reactionary to restore societies to their primitive state where social disciplines tended to encompass all individuals and individuals in their entirety.]

It is clear from Aron's other writing at the time that these words are a thinly veiled attack on Durkheimian social science and, associated with this, is an attack on the ideology of the Third Republic that could be said to have deployed Durkheimian social science to legitimate a socialist, totalitarian state.

Yet, Aron is not able to hold this line entirely. He immediately concedes that science can be seen to be 'partially' determined by social, historical and racial factors. He insists, however, that there is a fundamental difference between accepting that the character of science is shaped by its social milieu and accepting that its agenda can be determined by political authorities. As Aron comments:

> Dans le premier cas, la communauté de la science continue d'obéir, pour l'essentiel, à ses lois spécifiques. Dans l'autre, elle abdiquerait son autonomie et mettrait en péril, du même coup, sa vocation et ses progrès ultérieurs. (Weber, int. Aron, 1959 [1919/1922]: 17)
>
> [In the first instance, the scientific community continues to obey, in its essentials, its own specific laws. In the other, it would abdicate its autonomy and endanger, with one blow, its calling and its future developments.]

This argument led Aron to conclude that it would be fatal to deduce from the fact that social science is in part dependent on its social context

> [...] la conclusion que les sciences sociales ne sont que des idéologies de classes ou de races et que l'orthodoxie imposée par un Etat totalitaire ne diffère pas en nature de la libre recherche des sociétés pluralistes. Il existe, quoi qu'on en

> dise, *une communauté des sciences sociales*, moins autonome que la communauté des sciences naturelles mais malgré tout réelle. (Weber, int. Aron, 1959 [1919/1922]: 19)
>
> [[...] the conclusion that the social sciences are only the ideologies of classes or races and that the orthodoxy imposed by a totalitarian State doesn't differ in kind from the free research of pluralist societies. There exists, whatever one may say, a *social scientific community* which is less autonomous than the natural science community but, nonetheless, completely real.]

Aron proceeded to outline the constitutive rules of this community of the social sciences: first, the absence of restriction on research and the establishment of the facts themselves; second, the absence of restriction of any discussion and criticism of findings or methodologies; and third, the absence of any restriction of the right to disenchant reality. For Aron, the community of the social sciences has to retain the right to question what he called the 'mythologies' that dominate our behaviour whether these are imposed by communist or democratic states. He insisted:

> Par crainte d'être accusés d'antidémocratisme, ne nous arrêtons pas devant l'analyse des institutions parlementaires telles qu'elles fonctionnent à l'heure présente en Europe (Weber, int. Aron, 1959 [1919/1922]: 22)
>
> [Don't let us resist analysing parliamentary institutions as they currently function in Europe for fear of being accused of being anti-democratic.]

Indeed, by allowing free criticism of itself, democracy demonstrates its superiority.

I want to take two main points from Aron's introduction to Weber. The first point is that, although Aron had been appointed Professor of Sociology at the Sorbonne in 1955, his philosophy of social science was derived from his philosophy of history. His view of the participant historian related to Weber's view of the roles of the scientist and the politician in as much as Aron's view of participation was primarily that of the political scientist in politics. He tended to regard historical reality as an essentially *political* reality. Social-scientific explanation clarifies a subordinate domain of political reality and Aron's hostility to the Durkheimian tradition was that it sought to subordinate politics to social relations and to see sociology as the instrument for actualising individual and collective relations and of establishing a coherent, totalised social solidarity, which renders the political sphere moribund. Aron's subordination of social-scientific explanation was mirrored by his wish to subordinate social and cultural movements to changes brought about by 'legitimate', constitutional, political means. Hence, his hostility to the events of May 1968 and his use of his own terminology in describing the student revolt as a 'mythology'. The second point is related to this: the community of social science within which it is practised is an intrinsically autonomous community. To regard it as socially constructed would be to insert social-scientific explanation within a totalising Durkheimian social-scientific world view.

Aron's Conception of the Nature of Sociology as a Science

Aron devoted the first lecture of his *Dix-huit leçons sur la société industrielle* to an attempt to offer some 'general considerations on the nature of sociology' (Aron, 1962a: 13). He approached this task by trying to characterise the self-interrogations of sociologists by comparison with the self-interrogations of philosophers and political economists. Philosophers, Aron claimed, raise general questions without wanting to have anything to do with particular sciences, whereas political economists want to isolate one sector of global reality and subject this to scrutiny through the application of their own autonomous methodology. Sociology is caught between these two ambitions. As Aron put it, 'it wants to be a particular science and, at the same time, to analyse and understand society in its totality' (Aron, 1962a: 16). On the one view, sociology is just 'one discipline amongst a range of social disciplines' (Aron, 1962a: 19); but, on the other view, which Aron attributes to Durkheim, sociology aspires to embrace all the social sciences and 'to become the principle of their unity and the instrument of their synthesis' (Aron, 1962a: 20). For Aron, the former view is properly that of 'sociology', whereas the latter view is what he calls 'sociologism'. In France, according to Aron, the confusion has been dangerous and sociologism has usurped the functions of moral philosophy. Aron made it clear that he was hostile to sociologism, which – he thought – was embodied in the structure of the French educational system which was the consequence of the political adoption by the Third Republic of the post-Comtean sociologistic thinking of Durkheim. Nevertheless, he thought that any sociology which was content to limit itself to detailed enquiry was unsatisfactory. Detailed enquiry could be a means to the end of general understanding by articulating the similarities and differences between social systems in such a way that it would become possible 'to determine the fundamental types of social organisation, the subterranean logic of life in common' (Aron, 1962a: 25). This would be a universalisation which would be achieved in the understanding, deduced from particular enquiries, rather than a posited universalism immanently underpinning all forms of social life. He cited Lévi-Strauss's *Les structures élémentaires de la parenté* (Lévi-Strauss, 1968 [1949]) favourably as a 'model of sociological science' (Aron, 1962a: 24) in this mode, and he proceeded to argue that the sociologist should compare and contrast American and

Soviet economies and their political structures. Finally, in other words, Aron reached a view of sociology as a meta-science able to suggest sociologistic perceptions by carrying out detailed comparative examinations of economic and political sub-systems, understood as autonomous entities. Indeed, for Aron, the essential function of sociology, viewed in this way, was to establish whether economic behaviour itself has a universal logic or is conditioned by the political framework within which it is situated. Remaining loyal to Weber, Aron wanted to argue that sociology could demonstrate that there is no autonomous logic of economic behaviour, but his hostility to Durkheim made him unable to conceive of the possibility that the differences perceived sociologically might themselves be the products of autonomous social or cultural self-determinations within different contexts.

The 'Aronian' Research of Bourdieu and Passeron in the 1960s

Aron was most concerned to establish sociologically whether economic behaviour is apolitical. His own work had never been empirical, but his intention in establishing a Research Group was precisely to sponsor empirical investigations which would explore in detail aspects of the emergence of industrial society within alternative political systems. Bourdieu and Passeron had emerged deeply disenchanted out of the French higher education system. At the very beginning of the 1960s, they launched a project which, in Aronian terms, can be seen to have been an attempt to examine the logic of pedagogical relations in themselves and the implications of their operation within politically determined or managed educational systems. Initially, therefore, Bourdieu and Passeron were united in carrying out a research agenda that followed from Aron's views. In the early 1960s, they undertook research that, as Aron recommended, questioned whether aspects of French democracy in the Fifth Republic were true to the vision of an inclusive, socialist republic of the Third Republic. In particular, was the education system perpetuating the values and the privilege of the dominant classes and denying the cultures of the dominated? Were new technologies of the time, such as photography, allowing for the expression of indigenous culture or was there an increasingly homogenised culture imposed by the mass media? Were museums and art galleries perpetuating social exclusion, or were they the disguised instruments of state control? Were Malraux's motives in establishing the Maisons de la Culture essentially political in sustaining the subordination of popular culture to a state approved high culture?

Bourdieu and Passeron came to the study of education and culture not with the intention of contributing to the analysis of culture or education per se, but with the intention of considering how educational and cultural systems functioned politically. This explains their use of Aron's terminology in their attack on mass culture in 'Sociologues des mythologies et mythologies de sociologues' (Bourdieu and Passeron, 1963) as well as their interest in comparing educational systems within different political systems as evidenced by their contributions to *Education, développement et démocratie* (Castel and Passeron, 1967). The findings of the educational research of the early 1960s for which Bourdieu and Passeron are most famous were first released in a working paper of the Centre of 1964 entitled 'Les étudiants et leurs études' ['Students and their Studies'] (Bourdieu and Passeron, 1964a). These findings were the products of analyses of questionnaires returned by students of sociology and philosophy at the University of Lille and a range of other northern French universities.

In the same year, Bourdieu and Passeron published a book – *Les héritiers* [the inheritors] (Bourdieu and Passeron, 1964b) – which represented these findings with an interpretative gloss. In both forms, the research was aimed at analysing the socio-cultural processes of pedagogic communication without explicit consideration of the political structure of the French educational system within which the processes were situated. Yet, the implicitly Aronian dimension of their project is most clear from a publication of the Centre de sociologie européenne of 1967, which assembled papers which had been given in conferences organised by the Centre in Madrid in October 1964 and in Dubrovnik in October 1965. *Education, Développement et Démocratie* (Castel and Passeron, 1967) assembled papers on education in, amongst other regimes, those of Franco's Spain, Tito's Yugoslavia, de Gaulle's France, and the Greece of the Colonels. The collection was edited by Robert Castel and Jean-Claude Passeron. The Introduction to the collection contains a foreword by the editors and an essay by Bourdieu and Passeron entitled 'La comparabilité des systèmes d'enseignement' ['The Comparability of Systems of Education'], and there is a conclusion by the editors entitled 'Inégalités culturelles et politiques scolaires' ['Cultural Inequalities and Scholastic Politics']. These attempts to impose some interpretative order on contributions from researchers in various countries are all concerned to discuss the implications of attempting to adopt a comparative methodology. They express disquiet at the attempt to evaluate socialist educational systems in terms of capitalist and technocratic criteria – what we might call a kind of capitalist centrism –, but they also show anxiety at the inverse – the consequences of suggesting patterns of pedagogical relationship which might be thought to be independent of systemic context either as a result of a form of universal idealism or of autonomous culturalism. In particular, Castel and Passeron warn that 'monographic fidelity to cultural singularities' runs the risk of leading to 'sociological analysis with uncontrolled associations with a metaphysics of culture' (Castel and Passeron, 1967: 15) as in the case of Spengler, and they comment that this is fundamentally Hegelian.

To avoid these alternative traps, Castel and Passeron claim that any comparative analysis must be presented in tandem with an analysis of the principles of comparison in use and, in this way, they indicate the significance for the whole collection of the contribution made jointly by Bourdieu and Passeron. Castel and Passeron recommend what we have come to identify with Bourdieu's work – the rigorous introduction of a principle of reflexivity –, but I want to suggest that the approaches of Aron, Bourdieu and Passeron were diverging during the 1960s and that this divergence crystallised in their reactions to May 1968. Crudely, Aron retained a view of politics as diplomacy and of the primacy of politics understood as such. He would regard social action not as intrinsically political, but only as a variable in comparing political systems. Bourdieu's critique of structuralism led him to support immanent socio-cultural agency, running the risk of the culturalism described by Castel and Passeron and leading towards the totalitarianism of the social ascribed by Aron to Durkheim and the concomitant denial of the autonomy of politics as well as to what Passeron was to regard as clandestine Hegelianism. Attempting to resist the elements of transcendental idealism in Aron's position as well as the incipient culturalism of Bourdieu's, Passeron sought to map the autonomous logics of plural discourses, systems and institutions.

The Incipient Divergence between the Positions of Bourdieu and Passeron

As *normaliens*, both Bourdieu and Passeron had, of course, been trained philosophically. The incipient differences between their positions became apparent in the joint production of *Le métier de sociologue* (Bourdieu, Chamboredon and Passeron, 1968) in which they tried to set out the epistemological preliminaries for sociological enquiry. In a sub-section of their introduction – 'Epistémologie des sciences de l'homme et épistémologie des sciences de la nature' [epistemology of the human sciences and epistemology of the natural sciences] – they appeared to be in agreement that the legacy of the competing philosophies of social science of the nineteenth century offered a false dichotomy between positivism and hermeneutics and that the solution should be the establishment of an epistemology which would be particular to the social sciences. They described their proposal as follows:

> Pour dépasser ces débats académiques et les manières académiques de les dépasser, il faut soumettre la pratique scientifique à une réflexion qui, à la différence de la philosophie classique de la connaissance, s'applique non pas à

> la science faite, science *vraie* dont il faudrait établir les conditions de possibilité et de cohérence ou les titres de légitimité, mais à la science *se faisant*. (Bourdieu, Chamboredon and Passeron, 1968: 27, emphasis in original)
>
> [The way to move beyond these academic debates, and beyond the academic way of moving beyond them, is to subject scientific practice to a reflection which, unlike the classical philosophy of knowledge, is applied not to science that has been done – *true* science, for which one has to establish the conditions of possibility and coherence or the claims to legitimacy – but to science in progress. (Bourdieu, Chamboredon and Passeron, 1991: 8)]

As Passeron said to me in a conversation (unrecorded) in Marseille in September 2007, the production of the text of *Le métier de sociologue* was like the preparation of agreed doctrinal statements at the Councils of Nicea or Trent in the early church. The process showed him the disjunction between shared language and shared thought. The idea of submitting practical scientific research to systematic reflexion united Bourdieu and Passeron in as much as both were opposed to merely theoretical theory or speculative theorising, but their conceptions of reflexion were very different. Passeron – for instance, in 'La photographie parmi le personnel des usines Renault' [Photography amongst employees in Renault factories] Photography (Passeron, 1962) – had sought to analyse the emergent discourse of photographic criticism as manifest in everyday language, whereas Bourdieu was concerned with examining the institutionalisation of an aestheticism of photography in the growth of photographic clubs as social phenomena. Passeron was concerned to reflect on the deployment of linguistic categories in social-scientific research, whereas Bourdieu emphasised the need for social scientists to establish themselves collectively as an epistemic community. It is significant that the introduction ended with a passage that was deferential towards Durkheim, quoting from *The Rules of Sociological Method* (Durkheim, 1982 [1901]). Bourdieu, Chamboredon and Passeron concluded the introduction with the comment that

> [i]n short, the scientific community has to provide itself with specific forms of social interchange [...]. (Bourdieu, Chamboredon and Passeron, 1991: 77)

In other words, the uneasy compromise of *Le métier de sociologue* was that Passeron's inclination to subject social-scientific discourse per se to rigorous scrutiny was absorbed within a Durkheimian conception of the need socially to construct the community within which such scrutiny could occur. A fundamentally Weberian interest in rationality was absorbed within a conception of a socially constructed community which would have been anathema to Aron's understanding of a social-scientific community. My view is that Passeron's work retained this linguistic/logical orientation, as shown in *Les mots de la sociologie* (Passeron, 1980) and in *Le raisonnement sociologique* (Passeron, 1991), whereas Bourdieu's work took a turn towards philosophical anthropology, mixed with phenomenology and ontology, as indicated by the sub-title of *Réponses : Pour une anthropologie réflexive* (Bourdieu and Wacquant, 1992). Passeron retained his interest in language and reasoning, related to Husserl's *Logical Investigations* (Husserl, 1970 [1901]) and to Wittgenstein's *Tractatus Logico-Philosophicus*, as introduced by Bertrand Russell (Wittgenstein, int. Russell., 1961 [1922, 1921]). In other words, he was interested in the logistic rejection of psychologism and in the early developments of logical positivism. Bourdieu, by contrast, was probably more influenced by the late Husserl, whose position had been modified by contact with Heidegger, and by the late Wittgenstein of the *Logical Investigations* (Wittgenstein, 1963). Trained in a philosophical context that was primarily concerned with epistemology, Bourdieu and Passeron both became practising social scientists who found themselves analysing education and culture as a consequence of the political science and political orientations of their mentor, Raymond Aron.

Emerging Differences between Bourdieu and Passeron in Respect of the Analysis of Culture

Passeron's translation of *The Uses of Literacy* (Hoggart, 1957) was published as *La culture du pauvre* in 1970 (Hoggart, 1970 [1957]), that is to say after Hoggart had left the Centre for Contemporary Cultural Studies at the University of Birmingham, UK, and therefore precisely when the emergent English field of Cultural Studies was trying to shake off the legacy of the literary and textual tradition manifest in Hoggart's book. Passeron celebrates the way in which the *Uses of Literacy* practises the kind of sociology that is appropriate for the study of the working classes or the classes populaires. Precisely because Hoggart's book is essentially literary or particularly strong in registering working class language, Passeron tried to use Hoggart's work to support his contention that sociological analysis involves documenting the ways in which people articulate their own experiences linguistically, to support a kind of linguistic ethnomethodology, or, to relate this to a phrase used by Bourdieu, to support a linguistic analysis of texts of 'spontaneous sociology', like those supplied as appendices in *Travail et travailleurs en algérie* (Bourdieu, Darbel, Rivet and Seibel, 1963). I just want to make one point about Passeron's 'présentation' of the translation of *The Uses of Literacy* as *La culture du pauvre*. Passeron comments that one of the most original aspects of Hoggart's book is his capacity to question the image of the working classes and their values held by other classes. He notes:

> Sans doute, le passé de l'auteur, né et élevé dans une famille ouvrière, devenu boursier, puis universitaire et chercheur, le place-t-il dans une position particulièrement favorable pour apercevoir la signification de classe de ces jugements sur les classes populaires qui ont, dans les classes cultivées, toute l'opacité des 'évidences naturelles'. (Hoggart, 1970 [1957]: 17)
>
> [Undoubtedly, the author's past – born and brought up in a working-class family, receiving a scholarship, becoming an academic and a researcher – puts him in a particularly favourable situation to perceive the class significance of those judgements on the popular classes which, amongst the cultivated classes, have all the opacity of 'natural self-evidence'.]

Passeron recognises that Hoggart was a 'transfuge'. In this respect, Passeron recognised an affinity between himself and Hoggart and, at the same time, Bourdieu. The crucial difference, however, is that Passeron's solution is completely unlike that attempted by Bourdieu in his 'Célibat et condition paysanne' (Bourdieu, 1962). Bourdieu tried to engineer a conceptual encounter between the primary, unreflecting experience of Béarn peasants and the perspective on that experience which he had acquired as a social scientist who had attended Lévi-Strauss's seminars. Ten years later, Bourdieu was to articulate this encounter as a methodology when he adopted Bachelard's epistemological break to describe the three stages of theoretical knowledge, elaborated in *Esquisse d'une théorie de la pratique* (Bourdieu, 1972). By contrast, Passeron continues in his présentation:

> Mais, s'il est vrai que toute personnalité intellectuelle est socialement conditionnée et si aucune expérience de classe n'est capable d'engendrer par sa seule vertu l'attitude proprement scientifique (nulle grâce de naissance ne prédestinant jamais à l'objectivité de la perception sociologique, pas plus dans les classes privilégiées que dans les classes défavorisées, ou même dans les couches intellectuelles, n'en déplaise à Mannheim) […]. (Hoggart, 1970 [1957]: 17)
>
> [But, if it is true that every intellectual personality is socially conditioned and if no class experience is in itself capable of generating a properly scientific attitude (nothing ever predestining the objectivity of sociological perception thanks to birth, no more in the privileged classes than in the disadvantaged, *pace* Mannheim) […].]

In other words, scientific objectivity is not the preserve of any one class and is not socially constructed. All classes articulate their own self-understandings linguistically and these articulations have to be analysed intrinsically as 'science', rather than relatively as the products of different social groups.

This clear distinction between the positions taken by Passeron and Bourdieu at the end of the 1960s and early 1970s relates as well to the difference between them in relation to the interpretation of *La Reproduction* (Bourdieu and Passeron, 1970). It was the paper given by Bourdieu in England in 1970 as 'Reproduction culturelle et reproduction sociale' (Bourdieu, 1971), which consolidated the view that *La Reproduction* was arguing that cultural reproduction is an instrument in social reproduction, whereas Passeron's position had consistently been that there are autonomous logics in operation in both the cultural and the social spheres and that there is no universally formulatable causal connection between the two. The position which Bourdieu was developing became clear in the argument of *Esquisse* (Bourdieu, 1972), as further developed in the English translation as *Outline of a Theory of Practice* (Bourdieu, 1977), but in relation to class cultures it was, of course, most apparent in *La distinction* (1979). It was the publication of *La distinction* which stimulated the responses of Claude Grignon and Passeron, which were expressed in the text which they finally published together in 1989 as *Le savant et le populaire*, echoing the title of Aron's introduction to Weber's esssays. The book was the final version, barely altered, of seminars given in Marseille in 1982, and published by GIDES (Groupe inter-universitaire de documentation et d'enquêtes sociologiques [the inter-university group for documentation and sociological enquiries]) in 1983 and by CERCOM (Centre de Recherches sur Culture et Communication [Centre for Research on Culture and Communication]) in 1985. In the opening part of *Le savant et le populaire*, Passeron outlines the 'cultural relativism' position and the 'cultural legitimacy' position. He seems more inclined to expose Bourdieu as a cultural relativist and he suggests that the fallacy of Bourdieu's position was that he wrongly tried to adopt in France a cultural relativist position which had worked in Algeria. Cultural relativism applies in a context of 'pure alterity', but within one society there is, instead, a situation of 'altérité mêlée' [mixed alterity]. [Arguably, in parenthesis, in a global world, cultural relativism is now totally excluded since there is no possibility of any pure alterity and so, for Passeron, there is no defence remaining of Bourdieu's approach.] Passeron's main criticism of Bourdieu is the one to which I have already referred which he summarises again in the following way. Bourdieu acquiesced in a misreading of *La reproduction* which failed to acknowledge that

> [...] la connaissance des rapports de force entre groupes et classes n'apporte pas sur un plateau la clé de leurs rapports symboliques et du contenu de leurs cultures ou de leurs idéologies. (Grignon and Passeron, 1989, 27)

> [[...] the knowledge of the power relations between groups and classes does not dish out the key to their symbolic relations or to the content of their cultures or their ideologies.]

In place of a crude, Marxist schema to model the relations between culture and social class, Passeron proposes a second schema which has the possibility of integrating cultural analysis with ideological analysis. This schema represents diagrammatically the complex nature of socio-cultural analysis. As Passeron says:

> Une sociologie de la culture qui veut intégrer à ses analyses les faits de domination a toujours affaire à un circuit complexe d'interactions symboliques et de constitutions de symbolismes. (Grignon and Passeron, 1989: 29)
>
> [A sociology of culture which wants to integrate the facts of domination into its analyses is always involved in a complex circuit of symbolic interactions and constituted symbolisms.]

Passeron knows that his second schema is no more prescriptive or definitive than the first:

> Le schéma suggère évidemment l'apparence trompeuse d'un réseau routier que le chercheur pourrait parcourir sans problèmes. Ce n'est là qu'optimisme graphique. (Grignon and Passeron, 1989: 30)
>
> [The schema clearly suggests the mistaken appearance of a road network that the researcher can navigate without any problems. That is just graphical optimism.]

In other words, Passeron is in sympathy with Aron's criticism of Weber that he imposed a simplistic model on social reality, that is, a theoretical model which failed to do justice to the empirical complexities of society. To return to my starting point, my contention is that Passeron is equally in sympathy with Aron's more positive interpretation of Weber's position in balancing the commitments of science and politics. Passeron's second schema purports to offer a continuously self-modifying model of relations between culture and ideology, which itself is scientific and non-ideological. The autonomous status of science is not questioned and political convictions or commitments are of a different order. I am reminded of Paul Veyne's recent use of Weber to defend Foucault. Veyne (a close friend of Passeron) wrote:

> Si l'on cherche à cerner un type d'humanité, il y avait chez Foucault ce 'renoncement sceptique à trouver un sens au monde' dont parle Max Weber, qui y voyait avec quelque exagération une attitude 'commune à toutes les couches

intellectuelles de tous les temps.' (Veyne, 2008: 203, quoting Weber, 2006 [1910/1920]: 228)

[If we seek to discern a type of human nature, there was in Foucault that 'sceptical refusal to find meaning in the world' of which Weber spoke, who, with some exaggeration, saw in it an attitude which is 'common to all intellectual milieux at all times'.]

By contrast, Bourdieu tried to develop a conceptual framework which sought to represent the complexity of reality itself. Just as Passeron counteracts the Marxist schema logically, Bourdieu tried, by developing the concept of 'field', to moderate the crudity of a Marxist position. Bourdieu's contention was that there are in society relationally constructed or institutionalised 'fields' within which autonomous cultural analyses are exchanged whilst these fields are themselves socio-economically conditioned. Grignon accuses Bourdieu of evaluating dominated culture by the criteria of dominant culture, but the point of *Homo Academicus* (Bourdieu, 1984) is that Bourdieu deliberately situates the view of culture taken in *Distinction* as a function of his own position within the 'game of culture'.

Differences between Aron, Bourdieu and Passeron in Respect of Education

This is not the place to look fully at the work of the three men in respect of the sociology of education during the 1960s. I want to offer some bibliographic details and make a few comments as a prelude to some brief reference to the events of May 1968.

Aron wrote two articles specifically on education in this period. The first was 'Quelques problèmes des universités françaises' ['Some Problems of French Universities'], published in 1962 (Aron, 1962b). He made it clear that his interest was in the way in which European universities, as historic institutions, might adapt to the challenges of modern, industrial society. The problems of adaptation were to be resolved politically. He examined the ideological legacy in France, not of the medieval university but of the revolutionary and Napoleonic regimes, revised at the beginning of the Third Republic. He was highly critical of French universities, but he sought solutions in terms of management, governance, or legislative change. His second article was a paper given in June 1966 (Aron, 1966) at a conference of the *Institut international de planification de l'éducation* [International Institute for Educational Planning], thereby confirming his orientation towards the central, governmental planning of change.

As well as writing 'Les étudiants et leurs études' and *Les héritiers* in 1964, Bourdieu and Passeron wrote, with others under a pseudonym, an article in

Esprit in the same year entitled 'L'universitaire et son université' [professors and their universities] (Boupareytre, 1964). In 1965, they together wrote 'Langage et rapport au langage dans la situation pédagogique' and, with Monique de Saint-Martin, 'Les étudiants et la langue d'enseignement'[students and the language of teaching], both of which were issued as a working paper of the Centre, with the title *Rapport pédagogique et communication* [The pedagogic relationship and communication] (Bourdieu, Passeron and de Saint Martin, 1965) most of which was published in English translation in 1994 as *Academic Discourse* (Bourdieu, Passeron and de Saint Martin, 1994). The tendency of these joint papers was still to see the social or class differences of students as a variable to be considered in the analysis of pedagogic communication, but not yet to see the system within which the communication was occurring as something which itself should be subject to sociological analysis. Writing separately, Passeron produced a report in 1963 entitled 'Les étudiantes' [women students] (Passeron, 1963), which demonstrated that the language codes deployed by female students were the sources of pedagogically significant communicative variations and this view, perhaps, constituted a challenge to Bourdieu's inclination to define the student body as a social group exclusively in terms of its 'studentness', its gender-free situatedness. In 1967, Passeron published an article entitled 'La relation pédagogique dans le système d'enseignement [The pedagogical relationship in the teaching system]], in which he explicitly contended that the analysis of pedagogical relations was in danger of divorcing pedagogy 'from the institutional and social conditions in which it is accomplished' (Passeron, 1967: 149), and he proceeded to analyse instead the discourses of conservatism and innovation that were being deployed by those involved in educational reform. It was this discourse analysis that was also the basis of Passeron's contribution to a book that he published in 1966 with Gérald Antoine, entitled *La réforme de l'Université* [Reforming the university] (Antoine and Passeron, 1966). Passeron here compared the implementation of educational change at the beginning of the Third Republic, based upon the shared discourse of academics and legislators, with the difficulty of effecting change in the present when there was neither a shared discourse amongst academics nor a shared discourse between academics and administrators. Aron wrote a foreword to this book in which he recognised that the change by legislation which he favoured was predicated on a community of values which was currently lacking in France.

The May 'Events' of 1968

Aron used his position at Le Figaro to write pieces about the student revolt whilst it was happening. These were reproduced in a book which he published in September 1968, entitled *La révolution introuvable. Réflexions sur les événements de mai* [The unrealisable revolution. Reflections on the events of May]] (Aron, 1968). Fourteen short pieces, published between May 15th and June 28th, were collected as an appendix. The first, retrospective, part of the book offered reflections on the events, beginning with a statement about the nature of his involvement, which helps us steer a way through his intellectual response to the events, contextualising the contents of the appendix. On Friday, May 3rd, the University Rector called in the police to clear the Sorbonne, and there was a mass demonstration in the Latin Quarter. A week later, during the night of Friday 10th to Saturday 11th, there was a rising in the Latin Quarter following the breakdown of talks between the government and the students. The uprising was brutally repressed by the police. Aron recollects that he refused to write anything in Le Figaro in this first week of the Events. In the University, as he says, he 'belonged to the reformist and not the conservative party' (Aron, 1968: 21). As much as possible, he tried to abstain, not wanting to 'add to the confusion' nor to join those of his university colleagues who considered it their 'duty to accompany the students to the barricades' (Aron, 1968: 21). He was abroad in the United States from the 14th to the 23rd of May, honouring a long-standing commitment. Before leaving, he had written two 'Réflexions d'un universitaire' [Reflections of a professor], which were published on May 15th and 16th. In the first, he argued against the student view that their condition was universal, and he insisted that lecturing staff should force themselves 'patiently and modestly' to resolve problems which took particular forms in different countries in spite of 'certain common characteristics' (Aron, 1968: 159). In the second, he argued that the crisis of the university derived from the fact that student numbers had increased – something which had occurred in all industrial countries –, but that this had not been matched in France with the necessary disposition of resources.

What was articulated by students as an intrinsic shortcoming of a 'technocratic university' was actually the shortcoming of the modern state in failing to make provision for the kind of university entailed by its modernisation. Aron argued still for dialogue but he feared that the current events prefigured more danger than hope. The analysis offered in these first two articles was still reminiscent of his earlier lectures on industrial society and totalitarian and democratic political systems. On May 16th, Pompidou announced ominously that the government would 'do its duty' in the face of disorder. On the 18th, de Gaulle returned hastily from a visit to Roumania. The following week, the parliamentary left demanded the resignation of the government, but a motion of censure was defeated in the National Assembly on the 22nd. On Friday 24th, de Gaulle announced a referendum on participation, adding that he would resign if it were rejected. Aron cut short his trip to the United States, and he recollects that, on his return on May 23rd, there was 'apparently no government'. It was, therefore, as he puts it, no longer 'a question of writing then about the university' (Aron, 1968: 22–23). In his absence, the issues had escalated. His response escalated from that of a sociologist concerned with educational reform to that of a political philosopher confronting the problems of a modern social democracy. His method was historical. Rather than attempt a scientific analysis of contemporary events, Aron offered an account by analogy with the events of 1848 as recounted by Alexis de Tocqueville in a piece published on May 29th, entitled 'Immuable et changeante' [immutable and changing] – a title which deliberately echoed that of a book which Aron had written in 1958 on the eve of the adoption of the constitution of the Fifth Republic. On Thursday, May 30th, de Gaulle returned to Paris from a meeting in Germany and made a speech broadcast on radio and television in which he announced his refusal to withdraw and his decision to dissolve the National Assembly. When, as Aron comments, 'there was a government again, that is to say after May 30' (Aron, 1968: 23), he considered it his duty to continue pieces in his Le Figaro column, which were informed by the fact that he was also a university professor. The present circumstances demanded this, that is to say because 'there is such a confusion between university revolution and political revolution' (Aron, 1968: 23).

Aron's intention was to continue the political debate of May ex post facto, and the production of the book in September was an extension of this purpose. He compared the function of his book with that of his *La tragédie algérienne*, (Aron, 1958) which he had written in 1958 when de Gaulle had been recalled to power during the Algerian crisis. The aim was to be polemical. He had no pretention 'to impart the truth or the meaning of the event'. His objective was to 'demystify' and 'desacralise' it (Aron, 1968: 12). Aron's interventions had begun as contributions to debate about the reform of the university, but – after the beginning of June, culminating in the publication of his book in September – he broadened the discussion so as to offer an ideological critique, as a political philosopher, of the libertarian tendency in the French political tradition, which drew inspiration from the Jacobin communes of Paris of the 1790s, the 1848 revolution, and the Paris Commune of 1871.

The clearest evidence for Bourdieu's association with the Events of May 1968 is offered in the book published in the year of his death by two of his disciples – Franck Poupeau and Thierry Discepolo – entitled *Interventions,*

1961–2001. Science sociale et action politique (Bourdieu, 2002). They are concerned to show the continuity of Bourdieu's position from the early 1960s through to his opposition to neo-liberalism in the 1990s and, in particular, they reproduce two documents with which Bourdieu was associated, the first entitled *Appel à l'organisation d'états généraux de l'enseignement et de recherche* [Call for the organisation of Estates General of teaching and research] and the second entitled *Quelques indications pour une politique de démocratisation* [some suggestions for a democratisation policy]. The first document was the product of a meeting of a group of lecturers and researchers which took place on May 12th 'at the moment when, by their courage, the students have won a first battle' (Bourdieu, 2002: 63). It was most concerned to argue that there was a danger that the future of the university would be debated only by those who were the beneficiaries of the current system. In recommending the organisation of an Estates General which would provide a forum for those involved in education at all levels, from primary to higher education, the Call sought to ensure that the educational revolt would not be one within an autonomous, politically managed system, but would be transformed into a widespread social democratic revolution which would be operationalised by means adopted by the revolutionaries of 1789 in opposing the *Ancien Régime*. The second document outlines 16 principles to be followed in seeking to ensure that technocratic reform of the university does not reinforce existing social inequality. Together, these papers indicate the political implications of Bourdieu's sociocratic opposition to technocratic control of educational processes, and they do anticipate the position that he was to outline in *La noblesse d'état* (Bourdieu, 1989) as well as in the publications of Liber. Raisons d'Agir of the 1990s, especially *Quelques diagnostics et remèdes urgents pour une université en péril* (ARESER, 1997).

In 1966 Passeron moved to the University of Nantes and established a Department of Sociology there before accepting a post as Head of Sociology in 1968 at the new post-1968 University of Paris VIII at Vincennes, where he remained until 1977. He was committed to the institutionalisation of sociology and to the view that legislative changes would become effective if a receptive common discourse of educational innovation could be established. He was one of the seventy-eight signatories to the call for an Estates-General attributed, as we have seen, to Bourdieu, but it seems that Passeron had no further direct involvement with the Parisian events.

Conclusion

I have tried to sketch the three positions adopted in the 1960s by Aron, Passeron and Bourdieu. For me, the legacy of 1968 is encapsulated in the tension between these three positions, which is still our tension today. All three men wanted to be socio-politically engaged as scientists. Aron emphasised the necessity for political engagement and marginalised social activism. He sponsored sociological research in the hope of consolidating his political convictions through comparative analyses. Bourdieu and Passeron carried out these analyses. By exposing the extent to which pedagogical communication euphemised political domination, however, they autonomised the social and the cultural as arenas for a potential counter-politics, thereby undermining Aron's intention. Bourdieu sought to translate this sociological analysis into a blueprint for political action, based on the mobilisation of social movements. Passeron was to detach himself from Bourdieu's project in 1972 to concentrate, instead, on developing an epistemology of the social sciences, crystallised in *Le raisonnement sociologique* (1991)[2], so as to seek to understand philosophically the explanatory claims of those political and sociological discourses of which Aron and Bourdieu were opposed exponents.

Notes

1 This paper benefits from research which I am undertaking with the support of the ESRC on the work of Jean-Claude Passeron. I am also indebted to Simon Susen and Bryan S. Turner for their assistance and encouragement during the production of this text.
2 The revised edition of 2006 is currently being translated, to be published in 2010/11.

References

ARESER (Association de réflexion sur les enseignements supérieurs et la recherche [Association for reflection on higher education and research]) (1997) *Quelques diagnostics et remèdes urgents pour une université en péril*, Paris, Liber-Raisons d'Agir.

Antoine, Gérald and Jean-Claude Passeron (1966) *La réforme de l'université*, Paris: Calmann-Lévy.

Aron, Raymond (1935) *La sociologie allemande contemporaine*, Paris: Alcan.

Aron, Raymond (1948) *Le grand schisme*, Paris: Gallimard.

Aron, Raymond (1951) *Les guerres en chaîne*, Paris: Gallimard.

Aron, Raymond (1957) *La tragédie algérienne*, Paris: Plon.

Aron, Raymond (1964) *La lutte des classes. Nouvelles leçons sur les sociétés industrielles*, Paris: Gallimard.

Aron, Raymond (1962a) *Dix-huit leçons sur la société industrielle*, Paris: Gallimard.

Aron, Raymond (1962b) 'Quelques problèmes des universités françaises', *Archives européennes de sociologie* 1: 102–122.

Aron, Raymond (1965) *Démocratie et totalitarisme*, Paris: Gallimard.

Aron, Raymond (1966) 'Remarques sociologiques sur les notions de qualité et de quantité en fait d'éducation', Communication au colloque de l'Institut international de planification de l'éducation, June.

Aron, Raymond (1967 [1962]) *18 Lectures on Industrial Society*, trans. M. K. Bottomore, London: Weidenfeld and Nicolson.

Aron, Raymond (1967) *Les Etapes de la pensée sociologique*, Paris: Gallimard.
Aron, Raymond (1968) *La révolution introuvable. Réflexions sur les événements de Mai*, Paris: Fayard.
Aron, Raymond (1969) *D'une sainte Famille à l'autre : essai sur les marxismes imaginaires*, Paris: Gallimard.
Aron, Raymond (1990 [1983]) *Memoirs: Fifty Years of Political Thought*, trans. George Holoch, New York: Holmes and Meier.
Boupareytre, Émile [Pierre Bourdieu, Jean-Claude Passeron, Jean-Daniel Reynaud and Jean-René Treanton] (1964) 'L'universitaire et son université', *Esprit* 5–6: 834–847.
Bourdieu, Pierre (1958) *Sociologie de l'Algérie*, Paris: Presses Universitaires de France.
Bourdieu, Pierre (1961) *Sociologie de l'Algérie*, 2nd edition, Paris: Presses Universitaires de France.
Bourdieu, Pierre (1962 [1961]) *The Algerians*, Boston: Beacon Press.
Bourdieu, Pierre (1962) 'Célibat et condition paysanne', *Études rurales* 5–6: 32–136.
Bourdieu, Pierre (1971) 'Reproduction culturelle et reproduction sociale', *Information sur les sciences sociales* X(2): 45–99.
Bourdieu, Pierre (1972) *Esquisse d'une théorie de la pratique, précédé de trois études d'ethnologie kabyle*, Paris: Seuil.
Bourdieu, Pierre (1977 [1972]) *Outline of a Theory of Practice*, trans. Richard Nice, Cambridge: Cambridge University Press.
Bourdieu, Pierre (1979) *La distinction. Critique sociale du jugement*, Paris: Minuit.
Bourdieu, Pierre (1981) 'Décrire et prescrire. Note sur les conditions de possibilité et les limites de l'efficacité politique', *Actes de la recherche en sciences sociales* 38: 69–73.
Bourdieu, Pierre (1984) *Homo academicus*, Paris: Minuit.
Bourdieu, Pierre (1984 [1979]) *Distinction: A Social Critique of the Judgement of Taste*, trans. Richard Nice, Cambridge, Mass.: Harvard University Press.
Bourdieu, Pierre (1988 [1984]) *Homo Academicus*, trans. Peter Collier, Cambridge: Polity Press in association with Basil Blackwell.
Bourdieu, Pierre (1989) *La noblesse d'État. Grandes Écoles et esprit de corps*, Paris: Minuit.
Bourdieu, Pierre (1996 [1989]) *The State Nobility: Elite Schools in the Field of Power*, trans. Loretta Clough, Cambridge: Polity Press.
Bourdieu, Pierre (2002) *Interventions, 1961–2001. Science sociale et action politique*, textes choisis et présentés par Franck Poupeau et Thierry Discepolo, Marseille: Agone.
Bourdieu, Pierre, Jean-Claude Chamboredon and Jean-Claude Passeron (1968) *Le métier de sociologue. Préalables épistémologiques*, Paris: Éditions de l'École des Hautes Études en Sciences Sociales/Mouton.
Bourdieu, Pierre, Jean-Claude Chamboredon and Jean-Claude Passeron (1991 [1968]) *The Craft of Sociology: Epistemological Preliminaries*, trans. Richard Nice, edited by Beate Krais, Berlin: Walter de Gruyter.
Bourdieu, Pierre, Alain Darbel, Jean-Paul Rivet and Claude Seibel (1963) *Travail et travailleurs en Algérie*, Paris: Mouton.
Bourdieu, Pierre and Jean-Claude Passeron (1963) 'Sociologues des mythologies et mythologies de sociologues', *Les temps modernes* 211: 998–1021.
Bourdieu, Pierre and Jean-Claude Passeron (1964a) *Les étudiants et leurs études*, Cahiers du Centre de sociologie européenne, 1, Paris-The Hague: Mouton.
Bourdieu, Pierre and Jean-Claude Passeron (1964b) *Les héritiers. Les étudiants et la culture*, Paris: Minuit.
Bourdieu, Pierre and Jean-Claude Passeron (1965) « Langage et rapport au langage dans la situation pédagogique », in Pierre Bourdieu, Jean-Claude Passeron, Monique de Saint Martin, eds, 1965, 9–36.

Bourdieu, Pierre and Jean-Claude Passeron (1970) *La reproduction. Éléments pour une théorie du système d'enseignement*, Paris: Minuit.

Bourdieu, Pierre and Jean-Claude Passeron (1979 [1964]) *The Inheritors: French Students and their Relation to Culture*, trans. Richard Nice, Chicago: University of Chicago Press.

Bourdieu, Pierre and Jean-Claude Passeron (1990 [1977,1970]) *Reproduction in Education, Society and Culture*, trans. Richard Nice, 2nd Edition, London: Sage.

Bourdieu, Pierre, Jean-Claude Passeron and Michel Eliard (1964) *Les étudiants et leurs études*, Paris: Mouton.

Bourdieu, Pierre, Jean-Claude Passeron and Monique de Saint Martin (eds.) (1965) *Rapport pédagogique et communication*, Cahiers du Centre de sociologie européenne, 2, Paris-The Hague: Mouton.

Bourdieu, Pierre, Jean-Claude Passeron and Monique de Saint Martin (1994) *Academic Discourse: Linguistic Misunderstanding and Professorial Power*, trans. Richard Teese, Cambridge: Polity Press.

Bourdieu, Pierre and Loïc Wacquant (1992) *Réponses. Pour une anthropologie réflexive*, Paris: Seuil.

Bourdieu, Pierre and Loïc Wacquant (1992) *An Invitation to Reflexive Sociology*, Cambridge: Polity Press.

Castel, Robert and Jean-Claude Passeron (eds.) (1967) *Éducation, développement et démocratie*, Paris & The Hague: Mouton.

Durkheim, Émile (1982 [1901]) *The Rules of Sociological Method*, trans. W.D. Halls, 2nd edition, New York: Free Press.

Freund, Julien (1966) *Sociologie de Max Weber*, Paris: Presses Universitaires de France.

Grignon, Claude and Jean-Claude Passeron (1989) *Le savant et le populaire. Misérabilisme et populisme en sociologie et en littérature*, Paris: Gallimard/Seuil.

Hoggart, Richard (1957) *The Uses of Literacy: Aspects of Working-Class Life*, London: Chatto and Windus.

Hoggart, Richard (1970 [1957]) *La culture du pauvre*, trans. Jean-Claude Passeron, Paris: Minuit.

Husserl, Edmund (1970 [1954]) *The Crisis of European Sciences and Transcendental Phenomenology. An Introduction to Phenomenological Philosophy*, Evanston: Northwestern University Press.

Husserl, Edmund (1970 [1901]) *Logical Investigations*, trans. J.N. Findlay, 2nd edition, London: Routledge and Kegan Paul.

Husserl, Edmund (1977 [1950]) *Cartesian Meditations. An Introduction to Phenomenology*, The Hague: Martinus Nijhoff.

Lévi-Strauss, Claude (1968 [1949]) *Les structures élémentaires de la parenté*, nouv. éd. revue, Paris: Mouton.

Passeron, Jean-Claude (1962) 'La photographie parmi le personnel des usines Renault', Paris, Centre de sociologie européenne (internal working paper).

Passeron, Jean-Claude (1963) 'Les étudiantes', Paris: Centre de sociologie européenne (internal working paper).

Passeron, Jean-Claude (1967) 'La relation pédagogique dans le système d'enseignement', *Prospective* 14: 149–171.

Passeron, Jean-Claude (1980) *Les mots de la sociologie*, Nantes: University of Nantes.

Passeron, Jean-Claude (1991) *Le raisonnement sociologique. L'espace non poppérien du raisonnement naturel*, Paris: Nathan.

Passeron, Jean-Claude (2006 [1991]) *Le raisonnement sociologique. Un espace non poppérien de l'argumentation*, édition revue et augmentée, Paris: Albin Michel.

Passeron, Jean-Claude (2010/11 [2006]) *Sociological Reasoning. A Non-Popperian Space for Argument*, Oxford: Bardwell Press.

Veyne, Paul (2008) *Foucault. Sa pensée, sa personne*, Paris: Albin Michel.
Weber, Max (1919) *Wissenschaft als Beruf*, München: Duncker & Humboldt.
Weber, Max (1921) *Gesammelte Politische Schriften*, München: Duncker & Humboldt.
Weber, Max (1922) *Gesammelte Aufsätze zur Wissenschaftslehre*, Tübingen: Mohr.
Weber, Max (1959 [1919/1922]) *Le savant et le politique*, trans. J. Freund, Paris: Plon.
Weber, Max (1965) *Essais sur la théorie de la science*, trans. J. Freund, Paris: Plon.
Weber, Max (2006) *Sociologie des religions*, traduction de Jean-Pierre Grossein, introduction de Jean-Claude Passeron, Paris: Gallimard.
Wittgenstein, Ludwig (1961, int. Russell [1922, 1921]) *Tractatus Logico-Philosophicus*, London: Routledge and Kegan Paul.
Wittgenstein, Ludwig (1963) *Philosophical Investigations*, Oxford: Basil Blackwell.

CHAPTER FOURTEEN

Intellectual Critique and the Public Sphere: Between the Corporatism of the Universal and the *Realpolitik* of Reason

Yves Sintomer
Translated by Steven Corcoran

> But because what we propose to study above all is reality, it does not follow that we should give up the idea of improving it. We would esteem our research not worth the labour of a single hour if its interest were merely speculative. (Durkheim, *The Division of Labor in Society*, p. xxvi)

In the French edition of *The Weight of the World*, Bourdieu contends that the goal of his critical sociology is to 'open up possibilities for rational action to unmake or remake what history has made' (1999 [1993]: 187).[1] But what is 'rational action' in politics? And what potential contribution can intellectuals make to it? This last question is the one that I would like to address here, taking Bourdieu's own answers to it as my starting point. The aim will not be to analyse the concrete orientation of his public interventions, but instead to understand the type of articulation between political life and the intellectual world that he conceptualised. I have no philological ambitions of retracing Bourdieu's trajectory from the 1960s onwards. My intention is to focus on his theorisation of these issues during the last period of his life, from the moment he committed himself increasingly to the public realm (the turning point here is symbolised by the publication in 1993 of *The Weight of the World*, whose echo outside the academic world was considerable). After briefly defining the notion of the intellectual as it is used here, I will outline the essential characteristics of the Bourdieusian conception of engagement, as grounded in the concepts of 'corporatism of the universal' and the '*Realpolitik* of reason'. We will then see why this problematic, despite its stimulating character, risks falling into scientism, and why, by thinking with and against Bourdieu, it needs to be reformulated by means of its articulation with a socio-historical notion of the public sphere.

A *Realpolitik* of Reason

The word 'intellectual' possesses multiple meanings. The *Oxford Advanced Learner's Dictionary of Current English* defines it broadly as 'a person who is well educated and enjoys activities in which they have to think seriously about things'. In a more restricted sense, the word is often used to refer to those who exercise a profession in which intellectual activity is fundamental ('intellectual workers' by contrast to 'manual workers'). It can also take on a still more exclusive meaning and designation for those for whom reflection and artistic and literary creation is a profession. I would like here to uphold an even more circumscribed meaning, which stresses the one that Bourdieu gave to the word. I will employ the term 'intellectual' to designate that two-dimensional figure whose specific authority is earned in one of the cultural fields (scientific, artistic, and literary) and who invests his symbolic authority through his involvement in public affairs (1996 [1992]: 372). This definition does not follow as a matter of course, because it presupposes the historical thesis according to which the said intellectual is a modern invention that emerges only with the relative autonomisation of fields of culture. The definition, moreover, distinguishes intellectuals from figures who proclaim themselves intellectuals and have no academic or artistic recognition properly speaking, but are very present in a media scene, on which they depend heavily and in relation to which they therefore have no autonomy. Lastly, it designates a potential tension between the work of accumulation of specifically scientific or artistic capital and activities that enable the constitution of a 'politico-intellectual' capital with the public at large or a fraction of it. Each individual's time constraints and limited energy mean that every scientist or artist who decides to get involved in public affairs has to deal with this issue; and this is so irrespective of one's mode of engagement, as expert or fellow traveller in an institution (state, tribunal, party, social movement) or as a 'free' intellectual.

I will not go back over the concept of field again here, since it has already been dealt with abundantly. Instead, I will delve into two concepts which have remained relatively unanalysed thus far: the 'corporatism of the universal' and the '*Realpolitik* of reason'. To establish the first, Bourdieu had recourse to the paradigmatic example of the scientific field's achievement of (relative) autonomy in modernity in relation to the political or economic fields. According to him, this field becomes structured in such a way that lasting success in it is impossible to achieve by saying merely whatever. It is true that external social pressures continue to exert themselves and that power relations internal to the field (such as the weight of scientific bureaucracy) produce distortions whose effects are not relegated only to the margins. Nevertheless, in modern western democracies, recourse to social or political force turns out to be unable to prevent the better scientific arguments from winning out over the long term. The structure of the terrain of modern science demands a regulated and, to a certain extent, self-controlled competition. Those who appeal to bad arguments inevitably wind up disqualifying themselves in the eyes of their peers. By the same token, they lose the symbolic capital that comes with scientific prestige and find themselves handicapped in the competition of the search for truth. The agonistic relation which traverses the scientific field – like all the other fields – thus results in a sublimation of relations of power, since the agents have to place themselves in the service of reason and the universal if they are to be crowned with success. As Bourdieu puts it, '[t]he scientific field is a game in which you have to arm yourself with reason in order to win'. It is in this way that, far from being innate to 'man' or from following inevitably from the *a priori* conditions of human sociality, reason constitutes a historical and social product (1990 [1987]: 32).[2] The argument is, in some sense, a historicising rectification of the Kantian argument about the 'unsociable sociability' of human beings, and Bourdieu's Republic of Letters is evocative of the people of demons to which Kant alluded: instead of providence, however, specific social mechanisms constrain individuals to behave 'rationally' in determinate fields. In this way, it becomes possible to historicise reason without falling into relativism (2000 [1997]: 136). The scientific field constitutes a historical approximation of the ideal situation of communication. In Bourdieu's words, 'I do not think that reason is inscribed in the structure of the human spirit or in language. [...] Irrespective of what Habermas says, reason itself has a history: it did not fall from the heavens into our thinking and our language. The habitus (scientific or otherwise) is a transcendental, but it is an *historical transcendental*, which is partly connected with the structure and the history of the field' (1992: 188–189; 2000 [1997]: 110; 1997: 60).

This sociological argument, moreover, enables a coherent normative stance to be taken and its concepts take on the status of a 'normative description' (Bourdieu, 2000 [1997]: 140; 1996 [1992]: 214–274). Provided that the intellectual objectifies himself in a reflexive manner, that is, critically analyses his own interests and his own situation in the scientific field and society in general – his own historical unconscious – then he can, so the argument goes, lay claim to being a 'functionary of humanity'. To demonstrate the social conditions of the 'production of truth' in itself entails the actual existence of a 'politics of truth', one which aims precisely to 'defend and improve the functioning of the social universes in which rational principles are applied and truth comes into being' (1990 [1987]: 32). According to this view, then, the essential thing is to defend and increase the autonomy of the scientific field and its virtuous logic 'by strengthening the entry barriers, by rejecting the introduction and utilization of non-specific weapons, by favouring regulated forms of competition which are subject solely to the constraints of logical coherence and experimental verification' (1990 [1987]: 32). Bourdieu concludes his argument with a response to potential objections: 'This *Realpolitik* of reason will undoubtedly be suspected of corporatism. But it will be part of its task to prove, by the ends to which it puts the sorely won means of its autonomy, that it is a corporatism of the universal' (1996 [1992]: 348).

The social sciences have a particular role to play in the matter: via a socio-history of scientific practice, they bring to light the collusions or homologies between the structure of the scientific field and that of other fields, notably the economic and political fields. They enable us to discern the influences of the latter over scientific practices. They are therefore better at helping conceive how the latter can free themselves of the particular interests linked to this or that economic or political force, and how, by gaining in autonomy, they can gain in universality. It is in this precise sense that, at the end of his life, Bourdieu called for a 'politicisation of science' as opposed to the 'fatal' politicisation that would occur by importing polemics from the political into the scientific field (1997: 61). Bourdieu's definition of the intellectual does not only have analytic import, but it also contains a normative dimension. If a rigorous distinction has to be made between true intellectuals and 'media-intellectuals', the reason is that the latter, in abdicating their demands for the autonomy of the scientific field and without any legitimacy over it, go directly against the virtuous resort of scientists. And mere withdrawal into a purely academic position is likewise insufficient to guarantee the conditions of production so peculiar to scientists.

Had this been Bourdieu's only argument, it would, all in all, take us but a simple logical step further than the position that he previously advanced in the times when he firmly advised all collaborators against political involvement. Henceforth, the defence of the autonomy of science, a constant of Bourdieu's position, would be portrayed as requiring a certain 'politicisation', in a restricted sense. Bourdieu, however, makes a second argument. While the two concepts of the 'corporatism of the universal' and the '*Realpolitik* of reason' are closely interrelated, the latter distinguishes itself from the former insofar as it involves more than a simple defence of the autonomy of the scientific or artistic fields. It requires that the universal values that guide the logic of functioning of the latter, such as truth and authenticity, be reinvested in specifically political debates. From the 1990s onwards, Bourdieu began to endorse a broader sense of intellectual commitment. The critical intellectual, he wrote, is moved by a 'politics of purity', which is the 'perfect antithesis to the reason of state'.

This politics entails an assertion of the right to transgress the most sacred values of the political community, such as patriotism, 'in the name of values transcending those of citizenship or, if you will, in the name of a particular form of ethical and scientific universalism which can serve as a foundation not only for a sort of moral magisterium but also for a collective mobilisation to fight to promote these values' (1996 [1992]: 339–343).

It is this second step, at once theoretical and practical, which marks the real turning point with respect to his position in the 1970s. Hitherto, he had remained content to advance the notion that the social sciences, insofar as they proceed towards the unveiling of an otherwise masked reality, constitute a critique by the mere fact of their existence. By jealously demanding their independence in relation to political, economic, religious, etc., powers, the social sciences defend a liberty of judgement with respect to these latter; and by deconstructing the pseudo-evidences of the existing order, shot through with relations of domination, they contribute to putting such relations into question. In his later years, however, Bourdieu took things much further, advancing that critical intellectuals must reinvest positively in a politics of the universal values that are theirs in order to provide arguments for social movements.

Transcending the Political via Intellectual Critique?

From the 1990s onwards, the strength of Bourdieu's commitment is played out in his concept of the *Realpolitik* of reason (thus defined in its full scope). By dint of calling for scientists to mobilise politically and his own growing political involvement, he played a decisive role in public debate in the 1990s. He had not only joined the tradition of the great politically committed sociologists (Marx, Weber, and Durkheim), but also, although in a specific way, the heritage of the most famous French intellectuals, stretching from Voltaire to Jean-Paul Sartre, including Émile Zola, Michel Foucault and Simone de Beauvoir. He thereby acquired an immense politico-intellectual prestige. His role is not unrelated to that played by the Frankfurt School intellectuals in Germany. On this point, the closest figure to Bourdieu on the other side of the Rhine is Habermas. There can be little doubt, however, that Bourdieu had a proportionally far larger public echo. He influenced a whole generation of actors, both in the scientific field and social movements, and he contributed to a repoliticisation of the French university.

Nevertheless, the *Realpolitik* of reason raises two series of problems. On the one hand, in its cognitive dimension and its 'defensive' normative version (struggle for the autonomy of science), it tends to simplify, idealise and homogenise the fields of culture and, in particular, of the sciences. Indeed, social history provides us with a far more complex panorama of the dynamic of development of the sciences and technology, the driving force of which is irreducible to a progressive freeing in relation to other social relationships (Atten and Pestre, 2002; Pestre, 2003). Polarisation on the sole issue of the defence of scientific autonomy dissimulates the political dimension involved in the choice of research orientation or of the distribution of means making it possible to perform demonstrations of proof. It tends to disconnect research from public debates and prevents us from conceiving of a democratisation of sciences and technologies, whose topicality has nonetheless been extensively demonstrated over recent last years, including biomedical questions, controversies over nuclear power and research on the OGN gene (Callon, Lascoume and Barthes, 2001; Sclove, 1995).

In its 'offensive' dimension, the concept of the *Realpolitik* of reason presents an equally formidable problem: with which criteria is it possible to perform the conversion of 'universal' values of a cultural or scientific type into political values? How are we, for example, to go from an historical or sociological analysis of education or the social state to propositions for reform, that is, without getting involved in ethico-political debates? The social sciences can certainly contribute to deconstructing the self-evidences of such or such a policy by showing its contingency. In the 60s and 70s, to take only this example, the demonstration that the French school system reproduced social hierarchisations could in fact have a political effect, so long as the republican sense of equality through schooling constituted a broadly shared myth. Yet, in the name of what science or what art would it be possible to declare that one is for or against such and such a type of overhaul of the school or retirement system – that is, without further mobilising criteria that are, properly speaking, political? Bourdieu speaks of culture as an 'instrument of freedom presupposing liberty', in contrast to culture as 'thing-like and closed', that is, to 'dead' culture insofar as it is an 'instrument of domination and distinction'. From a similar perspective, he wrote that the 'liberation of women' had as its prior condition a culture that no longer functioned as 'a social relation of distinction' – something which makes women (and the dominated in general) into objects rather than subjects. Reacting to a rather regressive political conjuncture, he also warned against returning to the most primitive forms of barbarism in opposition to which all the democratic, parliamentary and notably judiciary institutions were built (1996 [1992]: 214–274 and 337–348; 1990c; 1993b). Now, what possible definition and conceptual status can notions such as the universal, democracy or liberty have? By implicitly maintaining – with Durkheim and against Weber – that normative positions can be deduced from cognitive reasoning while remaining positively 'scientific', Bourdieu reconciles science and morality at little cost by subordinating the latter to the former; he scientises politics by giving intellectuals a monopoly over the definition of the universal and, more broadly, of reason. Intellectual critique is then carried out from on high, without any real dialogue with the 'profane' actors of public life. Would it be at all surprising, then, if his privileged, even unique, styles of 'intellectual' or political writings came to be satirical pamphlets and magisterial lessons? Taken to an extreme, this orientation can lead to a modernised version of the myth of the cave, with the sociologist playing the role of the Platonic philosopher.

The risks of scientism are even greater as in his practice (if not in theory), Bourdieu progressively moves away from the figure of the 'specific intellectual', and closer to that of the 'universal intellectual'. Foucault theorised the former figure by arguing that scientists must involve themselves in public affairs, but can only do so with real legitimacy on the terrains in which they have specific competences. Foucault contrasted this figure to that of the universal intellectual, as embodied in Sartre, who himself deemed that he was able to intervene legitimately on the most varied of subjects in the name of the privileged place that he occupied in society or in that of a general theory able to establish the prolegomena for all possible political questions (1980 [1976]). Universal intellectuals have traditionally been philosophers or writers. Yet, by elaborating a general theory of society, by basing himself on the works of collaborators that touch on nearly all the aspects of the contemporary world, and indeed by laying claim to a privileged place for intellectuals in society in the name of the corporatism of the universal, did Bourdieu not also end up transforming himself into a universal intellectual, the very position he had once severely criticised? In the last years of life, Bourdieu adopted stances on practically every issue, whether directly or through close associates who benefitted from his symbolic capital. The collective intellectual that he gathered around him behaved like a universal intellectual, while nonetheless denying the position he very occupied.

The Public Sphere and the Corporatism of the Universal

Faced with the cognitive and normative difficulties of an approach, which, by intending to politicise science, threatens to become a scientisation of politics, is it not possible to adopt another path, with Bourdieu and against him? For this, it is necessary to take up a threefold guiding thread. On the one hand, at issue is to uphold the sound idea of the historicity of reason by inquiring into the social apparatuses which permit the development of rational processes. On the other hand, it is necessary to follow Bourdieu by avoiding all withdrawal into an 'apolitical' science and assuming intellectual involvement in the problems of society. Lastly, it is necessary to advance a mode of conversion, or at least a homology, between the pressures towards universalisation in the various fields that is cognitively convincing and normatively legitimate. Bourdieu sketched such a path in the third chapter of *Pascalian Meditations*, titled 'The Historical Foundations of Reason'. Pursuing it, however, would have involved major modifications to his global theoretical framework, and we are obliged to note that he did not proceed to make them. In fact, although the sociologist's evolution after *The Weight of the World* could appear as a veritable about-face with respect to the years in which he seemed to object to researchers undertaking any political activity, this turn masked fundamental continuities on the theoretical level, notably in his conception of science as *Aufklärung* and of the cut between science and common sense.

Two arguments seem particularly important for tackling the question of reason in history. The first sets out from an interrogation into the mechanisms of universalisation that render a corporatism of the universal possible in the scientific and artistic fields. How do 'bad' scientific productions or 'bad' works come to be deemed as such, and by what means are they recognised and rewarded? How do we arrive at adequate criteria, the means to renew them or to apply them, and a legitimacy so that the entirety of a field (as well as other fields, at least indirectly) accepts these criteria and the detailed judgements that they authorise? The explanation will naturally have to be complex; it cannot but vary according to historical conjunctures and no single mechanism could ever be made into the sole explanatory factor. Yet, it seems difficult to understand the dynamic of universalisation without going back over the historical emergence of the scientific and literary public spheres. Bourdieu alludes to this fact, notably, via the multiple references to Habermas strewn throughout his writings, but he never tackles the notion head on. It is doubtless necessary to adopt a realist socio-historical perspective on this public sphere and avoid conceiving all spheres on the same model. The history of science shows, notably, that it is imperative to contemplate the plurality of public spheres linked to the diverse disciplines in order to analyse the multiplicity between legitimate actors, types of dialogical confrontation and of apparatuses of objects on which they are based, or the modes of anchorage in cultural and national contexts. The criteria for proof and demonstrations, for example, are distinctly more rigorous and homogeneous in the mathematical sciences than in artistic and literary criticism, while the social sciences are situated in an intermediary position. What a collective considers 'universal' as the outcome of critique differs according to the type of public sphere, with dependency to local context being more or less strong depending on the case. The arts and many sciences do not really have a cumulative character.

It seems important, however, to have an ideal-type that aims at a characterisation of spheres in which the set of 'reasons' and positions are subject to critique, where bad arguments are at major risk of being disqualified, and in which veritably deliberative moments make possible dynamics that are not reducible to power relations that could be indifferent to the content of the arguments exchanged. Bourdieu comes closest to such a definition in the *Pascalian Meditations*. In it he writes that the social and human sciences 'make it possible to extend and radicalise the critical intention of Kantian rationalism [...] by helping to give sociological weapons to the free and generalised exercise of an epistemological critique of all by all, deriving from the field itself'. Here, then, competition appears to be part of 'the imperatives of rational polemics', with each of the participants having an interest in subordinating his egotistical interests 'to the rule of dialogic confrontation' (2000 [1997]: 119–120). Unfortunately, however, Bourdieu often goes from the notion of ideal-type to concrete description without due precaution, such that the latter ends up being generally idealised. His demonstration seems only to work if it is assumed that the reference point for the ideal of the scientific public sphere – that towards which all the others ought to aim in order to most effectively liberate the corporatism of the universal that they all harbour – is the model of pure mathematics.

Politics as a Corporatism of the Universal?

These reflections lead to a second argument bearing on the relation to establish between the corporatism of the universal and the political sphere. Are the social mechanisms that privilege reason and the universal restricted to the scientific field alone? Can politics not also be organised in such a way that it forms 'functionaries of humanity', in a way that the 'corporatism of the universal' prevails within it 'objectively'? Bourdieu gives two tendencially contradictory responses to this question.

On the one hand, similarly to the chapter from *Distinction* in which he deals with the political field, Bourdieu makes the general contention that agents in this field are only concerned with power struggles, and not with any universality comparable to that of the truth or of ethical authenticity. The scientific field tends 'to grant a practical primacy to the opposition between truth and error', and therefore 'an effective decision-making power to an agreement among specialists'. The political field, by contrast, is organised around the friend/enemy opposition and consequently tends to exclude the arbitrating invention of a third party (1990 [1987]: 831). Elsewhere, Bourdieu rejects the metaphor of war in his attempt to grasp the logic of the political, instead preferring that of the market, whose idea is presented through the terms of political offer and demand (1984 [1979]: 397–459).[3] In both cases, what appears to be excluded is the idea according to which public opinion can tend to play a role in public arbitration when a society is actually in the process of democratising and that this establishes a political public sphere. Moreover, the idea that democratic institutions, or at least some of them, can press the agents in struggle to adopt a universal stance is likewise excluded. Bourdieu (1984 [1979]: 27) is permanently tempted to reduce politics to the rivalry between elites for state power and to refuse citizens all critical political acumen – except in the form of access to knowledge popularised by sociologists and other scientists. Bourdieu endeavours to demonstrate that the idea of personal opinion is illusory, just like that of personal taste; that it is socially and historically determined, as also is opinion itself. It appears difficult that the opinion of citizens might, following the example of scientific knowledge, take up a certain distance in relation to that determination.[4] On this view, the corporatism of the universal driving intellectuals is unable to find any equivalent in civic life.

This first response that Bourdieu is tempted to give to the question of the relations between the corporatism of the universal and politics promotes an elitist view of the role of intellectuals: in a similar way to the avant-garde party once advocated by political movements inspired by Leninism, these latter purportedly have the monopoly on political interventions guided by the truth (or ethical purity). Such a politics is rather unconvincing, both from a cognitive and a normative viewpoint. Can a vibrant and institutionally guaranteed public sphere not constitute a potentially powerful vector of enlightened discussion about the problems of public life? Can the acts of scientists and writers find no echo in the action taken by ordinary citizens? Bourdieu himself recognises that the naturalised differences of the old order can be constituted 'as *political*, that is to say as likely to be contested and transformed' (1990: 26n.55; 2000 [1997]: 182–185). In this process, political reflexivity can echo what Bourdieu considers the specificity of social sciences: the critique of relations (and notably of relations of domination) which are reified as a second nature in everyday life. Moreover, it is no coincidence if one of the most positive evaluations of politicisation to be read in Bourdieu's work is expressed in an article dealing with masculine domination and feminist struggles: these latter are proof that the putting into question of social relations considered for centuries to be natural could stem from an emancipatory practice of everyday life, and in the political arena, well before critique in the field of science first became institutionalised (which does not mean that the latter cannot serve the former in a second stage). This is why the critique of state reason cannot be the exclusive prerogative of a scientific or artistic universalism, any more than it could be conducted in the name of universals that transcend public life. Quite to the contrary, a critique of state reason proves to be sharpest when undertaken in the name of the ideals of democracy. If we can grant Bourdieu the fact that human reason is thoroughly historical and that it resides 'in certain types of historical conditions, in certain social structures of dialogue and non-violent communication', then it must be added that such structures precisely constitute a primordial resort at the same time as an essential aim for every perspective of democratisation (1992: 174–201).

It is doubtless because he was cognisant of these objections that, in the last decade of his life, Bourdieu sketched a second response to the question of the relations between the corporatism of the universal and the political sphere. He began to consider that the political sphere can also be organised such that the practices deployed in it are always constrained to orient themselves toward a real universalisation. It is of interest to note the theoretical references under whose auspices Bourdieu carries out this analysis. On the one side stands Kant with his test of universality, which constitutes the point of anchorage on the basis of which an implicit claim is made for a normative type of universality. On the other hand, however, Bourdieu has no intention of endorsing any kind of moralisation of politics as founded on ahistorical presuppositions, as with Kant. To put the question in sociologically realist terms entails understanding that only a modification of the logic of the functioning of the political field will be able to carry along with it the development of a 'corporatism of the universal' in this domain: 'It would be a question of establishing social universes where, as in the Machiavellian ideal of the Republic, agents had an interest in virtue, disinterestedness, and devotion to public service and the common good. Political morality does not fall from heaven, and it is not innate to human nature. Only a *Realpolitik* of reason and morality can contribute favourably to the institution of a universe where all agents and their acts would be subject – notably through critique – to a kind of permanent test of universalisability which is practically instituted in the very logic of the field' (1998 [1994]: 144). Such a perspective is not purely utopian: history shows that dominant forces in struggle with one another have regularly availed themselves of the universal ('and, by dint of this, at least formally, [the] interests of the dominated') to the extent that they had to refer to it 'for the purposes of legitimation, or mobilization' (2000 [1997]: 103). Such a subordination to the universal, even if only outward, would enable the political field and, further still, the bureaucratic field and the state, to embody partially universalising rationales. As a result, the scientific field could be conceptualised as a 'reasonable utopia' serving as a model to 'indicate the principles of action aimed at promoting the equivalent, within the political field, of what is observed in the scientific field in its most autonomous forms: [...] a regulated competition, which would control itself [...] through social mechanisms capable of forcing agents to behave "rationally" and to sublimate their drives' (2000 [1997]: 126).

How are we to explain the fact that Bourdieu never went on to develop this intuition, that he counterbalanced it with opposed arguments until the very end, and that it never gave rise to an empirical research programme among his circle of collaborators or in the journal that he edited (2002b)? The above-mentioned absence of any ideal type of the public sphere no doubt heavily contributed to this. No doubt the limited scope of 'games of reason' or 'freedom' in the political field refers back to a pessimistic anthropology of the social bond, inherited from Weber much more than from Marx or Durkheim. Struggle and power relations, for Bourdieu, constitute the driving forces of all social relations, and this is so universally the case that the other relations do not merit being constituted as ideal types. The behaviour of individuals is, on this view, always 'interested' and therefore monological and strategico-instrumental – even as the types of interest vary and are not reducible to economic interest alone (1996 [1992]: 141–145; 1998 [1994]: 75–91). From this standpoint, conceptualising public sphere becomes understandably difficult, and the notion of corporatism of the universal tends to cast the process of universalisation as a result of strategic orientations rather than as the product of cooperation. Bourdieu recognised that not taking into account non-agonistic relations might constitute a real problem, but he relativised their place within social reality. For him, these relations are exceptional and based on what Aristotle calls *philia,* and as such can only be deployed within the family or between friends. Bourdieu adds that non-distorted communication, in the Habermasian sense, can only be attained in altogether extraordinary circumstances (1992). This statement, however, merely skirts the problem: a form of communication that is totally free of domination certainly is an exceptional phenomenon, but the same holds for situations in which only relations of force and symbolic or physical violence are at play to the exclusion of all cooperation between the persons concerned. The value of such categories lies in their ideality: they do not aim to grasp a human essence, and attempts to define some such essence can only end up in an interminable, rather fruitless quest. Forms of cooperation vary historically, just as do forms of domination, and they depend on the institution of determinate social mechanisms. This takes nothing away from the need to elaborate ideal types whose value is at once cognitive (they enable us to understand what, in a given situation, pertains to this or to that rationale) and normative (to put forward this or that and not another model also involves ethico-political arguments; basing oneself on a given model makes it possible to measure the gap separating it from reality; and lastly, the model furnishes a normative foundation for critique). Whenever Bourdieu gives a description of 'science', no doubt an ideal type is fundamentally at stake.[5] In some of his last writings he recognises this, but refrains from actually drawing any conclusions from it (2000 [1997]: 126; 2002b).[6]

In similar fashion, it is at once possible and necessary to put forward an ideal type of democracy that has a cognitive and normative import. It is clearly necessary to go beyond all 'provisional and deliberate reductionism', since this confines the social sciences to a strategy of suspicion and prohibits them from positively elaborating ideal types of historical freedom (1992: 115). To employ the terms of 'liberation' or 'emancipation' also entails recognising the legitimacy of normative discussions aiming to give depth and coherence to notions of freedom, political universality or justice. It is undoubtedly necessary for theories of justice to renounce all their transcendental pretensions and preoccupy themselves with the fact that politics – no matter how democratic – is necessarily irreducible to a social contract. Yet, for their part, the social sciences must make room for concrete studies and, each in their own theoretical field, for analytic concepts on which a reasoned normative reflection can be articulated. At stake, in particular, is to understand how democracy, without being the proper fate of mankind, can be instituted historically as a social mechanism that enhances rights, freedoms, and practices of universalisation. From this perspective, it is, for example, possible to conceive of rights as 'historical transcendentals'—to use one of Bourdieu's terms – that is to say, as socially instituted rules which favour an orientation towards an ethico-political universal. Similarly, it is also necessary to analyse the institutional mechanisms that, in the institutional political game, push or could push the various actors involved in the competition for power to defend the common good when they engage in the effective promotion of their own interests. Indeed, a whole field of reflections opens up in this regard, including everything from forms of ballot to legislative rules governing political competition, from modes of organisation to institutional structures for organising communication between elected members and citizens, and from the material infrastructures of civil society to the social characteristics of persons who devote themselves to politics.

A particular importance is assumed by reflections on an ideal type of public political sphere that take the diversity of its concrete forms into account (Fraser, 1992; Sintomer, 1998). Only such a notion can give conceptual meaning to the idea that the *Realpolitik* of reason can aim 'at favouring the setting up of non-distorted social structures of communication between the holders of power and the citizens' (2000 [1997]: 126). It alone is in a position to explicate the deployment of normative rationalities, which – while they may not claim a comparable objectivity or universality to a mathematical type of rationality – cannot be reduced to pure contingency or arbitrariness.[7] Lastly, the idea of a public political sphere enables us to understand better the homologies and differences between the various corporatisms of the universal capable of being instituted in the fields of politics, art and science. From the historical viewpoint of the *longue durée*, the various forms of public sphere are constituted according to a similar dynamic. Besides, in both the literary and political public spheres, we find a rather similar logic concerning the credibility of claims about the validity of statements (which may claim sincerity, authenticity, coherence and plausibility, but which can rarely be submitted to an analysis in terms of truth and error). In politics, there is also an observable tension between a logic 'of the quality' of the public sphere and a plebiscitary logic in which communication is emptied of any real argumentative content, and publicity marketing alone triumphs. A considerable historical and sociological literature already exists on these matters. For a large part, it simultaneously moves away from uniquely normative idealising views and from conceptions that, symmetrically, reduce public sphere to a manipulation of the masses by the power elite. These socio-historical works find a fulcrum in the renewal of a philosophical reflection on processes of deliberation that lay claim to realism.

Conclusion

As soon as the problematic of the corporatism of the universal is broadened to the political and a constellation of public spheres (scientific, literary and political) comes into theoretical consideration, it becomes possible to conceive the *Realpolitik* of reason differently to Bourdieu. It becomes possible to move away from a defence of the maximal autonomy of science and to avoid the failings of scientism in politics. It becomes possible to discard the idea that intellectual critique can be carried out from a putative bird's-eye view over the city: critical activity is an activity that can be shared, at least potentially, by both ordinary citizens and intellectuals, and the latter by no means have the monopoly over it. It is necessary to study the homologies and the gaps between scientific critique and artistic critique, intellectual critique and political critique, as well as the way in which they influence one another. On this basis, it becomes possible to envisage a genuine socio-history of intellectuals. The implications of such an approach are not limited to the cognitive dimension alone. On the back cover of the French edition of *The Weight of the World,* Bourdieu wrote: 'the reader will comprehend in closing this book that it offers another way of practicing politics'. However, there has to be yet another way of practising politics and the 'corporatism of the universal', one that is not the mere preserve of angels and *savants.* The social sciences have a duty to study the aspects whereby some political apparatuses promote a logic comparable to that which Bourdieu deems specific to a reflexive practice of the sociological interview (1999 [1993]: 608): the maximal reduction of the symbolic violence that accompanies communication between interlocutors of disparate social statuses.

Notes

1 Previous versions of this chapter have been published in Sintomer (1996) and Sintomer (2006).
2 See also Bourdieu (1996 [1992]: Postscript; 2000 [1997]; 2004 [2001]). Bourdieu extends his reasoning to the literary and artistic fields, which have also won their autonomy progressively over the course of recent centuries, and in which, by the same token, such strong values as 'ethic purity' are expressed.
3 These two possibilities were systematically developed by various currents inspired by Bourdieu in the French political sciences. See, on the one hand, Dobry (1992) and, on the other, Gaxie (1993) and Offerlé (1987).
4 It is true that, objecting to his adversaries' accusation of quietism, Bourdieu (1993 [1984]) retorts: 'Does that mean that one can only mobilize on the basis of illusions?' He adds that if opinion is socially determined, it is preferable to know it, before concluding with the following words: 'if we have some chance of having personal opinions, it is perhaps on condition that we know our opinions are not spontaneously so'. Bourdieu, however, leaves unanswered the question of knowing whether this veritably personal opinion, which implicitly refers to a reflexive autonomy, can be reached by agents situated in the political field. Reading the pages devoted to this field in *Distinction*, the reader is given cause to doubt it: the analysis bears uniquely on the conditioning of the *habitus* and of opinions, and passes in silence over anything that might lead towards a notion of the autonomous action and reflection of citizens.
5 Besides, it would be necessary to propose an ideal-type that operates somewhat differently to the scientific 'ideal', which takes further account of the potential contributions of mobilised citizens in its research orientation. Instead of basing oneself simply on the autonomy of the scientific field, this model would consider a certain opening up of the sciences out of their enclaves as a positive phenomenon. At the same time, it would be more pertinent cognitively in helping us to understand the contemporary evolution of relations between the sciences and the rest of society.
6 In the 1990s, Bourdieu directs his gaze further towards a 'comparative anthropology'. He thus attempts to extract a transhistorical law, namely that of the symbolic profit from which every individual would benefit if he put himself, at least outwardly, in the service of the universal. Bourdieu thereby supplements his philosophy of suspicion with a theory of legitimacy (Colliot-Thélène, 1995). This explication does not work to contradict the contention that advances in universalisation can only be the products of determinate social structures, and in particular of the institution of fields whose logic pushes the agents towards strategies of universalisation. Bourdieu simply presents this transhistorical law as a primary given, as a necessary condition for the appearance of fields with more virtuous logics: 'The genesis of a universe of this sort is not conceivable if one does not posit the motor, which is the universal recognition of the universal, that is, the official recognition of the primacy of the group and its interests over the individual and the individual's interests, which all groups profess in the very fact of affirming themselves as groups' (1998 [1994]: 89–90 and 141–144).
7 If Bourdieu could only conceive of politics on the mode of struggles between elites for power, thereby ruling out the idea of judgement from a third party, it was doubtless because he lacked this notion.

References

Atten, Michel and Dominique Pestre (2002) *Heinrich Hertz. L'administration de la preuve*, PUF, Paris.

Bourdieu, Pierre (1984 [1979]) *Distinction: A Social Critique of the Judgement of Taste*, transl. Richard Nice, London: Routledge.

Bourdieu, Pierre (1990 [1987]) *In Other words: Essays Towards a Reflexive Sociology*, trans. Matthew Adamson, Stanford: Stanford University Press.

Bourdieu, Pierre (1990) 'La domination masculine', *Actes de la recherche en sciences sociales* 84: 2–31.

Bourdieu, Pierre (1992) 'Doxa and Common Life', *New Left Review*, 191, January/February.

Bourdieu, Pierre (1993 [1984]) *Sociology in Question*, London: Sage.

Bourdieu, Pierre (1993b) 'Un entretien avec Pierre Bourdieu', *Le Monde*, 7 December.

Bourdieu, Pierre (1996 [1992]) *The Rules of Art: Genesis and Structure of the Literary Field*, trans. Susan Emanuel, Stanford: Stanford University Press.

Bourdieu, Pierre (1997) *Les usages sociaux de la science*, Paris: INRA Éditions.

Bourdieu, Pierre (1998 [1994]) *Practical Reason: On the Theory of Action*, trans. Randal Johnson, Stanford CA: Stanford University Press, 1998.

Bourdieu, Pierre (1999 [1993]) *The Weight of the World: Social Suffering in Contemporary Society*, trans. Priscilla Parkhurst Ferguson, London: Polity Press.

Bourdieu, Pierre (2000 [1997]) *Pascalian Meditations*, trans. Richard Nice, London: Polity Press.

Bourdieu, Pierre (2002a) *Propos sur le champ politique*, Lyon: Presses Universitaires de Lyon.

Bourdieu, Pierre (2002b) 'Science, politique et sciences sociales', in *Actes de la recherche en sciences sociales*, 141–142, March, Paris: Maison des sciences de l'homme.

Bourdieu, Pierre (2004 [2001]) *Science of Science and Reflexivity*, trans. Richard Nice, Chicago: University of Chicago Press.

Bourdieu, Pierre and Loïc Wacquant (1992) *An Invitation to Reflexive Sociology*, Cambridge: Polity Press.

Callon, Michel, Pierre Lascoume and Yannick Barthes (2001) *Agir dans un monde incertain. Essai sur la démocratie technique*, Paris: Éditions du Seuil.

Colliot-Thélène, Catherine (1995) 'La sociologie réflexive, l'anthropologie, l'histoire', *Critique*, August/September.

Dobry, Michel (1992) *Sociologie des crises politiques*, Paris: Presses de la FNSP.

Durkheim, Émile (1984 [1893]) *The Division of Labor in Society*, trans. W. D. Halls, 2nd Edition, New York: Free Press.

Fraser, Nancy (1992) 'Rethinking the Public Sphere: A Contribution to the Critique of Actually Existing Democracy', in Craigh Calhoun (ed.) *Habermas and the Public Sphere*, MIT Press, Cambridge/London.

Foucault, Michel (1980) 'Truth and Power', Interview with Alessandro Fontana and Pasquale Pasquino, in Colin Gordon (ed.) *Michel Foucault: Power/Knowledge*, transl. Colin Gordon, Leo Marshall, John Mepham and Kate Soper, New York/London: Harvester Wheatsheaf.

Gaxie, Daniel (1993) *La démocratie représentative*, Paris: Montchrestien.

Offerlé, Michel (1987) *Les partis politiques*, Paris: PUF.

Pestre, Dominique (2003) *Science, argent et politique. Un essai d'interprétation*, Paris: INRA éditions.

Sclove, Richard (1995) *Democracy and Technology*, New York and London: The Guilford Press.
Sintomer, Yves (1996) 'Le corporatisme de l'Universel et la cité', *Actuel Marx*, 20.
Sintomer, Yves (1998) 'Sociologie de l'espace public et corporatisme de l'universel', *L'homme et la société*, 4, Paris: L'Harmattan, pp. 7–19.
Sintomer, Yves (2006) 'La critique intellectuelle entre corporatisme de l'universel et espace public', in Hans-Peter Müller and Yves Sintomer (eds.) *Pierre Bourdieu. Théories et sens pratique*, Paris: La Découverte, pp. 207–222.

CHAPTER FIFTEEN

Practice as Temporalisation: Bourdieu and Economic Crisis

Lisa Adkins

Introduction

This chapter will examine the question of whether Bourdieu's social theory can be mobilised to understand our recent and ongoing global economic crisis. This may seem an odd question to pose on many fronts, not least because – and with the exception of markets for normatively defined cultural goods[1] – Bourdieu's corpus is rarely, if ever, called upon to engage with strictly economic processes and formations.[2] And this is the case despite the fact that Bourdieu (2005 [2000]) dedicated a whole volume to the study of the social structures of the economy and despite the fact that in his later, arguably more polemical, work (Bourdieu, 1998; 1999 [1993]; 2003 [2001]) he directly engaged with the political economy of neo-liberalism, mounting a sustained critique of what he termed the 'tyranny of the neo-liberal market'.

Yet, while this is so, Bourdieu's social theory is widely critiqued for its lack of traction in regard to economic processes, not least because of its inability to grasp the specificity of capitalist economic relations. Craig Calhoun (1993), for example, has argued that despite the emphasis we find in Bourdieu on the *forms* of capital (Bourdieu, 1986), what is striking is that nowhere in Bourdieu's social theory do we find an elaboration of the specificity of capitalist capital. Thus, while Bourdieu understands the various capitals he describes as comprising accumulated labour, he fails to specify what differentiates capitalist capital from such labour. More particularly, Bourdieu fails to elaborate the process of abstraction and quantification of labour into units of time, that is, the process of conversion of labour into exchangeable equivalents, which is both paradigmatic of and specific to capitalist social relations. Hence, whereas in Marx capitalist capital is understood as homogenous abstract units of labour time, in Bourdieu it is simply conceived of as accumulated labour (see Adkins, 2008). Understanding capital as congealed labour, Calhoun goes on, will never allow us to capture the specificity of capitalist capital – of how and why capitalism is able to constantly expand its reach and transcend its own limits and boundaries – since it is unable to grasp the extraordinary levels of convertibility encountered in capitalism, levels of convertibility that are precisely constituted in the very process of the production of abstract universal equivalents. Jon Beasley-Murray (2001) also observes that Bourdieu ignores the process of abstraction specific to capitalism, especially the conversion of living into abstract labour. Yet, while Calhoun is concerned that ignoring this process brackets the exponential rates of exchange specific to capitalist capital, Beasley-Murray is concerned that ignoring the process of abstraction amounts to a refusal to engage with the process of the production and accumulation of surplus value specific to capitalism, a refusal which amounts to a failure to confront the exploitation of human labour power characteristic of and inherent to capitalist production.

Given the apparent failure on the part of Bourdieu to confront the specificity of processes of capitalist accumulation, it is perhaps of little surprise that his general theoretical resources have not been put to use to engage with recent economic events. This is even less surprising if we consider that our current economic crisis is widely understood to concern a crisis of capitalism, indeed to concern a reaching of the limit point of a particular mode of capitalist accumulation, namely neo-liberal accumulation (see, for example, Law, 2009). In this context we might quite reasonably ask the following question: of what possible use is a social theory that fails to specify the dynamics of capitalism for understanding a crisis in those very dynamics? And, in as much as a crisis always implies social change and movement (Brown, 2005), we might add to this another question: how useful is a social theory which is concerned not primarily with crisis or change but predominately with stasis and social reproduction (Jenkins, 2002) for coming to terms with events which have been described as involving 'catastrophic generic change' (Poovey, 2009)?

It is also of little surprise that Bourdieu's later polemical work on neo-liberalism has not been put to use in regard to recent economic events. For not only has this part of his oeuvre been critiqued for a lack of sophistication and seen as a break from his own core socio-theoretical propositions (see, for example, McRobbie, 2002a),[3] but – more significantly for my concerns here – in his later works Bourdieu characterised neo-liberalism as doxic. Of what use, we might reasonably ask, is such an understanding when recent economic events suggest the end of that very doxa? We also might quite fairly ask of what use is a general social theory in relation to recent economic events, which rarely, if ever, touches on the issues that appear to be at the centre of economic crisis, including the performative power of socio-technical devices, especially the power of those devices and instruments concerned with financial calculation and measure (see Callon et al, 2007). Little wonder then that in existing accounts of recent economic events the work of Bourdieu rarely, if ever, features with the resources of what has been termed the 'new economic sociology' (McFall, 2009) being favoured not only above Bourdieu's approach but also above those approaches to the economy that might generally be located in the 'social embeddedness school' of economic sociology (Granovetter, 1985; Polanyi, 2001 [1957]).[4]

Nonetheless, despite the range of objections that could be raised in relation to thinking the economic crisis with and through the theoretical resources of Bourdieu, it is the contention of this chapter that in Bourdieu we can find important resources for this task, even if those resources may need certain refinements and modifications, and even if, at first sight, those resources appear to bear little connection to or resonance with recent economic events. The usefulness and relevance of these resources, however, may only be made explicit if we understand these events as concerning a reworking of time, an understanding that positions Bourdieu's understanding of temporality, and especially of practice as temporalisation, as rich and provocative, not only in regard to recent economic events, but also in regard to questions of economic futures. This chapter, therefore, contains two key interventions. The first is the claim that *recent economic events concern a crisis of time* or, and perhaps better said, a restructuring of time; and the second is the claim that *in Bourdieu we find unexpected resources that help us to elaborate this restructuring*. To lay out these two interventions it is necessary that I first turn to the issue of time and in particular the place of time in recent economic events.

Trading the Future?

A frequently rehearsed account of the financial actions and dealings that sparked our current global economic recession turns on a particular and normative account of time. Specifically, this is an account in which traders, dealers and finance capital in general are positioned as having engaged in an activity that *should not* have taken place, namely trading in the future at the expense of the present. Adams et al (2009), for instance, suggest that our current global economic recession was 'sparked by finance capital's delirious trade in futures and risks' (Adams et al, 2009: 254), a trade, which makes violently plain that our current moment is defined by a state of anticipation, that is, a thinking and living towards the future. The related credit-led financialisation of everyday life has been understood in similar terms, that is, as compelling forms of life and ways of being orientated towards and hinging on uncertain futures. A number of social phenomena are considered as evidence of the emergence anticipatory ways of life: consumers mortgaging their futures in the form of indebtedness to secure commodities in the here and now (Law, 2009); farmers obtaining credit for what might happen to their crops (Adams et al, 2009); company and organisation valuations not on the grounds of present assets but on the grounds of events yet to come (Marazzi, 2007); and calculations of the value of workers and workforces not on the basis of existing skills, experiences and capabilities but on potential ability, that is, on their ability to deal with events that are yet to take place (Sennett, 2006).

Similar to the financial dealers trading in (virtual and actual) futures, such anticipatory life forms are generally understood in no uncertain terms as negative. Adams et al (2009), for example, expose such a negativity via a set of reflections on strategies of refusal in regard to anticipation, while Sennett argues that the shift in skill he describes not only raises the spectre of uselessness, but also deprives people of a sense of narrative movement, that is, of the accumulation of experience and of connections between events in time. It also 'eschews sensate impressions, divides analyzing from believing, ignores the glue of emotional attachment, penalises digging deep' (Sennett, 2006: 121–122). I will return to the issue of the severing of connections between events in time as well as to the eschewing of sensate impressions, and for now I will also suspend any judgement regarding the imperative to anticipate. Instead, it seems important first to focus on the version of time that such accounts enact. For these are accounts that place the politics of time in particular and issues of temporality in general at the heart of our contemporary moment, a positioning of time with which a range of writers from a number of disciplines appear to agree (see, for example: Adam, 2004; Colebrook, 2009; Coleman, 2008; Edelman, 2005; Grosz, 2004). Yet, accounts of increasingly anticipatory forms of life also carry with them a further set of assumptions regarding time. These include the notion that the future should be at some distance from the present (or that a boundary should exist between the present and the future), the conjecture that the future can (and should be) protected via prudent action in the here and now, the assumption that the future should not be traded as a resource (that is, that it should not be commodified), and the supposition that the future should not determine the present. But most significantly, from the point of view of my concerns here, these accounts share two linked assumptions. First, they assume that the present – or, more precisely, a certain version of the present, one in which, on Sennett's account, experience can be accumulated and connections can be made between events in time – is being destroyed by a certain relationship to the future, namely by the injunction to anticipate. Second, they assume that the injunction towards thinking and living in the direction of the future is one which is relatively new or, at the very least, has intensified in our current moment.

Yet, many of these assumptions regarding time fly in the face of numerous sociological accounts of temporality. They pull against, for instance, Helga Nowotny's (1994) account not of a present under threat, undercut or destroyed by the future, but of a loss of temporal horizons. More specifically, they challenge Nowotny's thesis of the disappearance of the category of the future and the emergence of an *extended* present. Central to the disappearance of the future, Nowotny maintains, is the emergence of a present geared to accelerated innovation, a present, which 'devour[s] the future' (Nowotny, 1994: 11). Thus, she notes that a range of technologies and socio-technical devices have increased the permeability of the time boundary between present and future via facilitating temporal uncoupling and decentralisation. Such technologies and devices also produce different models of time and, in particular, generate presents that are detached from linearity. Indeed, as Nowotny remarks, with the end of an age in which the belief in linearity and progress were maintained by the time structure of industrial production 'the category of the future is losing much of its attractiveness' (1994: 11).

What is striking about this account is not only that it raises questions about the assumption that the present is being undercut by the future, but also that as a substantive sociological account of time, and especially of the changing boundaries between the past, present and future and, thus, of shifts in and to the categories and experience of time, it challenges some of the fundamental presuppositions regarding time found in accounts concerned with the rise of anticipation. Specifically, rather than assuming where boundaries between past present and future should be, or how time should be experienced, Nowotny's account alerts us to how these boundaries and experiences change, in short, to how these are pre-eminently sociological, rather than normative, issues. In fact, Nowotny's account makes clear that to make such normative assumptions regarding time is to close down the sociological imagination, indeed to assume that time itself should (and does) remain the same.

Anticipation: Time in the Making

But it is not just in substantive sociological accounts of temporal change but also in social theory that we can find challenges to the assumptions regarding time found in accounts of intensifying anticipation. While not particularly celebrated for his work on time, Bourdieu can be regarded as a thinker prepared to confront such challenges, particularly when insisting that the future is not a contingent possibility (a possible, which may or may not happen) or a distant horizon separated from the present, but always already present in the immediate present, a future that is always already there. As I have elaborated elsewhere (Adkins, 2009a), for Bourdieu the future is always already present in the immediate present because agents are ordinarily immersed in the forthcoming or, more precisely, agents practically and pre-reflexively anticipate the forthcoming as a routine part of action. Put differently, the future is always already present in the immediate present because *practice* – for Bourdieu, following Husserl (1931) – is *protensive* in character. Indeed, Bourdieu suggests that a pre-reflexive – that is, unconscious – aiming at the forthcoming is the most common form of the experience of time, although this experience is itself paradoxical, since, similar to the experience of the self-evidence of the familiar world, *time* does not offer itself to be felt or sensed and passes largely *unnoticed.* According to Bourdieu, then, time is – for the most part – *unexperienced.*

The ordinary practical anticipation of the forthcoming that Bourdieu proffers is particularly clear in the case of emotions, through which the body sees the forthcoming – the oncoming car or threatening dog – as something already there, that is, as something irremediable. In such instances, Bourdieu describes how 'the body is snatched by the forthcoming of the world' (Bourdieu, 2000 [1997]: 208). Yet, beyond these instances of fear, Bourdieu claims that similar processes are at work for mundane action. In a game of football, for instance, a good player positions himself or herself not where the ball is, but where the ball is about to land. In this instance, the forthcoming is not simply a possible, but it is already present in the configuration of the game, including the present positions and postures of teammates and opponents (Bourdieu, 2000 [1997]: 208).

For Bourdieu, however, the inscription of the future in the immediate present – or, put differently, the presence of the forthcoming in the configuration of the game – is not a simple given of practice;[5] rather, it is constituted in the relationship between the habitus and the social world, and more precisely, in the relationship between the dispositions, durable habits, schemes of appreciation and action with which agents are endowed (the habitus) and the tendencies of social fields. As is well rehearsed (see, for example, McNay, 1999), for Bourdieu fields are only fully viable if their logics are durably embedded in the dispositions of agents operating within them (Bourdieu, 1977 [1972]); that is, and to put it slightly differently, fields can only exist insofar as the unconscious and pre-reflexive dispositions, habits and schemes of agents are aligned with the objective principles of fields. Such schemes, Bourdieu writes, are 'the product of incorporation of the structures and tendencies of the world [...] [and] make it possible to adapt endlessly to partially modified contexts, and to construct the situation as a complex whole endowed with meaning, in a practical operation of quasi-bodily *anticipation* of the immanent tendencies of fields' (Bourdieu, 2000 [1997]: 139, emphasis in original). It is then because agents are incorporated in the world – that their dispositions are open to the very structures of the world – indeed that dispositions are the incorporated form of those structures, which enable a routine, pre-reflexive and practical anticipation of the future. And this is so because in the relationship between habitus and field the *future* is inscribed as an *objective* potential or trace in the immediate given. Specifically, 'what is to be done' is defined in the relationship between the structure of expectations constitutive of a particular habitus, and the structure of probabilities, which is constitutive of a given social space (a social field).

Bourdieu illustrates the practical anticipation of the forthcoming, engendered in the relationship between habitus and field, with reference to a variety of examples, but particularly relevant in the context of this chapter is the description of anticipation in the economic field that he provides in his book *The Social Structures of the Economy*.[6] In line with his general theorisation of social space, Bourdieu posits that to operate in the economic field agents must be endowed with the habits and dispositions of that field. That is, agents must be endowed with dispositions engendered by the incorporation of the experience of constant or recurring situations which are adapted to new, but not necessarily unprecedented, situations. Such engendering provides a practical mastery of situations, including situations of uncertainty, since the habitus 'grounds a relation to the future which is not that of a project, as an aiming for possible outcomes [...], but a relation of practical anticipation [...] grasping time-to-come as a quasi present (and not as a contingent future)' (Bourdieu, 2005 [2000]: 214). By virtue of the regularities inscribed in the recurrent games that are played out in it, the economic field therefore

> offers a predictable and calculable future and agents acquire in it transmissible skills and dispositions (sometimes called 'routines') which form the basis of practical anticipations that are at least roughly well founded. (Bourdieu, 2005 [2000]: 196)

Thus, just as agents operating in other fields practically anticipate the forthcoming, for agents in the economic field the future is always already present in the immediate present, allowing agents routinely to anticipate the forthcoming. Yet, and following Granovetter's (1985) insistence that economic action is always embedded in networks of social relations, Bourdieu warns that this practical anticipation of the future in the economic field – the grasping of time yet-to-come as a quasi-present – should not be understood – or, rather, misunderstood – to concern a rational calculus of risk, as economic science would suggest. Indeed, Bourdieu maintains that while economic orthodoxy will always reduce the practical mastery of situations of uncertainty to a rational calculus of risk, construing the anticipation of the behaviour of others as a calculation of the intent of opponents, understanding economic action and especially the practical anticipation of the future as engendered by the habitus – that is, by collective, historical and unconscious structures – throws the calculating agent of economic orthodoxy into radical doubt.[7]

I will return to the issue of time and the economic field, but for now it seems important to reflect on how Bourdieu's understanding of time and temporalisation raises challenges to accounts of increasingly anticipatory ways of life. At least four issues stand out here.

First, Bourdieu's insistence that ordinary action is anticipatory and that the future is already inscribed in the immediate present raises questions around the assumption, found in accounts of increasingly anticipatory ways of life, that the injunction to anticipate is relatively new and specific to our present moment. For in as much as ordinary action is necessarily anticipatory, how can it be claimed that action attuned to the forthcoming is specific to the present?

Second, Bourdieu's understanding of the inscription of the forthcoming in the immediate present surely also questions the assumption, found in accounts of the injunction to anticipate, that the present is being undercut or destroyed by the future. For if, as Bourdieu claims, the forthcoming is always and necessarily inscribed in the present, that is, if the present contains the future, how can it be claimed that the forthcoming can undercut and destabilise the present? How, for example, can the forthcoming undercut the accumulation of experience and compromise connections between events in time if the forthcoming is inscribed in those very practices?

Third, Bourdieu's account of time must surely make us question the normative assumptions in accounts of the injunction to anticipate that the future should be at some distance from the present, that a boundary should exist between the present and the future, and that the proper sequence of time is one in which the present precedes the future. For if the forthcoming is already present in the configuration of the game, how can such claims be upheld? How can we, for instance, uphold the claim that the proper sequence of time is one in which the future is at a distance from and comes after the present, when the future is already inscribed in ordinary practical action in the here and now?

Yet, perhaps the most significant – and fourth – challenge that Bourdieu's conception of time raises to accounts of increasingly anticipatory ways of life is the insistence that time is not an entity that simply passes. More specifically, for Bourdieu, time is not a simple medium through which or vessel in which events take place, nor does time operate externally to subjects and their actions. For far from practice simply taking place in time, for Bourdieu practice *makes* time. In short, Bourdieu insists that 'practice [is] temporalisation'

(Bourdieu, 2000 [1997]: 206). This insistence is of some significance when we consider that in accounts of increasingly anticipatory ways of life time and events (or practice) tend to be separated out. Thus, in Sennett's account of the undercutting of the present by the forthcoming, the present under threat is one in which connections can (and should) be made between events *in* time, that is, a present in which time operates and proceeds externally to events. Yet for Bourdieu events (or practices) do not only take place in time, but they also – more significantly – *make* time. As we have seen, the future, for example, is not separate from or an external horizon to practice but, and in as much as agents are endowed with the habitus adjusted to the field, is routinely constituted in practice (for instance, in a game of football). And while we can make use of Bourdieu to problematise the idea of a present in which time is external to events, the very notion of *practice as temporalisation* also makes it clear that the futures at issue in accounts of increasing anticipation – including the traded, mortgaged and contracted futures at issue in the global financial crisis – are not pre-existing blocks of yet-to-come time which have been (wrongly) subjected to certain practices (trading, contracting and mortgaging), as critics of the injunction to anticipate tend to assume. Whereas critics of anticipatory forms of life presuppose not only the latter, but also that the future is and should be a separate horizon from present practices and events, Bourdieu's notion of practice as temporalisation alerts us to the fact that traded, contracted and mortgaged futures are made in the present, that is, that they are in fact made in and through the very practices of trading, contracting and mortgaging.

Bourdieu's account of practice as temporalisation, however, does more than problematise the idea that the future has been, or can be, traded, and that, by implication, the recent financial crisis concerns such a trading. For it highlights a further normative assumption at work in critiques of the injunction to anticipate. Specifically, both Bourdieu's injunction that to perform practical acts is precisely to temporalise – that is, to make time – and the implications of this injunction for recent economic events – namely that practices such as trading, mortgaging and contracting do not stand outside of time or colonise existing futures, but make futures – make clear that critics of the injunction to anticipate are (problematically) objecting to the entanglement of economic practices with issues of time and temporalisation and demanding their separation. Indeed, we might speculate that the desire to separate out present and future on the part of such critics precisely concerns such a demand.

And it is not only Bourdieu's oeuvre that permits us to speculate this to be the case, but also the range of voices currently being heard which explicitly object to the entanglement of economic practice with time and demand their disentanglement. 'Don't mortgage our children's future', a US Republican senator recently barked in a CNN commentary critical of the Democratic government's economic stimulus plan for the US economy;[8] responding to the economic crisis, do not 'mortgage the future', the Bank for International Settlements warns governments, banks and consumers;[9] 'Gordon Brown is mortgaging our future' claim the UK's – formerly opposition – Conservative party;[10] while a journalist for the *The Times* newspaper claims that our future has been mortgaged by 'insane spendaholics', who she names as the then current UK Labour government.[11] Thus, it seems that it is not only financial traders and dealers who have problematically entangled economic practice and time, but also banks, governments and consumers.

Time is Money

Yet in response to such demands to separate out economic practice from time, we might, following Bourdieu, point out that economic practice – and in as much as it is *practice* – is always entangled with time, a point made particularly clear by the case of industrial capitalist production, where 'time is money' (Adam, 1994; Hassan, 2003; O'Carroll, 2008). Specifically, for capitalist industrial production, not only do rates of profit relate to rates of speed in production (where doing things faster and more efficiently produces increases in profits),[12] but those rates are measured in and as units of clock time, that is, in abstract, quantitative, homogenised and reversible units of the clock. Indeed, for the case of capitalist industrial production, not only are rates of profit and production measured in such units, but such time is hegemonic (Postone, 1993; Thompson, 1967). It is, moreover, precisely measurement in terms of abstract units of clock time that enables the exponential rates of exchange specific to industrial capitalism noted by Calhoun in his critique of Bourdieu's understanding of capital. In particular, the abstraction and quantification of labour into units of clock time, or the conversion of labour into exchangeable abstract equivalents, is the precise process which generates exponential rates of exchange, a conversion, which also allows the extraction of surplus from human labour, that is, the process by which capitalist exploitation of human labour takes place.

Thus, far from being disentangled from economic practice, time is central to and for such practice, an entanglement, which is made dramatically clear by the case of industrial capitalism. Yet, while we might posit – following Bourdieu – that economic practice will always concern temporalisation, and while the case of industrial capitalism unambiguously demonstrates the entanglement of economic practice with time, the case of industrial capitalism is – in a rather paradoxical fashion – of some significance for, and raises important challenges to, Bourdieu's theorisation of time. As we have seen for both Calhoun and Beasley-Murray, Bourdieu's failure to grasp the process of abstraction (the conversion of living labour into abstract and quantifiable units of time) specific to capitalist capital is ultimately a failure to confront the dynamics of capitalism, including processes of exploitation. But we might add to this and say that Bourdieu's general failure to elaborate the hegemony of clock time for the case of industrial capitalism, along with a failure to specify the operations and characteristics of that time, not only leads to a failure to confront the dynamics of capitalism, but confounds his insistence that time should not be understood as operating externally to subjects and their actions, as 'a thing with which we have a relationship of externality, that of a subject facing an object' (Bourdieu, 2000 [1997]: 206). This is so because, as a form of time, clock time is one arranged exogenously to practices and events, acting paradigmatically as an external measure of events, witnessed in measures such as production rates and targets, profit ratios and predictions, working day and working break lengths (Gilbert, 2007; Adkins, 2009b). And it does such measuring in abstract, quantitative, reversible, homogenous units. Contrary to Bourdieu's understanding of temporalisation as practice, in clock time phenomena and time are, in other words, separated out. In short, in clock time events do not make time but take place in time. Bourdieu's failure to recognise and elaborate the hegemony, operations and characteristics of clock time for industrial capitalism therefore not only – as Calhoun and Beasley-Murray observe – limits the ability of his social theory to capture the dynamics and specificities of capitalism, but also – and in as much as clock time operates externally to the events it attempts to measure – throws his account of time, of practice as temporalisation, into radical doubt.

So we have, or at least appear to have, a set of contradictions in regard to Bourdieu's understanding of time in general and in regard to time and economic practice in particular. On the one hand, and as I have already suggested, Bourdieu's understanding of practice as temporalisation permits us to cut through and problematise various normative assumptions concerning time, for example, that time should flow in one direction or another, or that there should be a certain sequencing of time, including the assumption that the future should operate as a distant horizon vis-à-vis present practices and events. In addition, Bourdieu's understanding that anticipation is a mundane feature of practice also warns that a degree of caution may be required around the claim that ways of life are increasingly anticipatory. The notion of practice as temporalisation also allows us to problematise the view that economic practices should (and can) be held at a distance from time and, therefore, question the view – expressed by all manner of voices in regard to the global financial crisis and its aftermath – that the future can be colonised, traded or commodified. Hence, as I have argued here, Bourdieu's social theory helps us to understand that, far from existing at a distance from economic presents, futures in general are made in practices, and financial futures in particular are made in economic practices, such as mortgaging, trading and contracting.

Yet while Bourdieu's social theory permits us to develop these kinds of insights, we might reasonably ask to what extent are they destabilised by his sidestepping of the issue of clock time and its hegemonic status in industrial capitalism. Does the bracketing of an abstract and 'externalist' form of time, one that moreover is at the very core of the logic and dynamics of capitalist accumulation, mean that Bourdieu's social theory is set to remain apt and germane for grasping issues of symbolic and cultural value and a rather blunt instrument in regard to economic practices, especially capitalist economic practices? Certainly, Calhoun and Beasley-Murray understand this to be the case. But while it may be correct to state that Bourdieu ignored and bracketed the hegemony of the clock and in so doing sidestepped a form of time which has radical implications for the status and relevance of his notion of practice as temporalisation, a closer look at the relationship between time and contemporary economic practices suggests that this bracketing may not be fatal. In fact, the nature of this relationship seems to suggest that, while it may well be the case that Bourdieu's social theory shot wide of the key dynamics and processes of industrial capitalism, for post-industrial or post-Fordist capitalism, this may be far from so. And this latter is the case because post-Fordist economic practices indicate an end to the hegemony of clock time and the emergence of a form of time in the economic field that is more akin to the conception of temporality that can be found in Bourdieu's analysis, that is, a form of time which is not simply a vessel for events but one in which time and events proceed together. In other words, the critical analysis of the relationship between time and contemporary economic practices suggests that while Bourdieu's social theory will never be a key resource for understanding the dynamics and processes of *industrial capitalism*, far greater traction can be found for the case of *post-Fordist capitalism*, including the recent and ongoing global economic crisis.

Money is Time

Consider, for example, the case of financial prediction. For many, financial prediction and related practices, such as economic forecasting and foreseeing, are increasingly blunt instruments, not least because of the novel forms of value unfolding in post-Fordist regimes of production which are not easily captured by such devices (see, for example, Marazzi, 2007). Indeed, the recent financial crisis – widely reported as unpredicted and unexpected, that is, as not amenable to instruments of prediction and foreseeing – seems to indicate that this view may well hold water. Yet, we can modify this view when we consider that in practices such as prediction and forecasting the relationship between time and events is not necessarily fixed but open to (and perhaps increasingly open to) *change and flux*. In a recent discussion of a specific predictive financial instrument, namely the yield curve of the US Treasury, Zaloom (2009) makes this shifting relation between time and events particularly clear. Specifically, Zaloom charts a shifting relationship between time and money, one where rather than standing outside of events, mapping and measuring the value of money, time is increasingly fused with money (and, hence, with events). In short, rather than acting as an external measure of events (as we encounter paradigmatically in clock time), in the practices associated with the yield curve, time unfolds with events.

As Zaloom explains, the yield curve of the US Treasury maps U.S. bonds' future value and is 'a widely used indicator of economic strength' (Zaloom, 2009: 247) both in the U.S. and internationally. The curve is a device for understanding risk and time in the U.S. Treasury market, and it does so by mapping treasury yields, that is, the relationship between interest rates and the time to maturity of a bond, a mapping which 'offers a way to understand the market's collective assessment of the future' (Zaloom, 2009: 247). While, as Zaloom describes, yield curve analysis had existed in the 1960s, its significance emerged in the 1970s and 1980s, that is, during a period of major transformation in global finance, including the floating of US currencies and interest rates on the open market following the collapse of the Bretton Woods agreement. Thus, rather than being fixed by the U.S. government, the market began to set the prices of dollars, bonds and interest rates. Before this shift, Zaloom goes on, bonds had been dealt as 'discrete packages of time' (Zaloom, 2009: 252), with traders being assigned to separate markets in two, five and ten-year bonds. Hence, for a two year bond, traders 'bought and sold the security looking at the risks that lay in the economy to the point of the bond's expiration' (Zaloom, 2009: 253). In short (and while Zaloom herself does not explain it in these terms), when the prices of dollars, bonds and interest rates were fixed, time and bonds were held as separate entities with bonds moving in and through time, and time acting as an external measure of yield and bond duration.

During the 1970s, however, the increasing deregulation of financial markets and especially market price setting shifted the relationship between time and money. Instead of acting as an external measure of financial objects, time became both part of those very objects and an object or event in and of itself. Zaloom describes, for instance, how as the market floating of price setting took place, and on receipt of the company's first computer, a mathematician working at a New York bond house used it to calculate the prices of bonds and even fractions of bonds and began trading on the basis of these calculations. Such calculations connected bonds that were previously traded as separate entities (for example, two and ten year bonds), a connection which crucially generated opportunities to exploit 'the relationships between future points in time' (2009: 253). In brief, such techniques 'generated profit making opportunities from temporal relationships' (2009: 252). Such practices therefore transformed the very materiality of bonds – instead of simply moving in and being measured by time, bonds themselves became time, indeed such practices transformed bonds from discrete objects moving *in* time into 'a continuum of moments' (Zaloom, 2009: 252). The unfixing of the price of dollars and interest rates therefore created a new relationship between time and phenomena, with the latter (such as bonds) becoming increasingly temporalised and temporalising. Indeed, in deregulated financial markets time itself emerged as an object of innovation. Thus, contrary to the case of industrial capitalism, where time is money, in deregulated finance markets, money has become time.

This previous point is crucial, for it allows us to see, once again, how the practices of financial traders, as well as of governments and consumers, have not involved a simple trade, commodification or colonisation of pre-existing futures; but rather that these practices relate to *a shift in time itself*. To be exact, in deregulated financial markets, time has ceased to operate as an external vessel for practice and has increasingly merged with events. And it is in this sense that we find resonances with Bourdieu's understanding of time. For just as Bourdieu insists that time is not a 'thing' in which events take place (that time is not something that simply 'passes') and that practice is temporalisation, in deregulated financial markets, *practices and events are both temporalised and temporalise*. In short, in deregulated financial markets, time has increasingly taken on the characteristics of the form of time theorised by Bourdieu: events and objects (such as bonds) have become forms of time, and time itself has become an object of both innovation and differentiation. While we might therefore rightly chastise Bourdieu for his lack of attention to the hegemony of clock time for the case of industrial capitalism and his lack of concern with the centrality of clock time for the very functioning of industrial capitalism, we find – perhaps ironically – that practice as temporalisation offers much purchase for contemporary economic practices, and we may even speculate about whether or not practice as temporalisation may be paradigmatic for post-Fordist regimes of production.

To be sure, Bourdieu had little, if anything, to say about time and financial practices; nonetheless, in an undeveloped aside in *The Social Structures of the Economy*, he noted how the liberalisation and deregulation of the financial sector tended 'to eliminate the time differentials that separated various national markets' (Bourdieu, 2005 [2000]: 224). While this comment was made in the context of a discussion on the political creation of what Bourdieu termed the 'global market', nonetheless it is suggestive that he understood – at least implicitly – that financial deregulation and liberalisation concerned a restructuring of time in the economic and financial field, one which I have described here as *a shift from the hegemony of clock time to practice as temporalisation.* This shift not only poses challenges to attempts to understand recent economic events via externalist and/or normative theories of time, but also raises a range of more general issues and questions for sociology as a discipline. It will be recalled, for instance, that Sennett laments the demise of narrative movement – that is, the accumulation of experience and of connections between events in time – and that he demands the reinstallation of a present in which such experience can be sensed. It will be recalled also that Sennett makes this case especially for economic practice. Yet, and in as much as it has been hypothesised here that in economic practice time and events increasingly unfold together and that events are not connected in time but are themselves forms of time, one might question whether or not such an experience is available to be either accumulated or sensed. Practice as temporalisation, therefore, raises the sociological spectre that experience may too have restructured, a prospect also gestured towards in Patricia Ticineto Clough's (2009) claim that social life is increasingly 'unexperienced', that is, increasingly beyond human meaning and interpretation, including narrative interpretation.

Conclusion

This chapter has argued that in Bourdieu's social theory we find unexpected and surprising resources to think through recent economic events. These resources, however, do not lie in the places that we might instinctively be drawn to think through such events. They do not lie, for example, in Bourdieu's understanding of the forms and structure of capital, in his understanding of the constitution and circulation of value, or in his later writings on the political economy of neo-liberalism. Instead, I have argued that it is in Bourdieu's writings on time, and especially on practice and temporalisation, that such resources are to be found. This is particularly so because, as illustrated in the previous analysis, post-Fordist economic practice – including, above all, financial economic practice – has contributed to the decline of the hegemony of clock time (under which practices and events take place in the shadow of the clock) and the emergence of practices and objects which are increasingly temporalised and temporalise. Yet this chapter has not sought to argue that we should (let alone attempted to) 'apply' or 'map' Bourdieu's writings on time to and onto recent economic events, for such an application or mapping is neither desirable nor helpful. Such methods would, for instance, leave the received terms of those events entirely intact. Instead, I have mobilised the resources of Bourdieu to understand these events in new terms. These new terms have not only allowed for an unsettling of many normative assumptions regarding the financial crisis and its aftermath, but they have also allowed events so often reported as unpredicted, unknowable, incalculable and inexplicable to become explicable. And in the face of the restructuring of time outlined here, it may well be that the work of sociologists will increasingly involve such procedures, indeed that, while once it was the job of sociologists to make the familiar strange, it is now their job to make the strange familiar.

Acknowledgments

This chapter was written during a period of sabbatical leave at the School of Philosophy and Social Inquiry at the University of Melbourne. I wish to thank the School and especially Associate Professor Helen Verran for their support during this period.

Notes

1 See, for example, Demaggio and Mukhtar (2004), Grenfell and Hardy (2007), and Lipstadt (2003).

2 An example of this – somewhat uncommon – view can be found in Lash (1993), who argues that the large-scale and general process of de-differentiation of economy and culture positions Bourdieu's social theory as particularly relevant for the contemporary economy or, more precisely, for the contemporary cultural economy.

3 As a contrast, see Calhoun (2006), who argues that, far from breaking with the principles of his general social theory, Bourdieu's critique of neo-liberalism is informed by his early ethnographic studies in Algeria and in particular by his studies of the economic and social transformations relating to French colonisation, especially those relating to Algeria's incorporation into capitalist economic relations. Thus, both in *The Social Structures of the Economy* and in *Firing Back*, Bourdieu parallels the social and economic transformations relating to the unification of the economic and financial field, aimed at by the juridical-political devices of neo-liberal policy, to those transformations concerning the unification of the economic field in the context of the colonial state.

4 The 'social embeddedness school' of economic sociology proposes that economic practices and events should be understood to be embedded in social relations, rather than to take place in the abstract. Bourdieu explicitly acknowledges his debt to this school, and specifically to Polanyi, in *The Social Structures of the Economy* (2005) when he argues that just as Polanyi observed to be the case for national markets, the 'global market' is a political creation, that is, a product of 'a more or less self-consciously concerted policy' (Bourdieu, 2005 [2000]: 225). Such policy, Bourdieu goes on, was implemented by a set of agents and institutions, and concerned the application of rules deliberately crafted for specific ends – specifically, trade liberalisation – involving the 'elimination of all national regulations restricting companies and their investments'

(Bourdieu, 2005 [2000]: 225). Bourdieu's debt to the 'social embeddedness school' is also registered in his acknowledgment (again, following Polanyi) that economic practice should be conceived of as a 'total social fact' (Bourdieu, 2005 [2000]: 2).

5 Bourdieu (2000 [1997]) elaborates how the inscription of the future in the immediate present is not a given of practice via the case of the chronically unemployed. The latter, he suggests, often exist with 'no future', or, to be more precise, experience time as purposeless and meaningless. For, without employment, the unemployed are deprived of an objective universe (deadlines, timetables, rates, targets and so on), which orientates and stimulates protensive practical action. In short, the chronically unemployed have 'no future' because they are excluded from the objective conditions (the pull of the field) that would allow for the practical making of time (see Adkins, 2009a).

6 Bourdieu explicitly conceives of the economy as a field, that is, as an autonomous structured space of positions, differentiated from other fields by virtue of the fact that it has its own properties. Moreover, the positions that comprise the field are constituted by accumulated capital, the volume and structure of which determines the 'structure of the field that determines them' (Bourdieu, 2005 [2000]: 193). Thus, the force attached to an agent depends on the volume and structure of capital that agents possess in different species: cultural, financial (potential or actual), technological, juridical, organisational, commercial, social and symbolic (Bourdieu, 2005 [2000]: 194). In brief, for the case of the economic field, and as in Bourdieu's general social theory, the structure of the distribution of capital determines the structure of the field.

7 For Bourdieu, understanding economic action via a philosophy of agents, action, time and the social world restores economics to 'its true vocation as a historical science' (2005 [2000]: 216), that is, as a discipline whose epistemological and ontological assumptions are highly contingent.

8 http://edition.cnn.com/2009/POLITICS/02/13/sanford.economy/index.html (accessed on 18th March 2010).

9 http://www.abc.net.au/lateline/content/2008/s2611909.htm (accessed on 30th March 2010).

10 http://www.coventryconservatives.com/index.php/news/brown_s_borrowing_bonanza_mortgages_nations_futu/ (accessed on 18th March 2010).

11 http://www.timesonline.co.uk/tol/comment/columnists/camilla_cavendish/article5941273.ece (accessed on 18th March 2010).

12 This principle does not necessarily always hold; see, for example: Sennett (2006), for the case of craft labour; and McRobbie (2002b), for the case of creative labour.

References

Adam, Barbara (1994) *Time and Social Theory*, Cambridge: Polity Press.

Adam, Barbara (2004) 'Towards a New Sociology of the Future' http://www.cardiff.ac.uk/socsi/futures/newsociologyofthefuture.pdf, accessed 14.03.09.

Adams, Vincanne, Michelle Murphy and Adele E. Clarke (2009) 'Anticipation: Technoscience, Life, Affect, Temporality', *Subjectivity* 28: 246–265.

Adkins, Lisa (2008) 'From Retroactivation to Futurity: The End of the Sexual Contract?', *Nordic Journal of Feminist and Gender Research* 16(3): 182–201.

Adkins, Lisa (2009a) 'Sociological Futures: From Clock Time to Event Time', *Sociological Research Online* 14(4): http://www.socresonline.org.uk/14/4/8.html.

Adkins, Lisa (2009b) 'Feminism After Measure', *Feminist Theory* 10(3): 1–17.

Beasley-Murray, Jon (2000) 'Value and Capital in Bourdieu and Marx', in Nicholas Brown and Imre Szeman (eds.) *Pierre Bourdieu: Fieldwork in Culture*, Lanham, MD: Rowman and Littlefield, pp. 100–119.

Bourdieu, Pierre (1977 [1972]) *Outline of a Theory of Practice*, trans. Richard Nice, Cambridge: Cambridge University Press.

Bourdieu, Pierre (1986) 'The Forms of Capital', in John C. Richardson (ed.) *Handbook of Theory and Research for the Sociology of Education*, New York: Greenwood, pp. 241–258.

Bourdieu, Pierre (1993 [1984]) *Sociology in Question*, trans. Richard Nice, London: Sage.

Bourdieu, Pierre (1998) *Acts of Resistance: Against the New Myths of Our Time*, trans. Richard Nice, Cambridge: Polity Press.

Bourdieu, Pierre (1999 [1993]) *The Weight of the World: Social Suffering in Contemporary Society*, trans. Priscilla Parkhurst Ferguson [et al.], Cambridge: Polity Press.

Bourdieu, Pierre (2000 [1997]) *Pascalian Meditations*, trans. Richard Nice, Cambridge: Polity Press.

Bourdieu, Pierre (2003 [2001]) *Firing Back: Against the Tyranny of the Market 2*, trans. Loïc Wacquant, London: Verso.

Bourdieu, Pierre (2005 [2000]) *The Social Structures of the Economy*, trans. Chris Turner, Cambridge: Polity Press.

Brown, Wendy (2005) *Edgework: Critical Essays on Knowledge and Politics*, Princeton, N.J.: Princeton University Press.

Calhoun, Craig (1993) 'Habitus, Field, and Capital: The Question of Historical Specificity', in Craig Calhoun, Edward LiPuma and Moishe Postone (eds.) *Bourdieu: Critical Perspectives*, Chicago: University of Chicago Press, pp. 61–88.

Calhoun, Craig (2006) 'Pierre Bourdieu and Social Transformation: Lessons from Algeria', *Development and Change* 37(6): 1403–1415.

Callon, Michel, Yuval Millo and Fabian Muniesa (eds.) (2007) *Market Devices*, Oxford: Blackwell.

Clough, Patricia (2009) 'The New Empiricism: Affect and Sociological Method', *European Journal of Social Theory* 12(1): 43–61.

Colebrook, Claire (2009) 'Stratigraphic Time, Women's Time', *Australian Feminist Studies* 24(59): 11–16.

Coleman, Rebecca (2008) 'Things that Stay', *Time and Society* 17(1): 85–102.

Dimaggio, Paul and Toqir Mukhtar (2004) 'Arts Participation as Cultural Capital in the United States, 1982–2002: Signs of Decline?', *Poetics* 32(2): 169–194.

Edelman, Lee (2005) *No Future: Queer Theory and the Death Drive*, Durham and London: Duke University Press.

Granovetter, Mark (1985) 'Economic Action and Social Structure: The Problem of Embeddedness', *American Journal of Sociology* 91(3): 481–510.

Grosz, Elizabeth (2004) *The Nick of Time: Politics, Evolution and the Untimely*, Durham, NC: Duke University Press.

Hassan, Robert (2003) 'Network Time and the New Knowledge Epoch', *Time and Society* 12(2–3): 225–241.

Husserl, Edmund (1931) *Ideas: General Introduction to Pure Phenomenology*, trans. W.R. Boyce Gibson, London: Allen and Unwin.

Jenkins, Richard (1992) *Pierre Bourdieu*, London: Routledge.

Lash, Scott (1993) 'Pierre Bourdieu: Cultural Economy and Social Change', in Craig Calhoun, Edward LiPuma and Moishe Postone (eds.) *Bourdieu: Critical Perspectives*, Chicago: University of Chicago Press, pp. 193–211.

Law, Alex (2009) 'The Callous Credit Nexous: Ideology and Compulsion in the Crisis of Neoliberalism', *Sociological Research Online* 14(4): http://www.socresonline.org.uk/14/4/5.html.

Lipstadt, Helene (2003) 'Can Art Professions be Bourdieuean Fields of Cultural Production? The Case of the Architecture Competition', *Cultural Studies* 17(3–4): 390–419.

Marazzi, Christian (2007) 'Rules for the Incommensurable', *SubStance* 36(1): 11–36.

McFall, Liz (2009) 'Devices and Desires: How Useful is the "New" Economic Sociology for Understanding Market Attachment?', *Sociology Compass* 3(2): 267–282.

McNay, Lois (1999) 'Gender, Habitus and the Field: Pierre Bourdieu and the Limits of Reflexivity', *Theory, Culture & Society* 16(1): 95–117.

McRobbie, Angela (2002a) 'A Mixed Bag of Misfortunes? Bourdieu's Weight of the World', *Theory, Culture & Society* 19(3): 129–138.

McRobbie, Angela (2002b) 'Clubs to Companies: Notes on the Decline of Political Culture in Speeded up Creative Worlds', *Cultural Studies* 16(4): 516–531.

Nowotny, Helga (2005 [1994]) *Time: The Modern and Postmodern Experience*, trans. Neville Plaice, Cambridge: Polity Press.

O'Carroll, Aileen (2008) 'Fuzzy Holes and Intangible Time: Time in a Knowledge Industry', *Time and Society* 17(2–3): 179–193.

Polanyi, Karl (2001 [1957]) *The Great Transformation*, foreword by R.M. MacIver, Boston: Beacon Press.

Poovey, Mary (2009) 'Understanding Global Interconnectedness: Catastrophic Generic Change', unpublished paper presented at the Nolte Center, University of Minnesota, 6th April 2009.

Postone, Moishe (1993) *Time, Labor, and Social Domination: A Reinterpretation of Marx's Critical Theory*, Cambridge: Cambridge University Press.

Sennett, Richard (2006) *The Culture of the New Capitalism*, New Haven: Yale University Press.

Thompson, E. P. (1967) 'Time, Work-Discipline and Industrial Capitalism', *Past and Present* 38: 56–97.

Zaloom, Caitlin (2009) 'How to Read the Future: The Yield Curve, Affect and Financial Prediction', *Public Culture* 21(2): 245–268.

AFTERWORD

Concluding Reflections on the Legacy of Pierre Bourdieu

Simon Susen

Approaching Pierre Bourdieu

Those who are unfamiliar, or barely familiar, with the writings of Pierre Bourdieu will find a useful and comprehensive introduction to his work in the opening chapter, entitled 'Between Structuralism and Theory of Practice: The Cultural Sociology of Pierre Bourdieu'. In it, Hans Joas and Wolfgang Knöbl provide us with a clear and accessible overview of some of the main philosophical and sociological themes that run through Bourdieu's writings. Joas and Knöbl centre their analysis on five interrelated concepts that play a pivotal role in Bourdieu's work: the concepts of (1) *practice*, (2) *action*, (3) *the social*, (4) *cultural sociology*, and (5) *social science*.

(1) The authors examine Bourdieu's concept of *practice* by focusing on one of his most influential early works, namely his *Outline of a Theory of Practice* (1977 [1972]). As explained by Joas and Knöbl, Bourdieu's theory of practice is based on a sympathetic but critical revision of Lévi-Strauss's anthropological structuralism through the proposal of an alternative, somewhat refined, form of structuralism, commonly described as 'genetic' or 'constructivist' structuralism. According to Joas and Knöbl, the paradigmatic transition from Lévi-Strauss's 'anthropological structuralism' to Bourdieu's 'genetic structuralism' contains a number of significant presuppositional shifts. (i) The *shift from 'rule following' to 'rule breaking'* is motivated by the insight that social actors do not always follow the rules imposed upon them by their social environment: the relative unpredictability of society is due to the ineluctable power of human agency. (ii) The *shift from 'structure' to 'action'* is justified considering the fact that social structures cannot exist without social action: the very possibility of society is contingent upon the constant interplay between social structure and social action. (iii) The *shift from 'theory' to 'practice'* is imperative to avoid falling into the

scholastic fallacy of treating 'the things of logic' as 'the logic of things' and thereby passing off 'the reality of the model' as 'the model of reality': a truly reflexive sociology, in the Bourdieusian sense, needs to recognise that human life is to be conceived of as an ensemble of social practices. (iv) The *shift from 'substantialism' to 'relationalism'* is based on the conviction that we need to replace the substantialist with the relationalist mode of thought in order to account for the fact that social fields are defined by contingent relations between, rather than by universal properties of, social actors: society is a relationally constructed reality. (v) The *shift from 'logocentric dichotomism' to 'homological holism'* permits us to transcend the counterproductive antinomy between objectivist and subjectivist approaches to the social: society emanates from the homological interplay between field-divided objectivities and habitus-specific subjectivities. Thus, from a Bourdieusian perspective, social practices are possible only through the homological interplay between positionally structured realms of objectivity and dispositionally constituted forms of subjectivity.

(2) Joas and Knöbl begin their examination of Bourdieu's concept of *action* by pointing out that the Bourdieusian model of human action differs from 'utilitarian' or 'economic' models in three respects: first, it conceives of human action in *relationalist*, rather than rationalist, terms; second, it studies human action in *contextualist*, rather than universalist, terms; and, third, it examines human action in *praxeological*, rather than transcendental, terms. If human action is always relationally, contextually, and praxeologically constituted, it cannot be reduced to the outcome of a largely self-sufficient, predominantly calculative, and merely cognitive subject. The *habitus* constitutes a dispositionally structured apparatus of perception, appreciation, and action. Its main function is to allow social actors to confront the field-specific imperatives thrown at them in a field-divided world. The social *field* denotes a positionally structured realm of socialisation, interaction, and competition. Its main function is to provide social actors with a practically defined framework in which to mobilise their habitus-specific resources in relation to a habitus-divided world. Different forms of *capital* describe different – objectively externalised and subjectively internalised – sources of material and symbolic power. The main function of (different types of) capital is to enable social actors to compete over material and symbolic resources in relationally constituted realms. A general theory of the economy of practices needs to account for the fact that the homological interplay between habitus-specific forms of subjectivity and field-differentiated forms of objectivity lies at the heart of the struggle over capital-based resources available in a given society.

(3) The two authors continue by reflecting upon Bourdieu's concept of *the social*. As they point out, *field*, *habitus*, and *capital* constitute the three conceptual cornerstones of the Bourdieusian architecture of the social. Yet, rather than

conceiving of these categories in isolation from each other, Bourdieusian analysis is concerned with exploring the various and often contradictory ways in which they are empirically interconnected. From a Bourdieusian perspective, the field can be regarded as the ontological foundation of the social: to be situated in different realms of social reality means to be embedded in different social fields. Social fields constitute the *espaces des possibles*, that is, the delimited and delimiting spaces of possibilities in which human actions take place. As Joas and Knöbl explain, Bourdieusian field theory and Luhmannian systems theory converge and diverge in three fundamental respects. They converge in emphasising that social fields – in the Bourdieusian sense – and social systems – in the Luhmannian sense – are characterised by their (i) constraining *ubiquity*, (ii) functional *differentiality*, and (iii) relative *autonomy*. Paradoxically, the two accounts also diverge in precisely these respects. (i) According to Bourdieu, the constraining ubiquity of social fields can be challenged through the generative power of social struggle and human agency. By contrast, according to Luhmann, there is little – if any – room for transformative malleability within social realms whose normative horizons are defined by systemic boundaries. (ii) From a Bourdieusian perspective, the functional differentiality of social fields is limited to the degree of evolutionary determinacy of a given society. Conversely, from a Luhmannian perspective, any kind of society has, in principle, the capacity to develop an infinite number of systemic realms that generate a potentially unlimited amount of spaces of delimited interactionality. (iii) Following Bourdieu, the relative autonomy of social fields is always subject to the hegemonic imperatives of a given type of society. Following Luhmann, social systems can, in principle, reproduce themselves without being dictated by the overarching imperatives of a dominant form of normativity.

(4) Joas and Knöbl provide us with useful insights into some of the key aspects of Bourdieu's notion of *cultural sociology*. Far from regarding culture as a neutral and disinterested affair, Bourdieu conceives of it as a vehicle of social distinction. Given the foundational status of our daily immersion in culture, the attainment of cultural capital is a precondition for the acquisition of other forms of capital. In other words, we obtain social, economic, political, linguistic, and educational forms of capital on condition that we have access to cultural capital. Ordinary actors can participate in social life only insofar as they are exposed to cultural fields, develop a cultural habitus, and acquire cultural capital. Since the human species is a socio-constructive species, the emergence of society is inconceivable without the creation of culture. In order to develop a cultural habitus and participate in a cultural field, we need to incorporate cultural capital. Culture is inevitably interest-laden because we can develop an interest in the world only if we develop an interest in culture, and culture is necessarily power-laden because access to culture is a precondition

for access to power. Symbolic power derives from people's generative capacity to convert the need for self-realisation into an endogenously mobilised resource of exogenously approved consecration.

(5) The authors conclude their chapter by reflecting on Bourdieu's remarkable influence on contemporary *social science.* They observe that Bourdieu's influence is particularly palpable in the Francophone, Germanophone, and Anglophone fields of social and political thought. (i) Probably more than in any other national tradition of sociology, the contemporary French academic field of sociology appears to be divided between 'the Bourdieusians' and 'the Boltanskians'; whereas the former are associated with the paradigm of *sociologie critique,* the latter are referred to as advocates of an alternative agenda commonly described as *sociologie de la critique* or, more recently, *sociologie pragmatique de la critique.* Bourdieusians tend to regard social science as a tool to uncover the underlying mechanisms that shape the hierarchical structuration of society. By contrast, Boltanskians tend to conceive of social science as a tool to make sense of the various disputes generated by ordinary actors when engaging in the discursive problematisation of society. (ii) In the contemporary German academic field of sociology, Bourdieusian conceptual frameworks are increasingly popular in empirical studies on life-style. This tendency reflects the sociological significance of actors' dependence on access to multiple forms of capital in differentiated societies: in order to enjoy the status of an empowered member of society we have no choice but to develop the capacity to acquire and mobilise capital-based resources that permit our subjectivity to relate to and act upon increasingly differentiated realms of objectivity. (iii) Despite the persisting paradigmatic predominance of economic and utilitarian approaches in the contemporary North American academic field of sociology, it appears to be more and more common to establish an elastic comfort zone between the utilitarian paradigm of 'rational action' in the market place and the relational paradigm of 'interest-laden action' in the social field. Social life, then, is driven by a permanent struggle over resources: cultural resources, economic resources, linguistic resources, educational resources, political resources, and symbolic resources. In short, the history of all hitherto existing society is the history of struggles over social resources. Ultimately, to have access to a legitimate habitus via the acquisition of legitimate capital and participation in a legitimate field means to have access to a legitimate life.

Bourdieu and Marx (I)

In the second chapter, entitled 'Pierre Bourdieu: Unorthodox Marxist?', Bridget Fowler defends the view that Bourdieu can be regarded as one of the great heirs of the Western Marxist tradition. Although she does not suggest that

Marx was the only classical sociologist whose oeuvre significantly influenced Bourdieu's writings, Fowler argues that Marx had a distinctive impact on Bourdieu and that the significance of this influence is often downplayed when examining Bourdieusian concepts such as field, habitus, and doxa. More specifically, she claims that Bourdieu's syntheses, which possess a masterly originality derived from a variety of intellectual traditions, were aimed at strengthening, rather than at undermining, Marx's historical materialism. Bourdieu neither abandoned nor repudiated Marx's materialist method, but rather converted it into a sociologically more complex and analytically more sophisticated approach, insisting upon the central importance of the ineluctable links between the material and the symbolic, the economic and the cultural, and the objective and the normative dimensions of social life.

Given his emphasis on the multidimensional constitution of human reality, it comes as no surprise that Bourdieu was strongly opposed to all forms of *Vulgärmarxismus*, which – as Fowler points out – fall into the traps of 'false radicalism' and 'mechanical materialism'. We are therefore confronted with a curious paradox: Bourdieu provides his most powerful critique of orthodox Marxism by adopting and developing Marx's own conceptual and methodological tools. He draws upon insights from Marxist thought whilst seeking to overcome some of its most significant shortcomings. In so doing, Bourdieu is firmly situated in the self-critical spirit of the Marxist project: just as 'it is essential to educate the educator himself' or herself, it is crucial to criticise the critic himself or herself (Marx, 2000/1977 [1845]: 172); and just as it is imperative to sociologise sociology itself, it is indispensable to reflect upon the process of reflection itself (Bourdieu, 1976: 104; 2001: 16, 19, and 220).

What, then, allows us to assume that Bourdieusian forms of reflection stand in the tradition of Marxist social analysis? To what extent can Bourdieu be regarded as one of the great inheritors of the Western Marxist tradition? As Fowler demonstrates on the basis of a close textual analysis, Marxian thought is an omnipresent feature in key areas of Bourdieu's writings. In order to illustrate this, the author focuses on six Bourdieusian themes: Algeria; education and class; the cultural field; struggles within the academic field; the problem of agency; and, finally, the idea of a general theory of cultural power. As Fowler outlines in the introductory part of her chapter, we can identify a number of theoretical concerns that feature centrally both in Marxian and in Bourdieusian social analysis. These overlapping theoretical concerns, which are instances of Bourdieu's debt to Marx, can be synthesised as follows.

(1) *Relationality:* The most obvious point of convergence between Marx and Bourdieu can be found in their shared conviction that human reality is the ensemble of social relations. From a sociological perspective, social life

is to be conceived of not in terms of transcendental essences or ahistorical abstractions, but in terms of spatiotemporally contingent relations between different people and between different groups of people.

(2) *Practice:* A further important meeting point between Marx and Bourdieu is the assumption that social life is essentially practical. Marx's historical materialism and Bourdieu's genetic structuralism constitute two macro-theoretical frameworks that are based on the presupposition that both the constitution and the evolution of society are shaped by the unfolding of interrelated social practices.

(3) *Capital:* Yet another shared concern in the works of Marx and Bourdieu is their critical engagement with the fact that, in stratified societies, access to social resources depends on access to capital. Bourdieu's differentiation between various forms of capital – such as economic, cultural, social, linguistic, and symbolic capital – does justice to the complexity of polycentrically organised realities in which social resources are not only asymmetrically distributed but also positionally externalised and dispositionally internalised.

(4) *Power:* In light of the fact that our ability to act upon the world is contingent upon our hierarchically defined position in the social space, Marx and Bourdieu aim to demonstrate that asymmetrically structured social relations are interest-laden power relations. Before we can imagine the possibility of a classless reality, we need to face up to the complexities arising from the structural divisions that permeate every class-ridden society.

(5) *Economic and Symbolic Power:* Both Marx and Bourdieu are holistic thinkers in that they stress the inseparability of the material and the cultural, the economic and the symbolic, and the objective and the normative dimensions of social life. Bourdieu's attempt to shift the emphasis from the study of economic power, which is central to early modern forms of orthodox Marxism, to the study of symbolic power, which is a key component of late modern versions of cultural Marxism, reflects the need to account for the sociological significance of people's capacity to acquire social power through both material and cultural resources. What is present in class is the power of social classification; what is present in culture is the power of social representation. Power-laden divisions in the world manifest themselves in interest-laden visions of the world.

(6) *Contradiction and Crisis:* In both Marx's and Bourdieu's writings, contradiction and crisis are considered as indivisible aspects of the social world. Regardless of whether – following Marx – we focus on the contradiction between the forces of production and the relations of production, or – following Bourdieu – we examine the contradiction between the orthodox discourses of dominant groups and the heterodox discourses of dominated groups, we cannot make sense of material and symbolic revolutions without recognising that structural and ideological

contradictions, which can lead to small-scale and large-scale social crises, are major driving forces of historical development.

(7) *Anti-Idealism:* As critical thinkers who are committed to the empirical investigation of social reality, both Marx and Bourdieu are deeply suspicious of philosophical idealism. The presuppositions underlying Marx's critique of German idealism are omnipresent in Bourdieu's critique of European idealism: Kant's transcendental account of reason and taste; Derrida's merely philosophical, and hence ultimately scholastic, attack on logocentrism; Foucault's obsession with free-floating *épistèmes*; Habermas's romantic belief in the socio-ontological preponderance of communicative action in the lifeworld; or Austin's meticulous study of language, which overestimates the power of words and underestimates the power of social roles. All of these philosophical projects are illustrative of scholastic attempts to study cognitive, discursive, or linguistic forces of human reality regardless of their socio-historical determinacy.

(8) *Science:* Just as Marx rejects a facile utopianism in the name of science, Bourdieu has little patience with postmodern relativism, insisting that a genuinely sociological study of human reality requires a scientific analysis of social relationality. From this perspective, neither ideal worlds, in which 'anything is possible', nor rainbow worlds, in which 'anything goes', contribute much – if anything – to the scientific world, in which 'everything is to be questioned'. Neither the *Idealpolitik* of utopian reason nor the *Provokationspolitik* of cynical reason can play a constructive role in the *Realpolitik* of scientific reason.

(9) *Theory and Practice:* For both Marx and Bourdieu, theorising for the sake of theorising can only lead to self-sufficient and pointless forms of knowledge production. Marx regards theory as an instrument that can become a material force when absorbed and mobilised by the masses, and Bourdieu considers sociology as a normative tool that can and should be used not only to undermine the disempowering effects of social domination but also to realise the empowering potentials of social emancipation.

Bourdieu and Marx (II)

The third chapter, 'From Marx to Bourdieu: The Limits of the Structuralism of Practice', was originally written in French by Bruno Karsenti and was translated into English by Simon Susen. It ties in with Bridget Fowler's conviction that the impact of Marx's historical materialism on Bourdieu's genetic structuralism cannot be overestimated. As the chapter's title suggests, Marxian thought can be regarded as an integral element of the Bourdieusian project. Thus, in order to make sense of the presuppositional underpinnings of the latter, we need to remind ourselves of the philosophical premises of the former. In relation to Bourdieu, the socio-ontological significance of these philosophical premises manifests itself in three of Marx's key concerns: first, in his concern with *anthropological distinctiveness*, which is rooted in humans' capacity to produce their own – materially constituted and symbolically mediated – means of subsistence; second, in his concern with *anthropological contradictions*, particularly those derived from the structural division between producers and non-producers; and, third, in his concern with *anthropological development*, which is inconceivable without the gradual differentiation between material labour and intellectual labour. Inspired by Marx's oeuvre, the whole point of Bourdieu's project is to replace the 'game of theory' with the 'reality of practice'. In the 'game of theory', the act of critical reflection is treated as independent of, and removed from, the empirical constitution of human life. By contrast, in the 'reality of practice', the act of critical reflection is experienced as both dependent upon and embedded within the relational production of social existence.

With the relational production of cultural life forms in mind, Karsenti provides a detailed analysis, on a number of levels, of the cornerstones of Bourdieu's structuralism of practice. Three levels of comparison between Marx and Bourdieu are particularly important. First, just as Marx insists upon the interwovenness of the material and the symbolic dimensions of social life, Bourdieu invites us to overcome the – arguably artificial and, in some respects, counterproductive – antinomy between objectivist and subjectivist approaches in the social sciences. Second, just as from a Marxian perspective the point is not only to interpret but also to transform the world, from a Bourdieusian perspective we need to move from the 'logic of theory' to the 'logic of practice' in order to account for our ineluctable situatedness within, rather than our imaginary detachment from, the world. And, third, just as in Marx we can find an unambiguous attempt to conceive of human consciousness in terms of social determinacy derived from the physical organisation of the world, in Bourdieu we are confronted with the task of shifting from the imaginary of cognitive detachment, celebrated in scholastic forms of philosophy, to the reality of bodily engagement, explored in reflexive forms of sociology. Hence, socio-analysis – as advocated by Bourdieu – is a form of sociological psychoanalysis, compelling us to comprehend the biographical condition of human individuality in relation to the historical condition of human society: every time we seek to throw ourselves at society by virtue of individual agency, society has already thrown itself at us by virtue of its relational determinacy. In fact, the 'belatedness' of the human condition explains the 'taken-for-grantedness' of human practices: our physical immersion in reality necessarily precedes our material and symbolic actions upon society.

Crucial to the paradigmatic shift from the scholastic illusion of 'cognitive detachment' to the critical reflection upon 'bodily engagement' is a normative issue: if we recognise that, as bodily beings, we are not only exposed to but also immersed in the structural contradictions of society, then we need to accept that the material and symbolic divisions by which we are surrounded are sources of separation *between* people that exist as classificatory schemes *within* people. Put differently, positional separations, which divide the social universe into competing groups and fields, manifest themselves in dispositional schemes of perception and appreciation, which impose themselves as quasi-naturalised resources upon all historically mediated forms of human action. To the extent that the positional divisions that exist in our society permeate the dispositional schemes that exist in our bodies, the structural contradictions that pervade the normative world have the power to colonise the corporeal apparatus that underlies our subjective world. There is no such thing as an innocent subject, for our inevitable immersion in the world compels us to internalise the contradictions of the world. Before we can create subversive forms of reflexivity and invent transformative modes of agency, we need to face up to the predominance of our bodily constituted complicity with established patterns of ideological and behavioural normativity.

Bourdieu and Durkheim

In the fourth chapter, 'Durkheim and Bourdieu: The Common Plinth and its Cracks', written in French by Loïc Wacquant and translated into English by Tarik Wareh, we move from Marx to another key figure in classical sociology whose writings have had an enormous impact on Bourdieu's work: Émile Durkheim. Rather than providing a sterile comparison between Durkheim and Bourdieu, and far from suggesting that Bourdieusian sociology represents a merely Durkheimian endeavour, Wacquant, whilst acknowledging the eclectic underpinnings of Bourdieu's work, offers a systematic and intellectually challenging account of four presuppositional pillars upon which both Durkheimian and Bourdieusian sociology are based. These four pillars, which according to Wacquant are omnipresent in the works of both Durkheim and Bourdieu, can be described as follows: (1) the attachment to *rationalism*, which manifests itself in the conviction that scientific knowledge can provide us with the conceptual and methodological tools that allow for a critical analysis of the social world; (2) the defence of the *undividedness of social science*, which is expressed in the categorical refusal of theoreticism; (3) the commitment to recognising the intimate link between *sociology and historiography*, which is articulated in the study of the socio-historical constitution of human existence; and (4) the recourse to *ethnology* as a privileged device for 'indirect experimentation', which is motivated by the idea that ethnological analysis can serve as a legitimate experimental technique of sociological investigation.

As stated above, Wacquant argues that the aforementioned concerns represent four normative pillars in the writings of both Durkheim and Bourdieu, particularly with regard to their respective conceptions of knowledge. According to both thinkers, sociological knowledge is by definition rationally motivated, scientifically oriented, historically informed, and ethnologically sensitive. Nevertheless, as Wacquant demonstrates, their epistemological frameworks not only converge but also diverge at various points.

(1) Both Durkheim and Bourdieu insist upon the *epistemological gap between ordinary and scientific knowledge*. Yet, whereas Durkheim seeks to free sociology from all presuppositional knowledge based on common sense, Bourdieu aims to construct an enlarged conception of the social, capable of accounting for the fact that insofar as the very possibility of society rests upon the homological interplay between field and habitus, the construction of a critical sociology depends on its capacity to explore the functional interplay between scientific types of reflexivity and ordinary forms of knowledgeability.

(2) Both thinkers highlight the *normative potentials of social science*, which are epitomised in a threefold refusal: (i) the refusal of worldly seductions, (ii) the refusal of confinement within the scholarly microcosm, and (iii) the refusal of disciplinary fragmentation and theoreticism. Paradoxically, however, the two scholars are both united and divided by this tripartite concern. (i) For Durkheim, the scientificity of sociology emanates from its purposive capacity to be guided by the rational search for objectivity. For Bourdieu, on the other hand, the scientificity of sociology derives from its contemplative capacity to embrace a self-critical position of reflexivity. (ii) Whereas Durkheim stresses the impersonal, and thus allegedly disinterested, constitution of scientific knowledge, Bourdieu emphasises the relational, and hence ultimately interest-laden, constitution of scientific knowledge. (iii) Durkheim opposes the scholastic celebration of theoreticism by reminding us of the objective prevalence of social facts. Bourdieu, by contrast, seeks to move from the 'logic of theory' to the 'logic of practice' by pointing at the powerful mystery of social acts.

(3) According to both Durkheim and Bourdieu, it is the task of social scientists to uncover the *historical constitution of the human condition*. The spatiotemporal contingency of the human condition can be illustrated on the basis of three forms of historicisation: (i) the historicisation of human agency, (ii) the historicisation of human society, and (iii) the historicisation of human knowledgeability. Yet, again – and again somewhat paradoxically – the two thinkers are not only united but also divided by this tripartite concern. (i) From a Durkheimian perspective, the creative power of human agency tends to be superseded by the constraining power of social factuality. From a Bourdieusian

perspective, however, the omnipresence of social factuality can be challenged by the unfolding of human agency. (ii) According to Durkheimian parameters, the preponderance of objectivity over subjectivity pervades the functional determinacy of every society. According to Bourdieusian parameters, it is the homology between positionally structured realms of objectivity and dispositionally constituted forms of subjectivity which permeates the relational determinacy of every society. (iii) In the Durkheimian universe, the validity of scientific knowledge hinges upon its objective capacity to rise above its own historicity. In the Bourdieusian universe, the validity of scientific knowledge rests upon its reflexive capacity to face up to its own historicity.

(4) Both Durkheim and Bourdieu favour *a posteriori* over *a priori* knowledge in that they are committed to the ethnological, rather than the logocentric, study of the social world; and both prefer *a fortiori* over *arbitrary* knowledge in that they are committed to scientific, rather than speculative, forms of reasoning. Yet, their respective conceptions of ethnologically informed validity also differ substantially from each other: whereas for Durkheim social-scientific research is oriented towards the discovery of irrefutable generalities that underlie the functioning of society, for Bourdieu social-scientific research cannot dispense with categorical openness to the potential refutability of all explanatory categories. In light of the above reflections we are obliged to recognise that, as Wacquant indicates in the title of his chapter, the common plinth beneath Durkheim and Bourdieu has significant cracks.

Bourdieu and Weber

Bourdieu was interviewed on several occasions in his career, and by now most of these interviews have been published and translated into English. The fifth chapter contains one that has not been previously translated into, let alone published in, English. This interview, conducted by Franz Schultheis and Andreas Pfeuffer, was published in German (see Bourdieu, 2000) one year after it took place in a café on Boulevard Saint-Germain in Paris in the spring of 1999. The interview was originally conducted in French, and we are grateful to Stephan Egger, the translator of the German publication, for providing us with both the original (French) audio version and the published (German) translation.

The title of this chapter anticipates the thematic focus of the interview: 'With Weber Against Weber: In Conversation With Pierre Bourdieu'. It is commonly accepted that some of the key elements of Marxian, Durkheimian, Weberian, and – to some extent – Simmelian sociology can be considered cornerstones of Bourdieusian thought. It is often suggested, however, that there is an imbalance between these 'classical' approaches in terms of their respective influence on the development of Bourdieu's oeuvre. More specifically, there is a pronounced tendency in the literature to presume or, in some cases, to demonstrate that both Marxian and Durkheimian sociology had a particularly strong impact on Bourdieu's work (see, for example, chapters 2, 3, and 4 in this volume). Yet, in comparison to the previous two influences, the impact that Weberian sociology had on Bourdieu remains not only widely underestimated but also to a significant extent underexplored.

This interview, hitherto largely unknown in the Anglophone world of social science, permits and indeed compels us to challenge the notion that Marx and Durkheim can be regarded as the 'primary' classical influences on Bourdieu's work, and that consequently Weber plays a somewhat 'secondary' role in his oeuvre. The elaborate responses given by Bourdieu in this interview illustrate not only that he had a far-reaching appreciation of Weber's writings, but also that Weberian sociology can be considered a *pierre angulaire* of the entire edifice of Bourdieusian thought. The interview covers a wide range of topics and touches upon issues related to some of Bourdieu's deepest concerns and convictions. The key assertions made in the interview shall be summarised here, somewhat provocatively, in *Eleven Theses on Bourdieu*:

1. *The chief defect of most hitherto existing forms of materialism in France (that of Althusser included) is the disregard of Weber.* Weber was not taken seriously by French Marxists because he was largely perceived as a conservative defender of 'methodological individualism' and 'bourgeois philosophy'.
2. *The question whether objective truth can be attributed to scientific thinking is not a question of theory but is a practical question.* Bourdieu makes this point clear when affirming that '[a]t the end of the day, the important thing is the research itself, that is, the research on the subject matter itself' (Bourdieu et al., 2011 [2000]: 117). In order to embark upon the study of society we need to engage with the reality of human practices.
3. *The orthodox materialist doctrine concerning changing circumstances and upbringing forgets that circumstances are changed through both material and symbolic struggles over the monopoly of legitimate power over worldly and sacred goods and that if, in principle, nothing 'must remain as it was'* (Bourdieu et al., 2011 [2000]: 121, italics added), *it is essential to socialise and resocialise the socialisers themselves.* If we can find one categorical imperative in Bourdieusian thought it is the notion that social arrangements are relatively arbitrary. Social reality 'does not *have to be* – that is, it is not *necessarily* – like this or like that' (Bourdieu et al., 2011 [2000]: 121, italics in original). From Bourdieu's constructivist perspective, 'great philosophical revolutions' cannot be dissociated from 'great social revolutions' (Bourdieu et al., 2011 [2000]: 120). The 'coincidence of the changing of circumstances and of human activity'

(Marx, 2000/1977 [1845]: 172) indicates that social actors cannot escape the homology between objectivity and subjectivity. They cannot step out of the socio-ontological interdependence between field-specific positions and habitus-specific dispositions. The homological interplay between objectivity and subjectivity underlies the construction of spatiotemporally specific arrangements in every society.

4. *Weber starts from the fact of the religious permeation of the world, of the duplication of the world into a religious world and a secular one.* Given that, throughout history, the constitution of society appears to be characterised by the intimate intertwinement of religious and secular modes of relating to and making sense of the world, a comprehensive social science needs to develop both a 'political economy of religion' and a 'critical anthropology of religion'. The former does justice to the fact that 'the symbolic' and 'the material' are two interdependent dimensions of the social world; the latter accounts for the fact that, in the long run, the social world can only survive as an enchanted – or at least quasi-enchanted – world. It is the meaning-donating function of religion which explains its pervasive power to deal with existential questions. As long as existential dilemmas are part of the human condition, religious – or at least quasi-religious – beliefs and practices will be an integral part of social life.
5. *Orthodox Marxists, not satisfied with abstract thinking, want concrete action; but they do not conceive of either abstract thinking or concrete action as field-specific and habitus-dependent practices.* Given the polycentric nature of complex societies, we need to recognise that different ways of making sense of and acting upon the world are positionally defined ways of being immersed in and dispositionally constituted ways of relating to the world. Polycentric social settings require centreless social theories.
6. *Every human being is situated in and constituted by an ensemble of social relations.* In order to understand both the positional and the dispositional determinacy of human actors, we need to capture the *relations* between them, for it is the contingent relations between, rather than the universal properties of, social actors which determine how they are situated in and relate to the world.
7. *If the 'religious sentiment' is itself a social product and if every religion emerges under particular social conditions, then it must be the task of a critical sociology of religion to shed light on both the material and the symbolic mechanisms that contribute to either the reproduction or the transformation of religious fields.* Religious fields, however, are to be conceived of not only as relations of feelings and meanings, but also as relations of power: a 'political economy of religion' needs to shed light on 'the stakes in the struggles over the monopoly of the legitimate power over the sacred goods' (Bourdieu et al., 2011 [2000]: 119 , italics removed) in order to understand that the power-laden nature of material relations

is impregnated with the interest-laden nature of symbolic relations, and vice versa.

8. *To recognise that all social life is essentially practical and that all human practices are essentially social means to acknowledge that society is practically lived.* It is because people have to live with one another that they encounter one another, and it is because they are situated in the world that they are invested in it.
9. *The highest point of orthodox materialism – that is, of materialism that does not comprehend the multilayered complexity of practical activity – is the reduction of sociorelational realities to socioeconomic ontologies.* Yet, the material and the symbolic are two *irreducible* components of the social world. There has never been a society whose mode of production could have been disentangled from its mode of signification, since all coexistentially established human arrangements are composed of materially constituted and symbolically mediated social relations.
10. *The standpoint of dogmatic philosophy is scholastic purism; the standpoint of critical sociology is reflexive eclecticism.* To engage in the critical exercise of reflexive eclecticism requires resisting the temptation of relying on intellectual inward-lookingness and thereby embarking upon a journey of transdisciplinary outward-lookingness. No tradition can possibly emerge without drawing on previously existing traditions. The success of a critical sociology depends on its capacity to overcome counterproductive boundaries between artificially divided epistemologies.
11. *Social actors reproduce the world in various ways; the point is to recognise their capacity to transform it.* Just as one cannot be situated in the world without perceiving the pervasive power of social constraints, 'one cannot make any progress without a respectful sense of freedom' (Bourdieu et al., 2011 [2000]: 117).

Bourdieu and Nietzsche

In the sixth chapter, 'Bourdieu and Nietzsche: Taste as a Struggle', Keijo Rahkonen offers an insightful comparison between Bourdieusian and Nietzschean thought, which fills a significant gap in the literature. Rahkonen's analysis is divided into five sections.

In the first section, Rahkonen examines *Bourdieu's conception of taste.* It is worth mentioning that Bourdieu was one of the first thinkers to provide a sociological account of taste. Although influential scholars such as Max Weber, Georg Simmel, Thorstein Veblen, and Norbert Elias clearly touched upon the concept of taste in their writings, none of them systematically explored its sociological significance. Hence, as Rahkonen – borrowing an expression from Loïc Wacquant – points out, Bourdieu's sociological account of taste, an elaborate version of which can be found in *Distinction*, can be described as a 'Copernican revolution in the study of taste'. Several philosophical accounts of taste – particularly those associated with Kantian thought – are based on the assumption that the nature of taste is transcendentally, and thus transhistorically, determined. By contrast, most sociological accounts of taste – notably those associated with Bourdieusian thought – put forward the idea that the constitution of taste is socially, and hence spatiotemporally, determined. Bourdieu differentiates between three different 'universes of taste': the realm of 'pure taste', oriented towards the consumption of 'highbrow culture' and mainly acquired by members of the dominant classes; the realm of 'average taste', directed towards the consumption of 'middlebrow culture' and particularly common amongst members of the middle classes; and the realm of 'popular taste', aimed at the consumption of 'lowbrow culture' and spread amongst members of the lower classes. In other words, the realm of human taste is impregnated with the relationally defined interplay between positionally structured forms of objectivity and dispositionally structured forms of subjectivity, which underlies the functioning of every stratified society.

In the second section, Rahkonen examines *Bourdieu's critique of Kant's conception of taste*. The Bourdieusian sociology of taste represents a radical critique of the Kantian philosophy of taste. From a Bourdieusian perspective, Kant's three famous critiques – the *Critique of Pure Reason*, the *Critique of Practical Reason*, and the *Critique of Judgement* – are deeply flawed for failing to take into consideration the social conditioning of reason and judgement. Kant's scholastic quest for aesthetic transcendentality disregards the ineluctable predominance of social relationality in the cultural construction of reality. If there is anything transcendental about the realm of aesthetics it is the fact that the transcendental itself is socially constituted. Rather than speculating about the analytical purity of theoretical reason, the moral universality of practical reason, or the transcendental lawfulness of aesthetic judgement, we need to examine the social determinacy of subjectivity in order to understand why our perception and appreciation of reality cannot escape the omnipresent power of human relationality. An interest-laden society generates interest-driven actors. How we perceive, appreciate, and act upon the world depends on how we are situated in the world in relation to others. Hence, taste is a matter not of disembodied or transhistorical subjectivity but of social determinacy.

In the third section, Rahkonen explores *Bourdieu's conceptions of taste and 'ressentiment' in relation to power*. From a Bourdieusian perspective, struggles over taste are struggles over power. If there is one truth about taste, it is that both its constitution and its meaning are constantly at stake in society. If taste is so powerful because it makes us perceive, appreciate, and act upon the world in particular ways, then neither access to nor cultivation of a particular taste can be dissociated from inclusion in or exclusion from symbolically mediated forms of social power. If we accept that no worldly situated subject can possibly escape the endogenous power of an exogenously determined apparatus of perception, appreciation, and action, then the classificatory schemes acquired by habitus-specific dispositions cannot be divorced from social struggles over field-specific positions. Given the interest-laden nature of our immersion in the social world, a truly reflexive sociology needs to be critical of itself: of its own schemes of classification, of its own programmes of perception, of its own agendas of appreciation; in short, as Rahkonen puts it, of its own 'ressentiments'.

The concern with the nature of 'ressentiment' leads Rahkonen, in the fourth section, to reflect upon *Nietzsche's conception of taste*. However one interprets the role of the concept of taste in Nietzsche's writings, there is little doubt that, from a Nietzschean perspective, not only 'power' and 'truth' but also 'power' and 'taste' are intimately interrelated: just as 'the will to power' cannot be disentangled from 'the will to truth', 'the will to power' cannot be dissociated from 'the will to taste'. What we *consider* to be either right or wrong is often what we *like* to be either right or wrong. The categorising powerfulness of taste is intertwined with the stratifying tastelessness of power. In Nietzsche's *Thus Spoke Zarathustra* we are reminded that 'all life is dispute over taste and tasting'. For, as we may add, 'all taste is dispute over life and living'.

And this is where, in the final section of Rahkonen's chapter, Bourdieu enters the stage again – this time together with Nietzsche. What, then, can we learn from *bringing Nietzsche and Bourdieu closer together*? Following Rahkonen, one of the most obvious features they have in common is their anti-Kantianism: both are opposed to Kant's arguably sterile and disembodied account of the subject in general and of taste in particular. To be precise, Nietzsche and Bourdieu share six anti-Kantian assumptions. First, taste is *interest-laden*: the symbolic differentiation between legitimate and illegitimate forms of taste emanates from the structural differentiation between dominant and dominated social groups, whose taken-for-grantedness of habitus-specific dispositions is permeated by the interest-ladenness of field-specific positions. Second, taste is *perspective-laden*: our perception of the world is contingent upon our position in the world. Third, taste is *context-laden*: before we can make sense of the world, we have to be situated in the world; and before we can develop a taste for the world, the world has to shape our taste. Fourth, taste is *culture-laden*: human subjectivity cannot escape the spatiotemporal determinacy of the intrinsic relationality which permeates all coexistential forms of human objectivity. Fifth, taste is *body-laden*: all socially acquired dispositions are bodily located traces of quasi-naturalised conditions. Sixth, taste is *power-laden*: the stratifying tastelessness of power nourishes the categorising powerfulness of taste. The tasteless empowerment of the powerfully tasteful goes hand in hand with the tasteless disempowerment of the powerfully tasteless. In short, the *Wille zum Geschmack* and the *Wille zur Macht* constitute two integral components of our *Wille zur Welt.*

Bourdieu and Elias

In the seventh chapter, Bowen Paulle, Bart van Heerikhuizen, and Mustafa Emirbayer discuss Bourdieu's somewhat ambiguous relation to the oeuvre of one of the most influential thinkers in modern sociology: Norbert Elias. The chapter, succinctly entitled 'Elias and Bourdieu', examines both points of convergence and points of divergence between these two thinkers. The authors insist, however, that such a comparative endeavour is motivated not by the pursuit of intellectual speculation but by the convictions that we can gain fruitful insights from bringing Bourdieu and Elias closer together and that we can learn important lessons from cross-fertilising their approaches. Thus, as the authors emphasise at the beginning of their chapter, their point is not only to shed light on the similarities and differences between Elias and Bourdieu, but also, and more importantly, to demonstrate that their perspectives yield a more comprehensive and more powerful sociological vision when considered together rather than separately.

The authors suggest that we can identify a number of reasons why the various affinities and commonalities between Elias and Bourdieu have not been a subject of debate in contemporary Anglophone sociology. First, there is the significant influence of diverging *historical contexts*: Elias's seminal works were produced in the years culminating in the Second World War; all of Bourdieu's influential works were produced a quarter-century after the Second World War. Second, there is the problem of an obvious *language barrier*: Elias's main works were written in German, whereas most of Bourdieu's oeuvre was written in French, and the English translations of their respective writings are not always of the most reliable quality. Third, there is the difference in *sociological emphasis*: while Elias studied long-term historical trends and developments spanning several centuries, Bourdieu focused on dynamics of social reproduction in particular historical contexts. Finally, there is the dividing question of the role of *sociological knowledge*: according to Elias, sociological knowledge is too specialised to have a significant use value in political matters; according to Bourdieu, it is the normative task of the reflexive sociologist not only to examine the social world but also to have a constructive and emancipatory impact on its development. There are multiple reasons why the idea of bringing the works of Elias and Bourdieu closer together is far from obvious. There are, however, also a number of striking affinities and commonalities between these two thinkers. Both were heavily influenced by continental sociologists such as Marx, Durkheim, and Weber, as well as by continental philosophers such as Husserl, Cassirer, and Heidegger. Both fought their way through the power-laden environment of academic institutions. And both had experienced and criticised the tangible consequences of social processes of inclusion and exclusion. Hence there are profound intellectual, biographical, and ideological similarities between the two thinkers. With both the differences and the similarities between Elias and Bourdieu in mind, the chapter explores key points of convergence and divergence between them by focusing on three concepts that feature centrally in their writings: *habitus*, *field*, and *power*.

How is this conceptual triad deployed by Bourdieu? We must first remind ourselves that, as Bourdieu insists, the notions of habitus, field, and capital are to be regarded as *interdependent* concepts in his architecture of society. In other words, habitus, field, and capital constitute three societal cornerstones, which cannot exist independently of each other. A socially competent actor is equipped with a habitus, immersed in different fields, and able to acquire different forms of capital. Regardless of whether we look at Bourdieu's earlier or later work, the ontological interdependence between these three cornerstones of the social is omnipresent in his writings: together, the dispositionally structured apparatus of the habitus, the positionally structured spaces of social fields, and the compositionally structured resources of capital form the relationally structured realm of society.

How is this conceptual triad deployed by Elias? In Elias's writings, habitus, field, and power are also conceived of as *interdependent*, but what meanings does he ascribe to these categories? The defining feature of a field, in the Eliasian sense, is that it describes a social space generated by relational dynamics with constantly shifting balances and imbalances of power. According to this view, a field is composed of chains or webs of interdependent actors and actions. Given the inescapable preponderance of relationally constructed fields in social life, all our actions are inevitably caught up in dynamic chains of interdependence and constantly shifting networks of power. One of the interesting features of the habitus is that its internally located and externally materialised steering mechanisms are the embodied manifestation of the fact that micro- and macro-sociological dynamics are intimately intertwined. Thus, the pervasive power of Elias's famous 'civilising process' is expressed in its capacity to shape the development of society by permeating every actor's subjectivity and thereby establish itself as a habitus-colonising reality. Yet, as Elias insists, the development of people's habitus often lags behind the transformation of social structures; and this is one of the reasons why macro-societal transformations normally need an enormous amount of time to insert themselves in people's day-to-day habits. The efficacy of social power consists in its capacity to assert the presence of its powerfulness as a subtle form of quotidian taken-for-grantedness. What is interesting from an Eliasian perspective, however, is that power is about both hierarchy *and* interdependence, competition *and* cooperation, subversion *and* compliance: not only do we all depend on other people, but we all depend on people who are objectively either more or less powerful than we are. In brief, to be immersed in social relations means to participate in the construction of power relations.

On the basis of these reflections, it seems justified to suggest that the works of Bourdieu and Elias are not as far apart as they may appear at first glance and that the conceptual triad of habitus, field, and power features centrally in their writings. In order to illustrate the tangible relevance of Bourdieu's and Elias's respective conceptual tools and sociological frameworks, Paulle, van Heerikhuizen, and Emirbayer use the example of sport, highlighting the fact that Bourdieu and Elias were the only influential sociologists of the twentieth century to take sport seriously and to regard it as a central and indeed illuminating element of modern social life. The authors argue that if we look at Bourdieu's and Elias's respective approaches to sport, it becomes obvious that there is an uncanny and far-reaching similarity between them. Above all, they share the view that sport can be seen as a social field in which emotional self-control and bodily self-discipline play a particularly important role in the mobilisation of resources, the normalisation of rules, the development of abilities, and the competition between actors. As such, the field of sport is a social field *par excellence*, because *all* social fields are relationally constructed and normatively codified spaces of possibilities with specific modes of functioning and competitive struggles over power. To suggest that the field is in the habitus because the habitus is in the field is to assume that the game is in the player because the player is in the game. The power of social actors depends on their practical capacity to determine not only the outcome but also the rules of the game.

Bourdieu and Adorno

In the eighth chapter, Simon Susen examines the transformation of culture in modern society by drawing upon the works of Pierre Bourdieu and Theodor W. Adorno. The chapter, entitled 'Bourdieu and Adorno on the Transformation of Culture in Modern Society: Towards a Critical Theory of Cultural Production', comprises four sections: the first provides some general reflections on the *concept of culture*; the second focuses on *Bourdieu's analysis of culture*, particularly his interest in the social functioning of the 'cultural economy'; the third centres on *Adorno's analysis of culture*, notably his concern with the social power of the 'culture industry'; and the fourth offers a *comparison* between Bourdieu and Adorno in relation to their respective accounts of the transformation of culture in modern society.

(1) With regard to the concept of culture, it is important to keep in mind that we can distinguish at least three interrelated meanings of culture: culture can be used as a *sociological*, *philosophical*, and *aesthetic* category. As a sociological category, the concept of culture refers to a specific *form of life* produced and reproduced by a given group of people. As such, it describes a spatiotemporally contingent mode of human coexistence: just as different life forms produce different cultures, different cultures produce different life forms. As a philosophical category, the concept of culture can be conceived of as a human *ideal*. As such, it designates a civilisational achievement of advanced societies, whose progressive development is determined by the transcendental power of 'the mind' or 'the spirit' and embodied in increasingly differentiated social institutions: the evolution of every society depends on the education of its members. As an aesthetic category, the concept of culture denotes a distinctively human expression of *artistic creativity*. As such, culture is a body of artistic and intellectual work and the vehicle for human creativity *par excellence*: culture is both a medium and an outcome of the distinctively human capacity to attach meaning to the world through the expressive power of artistic and intellectual production. In brief, the normative, purposive, and creative aspects of human life are realised through the sociological, philosophical, and aesthetic potentials of culture.

(2) Given the paradigmatic importance ascribed to the study of culture in his writings, Bourdieu's sociological theory can be regarded as a cultural theory. From a Bourdieusian perspective, there is no general theory of society without a general theory of culture. When examining Bourdieu's account of culture in general and his analysis of the cultural economy in particular, three social processes are particularly important: the *differentiation*, *commodification*, and *classification* of culture. (i) The differentiation of culture in the modern world manifests itself most significantly in the gradual separation between 'the field of restricted cultural production' and 'the field of large-scale cultural production'. Whereas the former – created and legitimated by the *société distinguée* – is destined for a public of producers of distinguished cultural goods, the latter – reproduced and legitimated by the *société massifiée* – is destined for a public of consumers of mainstream cultural goods. (ii) The commodification of culture in the modern world indicates that, under capitalism, symbolic goods have a two-faced reality: they have both a cultural use value and an economic exchange value. The degree of commodification of culture reflects the degree of colonisation of society by the market. The commodification of culture is problematic in that it reinforces the primacy of form over function, the prevalence of the mode of representation over the object of representation, the predominance of the signifier over the signified, and thus the preponderance of

appearance over substance. (iii) The classification of culture in modern society illustrates that symbolic struggles are power struggles over the distribution of legitimate resources. Legitimately situated actors are legitimately classified and legitimately classifying actors, able to mobilise the cultural resources of their subjectivity, which they acquire through their positionally determined and dispositionally mediated exposure to society. Patterns of cultural consumption need to generate patterns of aesthetic perception and appreciation in order to produce and reproduce patterns of social legitimation.

(3) It is difficult to overemphasise the complexity of Adorno's analysis of the transformation of culture in modern society. Yet, notwithstanding the complexity of his account, it is obvious that if there is one concept that features centrally in Adorno's social theory in general and in his cultural theory in particular, it is the notion of the culture industry. From an Adornian perspective, the rise of the culture industry is symptomatic of the changing nature of culture under late capitalism. In essence, the transformation of culture in modern society is reflected in three social processes: the *heteronomisation*, *commodification*, and *standardisation* of culture. (i) The heteronomisation of culture in the modern world is reflected in the fact that culture, although it never ceases to be an irreplaceable 'source of artistic creativity', is primarily used as a 'vehicle of systemic functionality'. In the totally administered world, which is mainly driven by instrumental rationality, culture is converted into an integrationist weapon of social domination. (ii) The commodification of culture in the modern world is illustrated in the fact that culture, whose true purpose is 'purposefulness without a purpose', becomes degraded to an existence oriented towards 'purposelessness for the purposes of the market'. Under late capitalism, even the most autonomous spheres of society can be heteronomised by the market. (iii) The standardisation of culture in the modern world suggests that we live in an increasingly synchronised and synchronising society in which the main function of culture is to serve as a 'machine of reproductive sociality', rather than as a 'realm of transformative individuality'. For, under late capitalism, the culture industry succeeds in imposing its systemic imperatives on the whole of society, thereby forcing culture to wear the standardised corset of the standardising market and transforming social entertainment, rather than social critique, into one of the main legitimating pillars of the social order.

(4) Although there are substantial differences between Bourdieusian and Adornian thought, the two perspectives share a number of fundamental assumptions about the nature and role of culture in modern society. As demonstrated in the final section of this chapter, the two approaches converge on at least five levels. (i) Given their concern with the relationship between *culture and economy*, both accounts shed light on the dynamic mechanisms underlying the commodification of culture in modern society: advanced

societies have developed omnipresent cultural economies and powerful culture industries. (ii) Determined to uncover the relationship between *culture and domination*, both accounts explore the interest-laden nature of the systemic functionalisation of culture in modern society: every economy of symbolic goods and cultural commodities is embedded in an economy of social power. (iii) Drawing our attention to the relationship between *culture and legitimacy*, both accounts remind us of the stratifying pervasiveness that underpins the classification of culture in modern society: struggles over cultural classification are struggles impregnated with social patterns of ideological legitimation. (iv) In light of the intimate relationship between *culture and history*, both accounts insist upon the spatiotemporal determinacy of every form of cultural specificity: culture is never forever. (v) Convinced that critical sociologists need to confront the normative task of reflecting upon the relationship between *culture and emancipation*, both accounts permit us to make sense not only of the disempowering consequences but also of the empowering potentials of the transformation of culture in modern society: emancipatory societies are inconceivable without emancipatory forms of culture.

Bourdieu and Honneth

In the ninth chapter, 'The Grammar of an Ambivalence', Mauro Basaure examines Bourdieu's influence on the critical theory developed by Axel Honneth. Basaure's main thesis is that Honneth's relation to Bourdieu is marked by a profound *ambivalence*: on the one hand, Bourdieu's work plays a pivotal role in Honneth's reformulation of critical theory, particularly regarding the view that social struggles are a motor of historical development; on the other hand, Honneth is deeply critical of Bourdieu's approach, accusing him of failing to account for the normative constitution of social life and of putting forward an overly pessimistic and essentially utilitarian conception of social action. In other words, while Honneth and Bourdieu converge in conceiving of social relations as power relations, Honneth criticises Bourdieu for not paying sufficient attention to the meaning-laden normativity that allows for the interactional functioning of society. Basaure proceeds in four steps: first, he presents the cornerstones of Honneth's theory of the struggle for recognition; second, he aims to explain why most commentators tend to ignore Honneth's sympathetic reading of Bourdieu; third, he analyses the impact of Bourdieusian thought on Honneth's theory of recognition; and, finally, he explores the common ground between Honnethian and Bourdieusian thought, in particular with regard to the role that Honneth and Bourdieu ascribe to struggles for recognition in their respective approaches to the social.

With regard to the first task, Basaure distinguishes three axes in Honneth's theory of the struggle for recognition: (i) a *moral-sociological* explicative axis, (ii) a *historico-philosophical* reconstructive axis, and (iii) a *political-sociological* axis. The first axis reflects the conceptual effort to account for *moral* motivations behind social actions (the micro-level of intersubjective relations based on reciprocal recognition processes); the second axis is concerned with wider *historical* processes of moral development (the macro-level of societal relations based on collective learning processes); and the third axis captures the *political* nature of social struggles and the ways in which they can contribute to the normative construction of antagonistic collectives (the normative level of social relations based on contestatory processes). Central to Honneth's theoretical framework is the assumption that all three axes have a moral dimension. Put differently, social struggles are by definition moral struggles, for every struggle over the constitution of society is concerned with the constitution of normativity. This is precisely where Honneth's main critique of Bourdieu comes into play: he accuses Bourdieu of paying insufficient attention to the moral dimension of social struggles.

With regard to the second task, Basaure argues that contemporary theories of social struggles are characterised by a failure to differentiate between two levels of analysis, namely between *the 'why'*, which is crucial to the moral-sociological axis, and *the 'how'*, which is central to the political-sociological axis. Basaure claims that, in Honneth's social theory, the former dimension is somewhat overdeveloped, while the latter aspect remains largely underdeveloped. And this appears to be one of the reasons why most commentators tend to ignore Honneth's sympathetic reading of Bourdieu: Honneth's emphasis on the normative nature of our daily search for various forms of social recognition seems irreconcilable with Bourdieu's insistence upon the strategic nature of our engagement in interest-laden forms of social action. However one tries to make sense of the relationship between these two positions, the Bourdieusian use of 'superstructural' concepts – such as 'interest', 'illusio', and 'doxa' – in relation to 'infrastructural' concepts – such as 'field', 'habitus', and 'capital' – suggests that conflicts over social power are driven by struggles over social recognition.

With regard to the third task, Basaure makes the point that, in Honneth's writings, the *political-sociological axis* is seen as embedded in the *moral-sociological axis*. Thus, within the Honnethian framework of social analysis, we are confronted with the assumption that 'the moral' is preponderant over 'the political': social relations are primarily conceived of as moral and normative, rather than as political and purposive. Central to Honneth's account of struggles for social recognition (*soziale Anerkennung*), however, is the profound ambivalence of the subject's dependence on social esteem (*soziale Wertschätzung*): just as the presence of social recognition allows for the empowerment of individuals, the absence of social recognition leads to their disempowerment. Individual or collective experiences that are characterised by feelings of social disrespect (*soziale Mißachtung*) are indicative of the fragility of human subjectivity: the human dependence on mechanisms of social recognition is so strong that the possibility of individual self-realisation is inconceivable without people's capacity to be integrated into society by establishing links based on reciprocity and intersubjectivity. Bourdieusian analysis is directly relevant to this moral-sociological explicative axis in that subjects dependent on reciprocal recognition are unavoidably interest-driven: we do not only depend on but we also have an interest in social recognition, because attainment of social esteem is a precondition for sustainable access to social power. Different social groups in different social fields struggle over different forms of social power by mobilising different resources of social recognition. All forms of capital – notably economic, cultural, political, educational, and linguistic capital – acquire social value if, and only if, they are convertible into at least a minimal degree of symbolic capital. The long-term sustainability of every field-specific form of normativity is contingent upon its capacity to obtain sufficient symbolic legitimacy to assert and, if possible, impose its general acceptability.

With regard to the fourth and final task of his chapter, namely the attempt to demonstrate that Bourdieusian thought is crucial to Honneth's sociology of recognition, Basaure asserts that Honneth has both *a 'broad' and a 'dynamic' conception of social struggle*: in the 'broad' sense, social struggles range from clearly visible and widely recognised collective movements in the public sphere to largely hidden and hardly problematised forms of conflict in the private sphere; in the 'dynamic' sense, social struggles change over time, and so do the ways in which they are discursively represented and politically interpreted. If we account not only for the eclectic but also for the processual nature of social struggles, then we need to accept that social conflicts over material and symbolic power, and the ways in which individual and collective actors make sense or fail to make sense of these conflicts, are constantly changing. Thus, a comprehensive critical theory needs to do justice to both the multifaceted and the dynamic nature of struggles for recognition and thereby shed light on the various ways in which the existential significance of social struggles manifests itself in the constant competition over material and symbolic resources.

Bourdieu and Religion

In his commentary on Bourdieu's engagement with the sociology of religion, Bryan S. Turner offers a comprehensive account of the strengths and weaknesses of Bourdieu's approach to religion. In essence, the chapter, which is entitled 'Pierre Bourdieu and the Sociology of Religion', is concerned with five issues: first, the relative decline of religion in the modern world; second, the apparent revival of religion in the contemporary world; third, recent attempts to reconcile secular with religious forms of reasoning; fourth, Bourdieu's account of religion; and, finally, the 'new paradigm' that has become increasingly influential in recent North American developments in the sociology of religion.

With regard to the first issue, the relative decline of religion in the modern world, Turner points out that the secularisation thesis can be regarded as a central and hitherto largely unquestioned element of classical sociological discourse. The secularisation thesis is based on the assumption that secularisation processes in modern societies contain five interrelated tendencies: industrialisation, differentiation, privatisation, welfarisation, and rationalisation. (i) The *industrialisation* of the social system has led to the weakening of face-to-face ties characteristic of traditional forms of religiously regulated societies. (ii) The *differentiation* of the social system into various coexisting and competing spheres – such as the state, the market, science, art, and religion – has degraded religion to only one field amongst other social fields. (iii) The *privatisation* of the social system has contributed to the gradual marginalisation of religion to the domestic sphere. (iv) The *welfarisation* of the social system – that is, the provision of social welfare by specialised institutions – has added to a significant improvement of living standards and contributed to a reduction of both short-term and long-term risks, undermining people's dependence on belief in the uncontrollable power of supernatural forces over empirical reality. (v) The *rationalisation* of the social system, driven by the gradual replacement of faith and superstition by reason and science, has resulted in the shift from the 'enchanted world' of traditional societies to the 'disenchanted world' of modern societies.

With regard to the second issue, the apparent revival of religion in the contemporary world, Turner reminds us that religion has far from disappeared and that, consequently, in recent years more and more sociologists and philosophers have concluded that religion needs to be taken seriously. Turner identifies some of the key developments associated with the revival of religion in late modern societies: the collapse of organised communism in the early 1990s, the subsequent decline of Marxism-Leninism as a quasi-religious ideology of the Eastern socialist bloc, the rise of globalisation, and the worldwide emergence of diasporic communities. Hence, whatever lies at the 'heart of the heartless world' in the contemporary context, there is substantial evidence to suggest that religion has not only survived the transition from traditional to modern society but that, in late modern society, in various parts of the world – particularly in America, Africa, and Asia, but also in some regions of continental Europe – it has expanded and gained increasing powers of adaptation, absorption, and transformation.

With regard to the third issue, concerning recent attempts to reconcile secular with religious forms of reasoning, Turner draws upon the work of Jürgen Habermas, who in his recent writings has made a sustained and vigorous effort to demonstrate that secular and religious citizens are capable of living peacefully side by side and that they are, furthermore, both morally and practically obliged to confront the challenge of establishing a fruitful dialogue between reason and faith. Secularists cannot ignore, let alone marginalise, religious practices and beliefs if they aim to be seriously involved in the construction of pluralistic and multicultural societies; at the same time, religious citizens cannot disregard, let alone demonise, secular ways of life and thought if they seek to be realistically engaged in the construction of maturing and reason-guided societies. Notwithstanding the question of whether, in late modern societies, either 'believing without belonging' or 'belonging without believing' is the predominant form of religious reproduction, there is little doubt that, in postsecular societies, there can be no 'reasoning without believing' just as there can be no 'believing without reasoning'.

With regard to the fourth issue, Bourdieu's account of religion, the obvious question to be asked is this: what, if anything, can we learn from Bourdieu's account of religion? Turner's answer to this question is, as he admits, somewhat paradoxical: on the one hand, it appears that Bourdieu's analysis of religion, developed in his small oeuvre of essays on religion, is not particularly insightful and is essentially a synthesis of Max Weber's sociological and Louis Althusser's philosophical interpretations of religion; on the other hand, Bourdieu's conceptual tools – such as habitus, field, and capital – do allow for the construction of a useful analytical framework that allows us to understand the sociological power of religion in terms of embodied practices, rather than in terms of disembodied beliefs. Turner argues that, given its functionalist undertones, Bourdieu's account of religion is based on a crude combination of the Marxian contention that religion serves as the 'opium of the people' used to obtain ideological acceptability, the Weberian notion that religion serves as an 'instrument of power struggles' oriented towards the attainment of social legitimacy, and the Althusserian view that religion serves as an 'ideological vehicle' mobilised for the control of people's subjectivity. From a Bourdieusian perspective, then, it is the task of a critical sociology of religion to explore the actual *practices and interests* of embodied actors situated in religious fields, rather than the formal *beliefs and doctrines* of disembodied subjects removed from those fields. According to this position, it is the ensemble of social relations which determines the ensemble of social beliefs. Despite Turner's appreciation of Bourdieu's approach to religion, he criticises Bourdieu for concentrating almost exclusively on field-specific positions and habitus-specific dispositions. In other words, he accuses Bourdieu of *overestimating* the reproductive mechanisms of social determinacy and *underestimating* the transformative potentials of social agency within religious fields. The argument is underscored by Turner's disappointment with Bourdieu's somewhat reductive reading, and partial misrepresentation, of Weber's sociology of religion.

With regard to the fifth issue, the 'new paradigm' prevalent in North American approaches to religion, the author turns his attention to a novel set of assumptions in the contemporary sociology of religion, epitomised by economic interpretations of religion. The shift from the 'old' European to the 'new' North American paradigm reflects a move away from an emphasis on *symbolic and ideological* dimensions to an emphasis on *economic and pragmatic* aspects of religious behaviour in advanced societies. This paradigmatic shift tends to be undertaken by focusing on three dimensions: (i) the *resilience* of religion in late modern, including secular, societies; (ii) the various social *functions* of religious and spiritual markets; and (iii) the cross-cultural *invariability* of religiously grounded demands for meaning. It is well known that Bourdieu was deeply critical of social-scientific approaches based on rational action theories. Nevertheless, somewhat counter-intuitively Turner draws our attention to the fact that there are striking similarities between Bourdieu's analysis of religious fields and the rational choice model of religious markets: both approaches move within a sociological comfort zone founded on economic concepts such as 'interests', 'stakes', and 'competition'. The economy of religious fields is inconceivable without a politics of religious markets. Whichever paradigm we subscribe to, however, we cannot ignore the existence of the functional dialectics of belief and practice: belief can only survive if embedded in and nourished by practice, just as practice can only survive if situated in and motivated by belief. Thus, from a Bourdieusian perspective, the sociology of religion describes another significant area of study that permits and indeed compels us to conceive of the apparent antinomy between 'the ideological' and 'the practical' as a socio-ontological unity.

Bourdieu and Habitus

In the eleventh chapter, 'Bourdieu's Sociological Fiction: A Phenomenological Reading of Habitus', Bruno Frère provides a detailed analysis of Bourdieu's conception of habitus. Frère points out that just as we need to be aware of the key strengths of Bourdieu's genetic-structuralist approach, we need to identify its main weaknesses. Hence it is possible to draw on Bourdieu's approach whilst developing it further and thereby overcoming its most significant shortcomings. Illustrating the complexity inherent in the analytical task of revising Bourdieu's genetic-structuralist approach to the social, Frère's chapter focuses on five accounts of the 'social actor': (1) Pierre Bourdieu's account of the 'homological actor', (2) Bernard Lahire's account of the 'plural actor', (3) Philippe Corcuff's account of the 'dynamic actor', (4) Merleau-Ponty's account of the 'bodily actor', and (5) Bruno Frère's own account of the 'imaginative actor'.

(1) With regard to Bourdieu's account of the 'homological actor', Frère remarks that arguably the most influential French sociologist of the late twentieth century has a tendency to privilege the reproductive and mechanical, over the transformative and creative, dimensions of social action. The fact that this is a common view in the literature, not only amongst those who are deeply critical of Bourdieu's work but also amongst those who sympathise with his approach, seems to indicate that Bourdieusian thought is particularly strong in terms of uncovering social mechanisms of reproduction and domination, but rather weak in terms of explaining social processes of transformation and emancipation. If, however, we are prepared to accept that the human proclivity towards creation and innovation as well as the human capacity of reflection and contemplation constitute integral components of ordinary social life, we are obliged to abandon a *determinist* view of the social, which fails to account for both the creative and the reflective potentials inherent in every ordinary subject. Although the whole point of Bourdieu's project is to overcome the counterproductive antinomy between objectivist and subjectivist approaches in the social sciences, his account of the 'homological actor' seems to suggest that he remains trapped in an objectivist-determinist paradigm of social action. According to this homological view, the dispositional constitution of every social actor is largely determined by the positional constitution of social fields.

(2) Seeking to move beyond Bourdieu's purportedly determinist conception of the social, Lahire puts forward an alternative model of social action, epitomised in the concept of the 'plural actor'. As Frère elucidates, Lahire's alternative approach allows us to account for three key features of subjectivity in complex societies: multiplicity, irreducibility, and autonomy. *Multiplicity* is a constitutive component of late modern subjectivity in that the diversity of dispositions incorporated by social actors corresponds to the plurality of positions located in social fields. *Irreducibility* is a pivotal aspect of late modern subjectivity in that the coexistence of various dispositions developed by social actors reflects the complexity of multidimensionally structured schemes of perception and action. *Autonomy* is an empowering element of late modern subjectivity in that individualist societies create 'dissonant profiles' which illustrate that people's attitudes, tastes, and practices do not necessarily correspond to one overriding (for example, socioeconomically defined)

disposition. In brief, unlike Bourdieu's 'homological actor', conceived of as a largely predictable entity determined by the correspondence between habitus and field, Lahire's 'plural actor' is an essentially unpredictable source of multi-causally determined agency in the fragmented landscape of centreless societies.

(3) In line with Lahire's insistence upon the multifaceted constitution of the 'plural actor', Corcuff puts forward the concept of the 'dynamic actor'. The most obvious feature of 'dynamic actors' is a 'malleable habitus', that is, a habitus capable of adjusting itself to the dynamic pace of life to which human actors situated in highly differentiated societies are almost inevitably exposed. As Frère points out, Corcuff's alternative perspective permits us to make sense of three key features of subjectivity in complex societies: reflexivity, creativity, and adaptability. Actors in complex societies have the potential to develop high degrees of *reflexivity* because the constant exposure to normative complexity requires not only the practical capacity to slip back and forth between different social roles played in particular social fields, but also the critical capacity to convert one's performative immersion in everyday forms of human agency into an object of reflection when trying to cope with role conflicts generated by the quotidian interactions taking place in differentiated societies. Actors in complex societies have the potential to develop high degrees of *creativity* because, in order to realise themselves through the development of their individuality, they are expected to be both competent carriers and self-determined creators of their identity. Actors in complex societies have the potential to develop high degrees of *adaptability* because, in order to find their individual place in the collective spaces constructed by different communities, they need to develop the ability to adjust to, and function in accordance with, various coexisting and often competing normativities. In short, unlike Bourdieu's 'homological actor', reducible to a largely reproductive element in a power-driven society, Corcuff's 'dynamic actor' is a transformative source of self-critical reflexivity, self-motivated creativity, and self-responsible adaptability in the fluid landscape of freedom-based societies.

(4) With the aim of overcoming the explanatory limitations arising from the philosophical obsession with the allegedly self-determining power of the 'rational actor', Bourdieu draws upon the works of phenomenological thinkers, in particular the writings of Edmund Husserl and Maurice Merleau-Ponty, to explore the sociological implications of the fact that every social actor is a 'bodily actor'. By centring his phenomenology on the body, rather than on consciousness, Merleau-Ponty shifts the emphasis from the rationalist concern with the subject's cognitive processing of and conscious control over the world to the phenomenological preoccupation with the actor's corporeal immersion in and unconscious absorption of the lifeworld. Regardless

of whether one favours an Aristotelian, a Husserlian, or a Bourdieusian conception of human subjectivity, one has to accept that these perspectives converge in acknowledging that the tangible power of the habitus stems from the dispositional structures which inhabit our bodies: the various positions that we occupy in the external world of society are worthless without the numerous dispositions that we carry within the internal world of our body. To accept the preponderance of the collective over the individual elements that inhabit our subjectivity, of the external over the internal facets that constitute interactional forms of objectivity, and of the unconscious over the conscious dimensions that permeate human reality means to face up to the omnipresence of society. Bourdieu's aphoristic statement that 'society is God' essentially suggests that, as members of humanity, we cannot escape the ubiquity of a relationally defined reality (Bourdieu, 2000 [1997]: 245). Given that we, as bodily entities, are physically exposed to the lawfulness, power-ladenness, and interest-drivenness of human reality, we are obliged to develop the practical capacity to cope with the material and the symbolic struggles over the normative arrangements that shape the development of society. The bodily constitution of the habitus makes the social appear natural to us: we are so used to absorbing, and thereby accepting, the givenness of the way things are that we – as bodily entities, nourished by the immersive power of everyday experience – tend to recognise the relative arbitrariness of social reality only when confronted with the crisis-ladenness of established patterns of normativity.

(5) Inspired by Bourdieu's account of the 'homological actor', Lahire's notion of the 'plural actor', Corcuff's interest in the 'dynamic actor', and Merleau-Ponty's examination of the 'bodily actor', Frère insists that we need to conceive of the human subject also as an 'imaginative actor'. With reference to the work of Cornelius Castoriadis, Frère introduces the idea of the 'sociological fiction' of the habitus: the imaginary institution of society is constantly constructed and reconstructed by the imaginary apparatus of the habitus. Frère's emphasis on the 'fictitious' constitution of the habitus is aimed not at suggesting that the habitus does not actually exist, but at drawing our attention to the fact that the habitus, as a perceptive and projective apparatus, has the power to bring things into being: for us, as perceiving and projecting entities, the normalisation of society is inconceivable without the externalising power of human subjectivity. As 'imaginative actors', we literally bring existence into being insofar as we project ourselves into the being of our existence. As Frère seeks to demonstrate in his own studies on social movements, it is by interacting with others that our need for expression *about* and working *upon* the world becomes a major resource that we need to mobilise in order to invent and reinvent our place *within* the world. A sociology that disregards the innovative power of imaginary

creativity cannot account for the developmental power of socio-historical contingency.

Bourdieu and Language

In the twelfth chapter, 'Overcoming Semiotic Structuralism: Language and Habitus in Bourdieu', Hans-Herbert Kögler provides an intellectually stimulating and analytically rigorous account of an ambitious philosophical project: the attempt to overcome some of the key pitfalls of semiotic structuralism by drawing on Bourdieu's theory of language and habitus. As illustrated in Kögler's essay, there is a noteworthy affinity between the 'linguistic turn' in philosophy – associated with the works of Saussure, Heidegger, Gadamer, Habermas, and Searle – and the 'reflexive turn' in sociology – associated with the writings of Bourdieu. The affinity is in the following sense: both paradigmatic turns are motivated by the insight that human actors, insofar as they are unavoidably immersed in particular socio-historical contexts, cannot escape the preponderance of implicitly reproduced and practically mobilised background horizons. Background horizons are socially powerful because they shape people's modes of perception, reflection, and action and, as a consequence, their spatiotemporally situated ways of relating to, making sense of, and acting upon the world.

However one conceives of the relation between necessity and freedom, objectivity and subjectivity, and structure and agency, it is imperative – as Kögler rightly insists – to explore the empowering potentials derived from one species-constitutive capacity: *intentional and reflexive agency*. The question that arises from recognising that we are not only motivationally and intentionally driven beings, but also reflexively and critically guided subjects is to what extent Bourdieu's notion of habitus allows us to account not only for the reproductive and habitual but also for the transformative and creative elements of human action. Even if we assume that Bourdieu is right to suggest that our linguistic habitus is embedded in and largely determined by our social habitus, it is far from clear to what extent the genetic-structuralist approach permits us to do justice to the relative autonomy of linguistically mediated forms of reflexivity.

After setting the scene and elucidating the complexity of the theoretical problems arising from Bourdieu's notion of habitus in relation to both social and linguistic practices, Kögler examines, in the first part of his chapter, the *explanatory limitations of the semiotic model of communication*. Drawing on Saussure's semiotic structuralism, Kögler argues that every language is based on a system of signs, which constitutes not only a unified duality between 'the signifier' and 'the signified' but also, more importantly, a communicative vehicle for intelligibly organised forms of intersubjectivity. From this perspective, a 'diachronic' view, which is primarily concerned with monological speech, needs to be replaced by a 'synchronic' view, which draws our attention to the importance of dialogical speech, when examining the very possibility of linguistically mediated forms of meaning: we need to focus on *shared* understandings, *shared* symbols, and *shared* meanings to make sense of the fact that our linguistic competence is primarily a social competence, that is, an interactive capacity developed through the constant exposure to and immersion in ordinary forms of intersubjectivity sustained through the linguistically mediated construction of mutual intelligibility. If, following Saussure's externalist rather than internalist model, the construction of linguistic meaning takes place 'between' rather than 'within' speakers, then we need to be aware of three levels of intertwinement: first, the intertwinement of interpretation (*know-that*) and application (*know-how*); second, the intertwinement of language-as-a-structure (*langue*) and language-as-a-process (*parole*); and, third, the intertwinement of intelligibility (*meaning*) and normativity (*values*). This is precisely where Bourdieu's work is helpful: from a sociological point of view, the internal organisation of a symbolic order is to be studied not as an autopoietic system of codes used by symmetrically situated subjects equipped with universally ingrained competences, but as an interest-laden market of signs mobilised by asymmetrically related actors divided by disproportionally available resources.

With this arguably Bourdieusian framework in mind, Kögler goes on to draw a broad distinction between two models of linguistic meaning: the first approach centres on the role of *validity claims*; the second approach focuses on the role of *practical dispositions*. Whereas the former is closely associated with Habermas's theory of universal pragmatics, the latter is particularly important in Bourdieu's theory of symbolic power. The main point that these two approaches have in common is their emphasis on the *performative* nature of linguistic practices: speakers need to speak – that is, they need to *use* language – in order to be part of a speech community. Yet, one of the key points that separate these two approaches from one another is the question of the main *function* that language plays in society. According to Habermas, people raise validity claims as linguistic subjects who have a deep-seated need to attribute meaning to their daily participation in the social *practices* of their lifeworlds: society can be reproduced and transformed only through communicative *action*. According to Bourdieu, people raise legitimacy claims as interest-driven actors who are determined to mobilise their habitus-specific resources to position themselves in relation to one another when immersed in *struggles* over material and symbolic power in different social fields: society is reproduced and transformed through strategic *competition*. According to Kögler, the epistemological discrepancy between these two positions is reflected in the *dialectic of normative reason and practical power*. Taking into account the respective merits of these models, a critical philosophy of language needs to shed light on the functional *ambivalence* of language: on the one hand, language is a vehicle for social normativity, communicative intelligibility, and critical reflexivity; on the other hand, language is a vehicle for social hierarchy, asymmetrical relationality, and surreptitious strategy. In short, language is both a communicative medium of rational action coordination and a purposive instrument of power-laden competition.

From a Bourdieusian perspective, we are obliged to reflect on the relationship between *language, habitus, and symbolic power*. Kögler's main thesis is that Bourdieu grounds the linguistic habitus in the social habitus. According to this view, linguistically mediated background assumptions are embedded in socially inculcated dispositions. Yet, the main problem with Bourdieu's conception of language is that, as Kögler insists, it underestimates the creative and critical potentials of linguistic actors. We need to account for the fact that subjects capable of speech and action are also capable of justification and reflection. A sociological approach that focuses almost exclusively on the relational determinacy and resourceful dispositionality of social actors fails to do justice to the anthropological specificity of linguistically mediated forms of intersubjectivity. Our *sens linguistique*, which inhabits our *sens pratique*, is not only a dispositional conglomerate, whose existence is indicative of our socially constituted determinacy, but also an empowering resource, which is indispensable to the development of our rationally grounded sense of autonomy.

In light of the empowering potentials inherent in rationally grounded forms of reflexivity, it is difficult to defend the – somewhat reductive – view that our linguistic habitus can be subordinated to our social habitus. The preponderance of social objectivity does not necessarily imply the preponderance of social heteronomy. As subjects capable of speech and reflection, we are able to develop a sense of linguistically grounded and rationally guided autonomy. To reduce the linguistic habitus to a mere subcategory of the social habitus means to treat linguistically mediated expressions of reflexivity as a peripheral element of exogenously determined forms of human agency. In opposition to this arguably 'sociologistic' perspective, Kögler makes a case for the view that there are at least three reasons why linguistically mediated forms of intentionality constitute an indispensable element of human agency. First, human beings are both *goal-oriented and value-rational* actors: the interdependence of purposive and substantive forms of rationality lies at the heart of every society. Second, human beings are both *immersive and reflexive* actors: the interdependence of doxic and discursive forms of rationality is fundamental to the daily unfolding of human performativity. Third, human beings are both *perspectival and transperspectival* actors: the interdependence of perspective-laden and perspective-taking forms of rationality is an indispensable moral driving force of human interactionality. In short, there is no ethical agency without linguistically mediated forms of reflexivity.

Bourdieu and Politics

The thirteenth chapter, written by Derek Robbins, is entitled 'Social Theory and Politics: Aron, Bourdieu and Passeron, and the Events of May 1968'. Derek Robbins is an established and internationally recognised scholar in the field of contemporary social and political theory, and his chapter is yet another example of his in-depth knowledge of twentieth century intellectual thought.

In the chapter's first section, Robbins provides us with a brief *mise-en-scène* by which he situates Aron, Bourdieu, and Passeron in their respective intellectual contexts. Particularly important with regard to Aron is the fact that from an early stage he maintained an intellectual and methodological commitment to the work of Max Weber. Due to this commitment to the Weberian view of the world, Aron's approach is based on the assumption that there is no genuine sociology of development without a critical philosophy of history, just as there is no professional separation between scientists and politicians without a conceptual distinction between objectivity and normativity. Yet, it is striking when reflecting on the works of Passeron and Bourdieu that, whilst both were philosophers by training, they became sociologists by choice. Given that both thinkers migrated from philosophy into sociology, Passeron and Bourdieu can be regarded as 'self-exiled intellectual emigrants', who escaped from the age-old discipline of philosophy, and as 'self-invited intellectual immigrants', who sought refuge in the juvenile discipline of sociology. With the motives for their intellectual migration from philosophy to sociology in mind, it is possible to understand Passeron and Bourdieu's radical critique of the 'scholastic gaze', that is, of the illusory philosophical pursuit of intellectual purity, universal validity, disinterested rationality, and value-neutrality. With their plea for a 'sociological gaze' in mind, one can make sense of their commitment to putting philosophy front and centre by insisting upon the socio-historical embeddedness of all forms of knowledge production.

In the chapter's second section, Robbins focuses on the work of Aron and proposes to examine his intellectual positions with regard to two concerns: the relationship between social science and political action, and the nature of sociology as a science. With regard to the first concern, the *relationship between social science and political action*, it comes as no surprise that Aron, as a Weberian, was a strong defender of the division between science and politics and, as a result, of a strict separation between the search for scientific validity and the search for political normativity. Although Aron – following Weber – regarded the historical nature of society as a constitutive component of human existence, he was opposed to historicist attempts to reduce the constitution of being to an evolutionary product of the hitherto-been. According to Aron, it is essential to preserve a notion of human freedom that allows us to recognise that our perceptions of the past do not necessarily shape, let alone determine, our actions in the future. Whatever may be one's view on the role of history in general and on the role of historical consciousness in particular, it seems indisputable that the disenchantment of worldly existence, triggered by the rise of modern society, is inextricably linked to the disenchantment of worldly knowledge, driven by the rise of modern science. With regard to Aron's second concern, the *nature of sociology as a science*, it is worth pointing out that – following Aron – there are two, fundamentally different, conceptions of sociology: one 'modest' and one 'ambitious' conception. According to the former, sociology is only one amongst a series of other social-scientific disciplines; according to the latter, sociology is the master discipline that both stands above and exists through other social-scientific disciplines. As Robbins remarks, Aron clearly favoured the former – that is, the 'realistic' – over the latter – that is, the 'sociologistic' – view. Thus he was concerned not to hypostatise 'the power of the social' into 'the fetish of the social'. Even if, due to its general commitment to exploring the nature and development of the social world, we conceive of sociology as both the most wide-ranging and the most ambitious discipline in the social sciences, we must not assume that it therefore possesses the epistemic monopoly over the systematic study of the functioning of society.

In the chapter's third section, Robbins sheds light on the – arguably 'Aronian' – nature of the research carried out by Bourdieu and Passeron in the 1960s. Profoundly disillusioned with the French higher education system and deeply critical of the exclusionary aspects of the presumably inclusionary French democracy, Bourdieu and Passeron developed a research agenda aimed at examining the underlying logic of both pedagogical and political relations in France and the ways in which they contributed to the actual reproduction, rather than the potential transformation, of established power relations. In essence, these studies demonstrated that in modern France the relative elasticity and stability of social domination was due to the interwovenness of symbolic and material, habitual and institutional, informal and formal, and cultural and economic resources of power. Yet, as Robbins insists, there were also some striking differences between Bourdieu and Passeron in terms of their respective approaches to the social. Bourdieu had a tendency to concentrate on the heteronomous, and thus ultimately reproductive, logic of field-dependent discourses, field-specific systems, and field-embedded institutions; conversely, Passeron was prepared to acknowledge the autonomous, and hence potentially transformative, logic of pluralised discourses, differentiated systems, and diversified institutions. Despite this not insignificant point of divergence derived from a normative discrepancy between different sociological presuppositions, Bourdieu and Passeron were united in their epistemologically inspired and methodologically justified ambition to overcome what they conceived of as artificial and counterproductive dichotomies: the oppositions between positivist and hermeneutic, naturalist and anti-naturalist, and empiricist and interpretivist approaches in the social sciences. Questioning the legitimacy of widely accepted antinomies in intellectual thought, Bourdieu and Passeron established themselves as two practising social scientists who, whilst sharing an educational background in philosophy, ended up developing an interest and expertise in sociology, particularly in the sociology of education and culture. As Robbins emphasises, their academic itineraries had been heavily influenced by Aron, notably by his practical engagement with politics and his intellectual interest in political science.

Finally, Robbins reminds us that, following in Aron's footsteps, Passeron and Bourdieu were politically engaged. They tried to link their commitment to politics with their commitment to science, and hence they sought to show both in their writings and in their actions that even if, in a classical Weberian fashion, one attempts to separate politics and science, the two spheres are inextricably interrelated. Practical questions concerning the political organisation of society cannot be separated from theoretical questions arising from the scientific study of society. Where both Bourdieu and Passeron clearly differed from Aron, however, was in their sustained efforts to bring to light the extent to which processes of pedagogical communication euphemised, and hence reproduced, mechanisms of political domination. More importantly, they differed from Aron in their radical, rather than conservative, beliefs in the liberating potentials of counter-cultures and counter-politics aimed at undermining the established doxa of the cultural and political mainstream of French society. From this perspective, a *raisonnement sociologique* can only have a constructive impact on society insofar as it conceives of itself as a *raisonnement politique*.

Bourdieu and the Public Sphere

In the fourteenth chapter, 'Intellectual Critique and the Public Sphere: Between the Corporatism of the Universal and the *Realpolitik* of Reason', Yves Sintomer discusses Bourdieu's account of the nature of scientific and intellectual thought. If, following Bourdieu, we conceive of critical sociology as a systematic attempt to uncover the underlying mechanisms that determine both the constitution and the evolution of the social world and if, furthermore, we consider this task to be a normative endeavour aimed at shedding light on both different sources of social domination and different resources of human emancipation, then the production of scientific knowledge is not an end in itself but an empowering tool that enables us to have a transformative impact on the world. Insisting on both the descriptive and the normative dimensions that permeate scientific and intellectual thought, Sintomer provides an insightful account of Bourdieu's sociology of reason, that is, of the systematic attempt to examine the social conditions underlying the rationally grounded production of knowledge. In essence, Sintomer's chapter offers a critical analysis of five types of reason: (1) intellectual reason, (2) scientific reason, (3) political reason, (4) critical reason, and (5) communicative reason.

(1) Reflecting upon the nature of *intellectual reason*, Sintomer identifies different denotative and connotative meanings of the word 'intellectual'. First, in the broadest sense, it can be used to refer to knowledgeable and cultured people, who are equipped with the necessary educational capital to immerse themselves in intellectual fields and thereby develop an intellectual habitus. Second, in a more restricted sense, the term is used to distinguish 'skilled labour' from 'manual labour', suggesting that the former is primarily cerebral whereas the latter is mainly physical in nature. Third, in an even narrower sense, the term can be employed to characterise professional academics and artists, for whom reflexivity and creativity constitute the *sine qua non* of their everyday existence. Finally, in an even more confined – and arguably Bourdieusian – sense, the term can be used to designate those people who have the symbolically, and often institutionally, conferred authority to participate in one of the three cultural fields *par excellence* – scientific, artistic, or literary – and defend their cultural legitimacy through the affirmation of their symbolic authority in the public realms of society. As Sintomer points out, it is this last meaning which is particularly important in making sense of the multifaceted ways in which the cultural field possesses the paradoxical capacity to convert its dependence on publicity into a privilege of collective privacy: in order to be part of a distinguished cultural group, one needs to master the distinguished cultural codes that allow one to relate to, and be recognised within, a distinguished cultural field.

(2) Examining the nature of *scientific reason*, Sintomer reminds us that one of the most remarkable achievements of the scientific field has always been its capacity to affirm its relative autonomy in relation to other powerful realms of society. If the lasting success of the scientific field manifests itself in its relative independence from other social fields, then the pervasive influence of scientific reason is expressed in its epistemic ability to distinguish itself from other forms of social rationality. Thus, the power of scientific reason is not only due to its – endogenously developed – explanatory capacity but also due to its – exogenously recognised – epistemic autonomy: in order for scientific rationality to be a source of enlightening knowledgeability it constantly needs

to affirm and demonstrate its relative independence from other – notably political, economic, and religious – forms of rationality. In Bourdieusian terms, the scientific game can be characterised as a 'corporatism of the universal' because it is based on the collectively negotiated search for universal truths. Nonetheless, in order to avoid the trap of epistemic transcendentalism or epistemic relativism, it is necessary to recognise both the historical embeddedness and the emancipatory progressiveness of scientific reason: just as particular life forms produce particular language games, particular language games produce particular life forms. The functional interdependence of scientifically motivated forms of rationality and scientifically shaped forms of society reflects the fruitful interplay between reason-guided language games and reason-guided life forms.

(3) Exploring the nature of *political reason*, Sintomer – following Bourdieu – puts forward the idea that the 'production of truth' can be conceived of as a 'politics of truth': given the social embeddedness of all knowledge claims and given the interest-ladenness of all social conditions, we cannot deny the intrinsic normativity that inhabits the most rigorously argued claims to epistemic validity and scientific objectivity. The '*Realpolitik* of reason', as Bourdieu calls it, is only sustainable insofar as it is guided by the '*Realvernunft* of politics', for a commitment to critical rationalism is worth nothing without a commitment to ethical pragmatism. As Sintomer – drawing on Bourdieu – insists, the 'corporatism of the universal' and the '*Realpolitik* of reason' are closely interrelated, for the scientific quest for defensible truth claims and the political quest for justifiable rightness claims are two integral components of the civilisational search for universally acceptable legitimacy claims. The politics of universal values, however, needs to face up to the interest-laden nature of all forms of normativity in order to recognise its own socio-historical determinacy.

(4) Exploring the nature of *critical reason*, Sintomer frames his analysis in terms of the relationship between the 'corporatism of the universal' and the 'public sphere', that is, in light of the emancipatory potentials inherent in all forms of rationality that are exposed to public scrutiny. By definition, the aforementioned types of reason – intellectual, scientific, and political – represent *critical* forms of reason. Yet, what are the constitutive features of such critical forms of reason? Inspired by Bourdieu's sociological critique of scholastic notions of reason in general and by his relentless attack on Kantian and Habermasian forms of abstract rationalism in particular, Sintomer brings five essential features of critical reason to our attention. First, critical reason is aware of its own *historicity*: a critical analysis of reason needs to examine the socio-historical contingency of all forms of rationality. Second, critical reason is capable of acknowledging its own *partiality*: a critical analysis of reason needs to explore the interest-laden normativity of all forms of rationality. Third, critical

reason does not hide away from its own *determinacy*: a critical analysis of reason needs to face up to the field-specific referentiality of all forms of rationality. Fourth, critical reason is prepared to put its own existence into perspective by recognising the enlightening power of epistemic *plurality*: a critical analysis of reason needs to accept the presuppositional elasticity underlying all forms of rationality. Finally, critical reason is inconceivable without a sustained reflection upon its own *contestability*: a critical analysis of reason needs to uncover the power-laden negotiability of all forms of rationality. In short, critical reason, in the Bourdieusian sense, demands the awareness of the social conditioning underlying all forms of action and reflection.

(5) In a Habermasian spirit, Sintomer offers critical reflections on Bourdieu's account of knowledge production, insisting on the emancipatory potentials inherent in social processes oriented towards mutual understanding, epitomised in what we may refer to as *communicative reason*. Despite the aforementioned strengths of the reflexive-sociological approach to knowledge production, Bourdieu's account of reason essentially suffers from three serious shortcomings: *determinism*, *scientism*, and *fatalism*. Bourdieu's tendency to conceive of rationality in terms of its field-immanent determinacy prevents him from accounting for the field-transcendent autonomy of both ordinary and scientific claims to epistemic validity: epistemic validity is partly, but not exclusively, determined by its field-specific legitimacy. Bourdieu's tendency to conceive of rationality in terms of a duality between mundane and methodical knowledgeability is based on the scientistic assumption that critical reflexivity represents a socio-professional privilege of intellectuals and experts, rather than a socio-ontological privilege of the human species. Yet, ordinary subjects capable of speech and action are also capable of reflection and action. Bourdieu's tendency to conceive of rationality in terms of strategic, rather than communicative, action is symptomatic of his fatalistic view of the social. A one-sided focus on the monological and purposive elements of social action oriented towards power and competition, however, proves incapable of doing justice to the emancipatory potentials inherent in the dialogical and communicative elements of social action oriented towards discussion and cooperation. In brief, a '*Realpolitik* of reason' should not only seek to recognise but also aim to realise the '*Realpotential* of reason'.

Bourdieu and Time

In the final chapter, 'Practice as Temporalisation: Bourdieu and Economic Crisis', Lisa Adkins assesses the relevance of Bourdieu's work to economic sociology in general and to the sociology of time in particular. Specifically, she asks to what extent Bourdieu's social theory can be a useful tool to make sense of the recent and ongoing global economic crisis. It is Adkins's contention that in Bourdieu's work we can find powerful resources to study economic crisis from a sociological perspective, but that the conceptual and methodological tools borrowed from a Bourdieusian framework need to be modified and refined to exploit their explanatory power in relation to the social and political analysis of contemporary issues.

Adkins identifies five main reasons why Bourdieu's work is not commonly used to analyse economic crises. (i) Despite his exploration of different types of capital – notably social, cultural, symbolic, and economic capital – nowhere in Bourdieu's writings can we find an attempt, however rudimentary, to elucidate the *specificity of capitalist capital.* (ii) Even though he insists upon the temporal constitution of the social world in general and of social fields in particular, Bourdieu does not examine the process of abstraction and quantification of labour into temporally structured units. Insofar as he fails to consider that under capitalism labour can be converted into exchangeable equivalents, Bourdieu does not account for the *specificity of capitalist labour appropriation.* (iii) While he is concerned with social processes of domination and exploitation, Bourdieu does not explore the social implications of the conversion of living labour into abstract labour (let alone of living into abstract forms of capital), which is central to the very functioning of capitalism as a social system; thus, he fails to do justice to the *specificity of capitalist abstraction.* (iv) Notwithstanding his general interest in the sociological significance of field-specific forms of crisis, usually triggered by a confrontation between orthodox and heterodox discourses as well as between dominant and dominated groups in a given social field, Bourdieu does not provide a set of explanatory tools capable of aiding our understanding of the *specificity of capitalist crisis.* (v) In spite of Bourdieu's emphasis on the dialectical nature of reproductive and transformative processes of social structuration, it is generally assumed that, within his theoretical framework of 'generic structuralism', the reproductive power of stasis remains prevalent over the transformative potential of crisis and that, as a consequence, Bourdieu's approach does not account for the *specificity of capitalist transformation.*

Adkins goes on to assert that, despite the aforementioned shortcomings, Bourdieu offers a number of conceptual resources that permit us to make sense of recent economic events, not only in terms of a *crisis of time* but also in terms of a *restructuring of time*. Drawing on Richard Sennett's critical account of the corrosive effects of late capitalism, she reminds us that the accumulation of flexibilised – that is, fragmented – experiences and the cultivation of weak – that is, opportunistic – ties in the post-Fordist economy have contributed to the construction of a world in which people find it increasingly difficult to develop a sense of narrative movement. Under the heading 'Trading the Future?', Adkins remarks that the post-Fordist universe is a world characterised by the radical renegotiation of temporal horizons. In a world dictated by the powerful dynamics of permanent scientific innovation, compulsive large-sale technologisation, and macro-societal transformation, the temporal boundaries between past, present, and future are constantly being reshaped and resignified towards emphases on situational contingency, historical indeterminacy, and societal uncertainty. Consequently, the looking-forwardness of the human condition is absorbed into the taken-for-grantedness of the post-Fordist condition.

This is where Bourdieu is helpful. Under the heading 'Anticipation: Time in the Making', Adkins discusses a Husserlian theme in Bourdieu's writings on time: according to Bourdieu, the future is always already existent in the immediate present, for human agents are ordinarily immersed in the forthcoming. Since human agents are equipped with predispositional schemes of perception and appreciation, which *anticipate* their positionally situated course of action, in the social world the always-still-to-be is part of the always-already-been just as the always-already-been is part of the always-still-to-be. In short, it is the *protensive* nature of practice which explains the *extensive* nature of the present. Human agents are condemned to anticipate the forthcoming *within* the world because they are obliged to impose their structured and structuring resources *upon* the world. The ineluctable preponderance of the predispositionally constituted and prereflexively executed nature of human agency is indicative of the protensive constitution of social temporality. The objective potentials that are always already inscribed in a given social field, constitute the background horizon of the subjective potentials that are still to be realised by a given social agent. To the extent that the *espace de possibles* is always a *temps de possibles*, the *possibles d'un espace* are always the *possibles du temps*: every spatially defined horizon of possibilities is also a temporally defined horizon of possibilities, and every possibility arising from a given social space is also a possibility emerging from a given social time. In other words, what is possible through a given human action is contingent upon the spatiotemporally constituted horizon of possibilities prescribed by a given social field.

If, as Adkins points out, we accept that the forthcoming is always already inscribed in the present, we have to be prepared to confront at least four issues: first, the injunction to anticipate may be an idiosyncratic feature of our present moment (*the socio-historical structuration of time*); second, to the degree that the forthcoming is capable of undercutting or destabilising the present, the former is preponderant over the latter (*the future-laden orientation of time*); third, given our simultaneous immersion in the temporal horizons of past, present, and future, we should conceive of human practices as being situated in a temporal continuum (*the fluid constitution of time*); and, fourth, rather than simply assuming that time makes practice, we also need to recognise that practice makes time (*the praxeological production of time*).

In the section entitled 'Time is Money', Adkins stresses the sociological importance of one of the underlying principles of the capitalist economy: to be able to do things faster and more efficiently than one's competitors is a precondition for increasing the profitability of one's business. The hegemonic mode of production, then, is also a hegemonic mode of temporalisation: rates of profit and production depend on profit-oriented and production-driven forms of temporalisation. The entanglement of economic practice with time obliges us, as critical sociologists, to reflect upon the ways in which societies are not only spatially but also temporally structured. Every mode of production requires a particular mode of temporalisation. The key issue when exploring the structuration of time in capitalist society is that, under the rule of clock time, social phenomena and social time are separated and hence – to use Adkins's formulation – *in clock time events do not make time but take place in time.* Rather than human practices determining time, time determines human practices.

In the section entitled 'Money is Time', Adkins examines the paradigmatic transformation of time in late modern societies. The slogan 'time is money' captures a central normative imperative of Fordist regimes of production: the more rapid and the more efficient, the more productive and the more profitable. By contrast, the slogan 'money is time' sums up a key normative imperative of post-Fordist regimes of production: the stronger and richer financially, the more flexible and powerful socially. Whereas under industrial capitalism time is money, in deregulated financial markets *money has become time.* Given that in the post-Fordist context, which is dictated by the pressing imperatives of the financial markets, time has ceased to operate as an external vessel for practice and has become increasingly merged with events, time itself has become a pivotal driving force of economic empowerment: in the post-Fordist world, the production of society is increasingly contingent upon the temporalisation of production. The question remains, however, to what extent the restructuration and resignification of time in the post-Fordist world have created a situation in which the experience of social life has become more abstract than in previous societies. If we now live in a world reproduced and kept alive through the collective experience of unexperienced experiences, then – as Adkins pertinently remarks – the participation in social life is potentially beyond meaning and interpretation. A society in which the control of time escapes the control of ordinary people is a society in which the search for meaning is increasingly shaped by the purposive power of systemic reproduction, rather than by the communicative power of everyday interaction. We certainly do not live in a timeless society, but we may live in a society without time.

Conclusion

From a range of authors and from a variety of perspectives, the chapters of this book provide a comprehensive and critical evaluation of the sociology of Pierre Bourdieu. Although they raise many difficult problems concerning Bourdieu's legacy, they illustrate the power and scope of his sociology in shaping our understanding of modern society, especially with regard to the sociological significance of field-specific struggles over various forms of power and different resources. It is obvious that Bourdieu borrowed extensively and openly from the writings of classical sociologists, notably from the works of Marx, Durkheim, and Weber. Yet, he also created a battery of concepts – such as 'field', 'habitus', and 'capital' – which have profoundly influenced, and will continue to stimulate, contemporary social and political analysis. These diverse contributions demonstrate the enduring importance of classical sociology, while recognising the creative and innovative energy that derives from Bourdieu's thought.

Acknowledgements

I am grateful to Bryan S. Turner and Elena Knox for their detailed comments on an earlier version of this Afterword.

References

Bourdieu, Pierre (1976) 'Le champ scientifique', *Actes de la recherche en sciences sociales* 8–9 [2–3]: 88–104.

Bourdieu, Pierre (1977 [1972]) *Outline of a Theory of Practice*, trans. Richard Nice, Cambridge: Cambridge University Press.

Bourdieu, Pierre (2000 [1997]) *Pascalian Meditations*, trans. Richard Nice, Cambridge: Polity Press.

Bourdieu, Pierre (2000) 'Mit Weber gegen Weber: Pierre Bourdieu im Gespräch', in Pierre Bourdieu, *Das religiöse Feld. Texte zur Ökonomie des Heilsgeschehens*, herausgegeben von Franz Schultheis, Andreas Pfeuffer und Stephan Egger, übersetzt von Stephan Egger, Konstanz: Universitätsverlag Konstanz, pp. 111–129.

Bourdieu, Pierre and Terry Eagleton (1992) 'Doxa and Common Life', *New Left Review* 191: 111–121.

Bourdieu, Pierre, Franz Schultheis and Andreas Pfeuffer (2011 [2000]) 'With Weber Against Weber: In Conversation With Pierre Bourdieu', in Simon Susen and Bryan S. Turner (eds.) *The Legacy of Pierre Bourdieu: Critical Essays*, trans. Simon Susen, London: Anthem Press, pp. 111–124.

Marx, Karl (2000/1977 [1845]) 'Theses on Feuerbach', in David McLellan (ed.) *Karl Marx: Selected Writings*, 2nd Edition, Oxford: Oxford University Press, pp. 171–174.

INDEX OF NAMES

INDEX OF SUBJECTS

CPSIA information can be obtained at www.ICGtesting.com
Printed in the USA
BVOW08s1702021213
337926BV00003B/14/P

9 781783 080724